Studies of the Max Planck Institute Luxembourg for International, European and Regulatory Procedural Law

edited by
Prof. Dr. Dres. h.c. Burkhard Hess
Prof. Dr. Hélène Ruiz Fabri

Volume 27

Hélène Ruiz Fabri | Valérie Rosoux | Alessandra Donati (Eds.)

Representing the Absent

Nomos

Max Planck Institute
LUXEMBOURG
for Procedural Law

Coverpicture: Photo Quentin Bertoux. Agence Vu

The Deutsche Nationalbibliothek lists this publication in the Deutsche Nationalbibliografie; detailed bibliographic data are available on the Internet at http://dnb.d-nb.de

ISBN 978-3-7560-1337-1 (Print)
978-3-7489-1864-6 (ePDF)

British Library Cataloguing-in-Publication Data
A catalogue record for this book is available from the British Library.

ISBN 978-3-7560-1337-1 (Print)
978-3-7489-1864-6 (ePDF)

Library of Congress Cataloging-in-Publication Data
Ruiz Fabri, Hélène | Rosoux, Valérie | Donati, Alessandra
Representing the Absent
Hélène Ruiz Fabri | Valérie Rosoux | Alessandra Donati (Eds.)
496 pp.
Includes bibliographic references.

ISBN 978-3-7560-1337-1 (Print)
978-3-7489-1864-6 (ePDF)

1st Edition 2023

Published by
Nomos Verlagsgesellschaft mbH & Co. KG
Waldseestraße 3–5 | 76530 Baden-Baden
www.nomos.de

Production of the printed version:
Nomos Verlagsgesellschaft mbH & Co. KG
Waldseestraße 3–5 | 76530 Baden-Baden

ISBN 978-3-7560-1337-1 (Print)
ISBN 978-3-7489-1864-6 (ePDF)
DOI https://doi.org/10.5771/9783748918646

Onlineversion
Nomos eLibrary

Table of Contents

Introduction

Alessandra Donati[*]*, Valérie Rosoux*[**] *and Hélène Ruiz Fabri*[***]

This book results from fascinating discussions triggered by the interdisciplinary seminars launched by Professor Hélène Ruiz Fabri at the Max Planck Institute Luxembourg for Procedural Law.[1] The general theme of these seminars concerned the scope and limits of various procedures put in place to give 'some kind of justice' to victims.[2] Despite the diversity of disciplines and topics, most analyses questioned multiple ways to 're-present' absent generations and move forward.[3] Some were devoted to past generations, while others dealt with future generations.[4] This led to the idea of focusing on the dimension of absence and 're-presentation'.

The 'absent' is a notion known in most legal systems. As a legal notion, primarily used in civil law, it refers to one who has left, either temporarily or permanently, their domicile or usual place of residence or business, or

---

* Alessandra Donati is *Réferendaire* (legal clerk) at the Court of Justice of the European Union and lecturer at the University of Luxembourg.

** Valérie Rosoux is a Research Director at the Belgian Fund for Scientific Research (FNRS) and a Professor at the University of Louvain, Belgium.

*** Hélène Ruiz Fabri is Professor of International Law at the Sorbonne Law School (University Paris 1 Panthéon-Sorbonne), on leave to be Director of the Max Planck Institute Luxembourg for Procedural Law.

1 See Hélène Ruiz Fabri (ed), *Max Planck Encyclopedia of International Procedural Law* (OUP – launched in 2019).

2 See Judith Shklar, *The Faces of Injustice* (Yale University Press 1990) and Diane Orentlicher, *Some Kind of Justice: The ICTY's Impact in Bosnia and Serbia* (OUP 2018).

3 On the presence of the absent, see Edith Goldbeter-Merinfeld, *Le deuil impossible* (De Boeck 2017) and Michaël Foessel, *Le temps de la consolation* (Seuil 2015) 293. On backward- and forward-looking outcomes processes, see William Zartman and Victor Kremenyuk (eds), *Peace versus Justice. Negotiating Forward-and Backward-Looking Outcomes* (Rowman & Littlefield 2005).

4 See, for instance: Valérie Rosoux, 'Memory, Cultural Heritage, and Legacies of Wars' in Fen Hampson, Alp Ozerdem and Jonathan Kent (eds), *Handbook of Peace, Security and Development* (Routledge 2020); and Valérie Rosoux, 'Negotiating on Behalf of Previous Generations: Justice in Post-Conflict Contexts' (2020) 25(1) International Negotiation 93; Alessandra Donati, *Le principe de précaution en droit de l'Union européenne* (Bruylant 2021).

whose whereabouts are not known and cannot be ascertained by diligent effort. And yet, the absent may have a family, own a business or property, for whom or which life has to go on. Being absent does not mean having no interest or stake. However, one recurring related issue is determining who can legally speak in the name of, or represent the absent. The project takes root in this idea and widens it by considering the issue of the representation of all those who are not there now, stretching from those who are not there anymore because they have disappeared, to those who are not there yet, because they have not yet appeared. Past and future generations are not only emblematic of both ends of the spectrum but also of the fact that absents can indeed have interests and would therefore need someone to speak in their name/represent them.

We organised two specific workshops to problematise the issue.[5] As suggested by numerous works in memory studies and environmental/climate law, a great deal is at stake. Millions of citizens are concerned by the existence – or lack – of procedures related to historical injustices[6] and/or the protection of future generations.[7]

The workshops aimed to understand and analyse, from an interdisciplinary perspective (law, philosophy, sociology, political science) and with a procedural focus, the commonalities and differences between the representation of past and future generations. In this regard, they examined the articulation, in the international arena, between judiciary and non-judiciary procedural techniques, both in terms of reparation (towards past generations) and prevention (towards future generations). They did so by combining theoretical analysis with the examination of some relevant case studies. This methodology was conceived to allow us to shed light on what we considered the common ground between the representation of past and future generations. This common ground is built around some common

5 The seminars took place on 12 June 2020 and 2 December 2020 at the Max Planck Institute Luxembourg for Procedural Law.

6 Adam B Lerner, *Collective Trauma and the Making of International Politics* (OUP 2022).

7 See Alberto Alemanno, 'Protecting the Future People's Future: How to Operationalize Present People's Unfulfilled Promises to Future Generations' (2023) European Journal of Risk Regulation (forthcoming) and Sonya Djemni-Wagner and Victoria Vanneau (eds), *Droit(s) des générations futures* (IERDJ 2023) <https://perma.cc/CE9G-MVAZ>. On the link between memory and future thinking, see Meymune N Topcu and William Hirst, 'Remembering a Nation's Past to Imagine its Future: The Role of Event Specificity, Phenomenology, Valence, and Perceived Agency' (2020) 46(3) J Exp Psychol Learn Mem Cogn 563.

principles (the principles of institutional continuity and temporal non-discrimination), some common obstacles (legitimacy, indeterminacy, conflicting interests) and some familiar procedural techniques (the representation *stricto sensu* of the absents and, more broadly, the procedural avenues to consider their interests).

Following this shared reflection, we identified the two guiding questions at the origin of all contributions to this book: (1) who do we consider as 'the absents'?; and (2) who represents them? We did not impose fixed once-and-for-all definitions and categories, but we shared some common understanding regarding the notions of absence and representation. We focused on two kinds of 'absent' parties: victims of political violence who belong to past generations and potential future victims to be protected. Similarly, we paid attention to both judiciary and non-judiciary procedures. This broad starting point allowed us to better circumscribe the notion of intergenerational justice.[8] The notion of generation has been largely studied by sociologists, historians, political scientists, and legal experts.[9] However, numerous questions still need to be explored.

Who can claim to be a legitimate guardian of past or future generations: official representatives, experts, families, or communities? Based on which criteria? Which relationship does the present generation entertain with past or future ones? Do they have specific legal and ethical obligations in this regard? Are these obligations only defined in terms of reparation and protection? Is harm transgenerational? Does the State play a specific role in defending the interests of past and future generations? When does reparation end? When does protection start? How can we correctly understand the combination between guilt, awareness, responsibility, equity, and

8 See: Edith Brown Weiss, *In Fairness to Future Generations: International Law, Common Patrimony and Intergenerational Equity* (OUP 1989); Edith Brown Weiss, 'Our Rights and Obligations to Future Generations for the Environment' (1990) 84 AJIL 198; Clara Sabbagh and Manfred Schmitt, *Handbook of Social Justice Theory and Research* (Springer 2016); Janna Thompson, 'Historical Injustice and Reparation: Justifying Claims of Descendants' (2001) 1 Ethics 114; Iñigo González-Ricoy and Axel Gosseries (eds), *Institutions for Future Generations* (OUP 2016).

9 Karl Mannheim, 'The Sociological Problem of Generations' in Paul Kecskemeti (ed), *Essays on the Sociology of Knowledge* (Routledge and Kegan Paul 1952); Jane Pichler, 'Mannheim's Sociology of Generations: An Undervalued Legacy' (1994) 45 British Journal of Sociology 481; 'Les générations' (1989) Vingtième Siècle. Revue d'histoire (special issue); Jean-François Sirinelli, 'Génération' in Claude Gauvard and Jean-Fraçois Sirinelli (eds), *Dictionnaire de l'historien* (PUF 2015) 299–301; Louis Chauvel, *Le destin des générations* (PUF 2010).

solidarity? All these questions show the need for a dialogue on these crucial but also polysemic notions.

Specificity of the Book

In the context of an avalanche of texts on historical and preventive responsibility, this book makes a unique contribution in three respects. Firstly, it seeks an articulation between the dynamics related to past and future victims. The notion of absence encompasses both figures and allows us to understand better the similarities and contrasts between both dynamics. At this stage, the scope and limits of procedures related to past and future injustices are studied in two separate fields: transitional justice and environmental/climate law. It is, therefore, useful to explore the interaction of the two. At first glance, the notion of intergenerational justice towards past and future generations might appear to refer to distinctive processes. However, as several chapters show, they are intimately connected. This book's underlying hypothesis is that arguments in favour of reparation towards past generations and protection towards future generations are not totally disconnected.

Secondly, the book gathers contributions from scholars anchored in law, political sciences, philosophy, ethics, and sociology. This interdisciplinary perspective provided challenging but also vibrant exchanges. The plurality of the approaches gathered in the book is indispensable to evaluating the significance and effectiveness of procedures enabling the representation of past and future generations. It also allows us to understand the multidimensional nature of the notion of generation.

Finally, the book's purpose is exploratory and pragmatic rather than prescriptive or normative. It is to analyse procedural choices and dilemmas and describe how judiciary and non-judiciary proceedings work. The intention is to raise and address questions regarding the scope and practical limits of concrete proceedings. To do so, it is fruitful to gather scholars coming not only from complementary disciplines but also from no less than four continents.

Taking the Longue Durée *Seriously*

When proceedings involve several generations, agreeing on what qualifies as injustice is difficult. As numerous chapters in this book indicate, the long-term effects of past violence on two, if not three, successive generations critically impact judiciary and non-judiciary processes. Taking into account the links between generations in such a *longue durée* is indispensable to apprehend the impact of past injustices and to frame the potential consequences of future ones.[10] It also allows one to question the loyalty to those considered to have been unfairly treated. It poses the legitimacy issue of engaging proceedings in the name of those who have suffered, or will suffer, injustice.

To address all these issues, not restricting the analysis to the legal dimension based on rights is decisive. Proceedings can also be described as rational games depending on the parties' interests. Admittedly, judiciary and non-judiciary processes related to reparation, compensation, or prevention can hardly be understood without considering power asymmetries, strategic postures, and diverging – if not contradictory – interests. Yet, these processes cannot be studied without considering the emotional dimension of these processes. The significance of emotions such as guilt, humiliation, anger, hatred and fear explains largely why these procedures cannot be reduced to any form of bargaining[11]. As well as considering rational dimensions (which remains critical), an understanding of procedures devoted to past and future injustices requires insight into psychological processes that scholars and practitioners do not always take seriously. The combination of these three dimensions (rights, interests, and emotions) constitutes the core of most analyses in the book.

The focus on the figure of 'the absent' allows us to question the appropriate time frame to achieve a form of intergenerational justice: should we consider immediate descendants of victims or adopt a longer-term approach? Likewise, should we pay attention only to the next generation

10 See Antoine Garapon, *Peut-on réparer l'histoire? Colonisation, Esclavage, Shoah* (Odile Jacob 2008); Lisa Ott, *Enforced Disappearance in International Law* (Intersentia 2011); Mariana Aguchar, *Discursive Processes of Intergenerational Transmission of Recent History* (Palgrave Macmillan 2016) and Grazyna Baranowska, *Rights of Families of Disappeared Persons. How International Bodies Address the Needs of Families of Disappeared Persons in Europe* (Intersentia 2021).

11 See Damien Short, *Reconciliation and Colonial Power. Indigeneous Rights in Australia* (Routledge 2008).

or for more? The answers given to these interrogations are decisive in determining who the ultimate beneficiaries of judiciary and non-judiciary proceedings are. Hence, should we consider that the most critical challenge, in all cases (even those that regard past injustices), is determining the decision that will best serve current and, above all, future generations? Can we consider past or future generations represented in the framework of current proceedings as victims?

Each of these questions demonstrates the need to combine the currently available methods to build bridges between the fields of memory studies, international law, transitional justice, and environmental/climate law – to name but a few.

Outlines of the Book

The book is divided into two main sections. The first refers to the figure of 'the absent' in the framework of proceedings related to past injustices. The second discusses the same figure from a future-thinking perspective. Both parties tend to emphasise the main variables that determine the negotiation processes at the international, national, regional, and local levels. They also attempt to underline lessons for practice and theory.

In the initial chapter, Stipe Odak offers stimulating 'conceptual starting points'. After distinguishing the 'past absent,' 'present absent,' and 'future absent,' he shows that the project of representing the figure of the absent (past, present, or future) is not without ambiguities. He also discusses the political and moral basis on which respect for past generations could be based and presents potential modes of representing the past absent.

Kritika Sharma completes this section with a legal analysis of 'intergenerational victimhood at the International Criminal Court (ICC)'. In focusing on the representatives of absent victims or indirect victims, she questions the lasting impact of unimpeded and rampant international crime. Her chapter analyses the intergenerational dimension of the victims' regime at the ICC. To do this, it explores the possibility of family members of victims participating in court proceedings and seeking reparations either as victims themselves or as successors of deceased victims.

Carlos J. Bichet Nicoletti concentrates on the past and future dimensions of the absent victim in international human rights adjudication. His contribution studies the contours of some of the decisions, procedural frameworks, and argumentative strategies used by regional human rights courts to provide some sort of redress in cases involving violations that can have intertemporal dimensions, either because the victims are not present or because the interests of future victims might also be at stake.

The chapter written by Fé de Jonge guides us in the field of critical archival studies. It interrogates the absence or 'presence of victims in the preservation, articulation and retrieval of the International Criminal Tribunal for the former Yugoslavia (ICTY) archives'. This case study allows us to observe the links between victim communities, international adjudicative mechanisms, and archives of mass atrocities.

The perspective adopted by Sandra M. Rios Oyola is sociological. She considers the notion of absence related to the victims of enforced disappearance who have been violently removed from public existence and made invisible. The chapter examines how families' activism allows the disappeared to continue being represented in the public sphere. The case of Colombia is particularly emblematic due to its large number of cases of enforced disappearance. It raises crucial questions that are relevant on all continents.

In her chapter, Lily Martinet wonders how we can 'untangle competing claims over colonial cultural objects'. Describing the processes of 'longing, belonging and owning', she adopts a critical perspective based on generations and historical injustice. Her main argument is that a shift needs to occur from a legal framework grounded in ownership and property rights focusing on States and cultural objects as assets to an approach integrating human rights and recognising communities as cultural bearers and items as components of a shared heritage.

The way to come to terms with the colonial past is also at the core of the chapter written by Valérie Rosoux. Her participation in the Special Commission established in 2020 by the Belgian Parliament to deal with its colonial past raises the issue of failure. The empirical analysis of this emblematic case study underlines the weight of 'the absents' and the difficulty of agreeing on the most appropriate way to represent and honour them. The tensions that characterise the work carried out by the Parliamentary Commission show how ambiguous the notion of 'absent' is.

The pitfalls and challenges related to the Belgian case studies are confirmed by the broader analysis carried out by I. William Zartman on 'negotiating the past: correcting or resurrecting?'. This chapter relates to a diversity of cases (from Native Americans to Namibia and Rwanda). It raises the question of whether it is the past, the intermediate, or then present situation that is being repaired. It also raises the question of numbers and apportionment and pays particular attention to the issue of restitution.

In the last chapter of the first section, Alexandra Harrington reflects on the notion of 'peace for the future' in studying 'the incorporation of future generations in peace treaties and reconciliation institutions'. She reminds us that such agreements and entities expressly include future generations in their motivations as well as provisions such as education and the development of a robust, rule-of-law-based justice system. The critical lens used for the chapter's analysis of peace agreements is that of the principle of prevention in the sense of agreements that are not only created to cause the cessation of hostilities in each State but also to prevent these hostilities from occurring again.

Harrington's chapter lies at the intersection between both parts of the book. The subsequent chapters are indeed all devoted to analysing the proceedings concerning the representation of future generations. They show that several instruments and institutions can be mobilised at different levels of regulation, whether at international, regional or national levels.

In her chapter on 'the rights of and obligations towards future generations', Yumiko Nakanishi examines the rights that could be granted to future generations, in terms of both fundamental rights and intergenerational rights and compares them with the obligations to protect assumed by the current generation towards future ones, with a particular focus on the obligations borne by States and private companies.

Alessandra Donati also focuses on future generations, but under EU law. She indicates that the protection of future generations under EU law should be ensured through a four-fold strategy based on the principle of sustainable development, the precautionary principle, the principle of solidarity between generations, and the principle of environmental non-regression.

In the chapter devoted to 'the greening of the Inter-American Court of Human Rights', Luisa Cortat Simonetti Goncalves stresses the evolution of the case law at the Inter-American Court of Human Rights. She dissects the interaction between human rights and rights to future generations. She provides some venues of reflection that would reinforce the protection of both the rights of current and future generations.

Marta Torre Schaub and Marcos de Armenteras Cabot present an empirical assessment of 'building climate law through intergenerational justice'. Their chapter examines the notion of intergenerational justice from the perspective of climate litigation by highlighting the tools and mechanisms that could be mobilised in this framework to consolidate the protection of future generations.

In the chapter devoted to the 'mechanisms available under the law of the sea to speak on behalf of future generations', Elena Ivanova pays attention to the protection and preservation of the marine environment and marine resources. She draws attention to the actions and tools through which future generations' interests could be voiced in the context of the law of the sea.

From a broader perspective, Rudolf Schuessler and Fritz Gillerke present a chapter entitled 'Voice and no votes for future citizens'. Their analysis questions the opportunity and feasibility of representing, in the context of democratic processes, future generations. Against this backdrop, they provide a critical assessment of the rights and the entitlements that the representatives of future generations should have in present political processes to implement their representation mandate.

The following chapter concentrates on 'democratic legitimacy, institutions for future generations and the problem of constitutional power'. In this study, Ludvig Beckham challenges the idea that future generations should always be given a voice in political decision-making to mitigate 'presentist' biases in democratic institutions. His main argument is that, although it may be feasible to include future generations by various mechanisms for proxy representation, they should not enjoy constitutional power.

From a practitioner's perspective, Marcel Szabo focuses on the Hungarian Ombudsman for Future Generations. This specific case study allows him to examine the institutional interpretation and implementation of the interests of future generations in Hungary, with particular consideration to the institution of the Hungarian Deputy Commissioner Responsible for the Protection of the Interests of Future Generations. The analysis is highly stimulating and questions how we can 'represent the interests of present and future generations at the same time'.

In the chapter entitled 'how to see the invisible? The 'methods' of the rights of nature to represent future generations', Michele Carducci and Silvia Bagni argue that, in the framework of our interconnected ecosystems, the recognition of the 'rights of Nature' is a powerful tool to also represent and protect the rights of future generations that will suffer the most from the degradation of the health and environmental conditions of the planet.

The last chapter entitled 'The recognition of the rights of nature in Latin America – The lost linkage with the rights of future generations' also focuses on the relationship between the rights of future generations and the 'rights of Nature'. In this study, Luis A. López Zamora outlines the reasons behind the recognition by the constitutions of several Latin America countries of the 'rights of Nature' and provides a critical assessment of their use to the benefit of future generations.

* *

*

We are thankful to all contributors for their excellent work and collaborative attitude. While we were unable to meet systematically in-person to share drafts and ideas as we had planned, we held one workshop online and one in hybrid format. Everyone was generous with their time and comments. We are delighted to have managed to attract such a wide range of authors in terms of disciplines, geographical origin and age. A subject of such global interest clearly deserved it.

We are also grateful to the Max Planck Institute Luxembourg for Procedural Law for its significant support to our work. Special thanks go to Nathalie Perrin and Dylan Siry for their constant support and devotion to the project.

1. Representing the Past Absent: Conceptual Starting Points

Stipe Odak[*]

Abstract: *The chapter analyses the notion of 'absence' in the political discourse on representation. Starting with the distinction between the 'past absent,' 'present absent,' and 'future absent,' the author outlines various senses and the implications of these terms. The focus is placed primarily on the 'past absent.' Numerous political projects attempt to draw their legitimacy from the claims that they represent the will of past generations or that they provide the work of justice for past victims. By showing the dangers and ambiguities inherent in such projects, the chapter discusses the political and moral basis on which respect for past generations could be based. Finally, presenting different ways of understanding the 'absence' (i.e., as an absence of biological lives, subjectivities, and political preferences), potential modes of representing the past absent are outlined.*

Introduction

'Preserve my Yugoslavia!' Bogoljub Jevtić claims these were the last words of the Yugoslav King Alexander I, pronounced only several minutes before he died, the victim of an assassination in Marseille in 1934. According to the footage of the event and medical reports, the King had lost consciousness only moments after the assassination, and it was thus very unlikely that he had time to say anything. The following day, those words nonetheless became an official slogan and a legitimation for preserving the Yugoslav project. Bogoljub Jevtić himself was soon appointed the head of the Council of Ministers and assumed the position of the protector of the dead king's will.[1]

In 1980, immediately after the death of Josip Broz Tito, the lifetime president of the second Yugoslavia, the state's Communist Party derived a catchphrase: 'I posle Tita – Tito' (Even after Tito, still Tito). The motto was meant to demonstrate that the will and spirit of the country's leader was not about to cease to exist; it was only to be transferred to new carriers.

In his speech at the opening of the 2017 Civilizations Forum, Turkish President Recep Tayyip Erdogan claimed that Alija Izetbegović, the former

---

* Dr Stipe Odak is a post-doctoral researcher and a lecturer at the Université catholique de Louvain (Belgium).

1 Dejan Ristić, *Zablude srpske istorije* (Vukotić Media 2020).

political leader of Bosniaks in Bosnia and Herzegovina, left the country to him as a bequest. According to Erdogan, just a day before his death, Izetbegović said the following: 'Tayyip, you are the descendants of the sultan Fatih; this country is given to you in testament. Protect it for that reason.'[2]

The claims for legitimate interpretations and representations of the past are not limited to individuals. In some cases, political leaders contend to represent the political will of the *collective absent*. Milorad Dodik, a member of the tripartite Bosnian-Herzegovinian presidency, frequently uses the memory of the genocide of Serbs in WWII as a legitimation for the existence (and even potential independence) of Republika Srpska, a federal entity in Bosnia and Herzegovina whose wartime leadership was convicted of war crimes at the International Criminal Tribunal for the former Yugoslavia (ICTY). During a speech in Donja Gradina in 2017, Dodik thus stated that Republika Srpska was a response to the sacrifice of numerous past generations of Serbs who died for their nation.[3] The implication of this speech was precisely that the absent generations of 'martyrs' provide moral warrants for the current political project.

What all these gestures have in common is the transference of the past political will to new appointees. As can be seen from this rather selective overview, the territories of the former Yugoslavia had more than a few of them. The assigned (or self-assigned) carriers of these political wills then see themselves not only as their guardians but also as the sole protectors of the continuity between the past and present. The problem, obviously, is that the political legitimacies derived from the claims on the past are anything but unequivocal.

The claims of *representing the absent* are commonplace in political discourse and are tied to three main groups: 1) past absent, 2) present absent, 3) future absent. As mentioned earlier, evocative claims of representing the will of the *past absent* are frequently used to consolidate power. Such examples, however, should not make us conclude prematurely that every claim of representing the absent is problematic. Concerns for past community members are also integral to the notion of heritage, tradition, and culture. Secondly, numerous initiatives aiming at giving voice to mar-

---

2 'Erdogan: Nikada nećemo ostaviti BiH koju mi je Alija dao u amanet' (*Klix.ba*, 21 October 2017) <https://www.klix.ba/vijesti/bih/erdogan-nikada-necemo-ostaviti-bih-koju-mi-je-alija-dao-u-amanet/171021079> accessed 19 July 2023.

3 Glas Srpske, 'Dodik: Stradanja ne bi bilo da smo 1941. imali Republiku Srpsku' (23 April 2017) <https://perma.cc/3ZK2-7SHS>.

ginalised groups can be characterised as advocacy for the *present absent*, i.e., for those *currently* excluded from political decision-making. Finally, the representation of the *future absent* concerns future generations. Such initiatives are often linked to ecological and developmental issues that will inevitably impact future humans. Some states have even appointed official representatives of future generations to voice their (envisaged) concerns. The Israeli Knesset has thereby established *the Commission for the Future Generations*, Hungary has appointed an *Ombudsman for Future Generations*, while France has introduced the *Constitutional Charter for the Environment.*

Therefore, the projects of representing the past, present, and future absent are not without ambiguities. Some of the questions that pertain to all of them are the following: Who exactly are the absent? Who can legitimately represent them? Are some of the 'absent' excluded from such projects? What aspects of the absent are represented – their lives, their subjectivities, or their preferences? To what extent can those be known, given the temporal and/or contextual distance? Why and to what degree should the present generations care about the absent?

In this article, I would like to bring some conceptual clarity to the discussion by addressing these issues. *In the first part*, I analyse the notions of present, past, and future absent (sections 1, 2, and 3). *The second part* examines the reasons for caring about the absent, particularly the past absent (section 4). In *the third part*, the focus is placed on the modalities of representing the absent (section 5). Finally, the scopes and limits of representing the absent are presented in the conclusion to this chapter.

1. The Present Absent

The 'absent' as a subject of rights can be interpreted in numerous ways. Before addressing the notion of the *past absent* and the *future absent*, let us first consider the category of the *present absent*. Unlike the other categories, the present absent are not chronologically distant. They are contemporary individuals (or groups) who are present holders of rights but are excluded from their enjoyment due to different circumstances. Here, we can include people who cannot articulate their preferences due to internal or external constraints (e.g., children) but also forcefully displaced people, institutionally confined individuals, and people in exile or hiding. While the latter have participated or will participate in political processes at some point(s) in their lives, they currently do not have any direct means to convey their opinions in public deliberations. They can thus be considered *absent* from standard procedures of decision-making. This, however, does not mean that those absent individuals are entirely voiceless. Sometimes, their concerns can be communicated through guardians or representatives (such is the case with children, for instance). The level of their indirect impact, moreover, varies drastically. A migrant caught in legal limbo shares with Edward Snowden a certain absence from political life, but their ability to influence political decisions indirectly are incomparable. There are activist groups who take a step further and include conceived but unborn children among the absent who need representation. Some other groups count animals among such subjects and thus endeavour to act as their proxies. Several examples will be provided below.

In 2000, Oxfam GB initiated the Indigenous People's Development Programme in Bangladesh. Together with 20 partner organisations, they aimed to support the political representation of indigenous Adibashi people, who are often discriminated against and excluded from political, economic, and cultural life.[4] This exemplifies a way to endorse the *present absent* in their attempts to achieve equality. Randall S. Abate takes a broader approach to representation. He collectively defines future generations, wildlife, and natural resources as 'voiceless.'[5] Those *voiceless groups* are most affected by global climate changes and should enjoy enhanced stewardship.[6] The best illustration of such attempts coming to fruition is the Te Awa Tupua (Whanganui River Claims Settlement) Bill, passed in March 2017 by the New Zealand Parliament, establishing the legal personhood of 'the Whanganui River from the mountains to the sea, incorporating all its physical and metaphysical elements.'[7] Te Awa Tapua, the Bill establishes, is 'a legal person and has all the rights, powers, duties, and liabilities of a legal person.'[8] The rights, powers, duties, liabilities, and responsibilities of the Whanganui River with all its essential elements are performed by a special

4 Bibhash Chakraborty and Ayesha Dastgir, 'Finding a Voice for the Voiceless: Indigenous People Gain Recognition in Bangladesh' (Oxfam GB 2018) <https://perma.cc/K59J-DZQR>.

5 Randall Abate, *Climate Change and the Voiceless* (CUP 2020).

6 ibid., 173–174.

7 The Parliament of New Zealand, 'Te Awa Tupua (Whanganui River Claims Settlement) Bill' (2017) para. 12 <https://www.legislation.govt.nz/bill/government/2016/0129/latest/whole.html#DLM6831458> accessed 22 February 2022.

8 ibid., para. 14.

two-person Office of Te Pou Tupua, which is 'the human face of Te Awa Tupua and act in the name of Te Awa Tupua.'[9] In order to avoid confusion, it is important to clarify that the legal personhood of Te Awa Tupua is not comprised solely of a river but also all the communities and elements integral to it, such as the iwi and hapū groups living nearby the Whanganui River.[10]Also in March 2017, the Uttarakhand High Court in India granted the status of legal minor to the Ganges and Yamuna rivers. The decision was later overturned by the Supreme Court of the Uttarakhand State.[11]

Tony Mifsud, the Malta Unborn Child Movement coordinator, suggested in 2012 that the state's Attorney General 'should recommend the introduction of an unborn child advocate to the government.'[12] In Mifsud's view, the role of this advocate should be to represent the interests 'of unborn children for protection to their lives and from harm, of any description, to their bodies.'[13] An example of those harms can be exposure to harmful toxins such as drugs and alcohol, and physical violence during pregnancy. The group thus strives to extend to the representation of the presently absent to potential future citizens in political terms and juridical procedures.

An anti-speciist group, Anonymous for the Voiceless, defines itself as a 'voice against history's largest and longest-standing injustice.'[14] The organisation aims to abolish 'all forms of non-human animal exploitation.'[15]

What all these organisations share is a conviction of representing the rights of constituents that are unjustly excluded from political considerations. All these actions are meant to represent the *present absent* in the political fora.

2. The Past Absent

The second category of the absent are the *past absent*. As was the case with the previous categories, here we can count not only dead humans but also past cultures, artefacts, or non-human forms of life. Species revival groups,

9 ibid., 18.2.
10 ibid., 13c-d.
11 A Vaidyanathan, 'No, Ganga And Yamuna Are Not Living Entities, Says Supreme Court' (*NDTV*, 7 July 2017) <https://perma.cc/J6KW-42LT>.
12 Tony Mifsud, 'Role of Unborn Child Advocate' (*Times of Malta*, 28 April 2012) <https://perma.cc/9K5Z-G6DD>.
13 ibid.
14 'Who We Are' (Anonymous for the Voiceless) < https://perma.cc/8DTX-QKYV>.
15 ibid.

for instance, gather scientists who aim at de-extinction, i.e., bringing extinct species to life through genetic engineering, and thus advocate for their interests. Most often, though, the notion of the past absent refers to dead individuals, people who used to be members of the polity but no longer are. We can deduce their wills or desires only indirectly. Generations preceding us have crystallised their political preferences through laws, institutions, norms, and elements of cultural heritage that define current life. We can infer, for instance, that previous generations meant certain political provisions to be stable and thus enshrined them in a constitution. By establishing national libraries and archives, we can assume they wanted to preserve national culture and heritage.

There are, however, at least three problems related to the representation of the past. *Firstly*, we can never be sure what the real political preferences of past generations were when it comes to the durability of their past projects. If past generations had founded a national petroleum company, should we respect their rights to use fossil oils for the betterment of society? Or were their preferences somehow vaguer – to use any available energy source for economic profit? We can only discern what past generations did in the past, but we have no way of knowing what their preferences under current, drastically different, circumstances would be. More fundamentally, we cannot know for sure if they even intended their wills or approaches to last beyond them. *Secondly*, the interests of the past generations are not necessarily compatible. Just like the present, the past was also a battlefield of ideas, political projects, and ideologies. Past individuals who built hydroelectric plants on a river or barriers to prevent its flooding would have very different worldviews and desires from those who believed that the river in question is a living entity and should flow unobstructed. *Thirdly*, it is unclear why and to what degree current generations owe respect to past generations regarding their political decisions and preferences concerning national legacy. I will return to this question of obligations towards past generations later in the chapter.

3. The Future Absent

The third category of the absent is the *future absent*, the upcoming generations, who are also the primary focus of the theories of intergenerational justice. A short clarification here is necessary. When I speak about the future absent, I have in mind the individuals, species, and creations, all of which *will exist* in the future but are currently absent. They should not be confused with currently existing beings and artefacts which will disappear in future, e.g., some extinct species of animals or languages that will become unused in future.

As is the case with the previous categories, the future absent primarily denotes future *human beings and groups*, those imagined generations that will live in the future but are not currently present as political subjects. Future generations, however, are in many ways, different from past generations. While the past generations did exist and participated in social developments, future generations exist only as a projection. While we can contend that we 'owe' something to past generations because we enjoy the benefits of their work, we cannot say the same about future generations. Therefore, the source of obligations towards the future absent must be somehow different – it cannot be based on their still non-existent acts, but on something that transcends every specific generation, some trans-temporal rights that every generation (current or future) needs to enjoy.

If there are such rights, we can argue that the *right to exist* should be the first among them. The right to exist, however, is predicated upon *the existence of an environment* which can support it. Therefore, current generations who have also inherited their environment should feel obliged to preserve it in such a condition that the future generations can exist and sustain themselves. This idea is based on the common stewardship of the Earth, according to which each generation should take into consideration those who come after them. While here we cannot talk about generational reciprocity, we can insist on upholding the common principle of respect. Samuel Freeman, following Rawls, writes:

> While this is not a principle of reciprocity – after all, future generations are not able to reciprocate the benefits we bestow on them by bestowing benefits on us – it resembles a principle of reciprocity in that it says in effect: 'Do unto future generations as you would have previous generations do unto you.'[16]

This Rawlsian 'golden rule' of intergenerational justice applies equally to the cultural legacy. People derive a great deal of meaning in their lives from the prospect of the future value of their work. In other words, our current cultural, artistic, spiritual, and material production is largely based

16 Samuel R Freeman, *Rawls* (Routledge 2007) 139.

on the idea that those products will be valuable even after our death. In that sense, current generations indirectly tie the value of their work to the future generations; current generations hope and assume that future generations will appreciate past achievements. If we could reasonably predict that art will disappear in two generations, much of the present artistic work would lose its appeal.[17]

In summary, the representation of the 'future absent' is first and foremost linked to the obligation to protect the environment and biosphere so that future generations can exist, flourish, and continue the civilisational developments achieved before them.

Now that we have a clearer outline of the differences between the past absent, present absent, and future absent, we can see that the political concerns regarding them are very different. The same can be said about the sources of moral and ethical responsibilities towards them. In the discussion that follows, I would like to focus primarily on the *past absent*. There, I will analyse the sources of moral obligations related to past generations, different forms of representing their interests, and the scopes and limits of the representation.

4. Why Should We Care About the Past Absent?

In the Gettysburg Address, one of the most famous speeches in American history, Abraham Lincoln addressed the soldiers of the Union, stating:

> We have come to dedicate a portion of that field, as a final resting-place for those who here gave their lives, that that nation might live. (...) It is for us the living, rather, to be dedicated here to the unfinished work which they who fought here have thus far so nobly advanced. (...) that

17 The premise, however, is tied to the belief that human legacy can only be preserved though future generations and that the only two possibilities of future human development are either destruction or procreation. Technological utopias make this problem even more complicated since they promise virtually limitless continuation of human lives through technological means, entirely decoupled from biological limitations. Those, still entirely fictional prospects nevertheless raise the question whether we owe existence to future generations at all if human culture can be preserved and developed though current individuals. This question is, however, beyond the scope of this paper. For a discussion on the significance of life-transcending interests, see: Janna Thompson, *Intergenerational Justice: Rights and Responsibilities in an Intergenerational Polity* (Routledge 2009) 43–50.

> we here highly resolve that these dead shall not have died in vain – that this nation, under God, shall have a new birth of freedom, and that government of the people, by the people, for the people, shall not perish from the earth.[18]

Lincoln's speech is, at the same time, one of the most famous invocations of dead lives given as a sacrifice to an idea, which thus serves as a guide for the future. Obligations towards past generations are often closely tied to the notion that past individuals gave their lives for certain goods and values. The fact that people are willing to die for something would suggest that the value in question is extremely precious – why would anyone sacrifice their life for something irrelevant? It is no matter of contestation whether some or even most of the dead saw their dying as a meaningful sacrifice for an idea or an ideal. Instead, the question is whether the loss of lives for the idea makes that very idea any more valuable than it would be without those losses. Should the amount of value that past generations had put into some idea – one can further ask – be judged based on their standards or according to standards we have today when many of the past values are reassessed?

The readiness to die, importantly, is not always a warrant of a generally appraised value. In October 1996, 39 members of the Heaven's Gate cult died for the idea of being subsequently abducted by aliens. In November 1978, more than 900 members of The Peoples Temple in Jonestown committed an act of 'revolutionary suicide' under the leadership of Jim Jones. In August 2021, The New York Times made a documentary *Dying in the Name of Vaccine Freedom,*[19] showing anti-vaccine individuals who prefer death to inoculation against a lethal pathogen. Thousands of individuals died for the idea of the Islamic Caliphate in recent years. In brief, people die in the name of all sorts of ideas daily. The relatives of dead sect members should be in no way obliged to respect the value or decisions of their predecessors. To put it more generally, the sole fact that a large number of people died for something does not incur any direct responsibility on their descendants.

An objection here could be that those descendants are in no way related to the circumstances that their predecessors deemed worthy to die for. People living in the USA today are still enjoying the benefits of the fights

18 Abraham Lincoln, 'The Gettysburg Address' (1863) <https://perma.cc/2V4E-BWU6>.

19 'Dying in the Name of Vaccine Freedom' (New York Times, 2021) <https://www.youtube.com/watch?v=pd8P12BXebo> accessed 7 November 2021.

and deaths under Lincoln's leadership. Contrary to this, the progeny of cult members does not live today in a small community that was supernaturally saved from the apocalypse. If the promises of their progenitors were indeed true, perhaps their obligations to continue previous ideologies would have been stronger? Is the current enjoyment of social and political benefits something that makes us indebted to those who created them?

While stronger, this argument is also not entirely convincing. Forefathers, for instance, might have died in a fight for a system that is comparatively worse than the alternatives available at the time. According to Encyclopedia Britannica, around 600 000 civilians and 406 000 soldiers from North Korea died during the Korean Wars.[20] It does not mean that current citizens of North Korea should feel obliged to respect the enduring revolutionary ideology or the regime, even though they live and 'benefit' from the system their forefathers created. While North Korean citizens could mourn the death of their compatriots, they should not be expected to treat their political preferences with any particular reverence. As a matter of fact, they might even feel resentment toward them. One could argue that current North Koreans do enjoy some benefits of living in a socially and politically organised community (in comparison to, let us say, complete anarchy), but those benefits should in no way prevent them from assessing freely and – if desired – abandoning the projects of their predecessors.

To put it concisely, the fact that a great number of people die for certain preferences should not guard those preferences against scrutiny. The question then naturally follows: Are there any reasons to treat the preferences of our predecessors with special reverence and not just as any other political opinion? A *conservative* argument favouring intergenerational obligations could be based on the idea of accumulated wisdom. If numerous generations valued specific ideas and if members of the society repeatedly died in defence of those ideals – the argument goes – we should consider that there might be something truly valuable therein, even if we do not see that value at that moment. While this does not prevent the *change itself*, it should curb *abrupt changes* in favour of extended social discussion. From the *liberal* perspective, however, scepticism towards the preferences of previous generations seems much sharper. I turn to those perspectives in the following sections.

20 Allan R Millett, 'Korean War: 1950–1953', Encyclopedia Britannica (18 July 2023) <https://perma.cc/P6PA-USV2>.

4.1. Every Generation Is a Separate Nation

Both Thomas Jefferson and Thomas Paine strongly opposed the idea of intergenerational decision-binding. To Thomas Paine, '[e]very age and generation must be as free to act for itself in all cases as the age and generations which preceded it.'[21] In his correspondence with James Madison, Jefferson famously stated that 'one generation is to another as one independent nation to another.'[22] Since the '*earth belongs in usufruct to the living*,' he added, 'the dead have neither powers nor rights over it.'[23] Jefferson thus proposed the expiration of all socially binding laws after the end of the average lifespan of the generation that made them, which was 19 years at his time.[24]

In both of those positions, however, there is already a latent key for interpreting intergenerational responsibility for *future generations*. Paine's stance that each generation should be free to act for itself assumes that each generation possesses the freedom to make independent decisions. The idea of freedom, in this case, is binary – either one possesses it or not. If we take a different view and see freedom as a continuous variable, we can speak of various degrees of freedom. In this perspective, the whole calculation changes. Even if we accept that future generations should be free to act for themselves, we must still acknowledge that the degrees of freedom to exercise such rights are partially defined by previous generations. The destruction of natural resources in one generation, for example, directly limits the degrees of freedom for future economic decisions. Consequently, Jefferson's position that the earth 'belongs in usufruct to the living' is viable only if we take for granted that every generation has the same ability to exercise the usufruct from the land. If the land becomes inhabitable, then the very idea of usufruct becomes void. In other words, the ability to usufruct the land is a matter of degrees, influenced significantly by previous generations.

While future generations might not have rights as they do not exist yet, we can defend their right indirectly – by defending the principle that *every generation should inherit the proper conditions for exercising their*

21 Thomas Paine, 'Rights of Man: Being an Answer to Mr. Burke's Attack on the French Revolution' (1860) <https://perma.cc/66FL-DLCS>.

22 Thomas Jefferson, 'To James Madison from Thomas Jefferson, 6 September 1789' (1789) <https://perma.cc/DZR2-TLYX>.

23 ibid. (emphasis in original).

24 ibid.

rights. The devastation of the environment beyond the point of natural recovery and above reasonable expectation of human adaptability would hence destroy the very basis for the exercise of freedom, even at its minimal degree. Thus, in order to ensure that any potential future subject can truly be a subject of freedoms and rights, we need first to ensure the conditions that make them possible. Even if we do not accept that future subjects have rights as of now, we can admit that they should have the ability to enjoy their rights once they become subjects.

But what argument shall we put forward in defence of the respect for the preferences of the *past generations*? Jefferson's concept of self-expiring laws exemplifies the liberal opposition to the idea that the will of past generations should bind future citizens. In his response to the said proposal, Madison offered several objections. Some objections are purely pragmatic: constant laws change would bring political instability and legislative confusion, particularly regarding property laws.[25] To that, he adds another argument, founded on emotions, indicating that a political community develops a special reverence for stable laws and institutions over time. Finally, Madison introduces the idea of a debt, based on the benefits that current generations enjoy and cannot reasonably repay within 19 years:

> Debts may be incurred for purposes which interest the unborn, as well as the living: such are debts for repelling a conquest, the evils of which descend through many generations. (...) The term of 19 years might not be sufficient for discharging the debts in either of these cases. There seems then to be a foundation in the nature of things, in the relation which one generation bears to another, for the descent of obligations from one to another. Equity requires it. Mutual good is promoted by it. All that is indispensable in adjusting the account between the dead & the living is to see that the debits against the latter do not exceed the advances made by the former.[26]

What Madison meant when stating that intergenerational debt is founded in the 'nature of things' is not entirely clear. He seems to suggest that there should be a natural sense of gratitude in present generations for the benefits they inherited from their predecessors (such as repelling of a conquest). However, Madison still adds an important clause: the debt of the living

25 James Madison, 'From James Madison to Thomas Jefferson, 4 February 1970' (1970) <https://perma.cc/8DE6-XNTJ>.

26 ibid.

should not exceed the advances of the predecessors. In other words, the present generation's debt towards their predecessors should be proportional to the benefits they inherited. The problem here lies precisely in the assessment of those benefits and debts. As I mentioned above, the current living could estimate that they have inherited more harm than benefits from their predecessors. If we based our argumentation on the idea of reciprocity, then past generations would be indebted to the current ones, which is obviously impossible. The argument from gratitude can thus be transposed to the following one: Current generations should respect the legacy of the past generations to the degree that they positively examine that very legacy. When rephrased, the argument requires no special reverence for the past generation since the degree of gratitude is a function of current evaluations, not something that precedes them.

Primoratz and Pavković, while contending in favour of patriotism, recognise a potential clash between liberal principles and automatic duties that would potentially follow from past sacrifices:

> We are surely entitled to make up our own minds about which goods are worthy of being maintained. So if we do decide to maintain an inheritance provided by our predecessors this must be because we find it desirable and not because of anything that our predecessors did or could have demanded.[27]

For the authors, the sacrifices of the past generations cannot be the primary but only *an additional reason* to support certain political decisions:

> Lincoln assumed that the desirability of a free democratic society was a good enough reason to maintain it, but this does not exclude the possibility that the sacrifices of the dead also give citizens a reason to carry it on. The fact that there can be more than one motivation for bringing about a wanted goal might be regarded as fortunate. If one fails another might achieve the result.[28]

Therefore, past desires and sacrifices oblige only insofar as the original ideals for which they were made are, on their own merit, still important. If those ideals at some later point become widely rejected (e.g., racial

27 Igor Primoratz and Aleksandar Pavković, *Patriotism: Philosophical and Political Perspectives* (Ashgate 2008) 153.
28 ibid., 154.

divisions or a caste system), then no amount of former sacrifice could supplement their inherent deficiencies.

Until this point, we have discussed political orientations and policies, something that can be respected, deliberated, and changed. No matter which stance we take, the fact remains that future generations have the ability to alter the course of political life. In other words, they are placed in a position of determining whether they should continue past projects (if they are deemed worthy) or not.

There is another segment of the obligation towards the past, which is much less voluntary and pertains to the notion of guilt and responsibility for past abuses. Even if we make a radical turn regarding the choices made by the previous generation, the idea is, we should still have a moral obligation to deal with the legacy of their crimes. Why – we might ask – should a political community be free to cut ties with past generations' decisions but not with their abuses? Jaspers and Arendt, in different ways, articulate that the responsibility for past abuses is a form of 'liability predicated on the duties of citizenship.'[29] Participation in citizenship would thus imply taking responsibility for the past actions of the political community, even if they did not involve any degree of personal agency.

In both cases, however, the overreaching idea is that citizenship (mostly inherited) brings certain moral obligations. The problem with this argument is that it sees moral obligations as a function that stems from belonging to a particular state. If it were the case that the citizenship changed after the fall of a regime, what would then be the source of political responsibility? I would instead suggest that political responsibility should follow directly from the demands of justice to respect all individuals equally. The sympathetic relationships of citizenship or nationhood can thus only be a supplementary reason for upholding those duties.

It follows that the duty of providing reparations does not need to be understood as a way of 'paying' for past sins but simply as a way of treating all citizens equally. Suppose individuals and/or groups of people are negatively affected by the legacy of some past decision. In that case, current polity members should feel obliged to remove those obstacles, regardless of whether they feel continuity with the past or not. This is simply another way to put forward an argument from the Rawlsian veil of

29 Andrew Schaap, 'Guilty Subjects and Political Responsibility: Arendt, Jaspers and the Resonance of the 'German Question' in Politics of Reconciliation' (2001) 49(4) Political Studies 749, 750.

ignorance. Often-heard quasi-theological talk about the 'sins of the Fathers' or the 'nation's original sin' is more confusing than helpful in articulating justice. The problem here is that the idea of sin implicitly opens a space for another related theological idea – the Messianic expiation of the sins. In such cases, some autocratic individual, a group, or even a generation imbues themselves with supra-political power to transform or supplement the mistakes of previous generations.

Some authors tie the obligation to provide redress to the sense of pride that members of the nation feel. In the same way, they feel entitled to participate in pride and victories of the nation, the argument goes, community members should partake in the feeling of shame, guilt, and duties to correct the injustices. Abdel-Nour thus claims the following:

> *[N]ational responsibility is actively incurred by individuals with every proud thought they have and every proud statement they make about the achievements of their nation. This, however, is also the limit of their national responsibility, which only extends to the actions that have historically brought about the objects of their national pride.*[30]

But let us imagine a situation in which a community makes a radical break with the past. What should be the base of their political responsibilities once there are no more ties of pride-cum-shame or genealogies of the assumed original sins? Revolutionary governments, for instance, are based on the premise of a radical rupture with the past. Should they nonetheless feel obliged to uplift polity members suffering the consequences of past discrimination? If we base our arguments on the sins of the *past absent*, post-revolutionary citizens who feel no connection whatsoever with the past generations could be easily dispensed of any responsibility towards the legacy of the abuses. They might even feel that they were also victims of the past regime. What would the source of obligations for uplifting the groups that suffer especially strong consequences of past abuses then be?

The case of Roma people during WWII in the Independent State of Croatia is particularly telling in this respect. Together with Jews, they were proportionally the largest victims of state-sanctioned genocide. Communist Yugoslavia, which incorporated all the territories of the former Independent State of Croatia, saw itself in complete discontinuity with the ideology, identification, nationhood, and acts of the Independent State of Croatia.

30 Farid Abdel-Nour, 'National Responsibility' (2003) 31(5) Political Theory 693, 703 (Emphasis in original).

The arguments from the 'original sin' or the prevalence of 'national pride' would offer little support in this case. Why would a new state, based on a revolutionary movement that actively fought against the previous government, feel any guilt for the 'sins' of the past regime?

Let's take another route based on the obligation to provide all citizens with equal opportunities to participate in political life. Then, we can contend more strongly that Yugoslavia had an obligation to address particular challenges that the Roma community suffered due to the preceding genocide under a different government. This, of course, involves dealing with potential remnants of the ideology on which this discrimination was based.

In short, I find the arguments that base the responsibility for the actions of the *past absent* based on citizenship or experienced emotions partially lacking. This is because political communities can radically break the ties of citizenship and emotions with the previous generations. But even in cases of radical rupture with the past, polities still feel obliged to carry the responsibility for the legacy of past discrimination. Although the emotional or sympathetic feelings towards past generations could be a supplementary reason, I argue, they cannot be the primary moral and political bases for the responsibility towards the past. The primary reason, I suggest, should be the demand to ensure equal opportunities for all citizens to participate in political life. This obligation remains active even in cases of a radical break from the past.

Dealing with the past also includes processes of remembering and documenting past abuses (contra denial and forgetting), as well as ensuring non-repetition of crimes. Yet, once again, the importance of remembering and documenting the past cannot be dependent on the existence of past abuses. Responsible remembrance (which stands in contrast to censorship or embellished past) is the best way to make reliable links between past and present conditions, and make reasonable predictions about the future. Remembering correctly should therefore be a principle that, in itself, requires recognition and preservation.

Regardless of the grounds for representation of the past absent, the question of how we represent the past remains unclear. The issue itself is dependent on the other concern, which asks: What is exactly *absent* in the *absent past*? I address these points in the following section.

5. How Do We Represent the Past Absent?

There are at least three different possibilities of interpreting the 'absence' in the 'past absent':

1) The absence of biological lives
2) The absence of subjectivities
3) The absence of preferences

Each of these options is consequential for the choices and possibilities of representation.

1. *The absence of biological lives* means that one portion of the population is absent today as a direct consequence of some previous acts they caried out or suffered. In that sense, the Jewish saying 'whoever kills one person, kills the whole world' is telling because it suggests that one killed individual could potentially have had uncountable progeny. While there is no possible remedy for this loss, the absence of those lives can be represented by memorials and through education. The *Children's Memorial* in *Yad Vashem* is a good example of the artistic representation of the absent. Five candles surrounded by mirrors create endless reflections while the names of child Holocaust victims are being constantly recited. The monument's message is simultaneously poignant and illustrative – even a small number of killed individuals could have been reflected in endless upcoming lives. The flames of those candles in mirrors thus show the absence – the reflection is observable, but it is only ephemeral; it can be felt but it is not materially present. Every year, Bosnian-Herzegovinian artist Aida Šehović performs absence by filling up 8372 cups of coffee, commemorating victims of the Srebrenica genocide. Those coffees, left untouched, symbolise and thus render visible the biological absence of people from the intimate sphere of their families and friends.
2. *The absence of subjectivities* goes one step beyond the absence of biological lives. It says that the people killed are not just a number or a demographic loss but something more – each represents an independent subjectivity, a rich universe of life and meaning taken away. Representation of this loss is also most visible in museums and memorial institutions. For example, the Holocaust exhibition at the United States Holocaust Memorial Museum gives visitors 'ID Cards' with basic details of a Holocaust victim. Those small booklets narrate the history of the Holocaust through personal stories, through subjective experiences of individuals.

In that way, the exhibit aims to reconstruct the absent subjectivities of past victims that were forcefully erased. DeSilva's, *In Memory's Kitchen,* is another example of how one part of a personal inheritance can be continued through acts of performative justice.[31] One female inmate in Theresienstadt collected recipes in a book meant to preserve their culinary heritage, transmitted over generations, from imminent destruction. The book's publication was motivated by a desire to pay homage to the creativity and legacy of imprisoned women by recreating their recipes. Therefore, the culinary work becomes a memory work through which a part of the subjectivity of forcefully killed women is remembered and thus represented again.[32]

3. Finally, the *absence of preferences* means that past generations had some political preferences that still affect our public lives. The reconstruction and representation of those preferences would then mean that current generations are responsible for past ones. In political discourse, the idea of representing the absent is frequently tied precisely to this last notion of *absent political preferences.* Clearly, those three forms of absence are mutually interconnected. The absence of preferences requires the absence of biological lives and the absence of subjectivity. Yet, I still believe it is analytically useful to differentiate between them. Namely, the reconstruction of preferences often implies a hierarchy among the past absent. Nobody ever talks about the need to reconstruct the political preferences of those judged to be on the 'wrong side of history.' While national monuments can be erected in order to represent the biological absence of dead community members (both perpetrators and victims), this is not the case with the representation of political preferences. Maya Lin's design for the *National Veteran Memorial* in Washington, DC, was one of the rare attempts to represent the loss of soldiers' lives without political connotations, neither positive nor negative. Conversely, when it comes to the representation of past political preferences, we are implicitly operating with the notion of the *deserving absent,* those who deserve respect and merit the continuation of their projects. Only the preferences of the *deserving absent* – it follows – are to be represented and, to a certain degree, respected.

31 Cf, Stipe Odak, 'Post-Conflict Memory as Performative Justice' (2021) Peace Review 1. The quoted book is the following: Cara DeSilva, *In memory's kitchen: A legacy from the women of Terezin* (J. Aronson 1996).

32 Cf, ibid.

It is important to restate that representing *the past absent*, in any form, is ambiguous. While it can be done as a form of memory work, it can also take the form of political propaganda. The cases in which politicians purport to speak in the names of past victims, assuming the prerogatives of interpreting their desires, are especially problematic. Every generation is inherently heterogeneous when it comes to interests and preferences. This is why the representation of the past absent, in all its pluriformity, should be an inclusive task for the community. Just as the literary tradition is best served not when imitated but when creatively encountered, representation of the past absent cannot be limited to replicating past decisions but their application to the current demands of social life.

Conclusion: Limits and Scopes of Representation

Procrustes, in Greek mythology, was a bandit who had only one size of bed. He forced all his victims to fit in it and thus cut the legs of those too tall and extended the limbs of those too short.

The meaning of the *past in its pastness* always escapes us. Even if we could potentially know all the social and political desires of the past generations, replicating them to the current situation would do them no service. Since the past norms and preferences were developed as a response to their context, what needs to be preserved is not only in the *content* of those preferences but also the *mechanism of their evolution*. In other words, faithfulness to a tradition requires respect not just towards heritage but also towards the adaptability and development of the same heritage. This is no different from the political representation of past individuals and groups.

Representation of the past absent, in other words, cannot simply be the continuation or a 'reconstruction' of the past. Instead, social and political projects of past generations should be judged on their inherent value and re-contextualised with respect to new circumstances. Reverence for the past and emotional links with previous generations can only serve as an additional reason which warrants due admiration for the past but does not guarantee its uncritical continuation. When it comes to the responsibility for past crimes, the duty for reparations should be based on the obligation to allow every citizen equal participation in social and political life. This principle should be upheld even in polities that declare a radical break with the previous one, thus feeling no connections of pride or shame related to the past regime. Finally, the acts representing the past can vary, depending on our understanding of the absence. If we are talking about the absence of biological lives or subjectivities, the representation can be achieved through measures of remembrance, commemoration, or performative justice. On the other hand, representation of absent political preferences requires new articulation of those preferences, necessitating the interpretative engagement of the whole community. Special attention should be paid to preventing the misuse of the past in ideological projects that promote antagonisms, further social cleavages, and incite violence. Similar caution should be exercised in projects attempting to represent *the present* and *future absent.* For the sake of justice, political decision-making should be as inclusive as possible, thus the need for attentiveness towards those excluded and marginalised (*present absent*). Our current interest, furthermore, should be balanced by care for the ability of future generations to exist and implement their interests, although they might differ from ours. Besides sensitivity, all these projects require a great deal of humility, primarily when it comes to the interpretation of preferences of those different from us, be it different species such as animals, different phenomena such as rivers, or culturally and/or chronologically distant humans. Their differences are not something that we can eliminate by increasing current efforts to understand them. The difference of the different is irreducible. While we are invited to interpret the preferences of those who are different, the attempts to define them unequivocally would resemble Procrustean's one-size-fits-all bed.

2. Representatives of Absent Victims or Indirect Victims? An Analysis of Intergenerational Victimhood at the International Criminal Court (ICC)

Kritika Sharma[*]

Abstract: *Given the undeniable lasting impact that international crime can and does effectuate, affecting generations who witness and experience its effects, this chapter focuses on intergenerational victimhood, in the context of International Criminal Court (ICC) proceedings. Based on an analysis which explores whether family members of victims, (including deceased victims), can participate and seek reparation, this chapter provides three key findings. First, that family members of victims can participate and seek reparations in two capacities: as victims themselves or as successors of deceased victims. Second, that this position remains unchanged irrespective of the category of victims as victims of a situation or victims of crimes. Third, that this remains further unaffected by the four categories of crimes that the victim has been subjected to. However, the chapter argues, that the underlying crimes may have an impact on the exact form of participation or reparation sought, particularly with respect to sexual and gender-based crimes, in the case of children born out of rape.*

1. Recognition of Victimhood Through the Generations by the International Criminal Court (ICC): Introduction

The lasting impact of unimpeded and rampant international crime has seldom been disputed.[1] Any analysis of the modalities that allow victims, access to the International Criminal Court (ICC), would be incomplete if it overlooked this intergenerational or transgenerational[2] dimension to international crime and the harm that ensues as a result. This chapter aims at focusing on this intergenerational or transgenerational aspect of the victims' regime at the ICC in particular. To do this, this chapter involves an analysis of the possibility of family members of victims participating in court proceedings and seeking reparations either as victims themselves or as successors of deceased victims. As part of this analysis, this chapter

* Kritika Sharma is a Research Fellow at the Max Planck Institute Luxembourg for Procedural Law.

1 See: Regina E Rauxloh, 'Good Intentions and Bad Consequences: The General Assistance Mandate of the Trust Fund for Victims of the ICC' (2021) 34(1) Leiden Journal of International Law 203, 203–204.

2 The terms intergenerational and transgenerational have been used synonymously throughout this chapter.

asks and attempts to answer three questions in particular. First, whether family members of victims can participate in proceedings before the Court under any circumstance, whether as victims themselves or successors of victims, and seek reparations. Second, whether the answer would remain unchanged irrespective of whether the victims are victims of a situation or victims of crimes. Third, whether in the case of victims of crimes, the applicable position both for participation and reparation remains unchanged irrespective of the crime in question. For this last part of the analysis, other than the four categories of international crime under Article 5 of the Rome Statute, this hapter also studies the impact of the different underlying acts, relying on the example of sexual and gender-based crimes in particular. This is with a view to determining whether the rights of family members to participate and seek reparation, if any, remain unaffected by the specific crimes and underlying acts that the (deceased) victims were subjected to.

For the purpose of this chapter, the 'absent' signifies deceased victims as well as the children of victims, who may either have had no agency at the time the crimes were committed or were born as a result of these crimes or after. Thus, the chapter refers to the present generation as victims of the crime, and those present at the time of the commission of these crimes. Future generations refer to the children, grandchildren, and great grandchildren of these victims. For this chapter, there is no limitation in the number of generations that qualify as future generations, other than those applicable *vis-à-vis* the jurisdictional limits of the ICC. This aspect is discussed in detail later in the chapter. Past generations refer to deceased victims, irrespective of whether or not their death was a result of the crimes perpetrated. This includes both sets of deceased victims, those who died after initiating proceedings before the Court and those who died prior thereto.

2. 'Victims' before the International Criminal Court: Eligibility Criteria and Relevant Factors (or Pre-requisites)

In the two decades since its establishment, the ICC has developed a multifarious regime governing the status and rights of victims before the Court. This refers to both, victims of situations before the Court as well as victims of specific cases pursued by the Office of the Prosecutor (OTP), also referred to as 'victims of crimes'. This regime, developed through the Court's albeit fragmented jurisprudence, adds colour to Articles 68 and 75 of the Rome Statute, which cater for victim participation and reparation respectively. *Vis-à-vis* the former, Article 68(3) states that:

> [w]here the personal interests of the victims are affected, the Court shall permit their views and concerns to be presented and considered at stages of the proceedings determined to be appropriate by the Court and in a manner which is not prejudicial to or inconsistent with the rights of the accused and a fair and impartial trial. Such views and concerns may be presented by the legal representatives of the victims where the Court considers it appropriate, in accordance with the Rules of Procedure and Evidence.[3]

Article 68(3) thus acts as the sole legal provision under the Statute on victim participation while Article 75 acts as its equivalent *vis-à-vis* reparation. Article 75(1) states that:

> [t]he Court shall establish principles relating to reparations to, or in respect of, victims, including restitution, compensation and rehabilitation. On this basis, in its decision the Court may, either upon request or on its own motion in exceptional circumstances, determine the scope and extent of any damage, loss and injury to, or in respect of, victims and will state the principles on which it is acting.[4]

Instead of 'principles relating to or in respect of victims', the French text of Article 75 specifically mentions '*principes applicables aux formes de réparation… à accorder aux victimes ou à leurs ayants droit*'. Irrespective of this, while the French text appears clearer in this regard, both versions arguably cater for an action on behalf of a victim.

While on participation, Article 68 talks of personal interests of victims and on reparation, Article 75 envisages reparations to victims and the determination of the 'scope and extent of any damage, loss and injury' to victims, both provisions lack a definition of 'victims'. The Rules of Procedure and Evidence of the ICC assist with this, albeit slightly. Rule 85 defines the term 'victims' for the purpose of both the Statute and the Rules themselves. This definition is twofold. According to this, natural persons qualify as victims if they 'have suffered harm as a result of the commission of any crime within the jurisdiction of the Court'.[5] This places the Court in a position

3 Art 68(3), Rome Statute of the International Criminal Court.
4 Art 75(1), Rome Statute of the International Criminal Court.
5 Rule 85(a), Rules of Procedure and Evidence of the International Criminal Court.

to determine the scope of 'harm' suffered by each of these individuals and whether it is linked to the crimes within the Court's jurisdiction, ie a causal nexus. *Prima facie,* harm does not appear to have been limited here to direct harm.

According to Rule 85, organisations can equally be categorised as victims if they 'have sustained direct harm to any of their property which is dedicated to religion, education, art or science or charitable purposes, and to their historic monuments, hospitals and other places and objects for humanitarian purposes'.[6] Thus, read together, the immediate variance between the provisions for the qualification of individuals as victims and that of organisations, is that the harm sustained by the latter is clearly limited to direct harm. Further yet, the direct harm that organisations suffer as a result of crimes within the Court's jurisdiction must be specifically sustained by property that is dedicated to a specific purpose listed under Rule 85 which appears to effectively exclude organizations dedicated to purely economic purposes, or economic organizations. The application forms for participation as victims usually differ for individuals and organisations.

2.1. Recognition as a Victim and the Resultant Consequences

While the sheer scale and nature of international crime often, if not always, results in mass victimization, official recognition as a victim before the ICC is much narrower in scope.[7] As mentioned earlier, recognition as a victim is limited to the situations and cases being investigated and prosecuted at the Court. Further, such recognition is limited by its objectives. These are to allow victims a voice through participation in the proceedings before the Court and to seek reparation for the harm they suffered. While victims can both participate generally in proceedings and seek reparations, the application process for the two stages is separate irrespective of any overlap in eligibility criteria. The rights that ensue from official recognition as a victim thus vary, based on whether this recognition pertains to participation or reparation. Maintaining the distinction between these two stages, the Court has stated on occasion that, 'victim participation at the ICC does not *per se* involve a request for reparations, but rather only the possibility for victims

6 Rule 85(b), Rules of Procedure and Evidence of the International Criminal Court.
7 See for eg *vis-à-vis* the 'reparation gap', Rauxloh (n 1) 204.

to have their views and concerns heard on matters affecting their *personal* interests.'[8]

While the Statute and the Rules are not particularly verbose on who qualifies as a victim other than the definition that Rule 85 has to offer, the Court has dealt with this on several occasions. The definition and role of victims *vis-à-vis* participation was dealt with by the Trial Chamber in the Court's first case, *The Prosecutor v Lubanga*. This however was not the first decision of the Court concerning the participation of victims. The first decision was instead that of the Pre-Trial Chamber in *The Situation of the Democratic Republic of Congo*, where amongst other issues the Court discussed and distinguished the concepts of victims of the situation and victims of a case.[9] The key question that the Pre-Trial Chamber dealt with in that decision was whether victims could participate in proceedings at the investigation stage.[10]

In 2006, in the case of *The Prosecutor v Lubanga*, the Pre-Trial Chamber determined that individuals could qualify as victims if they fulfilled the four criteria listed under Rule 85.[11] As per the Pre-Trial Chamber's interpretation, these four criteria required that 'the victim must be a natural person; that he/she has suffered harm; that the crime from which the harm resulted must fall within the jurisdiction of the Court and that there must be a causal link between the crime and harm'.[12] In this decision the Pre-Trial Chamber reinforced its previous view that in order to qualify as victims, individuals had to demonstrate a *sufficient* causal link between the harm they suffered and the crimes that 'there are reasonable grounds to believe' that the accused 'bears criminal responsibility and for which the Chamber

8 Megan Hirst, 'Termination of Victim Participation' in Kinga Tibori-Szabó and Megan Hirst (eds), *Victim Participation in International Criminal Justice: Practitioners' Guide* (Springer 2017) 422.

9 *The Situation in the Democratic Republic of the Congo, Decision on the Applications for Participation in the Proceedings of VPRS 1, VPRS 2, VPRS 3, VPRS 4, VPRS 5 and VPRS 6*, Pre-Trial Chamber I, 17 January 2006, ICC-01/04–101-tEN-Corr, 17.

10 ibid., 7.

11 *The Prosecutor v Thomas Lubanga Dyilo, Decision on the Applications for the Participation in the Proceedings of a/0001/06, a/0002/06 in the case of the Prosecutor v Thomas Lubanga Dyilo and of the investigation in the Democratic Republic of the Congo*, Pre-Trial Chamber I, 28 July 2006, ICC-01/04–01/06–228-tEN, 7.

12 ibid.

has issued an arrest warrant'.[13] In the view of the Pre-Trial Chamber, a causal link as per Rule 85

> at the case stage, is substantiated when the victim, and where applicable, close family or dependents, provides sufficient evidence to allow it to be established that the victim has suffered harm directly linked to the crimes contained in the arrest warrant or that the victim has suffered harm whilst intervening to help direct victims of the case or to prevent the latter from becoming victims because of the commission of these crimes.[14]

Essentially, in its decision the Pre-Trial Chamber foresaw two possibilities. First that the applicant demonstrated evidence to establish they suffered harm as a *direct* result or 'directly linked' to the crimes listed under the arrest warrant against the accused.[15] Second and alternatively, that the harm was a result of an intervention to help 'direct victims' of the crimes.[16] Thus, while not in so many words, the Court appears to acknowledge two categories of victims, direct and indirect. The Court relies on both, the 'Declaration of Basic Principles of Justice for Victims of Crime and Abuse of Power', as well as the 'Basic Principles and Guidelines on the Right to a Remedy and Reparation for Victims of Gross Violations of International Human Rights Law and Serious Violations of International Humanitarian Law'.[17] This concept of dividing victims into direct and indirect victims was later developed more explicitly through the Court's jurisprudence as discussed under the section on 'direct versus indirect victims below'.

---

13 *The Prosecutor v Thomas Lubanga Dyilo, Decision on the Applications for the Participation in the Proceedings of a/0001/06, a/0002/06 in the case of the Prosecutor v Thomas Lubanga Dyilo and of the investigation in the Democratic Republic of the Congo,* Pre-Trial Chamber I, 28 July 2006, ICC-01/04–01/06–228-tEN, p.9; relying on its decision in, *The Prosecutor v Thomas Lubanga Dyilo, Decision on the Applications for Participation in the Proceedings Submitted by VPRS 1 to VPRS 6 in the Case the Prosecutor v Thomas Lubanga Dyilo,* Pre-Trial Chamber I, 29 June 2006, ICC-01/04–01/06–172-tEN, 6.

14 ibid., 7–8.

15 ibid.

16 ibid.

17 ibid., citing, Declaration of Basic Principles of Justice for Victims of Crime and Abuse of Power', United Nations General Assembly, 29 November 1985, UN Doc No A/RES/40/34; Basic Principles and Guidelines on the Right to a Remedy and Reparation for Victims of Gross Violations of International Human Rights Law and Serious Violations of International Humanitarian Law', Human Rights Commission, 19 April 2005, Resolution 2005/35.

In the situation of Uganda, Pre-Trial Chamber II determined the criteria for participation of victims slightly differently. The Pre-Trial Chamber stated that an assessment was to be undertaken 'by analysing (i) whether the identity of the applicant as a natural person appears duly established; (ii) whether the events described by each applicant constitute a crime within the jurisdiction of the Court; (iii) whether the applicant claims to have suffered harm; and (iv) most crucially, whether such harm appears to have arisen "as a result" of the event constituting a crime within the jurisdiction of the Court'.[18] This approach appears to have been applied so far by the Court, in its subjective analysis of 'victimhood' for the purpose of court proceedings. Similarly, *in The Prosecutor v Ntaganda*, the Court reiterated these criteria with the slight difference of requiring that there be a 'direct causal nexus between the crime and the harm', and that this be a crime for which the defendant was convicted.[19]

2.2. Family Members as Successors of Deceased Victims

Over the years, the Court has received applications for both participation and reparation by family members of victims.[20] These applications have been in different capacities, either as successors of deceased victims, or as victims themselves. This section engages with the former while the latter position is discussed under the section on 'family members of victims as victims themselves'. In order to address the position of family members as successors of deceased victims and the ensuing rights of this status, this section starts with an analysis of the legal standing of deceased persons as

---

18 *Situation in Uganda, Decision on victims' applications for participation a/0010/06, a/0064/06 to a/0070/06, a/0081/06 to a/0104/06 and a/0111/06 to a/0127/06,* Pre-Trial Chamber II, 10 August 2007, ICC-02/04-101, 10.

19 *The Prosecutor v Bosco Ntaganda, Reparations Order,* Trial Chamber VI, 8 March 2021, ICC-01/04-02/06-2659, 15. In response to the appeal filed against this decision, the Appeals Chamber in its decision reiterated its stance in *The Prosecutor v Lubanga,* on the issue of causation and stated that, '[t]he standard of causation is a "but/for" relationship between the crime and the harm and, moreover, it is required that the crimes for which Mr Lubanga was convicted were the "proximate cause" of the harm for which reparations are sought.' See *The Prosecutor v Bosco* Ntaganda, *Judgment on the appeals against the decision of Trial Chamber VI of 8 March 2021 entitled "Reparations Order"* 12 September 2022, ICC-01/04-02/06-2782, para 650.

20 See for example, Héctor Olásolo and Alejandro Kiss, 'The Role of Victims in Criminal Proceedings before the International Criminal Court' (2010) 81(1-2) Revue internationale de droit pénal 125, 128.

victims before the Court and then deals with two situations where these persons can be represented by successors. First, in situations where the primary victim dies after initiating the original action; and second, where the primary victim is deceased prior to the commencement of the original proceedings.

2.2.1. Legal Standing of Deceased Persons as 'Victims'

Since the Rules of Procedure and Evidence stipulate that natural persons can qualify as victims before the Court, whether or not deceased persons can be categorised as victims has largely been dependent on the Court's interpretation of the term 'natural persons'. The Court has thus far not been uniform in its treatment of this question.[21] However gradually, its jurisprudence on the matter highlights patterns in the Court's treatment of the issue. At the Pre-Trial stage itself the Court has had varied approaches to this question. One approach has been to reject applications on behalf of deceased persons, in light of the fact that they are not 'natural persons' in the view of the Court.[22] Another, has been to consider such applications where the applicants themselves allege harm as a result of the death of a relative. This is analysed in greater detail under the section on family members as victims themselves.

A different Pre-Trial Chamber took a third approach whereby it decided that a victim who died as a result of a crime within the jurisdiction of the Court could be granted the status of a victim if an application to this effect was filed by the deceased victims' successor. In *The Prosecutor v Jean-Pierre Bemba Gombo*, the Pre-Trial Chamber, decided that it was possible for deceased persons to be represented as victims if the following three criteria were fulfilled: 'that (1) the deceased was a natural person, (2) the death of the person appears to have been caused by a crime within the jurisdiction of the Court and (3) a written application on behalf of the

21 ibid., 128–129.

22 *The Situation in Darfur, Corrigendum to Decision on the Applications for Participation in the Proceedings of Applicants a/001/06 to a/0015/06, a/0021/07, a/0023/07 to a/0033/07 and a 0035/07 to a/0038/07,* Pre-Trial Chamber I, 14 December 2007, ICC-02/05-111-Corr, p.18; *The Prosecutor v Germain Katanga and Mathieu Ngudjolo Chui, Decision on the 97 Applications for Participation at the Pre-Trial Stage of the Case,* Pre-Trial Chamber I, 10 June 2008, ICC-01/04-01/07-579, 25.

deceased person has been submitted by his or her successor'.[23] Thus, basing itself on an interpretation which in the view of the Pre-Trial Chamber was 'in conformity with internationally recognized human rights and related jurisprudence', the Chamber found it 'self-evident that a victim does not cease to be a victim because of his or her death'.[24] The Chamber appeared to rely on the jurisprudence of the Inter-American Court of Human Rights and European Court of Human Rights for this.[25] However, perhaps it ought to be noted here that, the application that the Chamber dealt with appeared to have been made both on behalf of the applicant having sustained harm as a result of the death of her father as well as the harm her deceased father had sustained.[26] It seems unclear if the Chamber's decision would have been the same had the applicant not had the status of a victim herself.

Trial Chambers appear to have been similarly divided on the issue and have taken different approaches in this regard. For example, one approach has been to allow deceased victims to be represented in proceedings if they died after submitting their application to be treated as a victim in the proceedings.[27] Most of the Trial Chambers' engagement with this issue has in fact been whilst disposing requests for resumption of action on behalf of deceased victims.

2.2.2. Resumption of Action on Behalf of a Deceased Victim

As mentioned above, a significant portion of the applications submitted to the Court on behalf of deceased victims has been for the resumption of action initiated prior to the death of these victims. Thus, the objective of these applications is to not allow proceedings to abate on the death of the victims who initiated it. Arguably, this has been in line with the Statute's objective to ensure that proceedings remain informed by the views of the victims, and that the views of eligible victims are not silenced in cases where the victims have since died. Such applications do not constitute new

---

23 *The Prosecutor v Jean-Pierre Bemba Gombo, Fourth Decision on Victims' Participation,* Pre-Trial Chamber III, 12 December 2008, ICC-01/05-01/08-320, 15.

24 ibid.

25 ibid., 16, citing IACtHR, *Case of Aloeboetoe et al v Suriname,* Judgment of 10 September 1993, para 54; and IACtHR, *Case of Garrido and Baigorria v Argentina,* Judgment of 27 August 1998, para 50; and *Keenan v The United Kingdom,* Judgment of 3 April 2001, Application no 27229/95, paras 135 et seq.

26 ibid., 15–17.

27 This appears to be based on the Court's interpretation of Rule 89(3). See Olásolo and Kiss (n 20) 130.

applications as victims or amount to initiation of new proceedings before the Court.

The Court has dealt with this issue on several occasions. While the Court now has a relatively consistent approach towards such matters, this was definitely not the case initially, since the Court's earlier jurisprudence on the matter was quite fragmented. Starting with the case of *The Prosecutor v Germain Katanga and Mathieu Ngudjolo Chui,* in which the Trial Chamber allowed a 'close relative' to resume participation on behalf of the deceased victim who had previously been participating in the course of proceedings.[28] However, in this case the Chamber clarified that the successor's participation would be limited to being 'on behalf of the deceased victim and within the limits of the views and concerns expressed by the victim in his or her initial application'.[29] For such resumed participation, the Trial Chamber asked that applicants furnish proof: '(i) of the death of the participating victim (usually by death certificate), (ii) of the family relationship between the deceased and the person wishing to resume the participation, and (iii) that the deceased victim's family have specifically mandated the person to continue the deceased victim's participation before the ICC'.[30] However, this was the subject of an appeal and the Appeals Chamber disagreed with the approach of the Trial Chamber. In the appeal, the Appeals Chamber dealt with the issue of whether deceased victims ought to be removed from the list of participating victims, as well as that of resumption of participation on behalf of deceased victims.[31] The Appeals Chamber noted that while the defence did not '*per se* object to the resumption of participation of deceased victims', the defence did nonetheless, 'object to the "excessive" delay in resuming participation on behalf of certain victims who have long since died'.[32] While the defence in this instance requested that a 'time bar' be placed on applications for the resumption of participation, the Appeals Chamber instead did not deem the 'resumption of a deceased victim's participation by an heir/successor' appropriate.[33]

---

28 Hirst (n 8) 420–421.

29 ibid., 421.

30 ibid.

31 *The Prosecutor v Mathieu Ngudjolo Chui, Decision on the participation of anonymous victims in the appeal and on the maintenance of deceased victims on the list of participating victims,* Appeals Chamber, 23 September 2013, ICC-01/04-02/12-140, 10–13.

32 ibid., 12.

33 ibid., 12–13.

The Chamber based its view on the understanding that '[v]ictims who are deceased can no longer be said to be participating' and that as far as their views and/or concerns that had been expressed by them prior to their death were concerned, these would not be disregarded by the Court. Thus, the Chamber appeared steadfast that, while the views of victims as expressed by them during the proceedings prior to their death would continue to be a part of the court record, allowing successors to resume participating on their behalf was not appropriate. Accordingly, the Appeals Chamber asked the Registrar to remove deceased victims and any representatives thereof from the list of participating victims in this case.[34] However, whilst stating that the Chamber found the resumption of participation on behalf of a deceased victim inappropriate, the Chamber nonetheless cautioned that '[t]his is without prejudice to any determination on the resumption of participation on behalf of deceased victims in relation to reparation proceedings.'[35] Thus, clearly the Court did not seem intent on limiting the right of succession to claims for reparation *per se*.

This question was revisited in the case of *The Prosecutor v Germain Katanga* where family members of deceased victims requested that they succeed these victims and 'continue the action initiated by those victims'.[36] The defence did not oppose the application in question in this instance, as noted by the Trial Chamber[37], which acknowledged that, 'the close relatives of a victim authorised to participate in the proceedings and who is now deceased may decide to continue the action initiated by the victim before the Court, but that they may do so only on behalf of the deceased victim and within the limits of the views and concerns expressed by the victim in his or her initial application'.[38] In addition to the limitation that this caveat places on the resumption of action by successors of deceased victims, the Chamber also required that such persons acting on behalf of a deceased

34 ibid., 13.

35 ibid.

36 *Le procurer c Germain Katanga, Demande de reprise des actions introduites par les victimes a/0170/08 et a/0294/09,* La chambre de première instance II, 13 janvier 2015, ICC-01/04–01/07–3515-Red; *The Prosecutor v Germain Katanga, Decision on the applications for resumption of action submitted by the family members of deceased victims a/0170/08 and a/0294/09,* Trial Chamber II, 11 May 2015, ICC-01/04–01/07–3547-tENG.

37 *The Prosecutor v Germain Katanga, Decision on the applications for resumption of action submitted by the family members of deceased victims a/0170/08 and a/0294/09,* Trial Chamber II, 11 May 2015, ICC-01/04–01/07–3547-tENG, 4.

38 ibid.

victim furnish evidence as to the death of the deceased victim, their relationship to the deceased victim and authorisation or 'appointment by' the deceased victim's family. These three conditions are identical to the Court's previous rulings on the matter as discussed above. Whilst seemingly at odds with the Appeals Chamber's approach in *The Prosecutor v Mathieu Ngudjolo Chui*, the Trial Chamber granted these individuals permission to resume action on behalf of the deceased victims, and also specified that its decision was 'without prejudice to the Chamber's order pursuant to article 75 of the Statute, which will decide as to the award of reparations'.[39]

Then, in 2015, the Trial Chamber in *The Prosecutor v Bosco Ntaganda* dealt with a request by the spouse of a deceased victim who asked the Court for permission 'to resume the action initiated before the Court by her deceased husband'.[40] The defence objected to this application, arguing that the evidence furnished by the applicant fell short of the requirements set out previously by the Court for the resumption of action on behalf of deceased victims. The Chamber granted this request. In granting the request to resume action on behalf of the deceased victim, the Chamber relied on the earlier three requirements specified in *The Prosecutor v Katanga*. In this case in particular, while the applicant furnished proof with respect to the first two criteria, *vis-à-vis* the third, ie appointment by the victim's family, the Court specified that this was 'where the applicant cannot easily be presumed to be entitled to continue the action or represent the family'.[41] The Court unambiguously clarified that 'such a presumption can, for example, be drawn where the applicant is: the spouse of a deceased victim; an only surviving child of a deceased victim, where the child has reached the age of eighteen and the deceased victim was either unmarried or the victim's spouse is already deceased; or the parents of an unmarried deceased victim who either has no children or whose children are below the age of eighteen'.[42] Further, in this case the Trial Chamber attempted at further simplifying and standardising the process for resumption of action by family members on behalf of deceased victims through the use of standardised forms and templates.[43] The Trial Chamber appears to have

39 ibid., 6.

40 *The Prosecutor v Bosco Ntaganda, Fourth decision on victims' participation in trial proceedings*, Trial Chamber VI, 1 September 2015, ICC-01/04–02/06–805, 3.

41 ibid., 5.

42 ibid.

43 ibid., 6–7.

made no reference to the Appeals Chamber's decision in *The Prosecutor v Mathieu Ngudjolo Chui.*

The Court dealt with this issue again in 2016 in *The Prosecutor v Jean-Pierre Bemba Gombo*, where a request was made for the resumption of action by the successors of several deceased victims.[44] The defence requested that the applicants be asked to provide further information *viz* 'the requirements for the participation by family members of deceased victims'.[45] After such further submissions were filed by the legal representative for the victims, the defence then asked the Chamber to reject the request for resumption on the basis that the supporting documents fell short of the requirements for 'continued representation'.[46] The defence cited the Appeals Chamber's decision in *The Prosecutor v Mathieu Ngudjolo Chui* wherein 'the resumption of a deceased victim's action by a successor was not deemed appropriate'.[47] In addition, the defence stated that, in light of the jurisprudence of the Court, applications on behalf of a victim can only be introduced in cases where the victim has consented to this or in a situation where such application is 'on behalf of a child or a disabled person'.[48] Further, the defence argued that any applications made on behalf of deceased ought to be rejected if the applicant did not allege any moral harm that resulted from the death of the deceased person, and that any relatives of deceased persons could only participate if they demonstrated personal harm suffered 'as a result of an incident falling within the parameters of the confirmed charges'.[49] However, it was argued by the legal representative for the victims that the defence argument fused together two distinct procedures; application for resumption of actions by a successor versus that of an application as a new victim.[50] In light of this not being a new application for victim participation, the Chamber did not find the defence's argument of

44 *The Prosecutor v Jean-Pierre Bemba Gombo, Decision on 'Requête relative à la reprise des actions introduites devant la Cour par des victimes décédées',* Trial Chamber III, 24 March 2016, ICC-01/05-01/08-3346, 3.

45 ibid., 3–4.

46 ibid., 5.

47 ibid., 8.

48 ibid.

49 ibid.

50 ibid., 9–10.

relevance.[51] The Trial Chamber in this case, thus followed the jurisprudence of Trial Chambers II and VI in this regard.[52]

Further, and specifically in relation to the defence's reliance on the Appeals Chamber's decision in *The Prosecutor v Mathieu Ngudjolo Chui,* the Trial Chamber stated that that decision pertained to appellate proceedings and was specifically 'without prejudice to any determination on behalf of deceased victims in relation to reparation proceedings'.[53] Thus, the Chamber found that since the present instance involved the 'sentencing and reparations stage', its decision to allow resumption of action applications was not contrary to the Appeals Chamber's decision.[54] Dissimilar to the approach of Trial Chamber VI in *the Prosecutor v Ntaganda* however, the Trial Chamber in this case stated that all three conditions including the third, which involved a mandate by the family of the deceased victim, were necessary to grant a request for a resumption of action.[55] However, the Chamber appeared to be of the view that the assessment of this criterion, of a specific mandate, had to be case based. In this instance, the Chamber found that, contrary to the arguments of the defence, 'the family link or other close connection between the Successor and the Deceased Victim is confirmed by the *jugement d'homologation*' and that '[i]ndeed the *jugement d'homologation* validates the decision of the *Conseil de famille*, composed of family members, nominating a person among its members to act as successor.'[56] This is in conformity with the Court's contextual approach towards the concept of family members.[57]

Notwithstanding its decision in this case, the Chamber asked that future applications for resumption of action include the 'specific family relationship or other close connection between the Successor and the deceased

51 ibid., 13.
52 ibid., 14.
53 ibid., 14–15.
54 ibid.
55 ibid., 15.
56 *The Prosecutor v Jean-Pierre Bemba Gombo, Decision on 'Requête relative à la reprise des actions introduites devant la Cour par des victimes décédées',* Trial Chamber III, 24 March 2016, ICC-01/05-01/08-3346, 19–20.
57 See for example, Luke Moffett and Clara Sandoval, 'Tilting at Windmills: Reparations and the International Criminal Court' (2021) 34(3) Leiden Journal of International Law 749, 755.

person' directly in each of the applications.[58] In this case, the Trial Chamber considered this issue, of resumption of action, in an instance where the deceased person had previously been admitted as a victim in the proceedings. Nevertheless, the Court's analysis does not exclude the possibility of family members acting on behalf of a deceased victim in the absence of such pre-existing participation by the deceased person prior to their death. Lastly, in its decision, the Trial Chamber also clarified that a declaration made prior to their death, 'that they were only seeking reparations for themselves', did not preclude the resumption of such actions by their successors.[59] The Chamber also specified a simplified procedure for future resumption of action requests similar to that recommended by Trial Chamber VI in *The Prosecutor v Bosco Ntaganda.* In connection to this procedure for future requests, the Chamber also made reference to a template for a 'resumption of action' application form which was annexed to the Chamber's decision.[60]

Subsequent to this decision, Trial Chamber II dealt with a similar request in *The Prosecutor v Germain Katanga* in December 2016.[61] In this instance, the legal representative of the victims requested that a successor of a deceased victim be allowed to resume action on behalf of the deceased victim.[62] In its response to the legal representative of victims' filing, the defence did not object to the resumption of action request.[63] The Trial Chamber reinforced its previous decision and recalled 'that close relatives of a victim who was authorised to participate in trial proceedings but who has died in the course of the trial may continue the action which the latter initiated before the Court'.[64] In allowing this request, the Chamber

58 *The Prosecutor v Jean-Pierre Bemba Gombo, Decision on 'Requête relative à la reprise des actions introduites devant la Cour par des victimes décédées',* Trial Chamber III, 24 March 2016, ICC-01/05-01/08-3346, 20.

59 ibid.

60 *The Prosecutor v Jean-Pierre Bemba Gombo, Decision on 'Requête relative à la reprise des actions introduites devant la Cour par des victimes décédées',* Trial Chamber III, 24 March 2016, ICC-01/05-01/08-3346, 28; Annex B, *Template for "Resumption of Action Form" to be prepared by the Registry,* 24 March 2016, ICC-01/05-01/08-3346-AnxB.

61 *The Prosecutor v Germain Katanga, Decision on the Application for Resumption of Action Submitted by a Relative of Deceased Victim a/0265/09 and the Appointment of a New Representative for Victim A/0071/08,* 12 December 2016, ICC-01/04-01/07-3721-tENG.

62 ibid., 3.

63 ibid., 4.

64 ibid.

reinforced its previously established principles for the resumption of action, including that such action be limited to the same confines as the deceased victim's application and that the application had to establish that they fulfilled the three pre-requisites for such applications.[65]

Despite the disjointed nature of the Court's early jurisprudence on the matter, this right of resumption of action appears to have been consistently upheld by various Trial Chambers of the Court ever since, irrespective of the Appeals Chamber's decision in 2013. Objections to such action on behalf of the defence for instance have related predominantly to the time taken for such proceedings. As discussed above, on at least one occasion the defence asked that a time limit be imposed for such action.[66] In *The Prosecutor v Al Mahdi,* The Trial Chamber's reparations order was partly amended by the Appeals Chamber on 8 March 2018.[67] While the issue of deceased victims does not appear to have been addressed through the reparations order and the amended order in this case, it did arise after these decisions. This was in the form of a request by a family member of an applicant for reparations who was then deceased, to be able to 'succeed the victim for purposes of the reparations award'.[68] In this instance it had been argued that the victim's individual request for reparation had already been granted by the Trust Fund for Victims and that accordingly it was requested 'that the designated successor can benefit from the reparations

65 *The Prosecutor v Germain Katanga, Decision on the Application for Resumption of Action Submitted by a Relative of Deceased Victim a/0265/09 and the Appointment of a New Representative for Victim A/0071/08*, 12 December 2016, ICC-01/04–01/07–3721-tENG, 4–5.

66 *The Prosecutor v Mathieu Ngudjolo Chui, Decision on the participation of anonymous victims in the appeal and on the maintenance of deceased victims on the list of participating victims,* Appeals Chamber, 23 September 2013, ICC-01/04–02/12–140, 12.

67 *The Prosecutor v Ahmad Al Faqi Al Mahdi, Reparations Order,* Trial Chamber VIII, 17 August 2017, ICC-01/12–01/15–236; *The Prosecutor v Ahmad Al Faqi Al Mahdi, Judgment on the appeal of the victims against the "Reparations Order",* Appeals Chamber, 8 March 2018, ICC-01/12–01/15–259-Red2.

68 *The Prosecutor v Ahmad Al Faqi Al Mahdi, Decision on the LRV Request for Resumption of Action for Deceased Victim a/20519/19,* Trial Chamber VIII, 21 April 2020, ICC-01/12–01/15–357, p.3 citing *le procurer c Ahmad Al Faqi Al Mahdi, demande de reprise d'action introduite par la victim a/20519/19,* Chambre de première instance VIII, 3 avril 2020, ICC-01/12–01/15–355.

award accorded to the victim'.[69] Accordingly, in support of the request the representative of victims submitted evidence to establish that the victim in question was deceased; that the proposed successor was a 'family relation' to the deceased victim; and that the family of the deceased victim had 'designated the person to resume the action initiated by [the deceased victim]'.[70] Seeing that these conditions appear to have been met, and in light of the fact that the Chamber had granted a similar request in 2017[71] when these three conditions had been met, the Chamber granted the request.[72] In the particular circumstances of this case, the Chamber was of the view that 'the entitlement to the reparations award granted to the victim is not terminated by the victim's death' and that '[t]herefore, if the conditions mentioned above are met, a designated family member is eligible to become beneficiary of the reparations award'.[73]

In its Reparations Order in *The Prosecutor v Bosco Ntaganda,* the Trial Chamber stated unambiguously that, '[i]n the event that a victim who was found eligible for reparations dies before receiving them, the victim's descendants or successors shall be equally entitled to them.'[74] In doing this, the Chamber relied on the Court's previous jurisprudence on the matter. Specifically, the Chamber relied on the decisions of Pre-Trial Chamber III in *The Prosecutor v Jean-Pierre Bemba Gombo* and of Trial Chamber II in *The Prosecutor v Germain Katanga*, as well as the jurisprudence of other courts that these Trial Chambers cited in their decisions. Therefore, the position of the Court thus far with the exception of a few decisions which the Court appears to have consistently deviated from since, appears to be to allow the resumption of action by successors of deceased victims. While this *per se* shows that the Court has appeared willing to allow requests for resumption in all stages of the proceedings whether with a view to

69 *The Prosecutor v Ahmad Al Faqi Al Mahdi, Decision on the LRV Request for Resumption of Action for Deceased Victim a/20519/19,* Trial Chamber VIII, 21 April 2020, ICC-01/12-01/15-357, 3.

70 ibid.

71 *The Prosecutor v Ahmad Al Faqi Al Mahdi, Decision on LRV Request for Resumption of Action for Deceased Victim a/35084/16,* Trial Chamber VIII, 2 June 2017, ICC-01/12-01/15-223, 3–4.

72 *The Prosecutor v Ahmad Al Faqi Al Mahdi, Decision on the LRV Request for Resumption of Action for Deceased Victim a/20519/19,* Trial Chamber VIII, 21 April 2020, ICC-01/12-01/15-357, 3–4.

73 ibid.

74 *The Prosecutor v Bosco Ntaganda, Reparations Order,* Trial Chamber VI, 8 March 2021, ICC-01/04-02/06-2659, 18.

simply participate or seek reparation, the rights ensuing from the grant of such requests are not unfettered. Any participation or action pursuant to resumption requests are confined by the original contours of participation or action granted to the deceased victim. Further, requests for resumption are subject to the three general criteria discussed above. While the Court plays a role in granting such requests, based on the jurisprudence and practice of the Court thus far, such requests would essentially now be dealt with by the Registry similar to other applications, with the Court playing an affirmational role in the grant of these requests.

2.3. Family Members of Victims as Victims Themselves

While resumption of action requests represent a significant portion of the Court's interaction with the requests by family members to participate in proceedings and seek reparations, such requests on behalf of deceased victims are not the only means through which such individuals can participate in court proceedings and seek reparations. The Court's jurisprudence on the subject also caters for family members of victims including family members of deceased victims to participate and seek reparation before the Court as victims themselves. The evolution of this recognition is intertwined with the Court's interpretation of the concept of victimhood. A key aspect of this, is the Court's acknowledgment of the possibility of both direct and indirect victims. In turn, this understanding is based on its acknowledgment that harm suffered by victims can be either direct or indirect as discussed in the following section.

2.3.1. Direct Versus Indirect Victims

Whether an individual qualifies as a direct victim appears to hinge on the harm they suffered and whether it was direct or indirect.[75] The question appeared to have arisen in *The Prosecutor v Thomas Lubanga Dyilo*, where

75 This harm whether direct or indirect must be personal to the victim and can be 'material, physical and psychological'. See *The Prosecutor v Thomas Lubanga Dyilo, Judgment on the appeals against the 'Decision establishing the principles and procedures to be applied to reparations' of 7 August 2012 with AMENDED order for reparations (Annex A), Annex A, Order for Reparations (amended)*, Appeals Chamber, 3 March 2015, ICC-01/04–01/06–3129-AnxA, 3.

the Registry asked the Chamber for advice on around 200 applications submitted by individuals claiming to have suffered harm as a result of the crimes committed by the child soldiers who themselves were direct victims in this case.[76] On this matter, the Appeals Chamber held that what was a pre-requisite was that the alleged harm had to be *personal* to the victim.[77]

The definition of victims unambiguously limits the kind of harm sustained by organisations to direct harm. The absence of a similar limitation indicates the deliberate inclusion of both direct and indirect harm sustained by natural persons. Nonetheless, the Court has, on occasion required the causal link between the harm suffered and crimes committed to be direct, at least in part, with the exception of situations where persons suffer harm whilst assisting 'direct victims'. In *The Prosecutor v Thomas Lubanga Dyilo*, as stated above, Pre-Trial Chamber I required, that to establish that the causal link stipulated under Rule 85, an individual had to 'provide sufficient evidence to establish that that person has suffered harm directly linked to the crimes set out in the arrest warrant' unless such person 'suffered harm by intervening to assist the direct victims in the case'.[78] The person would have to similarly provide sufficient evidence for the latter. Thus, while it has been argued that through this, the Court on occasion overlooked this distinction and limited the scope of 'victimhood' for natural persons, the inclusion of harm suffered whilst intervening to assist direct victims appears to maintain this wider scope. Nonetheless, it comes with the effect of dividing these victims into direct and indirect victims. However, the ambit of indirect victims has since been interpreted in a broader manner, so as to include family members of victims of crimes where such individuals suffer personal harm as a result of their relationship to direct victims of crimes.

The two categories of direct and indirect victims are also referred to at the reparation stage of the proceedings. In *The Prosecutor v Bosco Ntaganda*, the Trial Chamber clearly distinguished successors of deceased victims who died before receiving reparations and 'indirect victims who suffered personal harm'. The latter according to the Trial chamber, were 'entitled to

76 Olásolo and Kiss (n 20) 135, fn 32.

77 ibid., H136.

78 *The Prosecutor v Thomas Lubanga Dyilo, Decision on the Applications for Participation in the Proceedings of a/0001/06, a/0002/06 and a/0003/06 in the case of the Prosecutor v Thomas Lubanga Dyilo and of the investigation in the Democratic Republic of the Congo*, Pre-Trial Chamber I, 28 July 2006, ICC-01/04–01/06–228-tEN, 8–9.

reparations on their own right, regardless of whether they are the rightful successors of the deceased victim'.[79] In this case, the Trial Chamber maintained the distinction between direct and indirect victims.[80] The Court defined direct victims as 'those whose harm is the result of the commission of a crime for which the defendant was convicted'.[81] On the other hand, the Court defined indirect victims as 'those who suffer harm as a result of the harm suffered by the direct victims'.[82] While deliberating whether the Trial Chamber in this decision, erred in what the defence alleged amounted to 'the creation of a new category of indirect victims including persons who did not have a close personal relationship with the victim, who was nevertheless of significant importance in the lives', the Appeals Chamber upheld this distinction of direct and indirect victims.[83] The Appeals Chamber did not find an error on the part of the Trial Chamber in this regard and dismissed this ground of the defence's appeal.[84]

The Court's decision in *Ntaganda* thus, stated unambiguously that, natural persons could be either direct or indirect victims, 'provided they suffered a personal but not necessarily direct harm'.[85] This approach thus falls in line with the steadily growing jurisprudence of the Court that emphasises on the 'personal' nature of harm. In order to qualify for either, as a direct or an indirect victim, the individual thus has to demonstrate a causal nexus between the personal harm suffered, whether direct or indirect.[86] Previously, whilst hearing an appeal against a decision concerning participation, the Appeals Chamber agreed with the Trial Chamber's interpretation that there could be direct as well as indirect victims *viz* the context of Court proceedings. The Appeals Chamber further elaborated its understanding

79 *The Prosecutor v Bosco Ntaganda, Reparations Order,* Trial Chamber VI, 8 March 2021, ICC-01/04-02-2659, 18 citing as an example, Inter-American Court of Human Rights, *Case of Juan Humberto Sánchez v Honduras,* Series C No 102, para 66.

80 ibid., 54.

81 ibid., 16.

82 ibid.

83 *The Prosecutor v Bosco* Ntaganda, *Judgment on the appeals against the decision of Trial Chamber VI of 8 March 2021 entitled "Reparations Order"* 12 September 2022, ICC-01/04-02/06-2782, paras 18, 591. In para 18 of this decision, the Appeals Chamber acknowledges that 'the criteria for classification as a direct or indirect victim are indeed legal criteria that have been determined by the Trial Chamber and in this judgment [...]'.

84 ibid., para 640.

85 ibid.

86 ibid.

of this statement. According to the Appeals Chamber, '[h]arm suffered by one victim as a result of the commission of a crime within the jurisdiction of the Court can give rise to harm suffered by other victims', and that '[t]his is evident for instance, when there is a close personal relationship between the victims such as the relationship between a child soldier and the parents of that child'.[87] Thus, in the view of the Appeals Chamber, '[t]he recruitment of a child soldier may result in personal suffering of both the child concerned and the parents of that child.'[88] The Appeals Chamber stated clearly that it was not therefore necessary for the harm suffered to be direct harm, however, what remained essential was that the harm be personal to the victim.[89]

In doing this, the Chamber relies on the principles set out for this by the Appeals Chamber thus including within the ambit of indirect victims each of the four subcategories recognised in that decision.[90] Therefore, accordingly the Trial Chamber recognised four categories of indirect victims: 'i. the family members of direct victims, ii. anyone who attempted to prevent the commission of one or more of the crimes under consideration, iii. individuals who suffered harm when helping or intervening on behalf of direct victims, and iv. other persons who suffered personal harm as a result of these offences'.[91]

Perhaps, crucial in appreciating the impact of the Court's decision to acknowledge the category of indirect victims, is the fact that both direct and indirect victims are entitled to receive reparations. Thus, by adopting

---

87 *The Prosecutor v Thomas Lubanga Dyilo, Judgement on the appeals of The Prosecutor and The Defence against Trial Chamber I's Decision on Victims' Participation of 18 January 2008,* Appeals Chamber, 11 July 2008, ICC-01/04-01/06-1432, 13–14. In *The Prosecutor v Ntaganda,* the Appeals Chamber clarified that the Court in its jurisprudence 'has referred to the demonstration of a close personal relationship as being *one* way of proving harm', and that therefore 'it has not expressly closed the door to other ways in which this can be done'. See *The Prosecutor v Bosco* Ntaganda, *Judgment on the appeals against the decision of Trial Chamber VI of 8 March 2021 entitled "Reparations Order"* 12 September 2022, ICC-01/04-02/06-2782, para 622.

88 *The Prosecutor v Thomas Lubanga Dyilo*, ibid., 14.

89 ibid., 15.

90 *The Prosecutor v Bosco Ntaganda, Reparations Order,* Trial Chamber VI, 8 March 2021, ICC-01/04-02-2659, 46.

91 ibid., 17; *The Prosecutor v Thomas Lubanga Dyilo, Judgment on the appeals against the 'Decision establishing the principles and procedures to be applied to reparations' of 7 August 2012 with AMENDED order for reparations (Annex A), Annex A, Order for Reparations (amended),* Appeals Chamber, 3 March 2015, ICC-01/04-01/06-3129-AnxA, 2.

this twofold interpretation of victimhood, the Court arguably caters for intergenerational access to reparations for international crime. This is particularly the case in *The Prosecutor v Bosco Ntaganda,* where the Court, as discussed below, recognises 'transgenerational harm' as a specific category of harm. The Trial Chamber in *Ntaganda*, also stated that it was possible for a person to 'qualify simultaneously as a direct and as an indirect victim, on the basis of different crimes for which the defendant was convicted, and therefore may seek reparations for the different harms suffered'.[92] An example of this based on the observations of the Trial Chamber, is children born out of rape. The Chamber stated that 'although children born out of rape are considered direct victims, they may have also suffered transgenerational harm as indirect victims.'[93] The status of children born out of rape and their claim to reparation is specifically dealt with below. However, this decision by the Trial Chamber was appealed by the defence and one group of victims. The Appeals Chamber upheld the Trial Chamber's finding *viz* children born out of rape,[94] while *vis-à-vis* the concept of transgenerational harm, the Appeals Chamber found that the Trial Chamber had erred and remanded the issue back to the Trial Chamber to 'assess and properly reason the matter [...].'[95]

2.3.2. Types of Harm

Whilst establishing its principles on reparations, the Court has defined 'harm' as denoting 'hurt, injury and damage', stating that it need not be 'direct, but it must have been personal to the victim'.[96] According to the Court, such harm might be 'material, physical and psychological'.[97] The Court's decision to acknowledge specifically the multiplicity of harm and the various forms of its manifestation can reasonably be interpreted as

---

92 *The Prosecutor v Bosco Ntaganda, Reparations Order,* Trial Chamber VI, 8 March 2021, ICC-01/04-02-2659, 17.

93 ibid., 66.

94 *The Prosecutor v Bosco* Ntaganda, *Judgment on the appeals against the decision of Trial Chamber VI of 8 March 2021 entitled "Reparations Order"* 12 September 2022, ICC-01/04-02/06-2782, para 642.

95 ibid., para 493.

96 *The Prosecutor v Thomas Lubanga Dyilo, Judgment on the appeals against the 'Decision establishing the principles and procedures to be applied to reparations' of 7 August 2012 with AMENDED order for reparations (Annex A), Annex A, Order for Reparations (amended),* Appeals Chamber, 3 March 2015, ICC-01/04-01/06-3129-AnxA, 3.

97 ibid.

having led it to recognise the different categories of victims mentioned above.

Although the decision is the subject of an appeal, and the matter is to be decided by the Trial Chamber, particularly in view of 'the issue of scientific certainty as to the concept' and 'whether it is appropriate to award reparations at the ICC as well as any applicable evidentiary requirements for this', the Court's jurisprudence now makes an express reference to 'transgenerational harm'. Relying on the Trial Chamber's Decision in *The Prosecutor v Germain Katanga*, the Trial Chamber in *The Prosecutor v Ntaganda* defined transgenerational harm as 'a phenomenon, whereby social violence is passed on from ascendants to descendants with traumatic consequences for the latter'.[98] The Court went on further to state that:

> [i]t is characterised by the existence of an intergenerational cycle of dysfunction that traumatised parents set in motion, handing-down trauma by acting as violent and neglectful caretakers deforming the psyche and impacting the next generation. Traumatised parents, who live in constant and unresolved fear, unconsciously adopt a frightening behaviour. This affects their children's emotional behaviour, attachment, and well-being, increasing the risk that they will suffer post-traumatic stress disorders, mood disorders, and anxiety issues. It is argued that the noxious effects of trauma may be transmitted from one generation to the next, with a potential impact on the structure and mental health of families across generations.[99]

The Trial Chamber in *Ntaganda* also speaks of 'mass victimisation, affecting victims as members of families and entire communities'.[100] Consistent with previous jurisprudence, the Trial Chamber clarified that, such harm, as well as transgenerational harm 'shall be personally suffered by the victim'.[101] The Chamber also stated that children of direct victims might have suffered transgenerational harm, irrespective of the date on which they were born, provided they establish that they suffered such a harm as a result of the crimes that the accused was convicted of.[102] The actual qualification

98 *The Prosecutor v Bosco Ntaganda, Reparations Order,* Trial Chamber VI, 8 March 2021, ICC-01/04-02-2659, 30.

99 ibid.

100 *The Prosecutor v Bosco Ntaganda, Reparations Order,* Trial Chamber VI, 8 March 2021, ICC-01/04-02-2659, 30–31.

101 ibid., 31.

102 ibid., 66.

of individuals as victims of transgenerational harm or other indirect harm remains contingent on a subjective analysis of the personal harm that they have suffered. Moreover, in light of the Appeals Chamber's decision, the Trial Chamber will now have to reassess this category of harm and the standards applicable to the concept. Notwithstanding this, the principles set out by the Court, and its reference to these distinct categories of harm, present an opportunity to broaden access to the Court for such victims of crimes. Further, arguably, such recognition could also have symbolic value. Irrespective of that, practical advantages of this approach would definitely require the consistent application of these principles on a case-to-case basis in combination with coordinated approaches to logistical challenges that might arise. Given the multiple organs that are involved, particularly in the reparation process at the ICC, such coordinated approaches would be crucial for any successful implementation of reparation orders.

3. Differentiated Claims on the Basis of Different Categories of Victims and Different Categories of Crimes?

The previous sections of this Chapter reveal the different avenues for the representation of deceased victims in court proceedings and the rights of family members as successors and victims themselves. Based on this analysis, it is possible for family members to represent deceased victims through resumption of action requests in situations where the victim initiated proceedings prior to their death. However, it is also possible for family members to both, participate in proceedings and seek reparations as victims themselves. In most instances, this is as indirect victims. While initially disjointed, the Court's jurisprudence has now established two distinct sets of criteria for applications by family members for these two avenues. While the analysis based on these two criteria remains subjective, it offers insight as to the broad principles applied to these categories and recognition of victimhood before the Court. This section instead analyses the second question underlying this Chapter, of whether this position remains unaffected irrespective of (i) whether such victims are victims of situations or victims of a crime; and (ii) the category of crimes and underlying acts that the victims were subject to.

3.1. Victims of a Situation Versus Victims of a Crime

Other than the distinction between direct and indirect victims, which, as discussed above do not restrict access to the Court to the latter, the Court also categorises victims into victims of the situation and victims of crimes. This distinction originated whilst the Court considered whether, or not, it was possible for victims to participate in proceedings at the investigation stage.[103] Seeing this as possible and taking into consideration that the law applicable to the Court distinguishes cases and situations from a procedural perspective, the Court chose to maintain this distinction in its recognition of victims. Accordingly, the Court specified '[i]n light of this distinction, the chamber considers that, during the stage of investigation of a situation, the status of victim will be accorded to applicants who seem to meet the definition of victims set out in rule 85 of the Rules of Procedure and Evidence in relation to the situation in question. At the case stage, the status of victim will be accorded only to applicants who seem to meet the definition of victims set out in rule 85 in relation to the relevant case.'[104] Thus, essentially this division represents the procedural division at the Court between a situation and a specific case.

Prima facie this distinction does not appear to give rise to differentiated claims by family members whether as successors or victims themselves. Arguably, this distinction of victims of the situation and victims of crimes is less relevant *vis-à-vis* the issue of continued participation on behalf of deceased victims within proceedings, since in such cases it is the status of the deceased victim, and their original action, which will be continued through resumption proceedings. Similarly, in cases where family members of victims apply as victims themselves, their status as victims of a situation or of a crime will depend on the stage of the proceedings. Their particular status, as a family member of a victim ought not to alter the procedure for their recognition as victims.

103 *Situation in the Democratic Republic of the Congo, Decision on the Applications for Participation in the Proceedings of VPRS 1, VPRS 2, VPRS 3, VPRS 4, VPRS 5 and VPRS 6*, Pre-Trial Chamber I, 17 January 2006, ICC-01/04–101-tEN-Corr.

104 ibid., 17.

3.2. Difference in Legal Status Based on the Category of Crime and Underlying Acts

This section considers the third question that this Chapter set out to address – whether the different categories of crimes and underlying acts victims have been subject to, alter the status of family members as successors of deceased victims or victims themselves. Irrespective of whether family members apply for recognition as successors of deceased victims or as victims themselves, their eligibility as outlined in the sections above, remains unchanged by the category of crime that the individual was a victim of. Thus, the four categories of crimes, genocide, crimes against humanity, war crimes and aggression, do not directly affect the position of family members either as victims or as successors of deceased victims before the Court. The resumption of action applications that the Court has dealt with thus far, have dealt with such requests without allotting any weight or distinct treatment to the particular category of crime. Again, with the caveat that in resumption of action proceedings, any continued proceedings must be limited by the confines of the original action.

Specifically in the context of resumption proceedings, there is nothing in the jurisprudence of the Court to indicate its inclination to treat such requests differently based on specific categories of crimes. Nor is there any evidence to indicate that the Court is inclined to allot such differentiated treatment to requests by family members of victims as victims themselves, on the basis of the four categories of crimes within the Court's jurisdiction. Irrespective of this indifference to the categories of crimes, the same cannot be said for the effect of *underlying acts* to such crimes. First it is important to clarify that similar to the analysis above, a study of the impact of the different categories of underlying acts listed under the Statute on resumption of action requests, reveals that the Court does not treat these requests any differently on this basis. Thus, it is crucial to recognize that these different categories of underlying acts warrant differentiated treatment only in instances where the Court determines the status of family members of victims *as victims themselves*. This is particularly because of the Court's treatment of harm as a result of certain crimes, particularly in the context of sexual and gender-based crimes. This is specifically in view of the Court's categorisation of children born out of rape and sexual slavery as direct victims. This is discussed in further detail in the section below.

3.3. Children Born out of Rape and Sexual Slavery as Victims at the ICC

In its reparations order in *The Prosecutor v Ntaganda,* the Court noted the distinction between direct and indirect victims and deliberately held that children born out of rape and sexual slavery were direct victims of the crime.[105] This was upheld by the Appeals Chamber.[106] Prior to its decision in *Ntaganda,* children born out of rape, as children of direct victims of the crime, would have been eligible to participate in court proceedings and seek reparations as indirect victims. Thus, their position would have been similar to children of victims of other underlying acts such as torture, murder or deportation. However, in light of this decision, should it be followed subsequently, the Court could be required to recognize at least three generations of victims of certain sexual and gender-based crimes, in view of the Court's recognition of children born out of rape as direct victims. This is since pursuant to this decision, family members of children born out of rape *could* qualify as indirect victims.[107] Arguably, in situations where it was urged that grandparents of children born out of rape were primary carers for such children, in light of the jurisprudence of the Court, should these individuals demonstrate the requisite evidence pertaining to harm and its causal nexus to the crimes charged, in theory they could also qualify as victims. The Court clarified however, that children of victims of rape and other sexual and gender-based crimes, other than children born out of rape could still be eligible as indirect victims of the crime, similar to children of victims of other crimes.

It should be noted that both expert reports in *Ntaganda* recommended the inclusion of children born out of rape as victims. In fact, in *Ntaganda,* *vis-à-vis* transgenerational harm and harm suffered by children born out of rape, the Chamber appears to have adopted a stronger approach than the one recommended by the Expert Report on reparations. According to this report, transgenerational harm, which ought to be considered in this case, would include 'physical and psychological harm suffered by children of former child soldiers and physical, psychological and material harm

105 *The Prosecutor v Bosco Ntaganda, Reparations Order,* Trial Chamber VI, 8 March 2021, ICC-01/04–02/06–2659, 46.

106 *The Prosecutor v Bosco* Ntaganda, *Judgment on the appeals against the decision of Trial Chamber VI of 8 March 2021 entitled "Reparations Order"* 12 September 2022, ICC-01/04–02/06–2782, para 642.

107 ibid., para 660.

suffered by children born out of rape'.[108] This approach recommended by the experts would have resulted in children born out of rape being eligible as indirect victims. However, contrary to this, the Trial Chamber was firm in stating that 'in light of the circumstances of the case, children born out of rape and sexual slavery may qualify as direct victims, as the harm they suffered is a direct result of the commission of the crimes of rape and sexual slavery'.[109] The manner in which the Court framed this, highlights that irrespective of the principle that Court emphasised, this assessment remains subjective.

Prior to the Court's decision in *The Prosecutor v Ntaganda*, in *The Prosecutor v Jean-Pierre Bemba Gombo*, where the Court handed out its first conviction for sexual violence and gender-based crimes, later overturned by the Appeals Chamber, an expert report made several recommendations to the Court *vis-à-vis* reparations in the case. In their report, the experts specifically mentioned the different types of harm that children born out of rape suffer. Other than stating that '[f]amily members of eligible victims of rape and murder are also eligible for reparations', the experts specifically stated that, '[t]he Court may consider opening a new filing period for surviving victims of rape and children born of rape'.[110]

4. *Recognising the Past and the Future – Recognition of 'Intergenerational Victimhood': Conclusion*

While the initial jurisprudence of the ICC on the question of whether or not deceased persons could be victims before the Court appeared divided,[111] a substantial volume of litigation on the subject ever since, has allowed greater clarity on the matter. As discussed in this Chapter, the jurisprudence of the Court caters for deceased victims to be represented in Court by their successors in situations where such victims had initiated proceedings

108 *The Prosecutor v Bosco Ntaganda, Experts Report on Reparation, Presented to Trial Chamber VI, International Criminal Court,* 29 October 2020, ICC-01/04–02/06–2623-Anxl-Red2, 49.

109 *The Prosecutor v Bosco Ntaganda, Reparations Order,* Trial Chamber VI, 8 March 2021, ICC-01/04–02/06–2659, 46.

110 *The Prosecutor v Jean-Pierre Bemba Gombo, Expert Report on Reparation, Presented to Trial Chamber III, International Criminal Court,* 20 November 2017, ICC-01/05–01/08–3575-Anx-Corr2-Red, 91.

111 See for example, William A Schabas, *The International Criminal Court: A Commentary on the Rome Statute* (OUP 2016) 1063.

before the Court prior to their death. For this, successors are required to demonstrate proof of death of the deceased victim, proof of familial relationship and in most cases a mandate by the deceased victim's family to act on the deceased victim's behalf. Irrespective of this, any action in this capacity represents a continuation of proceedings and does not amount to the recognition of a new victim within the proceedings. However, the Court has at least on one occasion, hinted at the possibility of new applications being filed on behalf of deceased victims.

While not *on behalf* of deceased victims, children of deceased victims and other family members[112] of deceased victims are entitled to both participate in proceedings and seek reparations at the ICC. According to the Court, they can do this by qualifying as 'indirect victims'. As highlighted through decisions by the Court in the past, the difference between the two categories of victims, direct and indirect, is that while both categories suffer harm, the harm that indirect victims suffer is usually as a result of their relationship to direct victims.[113] This excludes children born out of rape or other sexual and gender-based crimes such as sexual slavery, where the defendant has been convicted of these crimes. Such children qualify as direct victims, which automatically entitles their children the *possibility* of qualifying as indirect victims themselves.

The case of *The Prosecutor v Dominic Ongwen* particularly highlights the issue of claims for victim participation and reparation by or on behalf of children. While the case has not reached the stage of reparations, the crimes that the defendant has been convicted of in this case, including both crimes

---

112 The Court's approach towards the concept of family and family has been informed by contextual interpretations, see for example the Court's decision in *The Prosecutor v Bosco Ntaganda*, where the Court held that 'due regard ought to be given to the applicable social and familial structures in the affected communities'. See *The Prosecutor v Bosco Ntaganda, Reparations Order,* Trial Chamber VI, 8 March 2021, ICC-01/04–02/06–2659, 46.

113 In the appeal against the reparations order in *The Prosecutor v Germain Katanga*, the Appeals Chamber stated that '[o]ne way in which an indirect victim may satisfy these requirements is by demonstrating a 'close personal relationship' with the direct victim, supported by evidence and established on a balance of probabilities. Establishing a close relationship may prove both the harm and that the harm resulted from the crimes committed.' See *The Prosecutor v Germain Katanga, Judgment on the appeals against the order of Trial Chamber II of 24 March 2017 entitled "Order for Reparations pursuant to Article 75 of the Statute",* Appeals Chamber, 8 March 2018, ICC-01/04–01/07–3778-Red, p.51; cited in *The Prosecutor v Bosco Ntaganda, Reparations Order,* Trial Chamber VI, 8 March 2021, ICC-01/04–02/06–2659, 47.

against humanity and war crimes of forced pregnancy,[114] highlight issues pertaining to the status of children as victims before the Court. In this case, the Prosecutor has referred to 'children born in captivity' as a distinct category of victims whilst referring to those born as a result of 'forced marriages'.[115] In light of this, the Court's impending decision on reparations could further develop and clarify the status of children as victims and intergenerational victimhood more generally.

The Court has in its past jurisprudence explicitly recognised the intergenerational aspects of harm. This might explain its analogous acceptance of several generations of victims of international crime. In view of the crimes that the Court was established to prosecute, and those currently being prosecuted, the Court's reference to transgenerational and multifaceted forms of harm represents a welcome, if not warranted, development in its jurisprudence. However, given that the decision concerning the concept of 'transgenerational harm' now rests with the Trial Chamber, the subsisting uncertainty on the matter might thus benefit from further clarification.

However, a clear factor for what remains a subjective analysis of victimhood, is that the harm suffered whether transgenerational or direct, must be 'personal'. The significance of the Court's insistence on *personal* harm being suffered by the victims, together with its conscious decision to include children born out of rape as direct victims should perhaps be viewed as steps in the same direction. It demonstrates a cognisant move by the Court towards recognising such individuals as direct victims and the emphasis that the harm suffered by victims is personal. While the decision to limit the kinds of harm suffered whether direct or indirect to personal harm could have been motivated by a strict or narrow interpretation of the Statute, as a consequence it has, in the least, the symbolic effect of acknowledging that each of these admitted victims have suffered harm personally and that they are not designated victims purely by surviving victims, who have since died (or as the successors of deceased victims).

---

114 *The Prosecutor v Dominic Ongwen, Trial Judgment,* Trial Chamber IX, 4 February 2021, ICC-02/04-01/15-1762-Red, 1052–1053.

115 *The Prosecutor v Dominic Ongwen, Statement of the Prosecutor of the International Criminal Court, Fatou Bensouda, at the opening of Trial in the case against Dominic Ongwen,* 6 December 2016 <https://perma.cc/Q3NG-P3SS>.

3. Exploring the Past and Future Dimensions of the Absent Victim in International Human Rights Adjudication

*Carlos J. Bichet Nicoletti**

Abstract: *This chapter studies the contours of some of the decisions, procedural frameworks, and argumentative strategies used by regional human rights courts to provide some sort of redress in cases involving violations that can have intertemporal dimensions, either because the victims are not present or because the interests of future victims might also be at stake. To do so, it first analyses who can be considered a victim in regional human rights courts, then proceeds to construct the idea of the 'absent victim' as a subject of the decision using insights from green criminology and victimology, and lastly, maps out certain ways in which courts might deal with these issues. It argues that the robust case law of the Inter-American Court of Human Rights regarding guarantees of non-repetition as a form of reparation and the introduction of pilot judgements that deal with structural issues with a forward-looking scope by the European Court of Human Rights, might have the potential for dealing with the interests of absent victims.*

Introduction

Regional human rights courts must adjudicate complex causes involving the violation of fundamental rights recognised in their constitutive documents and rules of procedure. The determination of who can claim to be a victim before these adjudicative bodies is regulated by their rules on standing, admissibility, and jurisdiction. However, certain cases speak to constituencies beyond the confines of the courtroom. Cases involving grave violations of human rights (eg enforced disappearances), environmental and collective property issues, climate change litigation and its human rights impacts, and situations of systematic injustice which are attached to intergenerational harm and trauma, have several implications for victims beyond those that are formally and exclusively recognised as such due to procedural constraints and limitations.

Some victims of injustices and human rights violations are simply not present in cases that are formally adjudicated by these courts. This could be, for instance, because the case deals with enforced disappearances, which as a crime entails in its substance 'the projection of human suffering

* Dr. Carlos J. Bichet Nicoletti is Assistant Professor, Universidad de Panamá, Facultad de Derecho y Ciencias Políticas.

in time',[1] or simply because the scope of victimisation in cases dealing with environmental damage necessarily affects future generations. In the former set of cases, the victims are not present in the courtroom but through forms of legal and formal representation; in the latter set of cases, the scope of the future repercussions of harmful actions will continue affecting people through generations, sometimes in unforeseen ways. Nonetheless, the experiences, trauma, and implications of these 'absent victims' – past and future – are, and should be, relevant contextual elements of the decisions taken by human rights courts.

This chapter explores these past and present dimensions of absent victimhood in regional human rights courts. It studies the contours of some of the decisions, procedural frameworks, and argumentative strategies used by these courts to provide some sort of redress in cases involving violations that can have intertemporal dimensions, either because the victims are not present or because the interests of future victims might also be at stake. To do so, the first section analyses who can be considered a victim in regional human rights courts, then proceeds to construct the idea of the 'absent victim' as a subject of the decision, and lastly, maps out certain ways in which courts might deal with these issues. In particular, the section argues that the robust case law of the Inter-American Court of Human Rights (IACtHR) regarding guarantees of non-repetition as a form of reparation and the introduction of pilot judgements that deal with structural issues with a forward-looking scope by the European Court of Human Rights (ECtHR), might have the potential for dealing with the interests of absent victims, particularly in the cases of intergenerational justice. The determination *per se* of what those interests of the absent victim may constitute and how current judges would ascertain them is not considered in this contribution. Nonetheless, it is worth highlighting that in the realm of law and emotions, judicial empathy[2] plays an important role in the determination of those interests. As noted by Hoffamn: [t]he challenge to the empathic imagination is to be moved by thinking or reading about the consequences of the litigation for absent – often completely unknown or even unborn – others

1 Antônio Augusto Cançado Trindade, 'Enforced Disappearances of Persons as a Violation of Jus Cogens: The Contribution of the Jurisprudence of the Inter-American Court of Human Rights' (2012) Nordic Journal of International Law 507, 521.

2 See: Richard Posner, 'Emotion vs Emotionalism in Law' in Susan Bandes (ed), *The Passions of Law* (New York University Press 1999).

who will be affected by your decision.'[3] Thus, any available procedural pathway for the representation of the absent in the legal process will require not only being informed by insights of green victimology and its particular concern for intergenerational justice, but also a degree of empathy from judges and decision makers in determining the protection of their interests.

As outlined above, the aim of this chapter is narrow and limited to the exploration of certain procedural avenues by which the interests of absent victims can be represented in international proceedings. There might certainly be other procedural devices worth exploring, but here special reference is made to guarantees of non-repetition and pilot judgements. Moreover, against the backdrop of the interdisciplinary endeavour undertaken in this volume, diverging understandings of what constitutes a generation, the 'absent', and even intergenerational justice can indeed present a challenge for construing a common and interchangeable vernacular amongst contributions, more so if they are informed by heterogeneous disciplinary epistemologies. What is expressed in this chapter is a much humbler endeavour; it recognizes the formal limits of the law in ascribing international responsibility in the adjudication of human rights claims. Within these formal limits, in certain cases and through certain procedural devices, direct and indirect redress can be found for absent victims. These can be past and present, belonging to the same or different generations, and in their quest for redress, there might be an impact on how we can understand the adjudication of intergenerational claims, indistinctive of what that might precisely mean for different disciplines and people.

1. Victims in International Human Rights Law

The concept of victim is impregnated with ambiguity, vagueness, semantic polyvalence and cultural polysemy.[4] The definition of victim is related, amongst other things, to theoretical conceptions developed by victimology, criminal law, criminology, and international human rights law; and involves discussions about who are the victimisers or perpetrators, the causes of victimisation, the legal and social definition of victims, and the

3 Martin L Hoffman, 'Empathy, Justice and Law' in Amy Coplan and Peter Goldie (eds), *Empathy: Philosophical and Psychological Perspectives* (OUP 2011) 252.

4 Alán Arias Marín, 'Teoría Crítica y Derechos Humanos: Hacia un Concepto Crítico de Víctima' (2012) Nómadas. Revista Crítica de Ciencias Sociales y Jurídicas 18.

characteristics that surround them. In this regard, Ezzat Fattah argues that in each society, there is constant construction and deconstruction of the concept of victim depending on various social attitudes.[5] For the purposes of our analysis in the present chapter, the same conceptual variables apply, in addition to the jurisdictional and standing requirements of each international court or tribunal.

In the field of international human rights law, the concept of victim is based on the existence of an injured party. Specifically, an individual or groups of individuals who have suffered a detriment to their rights. This concept is based on a damage to the physical, psychological and/or moral integrity, which may or may not have a patrimonial content, going from the direct victim to his or her family, relatives, and society. Under this premise, the victim is part of a social and family network which is affected because of the violations committed against the direct victim. For example, the family members and relatives of those who have been victims of disappearance, torture, homicide, or extrajudicial executions; although they are not the ones who personally suffer such events, they are affected not only by the pain, anguish and anxiety generated by these situations but also suffer economic losses.

At the universal level, a definition of victim can be found in the Declaration of Basic Principles of Justice for Victims of Crime and Abuse of Power. The Declaration, adopted by the UN General Assembly in 1985, states that:

1. "Victims" means persons who, individually or collectively, have suffered harm, including physical or mental injury, emotional suffering, economic loss or substantial impairment of their fundamental rights, through acts or omissions that are in violation of criminal laws operative within Member States, including those laws proscribing criminal abuse of power.
2. A person may be considered a victim, under this Declaration, regardless of whether the perpetrator is identified, apprehended, prosecuted or convicted and regardless of the familial relationship between the perpetrator and the victim. The term "victim" also includes, where appropriate, the immediate family or dependents of the direct victim.[6]

---

5 Ezzat Fattah, 'The Evolution of a Young, Promising Discipline. Sixty Years of Victimology, a Retrospective and Prospective Look' in Shlomo Giora Shoham, Paul Kneppet and Martin Kett (eds), *International Handbook of Victimology* (Routledge 2010) 49.

6 UNGA Res 40/34 (29 November 1985).

Arguably, the Declaration marks a starting point in international human rights law insofar as, for the first time, the UN organ of the hierarchy of the General Assembly dealt with victims as an independent category through a soft law instrument, defining the concept and establishing rights such as access to justice and fair treatment, and assistance. Subsequently, the 2005 UN Basic Principles and Guidelines on the Right to a Remedy and Reparations for Victims of Gross Violations of International Human Rights Law and Serious Violations of International Humanitarian Law further expanded the concept of victim to institute an accountability framework that included access to justice, truth, reparation, and guarantees of non-repetition as an obligation for states and a right for victims.[7]

Moreover, beyond the need for a general definition of victim, a more functional approach is the recognition that there are different descriptive categories derived from a plurality of international instruments referring to different groups of persons protected by international human rights law.[8] In this context, Fernández de Casadevante, recognizing that there is no single definition of victim in international law, states that:

> (...) the international norms actually related to victims fall into several categories: victims of crime, victims of abuse of power, victims of gross violations of international human rights law, victims of serious violations of international humanitarian law, victims of enforced disappearance, victims of violations of international criminal law, victims of trafficking and victims of terrorism.[9]

Thus, although a general concept of victim cannot be derived from international human rights law, it must be analyzed within the piecemeal approach provided by an array of international instruments that establish specific recognition for different groups of persons as victims and from which specific rights and duties derive, depending on a case-by-case basis. This general or specific recognition will have repercussions on procedural issues, particularly those related to *jus standi* and the possibility of seeking redress and remedies for human rights violations.

7 UNGA Res 60/147 (16 December 2005).

8 That is, women, children and adolescents, migrants, persons deprived of liberty, elderly persons, forcibly disappeared persons, persons with disabilities.

9 Carlos Fernández de Casadevante Romani, *International Law of Victims* (Springer 2012) 39.

1.1. Victims in the Inter-American System of Human Rights

Neither the American Convention of Human Rights nor the Rules of Procedure of the Inter-American Commission of Human Rights provide a definition of victim. Regarding *jus standi,* the Convention only specifies under Article 44 that 'any person or group of persons, or any nongovernmental entity legally recognized in one or more member States of the Organization, may lodge petitions with the Commission'. Article 46.1(d) further States that an admissibility requirement is that 'the petition contains the name, nationality, profession, domicile and signature of the persons or legal representatives that are lodging the petition.'

It is in Article 2 of the Rules of Procedure of the IACtHR that we find a characterisation of the term victim within the Inter-American System of Human Rights. Said provision states that 'the term victim refers to a person whose rights have been violated, according to a judgement emitted by the Court.'[10]

Moreover, according to Article 35.2. of the Court's Rules of Procedure: 'When it has not been possible to identify one or more of the alleged victims who figure in the facts of the case because it concerns massive or collective violations, the Tribunal shall decide whether to consider those individuals as victims.'[11] This provision has opened the possibility for the subsequent inclusion of other victims in the proceedings when the lack of identification can be justified. In a sense, these identifiable potential victims can be referred to as future victims, given the fact that they are only going to be individualized at a future stage of the proceedings, but the impact the case is going to have on their rights can be reasonably foreseen. Furthermore, these provisions have also helped the Court go beyond the limitation of the notion of 'injured party' that is originally found in Article 63.1 of the American Convention on Human Rights for the purpose of awarding reparations.[12]

---

10 Rules of Procedure of the Inter-American Court of Human Rights, approved by the Court during its LXXXV Regular Period of Sessions from November 16 to 28, 2009, available at <https://perma.cc/5Q93-62CQ>.

11 ibid.

12 For a recount on the evolution of how the IACtHR has dealt with interpreting the term 'injured party' *vis-à-vis* the concept of 'victims', see: Clara Sandoval Villalba, 'The Concepts of "Injured Party and "Victims" of Gross Human Rights Violations in the Jurisprudence of the Inter-American Court of Human Rights' in Carla Ferstman,

Based on this, the Inter-American Court has extended the scope for the determination of victims to those that are unknown but potentially identifiable. In *Plan de Sanchez Massacre v Guatemala,* the Court recognised as victims those initially mentioned by the Commission 'and those that may subsequently be identified since the complexities and difficulties faced in identifying them lead to the presumption that there may be victims yet to be identified.'[13] Later, this possibility was further interpreted to include members of entire communities in the case of reparations orders that included collective measures. Particularly, in the *Case of the Saramaka People v Suriname*, the Court categorically stated that:

> (...) given the size and geographic diversity of the Saramaka people, and particularly the collective nature of reparations to be ordered in the present case, the Court does not find it necessary in the instant case to individually name the members of the Saramaka people in order to recognize them as the injured party. Nevertheless, the Court observes that the members of the Saramaka people are identifiable in accordance with Saramaka customary law (...)[14]

In the words of Sandoval-Villalba, the use of the term 'injured party', as shown in the above-cited quote from the Saramaka case, can be considered 'an umbrella term that covers: victims (direct and indirect); potential victims; the next of kin of the victims as successors/heirs; dependents; and members of communities.'[15] This open-ended characterisation of the term victim for the purposes of reparations has led to general descriptions of the Court as victim-centered or victim-oriented in specialised scholarship.[16]

1.2. Victims in the European System of Human Rights

In comparison with other regional human rights systems which can be considered as having more lax rules regarding the standing of the petitioners,

Mariana Goetz and Alan Stephens (eds), *Reparations for Victims of Genocide, War Crimes and Crimes Against Humanity* (Martinus Nijhoff 2009).

13 *Case of Plan de Sanchez Massacre v. Guatemala*, Judgement on Merits, 29 April 2004, para. 47.

14 *Case of the Saramaka People v Suriname*, (2007) IACHR Series C No 172, para. 188.

15 Sandoval Villalba (n 12) 280.

16 See: Thomas Antkowiak, 'An Emerging Mandate for International Courts: Victim-Centered Remedies and Restorative Justice' (2011) 47 Stanford Journal of International Law 279.

the determination of who can claim to be a victim is of paramount importance in the European system of Human Rights. Article 34 of the European Convention on Human Rights (ECHR) states that: '[t]he Court may receive applications from any person, non-governmental organization or group of individuals claiming to be the victim of a violation (...) of the rights set forth in the Convention' or its Protocols by one of the State parties. This presupposes that a requirement for admissibility is directly linked to the applicant claiming to be affected or harmed by the circumstances of the case. The so-called 'victim requirement' is, thus, one of the pre-conditions for admissibility in the ECHR system in the case of individual applications.

In this context, it is important to point out that the victim requirement should be interpreted in accordance with the circumstances of the case. The Court has warned that an 'excessively formalistic, interpretation of that concept [the term 'victim'] would make protection of the rights guaranteed by the Convention ineffectual and illusory,'[17] and that the term victim in Article 34 must be 'interpreted in an evolutive manner in the light of conditions in contemporary society.'[18]

The ECtHR has recognised different categories of victims, mainly direct, indirect, and potential victims.[19] Direct victims are those where the applicant can show that he or she was 'directly affected' by the measure or order issued by the State party and which constitutes the alleged violation.[20] Usually, one of the benchmarks used by the Court to assess whether the applicant is a direct victim is his or her participation in the domestic proceedings. Nonetheless, this criterion is not of rigid application, and there are cases where the Court, due to specific circumstances, has recognised victims that have not participated in domestic proceedings as direct victims for the purpose of Article 34.[21]

---

17 *Gorraiz Lizarraga and Others v Spain* App no. 62543/00 (ECtHR, 27 April 2004) para. 38.

18 ibid.

19 See: ECHR, Practical Guide on Admissibility Criteria, updated 1 August 2021 <https://www.echr.coe.int/documents/admissibility_guide_eng.pdf> accessed 20 October 2021; Vassilisa Tzevelekos, 'Standing: European Court of Human Rights (ECtHR)' in Hélène Ruiz Fabri (ed), *Max Planck Encyclopedia of International Procedural Law* (OUP 2019).

20 See: *Tanase v Moldova* App no. 7/08 (ECtHR, 27 April 2010) para. 104; *Burden v United Kingdom* App no. 13378/07 (ECtHR, 29 April 2008) para. 33; *Lambert and Others v France* App no. 46043/14 (ECtHR, 5 June 2015) para. 89.

21 See: *Beizaras and Levickas v Lithuania* App no. 41288/15 (ECtHR, 14 January 2020) paras 78–81.

In terms of indirect victims, the Strasbourg Court has allowed the next-of-kin to present applications, predominantly in cases involving death or disappearance under Article 2 of the European Convention. These next-of-kin have included close family members, such as parents[22] of a dead or disappeared person, children,[23] siblings,[24] married and unmarried partners,[25] and even nephews.[26]

The ECtHR has also stated that Article 34 of the Convention does not allow for an *actio popularis* or *in abstracto* complaints.[27] Nonetheless, the Court has recognised that an applicant may be considered a potential victim in light of certain circumstances. For instance, in a case where specific legislation would criminalise homosexual acts, the mere existence of the law was considered as putting the applicant in a situation of potential affectation;[28] or in the case of an applicant who could not assert whether potentially violating legislation had been applied to him due to the secret character of the measures,[29] and even in cases where legislation permitting secret surveillance measures can affect an applicant who has no accessible remedy to challenge it.[30] In these kinds of cases, the prospective victim must present 'reasonable and convincing evidence of the potential violation; mere suspicion or conjecture is insufficient.'[31]

In contrast with the Inter-American System, the fact that the qualification of a victim is decided within the context of issues of admissibility leaves

22 See: *Ramsahai and Others v the Netherlands* App no. 52391/99 (ECtHR, 15 May 2007).

23 See: *McKerr v United Kingdom* App no. 28883/95 (ECtHR, 4 May 2001).

24 See: *Andronicu and Constantinou v Cyprus* App no. 25052/94 (ECtHR, 9 October 1997).

25 For married partners see: *McCann v United Kingdom* App no. 18984/91 (ECtHR, 27 September 1995). For unmarried partners see: *Velikova v Bulgaria* App no. 41488/98 (ECtHR, 18 May 2000).

26 See: *Abdullah Yasa and Others v Turkey* App no. 44827/08 (ECtHR, 16 July 2013).

27 See: *Centre for Legal Resources on behalf of Valentin Campeanu v Romania* App no. 47848/08 (ECtHR, 14 July 2014) para. 101.

28 *Dudgeon v United Kingdom* App no. 7525/76 (ECtHR, 22 October 1981) para. 41.

29 *Klass and Others v Germany* App no. 5029/71 (ECtHR, 6 September 1978) paras 33–34.

30 See: *Roman Zakharov v Russia* App no. 47143/06 (ECtHR 4 December 2015) paras 173–79; *Centrum för rättvisa v Sweden* App no. 35252/08 (ECtHR, 25 May 2021) paras 166–77.

31 *Centre for Legal Resources on behalf of Valentin Campeanu v Romania*, para. 101; *Tauira and 18 Others v France*, Commission decision of 4 December 1995, DR 83-B, 130; *Senator Lines GmbH v Ausria, Belgium, Denmark and others*, Grand Chamber, Decision of Admissibility, 10 March 2004.

little to discuss regarding the scope of who can be considered a victim at the stage of reparations.

1.3. Victims in the African System of Human Rights

Neither the African Charter of Human and Peoples' Rights, nor the Protocol for the Establishment of the Court, or even the Rules of Procedure, make any specific reference to victims. However, regarding the conditions for admissibility of a case, it is important to point out that by virtue of Article 6.2 of the Protocol for the Establishment of the African Court of Human and Peoples' Rights (ACtHPR), both the African Commission and the Court share the same criteria, found in Article 56 of the Charter. The latter Article simply stipulates that the petition should indicate the name of the authors, even if they request to maintain anonymity further in the proceedings. Applicant and victim should not be understood as necessarily the same person or persons, as it has been recognised that the African System has an open system of *actio popularis* that presupposes that anyone could action before the system and set it in motion.

On this last point, the African Commission has stated in the *Case of Article 19 v Eritrea* that:

> In the consideration of communications, the African Commission has adopted an actio popularis approach where the author of a communication need not know or have any relationship with the victim. This is to enable poor victims of human rights violations on the continent to receive assistance from NGOs and individuals far removed from their locality. All the author needs to do is to comply with the requirements of Article 56.[32]

Regarding access to the African Court, individuals can have indirect access through the Commission, or, if the case concerns a State Party to the Protocol that has made a declaration under its Article 34.6, individuals or NGOs with Observer Status before the Commission, irrespective of whether they are the injured parties or victims, can petition the Court directly.

In an African Court document entitled 'Fact Sheet on Filing Reparations Claims', the Court has implied recognition for direct and indirect victims by stating that the term victim can encompass:

32 *Article 19 v State of Eritrea*, Communication No 275/2003, 30 May 2007, para. 65.

> Person(s) who individually or collectively suffered harm, including physical or mental injury, emotional suffering, economic loss or impairment of their fundamental rights, through acts or omissions that constitute violations of international human rights law. Where appropriate, and in accordance with domestic law, the term "victim" also includes the immediate family or dependents of the direct victim and persons who have suffered harm in intervening to assist victims in distress or to prevent victimization.[33]

Furthermore, victims can also be entire communities, peoples' or groups with a common identity,[34] a staple of the African System for the protection of human rights, which places a strong emphasis on the collective scope of action.

1.4. The 'Absent Victim' and Human Rights Adjudication

When adjudicating complex cases, international human rights courts deal with scopes of victimhood that are not necessarily present at the moment that a particular claim is litigated. These claims can be either backward-looking in the sense that they focus on past victims or can be forward-looking in the sense that the actions caused in the scope of the claim might affect potential victims in the future. At these crossroads, issues involving claims of intergenerational justice (i.e. what is owed to past and future generations) overlap with the representation of the interests of the absent victims in judicial proceedings (past and potential). This, in turn, intersects with procedural institutions such as standing, jurisdiction, and the right to a remedy in the form of reparations, as we have seen from the brief analysis above regarding how human rights courts tackle these issues in the scope of their particular legal frameworks. Combined, all these aspects have an important effect on the narrative construction of who – or in whose name- can claim to be a victim of human rights violations and be recognised as such. For instance, groups of victims might coalesce in the identity of shared trauma and might remain united through their claims of redress or the scope of the decisions and judgements.

33 Fact Sheet on Filing Reparation Claims, Adopted during the Fifty-Third Ordinary Session of the African Court on Human and Peoples' Rights, 10 June – 5 July 2019, Arusha, Tanzania available at <https://perma.cc/JZ3S-UHQ8>.

34 ibid.

Decisions by international human rights courts more often than not construct narratives that, in some cases, impact the way we see victims. These narratives emerge from the judicial discourse that seeks to generate identity ties that in turn forge a chain of personal, social and cultural meanings. Thus, these narratives influence the judicial decision-making process and vice versa. Mirta Antonelli has described the process of this narrative construction as:

> (...) the specifically temporal dimension through which social actors assign meaning to life, individual and collective, linking-suturing time as narrative: memories (symbolic approximations of the past), future (imaginary projections of the future), both from the present as a point of articulation of a particular historical consciousness.[35]

Furthermore, and adding an intertemporal layer to the narrative legal process, as pointed out by Ezzat Fattah: 'the most important right of crime victims is the right to be protected against future victimization, yet this is a social, not a legal right, and it rarely, if ever, figures on the victims' rights agenda'[36]. Thus, international human rights law and victims' movements might be well served by different disciplines and understandings in analysing and assessing forms of victimhood. For instance, the field of environmental victimology includes future generations as victims of environmental degradation. Christopher Williams, one of the first scholars to explain environmental victimisation, defines environmental victims as:

> Those of past, present or future generations who are injured as a consequence of change to the chemical, physical, microbiological, or

---

35 Mirta Alejandra Antonelli, 'Mineria transnacional y dispositivos de intervención en la cultura: La gestión del paradigma hegemónico de la "minería responsable y desarrollo sostenible"' in Maristella Svampa and Mirta Alejandra Antonelli (eds), *Minería transnacional, narrativas del desarrollo y resistencias sociales* (Editoral Biblos 2009) 72. [Translation by the author from the original Spanish: '(...) la dimensión específicamente temporal mediante la cual los actores sociales le asignan sentido a la vida, individual y colectiva, eslabonando-suturando el tiempo como narración: memorias (aproximaciones simbólicas del pasado), porvenir (proyecciones imaginarias de futuro), ambas desde el presente como punto de articulación de una particular conciencia histórica.']

36 Fattah (n 5) 69.

> psychosocial environment, brought about by deliberate or reckless individual or collective human act or act of omission.[37]

As outlined above, certain forms of victimization are, in turn, related to an intergenerational component. For example, environmental degradation caused by toxic substances has serious intertemporal consequences. It not only jeopardizes the current health of the environment but has devastating consequences for future generations.[38] As Williams cautions in this context, any community comprises more than one generation; therefore, rights and responsibilities must be the same for all generations.[39] Thus clearly linking intergenerational justice with the protracted forms of harm found in environmental damage.

Although in these cases, it is not easy to identify future generations as current victims, it is clear that given the profound impact on the current environment, the same environmental conditions that exist today will not be available in the coming years.[40] In the words of Richard Hiskes:

> The interconnection of modern life is never more apparent nor better understood than in the context of environmental degradation and the need for preservation. Our natural environment is the singular physical manifestation of our connectedness both with our contemporaries and also with those who in their own future will inherit our space, our land, our air, water, and soil.[41]

This indicates that the damage related to toxic industries goes beyond the orbit of the collective, actual and present, to the collective, potential, and future. Consequently, those who are currently losing control over the

---

37 Christopher Williams, 'Environmental Victimization and Violence' (1996) 1(3) Aggression and Violent Behavior 191, 194.

38 UN Human Rights Council, Thirty-ninth session,10–28 September 2018, Report of the Special Rapporteur on the implications for human rights of the environmentally sound management and disposal of hazardous substances and wastes (3 August 2018) UN Doc A/HRC/39/48, para. 8.

39 Williams (n 37) 194.

40 See: Eileen Skinnider, *Victims of Environmental Crime – Mapping the Issues* (The International Centre for Criminal Law Reform and Criminal Justice Policy 2011) 2 <https://perma.cc/W79N-RB9Y>; Antony Pemberton, 'Environmental Victims and Criminal Justice: Proceed with Caution' in Toine Spapens, Rob White and Marieke Kluin (eds), *Environmental Crime and its Victims: Perspectives within Green Criminology* (Routledge 2014) 69.

41 Richard P Hiskes, *The Human Right to a Green Future: Environmental Rights and Intergenerational Justice* (CUP 2008) 66.

natural resources that have belonged to them for centuries affect the legitimate inheritance of future generations.[42] Ultimately, future generations suffer damage inasmuch as they will not be able to benefit from natural resources in the way that present generations have.[43] Of course this does not necessarily entail a right to access resources in the same capacity for future generations, the resources might not be available on the first place or what can be understood to be a valuable resource might change depending on new technologies and notions of productivity. As espoused by the International Law Association's 'New Delhi Declaration': 'benefit' in this context is to be understood in its broadest meaning as including, inter alia, economic, environmental, social and intrinsic benefit.'[44]

Moreover, the environmental damage can be direct or indirect, individual or collective, and occur in the short, medium or long term.[45] For instance, when the damage takes years to happen,[46] and the vast majority of people affected are not always aware of their own victimisation,[47] it could take years to identify the health and environmental effects.[48] The damage can be diffuse and difficult to detect.[49] Thus, as Skinnider outlines, '[f]uture generations are thus an important category of potential victims of environmental crimes'[50], in general and one could add, a potential subset of victims of human rights violations requiring domestic or international redress.

---

42 Rob White, *Transnational Environmental Crime: Toward and Eco-Global Criminology* (Routledge 2011) 113.

43 Skinnider (n 40) 35–39.

44 Article 2.2, *New Delhi Declaration on Principles of International Law Relating to Sustainable Development*, International Law Association, 70th Conference 2–6 April 2002.

45 ibid., 34; White (n 42) 116.

46 Lorenzo Natali, 'A Critical Gaze on Environmental Victimization' in Ragnhild A Sollund (ed), *Green Harms and Crimes: Criminological Perspectives* (Palgrave Macmillan 2015) 68.

47 Matthew Hall, *Victims of Environmental Harm: Rights, Recognition and Redress under National and International Law* (Routledge 2013) 26; Matthew Hall and Gema Varona, 'La Victimología Verde como Especia de Encuentro para. Repensar la Otredad más allá de la Posesión' (2018) 7 Revista de Victimología/Journal of Victimology 108, 112; Report of the Special Rapporteur on the implications for human rights of the environmentally sound management and disposal of hazardous substances and wastes, 7 October 2019, UN Doc A/74/480, para. 44; Skinnider (n 40) 25.

48 Pemberton (n 40) 68.

49 Skinnider (n 40) 2; Matthew Hall, 'Exploring the Cultural Dimensions of Environmental Victimization' (2017) 3 Palgrave Communications 1, 2; Rob White, *Crimes Against Nature: Environmental Criminology and Ecological Justice* (Willan Publishing 2008) 197.

50 Skinnider (n 40) 39.

At the same time, public interest environmental litigation has been used to establish future generations as victims of environmental crime[51] with the aim to ensure that they would be able to enjoy a high quality of the environment and natural resources.[52]

In the same way, as the legal narrative might contribute to the construction of the victimised collective and the self-appraisal of the individual as part of it, those who are left out of the group because of procedural or substantive constraints might constitute in and of themselves another group of direct, indirect, or potential victims. This is how the absent victim is construed beyond the confines of the courtroom. Fields such as victimology, green criminology, or socio-legal studies are way ahead of international human rights law in the identification of these issues and in recognition of how legal interventions affect these victims in an intertemporal dimension. In this sense, the interdisciplinary lens is warranted to adapt and reframe international human rights law to the challenges that the representation of absent generations (past and future) might pose in situations of environmental justice, climate change litigation, or gross and systematic human rights violations. Whilst the next sections focus on future absent victims, the same is applicable to past victims. As we have seen from the above discussion on victimhood in different systems of protection, the absent victim, no longer present because of death or other circumstances, can be vicariously represented by the next-of-kin. Nonetheless, in cases involving mass violations, redress mechanisms that affect society as a whole can have an impact beyond the parties recognised as such in decisions of human rights courts.

2. Redress for Absent Victims in Human Rights Courts

For lack of a better term, this section is called 'redress for absent victims.' At face value, this would seem to imply some sort of logical flow that presupposes a first step of determination of what an absent victim is and then a next logical step that would entail a tribunal or judge that actively interprets the law in an effort to provide some sort of remedy. The construction of the notion of absent victim and the possible impacts that a judgement can

51 Rob White, 'Green Victimology and Non-Human Victims' (2018) 24(2) International Review of Victimology 239, 242.

52 Hiskes (n 41) 92.

have then, requires a more dialectical relationship, nonetheless. The present section explores two instances where, in seeking redress for a particular case at hand, the decisions of courts have an impact on absent victims, even if not initially foreseen. Guarantees of non-repetition and pilot judgements are two procedural avenues that have structural connotations. They aim at changing situations that are, *per se,* states of systematic and structural injustice. In doing so, they provide redress not only to present victims recognized in the proceedings but also to future and potential victims.

2.1. Guarantees of Non-Repetition and Absent Victims

The basis for establishing reparations in the sphere of the IACtHR is Article 63.1 of the American Convention on Human Rights (ACHR). According to this Article, the Inter-American System has gone beyond a simple concept of reparation. It has referred to all its history of integral reparations as provisions that tend to return the victims to the situation they were in before the human rights violation occurred or, if not, to reduce the effects of such violation as far as possible.[53] In this regard, the Inter-American System implements restitution, compensation, rehabilitation, satisfaction and guarantees of non-repetition as reparation measures.

In the context of protecting the absent victims, guarantees of non-repetition take an important role. Guarantees of non-repetition intend to have a wider impact on society and prevent a repetition of similar human rights violations. Thus, they focus on the future, not the past. The Inter-American Court has established through its decisions:

> (...), according to the general obligation established in Article 1(1) of the Convention, the State has the obligation to take all necessary steps to ensure that these grave violations are not repeated, an obligation whose fulfillment benefits society as a whole.[54]

According to Schönsteiner, in many cases these guarantees can take the form of legislative measures that aim to remedy structural and systematic

53 Juana Inés Acosta López and Diana Bravo Rubio, 'El cumplimiento de los fines de reparación integral de las medidas ordenadas por la Corte Interamericana de Derechos Humanos: énfasis en la experiencia colombiana' (2008) International Law: Revista Colombiana de Derecho Internacional 323, 332.

54 *Case of Trujillo-Oroza v Bolivia,* Judgement (Reparations and Costs), 27 February 2002, para. 110.

human rights violations.[55] For instance, the Inter-American Court ordered Guatemala to reform its Criminal Code in relation to the treatment of prisoners who allegedly represent a danger to society at large,[56] its definition of the crime of abduction and the forms of criminal penalties.[57] In other cases, the Court has even ordered a State to implement a constitutional amendment[58] or sweeping legal reforms in relation to extrajudicial executions.[59]

However, guarantees of non-repetition go beyond legislative or constitutional reform. For instance, in the case of *González and others ('Cotton Field') v Mexico*, the IACtHR ordered that the State shall standardize all its protocols to investigate cases related to disappearances, sexual violence and homicides of women (femicides) according to the Istanbul Protocol and other international standards based on a gender perspective.[60] In addition, the Court prescribed that Mexico had to continue implementing programs and courses of education and training in human rights and gender.[61] In other decisions, such as the case of *Guerrero, Molina and others v. Venezuela, Massacre of Mozote and Nearby Places v. El Salvador*, and *Yarce and others v. Colombia,* the Court also ordered the respondent States to conduct training, programs and projects on human rights to build capacity and knowledge among different public officials and society at large.[62] In the case of *Ramírez Escobar and others v Guatemala*, the Inter-American Court prescribed that the State had to adopt the necessary measures to create

55 Judith Schönsteiner, 'Dissuasive Measures and the "Society as a Whole": A Working Theory of Reparations in the Inter-American Court of Human Rights' (2007) 23(1) American University International Law Review 127, 147.

56 *Case of Fermin Ramirez v Guatemala*, Judgement (Merits, Reparations and Costs), 20 June 2005, para. 138.8.

57 *Case of Raxcaco-Reyes v Guatemala*, Judgement (Merits, Reparations and Costs), 15 September 2005, para. 145.5.

58 *Case of the 'Last Temptation of Christ' (Olmedo-Bustos et al) v Chile*, Judgement (Merits, Reparations and Costs), 5 February 2001, para. 103.4.

59 *Case of Barrios Altos v Peru*, Judgement (Reparations and Costs), 30 November 2001, para. 50.5.

60 *Case of Gonzalez et al. ('Cotton Field') v Mexico*, Judgement (Preliminary Objection, Merits, Reparations, and Costs), 16 November 2009, para. 502.

61 ibid., paras 541–543.

62 See: *Caso Guerrero, Molina y Otros v Venezuela*, Sentencia (Fondo, Reparaciones y Costas), 3 de Junio de 2021, para. 181; *Case of the Massacres of El Mozote and Nearby Places v El Salvador*, Judgement (Merits, Reparations and Costs), 25 October 2012, para. 369; *Caso Yarce y Otras v Colombia*, Sentencia (Excepcion Preliminar, Fondo, Reparaciones y Costas), 22 de Noviembre de 2016, para. 350.

and implement an effective program to guarantee adequate supervision, inspection, and control of the institutionalization of minors.[63]

In certain cases, the line between guarantees of non-repetition and other measures of reparation can become blurred. Especially when the intent of the Court ordering a particular measure is tied to a general aim of providing a deterrent effect for society as a whole in the case of future violations. One good example of situations where this might happen is in cases linked with a procedural violation of the duty to investigate human rights violations and the positive obligations derived thereof for States. In the *Case of the Afro-descendant's Communities Displaced from the Cacarica River Basin v Colombia*, the IACtHR established this link between the duty to investigate and guarantees of non-repetition.[64] Even more poignantly, in the matter of *Beneficiaries of Late Norbert Zongo and others v Burkina Faso* before the African Court of Human and Peoples' Rights, the petitioners asked for the reopening of investigations on the assassination of Mr Zongo and his companions as a matter of guarantees of non-repetition in their submissions on reparations. The Court said that the measure could be characterized more as a matter of cessation but that, nonetheless, ordering the measure was in line with the jurisprudence of the African Commission of Human Rights and the UN Human Rights Committee as it would ensure that similar violations do not occur in the future.[65]

Returning to the Inter-American System, in many cases, the IACtHR, although not directly recognising an extended group of victims through measures of non-repetition, has gone beyond in protecting future generations or victims that were not represented during the proceedings. Thus, the Court has not expanded the scope of the 'victim' *per se* but has rather used reparations by chiefly referring to society's role in pursuing the aim of non-recurrence of human rights violations.[66]

An interesting example of how this phenomenon applies in the case of absent victims is the protracted action of the IACtHR in monitoring compliance with its decisions. On a very characteristic note, the Court remains

---

63 *Caso Ramirez Escobar y Otros v Guatemala*, Sentencia (Fondo, Reparaciones y Costas), 9 de Marzo de 2018, para. 408.

64 *Case of the Afro-Descendant Communities Displaced for the Cacarica River Basin (Operation Genesis) v Colombia,* Judgement (Preliminary objections, merits, reparations and costs), 20 November 2013, para. 370.

65 *Beneficiaries of Late Norbert Zongo and others v Burkina Faso*, Judgement on Reparations, 5 June 2015, App no. 013/2011, paras 101–106.

66 Schonsteiner (n 55) 138.

seized of the cases after it has taken decisions, periodically evaluating how the State complies with its orders. This is a form of judicial enforcement, lacking other political avenues for compliance, as with the ECtHR with the Council of Ministers. A case in point is that of *Velez Loor v Panama*. In that particular case, Panama recognized its international responsibility for a series of human rights violations against Mr Velez Loor, including a violation of his personal integrity and a lack of effective investigation on allegations of torture. Mr Velez Loor, an immigrant, was detained because of his migratory status in an ordinary detention facility for common criminals, something that the Court also found as a violation of several rights contained in the American Convention.[67]

The Court ordered as guarantees of non-repetition, amongst other things, that the State had to adopt administrative measures to ensure that in the future, those detained for their migratory status should be separated from those detained for ordinary crimes. It also ordered the State to improve its detention centres and penitentiary facilities (even those for ordinary crimes) to international standards.[68] By themselves, and taken in 2010, these orders for guarantees of non-repetition already have a strong projection in time that affect absent victims who are potentially protected from violations in the future. Nonetheless, the Court has remained seized of the matter in virtue of its powers to monitor compliance with its decisions and it has continued to issue provisional measures based on the original decision in June 2021, more than ten years after the original ruling on merits and reparations. These measures have gone as far as ordering the State of Panama to ensure the improvement of Panamanian detention centres to sanitary standards that help combat the Covid-19 pandemic.[69] The 2021 provisional measures even serve as a reminder to the Panamanian authorities that the migrant population has to be taken into consideration for Covid 19 vaccination schemes in light of the principle of equality and non-discrimination, without distinction of nationality and migratory status.[70]

It seems quite an exercise in judicial activism and expansive interpretation for a Court to take guarantees of non-repetition ordered in 2010 as the

67 *Case of Velez Loor v Panama*, Judgement (Preliminary Objections, Merits, Reparations and Costs), 23 November 2010, para. 210.

68 ibid., paras 271–276.

69 *Case of Velez Loor v Panama*, Medidas Provisionales, Resolución de la Corte Interamericana de Derechos Humanos, 24 de Junio de 2021, paras 26, 29 and 63.

70 ibid., para. 47.

basis for construing in 2021 an obligation for the State to (in attention to its capacities) provide for vaccination schemes to third-country nationals and improve its detention centres to sanitary standards that can help combat the Covid-19 pandemic. On the other side of the coin, this can also be seen as a perfect example of how guarantees of non-repetition can have a protracted effect in time on the protection of a group of potential victims that was not part of the original proceedings. Thus, it constitutes an avenue for safeguarding the interests of absent victims in general and specifically with the potential of addressing claims of intergenerational justice, such as those proceedings dealing with past generational redress (for instance, dealing with enforced disappearances) and those that have clear future-looking effects such as climate change and environmental protection litigations. In other words, as the *Case of Velez Loor* exemplifies, the IACtHR, through a broad understating and application of guarantees of non-repetition and the protracted effect of its procedure for monitoring compliance with its judgements, has opened the door for procedural pathways through which one can address intergenerational claims.

2.2. Pilot Judgements: Structural Decisions for Future Victims

Another mechanism that might prove promising in a reinterpretation of the victim that could provide redress for the absent is that of the pilot judgements adopted by the European Court of Human Rights. Depending on doctrinal leanings and institutional conceptions, pilot judgements can be described as answering to the constitutionalisation[71] of the ECHR system due to its structural character. They have even been labelled as a sort of 'human rights class action'.[72]

According to the ECtHR's case law, pilot judgments serve a dual function; they help to identify structural problems whilst at the same time inducing the State to take remedial action at the domestic level to resolve

71 Pilot judgements have been described as 'an emphatic expression of the constitutional turn' of the ECtHR. See: Wojciech Sadurski, 'Partnering with Strasbourg: Constitutionalisation of the European Court of Human Rights, the Accession of Central and East European States to the Council of Europe, and the Idea of Pilot Judgements' (2009) Human Rights Law Review 397, 450.

72 See: Tatiana Sainati, 'Human Rights Class Actions: Rethinking the Pilot-Judgment Procedure at the European Court of Human Rights' (2015) 56 Harvard International Law Journal 147.

the large number of cases that arise from these structural and systemic issues.[73] On the other hand, they also respond to the Court's need to manage its ever-increasing workload due to the repetitive nature of the cases that these structural problems create.[74] The increasing number of cases after the entry into force of Protocol 11 and their repetitive nature led to the issuance of the first pilot judgement in 2004 in the case of *Broniowski v Poland* concerning some 80 000 affected victims due to the lack of compensation faced by Polish citizens who had to abandon property beyond the Bug River (now in Ukrainian territory) after the Second World War.[75] Previously, the Committee of Ministers of the Council of Europe had identified repetitive cases and structural violations as a pressing issue for the Strasbourg system and had invited the Court 'to assist states in finding the appropriate solution.'[76]

It was not until 2011 that the Rules of Procedure of the Court were amended to provide a proper normative framework after the jurisprudential development. Rule 61 was introduced, stating that:

1. The Court may initiate a pilot-judgment procedure and adopt a pilot judgment where the facts of an application reveal in the Contracting Party concerned the existence of a structural or systemic problem or other similar dysfunction which has given rise or may give rise to similar applications.[77]

Furthermore, Rule 61 proceeds to acknowledge that the parties shall be consulted as to the existence and extent of the systemic and structural problems that may trigger the Court to activate a pilot judgement procedure and that these might be initiated on the Court's own motion, but also at the request of one of the parties. Since its initial creation, the Court has adjudicated pilot judgements in an array of issues deemed structural such as the violation of property rights due to inadequate provisions on rent-control,[78] problems with the restitution of nationalised or confiscated property

73 *Greens and M.T. v the United Kingdom* Apps no. 60041/08 and 60054/08 (ECtHR, 23 November 2010) paras 107–108.
74 Factsheet – Pilot Judgements, (ECtHR July 2021)<https://www.echr.coe.int/documents/fs_pilot_judgments_eng.pdf> accessed 26 October 2021.
75 See: *Broniowski v Poland* App no. 31443/96 (ECtHR, 22 June 2004).
76 Council of Europe, Resolution of the Committee of Ministers on judgments revealing an underlying systemic problem, Res (2004) 3.
77 ECtHR, Rule 61, Rules of Court, 18 October 2021 <https://perma.cc/TJZ4-W8LS>.
78 See: *Hutten-Czapska v Poland* App no. 35014/97 (ECtHR, 19 June 2006).

under communist regimes,[79] excessive length of domestic proceedings,[80] a blanket ban on voting for convicted prisoners,[81] and detention conditions that could be characterised as inhuman or degrading.[82]

Regarding a remedy and the rights of the victim, it can be interpreted that pilot judgements may have relevant implications for the right to individual application enshrined in Article 34 of the European Convention. This follows from the fact that under Rule 61(6), it is understood that the Court adjourns similar cases that pertain to the same issue after the delivery of the pilot judgement in order to give the respondent State the opportunity to implement remedial measures of a general character, thus limiting the rights of potential individual applicants. Nonetheless, Rule 61(3) and (4) require the Court to identify the structural and systemic problems and provide general measures in the operative provisions of the judgement. It states:

3. The Court shall in its pilot judgment identify both the nature of the structural or systemic problem or other dysfunction as established as well as the type of remedial measures which the Contracting Party concerned is required to take at the domestic level by virtue of the operative provisions of the judgment.
4. The Court may direct in the operative provisions of the pilot judgment that the remedial measures referred to in paragraph 3 above be adopted within a specified time, bearing in mind the nature of the measures required and the speed with which the problem which it has identified can be remedied at the domestic level.

By being part of the operative provisions of the Judgement and on the basis of Article 46 of the European Convention, these general measures cannot be labeled directly as forms of reparation under Article 41 of the

79 See: *Maria Atanasiu and Others v Romania* Apps no. 30767/05 and 33800/06 (ECtHR, 12 October 2010); *Manushaqe Puto and Others v Albania* Apps no. 604/07, 43628/07, 46684/07, 34770/09 (ECtHR, 31 July 2012).

80 See: *Rumpf v Germany* App no. 46344/06 (ECtHR, 2 September 2010); *Athanasiou and Others v Greece* App no. 50973/08 (ECtHR, 21 December 2010); *Ümmühan Kaplan v Turkey* App no. 24240/07 (ECtHR, 20 March 2012).

81 See: *Greens and M.T. v the United Kingdom* Apps no. 60041/08 and 60054/08 (ECtHR, 23 November 2010).

82 See: *Ananyev and Others v Russia* Apps no. 42525/07 and 60800/08 (ECtHR, 10 January 2012); *W.D. v Belgium* App no. 73548/13 (ECtHR, 6 September 2016); *Rezmives and Others v Romania* Apps no. 61467/12, 39516/13, 48213/13, and 68191/13 (ECtHR, 25 April 2017).

Convention. However, the resemblance in matters of impact with guarantees of non-repetition cannot be understated. Especially since the general measures ordered by pilot judgements tend to entail the adoption of legislative reform that would effectively promote non-recurrence in practice. As stated by Ichim:

> In essence, it is laudable that the Strasbourg mechanism has not tolerated mere assurances, but has endeavoured to provide effective guarantees of non-repetition, even if not labelled as such and even if not clearly demanded. In the context of the pilot-judgment procedure, the Court gives an express order to the respondent state to adopt and implement general measures. It is not simply an implied element of the execution phase, confined to political supervision.[83]

To be fair, the author further explains that while pilot judgement procedures are designed to act as a mechanism of redress for victims who are already affected by violations, guarantees of non-repetition are preventive in character and thus not directly analogous.[84] However, for the purposes of our analysis in the context of absent victims, it is clear that while their legal nature is not the same, both mechanisms can produce similar protracted effects for future absent victims. Both help construe a category of victim that is not necessarily present in the courtroom by addressing potential violations. Legal and administrative reform that tend to expedite access to justice or ameliorate conditions of detention and imprisonment – to mention just two examples of measures ordered by both the IACtHR and the ECtHR – might serve the purpose of potentially addressing intergenerational claims of justice by protecting the interests, albeit indirectly, of the absent.

Conclusions

Given the lack of mechanisms that could constitute a thorough and complete representation of the interests of those absent because either they are not with us anymore or they are not with us yet, a reinterpretation and reframing of certain procedural avenues in the context of human rights litigation can serve to provide a degree of protection that whilst not optimal,

83 Octavian Ichim, *Just Satisfaction under the European Convention on Human Rights* (CUP 2015) 253.

84 ibid., 254.

may constitute a starting point while political and international consensus is made elsewhere.

International human rights law and the mechanisms it provides can become a space for contestation and emancipation for the protection of the interests of the absent and even future and past generations. For that, a necessary reinterpretation and reimagination of the rules of procedure currently set up in international courts and tribunals against the background of certain disciplines such as victimology or green criminology, which already have strong considerations for intertemporal and intergenerational issues, is needed.

Current and future challenges such as climate change litigation, environmental protection, and the need to ensure a sustainable world for future generations require that legal action finds progressive ways to reinterpret existing normative structures in imaginative and performative ways that can ensure visibility and redress for victims. This chapter has sought to provide, in a succinct and limited way, how distinct legal institutions such as guarantees of non-repetition and pilot judgements can be reimagined in order to ensure those goals. Both, if analyzed from a socio-legal perspective, can help build redress for absent and potential victims.

4. Shared Memories, Shared Records, Shared Ownership: The Presence of Victims in the Preservation, Articulation, and Retrieval of the ICTY Archives

Fé de Jonge[*]

Abstract: *When the International Criminal Tribunal for the former Yugoslavia (ICTY) finalised its proceedings, its official records became the archives of the ICTY. As these archives contain all materials pertaining to the ICTY and its proceedings, they also hold the testimonies, artefacts, and experiences of victims which were used as evidence. Yet to view these as items with only evidentiary – or historical – value would be an oversimplification of their meaning to victims. However, this particular relationship between the ICTY, its archives, and victim communities has remained unaddressed. This chapter aims to fill this gap by examining and questioning the organisation, presentation, and accessibility of the archives, using the concept of conflict as property to situate this examination and critical archival studies to highlight the victim's position within these archives. Additionally, some considerations are presented which could facilitate the incorporation of victims and their needs in the organisation, presentation, and accessibility of the archives.*

1. Introduction

In 2009, it emerged that the Office of the Prosecutor of the International Criminal Tribunal for the former Yugoslavia (ICTY/Tribunal) had ordered the destruction of around 1000 artefacts found in the mass graves evidencing the massacre that took place after the fall of Srebrenica, Bosnia and Herzegovina, in 1995.[1] These artifacts, which included human tissue, personal belongings, and identification documents, presented a health risk due to decomposition, according to the Prosecutor's Office, and were destroyed in conformity with standard court procedure.[2] Victims and their relatives expressed their dismay, arguing that the items should have been returned to Bosnia and Herzegovina.[3] Hatidža Mehmedović, founder of the Mothers

* Fé de Jonge is a PhD candidate at the Grotius Centre for International Legal Studies, Leiden University (Netherlands).

1 Balkan Investigative Reporting Network, 'Srebrenica Artifacts Destroyed in The Hague' (*Balkan Insight*, 16 July 2009) <https://perma.cc/SW2T-W8CM>.

2 ibid.

3 Olivera Simić, 'Memorial Culture in the Former Yugoslavia: Mothers of Srebrenica and the Destruction of Artefacts by the ICTY' in Peter D Rush and Olivera Simić (eds), *The Arts of Transitional Justice: Culture, Activism, and Memory after Atrocity* (Springer

of Srebrenica – a foundation representing around 6000 victims and their relatives –, stated that, '[w]hat the Hague did is a crime. In Srebrenica, they killed our children and in the Hague, our memories.'[4]

While the Prosecutor's Office denied that the artifacts were the property of the Tribunal,[5] the items were in fact part of the United Nations (UN) official records. The official records of the ICTY include all evidentiary items, such as objects, audio-visual materials, and documents, as well as recordings of proceedings, judgments, orders, motions, transcripts, and other documentation produced by and for the Tribunal.[6] As the Tribunal is a subsidiary organ of the UN, these records are the legal property of the UN.[7] From a formal perspective then, perhaps the destruction of decomposing evidence does not raise too many questions. However, such a strictly formalistic approach towards matters that do not have a purely procedural meaning or character provokes a certain sense of unease. Another example that elicits a similar, and perhaps more tangible, sense of discomfort are the short videos featured on the ICTY's website under the heading 'Voices of the Victims'.[8] The videos, most of which display the full name of the victim witness and the crimes they suffered, contain excerpts of testimonies by these victim witnesses. The original audio is replaced with the English interpretation, and each video is accompanied by a quote from the testimony. Again, the audio-visual recordings of ICTY proceedings are part of the official records of the Tribunal and can therefore be used, as is the case here, to exhibit the work of the Tribunal. Once again, this partic-

---

2014) 161–162; Balkan Investigative Reporting Network, 'Loss of Srebrenica Victims' Possessions Shocks Families' (*Balkan Insight*, 13 May 2009) <https://perma.cc/ZR65-SE8F>; Balkan Investigative Reporting Network (n 1).

4 Simić (n 3) 161.

5 Balkan Investigative Reporting Network (n 3).

6 Iva Vukušić, 'The Archives of the International Criminal Tribunal for the Former Yugoslavia' (2013) 98 History 623, 626–629.

7 UNST 'United Nations Archives and Records Management' (26 June 1991) UN Doc ST/SGB/242; UNSC 'Report of the Secretary-General on the administrative and budgetary aspects of the options for possible locations for the archives of the International Tribunal for the Former Yugoslavia and the International Criminal Tribunal for Rwanda and the seat of the residual mechanism(s) for the Tribunals' (21 May 2009) UN Doc S/2009/258 6; UNSC Res 1966 (22 December 2010) UN Doc S/RES/1966 art 27(1); Trudy Huskamp Peterson, 'Temporary Courts, Permanent Records' (2006) 170 Special Report – United States Institute of Peace 2.

8 United Nations International Criminal Tribunal for the former Yugoslavia, 'Voice of the Victims' <https://www.icty.org/en/features/voice-of-the-victims> accessed 2 January 2022.

ular use of the official ICTY records might not be considered particularly controversial considering the objectives of the Tribunal, but to view these videos and other evidentiary materials as just that – *evidence* – would be an oversimplification of their content, meaning, and value. The records of the ICTY cannot solely be defined as those materials used before the Tribunal to present, defend, and judge cases. These records contain the experiences of individual victims, their stories, and memories. The Tribunal, in pursuit of its objective to achieve justice for the victims, took possession of these materials and presented them in the courtroom, acting as a representative of the victims. Yet by perceiving and treating the victims' stories as having a purely procedural function, the individuals behind these records became invisible. Experiences only became valuable to the extent that they could prove the commission of a crime, show the severity of this crime, or testify to the immorality of the defendant. The background of the individual victims behind the stories was relevant only to provide context to their testimony. While present in their legal capacity as witnesses, there was no room for their presence as victimised persons.

The unease which results from the treatment of these individual experiences as legal commodities, as legal evidence as well as legal possessions, was conceptualised in 1977 by Nils Christie in the understanding of conflict as property.[9] In his article, he offered a critique of the modern criminal justice process, in which official institutions and professionals have taken ownership of the original conflict that exists between perpetrator and victim. In these modern systems, the state has taken on the role of victim representative, speaks on their behalf, presents their case, and receives reparations. The person of the victim has been removed from the process, and the original conflict has now become property of the state. Christie's critique, as well as his appeal to return ownership of the conflict to the victim and restore the victim's central position within the criminal justice process, has had profound effects on the development of restorative justice practices within domestic criminal justice systems.[10] These ideas also impacted the field of international criminal justice, which resulted, inter alia, in the creation of a multitude of offices within the permanent International Criminal Court (ICC) focused on victim representation, participation and

9 Nils Christie, 'Conflicts As Property' (1977) 17(1) British Journal of Criminology 1.

10 William R Wood and Masahiro Suzuki, 'Are Conflicts Property? Re-Examining the Ownership of Conflict in Restorative Justice' (2020) 29 Social & Legal Studies 903, 904.

reparation.[11] This shift in thinking within criminal justice, and the accompanying institutional changes, have received much attention from international legal scholars who chronicled these developments, from the absence of victims in the proceedings of the ad hoc Tribunals to the participation and representation of victims in ICC proceedings.[12] Even after the ICTY closed its doors, the Tribunal remained a thankful source of academic reflection and lessons for the future.[13]

Nevertheless, even though active proceedings before the ICTY have ceased, this does not mean that the ICTY, and in particular its relationship with victim communities, has become a subject with only historical importance. While the ICTY finalised its proceedings in December 2017, its remaining functions were transferred to the International Residual Mechanism for Criminal Tribunals (IRMCT/Mechanism), established in 2010.[14] Due to the closure of the ICTY, its legal records now constitute the official archives of the Tribunal and are currently being managed by the IRMCT, which carries responsibility for, inter alia, the preservation, accessibility, declassification, and protection of the archives.[15] Therefore, the records continue to exist, but now under the auspices of the IRMCT. The stories, experiences, and memories contained in these records of course continue to exist as well, but similarly remain under the authority of the Mechanism. Thus, Christie's critique, even if originally focused on active criminal proceedings, continues to be applicable here as ownership of the original conflict has been transferred from the ICTY to the IRMCT. The absence of

---

11 Victims Participation and Reparations Section, *Victims before the International Criminal Court: A Guide for the Participation of Victims in the Proceedings of the ICC* (International Criminal Court 2020).

12 See, *inter alia*, Ilaria Bottigliero, Redress for Victims of Crimes Under International Law (Springer Netherlands 2004) 193–248; Emily Haslam, 'Victim Participation at the International Criminal Court: A Triumph of Hope Over Experience' in Dominic McGoldrick and Peter Rowe (eds), *The Permanent International Criminal Court: Legal and Policy Issues* (Hart Publishing 2004); Luke Moffett, *Justice for Victims before the International Criminal Court* (Routledge 2014); Christoph Safferling and Gurgen Petrossian, *Victims Before the International Criminal Court: Definition, Participation, Reparation* (Springer 2021).

13 See, for example, Carsten Stahn and others (eds), *Legacies of the International Criminal Tribunal for the Former Yugoslavia: A Multidisciplinary Approach* (1st edn, OUP 2020).

14 UNSC Res 1966 (22 December 2010), UN Doc S/RES/1966.

15 ibid., art 27(2) and (3); UNSC 'Report of the Secretary-General' (21 May 2009) UN Doc S/2009/258 22; IRMCT, 'Archives' <https://www.irmct.org/en/archives> accessed 3 January 2022.

the person of the victim in the ICTY's proceedings has received extensive scholarly attention, yet the question of whether this absence persists in the Tribunal's archives has remained unaddressed. This chapter aims to fill this gap by examining how victims are represented in the Tribunal's archives, using the concept of conflict as property to situate this examination and critical archival studies to question the victim's position – or lack thereof – within the archives.

This chapter proceeds as follows. The next section first explains the theory of conflict as property, the context within which it was first developed, and its relevance to this study. This section also briefly explains the field of critical archival studies and how it is used here to structure the dissection of the ICTY archives. Subsequently, three different aspects of the archives are examined, namely their organisation, presentation, and accessibility, focusing attention on the presence, or absence, of the victims in these three areas. The final section proposes a number of ways in which the discussion on the relationship between victim communities, international adjudicative mechanisms, and archives of mass atrocities can be continued and further developed.

2. Conflict as Property

As stated previously, the understanding of conflict as property was first developed in 1977 by Nils Christie, in an article published in the British Journal of Criminology. Christie argues that, in our modern criminal justice systems, victims, perpetrators, and the wider community have been side-lined in the resolution of their own conflicts. As the criminal justice system, and in particular criminal trials, became increasingly formalised and institutionalised, the original parties to the conflict became increasingly disconnected from the process of conflict resolution. This distance has manifested itself in the physical removal of the process from the location where the original conflict arose, and from the homes of the victims and offenders, to centralised, imposing, and often difficult to navigate court buildings situated in the administrative centre of the nearby town or city.[16] In addition, a figurative distance has been created by the indirect representation of the parties to the conflict. Victims no longer represent themselves

16 Christie (n 9) 2–3.

but are represented by the state. The state presents their grievances, demands a punishment, and receives reparations. While the offender is still officially a party in the modern criminal trial, often he will be represented by a lawyer.[17] The centralisation of the criminal justice process has meant that there is no longer any room for the interests of the community in which the crime occurred – this has been replaced by the interests of society as a whole. In sum, the formalisation of the criminal process has meant that the original parties to the conflict no longer own their conflict, as it has been taken over by the state and other professionals.[18] Christie argues that ownership of the conflict between offender and victim should be returned to those parties – and especially to the victim. This would entail, most importantly, direct participation of the parties to the conflict in its resolution. Not only does such direct participation allow the victim to personally confront the offender with the harm caused, but it also allows for a personalised resolution of the conflict and tailored forms of redress. Furthermore, direct participation presents parties with the opportunity to address wider and underlying societal problems – thereby encouraging participation in public life.[19] In order to have a system in which victims could once more have control and ownership of their conflict, Christie proposed the creation of informal neighbourhood courts. These courts would be composed of peers who would represent themselves and who would strive to find a solution among themselves – avoiding professionals and professionalisation at all costs. The victim would take centre stage in proceedings before these courts, and the conflict resolution process would focus on the victim's situation, their grievances, and their needs regarding reparations.[20]

While Christie's ideal of replacing the formal court system with informal neighbourhood courts never materialised, his article made an important contribution to the field of restorative justice. This field centres around the idea that justice processes should provide perpetrators and victims with the opportunity to come face to face – to allow them to communicate about the harm suffered and to agree on the appropriate form of redress.[21] Since the article's publication in 1977, substantial changes have been introduced

17 ibid.
18 ibid., 7.
19 ibid., 7–9.
20 ibid., 10–12.
21 Wood and Suzuki (n 10) 903–904.

in many national criminal justice systems to provide for various forms of victim participation in trial proceedings and for effective means of reparation.[22] Eventually, the field of international criminal justice also became infused with these ideas, with international legal scholars and practitioners reiterating the importance of victim participation and redress in order to truly achieve the objectives of international criminal justice.[23] In this light, the ad hoc Tribunals were heavily criticised for not granting victims an official position or effective means of reparations,[24] despite two of the core objectives – and stated achievements – of the ICTY being the ability to give a voice and bring justice to the victims.[25]

Even though Christie's article, and general scholarship on the relationship between the ICTY and its victim communities, focus on the role of victims in criminal proceedings, the ICTY archives present an important opportunity to examine the question of ownership of conflict after judicial proceedings have ended. In his article, Christie does not provide a definition of either *conflict* or *property*, but William Wood and Masahiro Suzuki understand these terms, not as strictly legal concepts, but as describing certain social relations.[26] The term *conflict*, then, refers both to conduct that the state has classified as unlawful, and to the sequence of events that causes friction as well as societal or personal harm. Wood and Suzuki interpret the term *property* as the ability of the direct parties to the conflict to take charge of the conflict and to decide on the consequences of the harm inflicted.[27] Still, as the meaning of these two terms is determined specifically and solely in reference to the criminal justice process, this is a

---

22 ibid.

23 David Donat-Cattin, 'Article 68 Protection of the Victims and Witnesses and Their Participation in the Proceedings' in Otto Triffterer (ed), *Commentary on the Rome Statute of the International Criminal Court: Observers' Notes, Article by Article* (Nomos 1999) 1682–1683; Haslam (n 12) 318–319; Moffett (n 12) 24–49; Safferling and Petrossian (n 12) 1–4.

24 Bottigliero (n 12) 196–211; Haslam (n 12) 320; Claude Jorda and Jérôme de Hemptinne, 'The Status and the Role of the Victim' in Antonio Cassese and others (eds), *The Rome Statute of the International Criminal Court: A Commentary, vol II* (OUP 2004) 1387–1390; Moffett (n 12) 67–85.

25 United Nations International Criminal Tribunal for the former Yugoslavia, 'Achievements' <https://www.icty.org/en/about/tribunal/achievements> accessed 3 January 2022; Amanda Potts and Anne Lise Kjær, 'Constructing Achievement in the International Criminal Tribunal for the Former Yugoslavia (ICTY): A Corpus-Based Critical Discourse Analysis' (2016) 29 International Journal for the Semiotics of Law 525.

26 Wood and Suzuki (n 10) 905.

27 ibid.

relatively restrictive interpretation. Conflict does not necessarily end with the completion of a criminal trial and the classification of certain conduct as unlawful and harmful. Conflict also manifests itself through the victim's intangible experience of the conduct, their testimony and memory, and through physical artifacts that are now intrinsically linked to the conduct, and which connect perpetrator and victim. These tangible and intangible objects evidence the existence of conflict – not just to a legal court, but also to victims, their relatives, and their community. Subsequently, having ownership of the conflict means having the ability to exercise control over these objects; it includes the ability to hold them, to hide, erase, or enshrine them, to reproduce and broadcast them. Thus, having control over these objects inevitably means having a high degree of power over them. In the case of the ICTY, while the victims and their relatives were the original owners of many of these objects, partial or complete ownership was transferred to the ICTY – sometimes without direct or explicit consent from the original owners. The ICTY thereby gained sole control over these objects and therefore holds power over them. This is problematic, because the objectives and interests of the actors involved do not necessarily align. The interests and objectives of the victims and the ICTY, which are often presumed to overlap, are likely to diverge on certain points – and even the interests of victims are not necessarily homogenous. Even when there is overlap, ideas about the manner in which these interests and objectives should be protected can diverge. Exclusive ownership of the ICTY archives, as granted to the IRMCT, leaves little room for the consideration and protection of the interests of victims.

The problems inherent in such exclusionary ownership, and related issues of power, inequality, and contention in historic recordkeeping, can best be examined within the framework of critical archival studies. While it is beyond the scope of this chapter to comprehensively discuss this particular branch of archival studies, it suffices to state here that the aim of critical archival studies is to identify inequalities, power imbalances, silences, and absences, not only in the structure of archives, but also, and perhaps more importantly, in the creation, management, and availability of archives.[28] These studies reject the understanding of archives as neutral depots of

28 See, *inter alia*, Michelle Caswell, Ricardo Punzalan and T-Kay Sangwand, 'Critical Archival Studies: An Introduction' (2017) 1 Journal of Critical Library and Information Studies 1; Eric Ketelaar, 'Tacit Narratives: The Meanings of Archives' (2001) 1 Archival Science 131; Joan M Schwartz and Terry Cook, 'Archives, Records, and Power: The Making of Modern Memory' (2002) 2 Archival Science 1; Terry Cook,

information about the past, and instead reframe them as institutions of power which can create and maintain inequality. A subsequent goal of such research is to offer practical tools with which to change existing archival practices. Following this approach, the next section of this chapter critically examines the organisation, presentation, and accessibility of the ICTY archives, by identifying issues within these three areas that testify to the existence of power imbalances in the exercise of ownership of the archives. Such an approach, in turn, allows for the identification and interrogation of silences, absences, and vacant spaces where the victim should be present, and for the articulation of a set of possible solutions.

3. The ICTY Archives as Touchstones of Memory

Laura Miller states that archives are 'touchstones upon which memories may be retrieved, preserved, and articulated.'[29] The three areas of accessibility, organisation, and presentation speak to the core of any archive, and it is in these three areas that the official institutions, whether it be the UN, the ICTY, or the IRMCT, can and do exhibit their power. It is also in these three areas that tensions, inequalities, and power imbalances in the relationship between the archives and victim communities arise, and in which the absence of the victim is most tangible. Therefore, this section examines each of these three aspects of the ICTY archives separately, whilst paying particular attention to the presence of the victim within these three areas.

3.1. Organisation

Before assessing the presentation and accessibility of the ICTY archives, an understanding and appraisal of their organisation is needed. In order to understand the current structures of the ICTY archives, it is imperative to examine the processes that preceded the eventual establishment of the archives, during which the framework and core principles of the archives were developed. The presence, or absence, of the person of the victim in

---

'The Archive(s) Is a Foreign Country: Historians, Archivists, and the Changing Archival Landscape' (2011) 74 The American Archivist 600.

29 Laura Millar, 'Touchstones: Considering the Relationship between Memory and Archives' (2006) 61 Archivaria 105, Abstract.

this process can explain the position of the victim in the current organisation of the ICTY archives.

The process which led to the eventual creation of the ICTY archives was an integral part of the inception of the IRMCT, which was founded in 2010 by the UN Security Council (UNSC).[30] Already in 2000, the Informal Working Group on the International Tribunals (the Working Group) was created, which consisted of a number of legal advisors from UNSC member states.[31] This working group consulted with both the ICTY and the International Criminal Tribunal for Rwanda (ICTR), on the completion strategies of both Tribunals and the responsibility for remaining residual functions.[32] In 2007, both ad hoc Tribunals submitted a report with their views on the creation of a residual mechanism to the UN Security Council.[33] Around the same time, the Registrars of both Tribunals established the Advisory Committee on Archives (the Advisory Committee), which specifically examined the question of the Tribunals' archives.[34] Consultations between the Working Group, the Advisory Committee, and officials from both Tribunals eventually resulted in a statement by the President of the UN Security Council in December 2008.[35] In this statement, the President acknowledges the need for an ad hoc mechanism that would be able to take over and carry out the residual functions of both Tribunals. Furthermore, the President requests the UN Secretary-General to draft a report on administrative and budgetary considerations for a number of possible locations which could house the residual mechanism and the Tribunals' archives.[36] While the reports from the Working Group and the Advisory Committee are not publicly available, the 2009 Report of the UN

30 UNSC Res 1966 (22 December 2020) UN Doc S/Res/1966.
31 UNSC 'Letter dated 19 December 2008 from the Permanent Representative of Belgium to the United Nations addressed to the President of the Security Council' (31 December 2008) UN Doc S/2008/849 1.
32 Konrad G Büehler, 'The Role of the UN Security Council in Preserving the Legacy of the Tribunals: Establishment of a Residual Mechanism and Preservation of Archives' in Richard H Steinberg (ed), *Assessing the Legacy of the ICTY* (Martinus Nijhoff Publishers 2011) 59–60.
33 UNSC 'Letter dated 19 December 2008' (31 December 2008) UN Doc S/2008/849 1.
34 ICTY Registry 'Tribunals launch Archiving Study' (9 October 2007) Press Release LM/MOW/ PR1189e; UNSC 'Letter dated 19 December 2008' (31 December 2008) UN Doc S/2008/849 2.
35 UNSC 'Statement by the President of the Security Council' (19 December 2008) UN Doc S/PRST/2008/47.
36 ibid.

Secretary-General on the administrative and budgetary aspects of the options for possible locations for the archives of the ICTY and ICTR and the seat of the residual mechanism(s) for the Tribunals (the Report), is freely accessible.[37] The Report contains considerations and recommendations on a number of issues related to the functions, budget, and location of the residual mechanism. With regard to the functions of the mechanism, the Report states that the Tribunals identified eight core duties – of which the maintenance of their archives is a principal one.[38] According to the Report, the choices regarding the location and composition of the Tribunals' archives are influenced by both the uses and users of the archives, as well as a number of other factors, including costs, archival integrity, security, preservation, access, (de)classification, and technology.[39]

With regard to the uses of the ICTY archives, the Report references a 2007 bulletin by the UN Secretary-General on record-keeping and the management of the UN archives, which defines these archives as 'records to be permanently preserved for their administrative, fiscal, legal, historical or informational value.'[40] In broader terms, the Report stipulates that the archives have primary importance as a record of the Tribunals' judicial activities, and secondary importance for memory, education, and research.[41] The residual mechanism, as the institution that takes over the remaining judicial functions from the ICTY, and its various offices require direct, speedy, and secure access to the Tribunal's archives in order to perform those functions. This distinction between primary and secondary uses is also made by the Report with regard to the expected users of the archives.[42] Primary users are those whose work relates directly to the judicial activities of the Tribunals, and include judges, prosecutors, and defence counsel, as well as present and former staff members, and national authorities wishing to investigate and prosecute individuals indicted by the Tribunals. Victims, witnesses, relatives, and affected communities, as

37 UNSC 'Report of the Secretary-General on the administrative and budgetary aspects of the options for possible locations for the archives of the International Tribunal for the Former Yugoslavia and the International Criminal Tribunal for Rwanda and the seat of the residual mechanism(s) for the Tribunals' (21 May 2009) UN Doc S/2009/258.

38 UNSC 'Report of the Secretary-General' (21 May 2009) UN Doc S/2009/258, 6.

39 ibid., 44.

40 ibid., 12.

41 ibid., 12 and 14.

42 ibid., 14–15.

well as lawyers, researchers, journalists, and other courts and governments, are identified as secondary users, for whom the archives can also carry significance. However, according to the Report, even though these groups are identified as secondary users, these secondary users will become more important as the trials come to an end and the mechanism completes its residual functions – and can even become primary users.[43]

As stated earlier, these categories of primary and secondary uses and users were important factors in the decision-making process regarding the location and composition of the ICTY archives.[44] With regard to the location of the archives, the ICTY and the Advisory Committee agree in the Report that these should be located in Europe.[45] Multiple locations in Europe are considered in the Report, including Bosnia and Herzegovina, Serbia, and Croatia.[46] However, the ICTY and the Advisory Committee disagreed about the feasibility of locating the archives in one or more countries of the former Yugoslavia. While the Advisory Committee suggested that the UN should contemplate transferring physical custody – but not ownership – of the archives to one or more of these countries once the number of confidential documents had been significantly reduced, the ICTY considered this an option only if all confidential documents had been declassified and only if one location in the former Yugoslavia would be chosen.[47] The Report presents the respective arguments of both the Tribunal and the Advisory Committee, as well as the views of the governments of Bosnia and Herzegovina, Serbia, and Croatia on this question.[48] In the end, even though access to the archives is recognised in the Report as an important part of fostering reconciliation and memory,[49] none of the countries of the former Yugoslavia were chosen to permanently house the ICTY archives. With regard to the composition of the archives, the Report identifies three different types of records that will be stored in the archives: judicial records relating to the various cases, records that have been produced in the context of proceedings but which are not judicial records, and lastly, administrative records.[50] Judicial records are the records of each individual

43 ibid., 14–15.
44 ibid., 12 and 46.
45 ibid., 43–44.
46 ibid., 48–52.
47 ibid., 43–44.
48 ibid., 48–49.
49 ibid., 46.
50 ibid., 13.

case and include, inter alia, indictments, motions, correspondence, internal memoranda, orders, decisions, judgements, disclosure, exhibits, and transcripts, and the translations of these files. These records are produced by the different branches of the Tribunal, such as the Chambers, Prosecutor, Registry or Defence, but also by other actors, such as the accused, states, and amicus curiae. The second category are those records that are not related to any specific case or proceedings, but which are related to the overall judicial process. These records also originate from the various branches of the Tribunal and include, amongst others, evidentiary materials collected and kept by the Prosecutor which have not (yet) been used in proceedings, papers on the ICTY's policies and practices, annual reports and completion strategy reports, as well as meeting notes, correspondence, and personal records related to the defendants and witnesses. The final category of administrative records contains those files related to human resources, procurement, finance, and other administrative functions. The Report makes a further distinction between public files, temporary files, and confidential files which cannot be disclosed to the public.[51] According to the Report, duplicate files and those records that are deemed to have only temporary value can be destroyed.[52]

It is unclear if, and to what extent, individual victims, victim groups, or non-governmental organisations representing victim communities were asked to provide input for or comments on this Report. Regardless, the Report's distinction between primary and secondary uses and users confirms that victims were not placed at the forefront of the decision-making process. Overall, the fact that the form and organisation of the archives is determined, according to the Report, mainly by their use and users seems rather reductive. In other words, does the classification of victims – whose memories, whether psychical or otherwise, are now stored within this institution – simply as users of the archives who might wish to use these archives for their memory, do justice to their particular relationship with the ICTY's records? The Report does not consider this point.

With regard to the *uses* of the archives, while the Report does mention the archives' secondary value for memory, education, and research, it does not specify what is meant by the term memory.[53] Additionally, the Report refers to

---

51 ibid., 12–14.

52 ibid., 22.

53 The Report even mentions the 'duty of memory', without explaining what this duty entails. UNSC 'Report of the Secretary-General' (21 May 2009) UN Doc S/2009/258 49.

the aim of fostering reconciliation,[54] without explaining the role that the archives can and should play in this process – or in the process of memorialisation. Other important definitions are also missing from the Report. For example, the Report does not explain what qualifies as a temporary file, why its temporary status warrants destruction, and if and how other considerations play a role in its designation as a temporary file. For victims these could be essential questions – for example, did the items that were destroyed by the Office of the Prosecutor in 2005 and 2006 qualify as temporary files? The Report provides no further explanation here. As regards the *users* of the archives, while victims are specifically mentioned in the Report as users of the archives, they are grouped together with journalists and researchers, implying a common and overlapping interest in the ICTY archives. However, the relationship between victims and the ICTY is deeply personal – as opposed to the professional interest of journalists and researchers in the Tribunal's archives. This is not to say that journalists and researchers can never have a personal interest in the archives, but an immediate overlap between the interests of victims and those of journalists and researchers in this regard cannot be presumed. The fact that the Report does not acknowledge this important distinction and fails to recognise victims as a separate category of interested persons, shows the limited consideration that was given to this particular group of users. As a final point, the division between primary and secondary users seems counterintuitive in light of the Report's distinction between present and future uses and users. The Report clearly states that the primary users are only temporary users – whose use of the archives only lasts as long as active investigations and prosecutions are ongoing – while the Report expects that the secondary users will become the long-term users of the archives.[55] The choice to prioritise present users potentially creates a self-fulfilling prophecy; by having these primary users guide the decision-making process regarding the location and composition of the archives, these archives will meet the needs of those users and will be more accessible to them – thereby possibly preventing expected secondary users becoming primary users. This last issue in particular is further discussed below in the section on accessibility.

54 UNSC 'Report of the Secretary-General' (21 May 2009) UN Doc S/2009/258 46 and 55.
55 ibid., 15.

3.2. Presentation

More than a year and a half after the publication of the UN Secretary-General's 2009 Report, the UN Security Council adopted Resolution 1966, which establishes the International Residual Mechanism for Criminal Tribunals with two branches: one seated in The Hague for the ICTY, and one seated in Arusha for the ICTR.[56] As stated in the introduction of this chapter, Resolution 1966 assigns the management of the archives to the IRMCT and locates the ICTY archives with the Mechanism's branch in The Hague.[57] Information about the physical archives can be found on the website of the Mechanism, although locating the specific webpage on the archives within the Mechanism's website is not straightforward.[58] The English-language version of this webpage provides some general information about the contents and purpose of the archives, as well as information concerning access to the archives. Details about the physical archives located in The Hague are scarce – in fact, the physical address of the archives can only be found through the 'Frequently Asked Questions' webpage.[59] While the webpage does provide some practical information for those wishing to visit the archives, there is no description of the physical appearance of the archives and it is not immediately clear to outsiders that the archives are housed in the former ICTY building, now the seat of the IRMCT. Unfortunately, at the time of writing it was not possible to visit the archives in person due to COVID-19 related restrictions.[60] Additionally, the IRMCT website does not explain in much detail what is contained in the physical archives, only that it stores 'thousands of linear metres of physical records and more than 3 petabytes of digital records [...].'[61] Otherwise, the website reiterates the distinction made in the UN Secretary-General's Report between the three different categories of records. There is no detailed overview of the records held in the physical archives, or an online catalogue

---

56 UNSC Res 1966 (22 December 2020) UN Doc S/Res/1966 art 3.

57 ibid., art 27.

58 IRMCT (n 15). A visitor of the Mechanism's homepage has to click 'About' in the bar at the top of the page, and then choose 'Functions' within the 'About' bar. At the bottom of that page is a link to the 'Archives' webpage. The fact that the official website of the ICTY is still operational creates further confusion about the correct information channel.

59 IRMCT, 'Records and Archives – Frequently Asked Questions' <https://www.irmct.org/en/about/functions/archives/faq> accessed 5 January 2022.

60 IRMCT, 'Visits' <https://www.irmct.org/en/about/visits> accessed 3 February 2022.

61 IRMCT (n 15).

or other search tool through which to assess the contents of the physical archives.

However, in addition to the physical archives, there are a number of online databases which contain digital records. Most importantly, the Unified Court Records (UCR) database was launched in September 2020,[62] which contains the public court records of both ad hoc Tribunals and the IRMCT – corresponding to the first category of judicial records mentioned in the Report. According to the UCR User Guide, this database includes legal documents, such as indictments, motions, orders, decisions and judgments, as well as evidence submitted during proceedings, and transcripts and audio-visual recordings of hearings.[63] First-time visitors have to create an account before being able to use the UCR database. Subsequently, the database can be searched through keywords contained in either the title or full text of a record, and by entering a variety of other details, such as the name of the accused, case number, exhibit number, document source, document type, and date. While it is not possible to select the name of a particular victim-witness from a dropdown menu, as is possible with the names of the accused, a victim-witness's name can be used in a keyword search – but only when searching the full text of a record, as the names of victim-witnesses are not included in the title of records. It is also not possible to filter results on the basis of specific crimes, items of evidence, or the location where crimes were committed. In essence, the search function of the database is most accommodating to those users who are familiar with and search for the numerics assigned to files by the ICTY. In other words, the records in this database are named, filed, and categorised according to their legal value and can best be retrieved using this institutional classification. While this is a logical choice for legal institutions such as the ICTY and the IRMCT, it must be remembered that for victims and their relatives those records have a different value, one that is not properly captured by a legal or institutional classification.

The press release which announced the launch of the UCR seems to imply that the UCR will eventually replace two pre-existing databases, namely the ICTY Court Records (ICR) and the Judicial Records and Archives

62 IRMCT, 'Unified Court Records' (2020) <https://ucr.irmct.org/> accessed 3 January 2022; IRMCT, 'Mechanism Launches Unified Court Records Database' (1 September 2020) <https://perma.cc/BWX9-JAKX>.

63 IRMCT, Unified Court Records Database User Guide (IRMCT 2020) 3 <https://perma.cc/B2A3-YJXU>.

Database (JRAD).[64] The ICTY Court Records database is very similar to the UCR as this database also contains the public court records of the ICTY.[65] The ICR, which also requires the user to create an account before it can be accessed, essentially has the same search options as the UCR database – except that the ICR does not differentiate between title searches and full text searches. The ICR continues to be updated, as is evidenced by the dates of files uploaded on the 'Recently Posted Records' webpage of the database's website. Conversely, the JRAD used to be an internal database of the ICTY, which was gradually opened up to other, external users through access keys.[66] Currently, the homepage of the JRAD website states that this database contains the public judicial records of the ICTR and of the IRMCT itself – but not of the ICTY – and that the JRAD has not been updated since September 2020.[67] A final database of public judicial records is the Case Law Database (CLD) of the IRMCT, which contains just the judgments and decisions of the ICTY, ICTR, and the IRMCT.[68] It must be noted here that the original website of the ICTY is still live and accessible, and also contains some digital archival materials. For example, visitors can find the 'Voice of the Victims' videos mentioned in the introduction of this chapter there.

A very different database, which is not publicly accessible, is the Electronic Disclosure System (EDS),[69] which is managed by the Office of the Prosecutor. This database is a tool through which the Prosecutor can securely disclose evidence to the Defense and contains the record of materials collected during the investigation phase.[70] Those materials which have been presented by the Prosecutor at trial are often publicly accessible through either the UCR database or the ICTY Court Records – these files fall within the first category of judicial records as mentioned in the UN Secretary-General's Report. However, even some of those files that have been presented at trial are still not publicly available, because they have

64 'Mechanism Launches Unified Court Records Database' (n 62).

65 ICTY, 'ICTY Court Records' (2009) <http://icr.icty.org/> accessed 3 January 2022.

66 ICTY, *ICTY Manual on Developed Practices* (UNICRI Publisher 2009) 174 <https://perma.cc/NP9Q-VNTD>.

67 IRMCT, 'Judicial Records and Archives Database' (2015) <https://jrad.irmct.org/> accessed 5 January 2022.

68 IRMCT, 'Case Law Database' (nd) <https://cld.irmct.org/#> accessed 3 January 2022.

69 ICTY, 'Electronic Disclosure System' (2004) <https://eds.icty.org/> accessed 3 January 2022.

70 ICTY (n 66) 62–63; Vukušić (n 6) 627–630.

been classified as confidential by the Office of the Prosecutor. Files can be classified as confidential, for example because they contain information about the identity of protected witnesses, because they relate to closed trial sessions or because they are files that have been given to the Prosecutor in confidence.[71] Materials that have not been used at trial are not publicly accessible, as they may still be used in future cases before the IRMCT, or because they are considered unreliable.[72]

The contrast between the relatively little information that is available about the physical archives on the one hand, and the plurality in online databases on the other hand, may seem surprising. However, if one keeps in mind the classification of and distinction between uses and users of the archives as made in the UN Secretary-General's Report, this particular attention for digital accessibility becomes a more logical choice. If the primary users of the archives, at least in the short term, are considered to be those directly involved in the judicial work of the Tribunal or Mechanism, then quick, easy, and efficient access to those records is essential. For those actors, accessing the physical archives might be unnecessary if the contents of the records can just as successfully be retrieved online. In addition, the majority of those primary users might already be familiar with the physical archives, as these are located in the same building as the former Tribunal and the Mechanism. In light of this prioritisation of primary users, it is possible that familiarity with the ICTY and its premises is assumed, and thus additional information about the physical archives is deemed unnecessary. Regardless, while the IRMCT's management of the archives is stated to be based on openness and transparency,[73] this is not evident from the manner in which the archives are presented – especially to users who do not fall within the category of primary users. On the one hand, the absence of any substantial information about the physical archives means that, for those unfamiliar with the ICTY premises, its appearance and composition is left to the imagination. For those actors – and perhaps even more so for victims – the archives are located in an unknown building, in an unfamiliar city, in a faraway country. On the other hand, the variety of digital databases is overwhelming and confusing. Not only is it unclear what the differences between the various databases are, but there is also

71 UNSC 'Report of the Secretary-General' (21 May 2009) UN Doc S/2009/258 12–13.

72 Vukušić (n 6) 627–630.

73 IRMCT 'Access Policy for the Records held by the International Residual Mechanism for Criminal Tribunals' (4 January 2019) UN Doc MICT/17/Rev.1 art 7(1).

no comprehensive overview of the materials that are contained in these databases. Apart from the classified materials stored in the EDS by the Office of the Prosecutor, there are also judicial records from other branches of the Tribunal that cannot be accessed through any of the aforementioned databases, because they have been classified as confidential for a variety of reasons.[74] For victims, identifying and using those databases that might be relevant for them is challenging and not straightforward. Thus, the manner in which the archives and its contents are presented seems to be in line with the principles that also guided the creation and organisation of the archives – meaning the distinction between primary and secondary uses and users. Yet this manner of presentation also shapes the perception that those unfamiliar with the ICTY, the IRMCT, and its premises, have of these institutions. In turn, as is discussed below, all these factors severely impact the accessibility of the ICTY archives, especially for victims.

3.3. Accessibility

While public accessibility of the ICTY archives is one of the Mechanism's core guiding principles,[75] the previous sections on the organisation and presentation of the archives have identified a multitude of issues that directly affect the accessibility of the archives – particularly for victims. This section aims to concretise these issues by examining the accessibility of the ICTY records explicitly, distinguishing between the two ways in which these records can be accessed: in person, by visiting the ICTY archives in The Hague, and online, by using the digital databases previously discussed. There is, however, one overarching issue that impacts the accessibility of the archives as a whole: the absence of a comprehensive overview of the contents of the archives. This not only includes a survey of the different databases – including the physical archives – but also a description of the types of materials that can be accessed in each database, which databases overlap and what their differences are. Importantly, such a survey would also clarify which materials cannot be found in these databases, why not, and when they might be made available to the public. Subsequently, it remains a challenge to get a complete picture of the different databases and their respective purposes.

74 ibid., art 10(3).
75 ibid., art 7(1).

As described in the previous section, the physical ICTY archives are located in the same building as the Mechanism's branch in The Hague – namely, the former seat of the ICTY. While the ICTY and the Mechanism shared these premises until the ICTY closed its doors in 2017, the Mechanism has since become the sole occupant of the building.[76] The archives can be visited in person, although, as stated previously, not at the time of writing. A visit must be planned in advance, however, as the archives can only be accessed by appointment. Such an appointment can be made by filling out the 'Records and Archives Enquiry Form' on the website of the Mechanism, which requires the name and email of the visitor, as well as an explanation of the enquiry.[77] Some logistical information for those travelling to the archives, either by public transport or by car, is provided on a separate page.[78] The website also contains a 'Frequently Asked Questions' webpage, which answers inquiries about the nature of the archives, rules regarding the use of the records, and services provided by the archives.[79] In addition, this page provides guidance for those who are looking for information about specific witnesses, places, accused, fugitives, or the different branches of the Mechanism. Unfortunately, the 'Frequently Asked Questions' webpage does not include any information for those looking for specific victims, crimes, or items of evidence. It is important to note that all these pages, except for the Research Room Rules,[80] are also available in Bosnian, Croatian, and Serbian.[81] As such, the information that is available online does increase the accessibility of the archives for those victims, relatives and communities located in the countries of the former Yugoslavia. However, a major impediment remains the location of the physical archives. The ICTY archives are far removed from the affected communities, as was the ICTY itself when it was still operational. During this time, this distance was already considered to be a major obstacle to

76 UNSC 'Letter dated 18 November 2019 from the President of the International Residual Mechanism for Criminal Tribunals addressed to the President of the Security Council, Annex I: Assessment and progress report of the President of the International Residual Mechanism for Criminal Tribunals, Judge Carmel Agius, for the period from 16 May 2019 to 15 November 2019' (18 November 2019) UN Doc S/2019/888 6.

77 IRMCT, 'Records and Archives Enquiry Form' <https://www.irmct.org/en/records-enquiry> accessed 5 January 2022.

78 IRMCT, 'Directions' <https://www.irmct.org/en/news/directions> accessed 5 January 2022.

79 IRMCT (n 59).

80 IRMCT, 'Research Room Rules' <https://perma.cc/8KHX-DW24>.

81 These webpages are not available in Albanian or Macedonian.

the effective achievement of the Tribunal's objectives, and a recurring point of critique in writings on the ICTY.[82] This distance has remained due to the decision to locate the ICTY archives in the same building as the Tribunal. The location of the archives means that individuals from affected communities who wish to travel to The Hague can only do so if they have the necessary means – including financial resources, but also the time and ability to travel abroad. In this light, it must be kept in mind that, of all the affected countries, only Croatia is set to join the Schengen Area in 2023,[83] and while there are agreements which ease visa requirements for those visiting the EU from the other affected countries except Kosovo, this circumstance does present an extra obstacle.[84] Unfortunately, according to the Mechanism's 'Frequently Asked Questions' webpage, even though Mechanism staff can 'provide general advice and assist with simple searches for records', they are not able to help with detailed research inquests.[85] This implies that it is not possible for individuals unable to travel to The Hague to ask the Mechanism to conduct research in the archives for them – although it could be that exceptions are made in practice.

In addition, it should be noted that, apart from physical distance, there can also be a mental distance. In other words, the archives are located in a city and country that could be regarded as distant due to factual or perceived societal differences. Unfamiliarity with The Netherlands, or an understanding formed through limited exposure – for example due to its portrayal in local media or by public figures,[86] can create obstacles that are as palpable as geographical or logistical obstacles. Finally, it must be kept

82 William W Burke-White, 'Regionalization of International Criminal Law Enforcement: A Preliminary Exploration' (2003) 38 Texas International Law Journal 729; Laura A Dickinson, 'The Promise of Hybrid Courts' (2003) 97 American Journal of International Law 295; Stuart Ford, 'A Social Psychology Model of the Perceived Legitimacy of International Criminal Courts: Implications for the Success of Transitional Justice Mechanisms' (2012) 45 Vanderbilt Journal of Transnational Law 405; ICTY (n 66) 10.

83 Cory Bennett and Camille Gijs, 'Croatia to Join Schengen Free-Travel Zone in 2023' *POLITICO* (Washington, 8 December 2022) <https://perma.cc/UH97-Z5Z5>.

84 The European Travel Information and Authorisation System, 'ETIAS Visa Waiver Requirements' <https://www.etias.info/visa-requirements/> accessed 2 January 2022; SchengenVisa Info, 'Kosovars Travelling to Europe – EU Entry Requirements for Kosovan Citizens' <https://www.schengenvisainfo.com/kosovo/> accessed 15 September 2022.

85 IRMCT (n 59).

86 Refik Hodžić, 'A Long Road Yet to Reconciliation: The Impact of the ICTY on Reconciliation and Victims' Perceptions of Criminal Justice' in Steinberg (n 32).

in mind that the location of the archives in a building that served, and continues to serve, as a court also affects the accessibility of the archives. Court buildings are designed to convey the power of the law and instil respect, reverence, and awe in those who enter. They are by their very nature imposing, and the building housing the IRMCT and the ICTY archives is no different – even though it was originally built for an insurance company.[87] Of course, it would be impossible to ascertain whether these specific issues have in fact prevented victims or relatives from travelling to The Hague. Nevertheless, the distance between the ICTY itself and the affected communities had an undeniable impact on their relationship and on the legacy of the ICTY overall. It is hard to imagine that the continuation of this distance with regard to the archives does not have a similar, if not the same, effect on the victim communities.

With regard to online access to the ICTY records, the number of databases is overwhelming, and it is challenging to distinguish between the different sources and websites. While lawyers, researchers and other professionals might have the knowledge, resources, and time to sift through the different databases to find the one most relevant to them, the same cannot necessarily be said for victims or their relatives. Using those databases presumes, first of all, access to a computer with an internet connection to search and download, as well as software to read, watch, and listen to files. In addition, finding and using the relevant databases is anything but straightforward. Without relatively advanced knowledge of the ICTY, the Mechanism, and their organisation, it would be difficult to know where and how to start. As stated above, the webpage on the ICTY archives is well-hidden within the general website of the Mechanism. Searching for the ICTY archives by using a popular online search engine generates a list of potentially relevant results – but no source which lists and explains the different databases and allows users to compare them. Most likely, after some preliminary research through the official website of the Mechanism, users will arrive at the UCR, which is clearly structured to accommodate those first-category users as identified in the UN Secretary-General's Report. While the UCR User Guide is certainly of great help,[88] it is only available in English and seems to presume a certain level of knowledge about the

87 Rijksdienst voor het Cultureel Erfgoed, 'Monumentnummer: 530892 Churchillplein 1 2517 JW Te 's-Gravenhage' (Rijksmonumentenregister) <https://monumentenregister.cultureelerfgoed.nl/monumenten/530892> accessed 15 September 2022.

88 IRMCT (n 63).

ICTY, its structure, and its cases. Additionally, the User Guide and the database itself also presume pre-existing knowledge about the specific object of inquiry and, most importantly, its classification within the ICTY system. In order to generate results in the UCR database, a user must enter keywords and other details – such as a date, document type, case, or exhibit number. For those without the necessary knowledge who wish to locate a specific exhibit or file, it can be challenging to find the right combination of keywords and details. An incorrect combination can yield no results, or an overwhelming amount of most likely irrelevant results that the user has to sift through. None of the public databases provide any options to ask for assistance – there are no 'Help' buttons, no troubleshooting pages or online forms to ask questions. Another fact to consider is that, even though the UCR can be accessed in Bosnian, Croatian and Serbian, and the majority of files have corresponding translations, the titles of those files are not translated and remain in English. There are many of such seemingly minute issues, which together can create an insurmountable wall for those without the required knowledge and know-how.

Finally, access to the ICTY archives is limited, and to a certain extent justifiably so, to those records that are public. As stated above, the records that have not been disclosed due to a variety of reasons cannot be viewed by the public – including victims. According to Article 11 of the official Access Policy of the IRMCT, which is only available in English, requests for access to undisclosed files can be made to the Mechanism, but these have to meet a number of requirements.[89] First of all, Article 10(3) of the Access Policy lists several types of records that are exempt from disclosure, mostly because of their confidential nature or the security risks associated with their disclosure. According to Article 11(2), requests for access to classified judicial records not covered by the exceptions of Article 10(3) must be made in accordance with the procedures described in another document, namely the Practice Direction on Filings made before the International Residual Mechanism for Criminal Tribunals, which is a document detailing the rules regarding all filings made before the Mechanism.[90] However, it is unclear which articles of this document are applicable to disclosure requests. In addition to this requirement, Article 11(2) of the Access Policy also stipulates that requests for access to classified judicial records must be made pursuant

89 IRMCT (n 73) art 11.

90 IRMCT 'Practice Direction on Filings made before the International Residual Mechanism for Criminal Tribunals' (4 January 2019) UN Doc MICT/7/Rev.3.

to other applicable Rules and Practice Directions – without specifying which other rules and practice directions could be applicable. Article 11(3) states that requests to access other, non-judicial classified records have to be submitted to the Access Focal Points of either the Registry or the Office of the Prosecutor, as listed on the Mechanism's website. Disclosure requests may be submitted in English or French, according to Article 11(4). Disclosure requests can be denied by the Mechanism, inter alia, if the information requested is non-specific, too broad, does not exist, is not held by the Mechanism, cannot be found, or if the information cannot be located without extensive examination or research.[91] Therefore, a request for access has to specify the sought after materials or files, and it is thus presumed that the person submitting the request knows, first of all, that the files exist, secondly, that the files are contained in the archives, and thirdly, that these files have not yet been disclosed. For those who do not possess this information, submitting a request for access is not a viable option.

The above paragraphs have identified a variety of obstacles that those who do not possess the necessary knowledge and expertise, and in particular victims and their relatives, could face when trying to access the physical and digital archives of the ICTY. Again, the prioritisation of those identified as the primary users of the archives means that the archives are most accessible to those actors who are professionally connected to the Tribunal or the Mechanism, who possess the knowledge, skills, and means necessary to search the archives. While it would be interesting in this regard to examine statistics on the number, location, and background of the archives' users over the years, these figures will of course not reveal any information about those actors who wish to – but have been unable to – use the archives.

4. Restoring the Balance

In light of the above, one must conclude that the ICTY archives have been designed for a very specific target audience, and are consequently quite inaccessible – in a multitude of ways – for the uninitiated. Overall, the person of the victim specifically seems to be absent in the current structures of the archives. This absence is not caused by malice, ignorance, or even negligence. The discussion surrounding the creation and management of the archives, the online databases and websites, and the maintenance of

91 IRMCT (n 73) art 11(6).

the physical archives all testify to the importance of the archives, not just to a restricted group of professionals, but to the global community. The archives exist and they are public, and – to that extent – accessible. Yet their classification as a record of the ICTY, its proceedings, investigations, and administration, ignores the undeniable fact that these archives are also a record of its subject matter. In other words, if one considers the archives as a touchstone of memory, the ICTY archives are not only a memory of the Tribunal, but also of the Yugoslav Wars themselves. The archives contain the conflict which the ICTY was created to judge. While this may seem obvious, the multifaceted nature and meaning of the archives is not visible in the archives' organisation, presentation, or accessibility. However, adopting a wider, more in-depth view of the archives' meaning is highly important. Not only can incorporating this idea into the organisation and presentation of the ICTY archives improve their accessibility to victim communities, giving consideration and equal weight to different understandings of the archives can potentially provide these communities with a sense of ownership – over the archives, and over the conflict contained therein. Returning to Christie's argument, to regard conflict as property that belongs to victims of crime, and to acknowledge their status as the original owners of conflict, can return to these victims a sense of agency that was taken away by the crime. This reasoning can be extended to the records that remain after judicial proceedings have ended, which preserve, present, and prove the existence of the original conflict.

Importantly, it is not argued here that victims of crime own the records of judicial proceedings, nor is it the aim of this chapter to argue in favour of returning full ownership of the ICTY archives to the victim communities. It would not be feasible or realistic to propose such far-reaching institutional changes here. Rather, what this chapter proposes is first and foremost a change in mindset regarding the relationship between the remaining ICTY records and victim communities. This is by no means a quick, short-term, or straightforward undertaking. Building and maintaining a close relationship with affected communities was also the main objective of the ICTY's Outreach Programme, and it achieved mixed results.[92] Funding of the Programme came from external sources – not from the regular ICTY budget – which meant that the planning, organisation, and implementation of its

92 Petar Finci, 'Was It Worth It? A Look into the Results of the ICTY's Outreach Programme' in Stahn and others (n 13).

activities were determined by various donors. This, in turn, meant that it became almost impossible to adopt an overarching set of objectives and policies to guide the Programme, and that, consequently, assessments of the overall impact of the Programme's activities have been ad hoc and incomplete.[93] However, the ICTY's Outreach Programme was the first of its kind and when successful, its achievements were significant. For example, the translation of the ICTY website into the languages of the region was part of this Programme, and Petar Finci estimates that the majority of official information available in the region about the ICTY was distributed through the Outreach Programme.[94] Therefore, when considering any possible venues for improvement, it is important to be mindful, not only of budgetary, institutional, and logistical constraints which are likely to hamper the implementation of any proposed recommendations, but also of the measures that have already been taken to make the ICTY archives accessible to victim communities. Nevertheless, it would be neglectful to refrain from discussing potential improvements just because of these considerations, especially in light of the – presumably – infinite existence of the ICTY records. Furthermore, just as the ICTY and ICTR were the first of their kind, so are their archives. Subsequent institutions were, and continue to be, built on the foundations of these two tribunals, and, while imperfect, they have provided invaluable lessons for the future. Similarly, the management of their archives functions as a framework through which the interrelationship between mass atrocities, victims, adjudicative institutions and their records can be further developed.

A starting point could be consultations with victim communities in order to understand and chart the meanings that the ICTY archives might have for them. How do these communities perceive the archives, what is their relationship with them – if there is a relationship at all? Subsequent questions could focus on the desired relationship: what kind of relationship would these affected communities want to have with the archives, or, if necessary, what additional information, communication, or action would they require in order to express their needs and desires? Such consultations could be carried out in partnership with external research institutes or universities.[95] The outcomes of such research could then be used to further

93 ibid., 357–359.

94 ibid., 361 and 369.

95 In 2016, the ICTY Outreach Programme established a partnership with the Castleberry Peace Institute of the University of North Texas. See, ICTY, 'ICTY Launches

give expression to the differentiated nature and meaning of the archives. Distinguishing between these meanings, and giving them equal weight, can bring balance into the further decision-making process regarding the archives. In addition, institutional acknowledgment of the gaps that exist in the Mechanism's widely accepted, yet limited, understanding of the ICTY archives can initiate discussion on potential venues for improvement. Such discussion could be facilitated by, for example, a specialised UN working group. The activities of such a working group could be a recurring section in the annual reports or the biannual progress reports drafted each year by the IRMCT.[96] In cooperation with victim communities, or their representatives, this working group could draft long-term solutions based on a careful consideration of different interests and needs. In addition, if possible and feasible, this working group could be consulted or otherwise involved in decisions made regarding the archives – for example, concerning the archivalisation,[97] declassification, or destruction of certain records.

There are also smaller changes that could be implemented to counterbalance the current primacy of those first-category users and improve the accessibility of the archives for other users. A first step towards improved accessibility could be the creation of a chart or compendium of the different databases and their contents – which would be beneficial to all users. This compendium could also explain what is contained in the physical archives versus the digital archives, and in which situations a visit to the physical archives is to be preferred. This overview, and descriptions of the databases, could incorporate and distinguish between the different objectives that prospective users may have. Similarly, the Mechanism could provide more, and more accessible, information about the number and types of classified records that remain undisclosed. It could be that the majority of those records are of little interest to victims or their relatives, yet information about these records is scarce, difficult to find, and confusing for those unfamiliar with UN documentation and the lingo used therein. More generally, the Mechanism's website could be more inclusive in its presentation of the archives, taking into consideration the variety of potential users. One way to achieve this would be the creation of a digital research guide specific-

Report on the Witness Experience' (6 October 2016) <https://perma.cc/K2V5-42E93>.

96 IRMCT, 'Documents: Reports' <https://www.irmct.org/en/documents/reports> accessed 3 February 2022.

97 Ketelaar (n 28) 132–133.

ally tailored to the needs and knowledge of non-professional users of the archives. With regard to the physical archives, another possibility would be the publication of an online photo gallery of the actual archival rooms and stacks, online guided tours, or even an instructional video. Currently, visitors of the website of the Mechanism can view a number of online exhibitions which showcase a variety of evidentiary items and explain how these were used in judicial proceedings.[98] Even though these exhibitions seem to focus on the work of the Tribunals, rather than the underlying conflicts or the archives, such exhibitions are an excellent way to introduce the archives to the public and can bring these archives to life. With regard to the digital databases, one question that can only be answered by those who manage these databases and who have the required technical know-how, is whether their search engines can be adapted in order to better facilitate searches by non-professionals – and victims in particular. Unfortunately, it is beyond the scope of this chapter to examine this question further, but even adding a 'Frequently Asked Questions' webpage to each database, or a troubleshooting webpage, could be useful for users. An alternative solution would be to appoint a liaison officer who is tasked specifically with assisting those users who are unfamiliar with the ICTY, the Mechanism or the archives, or who are otherwise unable to access the archives themselves. This liaison officer could assist with specific searches, individual visits, or draft disclosure requests. Perhaps a chat function could be added to the webpage on the ICTY archives, which could be made available to users for a few hours per week. Of course, even those suggested changes that might seem minimal require time, money, and effort, and it is possible that some – or perhaps all – proposed solutions are unfeasible. Nevertheless, this section presented some preliminary ideas with the aim of inspiring further discussion and research on the relationship between victim communities, international adjudicative institutions, and their shared archives.

5. Conclusion

This chapter studied the ICTY archives in light of Christie's understanding of conflict as property, according to which the victims of the Yugoslav Wars are the original owners of the conflict that exists between them and those who committed mass atrocities. This conflict manifests itself in the experi-

98 'Archives' (n 14), bottom of the page.

ences, memories, and stories of these victims. However, the compilation, use, and preservation of these memories by the ICTY to realise its institutional purpose have resulted in a collection of records that contain not only the original conflict, but also the work of the ICTY. Following Christie's approach, this multifaceted meaning of the ICTY archives should mean that the victim communities and the ICTY – or, presently, the Mechanism – share ownership of these records. Nevertheless, officially the UN own these records, and they have tasked the Mechanism with managing the archives. This perception of the archives as solely the records of the ICTY and its proceedings is also reflected in the organisation, presentation, and accessibility of the archives, which mainly accommodate a limited group of professionals and not necessarily affected communities. Borrowing from the field of critical archival studies, this chapter explored the ways in which victim communities are absent in the current organisation, presentation, and accessibility of the ICTY archives, and how this ignores the plural meaning that these records have. Finally, this chapter proposed a number of recommendations for change which can restore the balance in the relationship between the Mechanism and the victims as shared owners of the conflict and its records. While not meant as an exhaustive, or even a particularly in-depth, list of suggestions, the hope of this author is that these ideas will encourage further debate on these questions of memories, archives, and ownership.

5. Absence and the Victim of Enforced Disappearance

Sandra M. Rios Oyola[*]

Abstract: *This chapter provides an in-depth analysis of enforced disappearances in Colombia, focusing on how the absence of victims is ingrained within the crime itself and how their families represent it. Victims are stripped of their political presence, yet they continue to be represented in the public sphere through family activism. Despite the peace agreement signed in 2016, the practice of enforced disappearance persisted, with a reported 2460 disappearances in just the first half of 2020. The chapter delves into the legal framework of enforced disappearance. It explores various strategies that oppressive regimes employ to conceal the existence of enforced disappearances and undermine the credibility of victims and their families. Furthermore, through the analysis of interviews conducted with members of transitional justice institutions and victims' associations, the chapter elaborates on families' public mobilisation, art, and participation in transitional justice mechanisms. Their public displays of private grief seek to enhance solidarity, combat the stigma associated with disappearance, and underscore the ongoing nature of the crime.*[1]

1. Introduction

Hannah Arendt defines 'appearance' as 'something that is being seen and heard by others as well as ourselves'.[2] While reality might differ from what appears, appearance constitutes being seen and heard in a political space; consequently, what does not appear does not exist in the political space. Appearing is a condition for political action. Victims of enforced disappearance are made invisible; they do not participate; they have been violently removed from public existence. The victim of a forced disappearance suffers the annulation of the possibility of political presence, although not of their representation. This chapter examines how the activism of families allows for the disappeared to continue being represented in the public sphere.

This chapter analyses how 'absence' is part of the crime of enforced disappearance and how it is represented by the families of the disappeared.

---

* Dr Sandra M. Rios Oyola is an Assistant Professor at the University College Roosevelt.

1 This research was possible thanks to a postdoctoral grant by the FNRS (National Fund of Scientific Research, Belgium) conducted at the Institute of Political Science Louvain-Europe, University of Louvain. The author's current affiliation is at University College Roosevelt, The Netherlands.

2 Hannah Arendt, *The Human Condition* (1st edn, University of Chicago Press 1998) 49.

In 2004, the International Convention for the Protection of All Persons from Enforced Disappearance stated that families are direct victims (Article 24). Relatives are also considered victims of enforced disappearance since their lives are affected by the uncertainty and suffering due to not knowing about the fate of their relatives. A permanent search marks their lives. The relatives of victims of enforced disappearance engage in political action that challenges the notion of the victim of enforced disappearance as absent from the political landscape. The chapter first presents the definitions of enforced disappearance in international humanitarian law and in domestic law in the case of Colombia, which has been selected due to its large number of cases of enforced disappearance. These cases took place during the history of the armed conflict and have been carried out both by state and non-state armed actors. The National Historical Memory Center reports 80 000 disappeared victims between 1970 and 2018.[3] The practice of enforced disappearance continued even after the signing of the peace agreement in 2016. Between January and June 2020, 2460 people were reported as disappeared.[4] Secondly, the chapter discusses the absence of the disappeared victims in terms of forced disappearance and social disappearance. Thirdly, it presents the actions of resistance to the (political) absence of victims of enforced disappearance through collective mobilisation, art/protest, and participation in transitional justice mechanisms. In this chapter, I present and analyse extracts of interviews conducted in 2016, 2019 and 2020 with members of transitional justice institutions and victims' associations in Colombia.

2. Enforced Disappearance, and Social Disappearance

The 1992 Declaration on the Protection of All Persons from Enforced Disappearance ('the 1992 Declaration') was the first international legal instrument to define enforced disappearance. It states that a victim of enforced disappearance is a person who is:

> arrested, detained or abducted against their will or otherwise deprived of their liberty by officials of different branches or levels of Government,

3 'Lo que sabemos de los desaparecidos en Colombia' (Centro Nacional de Memoria Histórica) <https://perma.cc/VN85-JWGW>.

4 Pompilio Peña Montoya, 'La desaparición: un crimen que pervive en Colombia' (*Hacemos Memoria*, 29 August 2020) <https://perma.cc/Z8T4-7S8A>.

> or by organised groups or private individuals acting on behalf of, or with the support, direct or indirect, consent or acquiescence of the Government, followed by a refusal to disclose the fate or whereabouts of the persons concerned or a refusal to acknowledge the deprivation of their liberty, which places such persons outside the protection of the law (emphasis is added).[5]

Article 2 of the International Convention for the Protection of All Persons from Enforced Disappearance ('the 2007 Convention') states that:

> enforced disappearance is considered to be the arrest, detention, abduction or any other form of deprivation of liberty by agents of the State or by persons or groups of persons acting with the authorization, support or acquiescence of the State, followed by a refusal to acknowledge the deprivation of liberty or by concealment of the fate or whereabouts of the disappeared person, which place such a person outside the protection of the law (emphasis is added).[6]

The definition that appears in the 1992 Declaration highlights the role of the government in its execution, and the 2007 Convention adds to this definition the 'concealment of the fate or whereabouts of the disappeared person' to explain the fact that the crime does not only consist of the removal of their liberty but the ongoing concealment, which requires an additional set of criminal practices. It also highlights that the deprivation of their liberty is not the only fate of the victims of enforced disappearance; other outcomes could also be death, mass graves, and the destruction of their body. The lack of certainty about the whereabouts of the disappeared person is one of the crucial characteristics and effects of enforced disappearance.

The notion of disappearance has not only been used to describe a criminal act but to explain the broader phenomenon of 'social disappearance'. This term, coined by Gatti, is used to refer to the social dynamics and institutions

5 UNCHR 'Declaration on the Protection of All Persons from Enforced Disappearance' (28 February 1992) E/CN.4/RES/1992/29 <https://perma.cc/QHB3-UXGN>.

6 UNGA 'International Convention for the Protection of All Persons from Enforced Disappearance' (20 December 2006), adopted by General Assembly resolution 61/177 on 12 January 2007, <https://www.refworld.org/docid/47fdfaeb0.html> accessed 19 November 2022.

that produce marginalisation and exclusion.[7] People at the margins of society are excluded due to their ethnicity, race, sexual orientation or social class. This position leaves them vulnerable to armed state actors and to illegal armed actors, such as in the case of migrants crossing deserts and trafficked women, among others. Victims of social disappearance 'may not be forcefully made to disappear through a paramilitary commando, but denied the protection of the state through other means, or by mere inaction'.[8] Although social and forced disappearances describe different types of practices, they are similar in terms of accountability. Schindel argues that this type of marginalisation creates existences detached from legal inscription and civil protection: 'these cases bring about the conjunction of absence from state records and from its obligations, invisibility from mainstream society, and pervasiveness of modes of existence in which people often navigate between legality and illegality and mostly endure extreme material conditions.'[9] Both social and forced disappearance also have in common the 'absence' as a means to deter people from state legal protection.

3. *International Framework regarding the definition of Enforced Disappearance*

The crime of enforced disappearance continues in countries such as Syria, China, The Democratic Republic of Congo, Mexico, Sri Lanka, Pakistan, Zimbabwe, and Colombia.[10] Forced disappearance has been used as a tool of terror, particularly by governments trying to repress political opponents or by armed groups and is one of the many tactics of control used by states across the globe. Enforced disappearance committed under a 'state of exception', when the state suspends constitutional protections and uses extra-legal sovereign violence to defeat a possible threat, is less common.

7 Gabriel Gatti, 'The Social Disappeared: Genealogy, Global Circulations, and (Possible) Uses of a Category for the Bad Life' (2020) 32(1) Public Culture 25.

8 Estela Schindel, 'Mobility and Disappearance: Transregional Threads, Historical Resonances' in Schindel Estal and Gabriel Gatti (eds), *Social Disappearance. Explorations Between Latin America and Eastern Europe* (Forum Transregionale Studien 2020) 22.

9 ibid., 23.

10 Amnesty International, 'Enforced Disappearances' <https://perma.cc/JWK9-8BSJ>; 'A Closer Look at Abductions and Forced Disappearances Across the Globe (*ReliefWeb*, 28 August 2020)' <https://perma.cc/XX8Q-G75E>.

However, enforced disappearance is not an 'aberration' or an extreme form of the state of 'exception' but rather a logical consequence of sovereignty as a politics of erasure. Bargu, following Agamben, argues that enforced disappearance is a form of invisible violence that is not exceptional but part of an '*invisible penal architechture*'.[11] The 'insurgent's body becomes the surface upon which sovereignty imprints its mark – a mark written with an ink that erases itself as well as the surface out of existence.'[12]

Although with limited enforcing power, international law establishes norms and customary practices to deter the violence moved by sovereign will. It also imposes on states the obligation to continuously search for the disappeared in order to alleviate the permanent suffering caused by victims' continuous absence (Guiding Principle 7, 2019).[13] According to the Guiding Principles (2019), the continuous nature of the obligation to search only comes to an end when the person is found. If the person is found alive, he or she should be placed under the protection of the law. If the person is not found alive he or she should be properly identified and returned to the family in a dignified manner. The search does not stop with the identification or punishment of the perpetrator. According to this view, the crime of forced disappearance is not affected by a particular statute of limitations or by the principle of non-retroactivity 'since this is a crime that is still being committed'.[14]

State actors have often perpetrated the practice of enforced disappearance in order to silence a group of people that were considered to be a threat to their power. The systematic use of these practices was initially documented in Nazi Germany and South America, where this strategy was insidious during the Dirty War in Argentina, resulting in the disappearance of 30 000 civilians. The Inter-American Commission on Human Rights (IACHR) devoted special attention to the situation in Chile and Argentina in the 1970s. In September 1979, the IACHR's visit to Argentina led to finding large and systematic evidence of forced disappearances, and 'it

11 Banu Bargu, 'Mobility and Disappearance: Transregional Threads, Historical Resonances' (2014) 23(1) *Qui Parle, Special Dossier: Rethinking Sovereignty and Capitalism* 35.

12 ibid., 62.

13 Committee on Enforced Disappearances, Guiding Principles for the Search for Disappeared Persons (28 August 2019).

14 Maria Clara, Galvis Patiño and Rainer Huhle, 'The Rights of the Victims of Enforced Disappearance Do Not Have an Expiration Date' (*Opinio Juris*, 7 July 2020) <https://perma.cc/UCV2-QWHH>.

also found clandestine detainees in an official prison'.[15] The demand for this crime to be addressed was high in the region, where families of the disappeared and other human rights associations were particularly active in insisting on the recognition of this complex form of human rights violation.

Furthermore, according to the Article 7 of the Rome Statute enforced disappearance of persons is included among crimes against humanity when committed as part of a widespread or systematic attack directed against any civilian population with knowledge of the attack. Article 7, para. 2 (i), defines the crime as:

> the arrest, detention or abduction of persons by, or with the authorization, support or acquiescence of, a State or a political organization, followed by a refusal to acknowledge that deprivation of freedom or to give information on the fate or whereabouts of those persons, <u>with the intention of</u> removing them from the protection of the law for a prolonged period of time (emphasis is added).[16]

The goal of the Rome Statute is that crimes against humanity, among other crimes, are tried, proving a crime against humanity requires providing evidence of a special intent. Consequently, the definition of enforced disappearance used in the Rome Statute emphasises intention, while the 1992 and 2007 definitions emphasise the lack of protection of the law as a consequence of forced disappearance. When a victim is being unjustly retained, and their retention, their fate, or whereabouts are concealed, he or she is factually removed from the protection of the law. The victim's absence produces uncertainty and harm. This removal occurs independently of the intention of the perpetrator.

The international legislation recognises enforced disappearance only when it is committed by a state agent. There is a particular type of harm caused by a crime of this nature when it is perpetrated by the state. When a state agent carries out the disappearance of a person, it does not only harm the person directly, but it has the enhanced effect of breaking the trust in the state because the perpetrator uses the state apparatus to make the disappearance occur and continue. For example, between 1983 and 1992,

15 Reed Brody and Felipe González, 'Nunca Más: An Analysis of International Instruments on "Disappearances"' (1997) 19(2) Human Rights Quarterly 365, 368.

16 UNGA, Rome Statute of the International Criminal Court (last amended 2010), 17 July 1998, <https://www.refworld.org/docid/3ae6b3a84.html> accessed 20 November 2022.

close to 3000 cases of forced disappearance of alleged terrorism suspects took place in Peru's central southern Andes.[17] Isaias-Rojas explains that this practice was more a form of state rule than a crime. Members of the official security forces arrested civilians citing the law and promised their relatives that they would return the person when their investigation was over. The testimonies of relatives of victims of enforced disappearance reveal how members of the state repeatedly promised them '*mañana vienes*' (you come tomorrow) for an answer about the location of the victim, but tomorrow would become 'never'.[18] The bureaucratic landscape was used to *disappear the disappearance*, to neglect it and to erode the reliability of the witnesses.[19] Rojas-Perez observes how rumour, suspicion, insinuation, and culpability were the signature of the state, casting suspicion on the relatives:

> 'The authorities insinuated that the disappearance could not be a random event; that if the victim was missing, it certainly was because he or she was involved in terrorism – the presupposition being, of course, that only terrorists ended up being disappeared at the hands of the state.'[20]

In sum, the mere removal of the person from the public or their absence is not enough to define it as enforced disappearance. The 2007 Convention establishes state authorship as a crucial element. The clandestine nature of the crime makes it difficult to prove, and the access to bureaucracies and other resources is such in the case of the state that it makes it into a particular type of crime of its own. The Rome Statute presents the intention of the state agent as a decisive variable. Disappearance is not the same as absence, but absence is an essential component of this crime.

There are also a number of instances not covered by the Rome Statute or by the 2007 Convention, such as the acts of enforced disappearance occurred in the Middle East and North African (MENA) states, where only six countries are bound by the Rome Statute.[21] For example, the International Commission on Missing Persons (ICMP), an intergovernmental organisation that addresses the issue of persons missing as a result of

17 Isaias Rojas-Perez, *Mourning Remains: State Atrocity, Exhumations, and Governing the Disappeared in Peru's Postwar Andes* (Stanford University Press 2017) 121.

18 ibid., 122.

19 ibid., 128.

20 ibid., 131.

21 MENA: Middle East and North African countries consist of Algeria, Bahrain, Egypt, Iran, Iraq, Israel, Jordan, Kuwait, Lebanon, Libya, Morocco, Oman, Qatar, Saudi Arabia, Syria, Tunisia, United Arab Emirates, and Yemen.

armed conflicts, violations of human rights, and natural disasters, estimates that between 250 000 and one million Iraqis have been missing since 2003.[22] Other cases that are not included are those committed by non-state actors. In practice, there has been increasing use of enforced disappearance as a legal category to describe this practice when committed by non-state actors. Calls for a reformulation of the conceptualisation of enforced disappearance in international law are met with mixed reactions. On the one hand, there is the tension that an ampliation of the term will make it less effective. On the other hand, victims of enforced disappearance by non-state actors have weaker legal protection than victims of enforced disappearance committed by state actors because the crimes they have suffered cannot be covered by international law.[23] For those reasons, in 2019, the Working Group on Enforced or Involuntary Disappearances (WGEID) decided to expand its mandate to include limited situations of disappearances by non-state actors.[24] The WGEID opened up its definition to the disappearance of migrating individuals in transit and in destination countries, which are a considerable group of people vulnerable to the crime of disappearance, although not committed directly by state actors.[25] In 2021, the WGEID continued to review acts committed by non-state actors that are the *de facto* authorities.[26] These non-state actors are entities that exercise at least some effective authority over some territory within a state. They 'intend to

---

22 OMCT, 'Families of Disappeared Still Awaiting Justice throughout the Middle East' (*World Organization against Torture*, 30 August 2021) <https://perma.cc/6CPS-BZL7>.

23 Anna Srovin Coralli, 'Non-State Actors and Enforced Disappearances Defining a Path Forward' (2021) Working Paper Geneva Academy 1 <https://perma.cc/K3SP-QTZ5>; see also Amrei Müller, 'Can Armed Non-state Actors Exercise Jurisdiction and Thus Become Human Rights Duty Bearers?' (2020) 20 Human Rights Law Review 269.

24 The Working Group is composed of five independent experts of balanced geographical representation. Together, they investigate individual cases and produce reports and opinions in order to assist families in determining the fate or whereabouts of their family members who are reportedly disappeared. The group serves as a channel of communication between family members of victims of enforced disappearance and other sources reporting cases of disappearances, and the Governments concerned.

25 United Nations, 'Report of the Working Group on Enforced or Involuntary Disappearances' (2016) A/HRC/33/51 <https://undocs.org/Home/Mobile?FinalSymbol=A%2FHRC%2F33%2F51&Language=E&DeviceType=Desktop&LangRequested=False> accessed 7 July 2023.

26 ACNUDH, 'Working Group on Enforced or Involuntary Disappearances Concludes its 125th Session' (2021) <https://perma.cc/5X6M-HQW9>.

represent the state of which it partially or completely controls the territory in the capacity of official government'.[27]

4. Domestic Legislation: the Colombian Case

The practice of enforced disappearance was in place for decades during the internal armed conflict. The disappearance of persons deemed a threat to the state was often justified under Article 28 of the 1886 Colombian constitution, which stated that:

> This provision does not prevent that even in time of peace, but having serious reasons to fear a disturbance of public order, persons against whom there are serious indications that they are undermining public peace be apprehended and detained by order of the government and with the prior opinion of the ministers.[28]

In Colombia, the state of exception was used for over 40 years. This was a juridical instrument that provided a legal framework for the war. As a result, Colombia, which is not traditionally considered an authoritarian state in the same vein as the regimes experienced in Argentina, Uruguay or Chile, had an authoritarian legal framework that operated in a democratic context. For example, the armed forces had wide competencies that were legitimate under the 1886 constitution: 'Article 170 of the Charter creates the Courts-Martial and the Military Tribunals for the military criminal jurisdiction as an integral part of the branch of public power in charge of administering justice'.[29]

Although there were some previous attempts at typifying the crime of enforced disappearance, it was until a new constitution was adopted in 1991 that Colombia started to prohibit enforced disappearances (Article 12).[30] Furthermore, Colombia is a signatory to the Inter-American Convention

27 Jonte Van Essen, 'De Facto Regimes in International Law' (2012) 28(74) Utrecht Journal of International and European Law 31.

28 Article 28, incise 20, the 1886 Colombian Constitution. See also: Centro Nacional de Memoria Histórica, *Normas y Dimensiones de La Desaparición Forzada En Colombia* (Tome I, Imprenta Nacional 2014) 53–54.

29 Centro Nacional de Memoria Histórica, *Normas y Dimensiones de La Desaparición Forzada En Colombia* (Tome I, Imprenta Nacional 2014).

30 'No one will be subjected to forced disappearance, torture or cruel, inhuman or degrading treatment or punishment', article 12 of the Political Constitution of Colombia (1991).

on Forced Disappearance of Persons, as well as the Rome Statute. In 2000, the country introduced Law 589 that presented the judicial framework for criminal investigations and the search for the whereabouts of the victims. This law explicitly criminalises the act of enforced disappearance and includes those acts committed by non-state actors. The Penal Code (Art 165) defined enforced disappearance as:

> the person ... who deprives another individual of his/her liberty, conceals them and refuses to acknowledge the deprivation of liberty or give information on the whereabouts of the person, thus removing that person from the protection of the law.[31]

Initially, the law only referred to those perpetrators who were members of an illegal group, but this was changed by the Constitutional Court's judgement C-317 of 2002 to include any particular actor.[32]

As a result of the humanitarian crisis brought by the massive crime of enforced disappearance, a number of institutions in charge of registering and searching for the disappeared were created. In 2007, the mandate (Decree 929 of 2007) for the National Commission for the Search of Disappeared Persons ('Search Commission') was created. The Search Commission formally included the Association of Families of Detained and Disappeared Persons (ASFADDES).[33] The National Search Plan (NSP) brought a better structure to the search for the disappeared and counted on the input of specialised non-governmental organisations such as EQUITAS. The most recent strategies are born out of the Peace Agreement between the government and the Fuerzas Armadas Revolucionarias de Colombia (FARC) signed in 2016, ie, the Search Unit for Disappeared People (SUDP), the Special Jurisdiction for Peace, and the Truth and Clarification Commission.[34] Although the SUDP is a humanitarian office in charge of the search for the disappeared, the other mechanisms also deal with the crime of forced disappearance. For example, one of the cases of the Special Jurisdic-

31 Colombian Criminal Code, Article165, Forced Disappearance.
32 Colombian Constitutional Court, Judgement C-317, 2 May 2002, MP Clara Inés Vargas.
33 Asfaddes, 2023, Nuestra Historia <https://perma.cc/6X8D-3D9S >.
34 Unidad de Busqueda de Personas dadas por Desaparecidas, 2023 <https://ubpdbusquedadesaparecidos.co/>.

tion for Peace is the 'Deaths unlawfully presented as combat casualties by State agents', which also covers cases of forced disappearance.[35]

5. The Social Effects of Enforced Disappearance

Enforced disappearance was the preferred tool of states that wanted to silence or eradicate any sign of organised opposition. The effects of this crime do not only affect the direct victim but also their relatives and their communities. Enforced disappearance was used against vulnerable communities that had been stigmatised as allies of the subversion, as had occurred during the Dirty War in Argentina and Chile. The state sought to create the political incapacitation of the opposition. Disappearance, together with torture, was used as a tool of state terror. Its effects created silence through fear, broke the trust in the institutions of the state, severely damaged the social fabric and affected the structure of society.[36]

The crime of enforced disappearance exerts multiple human rights violations simultaneously. According to the Inter-American Court of Human Rights, enforced disappearance goes against the article that forbids the crime in itself.[37] Forced disappearance also violates a person's dignity, personal freedom, the right to the protection of personal integrity, the protection against inhuman treatment (Art 5.1 and 5.2 American Convention of Human Rights), the right to life, the right to personal and legal safety. Enforced disappearance not only harms the direct victims but also their relatives, the groups that they belonged to, and society in general. It creates ontological insecurity since there is no certainty about the location of the victim, and it prevents the relatives from using the palliative resource of funerals since the remains are not found. In the absence of evidence or recognition that the victim has suffered any violation of their rights, it prevents the victim from being recognised as a victim under the law and consequently their rights are not protected.

35 Jurisdicción Especial para la Paz. 2023. Caso 03. Asesinatos y desapariciones forzadas presentados como bajas en combate por agentes del Estado <https://perma.cc/9DQA-2P4Z>.

36 Francisco Ferrandiz and Antonius C G M Robben, *Necropolitics: Mass Graves and Exhumations in the Age of Human Rights* (University of Pennsylvania Press 2015).

37 'Libertad de pensamiento y de expresión' (2021) 16 Cuadernillo de Jurisprudencia de la Corte Interamericana de Derechos Humanos <https://perma.cc/X8WG-YFYU>.

The crime of enforced disappearance generates uncertainty. The case *Anzualdo-Castro v. Peru*, presented by the Inter-American Court on 22 September 2009, highlights the effects of uncertainty on victims:

> [...] in cases of forced disappearance of persons, the victim is placed in a situation of legal uncertainty that prevents, impedes or eliminates the possibility of the individual to be entitled to or effectively exercise his or her rights in general, in one of the most serious forms of non-compliance with the State's duties to respect and guarantee human rights.[38]

The state, through its legal mechanisms, recognises the victim as a disappeared victim, which means that the victim has specific rights and is the subject of specific protocols. These mechanisms correspond to what Isaias-Rojas calls *necro-governmentality of postconflict*.[39] The government creates intelligible interpretations of unspeakable atrocities in order to create 'a controlled version of the past'. Enforced disappearance is a socio-legal construction that names a condition that is full of uncertainties. Instead of having the crime of disappearance defined by the victim's relatives' suffering or experience of distrust towards the government, the crime is defined in terms of the relationship of the victim to the state.

Cath Collins argues that the legal definition of enforced disappearance is an exercise in administering the absence, in naming the limbo in which the non-dead, not-there victim exists.[40] It is important for the victim's relatives to open up the definition of disappearance and the social dimensions of said crime to encompass its complex variety of dimensions.

In addition to the complex character of the offence, it is not possible to fully leave the effect of enforced disappearance in the past. It is an ongoing crime that does not stay in the past: it starts from the moment in which the victim was detained and removed from the system that protected their rights, and it lasts while the action of removal and their fate continues to be concealed, and the victim continues to be disappeared. This ongoing crime affects how the victims' relatives live their lives, which is often embedded in an exhausting ongoing search. The temporality of the state is different from that of the relatives. The state can live on through its institutions, but the lifespan of relatives is different, is limited and is more urgent.

---

38 *Anzualdo-Castro v. Peru*, 2009, IACHR, Ser. C No. 202, para. 101.

39 Isaias-Rojas (n 17) 18.

40 Cath Collins, 'The Reemergence of the Disappeared, the Role of Remains and the Forensic Gaze' (2020) 13(3) Memory Studies 322, 323.

In an interview with a psychologist, who had worked with 30 cases of forced disappearance involving elderly people, he argued that:

> One of our patients had died, and it was terrible for us because we had to find other ways to dignify [recognise] her struggle. We searched among her relatives because nobody had documented her search [for the disappeared victim]. She had been looking for her nephew (not even her son!) for over 25 years, 25 years and nobody else asked, nobody else looked for him, nobody took the case, nobody asked for him. She asked for compensation; she lived in conditions of extreme poverty.[41]

The temporality of the crime of enforced disappearance is twofold: it involves an ongoing crime and an ongoing search. In the case of Colombia, where the conflict lasted for over five decades, a temporality perspective involves an intergenerational component. Once the relatives who are searching for the disappeared victims die, their work in pursuing the search, but also the representation of the absent victims, runs the risk of dying with them.

The complexity of the crime of enforced disappearance relies on its concealment and denial by state institutions. Consequently, it is in the aftermath of dictatorships and authoritarian regimes that transitional justice mechanisms can bring the secrecy of the crimes to light. Exhumations and the knowledge obtained by forensic experts working on mass graves reveal the extent of the atrocities.[42] Truth commissions shed light on the participation of state actors in these crimes. Reparations aim to recognise the harm caused to the relatives. Despite the efforts to overcome the legacy of suffering and harm caused by forced disappearance, decades later, the clashing narratives about the past continue, demonstrating the horror that pervades societies after the use of enforced disappearance as a systemic and widespread practice. Even in the context of post-transition, the legacy of the state terror of enforced disappearance has a prominent effect on society. Protests and political confrontations continue. Robben explains this situation in the case of Argentina as 'a sign of the unmistakable characteristics

41 (Personal interview, 2019).

42 Sandra Milena Rios Oyola, 'Dignification of Victims Through Exhumations in Colombia' (2021) 22(4) Human Rights Review 483.

of a society that had not yet come to terms with the massive trauma in its recent past'.[43]

The process of restoring the disappeared victims' political presence, legal rights, and dignity implies the restoration of their legal rights, challenging their alleged absence in the public and political arena. This is a space that is not granted by the state to the victims as passive receptors of the state's recognition. The political process led by the associations of relatives creates the space that identifies and names the absence of their disappeared relatives and a space for their political representation. In South America, one way in which the disappeared regain political representation has been through the political mobilisation of their families; some of the most prominent groups are Las Madres de la Plaza de Mayo, Abuelas (Grandmothers), HIJOS (SONS), Familiares de Desaparecidos y Detenidos (Families of the Disappeared and Detained), Hermanos (Brothers) and Ex-detenidos Desaparecidos (Ex-detained Disappeared).

6. Representing the Disappeared Victims' Absence

The families are victims in their own right since they have continuously been harmed by the uncertainty and continuous grief of their disappeared loved ones. Nevertheless, one of the central elements for understanding how victims of forced disappearance are represented in the public and legal arenas is through families' activism. On this matter, Bargu claims that:

> The struggles of the families of the disappeared to make the disappeared visible, to keep alive the memory of those who have been subjected to the erasing violence of the state, are crucial in this regard. It is through their agency that the disappeared insistently establish their presence and point to the profound impossibility of sovereignty's ultimate closure into a totality.[44]

Kovras, in his comparative international work with cases of massive forced disappearance, argues that 'the innovative mobilisation of the families of the disappeared shaped the mechanisms of contemporary transitional jus-

43 Antonius C G M Robben, *Political Violence and Trauma in Argentina* (University of Pennsylvania Press 2005) 35.

44 Bargu (n 11) 66.

tice'.[45] These mechanisms range from the judicial response that prioritises criminal responsibility to the administrative and humanitarian response that prioritises finding the disappeared victims' remains or knowing their fate. The activism of families of the disappeared has had an essential role in advancing the recognition of the crime of enforced disappearance as a complex human rights violation and a crime against humanity.

From a sociological perspective, the families' public representation of their private grief has contributed to creating broader sentiments of solidarity towards the disappeared, combating the stigma that concealed the disappearance, and highlighting the ongoing character of the crime. The activism of grassroots organisations working for the disappeared (through grassroots memorials, political activism, legal battles, participation in search commissions, and public protest) bring emotions such as grief from the private to the public sphere. Humphrey and Valverde call this process 'political mourning' or 'a protest against unjust and untimely death'.[46] It defines the movement from private grief to public grief in order to demand accountability from the state. An added consequence of these works of political mourning is their challenge to the alleged absence of the disappeared victim. These works aim to reinstate the disappeared victims' presence in the public sphere.

In what follows, I present three different elements related to the representation of the absence of the disappeared victims by their families based on interviews with relevant stakeholders in Colombia. Most of the interviews have been analysed through thematic analysis techniques, and they have been selected from a sample of over fifty semi-structured interviews in a larger project on 'How do Transitional Justice Measures Contribute to the Restoration of Victims' Dignity'. I have analysed these acts of public mourning as demands of transitional justice from below, where the vernacularisation of the language of human rights and transitional justice is used by social movements.

The first element is related to the problem of representation. The families of the disappeared victims represent those directly affected (themselves, the disappeared victim) but also a more abstract notion of the victim. Those who are relatives of others who are part of their group of victims or associa-

45 Iosif Kovras, *Grassroots Activism and the Evolution of Transitional Justice: The Families of the Disappeared* (CUP 2017) 84.

46 Michael Humphrey and Estela Valverde, 'Human Rights, Victimhood, and Impunity: An Anthropology of Democracy in Argentina' (2007) 51(1) Social Analysis: The International Journal of Social and Cultural Practice 179, 181.

tion, but also of those who could not participate in the mobilisation. The relatives represent their own relatives who have forcefully disappeared, but also the rest who remain anonymous and whose families are not actively looking for them. One of the members of the Salón del Nunca Más in Granada Antioquia, whose brother was disappeared, commented that:

> I am not speaking for me, I speak for everyone, because there are many disappeared, in the cemetery who are NN [No Name]; here three bodies have been recovered as remains of false positives, this year and in the past.[47]

The second element is related to the legitimacy of the representation of the disappeared victims provided by the families. Since the representation is not only validated by their character as relatives of the disappeared, but they also represent those who are not their direct relatives, their legitimacy comes in terms of their expertise. Throughout their work of decades searching for the disappeared, families have obtained important and strong knowledge and networks with national and international humanitarian organisations. Camilo Delgado, member of the national truth commission, *Comisión para el Esclarecimiento de la Verdad – CEV,* explains the importance of the families' expertise:

> you can see the relatives speak in a very very technical manner, they have enough arguments and vocabulary to be understood by a civil servant. These were women that used to work in the fields, or were housewives, now they are completely empowered... it should not be necessary, some of them have found their children but others have not yet.[48]

The findings presented by the families are introduced in the mechanisms of transitional justice, such as the historical memory commissions. The following is an extract of an interview with a member of the National Center for Historical Memory (NCHM):

> Generally [in the context of] forced disappearances, they [the authorities] say that he [the victim] did not leave, that he fell in combat. In this case they [the authorities] had said that he [the soldier victim] had left with the guerrilla. But [the truth was] that he was a soldier and the comrades had disappeared him, then of course...
> S: his own comrades?

47 (Personal Interview, 2016).
48 (Personal Interview, 2019).

> NCHM: yes, I remember that it was a matter of personal problems between the commander and him, they disappeared him in a specific place and...
> S: did you discover that truth?
> NCHM: she told us [his mom].
> S: then she had already found out.
> NCHM: yes of course, we do that report in 2013, 2014, so she told us about her entire search journey.[49]

The third element is related to the impact of the mobilisation carried by the relatives of the disappeared to other sectors of civil society, creating transnational memory movements. For example, the activist group *Dexpierte* promotes the memorialisation of the disappeared through street art and graffiti. Ana Maria, a member of this group, explains:

> When we began with Dexpierte, to work on the faces of the disappeared or those killed by the state, it began first as a personal wish, that is, our first intervention we painted Jaime Garzón, Nicolás Neira victim of the Mobile Anti-Disturbances Squadron or Escuadrón Móvil Antidisturbios (ESMAD), Jaime Pardo Leal, Carlos, the one who was the manager of the courthouse cafeteria and we painted it on 32nd street and Caracas street. We began to call them memory actions in the street. The references we had were, let's say the actions that were carried out in Argentina, for example, marking of public space or that were carried out in Guatemala, etc.[50]

These three elements (inclusion, expertise, influence) allow the broadening of the actions of representation of the victims of forced disappearance by their relatives. The relatives mobilise for victims who are not only their direct relatives; they include other victims of these crimes. They become experts, and their expertise validates their work and is included in other forms of transitional justice, such as historical memory commissions and truth commissions. Most of them influence other civil society movements beyond their national borders.

---

49 (Personal Interview, 2019).
50 (Personal Interview, 2019).

7. Conclusion

Victims of enforced disappearance are not absent victims. Their removal from the protection of the law is both a reason and a consequence of the practice of enforced disappearance. Victims of enforced disappearance are also often victims of social disappearance; they are already located at the margins of society, suffering a lack of protection from the state. They are forcefully disappeared to silence their voice, particularly when they are considered to be a threat or opposition to the government. Forced disappearance is an additional form of state violence or the result of violence from non-state armed actors. Victims of enforced disappearance are in a liminal state of being and not being absent. The label of enforced disappeared as it appears in international law and in domestic law is a form of managing the suffering of victims, of naming a situation that is deemed ongoing and unspeakable.

The crime of enforced disappearance is ongoing; this characteristic provides it with a particular temporality that demands further exploration. In a context of prolonged conflict such as the Colombian conflict that has lasted over five decades, it is possible to talk about different generations of disappeared victims (direct victims and their relatives). Victims of enforced disappearance have met different levels of recognition by the state. They may have been ignored or prosecuted during the violent dynamics of the conflict; they may have been sequentially ignored by the state. In the later stages, the mobilisation of the families of the disappeared has been recognised, and their expertise has given them legitimacy. Their work has influenced other social movements and other areas of civil society, which has created a broader dimension of representation for the victims of enforced disappearance.

The activism of the families calls for the ongoing search not only of their sons, daughters, or other direct relatives but the search for all those who have disappeared in a particular context, either in the hands of the state (ie Argentina, Chile) or non-state actors (ie Mexico, Colombia). The legitimacy and power of the movement come from their bonds and public grief, which is directly affected by the disappearance of their loved ones. However, the effectiveness of their permanence in the public and political sphere comes from their authority as experts and their identification with other groups of victims of enforced disappearance. These bonds with different groups of civil society could strengthen the representation of the otherwise absent victims in the future.

6. Longing, Belonging and Owning: How to Untangle Competing Claims over Colonial Cultural Objects?

Lily Martinet[*]

Abstract: *This chapter proposes to explore, as a case study, the intergenerational dimension of issues raised by the displacement of tangible heritage during the colonial conquest and occupation. In essence, cultural heritage is intergenerational as it bridges together past and future generations.*
During colonisation, tangible cultural heritage was massively displaced. Western colonial powers took possession of the cultural items created and preserved by colonised people. As a result, present generations are unable to access and experience what should have been their own cultural heritage. This situation has led to a recurring debate on the restitution, or return, of cultural objects acquired during colonisation.
This chapter contributes to this debate by adopting a perspective focusing on generations and historical injustice rather than on the ownership of these objects.

***

'Which means that today, what you find
on museum shelves throughout the world is
nothing but trophies and plunder.
And all the African, Indian or Asian
objects that we admire were stolen off corpses.'[1]

In essence, cultural heritage is intergenerational as it bridges past and future generations. Present generations have received cultural heritage from previous generations and preserve it to pass it on to future generations, which are not yet born, when the time comes. A continuum is established through cultural heritage between past, present and future generations. What is passed on is not only the tangible aspect of cultural heritage but also the values, intentions, beliefs, memories, worldviews, knowledge and traditions it carries with it. If this transmission is halted or hampered, cultural heritage disappears, and the sense of identity and continuity it supports is lost. Transmission to future generations is, therefore, key to

---

* Dr Lily Martinet is an Officer in charge of intangible cultural heritage, French Ministry of Culture.

1 Eric Vuillard, *Sorrow of the Earth: Buffalo Bill, Sitting Bull and the Tragedy of Show Business* (Ann Jefferson tr, Pushkin Press 2016) 8.

understanding why States, communities and families invest resources to protect buildings, artefacts and cultural practices. Each generation is entrusted by its ancestors with the obligation of caring for this heritage to hand it on to their children. Thus, the duty to protect cultural heritage is owed at the same time to past and future generations. Moreover, cultural heritage forms the backdrop against which creativity flourishes. As the United Nations General Assembly sums it up, 'the cultural heritage of a people conditions the present and future flowering of its artistic values and its overall development'.[2]

During colonisation, tangible cultural heritage was massively displaced. Western colonial powers took possession of the cultural property created and preserved by colonised people. Several phenomena have contributed to this displacement. First, cultural objects were seized by violence during colonial conquest as trophies and loot.[3] Second, anthropologists and ethnologists who had embarked on scientific expeditions, stole,[4] bartered, and bought items from the communities they were studying. Scientists believed at the time that they were preserving the tangible manifestations of dying cultures. According to Marcel Mauss, the goal was 'to collect swiftly the largest quantity possible of objects that could disappear to fill up the museums that were recently born'.[5] Even so, this collecting 'frenzy'[6] not only pursued a scientific purpose since ethnographic missions were also carried

2 UNGA Res 3187 (XXVIII) (18 December 1973).

3 For an account of the looting of the palace of the Asante king Kofi Karikari, see: Kwame Anthony Appiah, *Cosmopolitanism: Ethics in a World of Strangers* (W.W. Norton & Co 2006) 115–116; for a presentation of the Maqdala expedition, see: Richard Pankhurst, 'Ethiopia, the Aksum Obelisk, and the Return of Africa's Cultural Heritage' (1999) 98 African Affairs 229, 229–232; and on British troops sacking the City of Benin in 1897 and looting its bronzes, see: Dan Hicks, *The Brutish Museums: the Benin Bronzes, Colonial Violence and Cultural Restitution* (Pluto Press 2020).

4 See, for instance, the description of the theft of sacred objects committed by the ethnographer Michel Leiris during the Dakar-Djibouti mission in his book: *L'Afrique fantôme* (Gallimard 1981) 103–104, 156; for a compilation of ethnographers snatching cultural objects, see: Sally Price, *Primitive Art in Civilized Places* (University of Chicago Press 1993) 70–75.

5 'Récolter au plus vite la plus grande quantité possible d'objets qui pouvaient disparaître et de peupler les musées qui venaient de naître', citation translated from French into English by the author from Marcel Mauss, *Manuel d'ethnographie* (4th edn, Payot 2002) 27.

6 Folarin Shyllon, 'Restitution to Sub-saharan Africa: The Booty and Captivity: A Study of Some of the Unsuccessful Efforts to Retrieve Cultural Objects Purloined in the Age of Imperialism in Africa' (2015) 20 Art Antiquity & Law 369.

out to legitimise colonisation.[7] Some museums were designed to showcase the power of European States and the bounty of colonial conquests. Once inside the collections of public institutions, objects became part of the cultural property of the colonising State, and their return now requires compliance with deaccessioning procedures.[8] Finally, once the colonised States became independent, cultural objects continued to flow out of the global South as a consequence of the trafficking of cultural property and the effects of the art market, which favours buyers from wealthy nations.[9]

In the case of sub-Saharan Africa, 90–95 per cent of the cultural heritage has been removed from the continent.[10] For instance, the Royal Museum for Central Africa in Belgium (also known as the Africa Museum) preserves more than 200 000 objects from the cultures of the Congo region, whereas the sum of the national inventories of the States of this area does not exceed 60 000 objects.[11] Items (sculptures, artefacts, ritual objects) displaced from colonised territories are currently in the collections of western cultural heritage institutions (libraries, museums, archives) or of private individuals, such as art collectors. As a result, a Parisian, for instance, may experience the diversity of the world's cultural heritage in a single day, while present generations in sub-Saharan Africa are unable to access their own cultural heritage. What is even more unsettling is that collections in the West may include duplicate objects that are never displayed but are stored away. Despite this colonial past, today these institutions carry out an essential role in the conservation and scientific study of the cultural heritage of humanity.

The plunder and misappropriation of these cultural elements have disrupted the transmission of the cultural heritage of colonised people, who are now considered as 'the absent' in the equation of restitution. Present generations are unable to access and experience what should have been their own cultural heritage. Instead of a cultural item being transmitted

---

7 Benoît de L'Estoile, *Le goût des autres : de l'Exposition coloniale aux Arts premiers* (Flammarion 2010) 77.

8 See for instance, in France, the principle of inalienability enshrined in art 451–5 of the *Code du patrimoine*.

9 Maureen Murphy, 'Éthique et politique de la restitution des biens culturels à l'Afrique : les enjeux d'une polémique' (2019) 2 Sociétés et Représentations 260, 267.

10 Alain Godonou, 'Musées, mémoire et universalité' in Lyndel V Prott (eds), *Témoins de l'histoire : Recueil de textes et documents relatifs au retour des objets culturels* (UNESCO 2011) 63.

11 Alain Godonou, 'À propos de l'universalité et du retour des biens culturels' (2007) 70 Africultures 114, 116.

from one generation to another, it is the memory of its loss, its absence, that is bequeathed. The void resulting from colonisation has created a growing longing for cultural objects that have been missing for decades. The past has not been forgotten, and it shapes the relationships between nations and people. Restitution is sought in part as a remedy for a people 'to recover part of its memory and identity'.[12] This situation has led to a recurring debate on the restitution, or return, of cultural objects acquired during colonisation, engaging a plurality of actors: States, communities, descendants, cultural institutions (museums, archives, libraries, universities), art dealers, private collectors.

This contribution will not rehash the international legal framework for restitutions,[13] nor will it delve into the latest developments[14] that took place in the wake of the report authored by Felwine Sarr and Bénédicte Savoy,[15] as there is a bountiful supply of excellent publications on these topics.[16] Rather, it proposes to enter this debate by adopting a critical perspective focusing on generations and historical injustice. One of the pitfalls of this debate is to frame it exclusively as an ownership issue and exclude its intergenerational character. The thesis supported in this paper is thus that

12 In the words of Amadou-Mahtar M'Bow, Director-General of UNESCO, 'A plea for the return of an irreplaceable cultural heritage to those who created it' (1978) 31 The Unesco Courrier 4, 5.

13 For a presentation in French of this framework in relation to African cultural heritage, see Lily Martinet, 'La restitution du patrimoine culturel africain : règles internationales applicables et pratiques nationales' (2019) 65 Annuaire Français de Droit International 675.

14 See, for instance, the *Guidelines for German Museums: Care of Collections from Colonial Contexts* (published in 2018, revised in 2019) <https://perma.cc/8BXL-5YKT>; the Guidance on the way forward for colonial collections published by the Dutch Advisory Committee on the National Policy Framework for Colonial Collections: *'Colonial Collections a Recognition of Injustice'* (2020) <https://www.raadvoorcultuur.nl/binaries/raadvoorcultuur/documenten/adviezen/2021/01/22/colonial-collection-and-a-recognition-of-injustice/Colonial+Collection+a+Recognition+of+Injustice.pdf> accessed 1 November 2021; the Arts Council England's guide published on 5 August 2022 'Restitution and Repatriation: A Practical Guide For Museums in England'; Ethical Principles for the Management and Restitution of Colonial Collections in Belgium (June 2021) <https://perma.cc/5PCB-CGAD> and the Belgian law 'Loi reconnaissant le caractère aliénable des biens liés au passé colonial de l'État belge et déterminant un cadre juridique pour leur restitution et leur retour' (3 July 2022).

15 Felwine Sarr and Bénédicte Savoy, *Rapport sur la restitution du patrimoine culturel africain. Vers une nouvelle éthique relationnelle* (2018) <https://perma.cc/8VYR-JJJ9>.

16 See as an example Evelien Campfens, 'The Bangwa Queen: Artifact or Heritage?' (2019) 26 International Journal of Cultural Property 75.

a shift needs to occur from a legal framework grounded in ownership and property rights focusing on States and cultural objects as assets, to an approach integrating human rights and recognising communities as cultural bearers and items as components of a shared heritage.

To defend this thesis, this chapter will first highlight the conceptual gap between cultural property and cultural heritage (1); it will then reveal the flaws of a framework for restitution designed on a State centric basis (2) and relying solely on ownership (3). With these observations in mind, this chapter will present how the rights of Indigenous Peoples (4) and the recognition of the interest of future generations (5) may help in untangling competing claims over colonial cultural objects and arrive at creative solutions.

1. The Need to Bridge Cultural Property with Cultural Heritage

An analysis of international instruments dealing with culture shows that the term 'generation' is found in connection with cultural heritage and diversity, but that this is not the case in norms adopted for the restitution of 'cultural property' and 'cultural objects'. For instance, the 1972 Convention Concerning the Protection of the World Cultural and Natural Heritage charges States with 'the duty of ensuring the identification, protection, conservation, presentation and transmission *to future generations* of the cultural and natural heritage'.[17] The 2003 Convention for the Safeguarding of the Intangible Cultural Heritage illustrates this understanding by defining intangible cultural heritage as 'the practices, representations, expressions, knowledge, skills' that are 'transmitted from generation to generation' by communities and groups.[18] The 2005 Convention on the Protection and Promotion of the Diversity of Cultural Expressions states similarly that 'the protection, promotion and maintenance of cultural diversity are an essential requirement for sustainable development for the benefit of present

17 Convention for the Protection of the World Cultural and Natural Heritage (adopted 16 November 1972, entered into force 17 December 1975) 1037 UNTS 151 (World Heritage Convention) art 4 (emphasis added).

18 Convention for the Safeguarding of the Intangible Cultural Heritage (adopted 17 October 2003, entered into force 20 April 2006) 2368 UNTS 3 (hereafter 2003 Convention) art 2.1.

and *future generations*'.[19] Furthermore, the International Council of Museums (ICOM) Code of Ethics for Museums provides that one of the core missions of museums is to pass on to future generations collections 'in as good and safe a condition practicable'.[20] As a corollary, the 1997 United Nations Educational, Scientific and Cultural Organization (UNESCO) Declaration on the Responsibilities of the Present Generations towards Future Generations invites present generations to 'preserve the cultural diversity of humankind' and to 'identify, protect and safeguard the tangible and intangible cultural heritage and to transmit this common heritage to *future generations*'.[21]

In contrast, the term generation is absent from instruments establishing rules for the restitution and repatriation of cultural property and objects, namely the Protocol to the Convention for the Protection of Cultural Property in the Event of Armed Conflict (1954), the Convention on the Means of Prohibiting and Preventing the Illicit Import, Export and Transfer of Ownership of Cultural Property (1970), and the International Institute for the Unification of Private Law (UNIDROIT) Convention on Stolen or Illegally Exported Cultural Objects (1995) (UNIDROIT Convention).[22] The concept of generation is surprisingly foreign to this branch of international cultural law, which focuses on cultural property and ownership. Intergenerational transmission is completely absent from the scope of these instruments, as they reduce cultural heritage to assets. The term 'heritage'

---

19 Convention on the Protection and Promotion of the Diversity of Cultural Expressions (adopted 20 October 2005, entered into force 18 March 2007) 2440 UNTS 311, art 6 (emphasis added).

20 ICOM Code of Ethics (adopted 4 November 1986, revised 8 October 2004) §2.18; see also art 6 of the Recommendation concerning the protection and promotion of museums and collections, their diversity and their role in society (adopted 17 November 2015) which defines heritage 'as a set of tangible and intangible values, and expressions that people select and identify, independently of ownership, as a reflection and expression of their identities, beliefs, knowledge and traditions, and living environments, deserving of protection and enhancement by *contemporary generations* and transmission to *future generations*' (emphasis added).

21 Declaration on the Responsibilities of the Present Generations Towards Future Generations (12 November 1997) art 7 (emphasis added).

22 Protocol to the Convention for the Protection of Cultural Property in the Event of Armed Conflict (adopted 14 May 1954, entered into force 7 August 1956) 249 UNTS 240 (Hague Convention); Convention on the Means of Prohibiting and Preventing the Illicit Import, Export and Transfer of Ownership of Cultural Property (adopted 14 November 1970, entered into force 24 April 1972) 823 UNTS 231; UNIDROIT Convention on Stolen or Illegally Exported Cultural Objects (adopted 24 June 1995, entered into force 1 July 1998) 24421 UNTS 457.

effectively conveys the process of inheriting from the past material that forms a shared cultural heritage, whereas 'property' and 'objects' underline property rights. As Lyndel V. Prott and Patrick J. O'Keffe put it:

> The fundamental policy behind property law has been seen as the protection of the rights of the possessor. [...] the fundamental policy behind cultural heritage law is protection of the heritage for the enjoyment of present and later generations.[23]

Notwithstanding these terminological differences, the taking of cultural property from its community of origin breaks the intergenerational chain of transmission of cultural heritage. For instance, the looting of a ceremonial sculpture will lead to the disappearance of the living heritage (traditional rituals, dances, prayers, songs) associated with it. Issues raised by the displacement of cultural objects during the colonial conquest and occupation undeniably have an intergenerational dimension, which cannot be embraced by an approach based solely on ownership.

Furthermore, the emphasis put on property disregards the social and cultural values that are associated with a cultural object. The 'translocation'[24] of objects, works of art, or artefacts from their context of creation to the West is not only a geographical displacement but also a transformation. In its community of origin, the item fulfils social, religious and symbolic functions, which are entirely lost when it enters the glass case of a museum or when it is commodified on the art market. In the space of the museum, objects are presented as art pieces or as ethnographic items that are displayed for their historical, aesthetic, and scientific value. An everyday object, like a spoon, is transformed by the museum's space. The cultural institution controls the discourse and interpretation of the object and its access. For instance, the sculpture dedicated to Gou, which is considered by the Fon people as the God of metal and by extension of war, whose protection requires sacrifices, meat, blood, and palm oil, is now exposed as a masterpiece at the Louvre in the Pavillon des Sessions.[25] The function of

23 Lyndel V Prott and Patrick J O'Keffe, '"Cultural Heritage" or "Cultural Property"?' (1992) 1(2) International Journal of Cultural Property 307, 309.

24 Sarr and Savoy (n 15) 25.

25 Gaëlle Beaujean-Baltzer, 'Du trophée à l'œuvre : parcours de cinq artefacts du royaume d'Abomey' (2007) 6 Gradhiva 70, 12 and 15.

the sculpture has changed from religious to aesthetic. The social dimension of cultural heritage is set aside in the cultural property paradigm.[26]

Moreover, the standard-setting instruments in this field are devoid of retroactivity,[27] which means that the vast majority of colonial objects plundered fall outside of their scope. Aware of this issue, in 1978 UNESCO tried to complete the Convention on the Means of Prohibiting and Preventing the Illicit Import, Export and Transfer of Ownership of Cultural Property (1970) by creating the Intergovernmental Committee for Promoting the Return of Cultural Property to its Countries of Origin or its Restitution in Case of Illicit Appropriation (the Committee). The purpose of the Committee was to facilitate bilateral negotiations for the restitution of 'cultural property', and its mandate includes:

> cultural property which has a fundamental significance from the point of view of the spiritual values and cultural heritage of the people [...] and which has been lost as a result of colonial or foreign occupation or as a result of illicit appropriation.[28]

Despite these honourable intentions, in practice, the Committee has scarcely been involved in the restitution of cultural objects. Less than ten requests have been lodged with it in more than forty years of existence.[29] Still, it is worth noting that several of these requests were successful.[30]

---

26 For an example of an ethnologist instructing a museum not to clean collected objects to preserve the traces of their social functions and of the sacrifices they were used for, see Valérie Perlès, 'L'expérience de Bernard Maupoil au Dahomey : entre science et engagement, un laboratoire pour l'ethnologie en milieu colonial' (2021) 32 Gradhiva 192.

27 It is still important to note that art 15 of the 1970 Convention on the Means of Prohibiting and Preventing the Illicit Import, Export and Transfer of Ownership of Cultural Property permits the conclusion of special agreements between parties regarding the restitution of cultural property removed before it entered into force.

28 Statutes of the Intergovernmental Committee for Promoting the Return of Cultural Property to its Countries of Origin or its Restitution in Case of Illicit Appropriation, UNESCO Reso 4/7.6/5, 24 (28 November 1978) art 3.2.

29 Elisabeth Lambert Abdelgawad, 'Le Comité intergouvernemental de l'UNESCO pour la promotion du retour de biens culturels à leur pays d'origine ou de restitution en cas d'appropriation illégale : un bilan assez mitigé' (2012) 1 Revue de science criminelle et de droit pénal comparé 265, 269.

30 UNESCO's website presents the different cases of returns and restitutions that occurred under the aegis of the Intergovernmental Committee for Promoting the Return of Cultural Property to its Countries of Origin or its Restitution in Case of Illicit Appropriation (see <https://perma.cc/38LR-5PY2 >).

2. Going Beyond a State-centric Framework

In addition, when ownership lies at the crux of the restitution debate, the conceptual framework is limited mainly to States.[31] As a result, requests for restitutions become a diplomatic matter that may be integrated into broader policies pursuing, among others, political and commercial agendas. For instance, France likes to ease the conclusion of contracts with restitutions. In 2011, France handed back manuscripts to the Republic of Korea, which were plundered in 1866 and kept in storage at the French National Library. This operation was part of commercial negotiations for the construction of a high-speed French train (TGV) in Korea.[32] More recently, in 2019, the sabre belonging to El Hadj Omar Tall was handed over by France to Senegal during a trip made by Edouard Philippe, the then prime minister of France. This trip also provided the occasion for France to sell weapons to the Government of Senegal.[33] Although restitutions may give a positive aura to States and help buff their soft power, unfortunately, States rarely pursue altruistic motives.

In addition, by limiting restitution to inter-State relations, voices of stakeholders, such as Indigenous People, local communities (whose delineation does not always overlap with States' borders), families or Diasporas are silenced. Non-governmental organisations advocating on behalf of Diasporas may support requests for restitution, such as the *Conseil représentatif des associations noires* (CRAN) in France.[34] The interests of these different stakeholders are not always aligned with each other. They may also be distinct from national interests. For instance, States may want to promote tourism by displaying returned artworks in museums, whereas communities might prefer to use them to perform traditional rituals. Some communities might wish, for example, to bury some returned items, like funerary objects. In this event, there is a need to balance the interest of humanity to preserve these objects and the respect that is due to the customs and beliefs of source communities. Restitution founded on ownership falls short when

31 The UNIDROIT Convention does mention tribal or indigenous communities (arts 5 and 7), but it has been ratified by only 48 States.

32 Raphael Contel, Anne Laure Bandle and Marc-André Renold, 'Affaire Manuscrits Coréens – France et Corée du Sud' (2013) Plateforme ArThemis – Centre du droit de l'art, Université de Genève <https://perma.cc/5ZZW-J3BW>.

33 Héléne Ferrarini and Damien Cuvillier, 'Privée de retour' (2021) 32 La Revue Dessinée 8, 36.

34 Murphy (n 9) 269.

competing claims are made on an item. The question of who is legitimate to represent past generations, is always answered in the same way: States.

This shortcoming may be illustrated by the case of the 2019 restitution of a whip and a bible belonging to Hendrik Witbooi, national hero and chief of the Nama tribes, by the German state of Baden-Württemberg to Namibia.[35] The bible and the whip were taken by the German army as trophies during a raid in 1893.[36] The objects were then donated to the Linden museum in Stuttgart.[37] In 2019, Germany decided to return these items to Namibia, where they would be preserved at first in the National Archives, awaiting transfer to a future museum that will be built in Gideon, Hendrik Witbooi's hometown.[38] This decision was challenged by the Nama Traditional Leaders Association (NATLA) and the descendants of Hendrik Witbooi, who strived to be involved in the restitution process.[39] The latter used a sentence, which sums up their claim: 'repatriation process, CANNOT BE ABOUT US, IF IT IS NOT WITH US'.[40] The NATLA argued notably that Namibian authorities were dominated by the Ovambo people and that they were not representative of all the tribes.[41] Furthermore, the restitution was contemporaneous with an action brought on behalf of members and descendants of the Ovaherero and Nama Peoples against Germany in the United States in connection with the genocide of the Ovaherero and Nama peoples.[42] These circumstances may have influenced the process of restitution. This case highlights the tensions that can be brought by restitution when actors who are linked by their past to a cultural object are excluded from the process, and interests diverge.

Another issue resulting from State-bias is the lack of transparency and publicity of inter-State negotiations. States present the modalities of the restitutions as a *fait accompli* to the public. The opacity of the diplomatic

35 Sandrine Blanchard and Daniel Pelz, 'Retour d'un fouet et d'une bible spoliés en Namibie' (*Deutsche Welle*, 28 February 2019) <https://perma.cc/65MF-TPHG>.

36 ibid.

37 Katherine Keener, 'German Museum to Repatriate Artefacts Previously Belonging to Namibian Hero' (*Art Critique*, 24 February 2019) <https://perma.cc/EP8V-9ANK>.

38 For a detailed account of the restitution, see Reinhart Kössler, 'The Bible and the Whip – Entanglements Around the Restitution of Robbed Heirlooms' (2019) 12 ABI working paper <https://perma.cc/U5YP-YNT2>.

39 Blanchard and Pelz (n 35).

40 Kössler (n 38) 2.

41 ibid.

42 United States District Court, SD New York. *Rukoro v Federal Republic of Germany*, 6 mars 2019, 363 F.Supp.3d 436.

process allows the Western States to cherry-pick which cultural objects they agree to part with and the ones that they hang on to. In 2020, for instance, France adopted a law to return twenty-six objects to Benin, which were part of the spoils of war when General Alfred Amédée Dodds was in command. Although this is a significant step for France, the sculpture devoted to Gou is not among them despite the request made for its restitution.[43] States are not always aware of the cultural significance attached to some objects in the collections of cultural institutions. Items that are not on display but stored away because they are humble or not spectacular may have immense significance for their community of origin.

3. The Absence of Nuances in an Ownership Framework

If ownership serves as a guide for restitution, then the issue boils down to whether the object was acquired lawfully or unlawfully. The provenance of the item and its ownership history will be examined to try and identify its rightful owner. This perspective gives rise to hackneyed arguments, such as the plunder of cultural property was perfectly legal, under international law, at the time. As an example, Neil McGregor, Director of the British Museum from 2002 to 2015, argued on the subject of the plunder of Benin City that it was terrible, but that at the time, it was also perfectly legal.[44] Another point supported by property law is that the possession of these cultural items has lasted for so long, that claims are time-barred or that ownership has been transferred to museums.[45] These arguments are very unsettling, as they are tainted by bad faith and do not recognise injustices committed in the past.

Furthermore, ownership does not take into account the context of an acquisition or the vulnerability of the original owner, i.e. of the past generation. Even when colonial objects were purchased, doubts may linger as to

43 Loi n°2020–1673 du 24 décembre 2020 relative à la restitution de biens culturels à la République du Bénin et à la République du Sénégal, published in the Journal Officiel of 26 December 2020. For an analysis of this law, see Christophe Doubovetzky, 'Les modalités de restitution de biens culturels en question : réflexion à partir de restitutions récentes' (2021) 30–34 La Semaine Juridique – édition Administrations et Collectivités Territoriale 1.

44 Corinne Hershkovitch and Didier Rykner, *La restitution des œuvres d'art : solutions et impasses* (Hazan 2011) 70.

45 Lucas Lixinski, 'Axum Stele' in Jessie Hohmann and Daniel Joyce (eds), *International Law's Objects* (OUP 2018) 137; Declaration on the importance and value of universal museums (2004).

the lawfulness of their acquisition. The power imbalance between colonised populations and ethnographers was such that it is hard to assess whether consent to sell an item was given by the rightful owner. Sally Price perfectly sums up this asymmetrical relationship:

> It is quite another thing, however, when a Western traveller in Africa spots an interesting looking wooden figure and offers to purchase it for a price that represents a negligible amount to the traveller and a large sum to the owner, in this situation, the buyer lacks understanding of the meaning of the object in its native context, the seller lacks understanding of its meaning in its new home, and there is no common ground in the evaluation of the price for which it has been exchanged.[46]

Moreover, Felwine Sarr and Bénédicte Savoy have compared the prices paid by the Dakar-Djibouti mission with those reached in auctions in France. For a certain type of mask, ethnographers would pay seven Francs (the 'price for a dozen eggs at that time') even though in the same year, similar items reached an average price of 200 francs at auctions.[47] 'In the field of Nazi-looted art, a sale by a Jewish owner to a Nazi official is considered as a "forced sale"'.[48] Should this position be adopted for colonial objects? In some cases, the nature of the transaction was construed differently by both parties. The ethnographer believed that a sale was taking place, while the community being studied understood that they were establishing a relationship of reciprocity.[49] For all of these reasons, there is a need to change the conceptual framework for restitution of colonial objects from a paradigm relying exclusively on ownership to one that integrates human rights aspects.[50]

46 Price (n 4) 78.
47 Sarr and Savoy (n 15) 56.
48 Campfens (n 16) fn 34.
49 de L'Estoile (n 7) 159.
50 On the cross-fertilisation between human rights and cultural heritage, see: Ana Filipa Vrdoljak, 'Human Rights and Illicit Trade in Cultural Objects' in Silvia Borelli and Federico Lenzerini (eds), *Cultural Heritage, Cultural Rights, Cultural Diversity* (Brill 2012).

4. Mainstreaming the Framework Built for Indigenous People

Since the end of the 20th Century, a new understanding of restitution has emerged in the field of human rights, thanks to the fight for Indigenous People's rights. This shift occurred relatively recently in international law with the adoption of the United Nations Declaration on the Rights of Indigenous Peoples (UNDRIP) in 2007.[51] This instrument directed States towards, on the one hand, the restitution of indigenous people's 'cultural, intellectual, religious and spiritual property taken without their free, prior and informed consent or in violation of their laws, traditions and customs' and, on the other hand, enabling 'access and/or repatriation of ceremonial objects and human remains in their possession through fair, transparent and effective mechanisms'.[52] This instrument also recognised the right of Indigenous People to use and control their ceremonial objects[53] and to 'maintain, control, protect and develop their cultural heritage, traditional knowledge and traditional cultural expressions.'[54] The UNDRIP has suffused international law. The Recommendation concerning the protection and promotion of museums and collections, their diversity and their role in society (2015) also invites States to 'take appropriate measures to encourage and facilitate dialogue and the building of constructive relationships between [...] museums and indigenous peoples concerning the management of [...] collections, and, where appropriate, return or restitution in accordance with applicable laws and policies'.[55]

Both instruments go beyond the relationship between States to link cultural objects with the social group that created them. These objects are more than simply movable property as they are the tangible manifestation of the cultural identity of a community. The issue of ownership remains, but it is superimposed to other considerations, such as access and use of

51 See also art 13 of the American Declaration on the Rights of Indigenous Peoples (adopted 15 June 2016) OEA/Ser.D/XXVI.19.

52 United Nations Declaration on the Rights of Indigenous Peoples (adopted on 13 September 2007) art 11.2. and 12.2.

53 ibid., art 12.1.

54 ibid., art 31.1.

55 Recommendation concerning the protection and promotion of museums and collections, their diversity and their role in society (adopted 17 November 2015) para. 18; see also UNESCO's Policy on Engaging with Indigenous Peoples (2018) para. 77 (r).

cultural objects to perpetuate traditions.[56] Gaining back control of these objects realises the right to access and enjoyment of cultural heritage.[57] Both of these rights are derived from the right to participate in cultural life.[58] Moreover, this evolution goes hand in hand with the progressive anchoring of cultural heritage in the human rights realm. The preamble of the Convention for the safeguarding of the intangible cultural heritage opens, for instance, with a triple reference to human rights,[59] which means that this instrument 'operates' within a human rights context.[60] In light of this, instruments adopted for the return of cultural property appear outdated when they exclude human rights from their scope.

Indigenous people have thus gained a special status in international law, grounding claims for access and restitution of cultural objects in human rights law. Under this approach, cultural objects should not be returned because they were unlawfully acquired but because they *belong* to communities that created and preserved them. What matters is no longer how the object was acquired but the meaning it has for a social group and the function it serves. Belonging understands cultural objects as the expression of cultural identity. In this context, the social, cultural and religious functions of the object are taken into account. Under this perspective, continuity may be established between past creators of these items and current stakeholders. The intergenerational nature of cultural heritage is acknowledged.

---

56 Human Rights Council, 'Report of the Independent Expert in the Field of Cultural Rights, Farida Shaheed' (21 March 2011) A/HRC/17/38, recommendation g.

57 ibid.

58 Several instruments recognise this right at the international and regional levels, see for instance the Universal Declaration on Human Rights (adopted 10 December 1948) UNGA Res 217 A (III) (UDHR) art 27.1; the International Covenant on Economic, Social and Cultural Rights (adopted 16 December 1966, entered into force 3 January 1976) 993 UNTS 3 (ICESCR) art 15.1.a; the International Covenant on Civil and Political Rights (adopted 16 December 1966, entered into force 23 March 1976) 999 UNTS 171 (ICCPR) art 27; the African Charter on Human and Peoples' Rights (adopted 27 June 1981, entered into force 21 October 1986) 1520 UNTS 217, art 17(2); and the Additional Protocol to the American Convention on Human Rights in the Area of Economic, Social and Cultural Rights ('Protocol of San Salvador') (adopted 17 November 1988, entered into force 16 November 1999) art 14.1.a.

59 2003 Convention (n 18), preamble para. 1.

60 Janet Blake, 'Part II Commentary, the Preamble' in Janet Blake and Lucas Lixinski (eds), *The 2003 UNESCO Intangible Heritage Convention: A Commentary* (OUP 2020) 24.

From a human rights approach, the applicable law can also incorporate customs and local laws. For instance, the inalienability of a ceremonial object[61] is admitted, meaning that the bond between a social group and its cultural heritage is not broken by its appropriation. This development is particularly interesting as the inalienability of public collections in France has served as a shield for decades to refuse the restitution of cultural objects. In this way, inalienability may become a double-edged sword. Furthermore, by switching from ownership rights to human rights, procedural hurdles, like the statute of limitations or standing, may be overcome.

Human rights law first of all provides procedural principles to handle restitutions, namely free, prior and informed consent, participation, fair, transparent and effective mechanisms. Secondly, it provides forums to discuss the return of cultural objects. Human rights law is able to handle competing claims involving different types of stakeholders: communities, States, and cultural heritage institutions. For instance, in 2018, the Yaqui People, an Indigenous People, submitted a request to the Expert Mechanism on the Rights of Indigenous people to intervene as a facilitator for the restitution of a consecrated ceremonial deer head, the Maaso Kova, which was held by the Swedish National Museum of World Culture.[62] Because of armed conflicts and deportation in the 19th and 20th Century, the Yaqui People are now divided into the Pascua Yaqui, a group living in the United States as a federally recognised tribe, and the Rio Yaqui living in Mexico. Which of these two groups has standing to claim ownership of the ceremonial deer head? The solution found to this puzzle was the establishment of the Maaso Kova Committee, which was composed of members designated by the traditional authorities of the Rio Yaqui, 'committee members from the Pascua Yaqui [...] persons who 'hold position of great importance within'' their culture and cosmovision, and representatives of the cultural societies of the Yaqui people including the Kolensias, which are 'entrusted with the care of the Maaso Kava'.[63] The Committee represented, therefore, secular

61 Expert Mechanism on the Rights of Indigenous Peoples, Repatriation of ceremonial objects, human remains and intangible cultural heritage under the United Nations Declaration on the Rights of Indigenous Peoples (21 July 2020) A/HRC/45/35, 3; see also for the inalienability of the Maaso Kavo Expert Mechanism on the Rights of Indigenous People, Technical Advisory Note – Repatriation request for the Yaqui Maaso Kova (16 June 2020) 14–15.

62 ibid., 1–17.

63 ibid., 11.

and spiritual authorities from both States.[64] It agreed that the ceremonial deer head should be returned to the Kolensias, who will then decide 'where it should come home to finally be at rest'.[65] In the end, an agreement was reached between the Maaso Kova Committee and the Swedish museum.[66]

The contributions of human rights law to the debate surrounding restitutions should not be limited to a 'traditional' or restrictive understanding of Indigenous People adapted to settler States, such as Canada or Australia, and excluding communities in Africa and Asia.[67] The Expert Mechanism on the Rights of Indigenous People notes in this sense that:

> it will be important for indigenous peoples in Africa to have their own interests acknowledged in this process [i.e. the French process to repatriate cultural objects taken from Africa] that seems presently designed to repatriate to national Governments, such as Benin.[68]

Furthermore, the new light shone by human rights on the issue of restitution should benefit other social groups, such as minorities and local communities. There is a need to mesh ownership and human rights law together.

5. Putting Future Generations at the Heart of the Process

The dispossession of cultural objects is a hurdle to safeguarding and perpetuating cultural practices, traditional knowledge and traditional cultural expressions. Restitution may revitalise cultural heritage and contribute to a renaissance. Due regard is given in this way to the intangible cultural heritage associated with these objects. Some States submit the return of objects to conservation conditions, which means that their social function may not be restored. For instance, a musical instrument collected by ethnographers and preserved in a sealed glass case, which will never be played again, does

64 Kristen Carpenter and Alexey Tsykarev, 'Indigenous Peoples and Diplomacy on the World Stage' (2019) 115 AJIL Unbound 118, 121.

65 Expert Mechanism on the Rights of Indigenous People, Technical Advisory Note – Repatriation request for the Yaqui Maaso Kova (n 61) 11.

66 Carpenter and Tsykarev (n 64) 121.

67 José Martinez Cobo, *Étude du problème de la discrimination à l'encontre des populations autochtones* (vol 5, Ecosoc 1981–1987), para. 379–380.

68 Expert Mechanism on the Rights of Indigenous People, Repatriation of ceremonial objects, human remains and intangible cultural heritage under the United Nations Declaration on the Rights of Indigenous Peoples (21 July 2020) 12.

not make sense from a living heritage perspective. Similarly, communities wish to care for their cultural objects, which may, in some cases, be considered living beings. They may want, for instance, to feed masks ritually. Yet, these customs may run counter to one of the primary functions of cultural institutions, which is to preserve and conserve tangible heritage to avoid its deterioration. Fortunately, new collaborative museum practices have emerged to balance these conflicting concerns.

For instance, from 2014 to 2018, the collaborative research project SAWA (Savoirs Autochtones Wayana-Apalaï de Guyane[69]) brought together the Wayana and Apalaï (Indigenous Peoples of Guiana), researchers and museum professionals.[70] The communities were not seeking restitution of items, as conservation is impossible because of the humid climate they live in. Items would swiftly rot away. The goal of the project was for communities to have access to recordings, pictures and objects significant to their culture which had been collected since the 18th Century by researchers, travellers, and explorers.[71] All the material and data collected at that time would have disappeared without the intervention of these scientific and cultural institutions.[72] The aim of the project was twofold: for the communities to repatriate the past to the present by studying the objects and the documents preserved in the institutions and return this cultural heritage to their peoples by granting them access to it.[73] Three museums agreed to welcome the team representing the communities: the Musée des Cultures Guyanaises, the musée du quai Branly – Jacques Chirac, and the Bonner Amerikas-Sammlung Museum.[74] This experience was mutually beneficial since when examining items, the team helped update, correct and complete information in the collection catalogues. In this project, restitution took place in a digital format with the creation of a digital portal designed with the participation of the communities.[75] Among the first contents chosen for restitution was a collective ritual called 'Marake', as the practice of this

69 In English: traditional knowledge Wayana-Apalaï of Guiana [our own translation].

70 Valentina Vapnarsky, 'Des communautés sources aux communautés d'experts' (2019–2020) 140 Culture et recherche 71.

71 ibid.

72 Éliane Camargo and others, 'L'Amazonie amérindienne dans l'ère du numérique : le portail multilingue WATAU' (2021) 12 Patrimoines du Sud 1, 2.

73 ibid., 3.

74 ibid., 15.

75 The portal is accessible at <https://watau.fr/s/watau-fra/page/accueil> accessed on 1 November 2021.

traditional cultural expression was diminishing.[76] Thus, the project was oriented from its inception towards future generations and the transmission of cultural heritage from the past to them.

As in this case, sometimes communities do not demand restitution[77] but reparation or access to the items and the information collected to maintain cultural expressions and pass them on to future generations. The Conference of the parties to the Convention on Biological Diversity has adopted interesting guidelines in respect of the restitution of information: the 2018 Rutzolijirisaxik Voluntary Guidelines for the Repatriation of Traditional Knowledge of Indigenous Peoples and Local Communities Relevant for the Conservation and Sustainable Use of Biological Diversity.[78] The Guidelines stress the need to develop enduring relationships with Indigenous Peoples and local communities[79] and to establish a team 'guided by a multi-stakeholder committee'.[80] One of the purposes the guidelines serve is the 'recovery, revitalisation, and protection of traditional knowledge'.[81] This point is crucial as colonisation, evangelisation, and the expansion of monotheistic religions have destroyed living heritage such as social practices and knowledge and practices concerning nature.[82] The return of cultural objects will not in itself revive this cultural heritage. Concentrating resources only on property rights while living traditional cultural expressions are dying is truly regrettable. It is as important for future generations to be able to enjoy the creation of past generations as it is for them to be able to extend them in the present and the future. In other words, present generations should be able to view the sculpture handed down to them by their ancestors and also carve new ones.

76 Vapnarsky (n 70) 72.

77 Article 3 of the Principles for Cooperation in the Mutual Protection and Transfer of Cultural Material) lists alternatives to the transfer of cultural material (loans, production of copies, and shared management and control) (adopted 4–8 June 2006, published in 13 International Journal of Cultural Property 409).

78 The Rutzolijirisaxik Voluntary Guidelines for the Repatriation of Traditional Knowledge of Indigenous Peoples and Local Communities Relevant for the Conservation and Sustainable Use of Biological Diversity (adopted 30 November 2018) CBD/COP/DEC/14/12.

79 ibid., art 17.d.

80 ibid., art 20.

81 ibid., art 9.

82 Alain Resnais, Chris Marker and Ghislain Cloquet, *Les statues meurent aussi* (1953).

Conclusion

Former colonial powers and cultural institutions are gradually departing from their position that, as guardians of a universal interest, they should keep colonial objects because they have the capacity and better means to preserve cultural heritage. The irony of States having destroyed tangible and intangible heritage through colonisation and deculturation policies imposing material conditions on the return of these objects, such as the construction of infrastructures, is especially cruel. States should stop imposing a European-centred, elitist, turned toward the past conception of cultural heritage to the rest of the world. Restitution should not be perceived simplistically, pushing objects across borders from one State to another. Each case needs to be carefully thought through taking into account historical injustices and the interest of future generations. The current ownership paradigm shaping international law should be complemented with a human rights-based approach to establish continuities in cultures. Although the debate about restitutions concentrates attention on the past, it should not eclipse the present and the future. Most of the cultures that created these beautiful objects have not disappeared despite what ethnographers thought.[83] Cultural institutions should open their doors to contemporary art[84] and crafts from these cultures. For instance, supporting living human treasures programs or artist residencies could help restore know-how and enhance traditional cultural expressions. The space freed in museums by the return of cultural objects could indeed be used to display works produced by present generations.[85] Lastly, restitution does not account for the decades these displaced objects were exploited. How can present generations repair and testify to the years of absence and the wealth accrued as a result of the taking of this cultural heritage? States and cultural institutions could, in addition to restitution, fund capacity building in former colonised States to preserve and safeguard tangible and intangible cultural heritage and promote creativity. In this way, a process of

83 Still some objects may be orphaned, meaning that their provenance is unknown, or in other cases, entire cultures have disappeared, see for example the presentation of the Nok culture by Folarin Shyllon, 'Negotiations for the Return of Nok Sculptures from France to Nigeria: An Unrighteous Conclusion' (2003) 8 Art Antiquity and Law 133.

84 See for instance the exhibit *Magiciens de la Terre* (Centre Culturel Pompidou 1989).

85 Vincent Négri, 'À propos du rapport Sarr/Savoy sur la restitution du patrimoine africain : lecture juridique d'une éthique relationnelle repensée', presentation given at Université Laval on 11 September 2019.

reconciliation going beyond the transfer of tangible heritage should be set into motion.

7. Coming to Terms with Belgium's Colonial Past: The Failure of the Parliamentary Commission

Valérie Rosoux[*]

Abstract: *The chapter explores the scope and limits of the Special Commission established in 2020 by the Belgian Parliament to deal with its colonial past. This case underlines the weight of the 'absents' and the difficulty of agreeing on the most appropriate way to represent and honour them. The starting point of this chapter is two successive participant observations in the framework of this Commission (panel of 10 experts in charge of writing the initial report, from August 2020 to November 2021, and panel of three experts in charge of writing the final report, from February 2021 until December 2022). This experience led to a succession of meetings within the Commission and with Belgian Afro-descendants' associations, former colonials' associations, and Burundian, Congolese, and Rwandan scholars and practitioners. Most of these meetings share common characteristics: the processes' distributive dimension, the dynamics' highly emotional character, and the pervasiveness of justice claims.*

***

'[F]or years on end he had listened to his professors,
he had learned the law and its interpretation,
he had tried to get a good grasp of criminal proceedings
– yet only today, only in his own first plea to the court,
did he understand that those
proceedings were really about something
quite different: abused human beings.'

Ferdinand von Schirach[1]

Introduction

In his bestseller *Der Fall Collini,* published in Germany in 2011, the lawyer-turned-author Ferdinand von Schirach questions the nexus between the intergenerational transmission of memory and the role of a judicial proceeding. The thriller starts with the brutal murder of a prominent industrialist

* Valérie Rosoux is a Research Director at the Belgian Fund for Scientific Research (FNRS) and a Professor at the University of Louvain, Belgium.

1 Ferdinand von Schirach, *L'affaire Collini* (Gallimard 2014) 101.

in one of Berlin's most exclusive hotels. The criminal, Fabrizio Collini, is a quiet, recently retired man who could not be suspected of hurting anyone. The puzzle of the novel is why he became a criminal. As his young advocate searches for clues, he discovers that the victim was responsible for shooting Italian partisans during World War II. The objective of this introduction is not to disclose the novel's storyline but to illustrate the procedural dimension of what is known in Germany as *Vergangenheitsbewältigung* (the process of dealing with the past). Interestingly, the novel's storyline resonates with its author's personal story. The grandfather of Ferdinand von Schirach was a Nazi who headed the Hitler Youth and was eventually sentenced to 20 years for crimes against humanity at the Nuremberg war trials.

This theme is far from new. From Deuteronomy to Hamlet, cohorts of murdered people's descendants are driven by the need for justice. Myths, tragedies, and real stories on all continents reveal the strength of loyalty that can bind individuals to unfairly treated and dead ancestors. They highlight the significance of individual and collective proceedings designed to deal with a 'difficult past'.[2] This chapter explores the scope and limits of one specific case study related to the past of millions of individuals, namely the Special Commission established in 2020 by the Belgian Parliament to deal with its colonial past. This case underlines the weight of the 'absents' and the difficulty of agreeing on the most appropriate way to represent and honour them. But, first and foremost, it forces us to address an initial question: who are the absents we are talking about? Most voices insist on the victims of colonial violence. Yet, as we will see, there is no consensus on the identity of those who should be central throughout the process. The tensions that characterise the work carried out by the Parliamentary Com-

2 See Martha Minow, *Between Vengeance and Forgiveness: Facing History after Genocide and Mass Violence* (Beacon Press 1998); Elazar Barkan, *The Guilt of Nations. Restitution and Negotiating Historical Injustices* (The Johns Hopkins University Press 2000); Patricia Hayner, *Unspeakable Truths: Confronting State Terror and Atrocity* (Routledge 2001); Nigel Biggar (ed), *Burying the Past. Making Peace and doing Justice after Civil Conflicts,* (Georgetown University Press 2003); John Torpey, *Making Whole What Has Been Smashed: On Reparation Politics* (Harvard University Press 2006); Jeff Olick, *The Politics of Regret: On Collective Memory and Historical Responsibility* (Routledge 2007); Christopher Daase and others, *Apology and Reconciliation in International Relations. The Importance of Being Sorry* (Routledge 2016).

mission show how ambiguous the notion of 'absent' is. It also questions the role played by the victims in the proceeding.[3]

The Belgian case is emblematic in four respects. First, the Belgian colonial period is often depicted as a textbook case because of the degree of brutalisation reached. Since the publication of Conrad's *Heart of Darkness*, King Leopold II has become one of the symbols of colonial brutality. In 2020, his statues were systematically targeted by the protests against racism that followed the death of George Floyd and the 'Black Lives Matter' movement. Besides the extent of colonial violence, the Belgian case is particularly significant for a second reason: the political nature of the Commission. It was composed of 19 Belgian Members of Parliament (MPs) representing all the elected political parties from the far right to the far left. Some were strongly in favour of the work being done by the Commission, while others were entirely opposed to it.

Third, the mandate of most commissions related to the colonial past focuses on a specific aspect of this past. In the Belgian case, the mandate of the Parliamentary Commission was extremely broad. It concerned not only past injustices (the crimes committed in Congo from 1885 to 1960 and in Burundi and Rwanda from 1919 to 1962) but also contemporary injustices (current discrimination against Afro-descendants in Belgium). This twofold ambition allows us to observe the pros and cons of a maximalist approach. The fourth reason that justifies the exemplary nature of the Belgian case is its unexpected outcome – or rather, lack of outcome. After two and a half years of readings, hearings, and negotiations at all levels, the members of the Parliamentary Commission failed to reach a political deal. The absence of consensual recommendations allows us to question the notion of failure.[4] Who decides what a failure is? Based on which criteria? Above all, when do

---

3 See Sandra Walklate, *Imagining the Victim of Crime* (McGraw-Hill 2007); Tshepo Madlingozi, 'On Transitional Justice Entrepreneurs and the Production of Victims' (2010) 2(2) Journal of Human Rights Practice 208; Inge Vanfaechem, Anthony Pemberton and Felix Mukwiza Ndahinda (eds), *Justice for Victims: Perspectives on Rights, Transitions and Reconciliation* (Routledge 2014); Cheryl Lawther, '"Let *Me* Telle *You*": Transitional Justice, Victimhood, and Dealing with a Contested Past' (2020) 30(6) Social & Legal Studies 890.

4 On failure, see Elizabeth A Cole, Valérie Rosoux and Lauren Van Metre, 'Deepening Understandings of Success and Failure in Post-conflict Reconciliation' (2022) 10(4) Peacebuilding 357, and Stipe Odak, 'Reevaluating Religious Understandings of Reconciliation: A Study in Bosnia and Herzegovina' (2022) 10(4) Peacebuilding 434.

we decide whether a procedure failed or not[5]? The Belgian case indicates that a political failure does not automatically mean the whole prospect was null and void.

The starting point of this chapter is two successive participant observations in the framework of this Commission. The first occurred from August 2020 to November 2021 (panel of 10 academics and civil society representatives in charge of writing the initial report, 689 p.). The second started in February 2021 until the end of the Special Commission's mandate in December 2022 (panel of three experts in charge of writing the final paper, 112 p.).[6] This experience led to a succession of weekly meetings within the groups of experts and the Commission and a series of encounters with Belgian Afro-descendants' associations, former colonials' associations, and Burundian, Congolese, and Rwandan scholars and practitioners. Most of these meetings share common characteristics: the processes' distributive dimension, the dynamics' highly emotional character, and the pervasiveness of justice claims. The tensions and even contradictions between protagonists forced me to examine my own beliefs, judgements, and practices and be particularly vigilant to their potential influence on the analyses.

The chapter is divided into three parts. The first underlines the specificities of the Belgian context. The second focuses on three major procedural choices made throughout the process. The third concentrates on the main constraints and challenges observed throughout the process.

1. Glorifying and Silencing the Past

Unlike French, Dutch, or British colonisation, the creation of the Congo was 'one man's personal adventure'.[7] Between 1885 and 1908, the *Etat Indépendant du Congo* (EIC – Congo Free State) was, in fact, the personal property of King Leopold II. Whereas in Belgium, his constitutional role prevented him from taking any public action without a minister's approval, in the colony, the King enjoyed power often described as absolute. Only in 1908, mainly due to international pressure, did the Congo officially become

5 See Cecilia Albin and Daniel Druckman, 'Procedures Matter: Justice and Effectiveness in International Trade Negotiations' (2014) 20(4) European Journal of International Relations 1014.

6 See the initial and final reports: <https://perma.cc/D48B-FNB> and <https://perma.cc/5KSQ-CWQ5>.

7 Jean Stengers, *Congo. Mythes et réalités* (Racine 2007) 45.

a Belgian colony. Second, the territory of Ruanda-Urundi was administered by Belgium from 1922 to 1962 without being a colony in the strict sense of the term. From 1916 to 1922, it was under military occupation and later became a Belgian-controlled Mandate under the League of Nations. After World War II, it became a United Nations trust territory.

Throughout the first half of the 20th century, Belgian authorities represented the colonial past in such a way as to glorify the country's achievements. Belgian school textbooks were remarkably similar to the equally uncritical *Petit Lavisse* schoolbook used by schoolchildren in France. All emphasis was placed on the benefits of colonisation since the concept of national identity made it inconceivable that crimes could be committed on behalf of the State. In the view of the Belgian authorities, Belgium's administration of a territory 80 times its size gave the impression to the outside world of the workings of a 'model colony'. No single reference was made to the widespread violations of humanitarian standards.

Following independence and the shedding of some illusions, Belgium's colonial history was scarcely referred to in official addresses. State representatives systematically erased the bitter criticisms that had been levelled against colonisation for decades. This concealment policy was excused either by the need to normalise relations with the former colony or by the slogan 'Africa for the Africans'. Far from the *Belgium caput mundi* approach,[8] the Belgian authorities tried to avoid even the slightest accusation of neo-colonialism. Within just a few decades, aspirations had changed completely. As former Belgian Prime Minister Jean-Luc Dehaene explained in May 1999, 'the colonial past is completely past... There is really no strong emotional link anymore. It does not move the people. It's part of the past. It's history.'[9] This observation was soon to be contradicted.

Three months later, the new government of Guy Verhofstadt would radically change this approach and encourage a critical acceptance of the country's colonial heritage. The new Minister of Foreign Affairs, Louis Michel, acknowledged that:

> 'former colonial powers, such as Belgium, owe a large part of their development to their former colonies', and that 'it was thanks to "these colonies" that we were able, in part, to create the country we are today,

8 Laurent Demoulin, *Ulysse Lumumba* (Talus d'approche 2000) 14.

9 Quoted in Stephen Bates, 'The Hidden Holocaust' *The Guardian* (London, 13 May 1999).

the twelfth richest country in the world – the fourth, if we follow the UN classification system.'[10]

In 2000, Belgian representatives launched a Parliamentary Commission to determine the exact circumstances of the murder of Patrice Lumumba and the possible implications of Belgian political responsibility therein.[11] The Commission report led to official apologies by the Minister for Foreign Affairs, who acknowledged the 'apathy' and 'cold indifference' of the Belgian government at the time.

This approach was again overturned in July 2004 with the appointment of a new Minister for Foreign Affairs, Karel De Gucht. His attitude was far from apologetic, and he took an admonishing tone in his speeches. During his official visits to Central Africa, Karel De Gucht stirred up intense controversies by referring explicitly to the devastating effects of corruption, impunity, and violence in the Democratic Republic of Congo (DRC). Rather than stressing Belgium's 'responsibility' towards its former colony, the talk was now of the need to stop being 'indulgent'.[12] Karel De Gucht wished to put aside any 'misplaced' feelings of guilt. By way of response to accusations of paternalism, he recalled that colonisation also involved 'mass literacy campaigns', 'the setting up of an educational system', and 'generalised health coverage'.[13]

This uncritical attitude would progressively come to be considered as inappropriate. In 2019, former Belgian Prime Minister Charles Michel apologised for the kidnapping, segregation, and forced adoption of thousands of mixed-race children throughout Belgian colonial Africa. One year later, the murder of George Floyd in Minneapolis and the subsequent 'Black Lives Matter' movement impacted the Belgian political scene. On 7 June 2020, a demonstration brought together more than 10 000 protestors in Brussels despite the restrictions imposed due to Covid 19. Three weeks later, King Philippe marked the 60th anniversary of the independence of the DRC, expressing his 'deepest regrets' for acts of violence and brutality inflicted

10 Liège, 28 February 2003.

11 Patrice Lumumba was the first Prime Minister of the independent Democratic Republic of the Congo. He was assassinated on 17 January 1961. See Ludo De Witte, *De Moord op Lumumba* (Van Halewijck 1999) and Jean Omasombo Tshonda, 'Commission Lumumba : difficile regard sur un passé' (2002) 22 Nieuwsbrief Belgische Vereniging van Afrikanisten 11.

12 Kinshasa, 21 April 2008.

13 Tervuren, 3 February 2005.

during his country's rule over the Congo (30 June 2020). At approximately the same time, the Belgian Parliament established the special Commission to confront its colonial past.[14]

The creation of the Parliamentary Commission resulted from a series of negotiation processes within and between political parties and civil society organisations. For decades, the small size of the Congolese, Rwandan, and Burundian diasporic groups in Belgium explained their marginal influence on the public debate. However, the progressive arrival of refugees from the African Great Lakes called into question the predominance of a white, Eurocentric perspective on the colonial past.[15] In 2004, a group of activists cut off the hand of a 'grateful Congolese' kneeling before Leopold II in a famous monument in Ostend. From 2010 on, with the renovation of the Royal Museum of Central Africa, the African diasporic groups in Belgium tried to take a leading role in the societal exploration of the colonial legacy.[16] Their voices were amplified in 2019 by the final report of the UN Working Group of Experts on People of African Descent.[17] This report urged Belgium to recognise the injustices of its colonial past and tackle the root causes of present-day racism. A couple of months later, during the June 2020 protests, colonial monuments were vandalised. Besides the King's letter to the Congolese Prime Minister, several colonial monuments were removed from public spaces in various cities and University campuses. For

14 The idea of a Parliamentary Commission dealing with the colonial past was not entirely new. It had been proposed several times since 2012 but was never supported by a majority of political parties.

15 Danièle Bentrovato and Karel Van Nieuwenhuyse, 'Confronting "Dark" Colonial Pasts: A Historical Analysis of Practices of Representation in Belgian and Congolese Schools, 1945–2015' (2020) 56(3) Paredagogica Historica 293.

16 The passage of a second generation of Afro-descendants living in Belgium reinforced the work of local activist groups, which had been active since the end of the 1980s (see the websites of Collectif Mémoire Coloniale, Bamako, Change (ASBL), Black Speaks Back (BSB), Decolonize Belgium and Hand in Hand Against Racism). On the evolution of the representations of colonialism shared by Congolese immigrants living in Belgium, see Ana Figueiredo, Géraldine Oldenhove and Laurent Licata, 'Collective Memories of Colonialism and Acculturation Dynamics Among Congolese Immigrants Living in Belgium' (2018) 62 International Journal of Intercultural Relations 80. The findings of this study are interesting: while older participants (grandparents) tend to evoke more positive memories of colonialism, younger generations (grandchildren) think more negatively of Belgian colonialism. As for the intermediate generation (parents), they present this past in a somewhat ambivalent way.

17 On the report, see <https://digitallibrary.un.org/record/568010?ln=en#record-files-collapse-header> accessed 7 July 2023.

decolonisation advocates, this succession of events created the momentum to raise the issue of past and enduring injustices.

The pace of the decisions that followed was swift. Ten days after the demonstration of 7 June, the speaker of the Federal Parliament announced that the House of Representatives had decided to hold hearings on the troubled history of Belgium in the Congo. The proposal obtained the support of all political parties, with the exception of the Flemish nationalist *Vlaams Belang.* According to the Parliament chair Patrick Dewael (Open VLD), Belgium needed truth and reconciliation. He, therefore, presented the South African Truth and Reconciliation Commission (TRC) as a model.[18] This reference may be surprising if one considers the numerous contrasts between the Belgian and South-African cases (regarding the nature of past violence, the political regime and, above all, the timing, as most of the South African witnesses were still alive at the moment of the TRC).

At this stage, three main procedural issues were discussed in the Federal Chamber. First, the precise terms of reference for the Commission: should it be the responsibility of an existing parliamentary committee or a new one set up for the occasion? Second, the mandate: should the agenda be restricted to the first colonial period (when the Congo was the personal property of Leopold II) or related to Belgium's entire colonial past? Third, the role of experts: should they come from academia and/or civil society militant groups? To address these questions, the members of the Commission found themselves facing all the tensions that undermine Belgian national identity: Catholics versus secularists, French speakers versus Dutch speakers, opponents versus defenders of the Royal Institution, and left-wing versus right-wing political parties.

The parliamentarians appointed a panel of ten experts in August. Their task was to prepare the work of the Commission in writing a report on historical issues (what are the historical consensus on colonisation, the grey areas, and the historical gaps?) and reconciliation mechanisms (what are the lessons learned from other countries that tried to deal with their colonial past?). Their mandate covered past and enduring injustices.[19] After this initial stage, the Commission structured its work in six main phases:

18 Alan Hope, 'Parliament approves commission on Belgium's colonial past' *Brussels Times* (Brussels, 17 June 2021).

19 The initial report was presented and defended at the Belgian Parliament on the 22nd of November 2021. To watch the video of all presentations and debates between the members of the Commission and the experts, see <https://www.lachambre.be/media/index.html?language=fr&sid=55U2243> accessed 7 July 2023.

(1) listening to representatives of Belgian civil society associations as well as Burundian, Congolese, and Rwandan representatives; (2) scope and limits of past initiatives such as the Lumumba Commission and the Commission devoted to the Metis who were victims of systematic segregation (*cf. infra*); (3) responsibilities of the monarchy, the Belgian state, the Church and the business community; (4) academic research and archives, whether in Belgium or Burundi, Congo or Rwanda; (5) reparations and reconciliation; (6) final report and negotiation of the recommendations.

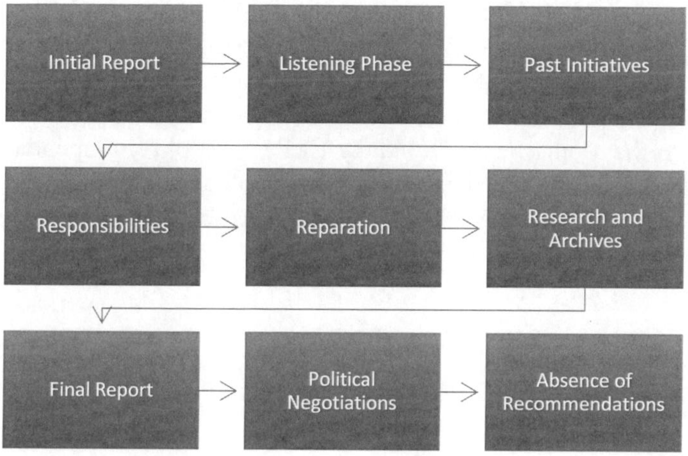

More than 150 witnesses, academics, artists, diplomats, and militants shared their views and expertise with the Parliament.[20] Their words and experiences were transcribed and videotaped. The same number of people (official representatives, academic experts, artists, representatives of civil society organisations, and students) met with the Belgian delegation of MPs who went to Kinshasa, Bujumbura, and Kigali in September 2022. Their expectations were systematically notified and reported to the Parliament. A list of 128 recommendations presented by the President of the Commission was officially published with the experts' final report in November 2022.

These recommendations covered all the issues analysed throughout the process, from research, archives, and international cooperation between

20 See the list of all sessions and hearings on the website of the federal Parliament: <https://www.lachambre.be/kvvcr/showpage.cfm?language=fr&section=/pri/congo&story=audition.xml> accessed 7 July 2023.

Belgium and its former colonies, to memorialisation, restitution, reparation, official apologies, and the fight against racism. Specific attention was paid to the commemoration of former Congolese combatants during World War I and World War II, the rehabilitation of Simon Kimbangu,[21] the restoration of the dignity of the victims of the human zoos,[22] and the school textbooks. Knowing that financial compensations were highly contentious among the political parties, one of the recommendations explicitly mentioned that the official apologies that the Belgian government and Parliament could present would not imply any financial reparation (recommendation 70). Nevertheless, this statement did not appease the tensions between the left and right parties. After six weeks of intense negotiation, there was no zone of potential agreement between the political parties of the majority in power: to the *Parti Socialiste* (PS), official apologies were unnegotiable requirements; to the *Mouvement réformateur* (MR), a list of recommendations that would mention official apologies was simply unacceptable. The absence of any agreement shows that the political parties preferred to take the risk of a 'zero recommendation' rather than conceding.

---

21 Simon Kimbangu is a central figure of the anti-colonial resistance in Congo. He was condemned to death (commuted to life imprisonment) in 1921. Mathieu Zana Etambala devoted an entire section of the initial report of the experts to this figure (pp. 154–185). For further information, see Diangienda Kuntima, *L'histoire du Kimbanguisme* (Éditions Kimbanguistes 1984).

22 Human zoos are among the most dramatic expressions of dehumanisation during the colonial period. The first 'negro village' in Belgium was created in Antwerp in 1885, with 12 Africans. Seven years later, Belgium organised a colonial exhibition in Tervuren as part of the Exposition Universelle. The so-called 'authentic villages' displayed 267 people brought from Congo. Seven of them died of cold or disease. Another village showed Congolese children going to school. Sixty children were brought to Belgium between 1891 and 1900 without their families. Twelve of them also died. On 2 December 2018, the Royal Museum for Central Africa inaugurated a commemorative plaque on this subject. In 1958, another human zoo was set up during the Exposition Universelle in Brussels. This time, 598 Congolese, including 197 children, were brought to this international exhibition. Many complained about the poor living conditions, the restrictions on their movements and contacts, and the daily abuse they faced during these 'mass spectacles'. More than six decades later, in 2021, the Royal Museum for Central Africa presented the exhibition 'Human Zoo'. Artists Teddy Mazina and Romeo Mivekannin invited the visitors to reflect on the impact of these human zoos. See Pascal Blanchard, Maarten Couttenier and Mathieu Zana Etambala, *Mensentuin. Koloniale tentoonstellingen wereldwijd* (Africa Musem 2021).

2. Major Procedural Choices

Proceedings related to reparation for historical injustices are often put into three main categories[23]. The first concerns individuals who were victims of an injustice committed many years ago. This can be illustrated by the compensation claims made by Aboriginal Australians who were abducted from their families when they were children. The second category covers injustices done to a community itself, such as seizing communal lands. In this case, the parties are not specific individuals but representatives of communities, nations, or groups. The third category results from the pressure of the individuals who are the descendants of victims of injustice.

These three categories were relevant in the framework of the Belgian Parliamentary Commission. Hearings devoted to the Metis were centred on individual witnesses who told their personal stories. The fate of those who were long stigmatised as the 'children of sin' is poignant. The stories of these direct witnesses to colonialism have been forgotten for decades. During the colonial period, interracial marriages were legally impossible as they threatened the division of power based on race. Children were taken from their African mothers and placed in Christian (mainly Catholic) boarding schools. At the time of independence, thousands of mixed-race children left Africa with a Belgian passport. Most of them were sent to Belgium where they were placed in adoptive families or children's homes. Many of them could never find their parents.[24] Besides this individual category, most hearings devoted to reparation focused on historical injustices done to entire communities in Congo, Rwanda, and Burundi. These injustices can be summarised by three main processes that were deeply interconnected: the destructuration, exploitation and segregation of the local population.[25]

---

23 See Janna Thompson, 'Justifying Claims of Descendants' (2001) 112(1) Ethics 114.

24 See Kathleen Ghequiere and Sibo Kanobana, *De bastaards van onze kolonie: Verzwegen verhalen van Belgische metissen* (Roularta 2010); Sarah Heynssens, *De kinderen van Save: Een geschiedenis tussen Afrika en België* (Uitgeverij Polis 2017); and Georges Kamanayo Kazungu, *Tussen twee werelden. Een leven in Europa en Afrika* (Uitgeverij Polis 2020).

25 On Belgian colonialism in Congo, see Didier Gondola, *The History of Congo* (Greenwood Publishing 2002); Georges Nzongola-Ntalaja, *The Congo from Leopold to Kabila: A People's History* (Zed Books 2007) and Isidore Ndaywel, *Nouvelle Histoire du Congo. Des origines à la République Démocratique* (Le Cri édition-Afrique Éditions 2008). On Belgian influence in Rwanda and Burundi, see Joseph Gahama, *Le Burundi sous l'administration belge. La période du Mandat, 1919–1939* (Karthala 1983); Melchior Mbonimpa, *Hutu, Tutsi, Twa: pour une société sans castes* (L'Harmattan

Knowing that the mandate of the Commission was not only centred on historical injustices but also on enduring discriminations against Afro-descendants, the members of the Commission faced a series of procedural questions. Three main sets of procedural choices were made throughout the process. The first covers agenda-setting. The second concerns the parties. The third is related to the principles of justice.

2.1. Agenda-setting: No Zone of Potential Agreement

The debates provoked by the creation of the Parliamentary Commission showed that the issues to be placed on the agenda were highly controversial. Most parties identified three main issues: truth, reconciliation, and justice. Regarding truth, two different opinions coexisted. For some, the truth about colonialism was already primarily known, 'the past is past', and it was therefore far more essential to concentrate on current and future national challenges. They emphasised the need to look forward and not backward.

Conversely, other parties considered the past still 'haunting' the present. They did not deny that most historians agree on the main aspects of Belgium's colonial past. Nonetheless, they argued that this academic knowledge was not sufficiently diffused and known within Belgian society. To them, it was crucial to modify school textbooks and launch a national debate on the topic.

As for reconciliation, the opinions were once again radically divergent. Some participants in the preliminary consultation initiated by the group of experts explained that there was no need for reconciliation since there was no conflict: 'The Congolese are not angry at us. Not at all.'[26] This position was far from consensual. In the Great Lakes, Congolese, Burundians, and Rwandans called for reconciliation based on the acknowledgement of the sombre aspects of colonisation, recalling some harrowing events such as the forced transfer of population or the denigration and progressive destruction of their ancestors' religious beliefs. In Belgium, Afro-descendants' associations systematically linked past and present discrimination, considering

1993); David Newbury, 'Precolonial Burundi and Rwanda: Local Loyalties, Regional Royalties' (2001) 34(2) The International Journal of African Historical Studies 271, and Deo Byanafashe and Paul Rutayisire (eds), *Histoire du Rwanda des origines à la fin du XXe siècle* (UNR-CNUR, 2011).

26 Brussels, 7 October 2020.

that past wrongdoings undermine the legitimacy of contemporary resource holdings and, therefore, justify the need for reparations. From this perspective, reconciliation could not be envisaged without structural changes. What they wanted was 'truth *and* justice'.[27]

In the triptych 'truth, reconciliation, justice', justice was the most divisive issue for two main reasons. First, there was no consensus on an overarching standard that defines what justice means. Even if all parties used the language of justice (from far-right to far-left parties), there was no zone of potential agreement between those who associated justice to redress and reparation and those who did not accept the appropriateness of apologies. The same comment can be made regarding restitution. Presented as a *sine qua non* condition of genuine decolonisation by some, they were not even tolerated as a potential option by others. Second, justice as an issue triggered intense emotions on all sides. Admittedly, a variety of positions existed. These cannot be reduced to a binary and brutal opposition between Blacks and Whites. Yet, detecting two viscerally opposed and almost caricatural attitudes at the extreme points of a long continuum is helpful.

On the one hand, most representatives of former colonialists' associations felt blamed, disrespected, and stigmatised based on current moral standards. They insisted that the events in question were not considered illegal at their time and that legal rules should not be applied retroactively.[28] Furthermore, they did not want to accept playing 'a tricky game' that would ultimately lead to an 'unfair and indecent' money transfer. To the spokespersons of Afro-descendants' associations, this attitude demonstrated that nothing had changed since colonial times. As far as they were concerned, official apologies were necessary but not sufficient. They would seem insincere and even obsequious if not accompanied by direct and immediate actions to stop current discrimination.

The *disputatio* between these two positions did not take the form of a rational debate but a deadlock characterised by anger, rage, resentment, shame, and guilt. Money was the ultimate bone of contention that all parties kept in mind, even though it was rarely made explicit. Most anti-racist militants called for an equitable redistribution of resources, while a vast majority of actors implicated in the colonial episode (first and second gen-

27 Brussels, discussion with representatives of *Change* on 16 February 2021.

28 On the limits of the principle of intertemporality, see Andreas Von Arnauld, 'How to Illegalize Past Injustices: Reinterpretrating the Rules of Intertemporality' (2021) 32(2) European Journal of International Law 401 and Michel Erpelding, 'Vers des réparations au titre du colonialisme?' (2022) 67 *Annuaire français de droit international* 1.

erations) categorically refused the idea of retrospective responsibility. These respective perceptions remained incompatible until the end of the process. Leaders of large companies active during the colonial period viewed any reference to compensation with suspicion.

In contrast, Afro-descendants' representatives repeated that current discrimination was directly related to the colonial past and needed, therefore, to be taken seriously into account. One of their strongest arguments resulted from the report of the UN Working Group of Experts on People of African Descent (2019). According to the experts, 'Belgium must recognise the true scope of the violence and injustice of its colonial past to tackle the root causes of present-day racism faced by people of African descent.'[29] This report led to an internal debate, within diasporic groups, about calculating past exploitation costs.[30] The questions that arose were: whose resources, and how much?

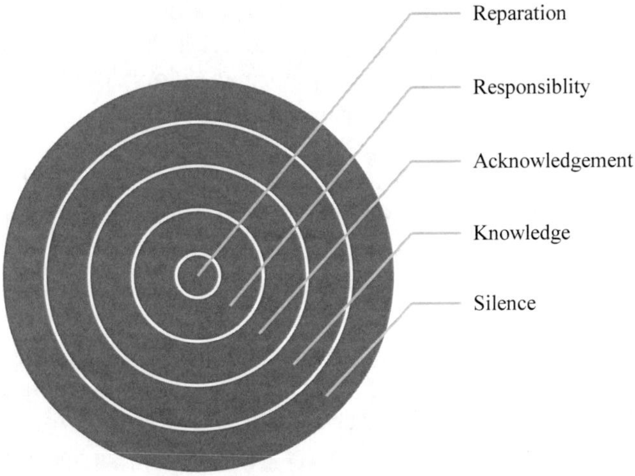

29 'We found clear evidence that racial discrimination is endemic in institutions in Belgium. People of African descent face discrimination in the enjoyment of economic, social, and cultural rights, including diversion from mainstream education into vocational schooling, 'downgrading' in employment opportunities and discrimination in the housing market'. See the full statement to the media by the United Nations Working Group of Experts on People of African Descent, on the conclusion of its official visit to Belgium, 4–11 February 2019 <https://perma.cc/3V3S-3JTZ>.

30 See Cecilia Albin, 'Negotiating International Cooperation: Global Public Goods and Fairness' (2003) 29 Review of International Studies 365.

2.2. Parties: Who can Speak on Behalf of the Absents?

Besides the agenda-setting, a second central interrogation was related to the legitimacy of the parties invited to participate in the process. This issue initially concerned the experts appointed by the Commission. The ten members of the first group of experts came from various backgrounds (history, political science, law and theology). The Commission aimed to avoid strictly technical expertise and to include academics, militants, and practitioners from the beginning of the process. Six members came from academia (in Belgium and the United States). The four other members were representatives of civil society associations (NGOs, diasporic associations, and churches in Burundi).[31] The selection made by the parliamentarians was immediately questioned in the national and international media. Various criticisms were made. The first came from civil society associations which criticised the Commission for the political nature of its selection.[32] Their main question can be summarised as: 'Why them, and not us?' The point made in this criticism did not only result from a potential competition between representatives of diasporic groups, it also revealed the gap between academic expertise and experience. As one young representative of a diasporic group said: 'We are the real experts! What is at stake is not an academic issue. It is our life.'[33] This reaction referred to persisting injustices faced by current Belgian Afro-descendants.

Besides this significant argument, the central polemic came from Kigali, where major concerns were expressed about two points. The first relates

31 The members of the panel were Zana Mathieu Etambala (historian at Leuven University), Gillian Mathys (historian at Ghent University), Elikia M'Bokolo (historian at the EHESS in Paris and professor at Kinshasa University), Anne Wetsi Mpoma (art historian and member of the anti-racist association *BAMKO*), Bishop Jean-Louis Nahimana, former president of the Burundian Truth Commission, Pierre-Luc Plasman (historian from the University of Louvain), Valérie Rosoux (philosopher and political scientist, professor at the University of Louvain – FNRS), Martien Schotsmans (lawyer, former director of the NGO *RCN Justice et Démocratie*, mainly active in the African Great Lakes), Laure Uwase (lawyer and member of the Rwandan diasporic association *Jambo*), and Sarah Van Beurden (historian and professor at Ohio State University).

32 On the limits of political appointments, see Jeremy Sarkin and Ram K. Bandari, 'Why Political Appointments to Truth Commissions Cause Difficulties for These Institutions: Using the Crisis in the Transitional Justice Process in Nepal to Understand how Matters of Legitimacy and Credibility Undermine Such Commissions' (2020) 12(2) Journal of Human Rights Practice 1.

33 Brussels, 16 February 2021.

to the absence of Rwandan representatives within the panel. The second regards the impartiality and moral integrity of one of the experts. To the Rwandan authorities, the appointment of one representative of the *Jambo* association was overtly politically and not done independently. Arguing that some members of *Jambo* deny the genocide of the Tutsi in Rwanda, they considered that the presence of one representative of this association within the experts' panel discredited the whole Commission. The tone of the criticisms expressed in the Rwandan media was sharp, as suggested by the terms used: 'outrage', 'disgrace to the Commission', 'usurpation of the expert title', and 'rubbing salt in a wound of a genocide survivor'.[34] Following this polemic, *Ibuka*, the association of survivors of the Tutsi genocide in Rwanda, and the Burundian collective refused to collaborate with the experts. As this initial tension reminds us, the challenge of reconciliation in the Great Lakes, and in Rwanda in particular, was directly reflected in the preparatory work of the Commission.

A second criticism came from 60 historians and colonial experts who expressed their scepticism about the presence of militant representatives among the experts and called for an independent report.[35] In amalgamating historians, lawyers, and representatives of diasporic groups, they said, the Commission took the risk of historical research being instrumentalised by political groups. According to them, the finality pursued by 'militants' or 'activists' is not to search for historical truth but to remain loyal to their group and to gain power. Along the same lines, the members of the Commission were also criticised for not including Rwandan and Burundian historians who could have contributed to avoiding any partial research posture. Lastly, some French historians explained that foreign historians should have also been selected to help Belgians and Congolese experts step back and consider Belgian national history with impartiality. In short, the experts' legitimacy was systematically questioned.

Beyond these polemics, the variety of the profiles chosen by the Commission impacted the concrete work of the experts' panel. The plurality of backgrounds and generations was undeniably a source of richness and reflexivity. Yet, it implied a 'taming process' between us. We were all were positioned on a continuum between two extreme points. For some, the main objective was to share research findings and clarify the potential

34 Emmanuel Ntirenganya, 'Outrage as Genocide Denier is Chosen Expert on Belgian Colonial Role in Rwanda' *The New Times* (Kigali, 8 August 2020).

35 'Eerst het onderzoek, dan het debat' *De Standaard* (Brussels, 17 August 2020).

options for the Commission members to make decisions. For others, the aim was to change the power asymmetry and convince the Commission members. After numerous discussions about the level of integration of our work, we decided that each expert would write a personal section of the report. This decision did not prevent us from collaborating and even co-signing some contributions. However, the guarantee that we could each share the findings we found relevant without compromising appeased the tension within the group.

This group adjustment required flexibility on all sides to establish our methodology and ethics and create sub-groups (history, reconciliation, links with diaspora). This initial phase led to a second phase of consultations conceived as a preliminary step to the consultations and hearings organised by the Commission. One of the objectives of the consultations (based on interviews and surveys) was to cope with the under-representation of historians of Congolese, Burundian and Rwandan origin in the group of experts. The message sent to the Commission was that experts from the Great Lakes could not be reduced to the role of local advisors or informants and needed to be on an equal footing with Belgian colleagues.

Besides the group of experts, the issue of legitimacy also concerned the participants in the public hearings. From a negotiation perspective, fairness implies bringing all parties to the negotiation table. Such ethics of equal participation favours inclusivity.[36] It also enhances the outcome's legitimacy and facilitates its implementation. Nonetheless, some diasporic groups, in particular did not agree to consider all parties as being on equal footing because it was time, they said, to listen to the voices of those who remained unheard for so long.[37] In their view, including former colonists' associations in the public hearings would reinforce a narrative that had been dominant in Belgium and the Great Lakes for more than a century and a half. The members of the Commission still decided to invite some representatives of the associations of former colonists to participate in the hearings.

The radically asymmetrical relations that characterised colonialism also raised difficult questions about the legitimate representatives of the colonised communities. Besides Afro-descendants living in Belgium, Con-

---

36 Nancy Fraser, 'From Redistribution to Recognition? Dilemmas of Justice in a 'Post Socialist' Age' in Cinthia Willett (ed), *Theorizing Multiculturalism: A Guide to the Current Debate* (Blackwell 1998); Onur Bakiner, *Truth Commissions. Memory, Power, and Legitimacy* (Penn University Press 2016).

37 Letter signed by 33 associations of Afro-descendants in Belgium, 8 July 2020.

golese, Burundian, and Rwandan official authorities considered themselves the legitimate spokespersons of all descendants of the colonised people. Their legitimacy seemed to be recognised by their Belgian counterparts, as was shown by the secret talks organised at the highest level regarding the restitution of archives, artistic or sacred pieces. However, their credibility was questioned by the descendants of the 'Congolese dynastic monarchs' who presented themselves as the 'genuine owners of the Congolese territory' for centuries.[38] As they explained, their ancestors were manipulated to sign treaties while they could neither read nor write. They were not even invited to participate in the conferences of Berlin in February 1885 and Brussels in November 1908 (at the time of the transfer of the rights of the Congo Free State by King Leopold II to Belgium). Three layers of victimhood completed this argument.[39] As far as they were concerned, 'the holders of ancestral power in the Congo constitute undeniably the cohort of the only victims' of the territorial conquests launched by Henry Morton Stanley from 1876 until 1879. They were also presented as 'the only victims of the transfer of the Congo Free State to Belgium.' And, for the third time, were 'the only victims of the independence' on 30 June 1960. Their conclusion was sharp: the Congolese monarchs should be 'the first, if not the only ones', to negotiate a justice based on the principles of restitution and rehabilitation.[40]

This competition between representatives of the absents indicates one of the peculiarities of the whole process: the systematic disqualification of the parties. In terms of legitimacy, academics were criticised by diasporic groups ('it is about us, and not about them'), Afro-descendant militants by former colonialists ('they want money and nothing else'), transitional justice experts by historians ('experts cannot get involved in politics'), Belgian experts by foreign ones ('they are not impartial'), White Belgian experts by some anti-racist militants ('they take our place'). This list could be extended. These tensions prefigured the incompatibilities that led to the impasse.

They also remind us that there was no consensus at all about the identity of the 'absents' that should be represented and honoured. Most voices con-

38 Letter signed by Marilyn Yav, S.A.I. Mwant-a-MWAD, Princess of the Mwant-a-YH-WH dynasty, Lunda Empire LUNDA (DRC, Angola, Zambia), 10 August 2020.

39 See Jean-Michel Chaumont, *La Concurrence des victimes. Génocide, identité, reconnaissance* (La Découverte 2002).

40 Marilyn Yav (n 38).

sidered that the *past absents* were the Congolese, Burundian and Rwandan victims of colonial violence. Yet, others highlighted the Belgian men and women who 'were sincerely committed and deeply attached to the Congo, Rwanda, or Burundi and their people.'[41] Hence, the role of the missionaries in the education of the local populations was stressed by some while highly criticised by others.[42] Further, numerous observers described the category of the *present absents*, namely the descendants of the colonised victims who still live in the Great Lakes. Various questions concerned them: why were they not massively involved in the procedure? Why did the Commission not launch a detailed questionnaire in the three countries? Why did the Commission only organise online hearings for participants coming from Africa? Lastly, the notion of *future absents* also made sense in this case study. To most Afro-descendant militants, their fight was oriented toward improving the living conditions of the next generation. This multiplicity of absents explains, to some extent, the confusion that characterised most of the interactions between parties.

2.3. Principles of Justice to Find their Rightful Place

This confusion was particularly palpable in the words and metaphors used by stakeholders. Almost all of them explained that they needed to find their rightful place. One of the requirements emphasised by Afro-descendants' representatives was the following: this time, they wanted to have *a place* at the negotiating table. In contrast to the Berlin Conference (1885), which was the monopoly of white leaders, in contrast to the Belgo-Congolese Round Table conference of 1960 (that led to Congolese independence), where Congolese voices were not heard, they wanted to be part of the process. As one Afro-descendant explained: 'It is because my father was not respected at the economic Round Table that we fight now.'[43] This argument explains why some groups did not agree on the principle of 'equality' according to which parties should receive identical or comparable treatment.

Similarly, they did not stress the principle of 'impartiality' since the purpose was precisely to compensate for decades of injustice. From this perspective, calling for impartiality would have been interpreted as a sym-

41 Speech of King Philippe in Kinshasa on 8 June 2022 <https://perma.cc/4J5K-BPP8>.
42 On this specific point, see the final report of the Commission's experts, 56–61.
43 Brussels, 10 October 2020.

bolic act of collaboration with past wrongdoers. Rather than insisting on impartiality, anti-racist groups underlined the necessity for all parties to assume their positionality, considering they were all 'partial and biased'.[44]

In reaction, former colonists' associations referred to the 'fair behaviour' principle. To them, fair hearings meant that each party had a chance to have an input into the process, from the initial stage to the final one. They also mentioned the notion of a rightful *place*. They did not deny the radical asymmetry that characterised colonial relationships. However, they could not accept losing their place and being rejected from the process. In addition to a fair hearing, they called for 'fair play' and complained of being systematically disqualified. They wanted to be 'equally well-placed' to participate in the process rather than being on the frontline.[45] To them, the process could not lead to protecting one set of interests at the expense of others.

To break the deadlock, the members of the Commission did not consider that some of the parties would be welcomed and others not. They focused on procedures and timing in particular. The question was no longer 'who is invited to participate in the process, and who is not?', but 'when shall we listen to each party?'. Sequencing was supposed to give a place to all and was eventually acceptable to all sides. Federal MPs conceived a primacy for descendants of colonised people. The listening sessions allowed them to hear some stories that had never been told before in such an official framework without interrupting them or raising questions, as is usually the case in Parliament. This active listening exercise took place before the waves of formal hearings.

Yet, this procedural choice was insufficient to prevent the sense of injustice underlined by all the parties. Afro-descendants living and often born in Belgium, insisted on the structural racism that directly results from colonialism. Congolese, Rwandan and Burundian participants in the consultation emphasised the brutality of colonial oppression. Former colonists and their descendants underlined the fact that they did not deserve moral disapprobation and they 'also have victims on [their] side'. Defenders of the royal institution argued that Leopold II was not a genocidist and that it was unfair to ruin his entire reputation by reducing a complex episode into a Manichean story. Representatives of the catholic church highlighted the 'positive aspects of the colonisation' and considered that missionaries could

44 Brussels, 25 September 2020.
45 Brian Barry, *Justice as Impartiality* (Clarendon Press 1995) 51.

not be blamed collectively. Representatives of active Belgian companies during the colonial period stressed that their action 'was perfectly fair at that time.'

These contradictions remind one of the importance of the historical perspective to avoid manipulations and denials. Nonetheless, as necessary as it can be, the work carried out by historians does not constitute a panacea. Their findings allow us to disqualify abusive readings of the past, but they do not give access to *the* Truth. In this respect, it would be naïve or totalitarian to try to impose *the* right narrative of the past. After mass atrocities, no fairytale narrative would homogenise the representations and emotions of all parties in presence. Groups in presence are too far apart to perceive the past similarly.[46]

3. *When Past and Present Devour Each Other*

The empirical analysis of one case study does not allow us to draw up general lessons for theory and practice. However, it raises general questions that might be relevant in other case studies. Three main challenges were unanimously emphasised in the experts' initial report: The Commission's duration, inclusiveness, and transparency.

'Let us not hurry.' These words were both explicitly and implicitly present in the consultations conducted by the experts. The transformation of the representations of the past implies a transformation of the representations of the other and, ultimately, a transformation of the representations of one's own group. This threefold evolution is a *sine qua non* condition for changing not only perceptions but also – and above all – concrete experiences in everyday life. Such evolution takes time. By choosing to consider the lasting impact of the colonial past, the Special Commission took seriously the intergenerational transmission of narratives and emotions linked to this past. It, therefore, launched a long-term project that could simply not be dealt with in a hurry. Far from the slogans calling for reconciliation 'as quickly as possible', the Commission dared to propose a long-term vision. A comparative analysis of approaches undertaken abroad shows that the work of memory that the Special Commission could stimulate resembles a mountain walk. It involves long, slow efforts, but it allows

46 See Judith N Shklar, *The Faces of Injustice* (Yale University Press 1990).

broadening the horizon and access to unexpected views – from which one no longer observes one single valley but several.

'Towards an inclusive future.' This objective was one of the wishes expressed in the responses to the initial questionnaire sent in the autumn of 2020. Echoing this, several representatives of civil society organisations complained that their involvement in the process was only 'superficial and late'. This aspect was a central, not peripheral, dimension of the approach. The inclusive nature of the process did not only concern all the communities present in Belgium, Burundi, Congo, and Rwanda but also all the generations involved. The initiatives taken abroad to deal with the colonial past show the strength of the resistance against any new official representation of the past. Therefore, it was vital to search for platforms outside the parliamentary framework and coordinate their actions with the Commission's work.

'Let's be transparent.' This demand has also been omnipresent since the creation of the Special Commission. The need for transparency in the decisions taken by the Parliament and by the members of the Commission was obvious. The Commission's founding resolution was adopted without prior public consultation. The initial meetings of the Commission took place behind closed doors. Criticism also stressed the lack of clear criteria for selecting the first expert group. To the experts, this call for transparency was critical in terms of democracy and ethics. It also concerned the effectiveness of the process: transparency could only strengthen the legitimacy and credibility of the Commission, the experts and victims heard, and of course, the final recommendations.

Were these three elements taken seriously by the Commission? (1) The Commission's members who were not in favour of the process considered that the duration of the process was far too long. They initially accepted the idea of a four-month mandate and eventually conceded an extension twice. Yet, if we take the Commission's initial goals seriously, the duration of the process was surprisingly short. The Commission's mandate was paradoxically maximalist in terms of goals and minimalist in terms of time, resources allocated to the Commission, and outreach efforts. The planned mission implied analysing past and current injustices related to the colonial past in Congo, Burundi, and Rwanda, a scenario to deal with the past fruitfully, and promoting a shared society favouring reconciliation. The Commission had just over than two years to attain these ambitious objectives. However, this process was multi-layered (experts' reports, listening sessions, hearings, official visits to the Great Lakes, and the negotiation process regarding the recommendations). Each of these stages required numerous adjustments. After massive violations of human rights, changing beliefs, representations, and emotions take time. Acknowledgement of the violence that was inflicted does not happen overnight. The ability to actively listen, understand, digest, and adapt, implies self-awareness. Designing and implementing a scenario based on equity and equality do not take months but years. Thus it could be wise to adopt a humble posture in favour of realistic – and not over-ambitious – mandates in the future.

(2) Like the length of the Commission, its degree of inclusiveness was seen as abusive by some and insufficient by others. On the one hand, political parties opposed to the approach argued that the bottom-up initiative that allowed the presence of civil society associations' representatives to be part of the first group of experts was inappropriate. On the other hand, many voices underlined that none of them was invited to participate in the conception of the Commission's methodology. In this regard, the process remained top-down and centralised around the MPs belonging to the majority in power. Moreover, no real action was taken throughout the process regarding outreach, either in Belgium or in the three relevant countries. However, all case studies demonstrate that outreach activities are decisive to favour a broader societal dialogue on the mandate, activities, and findings of the Commission, not only with victims and other stakeholders, but also with the broader public. The intensity of reactions towards the absence of concrete recommendations and actions indicates that this more comprehensive dialogue can admittedly be postponed but can hardly be avoided.

(3) The call for transparency impacted the process since the Commission selected the three members of the second group of experts and the participants in the hearings based on public calls. During the procedure, all hearings were public, translated into French or Dutch, and accessible online. From this perspective, the Commission could hardly be qualified as opaque. However, the ultimate negotiation that led to an impasse was not totally transparent. The absence of any ultimate recommendations forces us to question the political nature of the process. Was the choice of a Parliamentary Commission appropriate? The arguments in favour of this choice were initially twofold: (1) the legitimacy of all members of the Commission could hardly be called into question since they were all elected by Belgian citizens; (2) the official framework that characterises the Parliament was a signal of political will. However, the decisive role played by the presidents of most political parties demonstrates the pitfalls of this kind of process. The gap between the experience of most MPs who participated in the

hearings and debates for more than two years and the inflexible attitude of most presidents of political parties is striking. None of these presidents attended even a single session of the Commission. Beyond their positions, they shared one commonality. Their reference points were determined by short-term electoral concerns rather than a long-term vision of Belgium as a shared and open society. The next generation of citizens did not inspire their positions. They were defined by constituencies that differ immensely in their political, social, and economic statuses.

The limits of the Commission are clear. Yet, the absence of political recommendations cannot undo what has been done. An official debate has started. Witnesses' experiences and scientific findings were shared. All hearings were transcribed and videotaped. The Burundian, Congolese, and Rwandan official representatives, academic experts, artists, representatives of civil society organisations, and students who met the Parliamentary delegation in Bujumbura, Kinshasa, and Kigali will not be forgotten. Their emotions, criticisms, and /or expectations were systematically notified and reported to Parliament. Their messages and their legitimate hope cannot be erased.

Despite the political failure of the Commission, no one can deny that the succession of testimonies and analyses emphasised every Monday in Parliament was transformative. Several MPs – even among those who were not in favour of the proceeding – were deeply touched by the stories told week after week. Some realised, as in the novel by Ferdinand von Schirach, that the whole proceeding was fundamentally related to abused human beings. The opening of the Archives and the witnesses' personal memories gave them a place in the official narrative. In this regard, they are no longer absent.

Epilogue: When Memory Overflows

Living memory is never stagnant. It flows at a variable rate. A calm stream or a mountain waterfall that nobody can stop. It passes from one generation to the next. When blood has flowed, it floods. Case studies from all continents show that mass crimes inevitably lead to memory spills. Although it is possible to postpone them, it is illusory to try to escape them.

In some cases, denial allows us to do 'as if'. Amnesty, in other cases, claims to turn the page. But memory always resists. Unread ink turns to lead and requests time and attention. Far from any rush, only silence and concentration can gradually detect the unheard voices, the muzzled cries, and the despised murmurs. They all come to the surface. In these landscapes ravaged by violence, memory does not stop. Far from the easily detectable waterfalls, it digs, gnaws the ground, and finds its way. Underground, it slips away until it resurfaces. The phenomenon of resurgent rivers is striking. The large jet of water suddenly emerges in a calm, peaceful place with an unsuspected force.

This is the experience observed throughout the Parliamentary Commission. The voices of the absents come back and confuse the dialogue between actors and their descendants. Colonialism cannot be reduced to crime. But it is anchored in it. The massacres perpetrated in the Great Lakes have not been fully acknowledged. Unburied bodies are floating and waiting for the moment of rest. Swept along by the waters of memory, the disappeared take everything away and disrupt the priorities of the present. Contradictory interests and raw emotions are unleashed.

To stop this flow and slowly (re)build, procedures matter.

8. Negotiating the Past: Correcting or Resurrecting?

*I William Zartman**

Abstract: *Negotiating the past has its problems and is generally not recommended (Zartman & Kremenyuk 2005). Dealing with past grievances is a matter of mechanics and justice. It revives past grievances, weighing and interpreting the nature and degree of the past injustice in contemporary terms, and also does the same for the intervening period of time. It also raises the question of whether it is the past action that is being corrected or the impact of the past action, presumably cumulative, which means comparing an indicative against a conditional, i.e. what was the intervening situation and how is it to be judged against how it could have been in the absence of the grievance. Such actions tend to be one-sided, looking at the grievance only as perceived by the aggrieved, ignoring other elements in the past situation. Therefore, it raises the question of representation, which is a function of whether it is the past, the intermediate, or the present situation that is being repaired; it also raises the question of numbers and apportionment. Finally, there is the somewhat separate question of restitution: should the despoiled object be returned, what happens to the current beneficiaries, and how are current improvements to the despoiled property to be handled? Cases from Native Americans, Namibia, and Rwanda are examined along with other instances referenced.*

***

'Les absents ont toujours tort' (French proverb)
'Qui ne dit mot consent' (another French proverb)

This essay seeks to analyse the issues involved in furthering the concerns of the absents from the past in negotiation. It deals with two types of absents: those who have been wronged and seek redress, and those who have rights to pursue. To do so, it must examine the topic through its significant referents: representation, time, wrongs, rights, interests, legitimacy, reconciliation and justice. Essentially, it shows that absent parties, being absent, are no longer involved in negotiation, and that their only role is to have created information for present parties who claim present representation of past parties' interests and use it for their own interests. The result can legitimately be a recognition of past rights and wrongs. Material recognition can be paid only to the pasts' descendants who continue to be materially affected and can be negotiated conclusively. Non-material (memorial?)

* I William Zartman is a Professor Emeritus at the School of Advanced International Studies, John Hopkins University. He is a founding member and steering committee member for the International Negotiations network – German Institute for Global and Area Studies (PINGIGA).

recognition is more complicated and elusive; it is open to all claimants and can never be closed. The challenge then is to make the absents present.

Negotiation is a process of parties' combining their conflicting positions into a joint agreement,[1] using division (concession), exchange (compensation) or reframing (construction). It has been characterised as 'giving something to get something,' indicating that the parties give up something of their positions in order to buy movement that they accept as similar from the opponents. Mutual movement is typical; if one party makes all the concessions or movement and the other takes home all the bacon, it is an atypical negotiation or perhaps not even a negotiation at all; requitement is one of the norms of negotiation. Lastly, negotiation is carried out among parties, either directly or through their representatives.

But what if the negotiations do not involve a party, or at least a present party? Increasingly, negotiations involve parties of the future, on behalf of whom present parties negotiate. For example, heavy current expense in a government budget, such as the USD 1.9 trillion 'Covid bill' in the US, entails in fact enormous expenditure by future generations, who are in no way represented in the negotiations. Climate change negotiations continually invoke future generations, with little effort put into calculating their interests. Indeed, most negotiations are a gift – often poisoned – to future generations whether they like it or not; negotiators hope that their gift will be stable and that their agreement will provide the conflict or problem with an outcome of peace and justice, but it is for future generations unrepresented at the table to bear the burden of implementation and the realisation of its promise. Negotiated agreements are contingent promises and it is up to future parties to work out the contingency and verify the promise.

Yet these negotiations do not involve the absent futures as a party, that is, as a 'parti-cipant,' in the negotiations. At most they are carried out under the shadow of the future, much as negotiations to end a conflict are aimed at forestalling the return of the conflict in the future or, to put it otherwise, to achieve a better outcome for those who will be there in the future. The parties do give something to get something, such as giving up the expectation of victory in exchange for peace. However, it is not they that actually give and get, but the current negotiating parties on their behalf. Any action creates a future for future parties, but not by future parties.

1 I William Zartman, 'Negotiation as Joint Decision-Making' in I William Zartman (ed), *The Negotiation Process* (SAGE 1978).

Other negotiations involve past absents, with less of a clear custom or established procedure on how to handle them. They can neither give nor get, having already given and gotten all that they could, and that may be the problem. The only event in which to be involved would be over negotiations to alter that balance sheet, but even there it is not the absents who are involved but present parties speaking for them. Past absents leave a legacy that coming parties work out. Parties can be relieved of or compensated for that legacy if the relief or the compensation comes in time to correct the situation for the parties (or their immediate children) alive at the time and in that case they are not absent; how much later raises questions, which will be discussed below. An example could be a jail sentence or exoneration that is later found to be erroneous, and a correction is negotiated with the party. But in these cases, the party is not past but present in the negotiations, which returns the discussion to the matter of the past where the absents are not parties to a negotiation. They are no more stakeholders than they are shareholders, a distinction used to bring in the first circle of absents in the present.[2] Thus, the first principle in analysing past absents is that *past absents must be made present to negotiate.*

It is perhaps relevant to make a moral disclaimer at this point, lest the following discussion be taken to imply a disregard for the situation of past absents. The fact that past wrongs cannot be righted in the past does not make them any less wrong. The Kennedy brothers cannot be revived or restored even though their murders were morally and politically heinous. The fact that Hitler and Stalin cannot be punished for the Molotov-Ribbentrop Pact that erased Poland, among other things, does not make the agreement any more despicable; that situation can be righted, and it was, but not for the people of the past.

While the Kennedys cannot be restored to life or to politics, Poland can be – and has been – restored. Some individual citizens who last property have doubtless seen it returned or been compensated for it, some monuments and plaques have been erected, but life picks up with the restoration of Poland on the basis of the situation at the time of restoration. The same occurred in 1919 when Poland reappeared after 125 years' absence. Poles existed during these periods of absence, but the political entity and economy of Poland was absorbed by neighbors. Resuscitation was accomplished by

2 Maria Bonnafous-Boucher and Yvon Pesqueux, *Décider avec les parties prenantes* (Découverte 2006); Maria Bonnafous-Boucher and Jacob Dahl Rendtorff, *Stakeholder Theory* (Springer 2016).

descendants (shareholders) and 'stakeholders' (interested second parties) on both occasions. Essentially, the new (or renewed) corporate entity started out again where it was, the result of the balance sheet incurred in its absence.

1. Making the Absents Present in the United States

There seem to be only two ways to remove the status of absents: either to bring them back alive in the present or to meet them in the past. The first means carrying their line to one or more living descendants, converting their absence into presence and allowing for agreed closure by the present parties. The second means performing acts of material or memorial recognition open to a larger or unlimited audience, with acknowledgement or write-off only on behalf of but not from the absents. A few examples will illustrate these notions, realities being sharper but never as comprehensive as concepts.

A situation relevant to this discussion concerns the land of *Native Americans* which have been sequestered by the US federal government·.[3] By the doctrine of discovery, based on the European feudally-derived doctrine of conquest, Britain (and other European 'discovering' countries) had legal title to the land it 'discovered' and this power of sovereignty passed on to the United States upon independence and then, under the Constitution (art 1, §8, cl 3, the Interstate and Indian Commerce Clause) to the federal government.[4] Justice John Marshall defined the relationship with:

> domestic dependent nations...(who) occupy a territory to which we assert a title independent of their will. Meanwhile they are in a state of pupilage. Their relation to the United States resembles that of a ward to his guardian. They look to our government for protection; rely upon its kindness and its power, ...[5]

Many of the 'dependent nations' or tribes negotiated their landholdings with the federal government.

---

3 I am grateful to Katherine Nelson and David Smith for an understanding of this case. Katharine F Nelson, 'Resolving Native American Land Claims and the Eleventh Amendment: Changing the Balance of Power' (1994) 39(3) Villanova Law Review 525.

4 *Worcester v Georgia*, 31 US 515 (1832); *Johnson & Graham's Lessee v McIntosh*, 21 US 543 (1823); *Oneida Indian Nation v County of Oneida*, 414 US 661 (1974).

5 *Cherokee Nation v Georgia*, 30 US 1, 17 (1831).

But in 1887 Congress passed the Dawes Act that authorised the president 'to allot the lands in said reservations...to any Indian located thereon in quantities as follows: 160 acres to a head of family, 80 acres to adult single persons, and 40 acres to children', 'for agricultural and grazing purposes' to encourage them to become farmers subject to state laws, 'and, if they lived separate and apart from any tribe...and have adopted the habits of civilized life...to [become] a citizen of the United States'.[6] The federal government held in trust all grazing, oil, gas, and recreational leases or administered them through 'individual Indian money (IIM) accounts'. But over time the landowners received no or inadequate payments for the leases, and whatever payment was held for them in trust; the plots were too small and arid for farming or cattle raising, and gradually the owners sold them at low rates for an immediate return. The 155 million Indian-owned acres in 1881 dropped in half by 1900 and to a quarter in 1934. In 1996, Elouise Cobell, a Blackfeet Nation banker, launched a class action suit on behalf of over 300 000 landholders – the largest class action suit ever – against the Secretary of Interior to recover the sums held in trust by the federal government's Bureau of Indian Affairs (BIA) but withheld by 122 years of negligence or design (eventually *Cobell v. Salazar*[7]).

The suit, settled in 2009, raised innumerable and typical problems, which – politics aside, of course – may have helped delay its resolution for thirteen years of litigation including 10 trials, two judges, seven appeals, and 22 published decisions. Six generations of absent landowners had passed, and their inheritance had been fractionated by probate 'so that some parcels now have many hundreds – or even thousands – of owners,' which had made it difficult to reach agreement to develop, improve or lease the land.[8] At the time of the suit, 10 million acres contained 4.1 million fractionated interests in 99 000 land parcels.[9] A lawyer for the plaintiffs later claimed, 'I spent 7 or 8 years of my life trying to track down claimants and descendants.' The land itself was estimated at between 47 million and 54 million acres, and the lawsuit was designed to force the government

6 US Statutes at Large, XXIV, 386.

7 *Cobell v Salazar*, 573 US F.3d *808* (DC Cir. 2009) (Cobell XXII).

8 [8] Chris Edwards, 'Indian Lands, Indian Subsidies, and the Bureau of Indian Affairs' (*Downsizing the Federal Government*, 1 February 2012) <https://perma.cc/4S4G-TZPD>. In the US, 3-descendents fractionation yield 163 heirs in the sixth generation; 'Government Settles Indian Trust Fund Suit' (*Cultural Survival*, 14 December 2009) <https://perma.cc/B6R9-FZGG>.

9 Edwards (n 8).

either to fully account for the profits of the leases or to distribute them to the owners, a full accounting being impossible since the Department of Interior had either lost or destroyed many of the records (three previous cabinet secretaries for Interior and Treasury were held in contempt of court for failing to protect and provide adequate documentation.)[10] In sum, once the federal responsibility through the Bureau of Indian Affairs' (largely willful) mishandling was established, both the number of representatives of the absent landholders, the amount of their losses, the means of calculation of its value, and the allocation of any award, which lacked any firm basis, were open to negotiation.

It is reported that Judge Robertson brought the parties to his chambers in the summer of 2009 and said: 'You can litigate this for another 10 years or you can resolve it now. I want you to resolve it now'.[11] The value of the claims varied widely according to plaintiffs and scholars, from USD 47 billion demanded by the plaintiffs to USD 176 billion mentioned in press statements. Since tribal trust lands (three-quarters of the reservations' total acreage) are 80 percent less productive than fee-simple lands (5 % of the total) and individual trust lands (a fifth of the total) are 30–40 % less productive, the basis for an estimate of lost value is complex and uncertain.[12] In 2005, the US government proposed paying USD 7 billion as partial settlement; the plaintiffs requested USD 27.487 billion;[13] two years later, the government proposed USD 7 billion which the plaintiffs said was 'pennies on the dollar' and mentioned liability of over USD 100 billion.[14] After three months of negotiation in 2009 that followed a curious bargaining process of lowering totals to reach an agreement, the outcome was a USD 3.4 billion settlement, the largest such settlement ever for the US government. After legal and administrative fees, USD 1.4 billion was set aside for the plaintiffs, individuals who had an account open in the BIA as of 1994, who were

10 Cultural Survival (n 8).

11 Ari Shapiro, 'US in $3B Settlement with American Indians' (*NPR*, 8 December 2009) <https://perma.cc/ZSM9-MQ43>.

12 Terry L Anderson and Dean Lueck, 'Land Tenure and Productivity on Indian Reservations' (1992) 35(2) Journal of Law and Economics 427.

13 James Cason, 'Statement of James Cason, associate deputy secretary and Ross Swimmer, Special Trustee for American Indians on the Cobell Lawsuit' (*Department of the Interior – Office of Congressional and Legislative Affairs*, 26 July 2005) <https://perma.cc/V8KY-BKJH>.

14 Mary Clare Jalonik, 'Interior Proposes Settlement in Cobell Case' (*Bismarck Tribune*, 6 March 2007) <https://bismarcktribune.com/news/state-and-regional/article_e2586773-2cd9-5415-bdd3-a7d28ff5d455.html> accessed 7 July 2023.

expected to receive USD 1000 each; USD 1.9 billion went to individuals who wanted to sell their fractionated interests to the federal government to be turned over to the tribes as community lands, and USD 900 million was set aside for higher education scholarships, a common practice with Indian settlements. The settlement was the negotiation of a bad debt, paid on 10 cents or less to the dollar.

2. Making Absents Present in Africa

A case of absents for comparative relief concerning *German non-reparations to Namibians* killed and despoiled in 1904–1908, following a Herero and Nama resistance against the German colonisation of South West Africa, now Namibia. Germany launched an extirpation campaign against the two tribes, chasing them into the desert, poisoning and imprisoning those who remained, and killing 65 000 of the 80 000 Hereros and 10 000 of the 20 000 Namas. There are four questions involved.[15] The first is the matter of representation. Under internal pressure, Germany looked into negotiations in 2004 with the two tribes, who in 2007 petitioned inclusion; Germany found them locked into maximalist positions.[16] The Namibian government, composed of the national liberation movement turned single party, the South West Africa People's Orgnisation (SWAPO), which is primarily Ovambo, rejected the tribal associations, the Ovaherero Traditional Authority and the Nama Traditional Leaders Association, as non-representative. They then turned to the US court in a class action suit in 2007 but were rejected for non-jurisdiction, and then considered approaching the International Court. Instead, under pressure the government included a Ovaherero/Ovambanderu and Nama Council for Dialogue on the 1904–1908 Genocide (ONCD 1904–1908) that was willing to accept a role as a consultant body to the process. The Agreement finally reached between the two states was rejected by tribal representatives for agency as well as content.

---

15 Reinhart Kössler, *Namibia and Germany: Negotiating the Past* (University of Namibia Press 2016).

16 Rudolf Schüssler, 'Self-Centered Reconciliation: The German-Namibian Case' (2021) 50 PINPoints 31. Henning Melber, 'Germany and Namibia: Negotiating Genocide' (2020) 22(4) International Journal of Genocide Research 502.

The second issue, in time and in the negotiation process, is the game of the name. In part because of the past shadow of the word, it took until May 2021 for Germany to agree to the official use of the term 'genocide,' but it still refuses to refer to 'reparations' because 'the prevention and punishment of genocide [by the 1848 convention] does not apply retrospectively and cannot be the basis of [individual] financial claim,' whereas reparations open up endless possibilities of litigation and precedents for other cases involving Germany and other neighboring and colonial countries.[17]

The third issue is the 'Quantum' question. In 2005 Germany offered EUR 20 million in compensation over 10 years but the deal fell through in November; in 2015 it again offered EUR 10 million, presumably on different terms, but the negotiations on the issue stalled. The two states finally made an agreement in May 2021 for a EUR 1.1billion payment of EUR 36 million annually over 30 years, still rejecting the notion of reparations.[18] The payments are to be used for social and economic development including vocational training with a focus on Herero and Nama people but not specifically to them or to victims' descendants.[19] For these reasons, the agreement has been castigated by the tribal spokesmen, who claim the sum is inadequate, the representative inappropriate, the focus on training demeaning, and the reparations question still open. Analysts say that rising youth consciousness in Germany may yet make a return to the issue possible.

The fourth issue has not been addressed at all. Under colonisation, German settlers took over the land abandoned by their former Herero and Nama owners. Government policy has favored land recovery benefitting farming Ovambo people in the heavily populated north and little for the pastoral Herrero people in the northeast. As in former settler colonies in southern Africa and elsewhere, land redistribution is a highly political issue relating both to economics and historic identity. There is no accountability for the absent perpetrators, either of the genocide or – still present and visible – of the land usurpers.

The third case is again quite different. The absents are the 800 000 victims of the 1994 *Rwandan genocide*, primarily Tutsi. France did not commit the genocide but by its support, political and material, for the Hutu-domi-

17 Morimitsu Onishi and Melissa Eddy, 'A Forgotten Genocide' *The New York Times* (New York, 8 May 2021).

18 Philip Obermann, 'Germany Rules out financial reparations' (*The Guardian*, 21 May 2021) <https://perma.cc/Y24H-UELB>.

19 Alfred L Brody, *Reparations: Pro and Con* (OUP 2021).

nated regime in Rwanda associated with the Rwandan National Movement (MNR) and the ensuing *génocidaires* or *nguzu*, it made the killing possible. After the fact, genocide has been widely admitted and perpetrators have been pursued by the International Criminal Tribunal for Rwanda. The Rwanda regime has revived a traditional reconciliation institution of *gacaca* designed to air and meet the griefs of the survivors of the victims, although there have been charges that a frank and open exchange is absent and the institution is in Tutsi hands. French President Emmanuel Macron publicly acknowledged 'France's overwhelming responsibility' in the affair, standing next to the Rwandan President Paul Kagame, the Tutsi leader who ousted the MNR regime. The French government had commissioned a private Duclert report that established the record of responsibility.[20] The admission was greeted positively by Rwandan groups. However, some commentators have questioned the extent of the admission. French involvement was part of a policy of backing authoritarian regimes as a means of assuring good relations and French responsibility for stability in French-speaking Africa. The Kagame regime is a leading example of the same relationship with a repressive regime.[21] African critics stated that an appropriate recognition of the absents would be a future correction of the type of policy that underlay the support of the type of regime that engaged in genocide.

In the Native Indian case, the absents were brought to life, in some cases from 15 to 122 years (since 1887 or 1994) but they never were really absent, just ignored, having remained on the out-of-date BIA records. How the sums to be paid were negotiated down in a reverse bargaining process is not clear. The suit was not over the injustice of the law vis-à-vis the absents but over the neglect of its application. Payments were not updated to take the effects of economic conditions, back interest, inflation or opportunity costs into account.

In the Namibian case, none of the issues under negotiation has brought the absents back in any way. They celebrate an event, like a wake, and made (or sought to make) money out of it. Had they addressed the land issue, the

20 Mehdi Ba, 'Rwandan genocide was "a French political, institutional and moral failure" says Duclert Commission' (*The Africa Reports,* 29 March 2021) <https://perma.cc/66RB-NK8R>.

21 Achille Mbembe mentions 'France's "apparent blindness to tyranny"' in Barbara Wojazer and Melissa Bell, 'Macron Seeks Forgiveness for France's Role in Rwanda Genocide, But Stops Short of Apology' (*CNN World,* 2021) <https://perma.cc/Q9ME-6NP3>.

absents would appear and their confrontation with the presents would be more real. That may yet happen.

The Rwanda case shows the greatest distance between the absents and the presents, or really the futures. On the levels of legal naming and judicial retribution, the situation has been fully handled, if not settled. It is only on broader implications of policy and relations, twice removed, that the implications of the absents' situation is brought to the future.

3. Referent Principles

None of the component seven principles itemized below deal uniquely with the situation of the absents *per se*, but they frame such consideration. When discussing past absents, one is not considering their role in negotiations since they are absent, an unresurrectable situation. At most, one can consider their rights and wrongs as carried by a representative in the present. Thus, the past cannot be remedied or advanced in the past but only in the present, through the present situation of present parties with claims based on absents' losses and claims. In dealing with the value of such claims and negotiations, referents are crucial elements in framing the issue (Kaneman & Tversky). Such referents are involved in breaking down (analysing) the current issue, including rights (interests), wrongs, representation (standing), time, legitimacy, reconciliation, and justice, perhaps among others.

Rights including interests are a defining referent, concerning notably the issue of participation and the extent to which it can be restored. Presumably, the past absents had or would have or should have had the right to participate had they been present. That right is then reactivated by their representatives, discussed in the following section. However, if that right was absent along with them or not recognised, the first task is to establish it, again presumably by the claimant's representatives. The claim is made in the same terms as it would have been if the absents were present, in terms of damages and interests. The Poles can claim that they had the right to be present in the Molotov-Ribbentrop discussions since their existence was at stake, and in their absence, the negotiations were illegitimate. Denial of that right was one of the causes of World War II. Hereros and Namas can claim that a right to life and land existed for all time and that genocide now was extermination then, in concept even if not in legal language. Apartheid Blacks, American natives and American slaves can claim their rights as humans were not recognised and that by the same reasoning, apartheid, pupilage and slavery compacts were illegitimate. As a result the wronged groups had past rights that can be pursued by their representatives.

However, when such fundamental rights as existence as human beings or as a state are concerned, it should not only be the job of representatives but of all inheritors of the system to pursue them. Hence World War II was pursued by all the Allies, not just the Poles, and the end of apartheid and slavery is the challenge to all South Africans and Americans. These are clear cases: but what about the right of nations that are not yet states, such as Palestinians, Kurds,the Armenians in Nagorno Karabakh or Uighurs in China? The right of national (or state) self-determination has been firmly recognised but is obtainable only by intense violence. By the same token, another special group of absents with rights as human beings are the yet unborn, most of whom will not be absents in the future but some of whom are threatened with absence in their past. Not parties now themselves, they depend on their representative to insure the recognition of their right to life.[22]

Wrongs are defining elements in the consideration of absent parties. Most discussion of the past absents is triggered by a desire to right the wrongs of the past. It is not simply a question of suspended inheritance, as the discussion and the case to this point has indicated, but of a wrong condition of the estate at the very time of reckoning. Thus, it is not just a matter of updating the inheritance but of correcting the inheritance itself at the time of accounting. But should the books of the time be accepted at face value, without accrued interest and opportunity costs? However, there is no question of righting the wrong for the benefit of the wronged, since they are past, but of doing it for the benefit of present survivors. Beneficiaries are usually representatives of past absents but they also can include a larger group of present parties, when class action is possible, which is not the case in many legal systems.

Past wrongs cannot be used as an excuse to claim benefits for present parties other than immediate descendants. The notion is based on the fundamental idea that one is responsible for one's acts and that an individual can be held accountable only for them. Responsibility cannot be inherited or represented (and it is a good thing). There can be such a thing as collective responsibility in cases where the institutional or social collectivity is the agent; institutions and societies have longer lives than individuals and

22 Alveda King, 'Dr Mildred Jefferson: A Hero in the Pro-life Movement' (*The Washington Times*, 23 March 2021) <https://perma.cc/37MU-X423>.

so their responsibility is longer lasting, but then they are not absent parties. Without an official representative, there is no one to act for the wronged. Israel and the World Jewish Council were specifically designated as the representative of the holocaust victims for receiving German reparations, but the state of Namibia, rather than the tribal houses, arrogated for themselves the right of representation. There is not yet a representative for Sephardic Jews or Uighurs (Kurds on the other hand have at least three). The basic nature of individual responsibility is important in discussing rights and wrongs.

Representation is necessary for the past absents to be present again, to re-present their interests and grievances. It comes into play in regard to gaining a hearing so as to advance claims of the absent party, but also in regard to enjoyment of the results when the claims are heard. The most direct representatives are the direct descendants of the original absent party, however much fractioned and regardless of the intervening additions, as required, for example by the DAR for membership or the BIA for (belated) trust benefits. If the absents are a group, not simply direct descendants, a certain percentage (or number of qualifying ancestors) from the group might be required, leading to such categorisations as coloreds and octoroons; even in the presence of strict anti-miscegenation laws, leaks are frequent and have to be considered in some way. Unless the group is exclusively inbred, the extent of endogeneity requires specification. Thus, rights – and so, wrongs – can be inherited, as long as the line is not broken, but there is no statute of limitations, in law or in custom and no established rationale for extension. Any limitations or extension must be legislated for. This is an important conceptual and practical question and will keep on coming up in the discussion.

In the absence of direct descent, another type of representation would be through class action, as the Herero and Nama tried. In class action cases, the class is generally considered to be the group directly affected in the present, as the American Indian tribes, but the class could also be a human rights organisation interested in simply making the loss known rather than recouping any tangible benefits. The International League of human Rights (LIDH), the Catholic Church, the World Council of Churches, and their various national groups and members have been active and occasionally powerful in bringing to light the perpetrators and victims, by name, of atrocities in Brazil, Uruguay, Argentina, and Haiti; here the absents have been represented not to gain compensation but to pursue the perpetrators, who in turn have generally been represented by the military organisations as protectors. The most distant representation would be friends in court, without any direct link to the absents except support for their cause; unlike the others, this group would not have to worry about the degree to which it is related to the original absents, but would gain no benefits. Given this array of possibilities of representation, a specific criterion would have to be established with appropriate justification before the process can move ahead; the Namibian case illustrates the controversy.

Representation also concerns the calculation and allocation of benefits when the claims are awarded. Redress for past losses by absent parties are generally referred to as reparations, usually considered as tangible financial restorations. The basis of calculation is as complicated as the matter of apportionment. Would it be the victims' deficiency from a general standard at the time, or the victims' past condition updated by some growth factor to a present level, or the victims' level equalised to the average level at the time or at the present? The US government answered these questions by sticking to the recognised debt figures and awarded BIA trust money to each descendant. The calculation of the payment made to Israel for the victims of the holocaust on the basis of USD 3000 for each of the 500 000 holocaust survivors over 14 years, lowered in the 1962 agreement to USD 1 billion from West Germany (East Germany never paid its share);[23] another USD 2400 for 240 000 of the poorest survivors was added for Covid-19 (not expressly related to reparations). Apportionment of the reparation once made has its own logic which goes back to the above discussions of criteria for representation: fragmentated direct descent, group descent, or group membership.

In the case of the holocaust reparations, the state of Israel was the major representative of the victims (the World Jewish Council also for a small part) and used the funds for their collective welfare, whether they were descents or not. This role for the state of Namibia was rejected by the tribes affected, but it is not clear how the figures were arrived at. Yet the further question was also determinantal: if someone is to get rich as a result, who is to get poor? Who pays and why should they? In Germany, responsibility was generally accepted by the public and the (West) German state was the representative of the wrongdoers; the Namibian state, the US

23 Shoah Resource Center, The International School for Holocaust Studies, 'Reparations and Restitutions' (*Yad vashem*) <https://www.yadvashem.org/odot_pdf/microsoft%20word%20-%206419.pdf> accessed 7 July 2023; PG 'German Reparations to Israel: The 1952 Treaty and Its Effects' (1954) 10(6) The World Today 258.

federal government and the French state (at least for the moment) were the representatives in their cases. The American state has the responsibility toward the native Americans and paid USD 1.3 billion between 1945 and 1978 for seizing natives' land and another USD 3.4 billion for withheld payments on land that the BIA did not seize; there is no such representative for Black Americans nor is there any specific account of payment denied or assets withheld. Africans sold to European slavers about 90 % of those enslaved and shipped to the New World; about a quarter of US Southern white families bought and owned these slaves.

One relevant question is the motivation and expectation of the representative for representing the absent party. Representation of an absent party should be independent of the representative's own interests, lest the two become entangled and the one diluted.[24] However, since the absent party cannot benefit from the outcome of representation since it is absent, and the representative represents only interests derived from the absent party's losses and gains, it might even be expected to be motivated to represent in expectation of any such benefits. The only other reason for representing – and one that is prevalent and powerful in many cases – is altruistic, for the common good and the maintenance of a principle, including non-impunity or simply the right to life and property.

Time is also a referent for analysing the issue of past absents. In negotiations over the inheritance of a deceased party, the only absent party is the deceased, who has already indicated his/her position in the negotiations; present parties to an inheritance negotiate the estate left to them at the time of the deceased and may include generations as parties but only those who are present, the living survivors of the deceased. But the estate of earlier deceased or absent parties is beyond recall. If the condition (estate) of an absent party several generations previous were to be considered, the same questions on the value of the estate would arise. Would claims be based on the value of the condition of the absent at the time of decease, by current or original values? Or the value of the estate at present, including any growth or loss, in current values, and how is the investment or depreciation rate determine? As noted, these questions were avoided as unsolvable by the Native American Indian settlement The Biblical story of the servants who received either 3 talents, 2 talents, and 1 talent is apposite, although it does not establish a single growth rate (it suggests that the greater the

24 John Rawls, *A Theory of Justice* (Harvard University Press, Belknap Press 1971) 63; Cecilia Albin, *Justice and Fairness in International Negotiation* (CUP 2001) 28.

original sum, the higher the growth rate, but then the story is for illustrative and religious purposes only). No proposed answer to these questions is authoritative and there is no established rule of justice to authorise any particular answer.

But if apartheid and slavery, extermination and genocide, unremitted land claims and state dismemberment are over, what about their shadow? Shadows fade but can be revived; wounds become scars but can be reopened. But wherever it happens, it is for the benefit of the representatives, not of the absents or even of their memory. To avoid the recidivist memory, it is important to erase traces. The nostalgic representatives may have no interest in shelving the past, but the general public has a great interest in acknowledging the catastrophe and passing it on. Keeping the shadow under control depends much on positive actions in the meantime, between the event and the present. If little has changed, it is not the absents who are being recompensed but rather the presents representatives of themselves. But to the extent the absents' descendants have made progress since the event and overcome the wronging conditions – which clearly may take some time – the representatives have less and less of a claim on indemnification. There is no rule in law or logic by which to judge how long the shadow is as a justifiable argument for compensation, but it would likely involve the standard calculation: cost vs gain, loss at the time minus progress made to the general standard since then. But that does not settle the argument, it only gives a basis for debate and calculations. What is – or should be – clear is, again, that the beneficiaries are the representatives here present, and that the calculation of the formula refers to now, the present rather than the past or the future.

It is striking – but never considered – that the past is not made up solely of wrongs and losses.[25] Even wrongs have multiple consequences that need to be included when a balance sheet is drawn up and compensation calculated. Not to do so gives rise to feelings of victimization, that sees oneself as only a target of wrong and makes improvement impossible. Thus, it would be just, and important in quantitative terms, to consider opportunity gains as well as costs. Comparison with prior or alternative or full future situations can evaluate gains as well as losses to be included in the calculations. Repeated or gradual recovery of absents' interest opens the question of whether done is ever done. The BIA settlement was indicated

25 Robin Gregory and others, 'Methods for assessing social and cultural losses' (2023) 381(6657) Science 478.

as final, although challenging finality is only human, even if not legal (can the Namibian state indicate the case is closed when the tribes do not think so?). The German-Israeli agreement has a full-satisfaction clause, exempting specific personal claims; otherwise the demand could forever be repeated by future generations, since the issue is fully in the hands of present representatives. Milosevich has shown that without such a limit, the rerun of the claims can be eternal. If the US, *Brown v Board of Education* in 1954 was to have evened the scale, then Lyndon Johnson's New Society in the 1960s would have been definitive. Yet the issue of reparation still appears in the 2020s. The absents remain absent; it is the presents that raise the claims for their own benefit.

One curious and perhaps psychological characteristic of moving toward achievement of reparations for the absent past's condition is the final-push or approach-intensity effect (reverse of the approach-avoidance effect in negotiation).[26] As present parties move closer to the goal of eliminating the conditions of the past absent party after already making significant progress in that direction, representative present parties greatly intensify their efforts, magnify the past evils, and downplay past progress. The prospect theory finding that achieved gain is valued less than unrecovered loss registers a strong effect.[27] It may be an attempt not to slacken efforts and to overcome relaxation after past progress, or a benefit of the strengthened position made possible by the past progress, or an improved realisation that the full or oversubscribed goal is finally actually attainable, or a sharpened view of details as the end comes closer, or a heightened effort to overcome last-chance resistance that the heightened effort actually spurs (an approach-avoidance reaction), or all of these, that produce the effect and prolongs and intensifies the drive to realise the past absents' inheritance.

There has also been some discussion that reparations are not a restitution for a past condition but an initiation of an ongoing policy for the future, correcting condition of the past victims projected into the future, as in the criticism of the French position in regard to an African state like Rwanda.[28] This has been introduced as a meaning of reparations for XVIII-

26 Dean G Pruitt, 'When Is "Enough" Enough? Approach–Avoidance' in I William Zartman (ed), *How Negotiations End: Negotiating Behavior in the Endgame* (CUP 2019).

27 Amos Tversky and Daniel Kahneman, 'Judgment Under Uncertainty: Heuristics and Biases' (1974) 185(4157) Sciences New Series 1124.

28 Conor Friedersdorf, 'What do 2020 Candidates Mean When they Say "Reparations"?' (*The Atlantic*, 5 June 2019) <https://www.theatlantic.com/ideas/archive/2019/06/reparations-definition-2020-candidates/590863/> accessed 7 July 2023.

XIX century slavery and its aftermath in America but also as a consequence of the disclosure campaigns in authoritarian states such as South Africa and the Latin American republics where the identification of a repressive regime has been less disputed. In this understanding, the absent party is represented through a demand or promise for improvement of conditions as a consequence of its past deprivation. The demand is, in fact, independent of the past condition but is enhanced by it, a rather forward-looking projection of past deficiencies that aims at improving conditions for both descendants of the wronged party and for the rest of society, a kind of 'never again' response. This is perhaps the most diluted but most broadly beneficial notion of repayment for past wrongs, facing problems neither of calculation nor of apportionment. It is of course open to enormous battles over the degree of reform necessary for its accomplishment, as present parties dispute whether the past wrongs have already been sufficiently compensated and eliminated, and it returns the issue to the usual course of popular protest movements, which eventually die out in fatigue after a while after having achieved some but not all of its original promises.[29]

Legitimacy is one of the two underlying values of this inquiry. Can a party be held responsible by a value that was not in place at the time of the act? Such judgments are termed bills of attainder or ex post facto condemnations in the US Constitution (art 1 §9c) and are banned. If the representation of the absents is concerned with a general issue – slavery, apartheid, torture and disappearance – evaluation is a general moral judgment; if actual damage is the cause for remuneration, then more specific issues of quantitative evaluation are involved. In the latter case, the same questions of accounting apply: what is the basis of evaluating the failings of the absents' estate at that point? And then, how has it been evaluated. A major element in the answer depends on the source of values – by notions of legitimacy at the time or by current notions. The implied German contention that genocide was not recognised as genocide back then or the Guatemalan contention that subversion then should be recognised as subversion now should not cover the fact that herding victims into the desert and dropping them from airplanes is an inhuman action at any time, whereas death by duel cannot be considered murder a century later.

29 David Meyer, 'Civil Disobedience and Protest Cycles' in Jo Freeman and Victoria Johnson (eds), *Waves of Protest Social Movements Since the 1960s* (Rowman & Littlefield 1999). Doug McAdams, 'The Decline of the Civil Rights Movement' in Jo Freeman and Victoria Johnson (eds), *Waves of Protest Social Movements Since the 1960s* (Rowman & Littlefield 1999).

A contentious question in the matter of legitimacy, however, raises the reasons for which the past wrong was committed. The wrong may have been accepted by the norms of dominant society at the time (including the wronged parties at the time such as the South African or American Blacks or Native American Indians), judged wrong later on, or more narrowly imposed by the interests of an authoritarian regime, as in the case of military regimes in Latin America; in the latter case, the justifying norms were for the benefit of a repressive regime over much of society, the difference being in the degree of popular acquiescence to the system. Guilt maybe adjudged by revised standards later on, but it does not affect the fact that elements of the absent past were wronged, taking the discussion to the referent of representation.

When it is the whole system of governance or the social system that is responsible for condoning an action that is held reprehensible by later laws and mores, the legitimate criterion for responsibility may appear less clear, but it is nonetheless clear that a person cannot be held guilty for an act that was legal and legitimate at the time committed, even if that notion of legitimacy can itself be criticised later on. However, if the actor cannot be punished, the past actor's representative can be urged to seek acknowledgement, pardon and reconciliation at a later time.

There is no indication that a party wronged by current standards can be compensated for an action that was legal or legitimate at the time committed, and by what criteria? The change of standards does not involve any guilt in regard to the committing actor, merely a moral or legal evolution. Similarly, absent parties condemned at the time are exonerated because the standard of condemnation no longer holds. Women condemned of witchcraft in Salem Massachusetts in the XVII century were exonerated in 1711; women condemned between the XIV and the XIX centuries in Scotland were rehabilitated in 2021.[30] Disgusting though the condemnations were, there is no way the persecutors can be held accountable for their actions, nor can descendants of the condemned women sue for redress; statutory limitations have expired and, even if not statuted, accountability has to be fixed on a living person, and the rehabilitation of the "witches" brought no indemnification for their mistreatment.

30 Valentina Pop, 'Justice for the Victims of Witch Hunts, Old and New' (*Wall Street Journal*, 4 March 2021) <https://perma.cc/Z3RG-N4PD>.

Justice receives little attention in agreements on the issue of absent parties, probably because they are over-occupied by the plight of present parties. Although we are still searching for a commonly accepted meaning of the term applicable to all situations – and some have asserted rather strongly that such search is pointless and that justice in negotiation is situationally defined from among many meanings.[31]) – current attempts tend to land on such meanings as fairness[32] or envy-free[33] or some other twist on equality. This serves as good a starting point as any.

From the point of view of fairness or equality, the first cut at justice for absent parties is simple: all parties, present or absent, should have an equal chance of being heard, that is, absence should be mitigated. For the absents, if absence is not immediately correctable, this means representation at an effective level, interested in regard to the absent parties' interests, disinterested on the part of the representatives' own interests. Wrongs need redressing, rights need pursuing; but in neither case is the outcome automatically guaranteed, only the opportunity for equal presence before an appropriate decision-making agency- judicial or executive, voting, or negotiation.[34]

The simplicity disappears, however, when the absent party is more than a generation distant in time. The absence of the absent party can no longer be overcome, and its interests represented in current transaction. There is no justice for the distant absents, only for the shadow of their memory, and here the field is crowded. How many past memories should be corrected – Muslims and Jews in Spain (1492), Slavs at Kosovo (1381), Muslims in Algeria at many places including Setif (1948), Korean Pleasure Women in World War II, African Americans since 1619 and notably in Tulsa in 1921, and native Americans in 1815. Indeed, arguably every country has a time or incident in which the now-absents suffered a notable wrong, and in which their rights at the time remain unaddressed. Most of these events, and thousands others, have been relegated to history books, optimally duly acknowledged. It is interesting how many historical studies of awful doings

31 Lloyd Jensen and others, 'Negotiation as a Search for Justice' (1996) 1(1) International Negotiation 79.

32 Rawls (n 24).

33 Steven J Brams and Alan D Taylor, *Fair Division: From Cake-Cutting to Dispute Resolution* (CUP 1996).

34 Robert Dahl, 'Hierarchy, Democracy and Bargaining in Economics and Politics' in Robert Dahl and others (eds), *Research Frontiers in Politics and Government* (Brookings 1955); Zartman (n 1).

in the past appear in the Review section of any good Sunday papers without triggering a national protest to right the wrong (except Tulsa).

However, some have become roaring political causes. As such, they can never be fully satisfied and can forever be revived, even after long periods of somnolence. In an appropriate political context, they call for reparations, redress and revenge, ignited by eloquent appeals, from *Flanders Field* (1919) to Milosevic (1989) to al-Suri (2010) and ben Laden (2005); nothing can prevent such mad revivals. To many, there is no reconciliation possible, because reconciliation would be infidelity to the victims' (often relatives' or earlier ancestors'), grievances and unjust treatments and because those who committed the wrongs are no more present than the wronged and so apologies in their name by self-appointed representatives are fictitious and second-hand. Reconciliation is a reciprocal action, even though it involves separate individual decisions. Therefore, reconciliation with absent parties is not possible, whether they be the wronged or the wronging absent. Reconciliation can only be in the present.

This situation, finally, brings in an additional dimension not found in the previous type, a negative attachment or opprobrium. The previous elements were discussed and are handled in a business-like atmosphere; legal values are attached when appropriate, and rights and wrong claim a moral attachment, to which the representatives may or may not agree. Such is the atmosphere of any negotiation, and it colors the debate surrounding recent absents and their representatives. However, in cases of distant absents, who are in no way directly involved or benefit from the negotiations carried out in their name, there is an emotional element of shame that gives somber tones to the issue. What was done some time ago was not a single act in such cases, but a condition assented by all society (often with a few exceptional voices). Perhaps one should turn the description around and talk of situations that reflect social involvement, rather than emphasise the distant past as part of the definition. In any case, the situation is that of the holocaust as well as slavery, Armenians as well as Native Americans, apartheid victims and other colonised peoples, among others (in the case of the Hutu or the Korean women, it is the element of time and hence assignable guilt that differentiates). In each case of the type, the incident brings shame on the society which allowed – and indeed legitimised – the occurrence, a stain on history.

Shame belongs to the past, guilt is its present manifestation. It is here that the issue comes to its most extreme point. Shame is attached to a society that is now absent; guilt calls for justice and punishment. But who now is guilty? Just as the absents are no longer present, so it is with the perpetrators. Just as the wronged, being (long) absent cannot benefit from rectifications, so can the presents not pay for them or bear their guilt, an injustice in the present that would not rectify the injustice of the past. The inappropriate assignment of guilt has its costs, beyond any monetary burden on the non-guilty presents, resurrects not the damaged from the past but the damages to the present, where they are not being inflicted. Rather than healing the past it wounds the present, transposing the wounds of the past onto the present, ignoring any healing and restoration that has been accomplished in between. The only alternative to this juxtaposition of times is to operate in the present; the only thing those present can do is to make sure 'Never Again'.

4. Never Again

There is no easy way to square this circle. For absolutists who look back, history must be rewritten, evils reemphasised, statues torn down, and Once Before and Never Again written on everyone's forehead. For the relativists who look ahead, aware that Never Again was followed by Rwanda, the challenge is in prevention for the future, turning backs to the contentious past left among the absents and removing its causes for the future.[35] That is the more difficult of the two courses. But it can be done, not by erasing the past nor by memorialising it, but by making common projects that remove the separate identity of the wronged and wronging absents' heirs to make an indistinguishable just future.

35 Rudolf Schüssler, 'Reconciliation, Morality and Moral Compromise' in Valérie Rosoux and Mark Anstey (eds), *Negotiating Reconciliation in Peacemaking Quandaries of Relationship Building* (Springer 2017) 48–49; Valérie Rosoux, '*Time and Reconciliation: Dealing with Festering Wounds*' in Rosoux and Anstey (n 35) ; I William Zartman and Victor Kremenyuk (eds), *Peace vs Justice* (Rowman & Littlefield 2005).

9. Peace for the Future: The Incorporation of Future Generations in Peace Treaties and Reconciliation Institutions

Alexandra R. Harrington[*]

Abstract: *This chapter examines peace agreements and the statutes and findings of truth and reconciliation commissions from the lens of intergenerational justice and inclusion of future generations. The critical lens used for the chapter's analysis of peace agreements is that of the principle of prevention in the sense of agreements that are not only created to cause the cessation of hostilities in each State but rather to prevent these hostilities from occurring again in the future. To do this, the chapter stresses the ways that have been invoked to represent the interests of absent future generations by reducing the potential for renewal of hostilities by current or future societies. The chapter examines the ways in which environmental, economic, and educational provisions are constructed in order to determine how laws having a direct bearing on youth and future generations include these constituencies as rights holders, victims and beneficiaries of justice and peace.*

1. Introduction

Armed conflicts, be they relatively short or generational, have lasting – and typically destructive – impacts across all aspects of law and society. This includes impacts upon those who are absent in the discussions for peace, and peace time society, either because they were killed or disappeared as a result of the conflict or because they are members of future generations. Similar truths exist for institutionalised State violence against citizens, itself arguably a source of conflict and certainly a source of instability. Within the context of conflict-based impacts, perhaps the most potentially destructive are those to current youths and future generations who will suffer the immediate and long-term ramifications of violence, distrust, and community rupture, as well as environmental degradation and economic disruption. At the same time, the lack of acknowledgement and inclusion of those past absents who were harmed by the conflict at issue threatens to undermine the effort to move forward with peace by leaving open issues of law, justice and responsibility for these harms. Set against these impacts, the ways in which State and non-State actors involved in conflicts and institutionalised

* Dr. Alexandra R. Harrington is a Lecturer in Law at Lancaster University and Chair of the IUCN World Commission on Environmental Law's Agreement on Plastic Pollution Task Force.

violence response structure peace agreements, durable ceasefire agreements and institutions such as truth and reconciliation commissions and tribunals serve vital, and often under-appreciated, roles in ensuring the place of future generations in the immediate post-conflict setting and the long-term.

Indeed, each of these agreements – and the implementation mechanisms they create or operationalise – attempt to offer methods of addressing past traumas in ways that directly impact future generations from the perspective of national unity, identity, and societal understanding of the victims and the perpetrators of institutionalised violence and repression. At the same time, these agreements and mechanisms directly seek to allow individual, familial and community awareness of wrongs, reparations and reconciliation such that future generations will come into existence in their context and within the shadows of their abilities to promote or hinder healing. Even in instances where the mechanism is created to have a relatively short life-span or where the time period of the conflict is short, the durable legacies of trauma and suffering will last for generations. The same is true of the successes and failings of those entities seeking to bring transparency and justice to post-conflict law and life. Understood in this context, the article emphasises that harms committed against past generations and absents extend beyond this group of people and their immediate descendants into the present but instead are harms that translate to future absents as well. This is the result of the deep-seated and fundamental role that conflicts, violence, and absence play on the ability to achieve a holistic and entrenched peace that extends beyond the text of an agreement, or the time taken to draft it.

These are only some of the general ways in which peace treaties and reconciliation institutions incorporate future generations as impacted parties, rights holders, victims, and holders of expectations in post-conflict societies. In conjunction with this, many such agreements and entities expressly include future generations in their motivations as well as provisions such as education and the development of a robust, rule of law-based justice system. This chapter examines peace agreements and the statutes, rules and findings of truth and reconciliation commissions from the lens of intergenerational justice[1] and inclusion of future generations. The critical lens used for the chapter's analysis of peace agreements is that of the principle of

1 See Lukas Meyer, 'Intergenerational Justice' (2021) Stanford Encyclopedia of Philosophy <https://perma.cc/A6UC-GAS2>.

prevention in the sense of agreements that are not only created to cause the cessation of hostilities in each State but rather to prevent these hostilities from occurring again in the future. To do this, the chapter stresses the ways that have been invoked to represent the interests of absent future generations by reducing the potential for renewal of hostilities by current or future societies. The chapter begins with an examination of explicit references to children, young adults, and future generations throughout these instruments.[2] For the purposes of this discussion, the idea of future generations applies to those not yet born but whose existence is foreseeable in the short and long-term, including those born in the next year as well as the next decade and beyond. Following this, the chapter examines the ways in which environmental, economic, and educational provisions are constructed in order to determine how legal and policy areas having a direct bearing on youth and future generations are addressed to include these constituencies and rights holders, victims and beneficiaries of justice and peace.

Following these examinations, the chapter analyses areas of commonality and difference existing across the various instruments, jurisdictions, and types of conflict in order to establish trends for how children, youth, and future generations are included in fashioning a vision and order for peace. Not only is this an important research question, it is also a project with ramifications for how instruments and institutions of peace are created and conceived of moving forward.

2. *Peace Agreements, Intergenerational Equity and Intergenerational Justice*

There are numerous peace agreements to be reviewed and analysed, covering a broad range of times and timespans, geography, and underlying issues. Indeed, the agreements analysed include those relating to multi-generational conflicts, such as the more than five-decade long civil war in Colombia, to conflicts lasting a few months and those in between. This broad perspective is critical in assessing the commonalities and differences

2 For a discussion of the definition of 'child' as those from birth to age 18 as well as the differences between children and adolescents, notably in the context of participation in decision-making and civil life, see: Convention on the Rights of the Child (1989).

in how conflicts address intergenerational equity[3] and intergenerational justice[4] because it provides insights into the short and long-term impacts of conflict of future generations regardless the duration of the underlying conflict itself.

A core methodological element in this section and the following section is the decision to include agreements which ultimately did not lead to success in terms of their short and long-term implementation as well as those which have thus far resulted in significant progress toward peace. The rationale for this is that it is as important to analyse and learn from those instances in which efforts for peace have failed as those which have resulted in success, and that in each example there are vital lessons for how the voices of future generations are incorporated. Indeed, the chapter is founded on a belief that the lessons of failures can tell us as much as the lessons of successes in terms of preventing conflict, implementing justice, and incorporating the victims of conflict as more than passive recipients of assistance.

2.1. Explicit References to Children, Young Adults and Future Generations

Since it relates to a conflict that spanned over five decades, and thus was intergenerational as well as multigenerational, it is perhaps only appropriate that the Colombian Peace Agreement with the Revolutionary Armed Forces of Colombia/*Fuerzas Armadas Revolucionarias de Colombia* (FARC) includes explicit references to children, young adults and future generations. After all, many within the country have experienced the conflict both as children and as adults, parents, and grandparents. Such persons have a profound understanding of the entrenched nature of the conflict, as well as the devastation it has brought and can continue to bring across the generations.

In the preamble, the Colombian Peace Agreement expressly includes future generations as intended rights holders and beneficiaries under its terms, stating:

---

3 For a thorough discussion of the concept of intergenerational equity and the legal obligation to leave the Earth in the same condition as it was inherited, see Edith Brown Weiss, 'In Fairness to Future Generations and Sustainable Development' (1992) 8(1) American University International Law Review 19.

4 For perspectives on intergenerational justice as a moral imperative between two or more generations, see Meyer (n 1).

> [e]xtolling and enshrining the justice that is to come inasmuch as it acknowledges essential fundamental rights for new and future generations, such as the right to protected land, the right to the conservation of the human species, the right to be aware of one's origins and identity, the right to know the truth with regard to events occurring before one's birth, the right to exemption from liability for acts committed by earlier generations, the right to the preservation of freedom of choice, and other rights, notwithstanding the rights of victims of any age or generation to truth, justice and reparations.[5]

Although a preambular statement, this text provides significant insights into the ways in which children, youth, and multiple generations have suffered harm during the conflict, as well as the involved parties' shared understanding as to the means through which to address these issues. Thus, issues such as alienation from land – and concomitant recognition of land rights necessary to address this – play important roles beyond the preamble and throughout the Colombian Peace Agreement.[6]

Relatedly, the idea of recognising culpability for actions and activities under the terms of the Colombian Peace Agreement is tempered by the understanding that revelation of, and responsibility for, human rights and other legal abuses should be limited to impacting the individuals and generations directly involved.[7] This allows for a break of culpability such that current and future descendants are not subjected to stigmatisation, legal liability, or violence because of the actions and choices of their families and previous generations.[8] In theory, at least, this should be a method of ensuring the just application of the terms of the Colombian Peace Agreement without creating a reinforcing system of responsibility and retribution for generations to come.

The impacts of a generational conflict on the core aspects of personal life and identity, as well as the potential for their protection to cause conflicts with the rights of others to forget their past suffering, can be seen in these preambular statements as well.[9] These statements make it clear that youth and future generations have what might be called 'identity rights' and 'history

5 Final Agreement to End the Armed Conflict and Build a Stable and Lasting Peace (2016) (hereinafter 'Colombia Agreement').
6 ibid.
7 ibid.
8 ibid.
9 ibid.

rights' grounded in knowledge of their family backgrounds and circumstances of their families during the conflict as well as the right to know the truths of the conflict throughout its duration. The suggestion of 'identity rights' can be defined as the right to know one's identity, including family history, in both the positive and negative elements. For example, this would include: the ability of a child born of wartime rape to know the circumstances of his identity in terms of the facts of his conception; to know his identity as the child of a soldier, guerrilla or paramilitary member; and to know of his mother and her community. The suggestion of 'history rights' is quite similar, however this chapter argues that it is broader in terms of current and future generations having the right to know about the conflicts in their communities and country. This is, from the viewpoint of youth and future generations, essential for ensuring that the option of knowledge is available regardless of whether an individual makes the conscious decision to use or request it. Indeed, at the most granular level, there is an argument for identity and history rights as the core of effectively building peace because they provide a tool for knowledge and healing. In this context, it must be noted that law can favour healing in terms of fostering a system of rights and obligations to assist those damaged by conflict, provide solutions to bridge the divides caused by conflict, and ensure that there are equitable ways to address future claims through courts and regulatory systems that enfranchise society broadly. However, if these laws do not reflect the will of the people in any national setting, they face the real prospect of failing to advance healing because they cannot be enforced. In this context, and without careful and inclusive drafting, law can become a tool to undermine peace as much as it can be used to advance it.

At the same time, the construction of these rights is highly sensitive in that they are connected to trauma and acts of violence that are often easiest to leave buried in terms of victims and victimised communities. Certainly, the rights of the immediate victims, for example victims of rape or familial disappearance, to keep these facts and experiences hidden and not be forcibly retraumatised through their disclosure to new generations must be respected. Thus, an area of contestation can be observed between the rights and knowledge of the direct victims, families, and communities and those of current and future generations, with the inference being that current and future generations should be the primary beneficiaries of efforts to balance interests. There is, however, a real question regarding the potential for tensions between the interests of current generations and the interests of future generations, especially in terms of reconciliation mechanisms. This remains an open question, however it should be remembered that the ability of future generations to benefit from this or any peace agreement is necessarily predicated on the ability of current generations to honour and implement the agreement.

One of the most fundamental elements of the Colombian Peace Agreement in relation to children is the provision of protection and reincorporation for minors who were part of the FARC-EP at the time of signing and subsequently demobilised.[10] The Colombian Peace Agreement provides that these minors are to be afforded:

> [...]special care and protection measures... to ensure restitution of their rights with an equity-based approach, prioritizing their access to healthcare and education. These minors will be accorded all the rights, benefits and allowances established for the victims of the conflict as well as those deriving from their process of reincorporation in the terms contemplated in this Final Agreement and priority will be given to family reunification wherever possible, and to final placement in homes in their original communities or others of a similar nature, whilst at all times taking into account the best interests of the child. Follow-up of these programs shall be conducted by the National Reincorporation Council to coordinate with the competent state bodies, with the support of social or specialist organisations charged with carrying out oversight in the terms of Joint Communiqué No. 70... The programme must guarantee the full reincorporation of the minor and his or her psycho-social accompaniment, with the oversight of social or specialist organisations in the terms set out in Joint Communiqué No. 70, as well as the location of minors at temporary reception sites in municipalities near the TLZNs, guaranteeing the right to information for all participants, particularly children and adolescents.[11]

Thus, the Colombian Peace Agreement provides current generations of youth with access to core services necessary for their survival, future livelihoods, and ability to participate fully and meaningfully in their communities throughout their adult lives. It also recognises the rights and experiences of minors who have been drawn into the conflict and subsequently demo-

10 See Colombia Agreement (n 5) section 3.2.2.5.

11 ibid. Similar, though less comprehensive, terms are contained in the peace agreement for the Republic of Congo, 'The rehabilitation and reintegration into schools and universities of pupils and students, members of armed factions who are now signatories, having renounced violence, laid down their arms, and rejoined their place of education.' Agreement on Ending Hostilities in the Republic of Congo (1999) (i).

bilised as being linked with many of the same protections as those who are expressly classified as being direct victims of the conflict. In this way, the Colombian Peace Agreement recognises that there are child-combatants who will have a different legal and reincorporation situation than those who are victims *per se*, yet at the same time highlights that these children are, in themselves, victims of the conflict in a different way and still require specialised legal protections.

These provisions reflect efforts to balance the needs of child-combatants to be reunited with their families and to return to their communities on one hand, and the reality that such reunification and return might not be tenable for the families and communities involved given the activities of child-combatants during the conflict on the other. Through these balancing efforts, the Colombian Peace Agreement can be seen as furthering the rights of child-combatants and their descendants to participate in all aspects of public life and to return to the places with which they have a direct connection. At the same time, however, the Colombian Peace Agreement can be seen as ensuring that child-combatants are not reintroduced to communities in a way that would reignite former hostilities in the future. In this way, it seeks to protect future generations from the continued threat to new hostilities.

Throughout the Colombian Peace Agreement, there is a realisation of the multifaceted impacts children and young adults have suffered due to the prolonged and entrenched conflict.[12] As a result, children and young adults are included as vital constituencies for protection and inclusion, based on an understanding of their current vulnerabilities in conjunction with their status as paving the way for the next generations of Colombians.[13] As a reflection of this, while the Colombian Peace Agreement provides for a significant amnesty allowance, child abduction, the recruitment of minors, and the forced disappearance of minors were bars for those seeking to avail themselves of this opportunity.[14] Although these provisions cannot, of course, spare the minor victims of these activities or their families from the wrongs they have already suffered, such terms can be seen as validating the specialised nature of intergenerational harms caused by the taking of children and, where applicable, their forced participation in hostilities. This stresses the justice components of intergenerational concerns at the level

12 See Colombia Agreement (n 5).
13 ibid.
14 ibid., appx 1, Law on Amnesty, Pardon and Special Criminal Treatment.

of the individuals and families directly impacted, as well as at the level of future generations which have been deprived of members due to acts of those engaged in the conflict.

Further, in articulating the rights of victims of conflict and the role of the Special Jurisdiction for Peace, the Colombian Peace Agreement requires the use of 'an equity-based and gender-based approach... and in particular to the needs of women and children.'[15] In conjunction with this, the oversight mechanisms for the Colombian Peace Agreement and the institution for peace created under it were tasked with assessing and recognising the:

> [...] human and social impact of the conflict on society, including its impact on economic, social, cultural and environmental rights, and the different ways in which the conflict affected women, children, adolescents, youths and the elderly, persons on the basis of their religion, opinions or beliefs, persons with disabilities, indigenous peoples, rural communities, the Afro-Colombian, black, palenquero and raizal communities, the Roma community, the LGBTI community, displaced and exiled persons, human rights advocates, trade unionists, journalists, farmers, ranchers, traders and businessmen and -women, *inter alia*.[16]

Critical to the Colombian Peace Agreement is an emphasis on inclusion and extension of healthcare, education, housing, and general social policies that aim to address the idea of a poverty eradication throughout rural and urban areas.[17] Included in this is a specific recognition that healthcare must be geared toward serving women and children, particularly women before, during, and after pregnancy and young children in rural areas.[18] This can be seen as the result of increased scientific evidence regarding the durable effects of the entrenched conflict in Colombia on women and children.[19] Specific efforts to prevent the use of illicit substances by children, among many groups in society, are also essential elements for the protection of health and the reduction of the number of children becoming part of the criminal justice system.[20] Education is emphasised as essential to addressing the results of the multi-generational conflict throughout the Colombian

15 ibid., 5.1.
16 ibid., section 5.1.1.1.2.
17 ibid., section 1.3.2.
18 ibid., section 1.3.2.1.
19 ibid.
20 ibid., section 4.2.

Peace Agreement, and serves as a tool to ensure greater opportunity for children, young adults and future generations.[21] In the context of rural access to education, the Colombian Peace Agreement notes:

> [...] with the aim of providing a comprehensive service for early childhood, guaranteeing the coverage, quality and relevance of education, eradicating illiteracy in rural areas, helping the younger generation to remain part of the production sector in the countryside, and promoting involvement in rural development on the part of regional academic institutions, the National Government is to set up and implement the Special Rural Education Plan.[22]

Also in the rural context, the Agreement stresses the need to ensure labour protections and policies that simultaneously protect children from the negative consequences of child labour and adopt ILO standards on the protection of children legally in the workforce.[23]

Through these measures, there is an understanding that issues stemming from and underlying the conflict in Colombia were related in large part to pre-existing and emerging inequities and inequalities, and that a durable peace must be framed in ways which address these issues. The Colombian Peace Agreement's terms in this regard can be seen as furthering the idea that intergenerational equity and justice is not uniform and that future generations will have to address or find ways to overcome the inequities stemming from the conflict.

The contrast between multigenerational conflicts, such as in Colombia, and durable yet shorter-term conflicts can be quite striking. However, in many ways the instruments which ended these conflicts share many similarities. An example of this comes from the Arusha Accords of 2000, which sought to end the conflict in Burundi that extended for over a decade.[24] The conflict in Burundi was based largely on ethnicity- and identity-oriented persecution and violence connected to political strife and electoral disputes.[25]

Within the Arusha Accords, the newly established Charter of Freedoms for Burundi includes economic and social rights for children, protections

21 ibid., section 1.3.2.2.
22 ibid., 1.3.2.2.
23 ibid., 1.3.3.5.
24 See Arusha Peace and Reconciliation Agreement for Burundi (2000).
25 ibid.

against being used in conflict or as targets of conflict, and rights against detention in all but the most extreme circumstances.[26] Thus, even as it recognises efforts to entrench peace as part of the national practice, the Arusha Accords are aware that the potential for conflict continued to exist and that the need to protect children and future generations was vital to crafting systems which promote peace.

In the context of facilitated return for those who fled during the conflict, the Arusha Accords are clear that these returns must be made volitionally and with the dignity and potential vulnerability of women and children born in mind.[27] As in the context of Colombia, this reflects documented information regarding the impacts of conflict on these populations in Burundi, including the impacts of fleeing the conflict.[28] This is of particular note because the children returning to their mothers' communities include those who may be the product of wartime sexual violence and have suffered stigmatisation and abuse from these communities as a result. Those who returned were guaranteed rights, including educational access as well as housing, food and economic assistance while resettling in communities.[29]

Regardless of where they were located within the State, the Accords require that children be provided with primary and secondary school education access until age of 16 at the very earliest.[30] Additionally, the Accords require that '[t]he Government shall ensure, through special assistance, the protection, rehabilitation and advancement of vulnerable groups, namely child heads of families, orphans, street children, unaccompanied minors, traumatised children, widows, women heads of families, juvenile delinquents, the physically and mentally disabled, etc.'[31]

Further, the fundamental rights articulated in the Accords included that '[t]he State shall ensure the good management and utilisation of the nation's natural resources on a sustainable basis, conserving such resources for fu-

26 ibid., art 1.
27 ibid., art 2.
28 Shana Tabak, 'False Dichotomies of Transitional Justice: Gender, Conflicts and Combatants in Colombia' (2011) 44 NYU Journal of International Law and Policy 103; Paris A Cabello-Tijerina and Karen Quinones, 'The Relevance of the Territorial and Female Perspective in the Peace-Building in Colombia' (2018) 80 Revista de Ciencias Sociales.
29 Arusha Accords (n 24) art 4.
30 ibid., art 15.
31 ibid., art 10.

ture generations.'[32] In this way, it can be observed that the Arusha Accords are prospective as well as prescriptive in that they seek to ensure the preservation of resources which can be used for the stability and advancement of future generations in a way that advances intergenerational equity.

Additionally, in the Central African Republic's 2019 peace agreement, the principles for settlement of the conflict expressly include the involvement and incorporation of youth and women as well as their direct protection from violence and abuse.[33] The 2012 Kenyan peace agreement expressly incorporates the need to address unemployment of youth and adolescents as a necessary issue to address in order to create a stable environment for peace.[34]

These are a few of the many examples in which peace agreements expressly acknowledge the impacts of conflict and violence on children as vulnerable populations and as the embodiment of future generations. Often these methods of inclusion are part of the larger discussion of societal harm and also the need to generate thorough and meaningful reparations going forward. Additionally, many peace agreements make explicit reference to the use of education as a tool to address the root causes of conflict as well as to ensure that future generations will not be educated in theories of hatred.[35]

2.1.1. Implicit References to Children, Young Adults and Future Generations

In the preamble to the Arusha Accords for Burundi, discussed above, the Parties expressly state that the policies include:

> Reaffirming our unwavering determination to put an end to the root causes underlying the recurrent state of violence, bloodshed, insecurity, political instability, genocide and exclusion which is inflicting severe hardships and suffering on the people of Burundi, and seriously hampers the prospects for economic development and the attainment of equality and social justice in our country,

32 ibid., art 2.
33 Political Agreement for Peace and Reconciliation in the Central African Republic (2019) art 1.
34 National Accord and Reconciliation Act (2008) art II (D).
35 ibid.; Arusha Accords (n 24); Colombia Agreement (n 5).

> Reaffirming our commitment to shape a political order and a system of government inspired by the realities of our country and founded on the values of justice, democracy, good governance, pluralism, respect for the fundamental rights and freedoms of the individual, unity, solidarity, mutual understanding, tolerance and cooperation among the different ethnic groups within our society.[36]

Facially, these terms are very much oriented in the present and seek to address past wrongs which gave rise to the larger tensions underlying the conflict. And, indeed, there is a significant onus placed on present generations of adults, particularly policy-makers, to remedy the conditions which facilitated the conflict. However, reading these provisions carefully, it is clear that the intent of the Arusha Accords is not simply to stop the hostilities between warring sides and ensure peace in the present.[37] Rather, the intent is to ensure that a stable system is created for the present and the future to build upon in peace rather than to allow for cracks which could give rise to renewed hostilities.[38] These are to be considered efforts at achieving intergenerational equity and justice in the most fundamental sense of providing the next generation with a nation that is not based on conflict and has had the chance to heal before passing the nation on to the next generation.

Similarly, the peace agreement used in the Central African Republic stressed the need for reconciliation and healing to occur in order to address past and current violations and to ensure that these issues did not continue on into the future.[39] These elements work in conjunction with the more explicit terms of the preamble providing:

> *Recognizing* that the majority of the population of the Central African Republic is made up of children and women who have been deeply affected by the armed conflict, and that the full protection of their rights and the cessation of abuses and hostilities are objectives common to all Parties; and, convinced of the fundamental role of women of the Central African Republic in the prevention and resolution of conflicts and in building sustainable peace, and emphasizing their important con-

36 Arusha Agreement (n 24) preamble.
37 ibid.
38 ibid.
39 Political Agreement for Peace and Reconciliation in the Central African Republic (2019).

tribution to the efforts to find a definitive solution to end the crisis in the Central African Republic.[40]

Thus, there is an observed impact of the conflict on those who were most vulnerable to its predations at the same time that they represent those who offer the way for the future of society in the Central African Republic, particularly child and youth members of society. This is in recognition that children and youth might not have been the current generation of decision makers for the purposes of starting the conflict or bringing about the efforts for peace, but that they are the bearers of the scars of the same conflict and will bring them into their lives as future generations of decision makers and parents. Due to this relationship, the preambular text serves as a critical guide to understanding and implementing the terms of the peace agreement. This sentiment reflects the reality that those in past generations who are absent from the negotiation and implementation of the peace agreement who created and perpetuated the conflict should be held accountable in name if not in punishment and that the future generations of citizens, though absent in the present, are still included in the efforts to entrench peace.

In the Cote d'Ivoire, two civil wars occurred between 2002 and the end of 2011, although there are still ongoing tensions surrounding elections and related events.[41] These civil wars stemmed from a population that was – and continues to be – deeply divided over politics and political figures, and saw a number of major mass death events as well as deaths and acts of torture committed on all sides on a smaller yet continued scale. While there were periods of relative calm between the larger-scale events, this was still a conflict which raged for nearly a decade and continues to impact on societal stability.

The peace agreement for the Cote d'Ivoire contains a particularly important and pressing recognition of the impacts of an infrastructurally brutal conflict in terms of the issuance or reissuance of birth certificates and identity papers, as well as other forms of identification associated with them.[42] The importance of birth certificates and identity papers generally is an accepted premise of international human rights law as a right of the

40 ibid., preamble.

41 See Alexander Shipilov, 'Ten Years after the Ivorian Civil War (2002–2011): Reassessment of the Conflict' (2022) 29(1) South African Journal of International Affairs 45.

42 Abidjan Peace Agreement (2002) sect I.

child to be registered and to have a legal identity, and as a right of the parent to ensure that the child has a legal identity and ability to enjoy the rights to which the child is entitled.[43] Thus, by specifically including this provision in the terms of the peace agreement, the parties to the conflict in the Cote d'Ivoire enabled current and future generations of children to have rights regarding establishing their identity and, subsequently, the identities and rights of future generations. This is at the very core of intergenerational equity and justice concerns, which seek to ensure that there is parity between the generations and that the actions of one generation do not harm or prejudice the rights of future generations.

In El Salvador, conflict began in the 1970s and continued until 1992, and was largely centered on political differences between the dictatorial regime existing under a military coup led government and those opposing it.[44] These differences then translated into a long-term campaign of violence and intimidation between governmental authorities and the Farabundo Marti National Liberation Front during which governmental regime mechanisms were implicated in the atrocities committed as were governmentally affiliated groups and those working against the government.[45]

Reflecting the long-term role of the Salvadoran military as a main actor in the conflict and human rights violations stemming from it, the conclusion of the conflict sought to ensure that this would not happen again. Thus, the peace agreement for El Salvador contains significant requirements for changes to military policy and practice, including the immediate cessation of forcible recruitment for military service, which directly protects Salvadoran youth and adolescents.[46] This is certainly a present-focused activity that impacts on the children and youth who lived under constant threat of being drawn into armed hostilities although they were not members of the current generation of adults making these decisions. At the same time, it is impactful for intergenerational equity and justice because it ensures that future generations of adults and decision-makers will have the ability to participate in society as non-combatants and will not have suffered the same traumas as child soldiers face on a daily basis, both during and after the conflict.

---

43 See Convention on the Rights of the Child (n 2); International Covenant on Civil and Political Rights (1966).

44 Joaquin M Chavez, 'How Did the Civil War in El Salvador End?' (2015) 120(5) The American Historical Review 1784.

45 ibid.

46 Chapultepec Peace Accords (1992) art 11.

Through these examples, it becomes apparent that peace agreements, while outwardly seeking to end a current conflict, are inherently tools that incorporate and promote future generations because the termination of a conflict is done in contemplation of ending immediate harms and future harms. From this perspective, efforts at ending conflict – unless temporary in nature, such as a short-duration ceasefire – should be understood as intergenerational at their core because the cessation of conflict and the ways in which this is achieved through law and practice, have a durable impact on societies, their legacies, and histories. Indeed, the underlying motivation for seeking peace in most agreements is not only to end the damage suffered by current generations but also to protect future generations as well, thus bringing concepts of intergenerational equity, from the legal perspective, and intergenerational justice from the moral perspective, into the frame as a consistent element of concern. This can be seen in the texts of many peace agreements which reference aspirations for peace as including the cessation of contemporary conflicts in a way that addresses the causes of these conflicts so as to ensure they are not replicated in the future.[47]

3. *Truth and Reconciliation Mechanisms, Intergenerational Equity and Intergenerational Justice*

As previously noted, this section and the above section address truth and reconciliation mechanisms that are considered successful – for example through the adoption of their terms into laws and regulations – as well as those considered unsuccessful. Peace agreements are, as a matter of common practice, legally cognisable documents in which the parties commit to peace and to remedying the causes, drivers, and effects of conflict in a given setting. Truth and reconciliation mechanisms, however, occupy a distinct status between legally binding decisions – most commonly in the context of grants of amnesty within the reconciliation context – and findings and recommendations which function as guides for current and future legal activities.

In this section, it must be noted that the entities analysed as of the time of drafting have been truth and reconciliation commissions, however the

47 See, eg Arusha Accords (n 24); Political Agreement for Peace and Reconciliation in the Central African Republic (n 33).

full analysis of amnesty grants, public trials, and statements and evidence provided for reconciliation purposes has not yet been completed.

3.1. References to Children and Young Adults

Throughout the varying contours and legal parameters defining the findings of most truth and reconciliation mechanisms there is an explicit acknowledgment and discussion of violence and harm directed at children and young adults.

Examples of this include Chile, where it is noted that children were the victims of institutionalised violence, and that, overall, certain regions were home to violence and acts of disappearance against those aged 20 and below.[48] This must be framed against the decades of internal strife and by the dictatorial regime led by General Agusto Pinochet, which is well known for carrying out a brutal reign of repression regarding dissenting or potentially dissenting viewpoints and those espousing them.[49] As part of the effort at national healing and unity-building following the end of the Pinochet regime and the reintroduction of democratic government to Chile, the nation undertook a truth and reconciliation system which resulted in the generation of significant and wide-ranging findings relating to actions taken and their impacts.[50]

The Report of the Chilean National Commission on Truth and Reconciliation[51] notes instances in which parents were arrested or otherwise disappeared, in some cases their homes destroyed as well, and their children left to the mercy of neighbours, family members or religious orders for survival.[52] In other instances, pregnant women were arrested or otherwise disappeared and no record of their fate or the fate of their unborn children has been found.[53] Further, the Chilean Report stresses the number of instances in which children and young adults were witnesses to violence against parents, siblings, and extended family members, including the ex-

48 Report of the Chilean National Commission on Truth and Reconciliation (1990) (hereinafter 'Chilean Report') 178, 422–423, 873.
49 ibid.
50 ibid.
51 ibid.
52 ibid., 193, 395, 811.
53 ibid., 703, 743, 753, 811, 777, 785–786.

trajudicial killings of their family members.[54] In addition to being victims of targeted violence or targeted violence against family members, the Chile Report highlights the ways in which children and their families were collateral victims of violence, notably through indiscriminate or undisciplined discharge of firearms in the course of operations in a neighbourhood or nearby home.[55]

In some instances, it was found that children were arrested as a form of leverage against their parents or family members.[56] At the same time, the findings of many institutions demonstrate that children and young adults were also victims, intentionally or collaterally, of the groups which were fighting against governmental forces, even when these groups were ostensibly seeking to promote human rights and end abuses.[57] Through the use of these findings of fact, the Chilean Report sheds light on the ways in which individuals and society as a whole suffered harms which had a particularly deep and durable impact on the children and youth involved, whether they survived to adulthood or perished as minors.

In the vast majority of reports surveyed, education has been identified as a significant entity in ensuring that similar events do not recur and in the peace process, while at the same it has been seen as a major area where assistance to the family members of those killed, assaulted and disappeared is needed.[58] As stated in the Chilean Report:

> Our country needs the contribution of all its youth and particularly these young people who have been excluded from formal education by the facts and circumstances presented in the earlier chapters of this report. There is no need for a lengthy diagnosis. It is obvious that we need a vast creative and perhaps unprecedented effort in our country to find ways to make reparation in the realm of education before it is too late and the situation is irremediable. At the same time, the tasks of making reparation in the realm of education must be coordinated with the efforts to prevent human rights abuses and forge a culture respectful of human rights that we propose below.[59]

54 ibid., 255, 425, 663.
55 ibid., 197, 198, 728, 934.
56 ibid., 502, 742, 876.
57 ibid., 884, 914, 934, 958.
58 ibid., 1069.
59 ibid., 1069–1070.

While all acts of violence are inherently personal and individual in nature, as previously discussed, these acts also have broader familial and societal impacts. This has been repeatedly cited in the findings regarding decisions of governmental actors and insurgency groups across many States to target and victimise entire groups and communities, including children and young adults. In these contexts, children and young adults, especially young girls, have been victims of sexual violence, and frequently death or serious physical harm.[60] By recognising these harms and the need to address them through dedicated and tailored reparations, the Chilean Report legitimises and validates the harms suffered by minors. This is important in itself and takes on special significance in the context of ensuring that these minors are provided assistance as adults so that they can be active and engaged members of the current generation who raise and train children and youth of today and tomorrow.[61]

It is, perhaps, unnecessary to highlight the many ways in which successive generations of South Africans were impacted by the brutality of the apartheid regime which governed the nation for decades. Indeed, with the end of apartheid in 1994, the nation struggled to understand and heal the wounds of the system and these wounds are still endemic in the laws, rules and societal systems in the country today. Throughout the South African Truth and Reconciliation Commission Report, there are numerous references to violence against children and young adults by governmental forces and by civilian organisations operating at various points in the history of certain areas of the State.[62] This includes the massacres of children and young adults, as well as women who would typically lead families and elders who would serve as the connection between the past, present and future.[63] In so doing, the Report can be seen as a tool for acknowledgment and healing for current and future generations as well as for the ability of future generations to ensure that the spirit and rubrics of justice created in the post-apartheid process are maintained and advanced.

60 Chavez (n 44)
61 This was stressed in the Chilean Report's recognition and incorporation of 'the need to build the future' for those who suffered under the regime so that they can move on as part of society and family life. Chilean Report (n 48) 1020.
62 Report of the South African Truth and Reconciliation Commission (1998).
63 ibid.

3.2. Implicit References to Children, Young Adults and Future Generations

Poignantly, in many instances and across various States, the burden of keeping the memory of disappeared youth alive for current and future generations, and searching for them or their remains, has been undertaken by the grandparents, parents, and family members left behind. Highly visible examples of this include the Chilean Relatives of Persons Disappeared after Arrest,[64] and the Argentinian Las Abuelas del Plaza de Mayo.[65] In each example, the efforts of these groups emphasised the loss of the family members who suffered from the disappearance of adult loved ones as well as their inability to connect with the children and unborn relatives who were rendered absent because of their connection to disappeared family members. Thus, the losses here represented two types of absents – those who were integral to families and were removed without further explanation and those who were so young that they represented the future of a family, taking with them the future as well as the past and the present.

Indeed, in *Nunca Mas*, the Argentinian truth and reconciliation report, there are findings and discussions regarding the children and unborn children of those arrested, disappeared or killed, who were then taken by the regime and adopted by families loyal to it.[66] These findings expressly classify the taking of children as an act of terror committed by the State during the time period under review.[67] In many instances, these children were unaware of their real identities and the fate of their birth parents, and grandparents or other family members who sought them were unsuccessful for many years.[68] When these efforts proved successful, they brought with them justice for victims and their families as well as severe emotional and mental trauma for these now-adult children, who found the lives they lead to be based on falsehoods.[69] In other instances, however, children were constantly made aware of their family identities by their adoptive families, who saw their role as re-educating these children so that they would not adopt the political and social beliefs of their birth parents.[70]

---

64 See Chilean Report (n 48) 824.

65 CONADEP, *Nunca Mas: Report of the National Commission on the Disappearance of Peoples in Argentina* (1986) 150.

66 ibid., 148ff.

67 ibid., 32.

68 ibid.

69 ibid.

70 ibid.

Again, these experiences were found to have resulted in sustained emotional, mental – and often physical – trauma that carried into adulthood. All these situations, and the damage they have caused, can be seen as explicit references to children and adults, as well as implicit references regarding future generations, who will be indelibly impacted by the experiences of having family members in such situations or simply in a post-conflict society where these issues are still pervasive.[71]

At the same time, there is an intergenerational equity impact in the sense that there have been and continue to be generations who do not know their true identity and heritage, or that of their parents and purported families, and who carry that burden throughout life, transmitting it to the next generation in the process. The requirement in *Nunca Mas* that the Argentinian government assist with the reunification of families impacted by these practices is a significant step toward beginning the healing process and bridging the intergenerational chasm of identity, yet implementing it will not fully overcome the lasting damage caused or allow children to meet family members who are no longer living.[72] Thus, these references serve as a bridge between the absence of adults, arguably the absents of the past and present, and the absence of children and the unborn, arguably absents of the present and future. Each type of absent group carries with it a connection to current society and has a distinct place in the ability of a nation to heal, although part of the healing process must reflect the understanding of differences in loss and suffering due to these two forms of absents.

3.3. Implicit References to Intergenerational Equity and Intergenerational Justice

In the Charter establishing the Chilean Commission on Truth and Reconciliation, an essential element is the idea that '[t]hat only upon a foundation of truth will it be possible to meet the basic demands of justice and create the necessary conditions for achieving true national reconciliation.'[73] At the same time, the Charter emphasises that 'only the knowledge of the truth will restore the dignity of the victims in the public mind, allow their

71 ibid.
72 ibid., 23.
73 Chile, Supreme Decree No. 355 (25 April 1990).

relatives and mourners to honour them fittingly, and in some measure make it possible to make amends for the damage done.'[74] This is necessarily focused on the past, although at the same time the Chilean Report makes it clear that such a focus is necessary to facilitate the reparations that will allow Chilean society to move into the future with less conflict.[75] In this way, there is an implicit understanding that acknowledging the suffering of the past, particularly those who were disappeared, is an essential element for providing a more just and less contentious future for those generations yet to be born.

In the Chilean Report, there is an extensive discussion of the ways in which institutionalised violence and disappearances disrupted the lives of children themselves as well as the health, economic status and emotional status of their immediate family members.[76] The results are cited as manifesting in many ways, including inherent insecurity and fear, physical and psychological health issues, lack of access to or interest in education, and stigmatisation from multiple sectors.[77] Additionally, survivors' statements have demonstrated fears that the hatred and apathy which resulted from acts of violence against family members could become an intergenerational issue, destabilising individuals, communities and the prospects for a durable peace.[78] At the same time, the Report notes that the ability of victims and those they left behind to have children has been impacted as a result of the harms they suffered.[79] Further, the Chile Report demonstrates the various and multifaceted impacts of violence and disappearances on families, noting that in some instances these events caused the family to become quite close but in other instances it resulted in the breakdown of families and the ways in which they functioned.[80] This, as the Chilean Report notes, in turn, can be seen as creating an intergenerational impact that continues through to the present and can extend out to the future.

The creation of the South African Truth and Reconciliation Commission was premised upon a statute which sought to bring to light, address, and craft methods of reconciliation and reparation for the many forms of viol-

74 ibid.
75 See ibid.
76 See Chilean Report (n 48) 1005–1006.
77 ibid.
78 ibid., 1008.
79 ibid., 1007.
80 ibid., 1010.

ence and suffering experienced under the apartheid regime.[81] At the same time, it specifically included the actions of civilian groups and associated criminal organisations within its parameters in an effort to generate a robust reckoning for South African society.[82] As the preambular provisions state, 'it is deemed necessary to establish the truth in relation to past events as well as the motives for and circumstances in which gross violations of human rights have occurred, and to make the findings known in order to prevent a repetition of such acts in future.'[83] A primary objective for the South African Commission was:

> [...] to promote national unity and reconciliation in a spirit of understanding which transcends the conflicts and divisions of the past by-
> (a) establishing as complete a picture as possible of the causes, nature and extent of the gross violations of human rights which were committed during the period from 1 March 1960 to the cut-off date, including the antecedents, circumstances, factors and context of such violations, as well as the perspectives of the victims and the motives and perspectives of the persons responsible for the commission of the violations, by conducting investigations and holding hearings;
> (b) facilitating the granting of amnesty to persons who make full disclosure of all the relevant facts relating to acts associated with a political objective and comply with the requirements of this Act;
> (c) establishing and making known the fate or whereabouts of victims and by restoring the human and civil dignity of such victims by granting them an opportunity to relate their own accounts of the violations of which they are the victims, and by recommending reparation measures in respect of them [...].[84]

Additionally, the South African Truth and Reconciliation Commission Report highlights the pattern of denying non-white children and young adults access to education as creating a generational pattern of poverty and inability to engage in the economic life of the State.[85] At the same time, however, the South African Truth and Reconciliation Commission Report itself highlights the issues it faced as a result of a mandate that

81 Promotion of National Unity and Reconciliation, Act of 1995.
82 ibid.
83 ibid.
84 ibid., art 3.
85 See South Africa (n 62) v 1, 32, 64.

was largely focused on assessing the human rights violations committed against individuals and crafting methods of reconciliation and reparation for the perpetrators while failing to address the impacts of these actions on families and family members.[86] A unique element in the South African Truth and Reconciliation Commission fact-finding process was the express inclusion of children through methods including storytelling and artwork in order to ensure that they were able to participate without incurring further damage.[87]

In another example, while highly controversial in many ways, the use of the Gacaca justice system in Rwanda, which was identified as critical under the truth and reconciliation report, 'Rapport sur le Sommet National d'Unite et de Reconciliation', served to establish a link between the traditional tribal system and current and future concepts in intergenerational justice.[88] In addition, Rwanda has and continues to highlight the essential role of education across all ages and social groups in order to provide a shared understanding of the genocide as well as those who resisted it and allow society to move forward without carrying these lessons into future generations' consciousness.[89] Given the widespread use of sexual violence against women and girl children in Rwanda, the report further emphasises the need to implement significant mental and physical health provisions to assist the victims while also ensuring that they, and the children resulting from such violence, are protected from victimisation by society.[90] Similar concerns were also emphasised in the truth and reconciliation report and findings for Sierra Leone, where sexual crimes were a pervasive weapon of war and institutionalised violence against children as well as women.[91]

4. Conclusions

From a legal and societal perspective, peace is a commitment to and for future generations that also includes the recognition of past victims, especially those who are absent and can no longer speak for themselves or their

86 ibid., 367.
87 ibid., 423.
88 See Peace Agreement between the Government of the Republic of Rwanda and the Rwandese Patriotic Front (1993) 27–28.
89 ibid., 35–37.
90 ibid., 37.
91 Truth & Reconciliation Commission, *Witness to the Truth: Report of the Sierra Leone Truth and Reconciliation Commission* (2004) v1 141.

experiences. Although most often the result of an intense conflict in which the fabric of a society is stretched to its limits, and sometimes unravels, peace is the string which can bind the fabric of society together again. It is rare that any society speaks of peace as a luxury for the present generation alone to enjoy. At the end of a conflict, particularly an internal conflict, peace is a hard-fought decision reflecting the decision of multiple parties and a willingness to compromise for a collective good. Part of the collective good embodied in peace is, inevitably, the future and constructs relating to intergenerational equity and justice. Similarly, the commitment to peace is a commitment to truth and to methods of reconciliation that unearth often devastating realities and impacts on current generations of adults and children as well as on future generations of citizens and throughout society.

As this research demonstrates, while future generations and concepts of intergenerational equity and justice are often not discussed in these terms as such, they are the fundamental underpinning of peace mechanisms. Without a commitment to the future in law and policy, efforts to ensure the durability of peace agreements lack a centralised core. In coming to understand this, and in advancing the role of intergenerational equity and justice in peace agreements as well as the work of truth and reconciliation commissions and similar entities, it is critical that there be a balance between the need to move forward with the healing process and the need to ensure that victims have the chance for justice. In this context, justice is not only for the victims, their families and their communities in the present day but also can be seen as intergenerational justice in that it allows individuals and society to understand the past and ensure it is not repeated in the future.

10. The Rights of and Obligations towards Future Generations

*Yumiko Nakanishi**

Abstract: *In this chapter, the rights of future generations and obligations towards future generations in particular in the context of environmental protection in relation to climate change issues will be discussed. As for the relationship between the present generation and future generations, future generations transfer their rights to the present generation, so that their rights are represented by the present generation. Furthermore, the present generation has responsibility or obligations towards future generations. First, the rights of future generations will be discussed and will be explained, from where one can derive these rights. Second, the obligations of states towards future generations will be analysed, in examining climate change litigation, the question why states are obliged to protect the environment for future generations will be treated. Third, by considering legal documents and climate change judgments, the duties of the present generation towards future generations will be discussed.*

1. Introduction

Considerations about the rights or interests of future generations are not new. Early considerations were made in philosophical or ethical contexts. For example, John Rawls discussed intergenerational equity in his book '*Theory of justice*' in 1971,[1] and in 1988, Saladin and Zenger published a book, entitled '*Rechte künftiger Generationen [Rights of Future Generations]*'.[2] In addition, Hans Jonas's 1979 book '*Das Prinzip Verantwortung [the principle of responsibility]*'[3] indicated responsibility towards future generations. Later, Häberle pointed out that national debt and the disposal of radioactive waste are issues that simulate considerations about future generations.[4]I In March 2021, the German Constitutional Court gave a landmark judgment in the *Klimaschutzgesetz* (Climate Change Act) case,

* Yumiko Nakanishi is Professor of European Union Law at Graduate School of Law, Hitotsubashi University (Japan).

1 John Rawls, *Theory of Justice* (Belknap Press of Harvard University Press 1971).

2 Peter Saladin and Christoph Andreas Zenger, *Recht künftiger Generationen* (Helbing & Lichtenbahn 1988).

3 Hans Jonas, *Das Prinzip Verwantwortung* (Insel Verlag 1979).

4 Peter Häberle, 'A Constitutional Law for Future Generations – The 'Other' Form of the Social Contract: The Generation Contract' in Joerg Chet Tremmel, *Handbook of Intergenerational Justice* (Edward Elgar 2006) 215.

which is related to future generations.[5] In this case, the Court relied on its established case law related to nuclear power stations, in particular the 1978 *Kalkar* case[6] and the 1981 *Mühlheim-Kärlich* case.[7] Future generations have also been discussed regarding the pension system, national debt, chemicals, genetically modified organisms (GMOs) as well as nuclear energy related issues. In addition, regarding conservation of natural resources, Judge Cançado Trindade emphasised the importance of considering future generations in his separate opinion in the *Whaling in the Antarctic* case.[8] Currently, the concerns of future generations are receiving increasing attention in relation to climate change issues.

The amount of climate change litigation is increasing across the world. Children, young people and Non-Governmental Organisations (NGOs) are taking action before courts at national, regional and international level, playing an astonishing role as guardians not only of their own future interests but also of future generations and the earth. Climate change litigation is one of the most important mechanisms to induce states to protect the environment. Various courts have recently pronounced landmark judgments that oblige states to take measures to tackle climate change more efficiently and drastically. Such judgments enable us to recognise states' obligations towards future generations and may lead us to concretise the rights of future generations which have been considered as theoretical or ethical rights.

This book discusses 'representing the absent'. In this chapter, I will treat future generations as the absent. I will address the rights of future generations and obligations towards future generations in particular in the context of environmental protection in relation to climate change issues. I define future generations in the following way: future generations are composed of, young people who do not yet have the right to vote, and unborn people. Young people can also be considered to be part of the present generation. Thus, young people belong to both the present generation and

5 BVerfG, 1 BvR 2656/18, Beschluss des Ersten Senats vom 24. März 2021 [hereinafter '*Klimaschutzgesetz*'].

6 BVerfGE 49, 89, 2 BvL 8/77, Beschluß des Zweiten Senats vom 8. August 1978 [hereinafter '*Kalkar*'].

7 BVerfGE 53, 31, p. 57, 1 BvR 385/77, Beschluß des Ersten Senats vom 20. Dezember 1979 [hereinafter '*Mühlheim-Kärlich*'].

8 Separate Opinion of Judge Cançado Trindade, *Whaling in the Antarctic (Australia v Japan: New Zealand intervening)*, Merits, Judgment of 31 March 2014, (1994) ICJ Rep 226, 348.

future generations. The present generation is composed of people who are alive now, including governments, companies, and organisations. As for the relationship between the present generation and future generations, as I will explain later, future generations transfer their rights to the present generation, so that their rights are represented by the present generation. In addition, the present generation have responsibility or obligations towards future generations.

I will first discuss the rights of future generations and identify from where we can derive these rights. Second, I will analyse the obligations of states towards future generations. In examining climate change litigation, I explain why states are obliged to protect the environment for future generations. Third, by considering legal documents and climate change judgments, I will discuss the duties of the present generation towards future generations so that those rights and obligations do not remain fictitious and we might be able to concretise them.

2. Rights of Future Generations

2.1. Why Should Rights Be Discussed?

As unborn future generations cannot presently exercise their potential subjective rights, some authors argue that they do not have any subjective rights.[9] Calliess is an example here. In the *Klimaschutzgesetz* case, although the German Federal Constitutional Court accepted the legal standing of young people who claimed that their fundamental rights were being violated,[10] it confirmed that those plaintiffs did not claim the rights of unborn or future generations and additionally held that subjective fundamental rights did not belong to the latter.[11] The Court followed Calliess's argument.[12] Jakab has also discussed possible objections to the conceptualisation of sustainability as the 'rights of future generations' and concluded that the general attempt to posit the 'rights of future generations' is conceptually irreconcilable with the current language of rights.[13]

9 Christian Calliess, *Rechtsstaat und Umweltstaat* (Mohr Siebeck 2001) 119–120.
10 *Klimaschutzgesetz* (n 5) para. 90.
11 ibid., para. 109.
12 ibid.
13 András Jakab, 'Sustainability in European Constitutional Law' (2016) 16 MPIL Research Paper Series 1, 16–17, 27.

Even so, the rights of future generations should be discussed and be acknowledged. Stones states that 'right' has a meaning in ordinary legal language, and a society that speaks of the legal rights of the environment, for example, would tend to formally enact more environment-protecting legal rules.[14] Obligations and duties do not have the same force: a state's obligation towards future generations to protect the environment, and individuals' duty to consider future generations in exercising rights, are not equivalent to legal recognition of the rights of future generations. The rights approach offers a more stringent framework than the duties approach because rights grant generalised legal competence and are open-ended, whereas duties are usually broken down into specific rules of limited scope, and because the rights approach encourages the development of a new body of law.[15]

I will discuss the rights of future generations from three different perspectives in the following sections. First, I will discuss the existence of the fundamental rights of future generations. Second, I will consider the rights of future generations in intergenerational relations. Third, I will explain that future generations transfer their rights to the present generation and that these rights are represented by the present generation.

2.2. Existence of Fundamental Rights of Future Generations

2.2.1. Explicit Fundamental Rights of Future Generations

The 1776 Constitution of Virginia establishes 'a declaration of rights made by the good people of Virginia, assembled in full and free convention; which rights do pertain to them and their posterity, as the basis and foundation of government'.[16] However, most current national constitutions, including the EU treaties, have not yet explicitly established the rights of future generations. As a result, it is difficult to determine whether future

14 Christopher D Stone, 'Should Trees Have Standing-Toward Legal Rights for Natural Objects' (1972) 45(2) Sothern California Law Review 450, 488–489.

15 Susan Emmenegger and Axel Tschentscher, 'Taking Nature's Rights Seriously: The Long Way to Biocentrism in Environmental Law' (1994) 6(3) Georgetown International Environmental Law Review 545, 573; Cf Christopher D Stone (n 14) 488–489; Cf Anthony D'Amato and Sudhir K Chopra, 'Whales: Their Emerging Rights to Life (1991) 85(1) American Journal of International Law 21, 51.

16 The Constitution of Virginia, June 29, 1776, Bill of Rights: June 12, 1776, <https://perma.cc/HSS5-ZGSE>; underlined by author.

generations have the same subjective rights as the present generation. In this context, it is remarkable that the Japanese Constitution guarantees the fundamental rights of future generations. The Japanese Constitution was promulgated in 1946 and entered in force on 3 May 1947. The Constitution was drafted under the supervision of an American, Douglas MacArthur, after World War II and was based on the high ideals of the Japanese people and their strong determination to achieve lasting peace. This Constitution has never been amended, and it guarantees the rights of future generations.

Article 11 sentence 2 of the Constitution states that, '[the] fundamental human rights guaranteed to the people by this Constitution shall be conferred upon the people of this and future generations as eternal and inviolate rights.' This means that future generations as well as the present generation have fundamental rights according to this Article. Article 11 is located under chapter III 'Rights and Duties of the People'. Hatajiri comments that according to this Article, obligations towards future generations must be fulfilled in so far as not only current citizens, but also future generations, are able to enjoy the fundamental rights.[17] Furthermore, the preamble lays down, 'We, the Japanese people, [...] determined that we shall secure for ourselves and our posterity the fruits of peaceful cooperation'.[18] Article 13 provides for the right to pursue happiness. As the Japanese constitution has never been amended, this article has been used to adapt to social needs, and new fundamental rights such as the right of privacy have been established through interpretation. Thus, it can be also interpreted as, and is used as, a tool to make the government guarantee the right to environmental protection. Article 25 establishes the right to life, which is often used of to protect the environment. Kurokawa[19] indicates that these rights of future generations to environmental protection can be derived from individual provisions in combination with the preamble.

17 Tsuyoshi Hatajiri, *Peta Heberure no Kenpouron* [Constitutional theory of Peter Häberle] (in Japanese) (Chuodaigaku Shuppanbu 2021) 107–108.

18 Underlined by author.

19 Tetsushi Kurokawa, 'Kankyoho kara mita kokka no yakuwari to shoraisedai heno sekinin [the role of the state and obligations towards future generations from the aspect of environmental law]' (in Japanese) (2012) 74 Kohokenkyu [Journal of Public Law] 165.

Few constitutions explicitly establish the rights of future generations. However, this situation may change in the future.[20]

2.2.2. Implicit Fundamental Rights of Future Generations

Even if constitutions do not explicitly establish the fundamental rights of future generations, we can assume that they implicitly lay down such rights, using the 'social contract' idea.

In his book 'Du contrat social (the Social Contract)',[21] Rousseau establishes the concept of a social contract, a fictitious contract between the state and its citizens. Rousseau's idea contributed to the French revolution in 1789. During the revolution, the Declaration of the Rights of Man and of the Citizens was issued on 26 August 1789. The Declaration established that men are born and remain free and equal in rights, sovereignty lies in the citizens, and citizens have certain human rights. In this paper, I assume a fictitious social contract between states and future generations that is analogous to that described by Rousseau. National constitutions can be considered social contracts not only between past generations and the state and between the present generation and the state, but also between future generations and the state. Young people are both part of the present generation and future generations and have subjective rights. Obviously, unborn future generations will have subjective rights when they are born. Accordingly, the relationship between the state and future generations has not only been developing in the theoretical and ethical spheres, but also in the legal world. The development in the latter depends on national, regional, and international law.

2.3. The Rights of Future Generations in Intergenerational Relations

I take the stance that future generations have potential subjective rights, as some forward-looking authors have done. Using the concept 'planetary', Weiss indicates that '*planetary*' rights and obligations coexist in each gener-

20 For example, see Renan Araújo and Leonie Koessler, 'The Rise of the Constitutional Protection of Future Generations' (*Verfassungsblog*, 12 August 2022) <https://perma.cc/WDG3-TFBP>.

21 Jean-Jacques Rousseau, *Du Contrat Social* (first published 1762, Constant Bourquin 1947).

ation, and 'in the intergenerational dimension, the generations to which the obligations are owed are future generations, while the generations with which the rights are linked are past generations.'[22] Here, '*planetary*' rights and obligations imply that each generation is entitled to planetary quality comparable to that enjoyed by past generations and that they are required to maintain the quality of the planet. As a result, the rights of future generations are linked to the obligations of the present generation. Past generations, the present generation, and future generations are linked through planetary rights and obligations. In these intergenerational relations, intergenerational equity must be respected. These planetary rights have been translated to the right to a healthy environment or the right to life, in the legal language, while these planetary obligations have been translated to the duty on individuals to pay attention to future generations in exercising their rights.

The idea of intergenerational relations is concretised to some extent in the *Urgenda I* case.[23] In this case, the Dutch District Court referred to the principle of fairness between the present generation and future generations, although it did not recognise the rights of future generations. The Court pointed out that the principle of fairness means that 'the policy should not only start from what is most beneficial to the present generation at this moment, but also what this means for future generations, so that future generations are not exclusively and disproportionally burdened with the consequences of climate change'.[24]

2.4. Representation of Future Generations

I will explain how the rights of future generations can be represented and then will show concrete cases in climate change litigation in which future generations were represented.

22 Edith Brown Weiss, 'Our Rights and Obligations to Future Generations for the Environment' (1990) 84 The American Journal of International Law 198, 202.

23 The Hague District Court, *Urgenda Foundation v the State of the Netherlands*, Judgment of 24 June 2015, C/09/456689/HA ZA 13-1396 (English translation), ECLI:NL:RBDHA:2015:7196 [hereinafter '*Urgenda I*'].

24 ibid., para. 4.57.

2.4.1. Transfer of Rights of Future Generations to the Present Generation

Even if future generations have potential subjective rights, they cannot exercise them directly. They might thus transfer their rights to the present generation through an implicit intergenerational contract between the present generation and future generations. Häberle[25] considers an intergenerational contract to be 'another form' of the social contract. In reality, an increasing number of NGOs are representing future generations voluntarily, despite the lack of an explicit intergenerational contract. Thus, future generations not only have subjective rights, they can also exercise their rights in so far as they have representatives. In fact, whether future generations can get their interests represented depends only on the procedural law of each country. As I will mention below, NGOs represent interests of future generations before courts and (even if not always) are granted *locus standi*. Alternatively, some central authority or ombudsman can be established to take action on behalf of future generations. Acknowledgments of *locus standi* by courts depend on the procedural law of each country.

2.4.2. Climate Change Litigation

Recently, NGOs have been able to represent future generations in certain jurisdictions. In the Netherlands, the legal standing of environmental organisations can be easily accepted pursuant to Article 3:305a (Collective Actions) of the Dutch Civil Code (DCC), which establishes, 'a foundation or association with full legal capacity that, according to its articles of association, has the objection to protect specific interests, may bring to court a legal claim that intents to protect similar interests of other persons'.[26] This provision was introduced in 1994 to ensure a more effective and efficient legal protection of collective interests.[27] In *Urgenda I* in 2015,[28] the Hague District Court accepted the legal standing of the plaintiff, the Urgenda Foundation, which represented 886 individuals, to act on behalf of future as well as current generations. Urgenda filed a collective action claim

25 Häberle (n 4) 224.

26 As English version of the text, see <https://perma.cc/H43S-3ZLD>.

27 Berthy van den Broek and Liesbeth Enneking, 'Public Interest Litigation in the Netherlands: A Multidimensional Take on the Promotion of Environmental Interests by Private Parties through the Courts' (2014) 10(3) Utrecht Law Review 77, 84.

28 *Urgenda I* (n 23).

against the State before the Hague District Court. Urgenda represented the interests not only of current generations but also future generations of Dutch nationals. In the Netherlands, environmental organisations can take action before national courts without the existence of an identifiable group needing protection pursuant to the DCC. The Court positively recognised the meaning of representing the interests of future generations. First, the Court pointed out that Urgenda aims to achieve a more sustainable society according to Article 2 of its by-laws.[29] The Court then found that the phrase 'sustainable society' has an intergenerational dimension, referring to the definition of 'sustainability' in the Brundtland Report.[30] Furthermore, the Court ascertained that Urgenda strives to satisfy the interests of a sustainable society in defending the right of present and future generations' access to natural resources and a safe and healthy living environment.[31]

In *Milieudefensie et al. v Royal Dutch Shell* in 2021, the Hague District Court gave another landmark judgment regarding climate change.[32] The Court established that a private company should take responsibility for tackling climate change. The defendant was one of the world's biggest oil companies, Royal Dutch Shell. This case is notable because the Court again clearly acknowledged the legal standing of the plaintiffs representing future generations.

These two cases were won by the NGOs concerned. Article 3.305a of the DCC, which enables class action, allows public interest actions to be pursued before the Dutch Civil courts against public bodies as well as private companies. Thus, these cases demonstrate that the legal standing of NGOs is accepted in Dutch law and the interests which they represent are also acknowledged.

Intergenerational litigation, which represents future generations, is increasing not only in Europe, but also across the world. In *Juliana v U.S.*,[33] the plaintiffs were the non-profit organisation 'Our Children's Trust', to which young individuals belong, and climatologist James Hansen as a 'guardian for future generations'. The plaintiffs filed a lawsuit against the

---

29 ibid., para. 4.7.

30 World Commission on Environment and Development, *Our Common Future* (OUP 1987).

31 ibid., para. 4.8.

32 The Hague District Court, *Milieudefensie v Royal Dutch Shell*, Judgment of 26 May 2021, ECLI:NL:RBDHA:2021:5339 [hereinafter '*Milieudefensie*'].

33 United States District Court for the District of Oregon, *Juliana v United States*, April 8, 2016, 217 F. Supp. 3d 1224 [hereinafter '*Juliana*'].

United States government before the District Court of Oregon, insisting that the government had failed to take the necessary action to prevent CO_2 emissions. The plaintiffs asked the Court to order the government to take action to stabilise the climate system and protect vital resources for current and future generations. The plaintiffs alleged that emissions would lead to severe impacts on children and future generations and the government had thus violated their individual rights. The District Court acknowledged a substantive due process claim in the plaintiffs' assertions, stating that the government had a duty to protect public health and the 'government's public trust duties deeply ingrained in this country's [the US's] history'.

3. *States' Obligations towards Future Generations*

I have already approached the question of future generations from the perspective of their rights. In this section, I will instead approach the question of future generations from the perspective of state obligations.

Independently of whether constitutions establish the rights of future generations, states should take responsibility for future generations. In fact, some national constitutions do lay down states' obligations towards future generations and national courts have acknowledged these obligations more and more frequently. I will discuss why states should be obliged to take future generations into consideration and from where courts have derived states' obligations in climate litigation.

3.1. Why Should States take Future Generations into Consideration?

Young people who already have the right to vote can at least be involved in parliament's decision making by exercising voting rights. However, young people who do not yet have the right to vote and unborn people cannot participate in decision making because they could not exercise their subjective rights by themselves, even if they do have subjective rights. Kleiber points out that there is a structural political deficit here because future generations are disadvantaged compared to the present generation due to defective representation in the democratic process.[34] He also indicates that

34 Michael Kleiber, *Der grundrechtliche Schutz künftiger Generationen* (Mohr Siebeck 2014) 5.

the short-term legitimisation of current democracy brought about by short periods of office leads to a strong preference towards the present in politics at the expense of future generations. The state's long-term responsibility towards future generations, which does not depend on near-term benefits, is all the more important here because future generations cannot exercise their potential subjective rights.

Although future generations have subjective rights, they cannot exercise their rights by themselves. However, the need to protect future generations can be derived from the concept of intergenerational justice or equity, which is contained in the concept of sustainable development. Furthermore, a state's obligations to protect future generations are derived from the national constitution, which is considered to be a social contract between a state and its citizens. Appel suggests that an obligation to protect future generations might be derived from a combination of human dignity and trusteeship, and the constitution might be seen as the protection of the natural basis of life as a comprehensive social contract in which future generations participate as a fictional contract partner.[35] As I will explain in detail later, in the *Klimaschutzgesetz* case, the German Constitutional Court acknowledged that the State is responsible not only for the present generation but also for future generations under objective law when the state faces great dangers, such as climate change.[36]

The EU should also have obligations to protect future generations, in so far as the Member States transfer their competence to the EU. The obligations to protect future generations derive from the principle of sustainable development, which is a key principle of the EU. Acknowledging that Member States transfer their competence to the EU, Kube points out that the principle of sustainable development demands that the EU and Member states protect future generations.[37] In addition, the EU treaties themselves can also be considered as implicit social contracts between the EU and EU citizens because individuals are accepted as legal persons in the EU legal order, and they accordingly have rights and obligations. The EU treaties and the EU Charter of fundamental rights lay down the principle of sustainable development.

35 Ivo Appel, *Staatliche Zukunfts- und Entwicklungsvorsorge* (Mohr Siebeck 2005) 116.

36 *Klimaschutzgesetz* (n 5) para. 148.

37 Hanno Kube, 'Nachhaltigkeit und parlamentarische Demokratie' in Wolfgang Kahl (ed), *Nachhaltigkeit durch Organisation und Verfahren* (Mohr Siebeck 2016) 136, 157.

3.2. From Where do Courts Derive States' Obligations to Protect the Environment?

Tackling climate change is considered as a laboratory where new legal litigation is developed and tested.[38] Such litigation encompasses a model of society where we hope to live in future. Courts across the world have dealt with climate change litigation. Increased discussion and knowledge sharing around climate change litigation across the world leads to useful dialogues between applicants. NGOs exchange information across the world to strengthen their legal strategies.[39] Similarly, thanks to the availability of global discussions, judges around the world are increasingly influenced and informed by previous judgments and can also influence and inform future judgments.[40] For example, in the *Juliana v U.S.* case[41], the District Court of Oregon accepted the government's responsibility for CO2 emissions, referring to the judgment of the *Urgenda I* case by the Hague District Court. The US Appeals Court acknowledged this.[42] It is noteworthy that in the Climate Change Act case, the German Constitutional Court referred to the judgment of the US Appeals Court as well as the judgments of the *Urgenda I and II* cases in this context.[43] In the following I will show different climate litigations in the world. Courts have relied on a variety of legal instruments at national and international level in order to oblige states to tackle climate change.

3.2.1. The Duty of Care from National Law

In *Urgenda* I,[44] the Hague District Court in the Netherlands relied on the duty of care laid down in Article 21 of the Dutch Constitution, which states, 'It shall be the concern of the authorities to keep the country habitable and

38 Bruno Lasserre, 'L'environnement : les citoyens, le droit, les judges' (21 May 2021) <https://www.conseil-etat.fr/actualites/discours-et-interventions/l-environnement-les-citoyens-le-droit-les-juges-introduction-de-bruno-lasserre-vice-president-du-conseil-d-etat> accessed 28 November 2022.

39 Yann Aguila, 'Petite typologie des actions climatiques contre l'Etat' (2019) AJDA 1853.

40 ibid.

41 *Juliana* (n 33).

42 United States Court of Appeals for the Ninth Circuit, Judgment of 17 January 2020, No 18–36082, 19–20.

43 *Klimaschutzgesetz* (n 5), para. 203.

44 *Urgenda I* (n 23).

to protect and improve the environment', to find a state obligation towards *Urgenda*. It held that the Netherlands had failed to meet this duty of care by failing to take sufficient measures to prevent climate change. The Court acknowledged that the State had discretionary power under Article 21 of the Constitution to organise national climate policy, but that power is not unlimited.[45] Article 21 of the Constitution itself does not give rights to the present generation nor to future generations.[46] However, the State has a duty to care for the environment under this article. The State is obliged to take into account environment relevant principles in determining the scope of the duty of care.[47]

In another case that relied on the duty of care in Australia, eight high school students took class action before the Australian Federal Court, demanding that the Federal Environmental Minister should not approve coal mining projects. The Federal Court gave a landmark judgment on 27 May 2021.[48] Pursuant to the law of negligence, the Court recognised the duty of care of the Minister of the Environment not to harm young people and to protect them from foreseeable future climate damage in deciding on projects. Although this case is not directly linked with future generations, it is an example in which the Court acknowledged a state's duty of care towards young people.

3.2.2. Public Trust Doctrine

In the *Juliana v U.S.* case,[49] the District Court held that the government had a duty to protect public health and the 'government's public trust duties were deeply ingrained in this country's [the US's] history'. This decision was based on the public trust doctrine[50], which assigns the state responsibility for the integrity of a nation's public trust resources for future

45 ibid., paras 4.53 – 4.55.
46 ibid., para. 4.56.
47 ibid., para. 4.76.
48 Federal Court of Australia, *Sharma by her litigation representative Sister Marie Brigid Arthur v Minister for the Environment*, Judgment of 27 May 2021, (2021) FCA 560, VID 607/2020.
49 *Juliana* (n 33).
50 According to the Legal information Institute of Cornell Law School, 'public trust doctrine is a legal principle establishing that certain natural and cultural resources are preserved for public use'.

generations.[51] Lavorel commented regarding the opinion of Judge Aiken in the Julianna case that the judge relied on the concept of intergenerational vocation and found that federal authorities have an obligation to protect resources against damage and destruction and preserve capacities to provide ecological services for future generations.[52] Additionally, the Harvard Law Review case note[53] pointed out that the *Juliana v U.S.* case differed from ordinary environmental cases. The latter relied on common law tort theories or federal statutory law, in particular the 1970 Clean Air Act, while the former relied on unenumerated fundamental rights: constitutional rights to life, liberty and property.[54]

3.2.3. Human Rights

In *Urgenda II*, the Court of Appeal[55] relied on Articles 2 and 8 of the European Convention on Human Rights (ECHR) for the first time to find a positive state obligation to take action against climate change. It acknowledged that Article 2 ECHR is the right to life, which includes environment-related situations that affect or threaten to affect the right to life, and Article 8 ECHR protects the right to private life and family life and may also apply in environment-related situations.[56] The Court of Appeal held that the State has both positive and negative obligations relating to the interests protected by these articles including the positive obligation to take concrete measures to prevent a future violation of these interests.[57] It also held that it is appropriate to discuss the real threat of dangerous climate change, resulting in the serious risk that the present generation of Dutch nationals will be confronted with a loss of life and/or a disruption of family life and it follows from Articles 2 and 8 ECHR that the State has a duty to

51 Christiana Voigt, 'Introduction Climate Change as a Challenge for Global Governance, Courts and Human Rights' in Wolfgang Kahl and Marc-Philippe Weller (eds), *Climate Change Litigation* (Beck 2021) 9.

52 Sabine Lavorel, 'L'émergence d'une responsabilité climatique des États?' in Marta Torre-Schaub and others, *Quel(s) Droit(s) pour les changements climatiques?* (Mare & Martin 2018) 174–175.

53 '*Juliana v. United States*' (2021) 134(5) Harvard Law Review 1929.

54 ibid., 1929–1930.

55 The Hague Court of Appeal, Judgment of 9 October 2018, *the State of the Netherlands v Urgenda Foundation*, 200.178.245/01 (English translation), ECLI:EU:GHDHA:2018:2610.

56 ibid., para. 40.

57 ibid., para. 41.

protect against this real threat.[58] The Court of Appeal concluded that the State failed to fulfil its duty of care pursuant to Articles 2 and 8 ECHR by not demanding reduction of emissions by at least 25 % by the end of 2020.[59]

In *Urgenda III*, the Supreme Court ascertained that the State has a positive obligation to take measures to prevent climate change pursuant to Articles 2 and 8 ECHR.[60] In *Urgenda II* and *Urgenda III*, climate change issues can be linked to human rights – the right to life and the right to private and family life – and environmental organisations can rely on those rights before national courts. A landmark judgment such this one might have been possible because it was made in the Netherlands where the Constitution is open to international law and in particular to the ECHR.[61]

3.2.4. Protective Obligation from Fundamental Rights in the Constitution

Notably, the German Constitutional Court derived the state's objective obligation towards future generations from fundamental rights laid down in the German Constitution. First, the Court held that the State is obliged to protect against climate change based on the fundamental right in Article 2 para. 2 sentence 1 of the Grundgesetz (GG) (Basic Law).[62] Article 2 para. 2 sentence 1 lays down, 'Everyone shall have the right to life and physical integrity'.[63] The Court confirmed that Article 2 para. 2 sentence 1 contains a state's general obligation to protect life and physical integrity.[64] The Court held that this fundamental right not only protects against state intervention, it also includes the state's obligation to protectively and supportively guarantee the legal interests of life and physical integrity and to protect them against unlawful interferences. The Court explained that the protective obligations that derive from the objective function of the fundamental right belong to the subjective entitlement of the fundamental right (*subjektive*

58 ibid., para. 45.

59 ibid., para. 73.

60 The Supreme Court of the Netherlands, *the State of the Netherlands v Urgenda foundation*, Judgment of 20 December 2019, Number 19/00135, ECLI:NL:HR:2019:2006.

61 Cf, André Nollkaemper and Laura Burgers, 'A New Classic in Climate Change Litigation: The Dutch Supreme Court Decision in the Urgenda Case' (*EJILTalk!*, 6 January 2020) <https://perma.cc/RHH5-MJBV>.

62 *Klimaschutzgesetz* (n 5) para. 144.

63 Official translation by the Federal Ministry of Justice and Consumer Protection and the Federal Office of Justice <https://www.gesetze-im-internet.de/englisch_gg/>.

64 *Klimaschutzgesetz* (n 5) para. 145.

Grundrechtsberechtigung).[65] The Court then held that the state's obligation derived from Article 2 para. 2 sentence 1 GG does not only intervene when violations have already happened, but also when the obligation is directed towards the future.[66] Finally, the Court clarified that the obligation to protect life and physical integrity may constitute a protection obligation in relation to future generations as well.[67] The Court established a condition that this obligation applies only if irreversible development is at issue.[68] The Court added that such an intergenerational protection obligation can only be an objective law (not a subjective right) because future generations, neither as a whole nor as a sum of individuals, have legal capacity to enjoy fundamental rights.[69]

To this end, the Court referred to four previous judgments. The first is the judgement in the *Kalkar* case in 1978,[70] which concerned nuclear power stations. In this case, taking the risk of future damage into consideration, the Court held that pursuant to Article 1 para. 1 sentence 2 GG all state powers are obliged to not only respect human dignity but also to protect it.[71] The Court therefore held that the State is obliged to shape law so that the risk of violations of fundamental rights is reduced. In the *Mühlheim-Kärlich* case in 1981, which was also related to nuclear power stations, the Court held that Article 2 para. 2 not only protects the subjective right of defence against state intervention but that the state's obligation stands in a protective and supportive way for the legal interests of life and physical integrity derived from the objective substance of Article 2 para. 2.[72] In the third case, the Court referred to the first and second cases and confirmed that the state's obligation includes analysing future risks to fundamental rights.[73] Furthermore, the Court held that the state obligation derived from Article 2 para. 2 GG contains the obligation to tackle health risks from aircraft noise. The fourth case, which is related to the protection of non-smokers, also confirmed the existence of the State's obligation derived

65 ibid.
66 ibid., para. 146.
67 ibid.
68 ibid.
69 ibid.
70 *Kalkar* (n 6).
71 ibid., 141–142.
72 *Mühlheim-Kärlich* (n 7).
73 BVerfGE 56, 78, 1 BvR 612/72, Beschluß des Ersten Senats vom 14. Januar 1981.

from Article 2 para. 2 GG.[74] Those four judgments did not directly mention future generations, but took future risks regarding nuclear power stations, aircraft noise, and secondary smoking into account. All cases acknowledged the State's obligations from Article 1 or Article 2 GG. The ground-breaking climate protection judgment was based on established case law that dealt with future risks and acknowledged the State's protection obligation, which derives from the GG.

The Court concluded that the state's obligation to protect life and physical integrity against climate change may apply to future generations by referring to a 1986 article by Hasso Hofmann.[75] The article dealt with the state's protection obligation towards future generations in considering nuclear power stations.[76] In this article, Hofmann confirmed that future generations cannot have any entitlements. However, he argued that the state authority might not be allowed to force future generations to bear excessive burdens. He asserted that pursuant to Article 1 para. 1 sentence 1 GG the State is obliged not only to respect fundamental rights for the sake of human dignity, but also to protect them. He argued that the state must take appropriate defence measures when constitutional subjective fundamental rights are threatened by a third party. He contended that this objective or institutional effect of fundamental rights may apply for future generations who do not have a substantive entitlement to fundamental rights. Although he recognised that future generations cannot enjoy substantive rights, he argued that (objective) law may provide for the provisions for the protection of future generations. He concluded that the state's protection obligations derived from fundamental rights must exist independently from subjective entitlements. Furthermore, he argued that when the state faces an imminent public health risk that requires governmental measures to be taken, the state's protection obligation must extend into the future. He held that Article 2 para. 2 sentence 1 GG obliges the State to take measures against such dangers.

In addition, Appel, on whose literature the Court relied, also described that the state's obligation to respect constitutional objects of protection is an objective obligation and does not depend on whether certain people are

---

74 BVerfGE 121, 356, 1 BvR 3262/07, Urteil des Ersten Senats vom 30. Juli 2008.

75 *Klimaschutzgesetz* (n 5) para. 146.

76 Hasso Hofmann, 'Nachweltschutz als Verfassungsfrage' (1986) 19(4) Zeitschrift für Rechtspolitik 87, 88.

endangered. Thus, the state is obliged to protect constitutional objects of protection for future generations.[77]

3.2.5. Intertemporal Guarantees of Freedom

It is also noteworthy that for the first time, the German Constitutional Court introduced 'intertemporal guarantees of freedom'. In doing this, the Court transformed the theoretical concept of 'intergenerational equity' into a justiciable concept. In the Climate Protection Act case, most of the complainants were minors. The Court considered the guarantee of their freedom in the future, or their intertemporal guarantees of freedom. In doing so, the Court combined this concept with Article 20a GG.

First, the Court held that the fundamental rights of the complainants will continue to be protected against unreasonable impairments of freedom.[78] Then, it held that 'as intertemporal guarantees of freedom, fundamental rights afford the complainants protection against the greenhouse gas reduction burdens imposed by Article 20a GG being unilaterally offloaded onto the future'.[79] Article 20a GG lays down, '[m]indful also of its responsibility towards future generations, the state shall protect the natural foundations of life and animals by legislation and, in accordance with law and justice, by executive and judicial action, all within the framework of the constitutional order'. Article 20a GG does not establish a fundamental right, but Article 20a GG contains a constitutional provision that includes the elemental precepts.[80] Interference with fundamental rights can only be justified under constitutional law if relevant provisions comply with the elemental precepts and general constitutional principles of the GG.[81] Therefore, compatibility with Article 20a GG is a precondition to justify any interference with fundamental rights.[82] Furthermore, the Court held that fundamental rights in combination with Article 20a GG oblige the German legislator to ensure that 'the reduction burdens are not unevenly distributed over time and between generations to the detriment of the future'.[83] Based on the princi-

77 Appel (n 35) 117–118.
78 *Klimaschutzgesetz* (n 5) para. 117.
79 ibid., para. 183.
80 ibid., para. 190.
81 ibid., para. 189.
82 ibid., para. 190.
83 ibid., para. 192.

ple of proportionality, the Court also held that one generation must not be allowed to consume large portions of the CO2 budget while bearing a relatively minor share of the reduction effort.[84] The Court relied on the concept of intergenerational equity here. In addition, the Court clarified that the objective protection mandate derived from Article 20a GG includes the necessity to leave the natural foundations of life 'in such condition that future generations who wish to carry on preserving these foundations are not forced to engage in radical abstinence'.[85] As stated above, Article 20a GG does not create a fundamental right, but the Court held that Article 20a GG is a justiciable legal provision and is binding on the legislator, which is designed to commit to a political process favouring the ecological interests of future generations who will be particularly affected.[86] The Court went one step further regarding future generations, stating that based on Article 20a GG, environmental protection is now a matter of constitutional significance because future generations, who will be most affected, naturally have no voice of their own in shaping the current political agenda and that in light of these inherent limitations, Article 20a GG imposes substantive constraints on democratic decision making.[87] The Court relied on German literature to make this judgment, including Ivo Appel's 2005 book '*Staatliche Zukunfts- und Entwicklunsvorsorge*'. Appel stated that the interests of future generations should be taken into consideration by the present generation because the future generations cannot enunciate their interests in current political processes nor participate in current market development.[88] Kube also pointed out that although the principle of sustainable development requires the legislature to consider the interests of future generations, the will of future generations cannot be represented in parliament.[89] The Court acknowledged that Article 20a GG imposes a special duty of care on the legislator, including a responsibility for future generations.[90] In this case, the Court expanded the horizons of Article 20a GG for future generations by giving unprecedented importance to it.

84 ibid.
85 ibid., para. 193.
86 ibid., paras 197 and 205.
87 ibid., para. 206.
88 Appel (n 35) 75.
89 Kube (n 37) 143, 147, 157.
90 *Klimaschutzgesetz* (n 5) para. 229.

3.2.6. Obligations from the Paris Agreement

The Conseil d'État, the French Supreme Administrative Court, also pronounced a landmark judgment in 2020. In the *Grande Synthe* case, the Conseil d'État held that France is obliged to meet climate objectives and to transform obligations derived from the United Nations Framework Convention on Climate Change (UNFCCC) and the Paris Agreement into national law.[91] For the first time, it acknowledged that those obligations have a binding nature. The Conseil d'État held that the French government is obliged not only to meet these objectives, but also to account for how it meets them. Notably, the Court directly cited phrases including 'future generations', 'sustainable development' and 'equity' in referring to these documents.[92] The Court drew the state's obligation to take appropriate measures to combat climate change from the fact that the EU and France are bound by the UNFCCC and the Paris Agreement.[93] Furthermore, the Court held that the obligations derived from those international documents must be considered in interpreting the provisions of national law. Those documents must be fully effective in French law, even if they do not have any direct effect.[94] Finally, the Court held that the effective implementation of the principles set out in the UNFCCC and the Paris Agreement must be set by French national law.[95] Lasserre commented that the Conseil d'État had acknowledged an interpretive force for the first time and had taken a significant step in judging that the objectives of those documents are not simply programmatic, but binding.[96]

3.2.7. Etat de droit

According to the concept of 'Etat de droit' (the rule of law) in France, citizens play an important role as guardians of states' commitments.[97] In France there are two methods of taking action against the government; one is the 'action en responsabilité' (state responsibility action) and the other is the 'le recours pour excès de pouvoir' (appeal for misuse of power).

91 Conseil d'État, 19 novembre 2020, Grande Synthe, No 427301.
92 ibid., para. 9.
93 ibid., para. 12.
94 ibid.
95 ibid., para. 13.
96 Lasserre (n 38).
97 Aguila (n 39).

An example of the first method is *Affaire du Siècle* (the Case of the Century). Several NGOs – Oxfam France, Notre Affaire à Tous, Greenpeace and La Fondation pour la Nature et l'Homme – took action against the French Government before the administrative Tribunal of Paris. The Tribunal found that the Government had failed to exercise power ('la carence fautive').[98] According to Article 1246 of the French civil code, which is the legal foundation for reparation as any person responsible for ecological damage is required to repair it. Article 1248 lays down that the action for compensation for ecological damage is open to any person with standing and interest of action, and this can therefore include NGOs. The Tribunal held that the state had caused ecological damage caused by failing to comply with the obligations to combat climate change, and this failure had damaged the collective interests which the claimants defended. The Tribunal ordered the French state to pay the organisations the sum of one euro as compensation for their moral prejudice. In the case of *Affaire du Siècle*, episode 2 (the Case of the Century II), confirming that the reduction of CO_2 emission by the Government was not sufficient, the Court ordered the French government to repair the ecological damage until 31 December 2022 and to prevent further deterioration and to take measures as soon as possible.[99]

The aforementioned *Grande-Synthe* case is an example of the second method.

3.2.8. The Environmental Charter in France

The Environmental Charter can be a useful instrument to protect the environment for future generations. The Conseil Constitutionnel made an important judgment for environmental protection on 31 January 2020 in decision no 2019–823 QPC (la question prioritaire de constitutionalité),[100] in which it held that the protection of the environment is 'the common heritage of all mankind' and 'therefore constitutes an objective of constitutional values'.

98 Tribunal administratif de Paris, 3 février 2021, No 1904967, 1904968, 1904972, 1904976/4–1.

99 Tribunal administratif de Paris, 14 octobre 2021, No 1904967, 1904968, 1904972, 1904976/4–1.

100 Conseil Constitutionnel, 31 janvier 2020, Union des industries de la protection des plantes, No 2019–823 QPC, para. 4.

4. *Obligations of the Present Generation towards Future Generations*

4.1. The Present Generation and Future Generations

Climate change has been caused by anthropogenic emissions as the Intergovernmental Panel on Climate Change has made clear.[101] This means that not only the present generation, but also past generations have caused climate change through their activities. The present generation is thus the victimiser as well as the victim. The European Commission recognises that 'we are at a pivotal moment in the world's response to the climate and biodiversity emergencies and <u>we are the last generation</u> that can still act in time'.[102] Regarding the relationship between the present generation and future generations, Weiss states that 'intergenerational equity requires a new planetary ethos in which each generation views itself both in relation to past and future generations of the human species and as an integral part of the natural system' and furthermore that, 'each generation has a right to use the natural system for its own benefit but also an obligation to care for it so that future generations will inherit a robust planet in no worse condition than previous generations received it'.[103] Based on intergenerational equity, future generations should have the right to live in a healthy environment as the present generation has. The present generation has three types of obligations towards future generations. The first is to represent future generations, for example before courts. The second is to consider the interests of future generations in exercising fundamental rights. The third is to take positive actions for future generations.

In the first case, future generations confer competence on the present generation because they cannot exercise their subjective rights by themselves. The present generation is now taking action to address the irreparable man-made damage to nature. The present generation is obliged to make use of their competence for future generations. This has led to climate change litigation in which young people and NGOs represent future generations to request states to take more drastic and rapid measures to tackle climate change. Furthermore, citizens and courts act in tandem in order to

---

101 IPCC, the Sixth Assessment Report, 'Climate Change 2021: The Physical Science Basis', 6 August 2021.

102 The European Commission, COM(2021)550; underlined by author.

103 Edith Brown Weiss, 'In Fairness to Future Generations' (1990) 32(3) Environment 6, 31.

oblige states to protect environment and future generations. Citizens, and in particular NGOs, observe as guardians whether states respect their international commitments, and they take action before courts if necessary.[104] In the second case, the present generation has an obligation to maintain a healthy environment for future generations, that is to say, a duty to take care of the environment. That means that the present generation should take into account future generations in exercising their rights. Sometimes, the exercise of the rights by the present generation might deteriorate the interests of future generations. In this case, the present generation is under an obligation not to exercise their rights where this would lead to such a deterioration. In the third case, the present generation, which is composed of individuals and companies, should take positive action to protect the interests of future generations because the present generation as well as past generations has caused environmental damage.

These ideas based on intergenerational equity are concretised in some legal documents and climate change litigation. In the following sections, I will examine them in my discussion of the second and third type of obligations of the present generation.

4.2. Obligations of the Present Generation Towards Future Generations

4.2.1. Explicit Obligations of the Present Generations Towards Future Generations

Some legal documents from various countries explicitly specify the obligations of the present generations.

Japanese law is an example here. Article 97 of the Japanese Constitution, which is located under Chapter X 'Supreme Law', lays down, '(t)he fundamental human rights by this Constitution guaranteed to the people of Japan are fruits of the age-old struggle of humankind to be free; they have survived the many exacting tests for durability and are conferred upon this and future generations in trust, to be held for all time inviolate.' According to this provision, the trustees of the fundamental rights are the current and future generations. Interestingly, the beneficiary is all of humankind. The present generation enjoys the fundamental rights entrusted by past generations. The present generation may enjoy those fundamental rights

104 Aguila (n 39).

on the condition that it exercises them for the next generation and future generations.[105] As trustee, the present generation must preserve and hand over the fundamental rights as results to the next generation and future generations. Here, we can see intergenerational relations between past generations, the present generation and future generations regarding rights and obligations.

Furthermore, the concept of intergenerational equity is concretised in Japanese law.[106] The Japanese Basic Environmental Act, as the 'Constitution' of Japanese environmental law, was enacted in November 1993.[107] This Act establishes the obligations of companies and citizens and reflects the principles agreed at the Rio Summit of June 1992. The purpose of the Act is:

> to comprehensively and systematically promote policies for environmental conservation to ensure healthy and cultured living for both the present and future generations of the nation as well as to contribute to the welfare of mankind, through articulating the basic principles, clarifying the responsibilities of the State, local governments, corporations and citizens, and prescribing the basic policy considerations for environmental conservation (Art. 1).

The Act fully accepted the concept of sustainable development inserted into the Rio Declaration. Article 3 of the Basic Act provides that environmental conservation shall be conducted to ensure that present and future generations of human beings can enjoy the benefits of a healthy and productive environment. It is also noteworthy that the Act not only establishes state obligations (Article 6), and those of local governments (Article 7) but also those of companies (Article 8) and citizens (Article 9). According to Article 9 citizens are obliged to reduce the environmental impact associated with their daily lives to promote environmental conservation. Article 4 states that environmental conservation shall be conducted to ensure a sustainable society by obliging all people to share the burden of reducing their environmental impact fairly. In addition, Article 1 of the 1972 Japanese Conservation Act states that the purpose of the Act is 'to widely provide the citizens with the enjoyment of benefits of natural environments, as well

105 Hatajiri (n 17) 108.
106 Kurokawa (n 19) 163.
107 See, Yumiko Nakanishi, 'Introduction: The Impact of the International and European Union Environmental Law on Japanese Basic Environmental Law' in Yumiko Nakanishi (ed), *Contemporary Issues in Environmental Law* (Springer 2016) 4–6.

as to ensure inheriting this to future citizens, and with this, to contribute to secure the healthy and cultural life of the current and future citizens'. Article 2 of the 1989 Basic Act for Land indicates that the land is 'a finite, precious resources for citizens both at present and in the future. Article 3 para. 1 of the 2002 Japanese Law for the Promotion of Nature Restoration establishes that, 'Nature restoration shall be carried out appropriately for the purposes of maintaining and passing on a sound and bountiful national environment to <u>future generations</u>...'.[108]

National as well as international instruments increasingly concretise the intergenerational contract and establish the duties of the present generation to protect the environment for future generations. For example, the Bayern Constitution (a German State) of 1984 explicitly provides for the duty of the present generation towards future generations.[109] Article 141 establishes that, 'the protection of the natural basis of life shall be the duty of each individual and the state community, bearing in mind the responsibility for future generations'. In addition, the preamble of the French Charter for the environment states that 'the future and very existence of mankind are inextricably linked with its natural environment' and 'in order to ensure sustainable development, choices designed to meet the needs of the present generation should not jeopardise the ability of future generations'. The concept of intergenerational equity should be noted here. Article 2 of the French Environmental Charter provides that 'Every person has the duty to participate in the preservation and improvement'. Referring to this, the Conseil Constitutionnel held that compliance with the rights and duties set out in general terms under Articles 1 and 2 is a requirement not only for public bodies and administrative authorities but also for all persons: 'every person is under an obligation to exercise care that no damage to the environment results from his actions'.[110]

Additionally, members of the present generation have fundamental rights and can exercise them by themselves. However, individuals of the present generation cannot exercise their rights without limitations, and thus the exercise of their rights is connected to their responsibilities and duties to take future generations into consideration. Some documents state this explicitly. For example, Article 28 of the French Constitution of 24 June 1793 states that a generation cannot subject future generations to its laws. The pream-

108 Underlined by author.
109 Häberle enumerates other examples (n 4) 216–217.
110 Conseil Constitutionnel, 8 avril 2011, *M. Michel Z et autre*, No 2011–116 QPC, para. 5.

ble of the EU Charter of fundamental rights provides that the enjoyment of the EU's fundamental rights entails responsibilities and duties towards future generations.[111] Kitamura comments that Japanese environmental law, as discussed above, is based on an idea that the present generation should not maximise the use of resources and should rather take future generations into consideration in their use of resources.[112]

4.2.2. Obligations of Companies as the Present Generation

It can be argued that certain companies are responsible for climate change. Therefore, climate change litigation is pursued not only against states, but also against companies. In this context, in the *Milieudefensie v Royal Dutch Shell* case on 26 May 2021,[113] the Hague District Court gave another landmark judgment regarding climate change following its ground-breaking judgment regarding climate change in 2015. At that time, the Court had acknowledged that the State had violated its duty of care to take measures to prevent climate change. This time, in 2021, the Court established that a private company should take responsibility for tackling climate change. The defendant was one of the world's biggest oil companies, Royal Dutch Shell. Milieudefensie, six other environmental organisations and about 17 000 citizens participated in the proceedings as the plaintiff. Although Shell insisted that it had taken measures to reduce CO_2 emissions, the Court held that such measures were inadequate. This was a historic judgment because the Court determined that companies have certain responsibilities regarding climate protection. Companies that affect our society cannot longer ignore their social responsibilities. The Hague Court explicitly accepted the legal standing of Milieudefensie and other environmental organisations that represented current and future generations in the Netherlands based on Article 3:305a of the Dutch Civil Code, stating that 'the common interest of preventing dangerous climate change by reducing CO_2 emissions can be protected in a class action'.[114] We can see that the Court took future generations into consideration here. The Court relied on the unwritten standard of care established in Book 6 Section 162 Dutch Civil Code,

111 Häberle elaborated development of draft texts (n 4) 219–220.
112 Kitamura, *Kankyohou* [Environmental Law] (in Japanese) (2nd edn, Koubundo 2013) 10.
113 *Milieudefensie* (n 32).
114 ibid., paras 4.2.2. and 4.2.4.

'which means that acting in conflict with what is generally accepted according to unwritten law is unlawful'.[115] In addition, the Court stated that in its interpretation of the unwritten standard of care, it followed the UN Guiding Principle as soft law instrument, which set out the responsibilities of states and businesses in relation to human rights.[116] Furthermore, the Court held that Articles 2 and 8 ECHR and Articles 6 and 17 of the International Covenant on Civil and Political Rights (ICCPR) could not be directly invoked against Shell but these rights could be considered.[117] In this context, the Court referred to a case concerning the right to life as enshrined in Article 6 ICCPR,[118] and cited the following phrases of the UN Human Rights Committee: 'Furthermore, the Committee recalls that environmental degradation, climate change and unsustainable development constitute some of the most pressing and serious threats to the ability of present and future generations to enjoy the right of life'.[119] Significantly, the Court held that *Shell* is responsible for both current and future generations and is required to take measures to prevent climate change.[120]

This judgment is only the first example of legal interpretation of corporate social responsibility regarding climate change. Climate litigation is increasing across the world. In France, 14 local authorities and several NGOs sued the oil company Total before the tribunal of Nanterre (le tribunal judiciaire de Nanterre) on 28 January 2021. The tribunal rejected the allegation regarding the inadmissibility on the side of Total on 11 February 2021.[121] According to French law,[122] companies must respect the duty of vigilance (devoir de vigilance).

5. Concluding Remarks

In the second section of this chapter, I aimed to demonstrate the existence of the rights of future generations. Discussing such rights is difficult from

115 ibid., para. 4.4.1.
116 ibid., para. 4.4.11.
117 ibid., para. 4.4.9.
118 HRC 23 September 2020, CCPR/C/127/D/2728/2016 (Ioane Teitiota-New Zealand), section 9.4.
119 *Milieudefensie* (n 32) paras 4.4.9 and 4.4.10.
120 ibid., para. 4.4.54.
121 Tribunal Judiciaire de Nanterre, Ordonnance de mise en état, 11 février 2021.
122 Loi No 2017–399 du 27 mars 2017 relative au devoir de vigilance des sociétés mères et des entreprises donneuses d'ordre.

both a legal and general perspective because few constitutions explicitly establish the rights of future generations. However, it is important to discuss the rights of future generations to protect their interests. I explained why and how future generations have rights and that some national constitutions explicitly or implicitly lay down these rights of future generations. National constitutions can be considered as a social contract between future generations and the state, and unborn future generations will gain subjective rights when they are born (II.2). I also considered rights of future generations in the context of intergenerational relations (II.3). Furthermore, I discussed that future generations might transfer their rights to the present generation through an implicit intergenerational contract between the present generation and future generations (II. 4 (1)).

In sections III and IV, I dealt with obligations of the present generation towards future generations. I aimed to show the obligations of states towards future generations. I showed that states have or should have responsibility towards future generations. These obligations have been acknowledged before national courts, which have developed a variety of methods to create states' obligations towards future generations. Then, I clarified that not only states, but also individuals and companies have obligations towards future generations. The states' obligations have developed through climate change litigation by citizens and NGOs.

In climate change litigation, the defendants are usually states. In some cases, applicants have succeeded in obliging states to protect the environment. As a further and potentially more complex step, the obligations of companies as the present generation towards future generations should be recognised. The *Shell* case[123] highlighted the possibility of making a private companies' responsibilities towards future generations a legal duty. As a final step, which might be the hardest, we should consider the obligations of the present generation, or *our* own obligations towards future generations.

123 *Milieudefensie* (n 32).

11. Future Generations Under EU Law

*Alessandra Donati**

> *'Knowledge of the future is a contradiction in terms'*
> (Bernard De Jouvenel, *The Art of Conjecture*, 1967)

1. Introduction

'The future, for a long time, was a concept to which philosophers and jurists paid little attention. It was left to chance, to fate, or perhaps divine providence. So, alien to juristic thinking was the idea of caring about future generations.'[1] This was also the case under European Union (EU) law. Until very recently, future generations were barely present under EU law. The main exception was the preamble of the Charter of Fundamental Rights that stated that enjoyment of the rights of the Charter entails responsibilities and duties regarding other persons, the human community and future generations.

Today, this scenario is rapidly evolving. In the framework of the European Green Deal, the Commission sets forth the objective of launching a new growth strategy for the EU that will support the transition to a fair and prosperous society that responds to the challenges posed by climate change and environmental degradation, improving the quality of life of current and future generations.[2] The reference to upcoming generations is not limited to the text of the Green Deal but is also reiterated in some of the actions, strategies and legislative proposals implementing the Green Deal. As an example, in the Communication 'Fit for 55' adopted on 15

* Alessandra Donati is *Réferendaire* (legal clerk) at the Court of Justice of the European Union and lecturer at the University of Luxembourg. The views expressed in this chapter are personal and do not bind the institution for which she works.

1 Paolo Becchi, 'Our Responsibility Towards Future Generations' in Klaus Mathis (ed), *Efficiency, Sustainability, and Justice to Future Generations* (Springer 2011) 77.

2 Communication from the Commission to the European Parliament, the European Council, the Council, the European Economic and Social Committee and the Committee of the Regions, *The European Green Deal*, COM (2019) 640 final, 23–24.

July 2021, the Commission considers that next generations 'will bear the brunt of more frequent – and more intense – storms, wildfires, droughts and floods, as well as the conflicts that they could trigger around the world. Tackling these crises is, therefore, a matter of intergenerational and international solidarity.'[3] A reference to next generations is also provided for in the post-pandemic EU recovery plan that affirms that 'is the time for our European Union to get back to its feet and move forward together to repair damage from the crisis and prepare a better future for the next generation.'[4]

Considering the increasing references to the next/future generations, which legal instruments should be mobilised under EU law to represent their interests? To answer this question, it is first necessary to make a terminological clarification and specify the scope of my research.

First, concerning the terminology, EU law does not provide for a definition of future and next generations, and it does not indicate any criteria that might be considered to extrapolate such a definition. If the notion of next generations seems to suppose – compared to one of the future generations – an element of temporal proximity with regard to the current generations, it is difficult to clearly distinguish them. Moreover, it is doubtful whether the notions of next/future generations refer only to the current young generations or to the unborn children of the future with whom the current generations will, at least partially coexist or, even more widely, all the unborn children of the future. In the absence of any explicit reference, I will refrain for the purpose of this chapter from making a distinction between next and future generations, and I will refer broadly to future generations as also comprising the next ones. From this perspective, future generations include both today's children and the unborn children of the future with no temporal delimitation. Indeed, these populations share the same common

3 Communication from the Commission to the European Parliament, the European Council, the Council, the European Economic and Social Committee and the Committee of the Regions, *'Fit for 55': delivering the EU's 2030 Climate Target on the way to climate neutrality*, COM (2021) 550 final, 1.

4 Communication from the Commission to the European Parliament, the European Council, the Council, the European Economic and Social Committee and the Committee of the Regions, *Europe's moment: Repair and Prepare for the Next Generation*, COM/2020/456 final, 10. For other examples, see also: Communication from the Commission to the European Parliament, the European Council, the Council, the European Economic and Social Committee and the Committee of the Regions, *Pathway to a Healthy Planet for All EU Action Plan: 'Towards Zero Pollution for Air, Water and Soil'*, COM (2021) 400 final, 2.

vulnerability of inheriting a planet plagued by climate change, health and environmental crisis.

Second, concerning the object of my research, there are two ways of looking at the relationship between EU law and future generations. On the one hand, one can focus on the current generations and examine their obligation to protect future generations. On the other hand, one can concentrate on future generations and analyse their right to be protected by current generations. Despite the increasing interest expressed by scholars for the possibility of assigning rights to future generations,[5] I will limit my analysis to the obligations undertaken under EU law by the current generations to protect future ones. This choice is explained by the conviction that – even before exploring the interest and feasibility of granting rights to future generations – EU law already provides useful legal tools to enhance both today and in a long-term perspective the obligations of protection borne by the current generations. Of course, this approach is based on the assumption that, in the context of the current climate crisis, it is not enough to share resources and responsibilities between the members of the current generations, but it is also essential to ensure that future generations will be granted the opportunity of living in good health and environmental conditions.

In this framework, the core claim of this chapter is that the protection of future generations under EU law should be ensured through a four-fold strategy based on the following principles: the principle of sustainable development, the precautionary principle, the principle of solidarity between generations, and the principle of non-regression. Although the principles of sustainable development, precaution and solidarity between generations are already provided for under EU law, a claim is made for the introduction of the principle of non-regression. Against this backdrop, by referring to the main legislative, jurisprudential and scholarship contributions, I will examine, for each of these principles, their relevance and the main challenges that should be overcome to ensure the protection of future generations

5 Edith Brown Weiss, *In Fairness to Future Generations: International Law, Common Patrimony and Intergenerational Equity* (OUP 1989); Edith Brown Weiss, 'Our Rights and Obligations to Future Generations for the Environment' (1990) 84(1) AJIL 198; Anthony D'Amato, 'Do We Owe a Duty to Future Generations to Preserve the Global Environment?' (1990) 84(1) AJIL 190; Lothar Gündling, 'Our Responsibility to Future Generations' (1990) 84(1) AJIL 207; Emilie Gaillard, *Générations futures et droit privé : vers un droit des générations futures* (LGDJ 2011); Jan Linehan, *Giving Future Generations a Voice. Normative Frameworks, Institutions and Practice* (Edward Elgar 2021).

under EU law. It is out of the scope of this chapter to engage in a theoretical analysis aimed at examining the legal status of these principles under EU law. While my research is anchored in the analysis of existing EU legal sources, it also adopts a forward-looking approach aimed at nourishing future reflection on the tools that could be mobilised under EU law to better protect future generations.

Concerning the structure, Section 2 focuses on the principle of sustainable development, Section 3 on the precautionary principle, Section 4 on the principle of solidarity between generations, Section 5 on the principle of non-regression. Section 6 concludes.

2. The Principle of Sustainable Development

As this section will highlight, sustainable development is a key tool ensuring the protection of current and future generations against the risks posed by climate change and environmental degradation.

The theoretical foundation of the concept of sustainable development was first clarified in 1987 by the Commission on Environment and Development chaired by G Brundtland.[6] In his report, sustainable development is defined as the development that meets the needs of the present generation without compromising the ability of future generations to meet their own needs. It expresses the idea that living resources should not be so depleted that they cannot be renewed in the medium or long term.[7] While the definition given by the Brundtland report laid the groundwork for the definition of sustainable development, it did not clarify its content precisely. More than thirty years after the adoption of the report, the contours of the concept are still vague, and its meaning ambiguous.[8] Sustainable development remains one of the most debated international political and legal concepts.[9] Despite its vagueness, the concept of sustainable development is generally considered to be three-fold. It brings together three concerns: environmental, social and economic. This is stated in Article 3(3) Treaty on European Union (TEU):

6 Report of the World Commission on Environment and Development: Our Common Future, transmitted to the General Assembly as an Annex to Document A/42/427, Chapter 2. The Commission was set up by the Resolution 38/161 of the UN Assembly.

7 Michel Prieur, *Droit de l'environnement* (Bruylant 2014) 101.

8 Ludvig Krämer, *EU Environmental Law* (8th edn, Sweet & Maxwell 2016) 9.

9 Maria Lee, *EU Environmental Law, Governance and Decision-Making* (Hart Publishing 2014) 57.

> The Union shall work for the sustainable development of Europe based on balanced economic growth and price stability, a highly competitive social market economy, aiming at full employment and social progress, and a high level of protection and improvement of the quality of the environment.

As the European Commission underlines, sustainable development raises 'the question of reconciling economic development, social cohesion and environmental protection'.[10] It calls on public authorities to adopt a pro-active and integrated approach that preserves the economic, social and environmental balance of the planet.[11] From this perspective, sustainable development is a key legal tool for the protection of future generations since it 'institutionalises the recognition of future generations' interests to inherit a clean and healthy environment'.[12] In this regard, Article 2 of Regulation n° 2493/2000 specifies that:

> sustainable development means the improvement of the standard of living and welfare of the relevant population within the limits of the capacity of the ecosystems by maintaining natural assets and their biological diversity for the benefit of the present and future generations.[13]

Despite its importance, the principle of sustainable development gives rise only to an obligation of means and not an obligation of results under EU law. This conclusion stems from the interpretation of the EU Treaties. First of all, Article 11 Treaty on the Functioning of the European Union (TFEU) states that environmental protection requirements must be integrated into the definition and implementation of other policies and activities, in particular with a view to *promoting* sustainable development. The term *promote* refers to the idea of advancing, of making progress. Furthermore, Article 3(3) TEU provides that the Union shall *work* for sustainable development. The term *work* aims at indicating that EU institutions and Member States should act in such a way as to move towards the achievement of an object-

---

10 Communication from the Commission to the Council and the European Parliament, *The 2005 Review of the EU Sustainable Development Strategy 2005: Initial Stocktaking and Future Orientations*, COM/2005/0037 final, 1.

11 ibid.

12 Abate Randall, *Climate Change and the Voiceless, Protecting Future Generations, Wildlife and Natural Environment* (CUP 2019) 55.

13 Regulation (EC) No 2493/2000 of the European Parliament and of the Council of 7 November 2000 on measures to promote the full integration of the environmental dimension in the development process of developing countries, OJ 2000 L 288, 1–5.

ive over time, i.e. sustainable development. Finally, according to Article 3(5) TEU, the Union shall *contribute* to sustainable development, where the word *contribute* refers to the idea of taking part in the achievement of a result. Despite their linguistic differences, the verb *promote, work* and *contribute* convey the message that, according to the Treaties, the EU institutions have an obligation to initiate a process of sustainable development, but they are not obliged to achieve a specific result.[14]

To implement the principle of sustainable development, since 2001 the EU has adopted a sustainable development strategy.[15] However, it was only in 2019, with the enactment by the Commission of the European Green Deal, that the European sustainability strategy was significantly expanded and strengthened[16].

On the one hand, the expansion of the sustainability strategy is linked to the objective of the Green Deal. According to the Commission, the Green Deal is the:

> new growth strategy that aims to transform the EU into a fair and prosperous society, with a modern, resource-efficient and competitive economy where there are no net emissions of greenhouse gases in 2050 and where economic growth is decoupled from resource use. It also aims to protect, conserve and enhance the EU's natural capital, and protect the health and well-being of citizens from environment-related risks and impacts.[17]

To meet these objectives, the Green Deal aims to overcome the existing sectoral approaches to adopt an integrated perspective that will allow incorporating sustainability into all EU policies and actions. This is why starting from 2020, the Commission adopted several texts that make sustainability a

14 Gyula Bàndi, 'Principles of EU Environmental Law Including (the Objective of) Sustainable Development' in Maria Peeters and Mariolina Eliantonio, *Research Handbook on EU Environmental Law* (Elgar 2020) 39.

15 Communication from the Commission, *A Sustainable Europe for a Better World: A European Union Strategy for Sustainable Development*, COM (2001) 264 final amended in 2009 by Communication from the Commission to the European Parliament, the Council, the European Economic and Social Committee and the Committee of the Regions, *Mainstreaming sustainable development into EU policies: 2009 Review of the European Union Strategy for Sustainable* Development, COM (2009) 400 final.

16 Communication from the Commission to the European Parliament, the European Council, the European Economic and Social Committee and the Committee of the Regions, *The European Green Deal* (n 2).

17 ibid., 2.

pivotal element of European law in the fields of, *inter alia,* climate[18], food[19], biodiversity[20], energy[21], pollution[22], and deforestation.[23]

On the other hand, the strengthening of the strategy is linked to the choice of the legal instruments mobilised to meet the objective of sustainable development. In this respect, even if the majority of the actions and plans presented by the Commission still take the form of non-binding legal acts, the new European Climate Law adopted in June 2021 (Regulation (EU) 2021/1119)[24] gives an idea of the different level of ambition displayed by the EU decision-makers concerning the achievement of sustainability. In this regard, the European Climate Law sets out a binding objective of net reduction in greenhouse gas emissions by at least 55 % compared to 1990 levels by 2030 and of climate neutrality in the Union by 2050 (Article 1). To do so, the relevant Union institutions and the Member States shall take the necessary measures at Union and national level, respectively, to enable the collective achievement of these climate objectives, taking into account the importance of promoting both fairness and solidarity among the Member States and cost-effectiveness in achieving this objective (Article 2). By 30 September 2023, and every five years thereafter, the Commission shall assess the collective progress made by all Member States as well as the consistency of Union measures on these climate objectives (Article 6).

---

18 Regulation (EU) 2021/1119 of the European Parliament and of the Council of 30 June 2021 establishing the framework for achieving climate neutrality and amending Regulations (EC) No 401/2009 and (EU) 2018/1999 ('European Climate Law') OJ 2021 L 243, 1–17.

19 Communication from the Commission to the European Parliament, the European Council, the European Economic and Social Committee and the Committee of the Regions, *A Farm to Table Strategy for a Fair, Healthy and Environmentally Sound Food System*, COM (2020) 381 final.

20 Communication from the Commission to the European Parliament, the European Council, the European Economic and Social Committee and the Committee of the Regions, *EU Biodiversity Strategy 2030: Bringing nature into our lives*, COM (2020) 380 final.

21 European Commission, *Strategy for an integrated energy system*, July 8, 2020.

22 Communication from the Commission to the European Parliament, the European Council, the Council, the European Economic and Social Committee and the Committee of the Regions, *Pathway to a Healthy Planet for All EU Action Plan: 'Towards Zero Pollution for Air, Water and Soil'* (n 4).

23 European Commission, Proposal for a regulation of the European parliament and of the Council on the making available on the union market as well as export from the union of certain commodities and products associated with deforestation and forest degradation and repealing Regulation (EU) No 995/2010, COM/2021/706 final.

24 European Climate Law.

If the adoption of the Green Deal represents an important step forward for ensuring the protection of current and future generations against the risks posed by climate change and environmental degradation, a lot still remains to be done.

First, the strategies, actions and legislative proposals of the Commission shall go through the EU legislative procedure and the subsequent negotiation with the other EU institutions and the Member States.

Second, to be effective, the shift towards sustainability will require effective integration between economic, environmental and social laws and policies. This will not be easy since, these disciplines currently have very different scopes and functions. In addition, as underlined by the Commission, the transition shall be just, fair and inclusive. It must:

> put people first, and pay attention to the regions, industries and workers who will face the greatest challenges. Since it will bring substantial change, active public participation and confidence in the transition is paramount if policies are to work and be accepted. A new pact is needed to bring together citizens in all their diversity, with national, regional, local authorities, civil society and industry working closely with the EU's institutions and consultative bodies.[25]

Third, the scale of change needed to achieve the Green Deal's objective will require time to be implemented under EU law. Nevertheless, the time required to complete the transition towards sustainability might not be aligned with the urgency to act resulting from the fast depletion of climate and environmental conditions. According to the latest report by the European Environmental Agency in 2021, despite the efforts of Member States, biodiversity in the EU continues to decline and is facing significant deterioration due to overexploitation of land and unsustainable land management, as well as changes in the water regime, air quality, soil pollution and climate change.[26] Similarly, natural resources (water, oceans, forests) are increasingly threatened by human activities that jeopardise the balance of natural ecosystems. In addition, CO_2 emissions continued to rise in both 2018 and 2019 and only decreased in 2020 because of the restrictive

25 European Green Deal (n 2) 2.

26 European Environmental Agency, 'State of Nature in the EU – 2021' <https://perma.cc/BNC2-DNJH>.

measures adopted by the Member States in the context of the Covid-19 crisis.[27]

3. The Precautionary Principle

Provided for by Article 191 para. 2TFUE, the precautionary principle is a founding principle of the European environmental policy.[28] Moreover, since the *National Farmers' Union and the United Kingdom vs Commission* judgments of 5 May 1998,[29] both the Court of Justice (CJ) and the General Court (GC) have also repeatedly applied the precautionary principle in the field of public health.[30]

Although the precautionary principle directly aims to protect current generations by ensuring that decision-makers will pursue a high level of environmental and public health protection, it also takes into account, at least indirectly, future generations.

Indeed, precaution can be defined as a principle of anticipated action, which – in a context of risk and uncertainty for the environment and public health – requires the competent authorities (EU institutions and the Member States) to anticipate the traditional time for the adoption of a measure to protect the environment and public health.[31] This means that decision-makers shall not wait until the risk is certain, from a scientific point of view, but shall act before, when the risk is still uncertain.

When decision-makers act based on the precautionary principle, they do not know if and when the uncertain risk at stake may materialise. Risks affecting the environment and public health (eg chemicals, pesticides, endocrine disruptors, air pollution etc) do not occur immediately but usually have a long-time horizon and might acquire an intergenerational

---

27 'Global Carbon Project: Coronavirus Causes 'Record Fall' in Fossil-fuel Emissions in 2020' (Carbon Brief, 11 December 2020) <https://perma.cc/2URD-BMBT>.

28 For a detailed analysis of the precautionary principle under EU law, see Alessandra Donati, *Le principe de précaution en droit de l'Union européenne* (Bruylant 2021).

29 C-157/96, *National Farmers' Union*, CJEU, 5 May 1998, EU:C:1998:191; C-180/96 *United Kingdom/Commission*, CJEU, 5 May 1998, EU:C:1998:192.

30 C-132/03 *Codacons and Federconsumatori*, CJEU, 26 May 2005, EU:C:2005:310; C-504/04 *Agrarproduktion Staebelow*, CJEU, 12 January 2006, EU:C:2006:30; T-177/02 *Malagutti-Vezinhet*, GC 10 March 2004, EU:T:2004:72; T-539/10 *Acino vs Commission*, GC 7 March 2010, EU:T:2013:110.

31 Alessandra Donati, 'The Precautionary Principle under European Union Law' (2021) 49 Hitotsubashi Journal of Law and Politics 44.

dimension.[32] This means that, should they materialise, their negative consequences might be suffered by the ongoing and future generations. The long-term perspective of the uncertain risks explains the long-term dimension of the precautionary principle. Precaution is future-oriented.[33] It is a foresight principle that requests decision-makers to anticipate, as far as is possible, their action to ensure a high level of protection of the environment and public health. Therefore, by preventing the occurrence of major risks for the environment and public health that might jeopardise the objective of a high level of protection, the precautionary principle might be a useful tool to protect, at least indirectly, future generations. Indeed, the latter would be able to enjoy better environmental and health conditions that would not have been undermined by the occurrence of major risks.

However, to be effective towards current and future generations, the precautionary principle should be implemented by the decision-makers when the conditions for its application are met. Nonetheless, the precautionary principle was not applied in several sensitive cases concerning the environment or public health.[34] One example concerning the authorisation of glyphosate will clarify this issue. This example is not exhaustive but is particularly relevant to show the lack of implementation of the precautionary principle and understand the rationale behind this failure.

Glyphosate is an active substance used in the production of a herbicide. The risk of damage associated with the use of pesticides has a long-time horizon and might affect current and future generations. Developed by Monsanto in the 1970s under the brand name Roundup, glyphosate is now produced and sold under many other brand names. It is used in particular

32 Janelle Lamoreaux, 'Passing Down Pollution: (Inter)generational Toxicology and (Epi)genetic Environmental Health' (2021) 35(4) Med Anthropol 529; Jonathan Colmer and John Voorheis, 'The Grandkids Aren't Alright: the Intergenerational Effects of Prenatal Pollution Exposure' (2021) 1733 Discussion Paper – Centre For Economic Performance 1 <https://perma.cc/9WWG-N53D>.

33 Alexandre Kiss, 'L'irréversibilité et le droit des générations futures' (1998) Revue juridique de l'Environnement 49, 51; Anne Guégan, 'L'apport du principe de précaution au droit de la responsabilité civile' (2000) 2 Revue juridique de l'Environnement 147, 167.

34 For an analysis of the cases (including Covid-19, 5G and endocrine disruptors) where the precautionary principle was not applied by EU institutions, see: Alessandra Donati, 'Le principe de précaution : un outil de gestion des crises en droit de l'Union européenne?' (2020) 10 Journal de droit européen 430; Alessandra Donati, 'Droit européen et perturbateurs endocriniens: il est où le principe de précaution' (*blogdroiteuropéen*, 27 November 2018) <https://perma.cc/EL4T-V7EX>.

to fight against weeds. Glyphosate is at the centre of a major scientific controversy over its carcinogenic effect to humans. On the one hand, the International Agency for Research on Cancer (IARC) classified it as a probable human carcinogen in 2015;[35] on the other hand, the European Food Safety Agency (EFSA) and the European Chemicals Agency (ECHA) rejected the IARC's conclusions by downplaying the danger of glyphosate to humans.[36] In addition, the *Monsanto Papers*, internal Monsanto documents declassified by the US courts in 2017, appear to show that, as early as 1999, Monsanto was concerned about the carcinogenic effects of glyphosate and tried to obstruct the work of the IARC and other regulatory agencies in order to hide the scientific data proving the dangerous nature of this product for humans.[37] In Europe, the rules for pesticides are set forth in Regulation n° 1107/2009.[38] Under this regulation, active substances, including glyphosate, are subject to authorisation at the European level. After the expiry of the marketing authorisation for glyphosate and following an intense public debate, in December 2017, the European Commission granted its renewal for 5 years (Implementing Regulation n° 2017/2324).[39] The precautionary principle, which is enshrined in the TFEU and provided for in Regulation n° 1107/2009, is nevertheless ignored by the Implementing Regulation n° 2017/2324 renewing the approval of glyphosate, as the Commission makes no reference to this principle or to the scientific controversies surrounding it. However, all the conditions for its application were met: glyphosate presents a risk to public health that might materialise in

35 International Agency for Research on Cancer (IARC), 'IARC Monographs Volume 112: Evaluation of Five Organophosphate Insecticides and Herbicides' <https://perma.cc/7A99-Z7WV>.

36 European Food Safety Authority (EFSA), 'EFSA Statement regarding the EU Assessment of Glyphosate and the so Called 'Monsanto Papers' <https://perma.cc/ES3A-DKWJ>.

37 Stéphane Horel et Stéphane Foucart, '"Monsanto papers", désinformation organisée autour du glyphosate' *Le Monde* (Paris, 4 October 2017) <https://www.lemonde.fr/planete/article/2017/10/04/monsanto-papers-desinformation-organisee-autour-du-glyphosate_5195771_3244.html> accessed 24 July 2023.

38 Regulation (EC) No 1107/2009 of the European Parliament and of the Council of 21 October 2009 concerning the placing of plant protection products on the market and repealing Council Directives 79/117/EEC and 91/414/EEC, OJ 2009 L 309, 1.

39 Commission Implementing Regulation (EU) No 2017/2324 of 12 December 2017 renewing the approval of the active substance glyphosate in accordance with Regulation (EC) No 1107/2009 of the European Parliament and of the Council concerning the placing of plant protection products on the market and amending the Annex to Commission Implementing Regulation (EU) No 540/2011 OJ 2017 L 333, 10–16.

a short, long or even intergenerational time-period, and this risk is the subject of divergent scientific studies. Thus, in the presence of risk and scientific uncertainty and to ensure a high level of public health protection to the benefit of the ongoing and the current generations, the precautionary principle should have been applied.

Several attempts to have the Commission's decision overturned in the light of the precautionary principle have been made before the CJEU, but so far, they have not had the desired result.[40] Glyphosate remains in circulation under EU law at least until December 2023, when its authorisation expires, and the authorities will again be called upon to decide on the release of this herbicide. It remains to be seen whether the precautionary principle will be applied in a timely manner by policymakers this time.

How can we explain the failure by the EU decision-makers to apply the precautionary principle in the case of glyphosate? Despite the complexity of the case at stake – where legal, political, scientific and ethical considerations are deeply intertwined – and the difficulty to provide a straightforward answer, it is worth considering that when implementing the precautionary principle, decision-makers enjoy a broad discretionary power that is limited by their duty to comply with the obligation to take into account the results of the scientific assessment executed by scientific experts before the adoption of the precautionary measure and the other costs and benefits of the action.[41] Authorities are, therefore, substantially free to decide on the implementation of the precautionary principle, provided that they demonstrate that they have complied with the procedural requirements for its application.[42]

While the existence of such a discretionary power can be explained by the need to modulate the action to be taken on the basis of the very specific and variable characteristics of the risk and uncertainty involved, it could also justify the decision-makers' choice not to adopt a precautionary measure in a given situation. In that case, it will be up to the CJEU to verify whether the decision of the authorities is grounded since they have respected the procedural content of the precautionary principle. However, the intensity of the control exercised by the Court is limited. The CJEU

---

40 Alessandra Donati, 'The Glyphosate Saga – A Further but not a Final Step – the CJEU Confirms the Validity of the Regulation on Plant Protection Products in Light of the Precautionary Principle' (2020) 11(1) European Journal of Risk Regulation 148.

41 Donati (n 28) 191.

42 ibid.

refuses to substitute its assessment of the facts for that of the institutions and Member States to whom the Treaty has entrusted this task and limits the intensity of its review.[43] The Court considers that it is not required to resolve complex issues, which are a matter for the exercise of discretion by decision-makers.[44] Indeed, any further control could imply a dangerous shift in the boundary between the judge and the administrator.[45] In this sense, if it is up to the decision-makers to assess the scientific basis and the political importance of the risk in question, the judge must limit himself to verifying that the decision-makers have correctly used their discretionary power without carrying out a new assessment of the factual elements of the case. Therefore, the control exercised by the CJEU over the precautionary measures is limited to the verification of the existence of a manifest error of assessment or a misuse of powers by the political decision-makers, but does not aim at substituting the judge's assessment to that of the EU institutions.

To overcome the constraints linked to the application – and often as in the case of glyphosate, the failure to apply the precautionary principle – I propose two avenues of reflection.

First, it is through the extension of the procedural content of the precautionary principle that it could be possible to bind the discretionary power of the authorities by intensifying, at the same time, the standard of control exercised by the CJEU. This has been the trend in the case-law of the CJEU in recent years. A discreet development can be seen in the case-law concerning the precautionary principle.[46] In principle, the Court always states that it limits the standard of its review to the assessment of a manifest error of assessment. However, *de facto,* the Court sometimes carries out a reinforced judicial review. The strengthening of judicial review is reflected in the procedural deepening of the intensity of the review. Thus, by verifying that the authorities have complied with the procedural obligations governing the precautionary principle, the Court can examine whether the factual and legal elements on which the exercise of the discretionary power

---

43 T-105/96 *Pharos SA vs Commission*, GC, 17 February 1998, EU:T:1998:35, 69.

44 C-341/95, *Safety High Tech*, CJEU, 14 July 1998, EU:C:1998:353, 54.

45 Christine Noiville, 'Du juge guide au juge arbitre? Le rôle du juge face à l'expertise scientifique dans le contentieux de la précaution' in Eve Truilhé-Marengo (ed), *La relation juge-expert dans les contentieux sanitaires et environnementaux* (La Documentation française 2011) 82.

46 Alessandra Donati, 'Vers un renforcement du contrôle juridictionnel à la Cour de justice de l'Union européenne? L'exemple du contentieux du principe de précaution' (2020) 56(2–3) Cahiers de droit européen 629.

depends are present, and thus whether the precautionary principle has been correctly applied. For the Court, compliance with procedural obligations constitutes the primary *raison d'être* of the precautionary principle.[47]

On the basis of this jurisprudential development, it would be important for the European legislator to intervene in order to clarify the procedural content of the precautionary principle. While respecting the margin of appreciation that decision-makers enjoy in exercising their political power of choice in situations of risk and uncertainty, it would be important to better clarify the scope of the procedural obligations that mark the implementation of the precautionary principle. The procedure allows for the collection and organisation of the information needed to manage uncertain risks, and structures the way decisions are made. From this perspective, extended procedural obligations could be seen as a lever to strengthen the coherence, completeness and clarity of decisions based on the precautionary principle. Framed by procedural guidelines, the decision-making process leading to the adoption of a precautionary measure would thus become more legible since it would underpin a more explicit and analytical approach. The decision-making process would also be easier for the judge to review.

Second, the application of the precautionary principle crucially depends on the individual decision taken by the authorities in charge of risk prevention. The risks to be prevented do have an objective component (linked to the mathematical probability of occurrence of a risk) and a subjective component (which depends on the appreciation of the risk in question in each social, geographical, and economic context). The uncertainty that characterises these risks is a consequence of the lack of scientific information as perceived by the experts at the time the decision on the risk is taken. This means that recourse to the precautionary principle *ultimately* depends on the assessment by decision-makers and experts (commissioned by the authorities) of the extent and seriousness of the risk and uncertainty involved, and their balance with the other interests at stake. The tensions that arise during the implementation of the precautionary principle thus reflect what constitutes the major difficulty of anticipation, namely the definition of the acceptable and unacceptable risk. Because acceptability includes, in addition to its objective and rational elements, a strong psycho-

47 T-13/99, *Pfizer Animal Health vs Council*, GC, 11 September 2002, EU:T:2002:209,170–172.

logical content, its mechanical and rational delimitation is impossible[48]. However, the European model of decision-making in a context of risk and uncertainty is structured on the basis of the idea that decision-makers are rational agents who, in each case, make rational decisions that are a function of the level of risk established. For each decision, they, therefore, try to optimise the chosen level of protection by applying the precautionary principle if necessary.

The application of this principle is thus the consequence of a rational process organised around the static (and very theoretical) distinction between scientific risk assessment and political risk management. However, when they act to prevent the realisation of risk, the rational dimension of the decision is offset by the biases to which decision-makers are subject (inertia, optimism, loss aversion, etc), and their relevant trade-off. A more targeted and precise understanding of how these decisions are made could be a useful complement to try to strengthen the effectiveness of the implementation of the precautionary principle. For this, behavioural sciences could prove useful in an attempt to better understand and thus better regulate the adoption of a precautionary measure by the authorities. A large body of empirical research reveals that the assumption of strict rationality – that individuals are rational agents making a rational decision in every circumstance – is incorrect.[49] Individuals have limited cognitive resources and are affected by biases.[50] Therefore, while the rationality assumption can sometimes provide a realistic approximation, a more accurate view of human behaviour is a condition for the effectiveness of the law.[51] Behavioural analysis of law meets this need by providing an intermediate empirical basis between the theoretical abstractions of the rational actor model and the implicit intuitive and unstructured view of human behaviour as proposed by traditional legal research. Therefore, to foster a better application of the precautionary principle, in addition to traditional legal analysis, it would

48 Christine Noiville, 'La lente maturation du principe de précaution' (2007) 22 Recueil Dalloz 1514, 1515.

49 These studies have been popularised in books such as: Daniel Kahnmeman, *Thinking, Fast and Slow* (Farrar, Straus and Giroux 2011); Richard Thaler, *Misbehaving: How Economics Became Behavioral* (Norton 2015); Richard Thaler and Cass Sunstain, *Nudge: Improving Decisions About Health, Wealth, and Happiness* (Yale University Press 2008).

50 Avishalom Tor, 'The Fable of Entry: Bounded Rationality, Market Discipline, and Legal Policy' (2002) 101(2) Michigan Law Review 482.

51 Christine Jolls, Cass Sunstain and Richard Thaler, 'A Behavioral Approach to Law and Economics' (1998) 50 Stanford Law Review 1471, 1474–1475.

be important to learn from the behavioural sciences in order to understand better the logic, biases and limitations of the behaviour of authorities called upon to prevent the occurrence of a risk and to incorporate this knowledge into legal regulation.

4. The Principle of Solidarity Between Generations

In his 2016 speech on the State of the Union, the former president of the European Commission, Jean-Claude Juncker, affirmed that 'solidarity is the glue that keeps our Union together'.[52] Provided for by the EU Treaties in more than fifteen places (ranging from the energy policy to the policies on asylum, immigration and refugees, as well as the humanitarian and civil protection policies)[53], solidarity was identified very early by the CJEU as a general principle of EU law.[54] Moreover, the EU Charter of Fundamental rights which has the same value as the Treaties, considers that solidarity is an indivisible and universal founding value of the EU together with human dignity, freedom and equality.

Despite its multiple references, no specific definition of the principle of solidarity is provided for by the EU legislator or the CJEU.[55] Therefore, solidarity remains a vague and multifaceted principle whose content varies significantly depending on the specific EU policy that implements it. However, the different applications and definitions of the principle of solidarity

52 Jean-Claude Juncker, 'State of the Union 2016' <https://commission.europa.eu/strategy-and-policy/strategic-planning/state-union-addresses/state-union-speeches/state-union-2016_en> accessed 24 July 2023.

53 TEU Articles 2, 3(3), 5, 21, 24(2), 24(3), 31(1), 32. TFEU: Articles 78(1), 78(3), 80, 107(2)(b), 107(3)(a), 107(3)(b), 122(1), 194(1), 222.

54 C-63/90 and C-67/90, *Portuguese Republic and Kingdom of Spain vs Council of the European Communities*, CJEU, 13 October 1992; C-335/90 *Republic of Poland vs European Commission*, CJEU, 26 June 2012. On the principle of solidarity, see: Jenö Czuczai, 'The principle of solidarity in the EU legal order – some practical examples after Lisbon' in Jenö Czuczai and Frederik Naert, *The EU as a global actor – bridging legal theory and practice. Liber Amicorum in honour of Ricardo Gosalbo Bono* (Brill 2017); Peter Hipold, 'Understanding solidarity within the EU: an analysis of the islands of solidarity with particular regard to Monetary Union' (2015) 34 Yearbook of European Law 257; Helle Krunke, Hanne Petersen and Ian Manners, *Transnational Solidarity. Concept, Challenges and Opportunities* (CUP 2020).

55 Pieter Van Cleynenbreugel, 'Typologies of Solidarity in EU Law: a Non-shifting Landscape in the Wake of Economic Crises' in Andrea Biondi, Egle Dagilyte and Esin Küçük, *Solidarity in EU Law. A Legal Principle in the Making* (Elgar 2018) 13.

converge in the idea that solidarity triggers a duty of sharing resources with others in a spirit of mutual support.[56] In this sense, solidarity is anchored in the idea of dividing the advantages and burdens of an action equally and justly among the members of a community.[57]

A specific dimension of the principle of solidarity is the principle of solidarity between generations set forth by Article 3(3) TUE, according to which the Union 'shall combat social exclusion and discrimination, and shall promote social justice and protection, equality between women and men, solidarity between generations and protection of the rights of the child.' Besides its application concerning the relationship between members of the same generation (intra-generational solidarity), the principle of solidarity between generations has an intergenerational dimension. In this regard, it entails obligations of solidarity between the younger and the older generations of those living, including child-parent relationships, social participation of elderly people and children in communities, affordability of pensions and care of the elderly.[58]

Could it be possible to extend the notion of inter-generational solidarity to cover the relationship between the current generations and the future ones, by meaning here those that are not yet born? The question is important because, in the framework of the ongoing climate crisis and according to the objective of sustainability enshrined in the European treaties and in the European Green Deal, the assumption is made that it is not enough to share resources and responsibilities between the young and the older generations, but it is also essential to ensure that future generations will be granted the opportunity of living in good health and environmental conditions. In this view, humanity as a whole should form an intergenerational community in which all members would respect and care for each other, achieving the common goal of the survival of humankind.[59] Even if the answer to this question is still open, some references to the notion

---

56 Chris Hilson, 'EU Environmental Solidarity and the Ecological Consumer: Towards a Republican Citizenship' in Malcolm Ross and Yuri Borgmann-Prebil (eds), *Promoting Solidarity in the European Union* (OUP 2010) 136.

57 Cleynenbreugel (n 55) 17.

58 Decision No 940/2011/EU of the European Parliament and of the Council of 14 September 2011 on the European Year for Active Aging and Solidarity between Generations (2012), OJ 2011 L 246, 5; European Commission, *Renewed Social Agenda: Opportunities, Access and Solidarity in 21st Century Europe*, COM 412 (2008) 6.

59 United Nations, *General Assembly, Intergenerational solidarity and the needs of future generations. Report of the Secretary-General*, 15 August 2013, A/68/322, 3.

of solidarity towards future generations can already be found under EU law. For example, in the Communication, *Strategic Objectives 2005 – 2009, Europe 2010: A Partnership for European Renewal Prosperity, Solidarity and Security,*[60] the Commission states that 'solidarity needs a concrete expression, both at present and with future generations.' Furthermore, in the framework of the EU Green Deal, in the Communication '*Fit for 55: delivering the EU's 2030 Climate Target on the way to climate neutrality*', the Commission underlines that 'solidarity is a defining principle of the European Green Deal between generations, Member States, regions, rural and urban areas, and different parts of society', and that tackling the climate crisis is 'a matter of intergenerational and international solidarity'.[61]

In addition to these references, the interpretation of Article 222 TFEU might also play in favour of the extension of the principle of solidarity to include solidarity towards future generations. Article 222 TFEU provides that the Union and its Member States shall act jointly in a spirit of solidarity if a Member State is the object of a terrorist attack or the victim of a natural or man-made disaster. In this case, at the request of the Member State facing such an emergency, the other Member States shall assist it. Climate change represents a man-made disaster that might fall within the scope of application of Article 222 TFEU. If this is the case, why should the solidarity be limited to the current generations of the affected Member State? Would it not be possible to broaden it to include also the future generations of such Member State that will suffer the most from the negative consequences of climate change? Two further arguments might support this interpretation.

On the one hand, Article 37 of the EU Charter of Fundamental Rights – included in the chapter 'Solidarity' – states that 'a high level of environmental protection and the improvement of the quality of the environment must be integrated into the policies of the Union and ensured in accordance with the principle of sustainable development'. This means that, under the Charter of Fundamental Rights, the achievement of a high level of environmental protection in all EU policies is considered to be an expression

60 Communication from the Commission, *Strategic Objectives 2005–2009, Europe 2010: A Partnership for European Renewal Prosperity, Solidarity and Security*, COM (2005) 12 final, 8–9.

61 Communication from the Commission to the European Parliament, the European Council, the Council, the European Economic and Social Committee and the Committee of the Regions, 'Fit for 55': delivering the EU's 2030 Climate Target on the way to climate neutrality, *prec*, 1.

of solidarity. Yet, the pursuit of a high level of environmental protection should not be limited to the current generation but should also include future generations that are seriously threatened by the absence of a long-term protective approach in the environmental regulations adopted today. From this perspective, one might argue that the extension of the principle of solidarity to future generations would be a way of operationalising the objective of achieving a high level of environmental protection in the long-term.

On the other hand, beyond the scope of Article 222 and even before its adoption with the Treaty of Lisbon in 2007, solidarity was conceived as a crisis-management tool. It is, under situations of crisis, that such a principle evolved to embrace new applications that would respond better to the needs of the case at stake. For example, in the late 1970s and early 1980s, Europe faced a huge production crisis in the coal and steel industries. In this situation, the CJEU pushed forward the existing applications of the principle of solidarity by ruling that when seeking to spread the inevitable sacrifices entailed by the general crisis in the steel industry in an equitable manner among all undertakings in the community, a special system of production quotas could be established.[62] In a similar vein, solidarity was largely invoked in the framework of the financial crisis of 2008, the banking crisis in 2012, the migration crisis in 2015[63], and since 2019, the Covid-19 crisis.[64] In all these cases, the need to overcome the ongoing crisis, pushed the EU legislator and the CJEU to reflect on new applications of the principle of solidarity. In light of these considerations, could the ongoing climate crisis not be the occasion to push the application of the solidarity principle to new horizons by making it a key principle for the protection of future generations?

Although applying the principle of solidarity towards future generations would represent an important step further in the evolution of this principle, it would also present some challenges that would need to be addressed. The main one concerns the source of solidarity. Traditionally, solidarity has been interpreted as being linked, both from the spatial and temporal

62 C-276/80 *Ferriera Padana SpA vs Commission of the European Communities*, CJEU, 6 February 1982, EU:C:1982:57.

63 For an overview of the use of solidarity in the financial, banking and migration crisis see: Biondi, Dagilyte and Esin Küçük (n 55).

64 Kate Shaw and Pavel Repyeuski, 'Council Recommendation for Promoting Cooperation and Solidarity Amongst the Member States: A Far Enough Step?' (2021) 6(1) *European Papers* 189 <https://perma.cc/WG8Q-AQ8R>.

point of view, to the living generations of a nation-state. According to Habermas, solidarity emerged in the context of nation-state building and represented a cooperative effort from a shared political perspective to redeem relationships of justice that have been lost in the process of modern nation state-building.[65] From this perspective, the concept of solidarity expresses a state of mind in which a belief of 'sharedness' is translated into daily governance between the living members of a political community.[66] Against this backdrop, national identification – which entails a feeling of common interests, sameness or altruism between the living members of a community – is considered to be the main source of solidarity. National identification is also very often connected to the idea of reciprocity: we show solidarity in a way that also benefits the contributor.[67] The idea of reciprocity as a tenant of solidarity can be better explained with an example taken from the EU provisions governing the economic, social and territorial cohesion between the Member States. The driving motivation for economically strong Member States to act in solidarity is their conviction that market integration, which does not allow for wide disparities in prosperity levels among the Members States, will generate future returns. Stronger economies support the weaker economies to enable them to integrate into the common market, which in turn benefits the strong economies in many ways.[68]

Should the principle of solidarity be extended to future generations, the source of solidarity could not be national identification between the living members of a specific community, and rely on the idea of reciprocity. On the one hand, it would be necessary to substitute the narrow concept of national identification with a broader one of universal identification. Accordingly, the foundation for solidarity could be defined as a matter of safeguarding our ecosystems by taking care not to leave irreversible environmental damage to future generations.[69] On the other hand, solidarity should be detached from the idea of justice as reciprocity as we can neither expect anything from future generations nor know what their preferences

---

65 Jürgen Habermas, 'Democracy, Solidarity and the European Crisis (Lecture delivered at KU Leuven on 26 April 2013)' <https://perma.cc/BZ78-6RDN>.

66 ibid., 14.

67 Esin Küçük, 'Solidarity in EU Law: an Elusive Political Statement or a Legal Principle with Substance' in Biondi, Dagilyte and Küçük (n 55) 47.

68 ibid.

69 Marianne Takle, 'Common Concern for the Global Ecological Commons: Solidarity with Future Generations' (2021) 35(3) International Relations 403, 408.

will be[70]. In this regard, as underlined by Habermas, detached from its nation-state commitments, solidarity should reflect a fundamental value in accordance with which the advantages and burdens of any initiative are to be shared equally and justly among the affected members.[71] In this regard, future generations might be considered as members of a universal ecological community that should be taken into consideration while sharing the advantages and burdens of any decision taken today that might jeopardise the right to live on a healthy planet tomorrow.

5. The Principle of Non-regression

Is environmental law like a Penelope tapestry where what is done today is undone the next day?[72] Despite the remarkable development of EU environmental law that, in recent years, has been significantly expanded to achieve a higher level of protection, its accomplishments are not immutable. Therefore, diverging economic interests, a major health crisis like Covid-19, or a different political willingness might call environmental law into question by reducing the already set level of protection.[73] Of course, the regression in environmental protection may also be the result of the interpretation of EU law provided by the CJEU or the application ensured by the EU administration. On the one hand, the Court, by applying the principle of sustainable development, needs to reconcile environmental interests with economic and social ones. In this case, it may arbitrate in favour of non-environmental interests and thus undermine the progress of environmental law. On the other hand, by not applying the existing environmental regulations or not triggering the sanctions set forth by the law, the administration may contribute to the deterioration of the environment and thus to a regression in environmental protection. Whether the regression of environmental law comes from the law, the CJEU or the administration, the question arises as to whether it is inevitable or whether

70 ibid., 414.

71 Cleynenbreugel (n 55) 17.

72 François Ost, *La nature hors la loi – l'écologie à l'épreuve du droit* (Éditions La Découverte 2003) 115.

73 Michel Prieur, 'Le nouveau principe de non régression en droit de l'environnement' in Michel Prieur and Gonzalo Sozzo, *La non régression en droit de l'environnement* (Bruylant 2012) 5.

it may come up against some legal obstacles guaranteeing the non-regression.[74]

The principle of environmental non-regression answers to the need of protecting the acquired level of environmental protection. It translates the idea that the latter should not be reduced by the adoption of a subsequent act and that the highest level of environmental protection shall always be pursued. From this perspective, the principle of non-regression aims to ensure that the successive environmental law shall not undermine the high level of protection provided by the preceding one.[75] The goal of this principle is not to freeze acquired situations. The authority maintains its freedom to amend legislation, but only as long as it remains as protective as the previous one.[76] At first sight, the claim to legislate environmental law in perpetuity might seem pretentious. It also contradicts Thomas Paine's[77] thought that no country or parliament can bind posterity until the end of time and the content of Article 28 of the Declaration of the Rights of Men and Citizens of 24 June 1793 that considers that one generation cannot subject future generations to its own laws. Although these ideas can be explained by the willingness to protect the autonomy and self-determination of future generations, they reach their limits in the framework of the ongoing climate crisis. In this context, it is no longer a question of avoiding for future generations the burden of the regulations adopted by the previous ones, but on the contrary, of taking measures to protect the interest of future generations of inheriting a planet where its environmental conditions would be protected. The regression of environmental law decided today would, indeed, breach the interests of future generations since it would result in imposing a degraded environment on them. In this regard, by crystallising the achieved high level of environmental protection and guaranteeing its preservation over time, the principle of non-regression is a key tool for the protection of future generations.

At the international level, the principle of non-regression is still in the development phase, and it appears indirectly in some legal instruments. For example, the outcome document 'The future we want' adopted in 2012

74 ibid., 6.
75 Nathalie Hervé-Fournerau, 'Le principe de non régression environnementale en droit de l'Union européenne : entre idéalité et réalité normative' in Prieur and Sozzo (n 73) 199.
76 Christophe Krolik, 'Contribution à une méthodologie du principe de non-régression' in Prieur and Sozzo (n 73) 142.
77 Thomas Paine, *The Rights of Men* (London, 1791).

by the Rio+20 United Nations Conference on Sustainable Development, states that: 'it is critical that we *do not backtrack* from our commitment to the outcome of the United Nations Conference on Environment and Development.'[78] Moreover, the 2015 Paris Agreement provides under Article 4, paragraph 3, that each nationally determined contribution setting for national climate obligations will represent a *progression* beyond the Party's current nationally determined contribution and reflect its highest possible ambition.[79] In clearer terms, the project for a Pact for the Protection of Human Rights and the Environment[80] indicates that everyone has the right to a high level of protection of the state of the environment and to the *non-regression* of the levels of protection already achieved (Article 2).

Hardly envisaged in international law, the principle of non-regression is recognized, with some variations, by certain Member States in their national law. For instance, in France, the principle of non-regression was introduced in 2016. According to Article 2 of the law on biodiversity[81], the environmental code is completed with a principle of non-regression, according to which the protection of the environment can only be subject to constant improvement based on the current scientific and technical knowledge. In Belgium, the principle of non-regression is not enshrined in a legislative text and does not have an absolute value, but the Constitutional Court considers that Article 23 of the Constitution – which provides the right to a healthy environment – implies a non-regression obligation that prevents the competent legislator from significantly reducing the level of

78 United Nations, *The Future We Want – Outcome document of the United Nations Conference on Sustainable Development* (United Nations 2012) <https://perma.cc/64X3-AG5M>.

79 Conference of the Parties, *Paris Agreement,* Dec. 12, 2015 U.N. Doc. FCCC/CP/2015/L.9/Rev/1 (Dec. 12, 2015).

80 International Centre of Comparative Environmental Law, *Projet de Pacte international relatif au droit des êtres humains à l'environnement* <https://cidce.org/wp-content/uploads/2017/01/Projet-de-Pacte-international-relatif-au-droit-des-e%CC%82tres-humains-a%CC%80-l%E2%80%99environnement_16.II_.2017_FR.pdf> accessed 8 March 2022.

81 Law of 8 August 2016 for the recovery of biodiversity, nature and landscapes, n° 2016–1087.

protection afforded by the applicable legislation in the absence of general interest.[82]

Under EU law, the principle of environmental non-regression has not received formal consecration. Yet, the idea of non-regression of the general level of protection is already present in European social law. Implicitly, the TFEU recognises it in paragraph 3 of the preamble by referring to the objective of the *constant improvement* of the living and working conditions of Europeans. In addition, the principle of non-regression of the acquired level of protection is expressly recognised in Directive 1999/70/CE concerning the framework agreement on fixed-term work and Directive 2000/78 for equal treatment in employment and occupation.[83] In both cases, the Directives provide that their implementation shall under no circumstances constitute grounds for a reduction in the level of protection afforded at the EU level. In addition, the CJEU has recognised the principle of non-regression of the level of protection in some cases concerning the protection afforded to workers.[84] Eventually, the EU Parliament in its resolution of 29 September 2011 called for 'the recognition of the principle of non-regression in the context of environmental protection as well as fundamental rights.'[85]

The adoption under EU law of the principle of environmental non-regression would not only reflect the advancements made under EU social law but also complete the toolbox at the disposal of the EU institutions to ensure the protection of the environment in addition to the principles of sustainable development, precaution and solidarity. Not only would the EU legislator be able to work for a sustainable future by anticipating the risk at stake and promoting solidarity towards future generations, but it could also guarantee that the high level of protection pursued would not

---

82 Belgium Constitutional Court, 27 Janvier 2011, n° 8/2011. In this sense, see also Paul-Louis Suetens, 'Le droit à la protection d'un environnement sain (Article 23 de la Constitution belge)' in *Les hommes et l'environnement, en hommage à Alexandre Kiss* (Frison Roche 1998) 496.

83 Council Directive 1999/70/EC of 28 June 1999 concerning the framework agreement on fixed-term work concluded by ETUC, UNICE and CEEP OJ 1999 L 175, 43–48, Article 8(3); Council Directive 2000/78/EC of 27 November 2000 establishing a general framework for equal treatment in employment and occupation OJ 2000 L 303, 16–22, Article 8(2).

84 C-378/07 to C-380/07 *Kiriaki Angelidaki e.a. vs Organismos Nomarchiakis Autodioikisis Rethymnis e.a.*, CJEU, April 2009, EU:C:2009:250.

85 European Parliament, Resolution of 29 September 2011 on developing a common EU position ahead of the United Nations Conference on Sustainable Development (Rio+20), P7- TA(2011)0430, 97.

be jeopardised by the adoption of subsequent regressive legislation. From this perspective, the principle of non-regression would allow stabilising the environmental *acquis* and granting its legacy to future generations.

6. Conclusion

What do the principles of sustainable development, precaution, solidarity between generations and environmental non-regression have in common? Despite the complexity and evolving nature of these principles, I consider that they all have an inter-generational dimension and, if correctly applied in a timely manner, could contribute to the protection of future generations under EU law. First, the principle of sustainable development requests decision-makers to consider the needs of future generations when adopting environmental, social and economic decisions to preserve the possibility of future generations living on a healthy planet and responding to their own needs. Second, the precautionary principle binds decision-makers to anticipate the time of action by preventing the occurrence of scientifically uncertain risks that might jeopardise the environment and public health. Third, the principle of solidarity between generations invites the decision-makers to share resources (namely ecological resources) with future generations in a spirit of mutual support. Fourth, the principle of environmental non-regression aims at protecting the acquired level of environmental protection, and it translates the idea that the latter should not be reduced by the adoption of a subsequent act and that the highest level of environmental protection shall always be pursued.

By creating a connection between current and future generations, the principles of sustainable development, precaution, solidarity between generations and environmental non-regression seem to contribute to the progressive emergence of the principle of inter-generational equity under EU law. Professor Edith Brown Weiss proposed a well-known definition of this principle. According to her, the principle of inter-generational equity is based on the allocation of burdens and benefits across generations, and it entails three planetary obligations for the living generation.[86] First, each generation shall conserve the diversity of the natural and cultural resource base. Second, each generation shall maintain the quality of the planet

86 Weiss, *In Fairness to Future Generations* (n 5).

so that subsequent generations are entitled to a comparable level of that enjoyed by previous generations. This means that the present generation shall pass the planet on to future generations in no worse conditions than that in which it was received. Third, each generation shall provide its members with equitable rights of access to the legacy of past generations and conserve such access for future generations. While many acknowledge that humankind has a responsibility to take account of its actions for the future,[87] the principle of inter-generational equity has found only limited recognition in law. No direct references to this principle exist today under EU law. Yet, the Paris Agreement[88] – which represents the reference agreement for managing the climate crisis and inspires the legislation adopted under EU law – acknowledges in its preamble that climate change is a common concern of humankind and considers that when acting to address climate change, the parties should consider, *inter alia*, inter-generational equity.

Even if it is too early to assess whether the principle of inter-generational equity will effectively find a place under EU law, the principles of sustainable development, precaution, solidarity between generations and environmental non-regression already translate, under EU law, its main tenants by creating a set of protection obligations from the current generations to the future ones.

87 Wilfred Beckerman, 'The Impossibility of a Theory of Intergenerational Justice' in Joerg Chet Tremmel (eds), *Handbook of Intergenerational Justice* (Elgar 2006) 53.

88 Conference of the Parties, *Paris Agreement* (n 79).

12. The Greening of the Inter-American Court of Human Rights: Environmental Protection Possibilities for Future Generations

*Luisa Cortat Simonetti Gonçalves**

Abstract: *The protection of the right to a healthy environment differs greatly within the different human rights regional systems. Moreover, when it comes to discussing the rights of future generations, complexity increases. This chapter focuses on the Inter-American system and asks whether, in the context of its greening, the Rio Principles and the principles of institutional continuity and temporal non-discrimination could be used as interpretation methods to mainstream the intergenerational rights for a deeper environmental protection. Thus, the chapter clarifies the historical progression of the protection of the right to a healthy environment before the Inter-American system: going from the incompetence of the Court to exert its jurisdiction to an independent analysis of the right to a healthy environment. Despite the largely procedural nature of the discussion, the chapter goes beyond and justifies the possibility of including the protection of environmental rights of future generations from the perspective of substantive rights.*

1. Introduction

The right to a healthy environment is included in the extensive list of protected human rights under the Inter-American system. However, such environmental protection is excluded from the jurisdiction of the Inter-American Court of Human Rights ('the Court') and the Inter-American Commission on Human Rights (the Commission), at least as stated in the text of the Inter-American Convention on Human Rights ('the Convention'). More recently, through the process known as the greening of the Inter-American system, the so-called reflex protection – through the analysis of other human rights – has been made possible by the Commission and the Court. This means it has become possible to provide environmental protection when civil and political rights are violated due to poor environmental protection. From the early 2000s and onwards, especially after Resolution 12/85 in *Yanomami v Brazil* and after *Indigenous Community Awas Tingni Mayagna (Sumo) v Nicaragua*, this type of reflex protection

* Dr Luisa Cortat Simonetti Goncalves is a Course Director in Environmental Law at the Academy of European Law ERA, a Research Associate at the United Nations University FLORES, and a Supervisor of Master theses at the Maastricht Sustainability Institute (Maastricht University).

has been progressively accepted in case law and doctrine. Its consolidation came with the Court's *Advisory Opinion OC-23/17*.

This chapter will go one step further by addressing the issue of future generations. It is important to establish that I understand future generations, from a legal perspective, as both those that cannot yet speak for themselves (legally incompetent) – mainly for reasons of age –, and those that are not yet born and, thus, their physical existence is situated in the future. However, this chapter will focus on the second group since the discussion regarding their legal representation is more complex and, as yet, not settled. Still, aspects regarding the under-aged may be of great importance and might be recalled as grounds for the reasoning. Another relevant aspect dealt with is the perspective that the present generation is subject to a duty to protect rights and the environment for future generations.

Because of the current construction of environmental protection within the Inter-American human rights system, there is a need for identifiable harm caused to the rights – such as life or health – of a specific person or group of people. However, if only future generations will feel the harm, those absent still go unprotected, as the interconnection with civil or political rights is virtually impossible in those cases. Therefore, the chapter asks whether in the context of this greener Inter-American system, the Rio Principles – especially sustainable development and precautionary principles – and the principles of institutional continuity and temporal non-discrimination could be used as interpretation methods to mainstream the intergenerational rights for a more profound environmental protection from the Commission and the Court. This means analysing both material and procedural issues because, even if the materiality is proven possible, there is still the hurdle of representing those absents in a system that restricts access to the Court only to the Member States and the Commission.

To do so, the chapter is divided into four parts: Section 2 provides an overview of the greening of the Inter-American system and of the arguments and main cases that enabled it; Section 3 gives an overview of the procedural aspects involved in access to the Inter-American Commission and Court; Section 4 focuses on the analysis of the principles and their application in the construction of International Environmental Law; and Section 5 deals with the application of those principles in the explained scenario, to answer to the research question.

2. The Greening of the Inter-American System

Since 1988, the inter-American system has recognised the human right to a healthy environment. Article 11 of the Additional Protocol to the American Convention on Human Rights in the Area of Economic, Social and Cultural Rights (Protocol of San Salvador)[1] clearly states: '1. Everyone shall have the right to live in a healthy environment and to have access to basic public services. 2. The States Parties shall promote the protection, preservation, and improvement of the environment.' Nonetheless, the same Protocol does not include such a right among those that may have jurisdictional control of the Commission and the Court. In that sense, the text of Article 19, para. 6, reads:

> Any instance in which the rights established in paragraph a) of Article 8 and in Article 13 are violated by action directly attributable to a State Party to this Protocol may give rise, through participation of the Inter-American Commission on Human Rights and, when applicable, of the Inter-American Court of Human Rights, to application of the system of individual petitions governed by Article 44 through 51 and 61 through 69 of the American Convention on Human Rights.

Thus, being neither listed under the substantive part of the American Convention on Human Rights[2] nor included for jurisdictional purposes by the San Salvador Protocol, the right to a healthy environment cannot be directly demanded before the Inter-American Commission nor the Court.[3]

It is possible, however, to allege a violation of the right to a healthy environment when an offence causes a violation of one or more of the rights pro-

1 Additional Protocol to the American Convention on Human Rights in the Area of Economic, Social and Cultural Rights (Protocol of San Salvador), OAS Treaty Series No 69 (1988) (entered into force 16 November 1999) reprinted in Basic Documents Pertaining to Human Rights in the Inter-American System, OEA/Ser L V/II.82 Doc 6 Rev 1 at 67 (1992).

2 American Convention on Human Rights, OAS Treaty Series No 36, 1144 UNTS 123 (entered into force 18 July 1978) reprinted in Basic Documents Pertaining to Human Rights in the Inter-American System, OEA/Ser L V/II.82 Doc 6 Rev 1 at 25 (1992).

3 Christian Courtis, 'Proteção do ambiente por meio dos direitos consagrados na Convenção Americana' in Associação Interamericana para. a Defesa do Ambiente (AIDA) (ed), *Guia de Defesa Ambiental: construindo a estratégia para. o litígio de casos diante do Sistema Interamericano de Direitos Humanos* (AIDA 2010) 69.

tected by the American Declaration,[4] the Convention, or the selected rights of the San Salvador Protocol.[5] From the early 2000s onwards, this kind of reflex protection has been increasingly accepted in case law and doctrine, especially in connection with cases involving Article 26 of the American Convention, which protects the right to progressive development.

The first cases dealing with reflex environmental protection were Resolution n. 12/85 in *Yanomami v Brasil*[6] and the *Indigenous Community Awas Tingni Mayagna (Sumo) v Nicarágua*[7], respectively analysed by the Commission and the Court.

In the case *Yanomami v Brazil* – which preceded the San Salvador Protocol – the petition adduced that the government violated the rights of the Yanomami community when building a highway crossing their land and authorising the exploration of the land's resources by private parties. Those actions led outsiders to the land, who took contagious diseases to the indigenous people that were not treated due to lack of medical attention. The Commission, in Resolution n. 12/85, determined that the government violated the rights to life (Art. 4) and integrity (Art. 5) of the Convention in light of the environment as a human right and the rights to housing and health. The basis of the discussion was the environment, because the fundamental argument of the petitioners was the indiscriminate exploitation of resources. Consequently, the Commission based its decision on Article 27 of the International Covenant on Civil and Political Rights,[8] concluding

4 American Declaration of the Rights and Duties of Man, OAS Res XXX adopted by the Ninth International Conference of American States (1948) reprinted in Basic Documents Pertaining to Human Rights in the Inter-American System OEA/Ser L V/II.82 Doc 6 Rev 1 at 17 (1992).

5 Valerio de Oliveira Mazzuoli and Gustavo de Faria Moreira Teixeira, 'O direito internacional do meio ambiente e o greening da Convenção Americana sobre Direitos Humanos' (2012) 17(67) *Revista de Direito Ambiental (RDA)* 234; Gustavo de Faria Moreira Teixeira, *O Greening no Sistema Interamericano de Direitos Humanos* (Juruá 2011) 32.

6 Inter-American Commission on Human Rights, 'Resolution n.12/85 – Case n. 7615 Brazil', 5 March 1985. In Annual Report CIDH 1984–85, OEA/Ser L V/II.66 Doc 10 rev 1, 1 outubro, 1985, 24, 31 (Caso Yanomami).

7 *Caso Comunidade Mayagna (Sumo) Awas Tingni v Nicaragua*, Inter-American Court of Human Rights, Judgement, 31 August 2001, Series C, No 79 <https://perma.cc/KR58-QEMC>.

8 'Nos Estados em que existam minorias étnicas, religiosas ou linguísticas, não será negado o direito que assiste às pessoas que pertençam a essas minorias, em conjunto com os restantes membros do seu grupo, a ter a sua própria vida cultural, a professar e praticar a sua própria religião e a utilizar a sua própria língua'.

that the Brazilian State did not undertake the necessary care to prevent the severe social damage resulting from the invasion of the indigenous lands.

The *Indigenous Community Awas Tingni Mayagna (Sumo) v Nicaragua* case concerns over 600 people of such a community. In March 1992, due to a project of forest extraction, the Community Awas Tingni concluded a contract with the company MADENSA to determine the integral management of the forest, recognising certain rights of participation over the territory occupied by the Community due to its 'historical possession' thereof. Two years later, the Community, MADENSA, and the Ministry of Environment and Natural Resources of Nicaragua (MARENA) concluded a covenant in which the Ministry committed to facilitating the circumscription of the indigenous land. In March 1996, the State granted a 30-year concession for the forest management and use of approximately 62 000 hectares to the company SOLCARSA without consulting the Community. The members of the community called on several governmental agencies to stop the concession and, instead, circumscribe its territory. However, none of the requests were granted. The Inter-American Court decided that Nicaragua violated their rights to judicial protection (Art. 25) and property (Art. 21) under the American Convention.

The third relevant case that reinforces the case law for the reflex protection of environmental rights is *Yakye Axa v Paraguay*.[9] It concerns the international responsibility of the State for not guaranteeing the right to the ancestral property of the Yakye Axa Indigenous Community and the consequences thereof for over 300 people. At the end of the 19th century, large tracts of land of the Paraguayan Chaco were sold to British entrepreneurs, which led to the settlement of several missions of the Anglican Church in the region. Various cattle ranches were also established in the area, where the indigenous people that were there beforehand were employed. At the beginning of 1986, the members of the Yakye Axa community moved, due to the terrible living conditions they had to endure in the cattle ranches. However, this did not improve their situation, which is why, in 1993, they started domestic procedures to reclaim the land they considered their traditional habitat. None of the several appeals resulted. Since 1996, 28 to 57 families settled next to a highway, and the remainder of the members are spread around villages in the area. In the face of the lack of results

9 *Caso das comunidades indígenas Yakye Axa contra o Paraguai*, Inter-American Court of Human Rights, Judgement, 17 June 2005, Series C, No 125 <https://perma.cc/W776-RD4H>.

in the national judiciary, they brought the case before the Inter-American system, arguing violations of the rights to life (Art. 4), humane treatment (Art. 5), personal liberty (Art. 7), fair trial (Art. 8), of the child (Art. 19), property (Art. 21), and judicial protection (Art. 25), all from the American Convention. Violations of the San Salvador Protocol were also argued. Particularly to environmental issues, Article 11 of the Protocol was mentioned due to claims for access to clean water and sanitation to the traditional communities. In summary, the Court was asked to decide whether the basic means for the dignified life of the members of the Yakye Axa community were provided, including environmental and progress-related means. The Court concluded that they were not provided.

Despite being an indirect recognition of the right to a healthy environment in the competence of the Inter-American System, it is, nonetheless, perceptible. The core is that cases of environmental degradation may demonstrate situations in which fundamental rights are at risk of irreparable harm.[10] In other words, the international instruments of environmental protection – mainly the declarations of Stockholm 1972 and Rio 1992 –, together with Article 11 of the San Salvador Protocol and the provisions of the American Declaration and Convention, give legal ground for the indirect applicability of the right to a healthy environment within the Inter-American System.[11]

In that sense, other cases considered by the Court may also be included: *Community La Oroya v Peru*,[12] due to the effects of industrial pollution; *Claude Reyes and others v Chile*,[13] due to the State restriction in providing information to citizens about the ecological impacts of projects, as well as cases analysed by the Commission: *Community Kichwa de Sarayacu and its people v Ecuador*;[14] *Indigenous Maian Communities of the Toledo District v Belize*;[15] *Indigenous Communities San Mateo Huanchor v Peru*;[16] *Indigenous*

10 Oliveira Mazzuoli and Faria Moreira Teixeira (n 5) 237.

11 Faria Moreira Teixeira (n 5) 134.

12 CIDH, caso da comunidade de La Oroya contra o Peru, Relatório Anual de 2007, Cap.III, para. 46, OEA/Ser L /V/II.130 Doc 22Rev 1, de 29 de dez. de 2007.

13 Corte IDH, caso Claude Reyes e outros contra o Chile, sentença de 19 de set. de 2006, Série C, No 151.

14 CIDH, Informe de No 62/04, caso das comunidades indígenas Kichwa de Sarayacu e seus membros contra o Equador, de 13 de out. de 2004.

15 CIDH, Informe de No 40/04, caso de No 12.053 das comunidades indígenas Maias do Distrito de Toledo contra Belize, de 12 de out. de 2004.

16 CIDH, Informe de No 69/04, caso das comunidades indígenas San Mateo Huanchor contra o Peru, OEA/Ser L V/II.122 Doc 5 Rev 1, de 15 de out. de 2004.

Communities Ngöbe and its people v Panamá;[17] *Metropolitan Natural Park by Rodrigo Noriega v Panamá;*[18] *Indigenous Communities Mapuche Pehuence by Mercedes Julia Henteao Beroiza and others v Chile;*[19] *Inuit People v United States of America (USA);*[20] *Indigenous and Riverside Communities of the Xingu River v Brazil;*[21] and *Community La Oroya v Peru.*[22]

The interpretation of the Inter-American Court on this matter was consolidated in Advisory Opinion OC-23/17. On 14 March 2016, Colombia requested the Court to issue an Advisory Opinion whose 'essential question' was about how to interpret the American Convention when infrastructure projects may pose a risk of severe impact:

> on the marine environment of the Wider Caribbean Region and, consequently, the human habitat that is essential for the full exercise and enjoyment of the rights of the inhabitants of the coasts and/or islands of a State Party to the Pact, in light of the environmental laws established in treaties and customary international law applicable between the respective States.[23]

Thus, the Opinion addressed the scope of Articles 1(1) – obligation to respect rights, 4(1) – right to life, and 5(1) – right to humane treatment/personal integrity, all of the American Convention and in light of international environmental law. In the Court's own words, '[t]his Opinion constitutes one of the first opportunities this Court has to refer extensively to the State obligations arising from the need to protect the environment under the American Convention.'[24]

In summary, the Court concluded on a number of duties that States must comply with, derived from the obligations to respect and ensure the rights

17 CIDH, Informe de n No 75/09, caso das comunidades indígenas Ngöbe e seus membros contra o Panamá, de 5 de ago. de 2009.

18 CIDH, Informe de No 84/03, caso Parque Natural Metropolitano do Panamá, de 22 de out. de 2003.

19 CIDH, Informe de No 30/04, Solução Amistosa Mercedes Julia Huentes Beroiza, de 11 de mar. de 2004.

20 CIDH, Petição Inicial de No 1.413/05, caso do Povo Inuit contra os Estados Unidos da América (EUA).

21 CIDH, Solicitação de Medidas Cautelares de No 382/10, caso das comunidades tradicionais da bacia do Rio Xingu (Pará) contra o Brasil, de 11 de nov. de 2009.

22 CIDH, Informe de No 76/09, caso da comunidade de La Oroya contra o Peru, de 5 de ago. de 2009.

23 *Advisory Opinion OC-23/17,* Inter-American Court of Human Rights, 15 November 2017, para. 1 <https://perma.cc/KE5E-V3XY>.

24 ibid., para. 46.

to life and personal integrity in the context of environmental protection. Those include the obligation of:

- prevention, with duties to regulate, supervise and monitor, require and approve impact assessments on the environment, prepare a contingency plan and mitigate if environmental damage occurs;
- acting in accordance with the precautionary principle 'to protect the rights to life and to personal integrity in cases where there are plausible indications that an activity could result in serious or irreversible environmental damage, even in the absence of scientific certainty'[25];
- cooperation, with duties to notify, and to consult and negotiate with potentially affected States;
- ensuring the right of access to information and public participation, as well as the right of access to justice.

Finally, the Court's decision in *Indigenous Communities Members of the Lhaka Honhat (Our Land) Association v Argentina* in April 2020 was the first to analyse the right to a healthy environment independently. So, it no longer uses the reflex effect. Therefore, it is of great relevance to the analysis of cases.

The indigenous communities claimed ownership of lands in the Argentine province of Salta. For around 35 years, the State had made progress towards recognising indigenous land ownership, but implementing actions related to the indigenous territory had not yet been concluded. The relevant circumstances included the presence of non-indigenous settlers and various activities being carried out on these lands: livestock farming, installation of fences and illegal logging. The relevant facts also included civil works, activities and projects in the territory claimed.[26]

Specifically regarding the right to a healthy environment, the Court referred directly to Advisory Opinion OC-23/17 to state that it is an autonomous fundamental right.[27] The Court has also referred to the fact that Argentina recognises the right to a healthy environment in its Constitution and has ratified the international instruments relevant for recognising such a right within the Inter-American system. On those bases, the

25 ibid., para. 180.

26 *Case of the Indigenous Community of the Lhaka Honhat (Our Land) Association v Argentina,* Inter-American Court of Human Rights, Judgment of 6 January 2020, para. 46 <https://perma.cc/998V-MDHZ>.

27 ibid., para. 203.

Court established that the States must respect not only the right but also the obligation to ensure it.[28] In particular, the obligation to implement *ex ante* measures, based on the prevention principle, was, among other arguments, highlighted as international customary law by the Advisory Opinion. In the face of all that, the Court concluded that, besides harming the rights to take part in cultural life in relation to cultural identity, to adequate food, and water, the State of Argentina violated the right to a healthy environment in regard to the obligation to ensure the rights established in Article 1(1) of the American Convention.[29]

Therefore, the progressively greening path taken by the Inter-American Commission and Court already seems to indicate that it is worth looking in depth into the possibility of protecting the environmental rights of future generations. However, before finally drawing conclusions in this regard, the question of legal standing naturally emerges when talking about future generations. Hence, the next section will analyse the possibilities for accessing the Commission and the Court on behalf of future generations.

3. Access to the Inter-American Commission and Court

Before delving into the intergenerational aspect, it is interesting to analyse the discussions regarding transboundary environmental harm, which were also raised in Advisory Opinion OC-23/17. The latter explored the meaning and scope of the word jurisdiction (including transboundary) in Article 1(1) of the American Convention to determine State obligations in relation to environmental protection:

> For the purposes of Article 1(1) of the American Convention, it is understood that individuals whose rights under the Convention have been violated owing to transboundary harm are subject to the jurisdiction of the State of origin of the harm, because that State exercises effective control over the activities carried out in its territory or under its jurisdiction, in accordance with paragraphs 95 to 103 of this Opinion.

Thus, a first concern when discussing the judicialisation of the rights of future generations is jurisdiction, which has both geographical/spatial and chronological aspects. In that sense, it is relevant to understand trans-

28 ibid., paras 204–207.
29 ibid., para. 289.

boundary environmental impacts and how the Court may assess the State's responsibilities. It is largely settled by the Court that the obligations of States do not include harming the rights of people located outside their borders, but they may be liable for harm caused within their territory and inflicted outside. The key aspect here is whether or not the same reasoning applies to 'trans-chronological' harms.

From the jurisdictional perspective, we are dealing with two sides of the same coin, despite there being two discussions. 'State jurisdiction refers to the power of a state to affect persons, property, and circumstances within its territory'.[30] It should be recalled that, for the purposes of analysis in this chapter, we consider the absent (future) generations as those not yet born. Thus, when referring to the geographical aspect, the harm caused to people in another country is harm caused to someone outside the State's jurisdiction. One of the problems with protecting the rights of the generations not yet born could be considering that those are people out of the reach of jurisdictional power, even for damages that have already occurred and will impact or continue to impact until future generations come along. This might be true for other matters, but not for protecting people against harm to their environment-related rights. That is what the Advisory Opinion had already clarified in relation to spatial absence, with direct application of the reasoning to the time absence, considering that the core feature is the effective control over the harmful activity. The responsibility of a State is not linked with its territorial jurisdiction.

In other words, if it were a matter of discussing jurisdiction, the State where the transnational environmental harm originates would not be responsible for it. It is, however, a matter of effective control over harmful activity. Therefore, choosing the path of arguments related to jurisdiction for excluding the responsibility of the State makes no sense, neither for spatial nor for time discussions.

Still, the second and main concern when discussing the judicialisation of the rights of future generations is active legitimation. In this regard, two aspects must be considered: (i) the representation of the victims, which, in this case, are absent; (ii) the procedure within the Inter-American system, in which the victims access the Court through the action of the Commission.

30 Malcom Shaw, 'International Law: Jurisdiction' (*Britannica* 1998) <https://perma.cc/8YWB-9498>.

For the analysis of the representation of victims, the procedures in the case of deceased victims – or other victims that cannot act – may be of assistance. In those cases, victims are also absent, but they belonged to past generations. In those cases, the active legitimation can be exercised through procedural representation, i.e., by someone else on behalf of the victim. A complaint may then be presented either by a person with a private and personal connection with the victim or by the so-called indirect victims.[31] This means that the complaint may be submitted by:

> those that may allege that the violation caused them some harm, or that they have a valid personal interest in having the offence ceased. This is the case of parents and siblings presented as victims due to the passing of his/her relative [...].[32]

The critical difference, then, is no longer of a procedural nature but of a substantive nature: how should the harm be characterised?. Would it be possible to prove the violation of a human right or even an autonomous environmental harm when discussing the rights of people that do not yet exist?

A philosophical approach to the problem of granting rights to future people raises a strong objection, stating that

> The fact that future individuals do not yet exist seems to entail that they could not have rights; rights need to be ascribed to someone (as opposed to "floating in the air"). This would mean not only that the rights of future people are meaningless but even that no duties are owed to them. A full examination of this challenge therefore requires us to find out whether duties can make sense without correlative rights (and if so, what could still be the added value of rights), and whether such correlative rights are really out of reach in our context.[33]

31 See also: *X v France,* European Court of Human Rights, Application No 18020/91, Judgement, 31 March 1992 <www.echr.coe.int/echr/>; Irineu Cabral Barreto, *A Convenção Europeia dos Direitos do Homem anotada* (3rd edn, Coimbra Editora 2005); Jorge de Jesus Ferreira Alves, *A Convenção Europeia dos Direitos do Homem Anotada e Protocolos Adicionais Anotados* (Legis 2008).

32 André Pires Gontijo, 'O papel do sujeito perante os sistemas de proteção dos direitos humanos: a construção de uma esfera pública por meio do acesso universal como instrumento na luta contra violação dos direitos humanos' (2009) 49 Revista IIDH 107.

33 Axel Gosseries, 'On Future Generations' Future Rights' (2008) 16(4) The Journal of Political Philosophy 446.

Legally, however, the issue does not seem to be restricted to the existential discussion; it is related (i) to a group of people, identifiable or not, who at least at some level, have the nature of a social right – as recognized by the American Convention of Human Rights, under Article 26;[34] and (ii) to environmental principles, including the sustainable development principle, which have already been incorporated into the body of international customary law.

The relation to a group of people means that the rights of future generations can be compared to social rights due to their shared nature. Initially, this could be a problem for attempting protection under the Inter-American system, where the competence is restricted to civil and political rights. Thus, even with the greening of the Commission and the Court, it would be hard to characterise grounds for protection without a precise characterisation of violation of individual rights. The most recent developments, though, bring the right to a healthy environment, which is inherently social, to the scope of protection of the Inter-American system. Therefore, the nature of protected rights is no longer an obstacle to protecting future generations' environmental rights.

It follows that, in the same way as they may do for the violation of rights of multiple individuals or the violation of environmental rights of present generations, civil organisations may play an essential role in representing the absent – including future generations.

The relation to environmental principles, in turn, means that countries must respect the entirety of the sustainable development principle. It thus conveys the aspect of guaranteeing that future generations have the resources to fulfil their needs. Also, because of being customary law,[35] the principle of sustainable development may be brought before the Commission and the Court in accordance with the principle of good faith and the duty to modify the relevant internal legislation.

---

34 Under the paradigm of human rights protection at the Inter-American System, this is the consensual approach. Although different approaches are possible – and adopted in other systems – such a discussion is out of the scope of this chapter, which deals with the possibilities within the frame of the Inter-American System.

35 Pedro Ivo Diniz, 'Natureza Juridica do Desenvolvimento Sustentavel no Direito Internacional' (2015) 12(2) Revista de Direito Internacional 739.

3.1. Brief Note on the Criticism of the Environmental Control by the Inter-American Court

All arguments considered so far indicate not only the possibility, but also the need to enable the protection of the environmental rights of future generations under the Inter-American system by both the Commission and the Court. They are, however, largely based on the progressively increasing greening of the Inter-American System of Human Rights, against which there is also criticism. The most relevant one here is that the expansion of the competence towards environmental matters may engender a backlash effect that creates resistance from States, which may even lead to non-compliance by those who argue that they did not agree with such competence.

This discussion is even more sensitive and of higher relevance in the context of the rights of future generations, for which harms are potential instead of consummated. The more uncertainty involved, the more States might refrain from committing or complying. A common suggestion here is to differentiate clearly between rules and standards. This, having in mind that:

> rules are those legal commands which differentiate legal from illegal behavior in a simple and clear way. Standards, however, are general legal criteria which are unclear and fuzzy and require complicated judiciary decision making.[36]

In other words, when dealing with legal standards, more flexibility – and even activism – is both allowed and expected from the court.

Although this is a path whose exploration is outside of the scope of this chapter – mainly because of its political nature –, it is undoubtedly a discussion that must be included when searching for the protection of future generations' environmental rights under the Inter-American system.

4. Environmental Principles and Rights for Future Generations

This section focuses on the principles involved in protecting human rights in the context of environmental protection, namely, sustaable development, prevention, precaution, cooperation, institutional continuity, and temporal

36 Hans-Bernd Schaefer, 'Legal Rules and Standards', in Charles K Rowley and Friedrich Schneider (eds), *The Encyclopedia of Public Choice* (Springer 2005).

non-discrimination. As already briefly mentioned in the previous section, the environmental principles may already be considered, if not sources *per se* of international law, instruments for interpretation.[37]

Beyond the discussion of principles as a source of international law, there is a more recent understanding of the need to rebuild international law based on solidarity and that could also be applied. Such a perspective points out that there are:

> elements to approach the issue, from such a perspective and in a more satisfying way, on international jurisprudence and in the practice of States and international bodies, as well as in the more lucid legal doctrine. From such elements comes [...] the awakening of an universal legal consciousness [...] to rebuild, in the beginning of the XXI century, the International Law base in a new paradigm, no longer State-centered, but situating humankind in a central position and having present the problems that affect humankind as a whole.[38]

Still, only the more consolidated approach of applying the principles of international environmental law will be used.

a) Sustainable Development

The broader principle of sustainable development was first described as such by the Report of the Brundtland Commission in 1987: 'development that meets the needs of the present without compromising the ability of future generations to meet their own needs'.[39] Incorporating the concept adopted by the Brundtland Commission, Principle 4 of the 1992 Rio De-

37 See, eg: Antonio Augusto Cancado Trindade, *Principios do Direito Internacional Contemporaneo* (2nd edn, Brasilia – FUNAG 2017); Max Valverde Soto, 'General Principles of International Environmental Law' (1997) 3(1) ILSA Journal of International & Comparative Law 193; Winfried Lang, 'UN-Principles and International Environmental Law' (1999) 3 Max Planck UNYB 157 <https://perma.cc/869D-HK42>; Oscar Schachter, 'The Emergence of International Environmental Law' (1991) 44(2) Journal of International Affairs 457; Diniz (n 35).

38 Antonio Augusto Cancado Trindade, 'A Formação do Direito Internacional Contemporâneo: Reavaliação Crítica da Teoria Clássica de Suas "Fontes"' (2002) 29 Curso de Direito Internacional Organizado pelo Comitê Jurídico Interamericano 1, 60 <https://perma.cc/29SQ-PHJ5>.

39 Gro H Brundtland and others, 'Our Common Future: Report of the World Commission on Environment and Development', UN-Doc A/42/427 (United Nations 1987) <https://perma.cc/B5MA-QNXZ>.

claration on Environment and Development affirms that '[i]n order to achieve sustainable development, environmental protection shall constitute an integral part of the development process and cannot be considered in isolation from it'.[40]

No further arguments are needed for this chapter. As stated in the previous section, such an umbrella principle explicitly incorporates the rights of future generations – by unequivocally acknowledging them and their rights – into the international regulatory framework.

b) Prevention

Another basic principle is the prevention principle, established as number 11 of the 1992 Rio Declaration. It requires States to:

> enact effective environmental legislation. Environmental standards, management objectives and priorities should reflect the environmental and developmental context to which they apply. Standards applied by some countries may be inappropriate and of unwarranted economic and social cost to other countries, in particular developing countries.[41]

The principle of prevention requires action to be taken at an early stage and, if possible, before damage has actually occurred, leading to the prohibition of activities that (may) cause environmental damage. Therefore, it is in direct alignment with the purpose of preventing environmental damage from occurring to future generations.

c) Precaution

Together with the principle of prevention must always come the precautionary principle. The Rio Declaration expressly enshrined it under Principle 15:

> In order to protect the environment, the precautionary approach shall be widely applied by States according to their capabilities. Where there are threats of serious or irreversible damage, lack of full scientific certainty

40 United Nations Conference on Environment and Development, 'Rio Declaration on Environment and Development' UN-Doc A/CONF.151/5/Rev.1 (United Nations 1997).

41 ibid.

shall not be used as a reason for postponing cost-effective measures to prevent environmental degradation.[42]

The precautionary principle protects society from the potential risks associated with the current uncertainties about the impacts of behaviours and activities. This sheds light on the discussion about proving harm. Even in the face of uncertainties – including temporal uncertainties, as in the case of harm to future generations – environmental rights must be protected.

d) Cooperation

In several fields of international law, States have chosen to go beyond mere co-existence and the allocation and regulation of sovereign rights to cooperate. This is the case of protecting the environment. Those grounds allowed for the recognition that States are responsible for thinking globally about not harming the environment, making room for international instruments such as the Stockholm and the Rio Declarations. It also makes the existence of agreed supervisory and monitoring mechanisms possible, including the Convention on Long-Range Transboundary Air Pollution, the Convention on the Law of the Sea, the Vienna Convention for the Protection of the Ozone Layer, the amended Convention on Marine Pollution from Land-Based Sources, the Convention on Biological Diversity, the United Nations Framework Convention on Climate Change, among others.[43] Similarly, the principle of cooperation may provide enough basis for protecting the environmental rights of future generations, as long as States decide to cooperate to achieve such a goal.

e) Temporal Non-Discrimination and Institutional Continuity

Although the path towards its recognition was not easy, the principle of non-discrimination became a basilar one after the Second World War,[44]

---

42 ibid.

43 Malcom Shaw, 'International Law: International Cooperation' (*Britannica*, 1998) <https://perma.cc/9J6V-LUXA>; Rüdiger Wolfrum, 'International Law of Cooperation' in *Max Planck Encyclopedia of Public International Law* (OUP 2010).

44 Office of the High Commissioner for Human Rights and the International BAR Association, 'The Right to Equality and Non-Discrimination in the Administration of Justice' in *Human Rights in the Administration of Justice: A Manual on Human Rights for Judges, Prosecutors and Lawyers* (United Nations 2003) 634.

starting with the UN Charter (1945) and strengthened by the Universal Declaration of Human Rights. Accepting that there is an intergenerational (or temporal) aspect for non-discrimination is simply another way of applying the principle of intergenerational solidarity[45] and, thus, aiming at fully guaranteeing sustainable development.

The principle of institutional continuity refers to the recurring modes of action and organisational patterns within institutions. Although, theoretically, such continuity could serve both the negative purpose of reproducing flawed patterns or the positive purpose of pushing forward improved rights protection and standards of equality, the discussion about future generations should try to ensure it is positive, for instance, in attempting to perpetuate the principle of non-discrimination also on its temporal dimension.

This brief review of basic environmental principles, and their connection to the protection of rights – especially environmental rights – of future generations, reinforces the possibility of judicialising such protection in the international courts.

5. Concluding Remarks

All that considered, we can see a clear historical progression of the protection of the right to a healthy environment before the Inter-American system: going from the incompetence of the Court to exert its jurisdiction to an independent analysis of the right to a healthy environment. In such a context, the chapter goes beyond and justifies the possibility of including the protection of environmental rights of future generations from the perspective of substantive rights, especially when all the involved principles are considered.

Although the procedural aspects pose extra challenges, mainly the: (i) scope of jurisdiction; (ii) representation of the victims, which, in this case, are absent; and (iii) the procedure within the Inter-American system, in which the victims access the Court through the action of the Commission. However, all those are overcome in the context of protecting the right to a healthy environment. First, it is a matter of control over harmful activity

45 Marisa Quaresma dos Reis, 'The Principle of Intergenerational Solidarity in Reshaping Constitutional Rights and Obligations: An Example from Portugal' in Marie-Claire Cordonier Segger, Marcel Szabó and Alexandra R Harrington (eds), *Advancing Future Generations Rights through National Institutions* (CUP 2021).

and not a matter of national jurisdiction over a territory. Thus, in the same sense that territoriality plays no role on State responsibility when harm is transboundary, time constraints should play no role when harm transcends current generations. Second and third, the representation of absent victims is not a novelty. The reasoning here is similar to the necessity of representation when the absent are past generations – for instance, deceased victims. In the face of the international protection of sustainable development and the environmental dimension, the fact that the victims do not yet exist is not an impediment *per se*. To that, the precautionary principle even adds the factor that certainty of harm is not necessarily mandatory to address activities that pose risks to the environment.

Finally, the criticism of the expansion of the Commission and the Court's intervention in environmental matters should also be considered, mainly aiming at preventing resistance and non-compliance from States. This should not, however, obstruct the possibility of protecting the environmental rights of future generations through the Inter-American System of Human Rights.

13. Building Climate Law Through Intergenerational Justice: An Empirical Assessment

Marta Torre-Schaub[*] *and Marcos de Armenteras Cabot*[**]

Abstract: *Climate change is a global phenomenon with long-term consequences, including for those not yet born. In the same way, climate change has its origins in human activities (industrialization) that date back to the second half of the 19th century. Those who are no longer with us are also connected to the phenomenon. Climate change and absentees are therefore two intimately linked issues. From this angle, climate change is a major challenge for the realization of intergenerational justice. The impact of climate change on future generations depends on decisions taken today. Given the growing importance of climate change litigation as a mechanism for promoting action against climate change, this article analyses the relevance of intergenerational equity in such litigation. By examining case law linking intergenerational justice and climate change, this article explores the extent to which different legal mechanisms can be useful in protecting future generations from the climate crisis. In this sense, it examines the involvement of young people or representatives of future generations in the legal process, and how a broader interpretation of environmental law principles and fundamental rights may be relevant to extending the protection of future generations' interests and achieving intergenerational justice.*

Introduction

'The scientific evidence is unequivocal: climate change is a threat to human well-being and the health of the planet. Any further delay in concerted global action will miss a brief and rapidly closing window to secure a liveable future'[1]. The conclusion of the latest Intergovernmental Panel for Climate Change report is clear: climate change poses a threat to humankind, and time is running out. Time is an essential element in the fight against climate change. Current actions will affect those who will live in the future. It is urgent to drastically reduce global greenhouse gas emissions and carry out climate change adaptation policies.

---

* Marta Torres-Schaub is a Senior Professor Researcher at the University Paris 1 Panthéon-Sorbonne (France).

** Marcos de Armenteras Cabot is an Assistant Professor at the University of the Balearic Islands (Spain).

1 Hans-Otto Pörtner and others, 'Working Group II contribution to IPCC Sixth Assessment Report, Climate Change 2022: Impacts, Adaptation and Vulnerability, Summary For Policymakers' (2022) 35 <https://report.ipcc.ch/ar6/wg2/IPCC_AR6_WGII_FullReport.pdf> accessed on 20 July 2023.

In the last few years, climate litigation has emerged as a new regulatory tool[2] with different social actors aiming to trigger ambitious climate policies globally. The lack of ambitious action in recent decades and the 2015 entry into force of the Paris Agreement, which shifts States' obligations from *top-down* to *bottom-up* and, in so doing, empowers social actors to seek greater ambition within their jurisdiction. Consequently, climate litigation has expanded globally since then.[3] Climate change requires that we rethink the vincula of our past and present actions in both the near and distant future. Similar phenomena can be observed in climate litigation, where actions are framed in a time scale that brings past actions to future remote consequences.[4] This is why it is pertinent to account for the relevance of intergenerational relations when dealing with climate litigation: the concepts of 'intergenerational justice' – understood as the relationship between generations (overlapping in time or not) based on principles of justice – and 'future generations' – those who will live in the future but are not yet born- play an important role in the construction of the legal regime concerning the climate[5]. Consequently, inquiring about the role of 'absent' generations (past and future) within climate litigation, understood as a regulatory mechanism to help achieve climate justice objectives, may be central to accomplishing those goals.

This chapter aims to show how those 'absent' generations (future generations) are represented in climate change litigation. The main purpose is to analyse the different tools and legal mechanisms used and bring an understanding of the possible avenues to bring future protection to legal reasoning. In this sense, future generations can be invoked directly and indirectly in climate change litigation. The purpose of this chapter is to show how this direct and indirect invocation is done. We also analyse the legal and practical restraints to bringing 'absent generations' to climate litigation. Finally, we study the best courses of action to incorporate their interests and needs in litigation.

---

2 Jacqueline Peel and Hari M Osofsky, 'Litigation as a Climate Regulatory Tool' in Christina Voigt (ed), *International Judicial Practice on the Environment: Questions of Legitimacy* (CUP 2019).

3 Jacqueline Peel and Hari M Osofsky, 'Climate Change Litigation' (2020) 16(1) Annual Review of Law and Social Science 21. Currently there are more than 1550 cases across 38 countries.

4 Chris Hilson, 'Framing Time in Climate Change Litigation' (2017) 9(3) Oñati Socio-Legal Series 361.

5 Axel Gosseries, *What is Intergenerational Justice?* (Polity Press 2023).

To better illustrate our remarks, this chapter is divided into two parts: the first analyses the direct invocation of future generations in climate disputes (I). The second focuses on the indirect invocation of absent generations to better show how transgenerational justice is progressively put into place in climate disputes (II).

1. The Direct Invocations of Future Generations: On Standing and Representation

Bringing future generations to climate litigation may be one way to incorporate those who will experience the worst consequences of climate change into courts' decision-making. It has been observed that children have been joining the climate justice movement worldwide, coming to the forefront of public discussion.[6] The role of children in climate movements has also been replicated in the use of litigation as a strategy to influence national and international climate policies effectively.[7] Their involvement in climate litigation may serve as a mechanism to account for this futurability, which is also reflected in the invocation of the interests of future generations. The representation of future generations' interests emphasises the long-term impacts of climate change and its dangerous consequences for those who will live on the Earth in the future. Among climate litigation case-law, there is growing litigation where the connection between generations has been raised through the direct invocation of future generations. In this section, we will give an account of those cases where there has been a direct invocation of future generations through their representation by specific actors. We will first analyse the levers (1) through different examples, and

---

6 Marcos de Armenteras Cabot, 'La acción global por el clima y la importancia de los jóvenes en el movimiento por la justicia climática' (2021) 18 OXÍMORA Revista Internacional De Ética Y Política 153.

7 Among other cases it is worth mentioning *Duarte Agostinho and Others v Portugal and 32 Other States* App No 39371/20 (ECtHR, 13 November 2020), where six Portuguese children and young people brought a court case to the European Court of Human Rights (ECtHR) alleging violation of their human rights by not taking action against climate change. Also, in *Sacchi, et al. v Argentina, et al.* (11 November 2021) UN Doc CRC/C/88/D/104/2019), 16 children filed a petition before the United Nations Committee on the Rights of the Child alleging the violation of their rights under the United Nations Convention on the Rights of the Child, due their inaction to respond to climate change. For further reading on these cases, see Bridget Lewis, 'Children's Human Rights-based Climate Litigation at the Frontiers of Environmental and Children's Rights' (2021) 39(2) Nordic Journal of Human Rights 180.

then present the limitations in a second step (2). That will allow us to outline the actual value of the arguments for future generations.

1.1. Future Generations as a Core Argument: Levers

The invocation of future generations before the courts stems from the landmark *Oposa Minors* case ruled in the Philippines in 1993. It could be helpful to look at this jurisprudential development to highlight whether the representation of future generations in courts may or may not be relevant in climate litigation.

1.1.1. The Oposa Minors Case as a Landmark Illustration

On behalf of his son and a group of minors represented by their parents, Mr Oposa filed a civil suit against the Secretary of the Department of Environment and Natural Resources of the Philippines Government. The lawsuit filed by 43 children, also on behalf of future generations, claimed that the licences granted under the Timber Licensing Agreements violated the constitutional right to a healthy environment and ordinary environmental standards. The plaintiffs requested that the licences be cancelled and no further licences be granted. In its judgment in 1993, the Court accepted the plaintiffs' arguments, concluding that the licences contravened the duties and functions of the Department of Environment and that the environmental damage they caused violated its obligation to preserve the environment for future generations. In this regard, the Court first explicitly ruled on the possibility that the plaintiffs were also acting on behalf of future generations, thus:

> This case, however, has a special and novel element. Petitioners minors assert that they represent their generation as well as generations yet unborn. We find no difficulty in ruling that they can, for themselves, for others of their generation and for the succeeding generations, file a class suit. Their personality to sue on behalf of the succeeding generations can only be based on the concept of intergenerational responsibility insofar as the right to a balanced and healthful ecology is concerned.[8]

8 *Minors Oposa v Factoran* (Supreme Court of the Philippines, case No 101083, 224 SCRA 792, 30 July 1993).

In accepting the representation of future generations by Oposa *et al.*, the Court upholds not only the standing of minors but also that if the interests of future generations are at stake, they can be represented in the proceedings. As to the interpretation of the constitutional articles in relation to the protection of the environment, the Court considers that Article II of Section 16 of the Constitution (1987), despite being included in the section on the Declaration of Principles and Policies of the State, and not under the section on the Bill of Rights, does not mean that it does not have the same importance as any political and civil right protected under the latter, because despite being part of another category of rights, they are linked to 'self-preservation' and 'self-perpetuation'. The Court's interpretation that follows is highly suggestive. Thus, the Court considers that it would not be necessary for this fundamental right to be recognised in the Constitution. The Court further restates that the constituents included this fundamental right out of a fear that if the rights to a healthy environment and to health were not included as a state policy by the Constitution itself – thereby imposing obligations to preserve the environment and advance health protection – one day everything would be lost, not only for the present generation, but also for the generations to come. These generations will inherit nothing but a 'parched earth incapable of sustaining life'[9]. That is, the right to a balanced and healthy ecological system carries a correlative duty to refrain from damaging the environment and, consequently, the reasonable management and conservation of the country's forests. According to the Court, the ecological or environmental balance would be irreversibly disturbed without these forests.

For the case at hand, as some critics point out, the direct result of the judgment on the protection of the environment and the interests of future generations is not commensurate with the importance, scope and notoriety of the judgment[10]. The logging licences were not cancelled because the plaintiffs did not pursue the action, and the recognition of future generations as a party to the proceedings did not set a precedent. Moreover, the settled case law of the Supreme Court already allowed broad standing for any citizen, which raises the legal irrelevance that future generations were represented in the case. Thus, a key question will be whether the inclusion of future generations in the present case, taking into account the fact that

9 ibid., 9.

10 Dante Gatmayan, 'Illusion of Intergenerational Equity: Oposa v Factoran as Pyrrhic Victory' (2003) 15(3) Georgetown International Environmental Law Review 457.

minors could have brought their claim due to the recognised standing, has had any differentiating effect on the outcome of the case.

1.1.2. The Added Value of Standing for Future Generations

According to Gatmayan, it did not. In his view, in environmental protection cases, the distinction between present and future generations is irrelevant because it is impossible to protect the rights of future generations without protecting the rights of present generations.[11] The latter affirmation may be alien to the theoretical grounds of intergenerational justice since it is possible to imagine situations where the 'rights' or interests of future generations are protected, and those of the present generations are not. Thus, in arguing that it is not possible to protect the 'rights' of future generations without protecting the rights of present generations, the author ignores the fact that the protection for the benefit of future generations puts the focus on the fact that processes of ecological degradation have impacts that go beyond one generation of humans, and that cumulative impacts have effects on ecosystems in an interdependent manner – the degradation of one has an impact on others. For instance, harvesting timber for paper production can have both positive and negative impacts on the current generation, as they will not benefit from the ecosystem services provided by forests, but they will reap the economic benefits of the activity. Still, timber harvesting will also affect future generations by increasing the risk of degradation of the ecosystem in which they are located, losing natural sinks and emitting previously captured greenhouse gases, but the economic benefits for future generations will depend on how past generations have managed the economic benefits of the activity. The environmental effect of the activity is not immediate. Environmental degradation is generally a progressive process that tends towards the disappearance of the natural asset in question, which may occur in the long-term. According to this scheme, the protection of the interests of future generations, contrary to what Gatmayan argues, depends on what is decided politically in a balance between present and future interests, which may or may not be in conflict.

Furthermore, when accounting for intergenerational conflicts, the issue at stake is the tension between immediate and long-term interests. Thus, in the present case, we could argue that trade in timber for short-term gains, which has a positive impact on the country's economic revenues

11 ibid., 460.

and, consequently, may lead to safeguarding social rights, may also have perverse effects in the medium and long term. This is, in fact, the regulatory structure of environmental law: the authorisation of degradation and pollution within the limits considered appropriate at a given time. So, if only present generations were taken into account, we would have to include in the reasoning the total benefits, which would be represented by the social and economic benefits (from logging and the timber trade) and the immediate environmental consequences (the loss of part of the biodiversity). In contrast, if future generations – or an intergenerational perspective – were also taken into account, the analysis should include how this logging will affect the long term, how logging may impact the sustainability of dependent forests and ecosystems, whether the immediate benefits of the activity outweigh the potential intergenerational damage, or whether the immediate damage may be justified because the end result may be beneficial for future generations. That is, environmental restrictions viewed through the prism of immediate harm is a very restrictive way of understanding the process of ecological degradation.

However, the central question is not whether it is relevant or not to introduce an intergenerational perspective when interpreting environmental regulations but whether or not it is necessary to open the standing to future generations.

1.2. Is it then Necessary to Open Standing for Future Generations? Limits

In this sense, the Supreme Court of the Philippines again stressed the arguments it upheld in the *Oposa Minors* judgment in *Arigo v Swift* in 2014.[12] The Court affirmed the possibility that the claimants in the present case, minors, could bring a claim on their own behalf, on behalf of their generation and on behalf of future generations, based on intergenerational responsibility concerning the right to a balanced and healthy ecological system. Furthermore, it emphasised that the right of minors to a healthy environment also constitutes the fulfilment of an obligation to ensure the protection of such a right for future generations. However, in one of the concurring votes in the judgment, Judge Leonen held that the representation of future generations by present generations and the representation

12 *Arigo v Swift* (Supreme Court of the Philippines, case GR No 206510, 16 September 2014).

carried out by minors on behalf of their own generation 'allows an unrepresentative group to universally represent an entire population as well as an unborn generation by linking it to causes of action, arguments and grievances it did not choose' and thus 'unborn generations suffer the legal incapacity to assert a false or unwanted representation'.[13] In this sense, the judge distinguishes between collective actions as procedural devices that allow a genuine cause of action to be judicially considered despite the social costs and externalities involved, and class suits that seek to represent the entire population and generations to come. In his view, class suits are based on the constitutional protection of the people and the necessary constitutional protection of citizens. The latter should only be used in extraordinary situations. This opinion is based on the fact that, from his point of view, in environmental issues, the different interests at stake should be taken into account in a balanced way, and, therefore, legal standing should go hand in hand with sufficient and substantial individual interest and capacity.

1.2.1. The Real Utility of Representing the Future Generations in Climate Case Law

In a climate case in 2017,[14] the Supreme Court of the Philippines dismissed a lawsuit filed by a group of young people on their own behalf, the children of the present and the children of the future, against the Climate Change Commission, seeking protection of the right to a healthy environment to achieve emission reductions in mobility and transport under the provisions of the Constitution and an executive order on sustainable mobility. While dismissing the claim, the Court held that the rules of procedure in environmental cases liberalised the requirements for bringing an action. The Court had confirmed this in its previous case law. Still, it stated that the applicants did not prove that the Commission was directly guilty of violating environmental rules and that they had suffered direct or personal injury from such action or omission. However, Judge Leonen again issued a concurring opinion re-emphasising the need to limit the standing of the representation of future generations.[15] According to the Judge, allowing any

13 ibid.

14 *Segovia et al. v Climate Change Commission* (Supreme Court of the Philippines, GR No 211010, 7 March 2017).

15 *Segovia et al. v Climate Change Commission*, Concurring opinion of Justice Leonen (Supreme Court of the Philippines, GR No 211010, 7 March 2017).

person of the present generation to represent others who are not yet born poses three potential dangers:

> First, they run the risk of foreclosing arguments of others who are unable to take part in the suit, putting into question its representativeness. Second, varying interests may potentially result in arguments that are bordering on political issues, the resolutions of which do not fall upon this court. Third, automatically allowing a class or citizen's suit on behalf of minors and generations yet unborn may result in the oversimplification of what may be a complex issue, especially in light of the impossibility of determining future generations true interests on the matter.

It is for these reasons that Judge Leonen states that the *Oposa Minors* judgment opens up a dangerous practice since it binds those who are not capable of making decisions for themselves – either because they are minors or because they do not exist. Once the matter is *res judicata* and the interested agents come into existence or have the capacity to litigate for their interests, they will not be able to modify the judgment. In this sense, the judge objects that the present generation is fully entitled to dictate what is best for those who will exist at a different time and live under different conditions and argues that although the principle of intergenerational responsibility is very noble, it cannot be used to prevent and limit future generations from defending their own interests, since the present generation does not have the right 'to deprive future generations of both agency and autonomy'.

1.2.2. The Legitimacy of Representing Future Generations

The argument of Judge Leonen has a normative ground that is key. In his perspective, the problem would not be who can represent future generations and how but if it is legitimate to represent them. Noting that this argument, *mutatis mutandis*, may apply to any mechanism aiming to represent future generations, it would cancel any attempt to bring the interest of future generations to any decision-making authority. In this sense, depriving future generations of agency and autonomy is really the issue at stake in arguments about intergenerational justice: whether our actions can negatively affect future generations and the reasons we have to avoid doing so. The question is not about the legitimacy of decisions taken to improve the welfare of future generations, as we can give good or bad reasons for this and weigh up short, medium and long-term interests. The question is whether it is relevant or not to grant standing to future generations through a representative. The central question relies on the practical utility and the substantive relevance that the representation of future generations may have in climate case-law.

This question was also brought up in the case of *Juliana et al. v United States,*[16] where the scientist James Hansen served as a guardian of future generations. In this case, probably the one that has received the most public notoriety, a group of 21 young people, together with the organisation 'Earth Guardian' and 'Future Generations', represented by scientist James Hansen, sued the United States, its president, and the directors and heads of the various offices that had some responsibility for reducing greenhouse gas emissions, in the Federal District Court of Oregon. The plaintiffs asked the Court to compel the defendant to undertake greenhouse gas reductions to bring atmospheric CO_2 concentrations to no more than 350 ppm by 2100. The representation of future generations by Professor Hansen was accepted without questioning its capacity. However, it does not seem to have had any practical relevance. Thus, it is not so relevant to guarantee a broad procedural capacity that includes the representation of future generations in order to safeguard its interests. That is, the representation of future generations before courts may encourage courts to consider long-term impacts.[17] Nevertheless, it is the legal reasoning and not the representation the relevant factor to consider in these cases. Thus, mere 'representation' is not as appropriate as protecting the interests of future generations, whether by virtue of the principle of intergenerational equity, sustainable development, or considering the ultimate ends of environmental law. This is where the emphasis should be placed. The representation and standing of absentees are not decisive for the case at hand. The emphasis should be on the arguments and how it is possible to understand whether or not the current effects will impact the medium and long term. The legal interpretation can also take this into account. Thus, the representation of future generations

16 *Juliana, et al. v United States of America, et al.*, US 9th Cir. 947 F.3d 1159 (2020). Further reading: 'Juliana v United States Ninth Circuit Holds that Developing and Supervising Plan to Mitigate Anthropogenic Climate Change Would Exceed Remedial Powers of Article III Court' (2021) 134 Harvard Law Review 1929.

17 Humphreys notes that referring to future generations allows us to avoid entering into an analysis of more concrete and coherent responsibilities regarding the climate crisis. This is relevant; however, it is not trivial that in interpretative terms, in order to consider long-term impacts, it may be useful to trace the responsibility towards those that do not yet exist, but that are at the axiological core of the principles of environmental law. Stephen Humphreys, 'Against future generations' (2023) 33 (4). European Journal of International Law, 1061.

may have discursive weight. Since the legal force is seen in the arguments and not in whether or not there is a possibility for them to be represented, as it is possible that the interests of those who will live in the future can be commensurate without them having a representative before the court.

Additionally, it is apposite to mention the case brought in Colombia by a group of 25 children who filed a tutela action against different Colombian public bodies for their inaction on the deforestation of the Colombian Amazon. In this case, known as *Generaciones Futuras v Ministerio de Medio Ambiente et al.*, the claimants, all young people between the ages of 7 and 26 (in 2018), argued that the short, medium and long-term effects of deforestation in the Colombian Amazon put at risk the safeguarding of their rights in the present and the future. Thus, the plaintiffs consider that deforestation in the Amazon violates their right to enjoy a healthy environment today and puts their rights in the future at serious risk because deforestation is the leading cause of greenhouse gas emissions in Colombia.[18] The Supreme Court, overruling the Bogotá District Court decision,[19] accepted the plaintiffs' recourse to the tutela action, given the connection between a healthy environment and fundamental rights, considering that the damage caused by deforestation to the environment and the climate has been proved, which implies a transgression of the principle of intergenerational equity and a violation of the fundamental rights to water, air, dignified life and health, among others, in connection with the environment. For that, the court, among other measures, ordered the defendants to formulate a short, medium and long-term action plan to counteract the rate of deforestation in the Amazon to address the effects of climate change; it also ordered them, within five months, and with the active participation of the plaintiffs, the affected communities, scientific organisations or environmental research groups, and the interested population in general, to build an 'intergenerational pact for the life of the Colombian Amazon', in which measures would be adopted for the protection of the environment and the environment.[20]

18 Complaint filed on 29 January 2018 before the Superior Court of the Judicial District of Bogotá.

19 *Generaciones Futuras v Ministerio de Medio Ambiente et al.* (Superior Court of the Judicial District of Bogotá DC, 12 February 2018).

20 *Generaciones Futuras v Ministerio de Medio Ambiente et al.* (Supreme Court of Colombia, case No STC4360–2018, 5 April 2018).

In the case at hand, it is important to highlight two elements. Firstly, the definition of 'future generation' and its differentiation from the notion of 'absents'. In this case, unlike those mentioned above, the plaintiffs propose a definition of future generations in which they are included. Thus, they ask the Court to recognise their rights as a future generation. To this end, they define a generation as 'a group of people who, because of their simultaneous historical experiences, share, to a greater or lesser degree, a worldview, a historical consciousness and a collective identity, which is reflected in their attitudes and behaviour'.[21] With this, they state that the claimants have an average life expectancy of 78 years, expecting to live their adult life in the period 2041–2070 and part of their old age from 2071 onwards, a period where the annual temperature of the country could gradually increase by 1.6°C and 2.14°C.[22] Secondly, this configuration of the notion of 'future generation' is not equivalent to those who are not there, those who do not yet exist – the absent – but the projection of subjects who already exist in the future. This may lead to an ontological question about what we are in the present and what we will be in the future, but beyond that, what is relevant is how to deal with the impacts of climate change on those who are alive today and whose lives are projected to the end of the century. This, in addition to showing the semantic indeterminacy of 'future generation', also shows that there are already generations who will be alive at the end of the century and who will coexist throughout their lives with climate change and its consequences; furthermore, it casts doubt on the fact that the procedural capacity of future generations and their representation before the courts lack substantive relevance since the interpretation of future harms can be carried out without including future generations – those who do not exist – in the process.

2. An Emerging Path for Transgenerational Justice: The Indirect Invocation of Future Generations in Climate Change Litigation

Climate litigation is part of a time process that implies both a return to the past and a forecast of the future. The invocation of the 'absents', both

21 Complaint filed on 29 January 2018 before the Superior Court of the Judicial District of Bogotá. Note 269, Elisa Dulcey-Ruiz (2015) Generaciones y relaciones intergeneracionales. Envejecimiento y vejez. Siglo del hombre editores [Author's translation].

22 ibid.

because they are no longer there or because they have not yet been born, is often indirectly present in climate litigation. As we have shown in the first part of this article, 'absents' are frequently the future generations more than past generations. There is a fruitful path to build transgenerational justice through climate change litigation across the argument of future generations' interests[23]. An excellent recent example is provided by the decision of the Montana court in the United States, handed down on August 14, 2023. However, this is a first-instance decision, which is something of an exception[24]. Yet, this argument does not often appear directly, as we have seen, but more in an underlined way.

It is then an 'indirect' invocation that can be observed as part of the defendants' arguments. Despite this modality, the argument is strong and a core and powerful element in climate change litigation for defending the absents' – future generations – interests. As Article 4 of the Paris Agreement notes: countries 'must continue their efforts in reducing GHG emissions'. This indicates a progressive and forward-looking pathway. From a procedural point of view, the absents and, more precisely, future generations appear in two ways: the first is when it comes to constitutional arguments (1). The second is when other legal tools, such as National Plans, are used (2).[25] Finally, we will illustrate how environmental principles can be reinforced through the use of 'the absents' and, more specifically, of 'future generations' (3).

---

23 Marcos De Armenteras Cabot, 'Justicia intergeneracional derecho y litigio climatico', PHD Universitat Rovira i Virgili, Tarragona, Spain, July 2021; Catherine Redwell, 'Principles and emerging norms in International Law: Intra and Intergenerational Equity' in Cinnamon Carlarne, Kevin Gray and Richard Tarasofsky (eds), *The Oxford Handbook of International Climate Change Law* (OUP 2016).

24 *Held v Montana*, Montana First Judicial District Court, Lewis & Clarck County, 14 August 2023. A group of young people in Montana won a landmark lawsuit on Monday when a judge ruled that the state's failure to consider climate change when approving fossil fuel projects was unconstitutional, see <https://perma.cc/E9DV-XZHP>.

25 Marta Torre-Schaub, 'Climate Change Litigation in France: New Perspectives and Trends' in Ivano Alogna, Christine Bakker and Jean-Pierre Gauci (eds), *Climate Change Litigation: Global Perspectives* (Brill 2021); Marta Torre-Schaub, 'Climate Change Risk and Climate Justice: the High Administrative Court as Janus or Prometheus?' (2023) 14(1) *European Journal of Risk Regulation* 1.

2.1. The Construction of an Intergenerational Principle Through Constitutional Arguments

If future generations do not always appear as a specific group or precise community, several climate lawsuits carry the idea of intergenerational justice. The core values of national constitutions are usually at stake in those lawsuits.[26] Those values include fundamental and constitutional rights and freedoms such as the right to life, the right to property, and freedom of speech. Those rights are presented as being challenged by climate change and potentially in danger for present and future generations.

2.1.1. Using Constitutional Rights to Protect the Future

The *Urgenda* case, in its first instance ruled in 2015,[27] considered Article 20 of the Constitution of the Netherlands as an 'obligation for the State to improve the environment'. This case combines three instances (first, appeal and cassation) in the Netherlands between 2015 and 2019. It was a lawsuit brought by almost 900 citizens and the Urgenda Foundation against the Dutch government on the grounds that the government had not acted sufficiently to protect citizens against climate change and that the greenhouse gas reduction targets set by the State were well below those set by European Union law and the need not to exceed a dangerous level of global warming following the international targets resulting from the negotiations of the United Nations Framework Convention on Climate Change of 1992. All three decisions in this case ruled in favour of the defendants and considered that the State had failed in its duty of care to protect citizens against the dangers and risks of global warming. Among other arguments, the defendants asked the Court, based on Article 20 of the Constitution, to establish a constitutional ground for an obligation not only to protect the environment, but also to improve it. This idea of 'improvement' shall be interpreted as an obligation of 'non-regression' and a duty for the present generations to protect future generations.

26 Peel and Osofsky (n 3); Mary Robinson Foundation for Climate Justice, *Principles of Climate Justice* <https://perma.cc/8NDR-9QEP>; Marta Torre-Schaub (ed), *Justice climatique : Procès et actions* (CNRS 2020); Marta Torre-Schaub, 'Justice climatique, nouvelles tendances, nouvelles opportunité' (*IDDRI*, 30 June 2021) <https://perma.cc/7M76-7SPE>.

27 *Urgenda v the Netherlands* (Court of The Hague, case No C/09/456689/ HA ZA 13–1396, 24 June 2015).

Similarly, the *Juliana Olson* case[28] should be analysed as a decision that brings the issue of intergenerational justice to the forefront. This case was complex and presented many procedural obstacles. The decision went against the defendants, but the individual opinion of Judge Eiken about the 'constitutional right to a healthy environment' could be a strong base for future cases establishing environmental rights for the present and future generations. This case cannot, however, establish a model as later cases, for example, *Aji P v Washington* (2018), decided that: 'there is not a constitutional right to a healthy environment -including a right to a stable climate'[29]. The question in the United States jurisprudence is not settled and deserves attention to future jurisprudential developments in this field.

Returning to Europe, the *Greenpeace Nordic* decision ruled in 2018 recognised the foundation of a constitutional right for future cases even though the cause was dismissed.[30] The NGO Greenpeace brought a case before the Oslo District Court asking it to cancel the authorisation given by the Ministry for Petroleum and Energy to extract oil and gas from the Barents Sea. In the first petition, a coalition of environmental groups with Greenpeace sought a declaratory judgment from the Oslo District Court that Norway's Ministry for Petroleum and Energy violated the Norwegian constitution by issuing a block of oil and gas licenses for deep-sea extraction from sites in the Barents Sea. The NGO built this case based on constitutional arguments to preserve both present and future generations. The strongest argument used was Article 112 of the Norwegian Constitution, which establishes a 'right to an environment that is conducive to health and to a natural environment whose productivity and diversity are maintained.' The Oslo District Court ruled in favour of the Norwegian Government on 4 January 2018. The court recognised that Article 112 of the Constitution is a rights provision but found that the government did not violate any

28 *Juliana v United States* (Oregon District Court, case No 6:15-CV-01517-TC, 10 November 2016).

29 The 'Right to a stable climate' is the constitutional question asked by the lawcase *Juliana (Kelsey Cascadia Rose Juliana v the United States)*, brought before the State of Oleron's ninth Circuit Court in 2014. The main goal of the Paris Agreement (2015 and ratified by 193 states in 2016) is to stablize the climate system and avoid global warming up to +2°C or if possible under 1,5°C; see Marta Torre-Schaub, 'L'émergence d'un droit à un climat stable : une construction interdisciplinaire' in Marta Torre-Schaub (ed), *Droit et Changement climatique : Regards croisés à l'interdisciplinaire. Quelles réponses à l'urgence climatique?* (Mare & Martin 2020).

30 *Greenpeace Nordic and Nature & Youth v Ministry of Petroleum and Energy* (Oslo District Court, case No 16–166674TVI-OTIR/06, 4 January 2018).

relevant rights because it had fulfilled the necessary duties before making the licensing decision. Greenpeace Nordic and Nature and Youth appealed the decision alleging that '[t]he District Court erred in interpreting Article 112 in such a way that it limits the duty of the Norwegian government to guarantee the right to a healthy environment.'[31] On 22 January 2020, the Court of Appeal affirmed the District Court's ruling that the oil and gas licenses were valid. The Court held that the appellants could not show a violation of Article 112 in this instance, particularly because it is uncertain whether and to what extent the licenses would lead to increased greenhouse gas emissions. The plaintiffs appealed the decision on 24 February 2020. The Norwegian Supreme Court granted leave to appeal on 20 April. On 22 December 2020, the Supreme Court announced its decision rejecting the appeal and upholding the licenses for deep-sea extraction. Eleven of the 15 judges panel upheld the lower court's ruling. The Court reasoned that although the Norwegian constitution protects citizens from environmental and climate harms, the future emissions from exported oil were too uncertain to bar the granting of these petroleum exploration licenses. The plaintiffs referred the case to the European Court of Human Rights on 15 June 2021.[32] It seems probable that the capacity of the Norwegian government to protect its citizens, both present and future generations through its constitution will be discussed before the European Court.

2.1.2. Consolidating Intergenerational Justice

In Ireland, in the *Friends of the Irish Environment* case[33] ruled in 2017, 2019 and 2020, the final decision implied the recognition of an 'unwritten constitutional right to a healthy environment' and a 'just transition', both pointing to the necessity of prospective protection for the environment through the constitution.

But one the latest and undoubtedly most important case in that field is the decision ruled by the German Federal Constitutional Court in an Order

31 ibid.

32 Natalia Kobylarz, 'Derniers développements sur la question environnementale et climatique au sein des différents organes du Conseil de l'Europe' (2022) 1 Revue Internationale de Droit Comparé 63; Marta Torre-Schaub, 'La construction d'un droit fondamental à un climat stable : évolutions, difficultés et perspectives'(2022) 1 Revue Internationale de Droit Comparé 7.

33 *Friends of the Irish Environment v The Government of Ireland* (2020) IEHC 747.

of 24 March 2021.[34] This decision is considered a landmark judgment. It underlined several crucial questions.[35] First, it affirmed the necessity for the State to organise a 'fair distribution between generations of the burden of climate change budgets'. The second important point highlighted was the affirmation that the protection of citizens is 'intertemporal' and 'transnational', including its elementary preconditions, not only the freedoms exercised today but those infringed for future generations and people living in other countries. The third question referred to the acceptance of 'damage' to a future or 'infringements to a future' due to climate change. Another interesting issue was the recognition by the Court of the necessity of ensuring a 'fundamental right' to a 'subsistence level' or 'a bare minimum' for future generations. It also underlined the necessity to 'ensure future freedoms' for future generations. As several authors emphasise, this 'intergenerational approach' makes this decision one of the most successful and developed in the field[36].

2.2. Using National Plans and Programs to Protect Future Interests

Future generations and current young generations can also be protected in some cases through other legal tools. Temporal scheduling in public policies is also crucial to better 'prepare the future' and to more equitably distribute the burden of reducing greenhouse emissions and the risks generated by climate change. In this sense, two lawsuits illustrate this 'function' and show how future generations are already 'presents' in the judge's reasoning.

---

34 Bundesverfassungsgericht (German Constitutional Court), 24 March 2021, 1 BvR 2656/18, 1 BvR 96/20, 1 BvR 78/20, 1 BvR 288/20, 1 BvR 96/20, 1 BvR 78/20.

35 Felix Eckardt, 'Liberté, droits de l'homme, Accord de Paris et changement climatique : l'arrêt historique allemand sur le contentieux climatique' (2022) 1 Revue Internationale de Droit Comparé 81; Felix Eckardt, 'How Can Climate Litigation Help Fighting Climate Change?' (9 June 2021) <https://www.sciencespo.fr/fr/evenements/how-can-climate-litigation-help-fighting-climate-change> accessed 7 July 2023.

36 Joana Setzer and Keina Yoshida, 'The Trends and Challenges of Climate Change Litigation and Human Rights' (2020) 2 European Human Rights Law Review 161; Marcos De Armenteras Cabot (n 23); Felix Eckardt, 'How can climate litigation help fithting climate change?' (n 34); Marcos de Armenteras Cabot, 'El litigio clímático ante la responsabilidad intergeneracional' (2021) 44 Cuadernos Electrónicos de Filosofía del Derecho 1; Emilie Gaillard, 'L'historique déclinaison transgénérationnelle des devoirs fondamentaux envers les generations futures par le tribunal fédéral constitutionnel allemande' (2021) 7 Revue Environnement, Energie, Infrastructures 1–2.

The *Friends of the Irish Environment*[37] case judgment at the Supreme Court of Ireland in July 2020 had the question of the national climate plan as a central point. This plan is a programmatic law that designates the different activities and obligations of the State in terms of climate according to a specific time scale and deadlines (National Climate Plan). The NGO Friends of the Irish Environment challenged the plan on the grounds that it did not sufficiently protect the rights of citizens, given that the plan was not sufficiently ambitious in terms of the fight against climate change. This lack of ambition of the plan could become a source of violation of fundamental rights by not including the rights of future generations.

In the United Kingdom, the decision concerning the project of future enlargement of Heathrow Airport in London[38] allowed the judges to cast the National Plan of Transports in a new perspective in accordance with the Paris Agreement targets and, more generally, its content, including the principles of common and shared responsibilities and the sustainability principle. By those two principles, as previously stated, future generations' interests can be protected or, at least, taken into account. This case, divided into two decisions, obliged the authorities to justify their project of enlargement of the airport based on the need to remain in line with the Paris Agreement. The decision asserted that the authorities would have to justify any project involving the National Plan of Transports – as was the case for the project of enlargement of the airport – that the project will be compatible with the Paris Agreement statements.

The *Grand Synthe*[39] case in France, which was considered by the *Conseil d'Etat* in two different decisions (November 2020 and July 2021), is another example of this tendency. In this case, brought by the municipality of Grand Synthe and its mayor, the legality of climate planning (in particular, the Stratégy Nationale Bas Carbone – (SNBC) i.e., national climate plan) and

37 *Friends of the Irish Environment v The Government of Ireland* (2020) IEHC 747.

38 *R (Plan B Earth and others) v Secretary of State for Business, Energy and Industrial Strategy* (2018) EWHC 1892 (Queen's Benchs division decision); Court of Appeal, Civil Division, *Re: The Queen on the application of Plan B. Earth and Ors v Sec'y of State for Bus., Energy & Indus. Strategy and Anr* (25 January 2019) EWCA civ. C1/2018/1750 <https://perma.cc/TYX2-Y4EJ>.

39 *Commune de Grande-Synthe et Damien Carème c France* (French Conseil d'Etat, case No 427301, 1 July 2021) et CE, *Commune de Grande-Synthe et Damien Carème c France* (French Conseil d'Etat, case No 427301, 19 November 2020).

other legislative measures was challenged,[40] considering that they do not allow sufficient protection of the city of Grande Synthe against climate risks. In both decisions, the *Conseil d'Etat* considers that, on the one hand, the SNBC is indeed a text that creates obligations for the State. On the other hand, both decisions agree that the State has not made sufficient efforts to reduce emissions by following the current trajectory, which will not make it possible to achieve carbon neutrality by 2050 or else at the cost of immeasurable efforts for future generations.[41] In these decisions, future generations do not appear on the front line. How the State plans and programmes climate change mitigation (by reaching carbon neutrality by 2050) is the core question of this case. However, this discussion contributes to the debate on the protection of future generations by putting on the table the question of whether future generations will not have to make additional efforts to reduce their emissions in the event that today's efforts are insufficient.

The last decision in this case was handed down in May 2023[42]. For the third time, the Conseil d'Etat affirmed that the government had not fulfilled its climate obligations arising from legislative texts committing it to action at a more sustained pace than that stipulated. However, the High court has not yet determined that it is necessary to impose an astreinte on the administration at this stage, and has again set a 'grace' period for the government to deploy more ambitious climate action. Despite this somewhat

40 Christian Huglo and Théophile Bégel, 'Le recours de la commune de Grande-Synthe et de son maire contre l'insuffisance des actions mises en œuvre par l'Etat pour lutter contre le changement climatique' (2019) 5 Revue Environnement, Energie, Infrastructures 38; Remi Radiguet, 'Objectif de décision des émissions de gaz… à effet normatif?' (2020) La Semaine Juridique Administration et collectivités territoriales 28–33; Beatrice Parence and Judith Rochfeld, 'Tsunami juridique au Conseil d'Etat : Une première décision "climatique" historique' (2020) 49 La Semaine du Droit–Edition Générale 2138; Marta Torre-Schaub, 'Plainte de Grande-Synthe pour inaction climatique : pourquoi la décision du Conseil d'Etat fera date' *The Conversation* (Melbourne, 23 November 2020) <https://perma.cc/D36L-8DA9>; Marta Torre-Schaub, 'L'affaire de Grande Synthe, une première décision emblématique dans le contentieux climatique français' (2020) 12 Revue Environnement, Energie, Infrastructures 13; Hubert Delzangles, 'Le premier "recours climatique" en France : une affaire à suivre!' (2021) 4 l'Actualité Juridique Droit Administratif 217.

41 Marta Torre-Schaub, 'Les contentieux climatiques. Du passé vers l'avenir' (2022) 1 Revue française de droit administratif 75.

42 *Grande Synthe III*, Conseil d'Etat, 10 May 2023 <https://perma.cc/WG6F-S455>; see Jean-Marc Pastor, Dalloz Actualité, 17 mai 2023; Marta Torre-Schaub, 'Qui va doucement, ne va (peut-être pas) durement' (2023) 23 La Semaine Juridique, Commentaires.

timid decision, the Conseil d'Etat has also submitted a preliminary question to the Conseil Constitutionnel on whether certain legal provisions infringe the right to a healthy environment. Indirectly, once again, this fundamental right to a healthy environment is reappearing, like a sea serpent. This right, as we know, protects the environmental rights of present and future generations.

This type of dispute will very likely develop in the short to medium term, as most national climate plans do not seem to have lived up to the ambitions set by the objectives of the Paris Agreement. Let us briefly recall that these objectives include not exceeding global warming of 2° C and staying below 1.5° C if possible. This objective is developed by various domestic laws in terms of the temporality of reduction of emissions at various scales in time until 2050 to achieve the objective of carbon neutrality by that date. Therefore, all domestic laws or climate plans that do not allow these trajectories of reduction to be followed, do not sufficiently protect future generations and there will likely be successive litigation around this issue in the coming years.

The last point we wish to highlight here is the role that general environmental principles can play to protect future generations from climate change's negative effects.

2.3. Affirming Principles and Rights through Climate Change Litigation

The use of environmental legal principles to ensure the protection of future generations is frequent in climate change litigation. Several principles are often discussed as part of the cases. Some of these principles are interesting tools to protect future generations (a). In the same innovative way, in climate change litigation, human rights appear to be a promising path for ensuring sustainable protection for future generations.[43]

---

43 John Knox, UN Committee for Human Rights, 'Report of the Special Rapporteur on the Issue of Human Rights Obligations Relating to the Enjoyment of a Safe, Clean, Healthy and Sustainable Environment' (24 January 2018) U.N. Doc. A/HRC/37/58 §57, 52; UN Committee for Human Rights, 'Petition of Torres Strait Islanders to the United Nations Human Rights Committee Alleging Violations Stemming from Australia's Inaction on Climate Change' (13 May 2019); Cesar Rodriguez Garavito, 'International Human Rights and Climate Governance: Origins and Implications of a Climate-based Litigation' document presented during the Conference 'Climate Litigation Emergency' (NYU School of Law, 9–10 March 2020); Cesar Rodriguez Garavito,

2.3.1. Asserting Environmental Principles to Protect Future Generations' Interests

The principle of 'common and shared responsibilities' reflected in Article 2 of the CCNU and in the Paris Agreement gives an interesting 'frame' to think about both the past and the future. The past is reflected in the constant reference to the 1990 emission level and industrial activities to fix a 'starting point' for past responsibilities for developed countries concerning their past CO_2 emissions. This principle also appears in reference to 'human activities' as a cause of aggravation of global warming. The future is apparent in this principle because it gives a 'map' of the world, divided into 'developed' and 'developing' countries. This map proposes different time frames for emission levels, for timely reductions and for actual and future National Contributions (NC) for reducing global emissions on a domestic scale. This road map of the world, in terms of reduction obligations by countries, allows a new path for protecting future generations. To date, there are no climate cases concerning this particular principle. However, there will probably will be in the next few years, mostly regarding the developing and emerging economies countries of the Global South, which are particularly concerned by the dilemma for 'economic and industrial development' and 'sustainability and protection for the future generations'.

More explicitly referring to the future, the 'principle of sustainability' is also a very powerful tool for protecting future generations. In the first *Urgenda* decision ruled in 2015, an explicit reference to future generations appears clearly and constitutes one of the core arguments of the defendants. In its decision of June 2015, the Court of District of The Hague retakes this argument and develops it in a very interesting opinion. The decision asserts that the State does indeed have a duty to protect its citizens against

'Litigating the Climate Emergency: The Global Raise of Human-Based Litigation for Climate Action' in César Rodríguez Garavito (ed), *Litigating the Climate Emergency: How Human Rights, Courts and Legal Mobilisation Can Bolster Climate Action* (CUP 2022); Natalia Kobylarz, 'Balancing its Way Out of Strong Anthropocentrism: Integration of Ecological Minimum Standards in the European Court of Human Rights Fair Balance Review' (2022) Journal of Human Rights and the Environment 16; Helen Keller and Corina Heri, 'The Future is Now. Climate Cases Before the ECtHR' (2022) 40(1) Nordic Journal of Human Rights 153; Marta Torre-Schaub, 'The Future of European Climate Change Litigation. The Carême Case Before the European Court of Human Rights' (*Verfassungsblog*, 10 August 2022) <https://perma.cc/G7XW-U9LN>; Amelie Adam, Delphine Misonne and Marta Torre-Schaub, 'Chronique des contentieux climatiques et droits de l'homme' (2023) 1 Revue européenne des droits de l'homme.

the adverse effects of climate change, based on the sustainability principle. This principle, following the reasoning of the Court, implies a specific and reinforced obligation of duty for the Netherlands, as they are one of the leading countries in the developed world. This duty concerns both present generations and future generations.

In this particular case, the 'precautionary principle' is also visible. The judges develop an interesting use of this principle in the first *Urgenda* decision.[44] According to the judgment, the precautionary principle should be applied by the Dutch government to better protect citizens against future climate risks. Again, the protection of future generations is implied in this reasoning, and the interpretation of this principle concerning climate change opens up an interesting path for the protection of future generations.

Last but not least, the prevention principle plays an important role in 'preparing the future' and reaffirming rights to prevent future damage and risks. This preventive function as a basis for establishing a right for more robust protection appears in the *Friends of the Irish Environment* case of 2020, given the fact that the Irish Climate National Plan cannot prevent harm to human rights. Pushing this argument further, human rights should be interpreted broadly, including future generations' rights.

---

44 *Urgenda v the Netherlands* (Court of The Hague, case No C/09/456689/ HA ZA 13–1396, 24 June 2015); *Urgenda v the Netherlands* (Court of Appeal of The Hague, case No 200.178.245/01, 9 October 2018); *Urgenda v the Netherlands* (Dutch Supreme Court, case No 19/00135, 20 December 2019).

45 TA de Paris (Administrative Court of Paris), decisions of 3 February 2021, n°1904967, 1904968, 1904972, 1904976 Lexis Kiosque; 'L'affaire du siècle, une révolution pour la justice climatique? A propos de la décision du TA du 3 février 2021 (n° 1904967, 1904968, 1904972, 1904976/4–1)' (2021) 10 La Semaine juridique Générale 247; Marta Torre-Schaub, 'l'Affaire du siècle, une affaire à suivre' (2021) 3 Environnement, Energie, Infrastructures 10; Denis Mazeaud, 'L'affaire du siècle un petit pas vers le solidarisme climatique' (2021) 6 La Semaine juridique Générale JCP-G 139; Marta Torre-Schaub, 'Décryptage juridique de l'affaire du siècle' *The Conversation* (Melbourne, 10 February 2021) <https://perma.cc/95DT-D84B>; Marta Torre-Schaub and Pauline Bozo, 'L'affaire du siècle, un jugement en clair-obscur?' (2021)12 La Semaine Juridique Administrations et Collectivités territoriales 2088 at 31; Mathilde Hautereau-Boutonnet, 'L'affaire du siècle, de l'audace, encore de l'audace, toujours de l'audace!' (2021) 6 Recueil Dalloz 281; Marta Torre-Schaub, 'Climate Change Litigation in France' (n 24); Meryem Deffairi, 'Le préjudice écologique saisi par le juge administratif. Commentaire de la décision du Tribunal administratif de Paris du 3 février 2021, n°1904967, Notre affaire à tous' (2021) Droit administratif, comm. 28; Marta Torre-Schaub, 'Le contentieux climatique. Du passé vers le future' (2022) 1 Revue française de droit administratif 1; Marta Torre-Schaub, 'Dynamics, Prospects

In the recent judgment in France, *l'affaire du siècle*[45], the prevention principle[46] plays a core role in showing the way for the State to take responsibility for not having made enough efforts in the past to attend to the carbon-neutral goal set for 2050. This insufficient action by the State implies that in the years to come unless the trajectory is addressed, the considerable efforts that should be made to reduce emissions will be a significant burden and will become progressively more difficult to attain. Following this decision, to better ensure both a duty for the State to take climate obligations more seriously and, to better ensure a right to a future for all generations, long-term decisions have to be taken urgently and firmly to make it possible to achieve the target of carbon neutrality in the future.

2.3.2. How Duties and Rights Can Defend Future Interests

The obligation imposed by the 'duty of care', which appears explicitly in the 2015 *Urgenda* case, is reinforced in the decisions of 2018 by the Court of Appeals of The Hague and in 2019 in the final ruling by the Supreme Court. This principle is also present in two other lawsuits, the lawsuit against Shell[47] in the Netherlands, ruled in 2021, and the *Sharma* case, ruled in Australia the same year[48].

In *Millieudefensie against Shell* ruled in May 2021, plaintiffs used the argument of the 'duty of care' extended to private companies. They argued that given the Paris Agreement's goals and the scientific evidence regarding the dangers of climate change, Shell had a duty of care to take action to reduce its greenhouse gas emissions. Plaintiffs based this duty of care argument on Article 6:162 of the Dutch Civil Code and Articles 2 and 8 of the European Convention on Human Rights (ECHR), which guarantees the right to life (Article 2) and the right to private life, family life, home, and correspondence (Article 8). The plaintiffs' argument outlined the com-

---

and Trends in Climate Change Litigation. Making Climate Change a Priority in France' (2021) 22(8) German Law Review 1445; Julien Bétaille, 'Climate Litigation in France, a Reflection of Trends in Environmental Litigation' (2022) 22 *elni Review* 63; Marta Torre-Schaub, 'Climate Litigation in France. The High Administrative Court as Janus or Prometheus?' (2023) European Journal of Risk Regulation (forthcoming).

46 Marta Torre-Schaub, 'Le préjudice écologique au secours du climat, ombres et lumières' (2021) 11 La Semaine du Droit–Edition Générale 520.

47 *Milieudefensie et al. v Royal Dutch Shell* (Rechtbank Den Haag, No C/09/571932 / HA ZA 19–379, 26 May 2021).

48 *Sharma and others v Ministry of the Environment* (Federal Court of Australia 560, 27 May 2021).

pany's misleading statements on climate change and inadequate action to reduce climate change. They stand on Shell's unlawful endangerment of Dutch citizens and actions constituting hazardous negligence. Such behaviour will endanger both present and future generations. This duty implies the obligation of 'doing better in the future', and consequently conducting their activities making 'significant efforts' in reducing emissions. For the company, this implies paying special attention to future activities.

Even more illustrative of this trend is the *Sharma* case, filed on 8 September 2020 by eight young people before Australia's Federal Court to block a coal project. The lawsuit sought an injunction to stop the Australian Government from approving an extension of the Whitehaven Vickery coal mine. The plaintiffs claimed to represent all people under 18 and argued that the Federal Minister has a common law duty of care for young people. They further asserted that digging up and burning coal will exacerbate climate change and harm young people in the future. The plaintiffs sought an injunction to prevent the Minister from approving the project under the Environment Protection and Biodiversity Conservation Act (EPBC). The Court established a new duty of care to avoid causing personal harm to minors but declined to issue an injunction to force the Minister to block the coal mine extension. The applicants established that the Minister had a duty to take reasonable care to avoid causing personal injury to minors having the possibility, under s 130 and s 133 of the EPBC Act, to approve or not approve the project[49]. The judges, however, declined to issue an injunction, reasoning that the plaintiffs had not established that it was probable that the Minister would breach the duty of care in making the approval decision. This decision, even though the injunction was not approved, raised a number of questions about the scope of the duty, especially with regard to minors and future generations.

In the category of human rights[50] as a tool to protect future generations, a complaint filed by six young Portuguese people against 33 countries

---

49 *Sharma and others v Ministry of the Environment* (Federal Court of Australia 560, 27 May 2021).

50 Regarding the growing link between human rights and climate change litigation, see for example: Annalisa Savaresi and Joana Setzer, 'Mapping the Whole of the Moon: An Analysis of the Role of Human Rights in Climate Litigation' (2021) Journal of Human Rights and the Environment 1759 ss; Joana Setzer and Catherine Highman, *Global Trends in Climate Change Litigation: 2021 Snapshot* (Grantham Research Institute on Climate Change and the Environment and Centre for Climate Change Economics and Policy, London School of Economics and Political Science 2021);

before the European Court of Human Rights on 2 September 2020[51] is to be noted. Invoking the European Convention on Human Rights, the plaintiffs claim that their right to life is threatened by the effects of climate change (such as forest fires in Portugal), that their right to privacy includes their physical and mental well-being and that it is threatened by heat waves that force them to spend more time inside their homes. These circumstances lead them to point to the violation of their human rights based on the said Convention. Their request also points to the violation of Article 14 ECHR, which establishes the right to non-discrimination. This right should be interpreted in a 'temporal' way as a new path for protecting future interests and consolidating trans-generational justice.

In the same vein, another case was recently filed by the Union of Swiss Senior Women for Climate Protection against the Swiss Federal Council and others[52]. Previously, the Swiss Federal Court had dismissed the case on the grounds that the protection of fundamental rights sought by the applicants could not be claimed as long as the long-term temperature objective of the Paris Agreement had not been achieved. In March 2021, the Strasbourg Court decided to grant the application. The appeal is based on Articles 6, 2 and 8 of the ECHR (i.e., the right to an effective remedy, the right to life and the right to private and family life).

The latest case is the aforementioned decision by the Montana court, which found that the various legislative provisions concerning fossil fuels in the state of Montana were contrary to the state constitution[53]. The plaintiffs, a group of young people between the ages of 6 and 20, alleged that these legislative provisions violated their constitutional rights, including the right to a healthy environment and a stable climate[54]. More specifically, the

---

Joana Setzer and Lisa Vanhala, 'Climate Change Litigation: A Review of Research on Courts and Litigants in Climate Governance' (2019) 10(3) WIREs Climate Change 1; Setzer and Yoshida (n 35). About climate change litigation and human rights in the European Council context, see: Kobylarz (n 31); Keller and Heri (n 41); Marta Torre-Schaub (n 41); Misonne and Torre-Schaub (n 41).

51 *Cláudia Duarte Agostinho et autres c le Portugal et 32 autres États* App No 39371/20 (ECtHR, 13 November 2020); Chloe Farand, 'Six Portuguese Youth File "Unprecedented" Climate Lawsuit Against 33 Countries' (*Climate Home News*, 3 September 2020) <https://perma.cc/L5M8-ZDSR>.

52 *Association Aînées pour la protection du climat c Suisse Klimat Seniorinnen* App No 53600/20 (ECtHR, 27 October 2020).

53 *Held v Montana*, Montana First Judicial District Court, Lewis & Clarck County, 14 August 2023, <https://perma.cc/WB4G-QCXX>.

54 ibid.

decision finds that the various legislative provisions in question do not meet the conditions necessary to preserve the principle of prevention and fairness for the young applicants[55].

Once again, even if a direct reference to protect future generations does not appear in the cases we have analysed, it is nevertheless implied.[56] Those decisions show the necessity to consider future generations more and in a better way. Those cases also illustrate the imperious necessity of thinking about climate action in the medium and long term, not just in the short term. The 'future' of future generations is clearly at stake when it comes to climate change's adverse effects.

The cases we have presented show the necessity of including future generations' rights in the law. Above all the cases cited here, we highlighted the need for more inclusive legal methods in order to better protect future generations and the continuity of Humankind.

***

Concluding Remarks

Climate change litigation can contribute to enhancing the importance of protecting future generations. Even when it is not invoked directly, the emerging obligation of 'thinking on the future' and 'protecting the future' opens up a new pathway in several cases. Some environmental law principles are opening up and reaffirming themselves to rethink the future. The younger generation's interest in climate issues is growing. This interest can be seen in a number of ways. In some cases, these are classic mobilizations (strikes, demonstrations, exhibitions). In others, the action goes further and takes more active forms of protest (symbolic attacks on activities considered superfluous and contrary to a proactive commitment to climate protection). In other situations, youth smobilizations take the form of petitions for advisory opinions to international bodies dedicated to the protection of children (United Nations Committee of the Rights of

55 ibid., 102, point 9.

56 Marta Torre-Schaub, 'Les dynamiques juridiques et judiciaires de la gouvernance climatique. Libres propos autour de la construction d'un droit du changement climatique' (2021) 22 Revue juridique d'Assas 35; Marta Torre-Schaub, 'Dynamics, Prospects and Trends in Climate Change Litigation. Making Climate Change Emergency a Priority in France' (2021) 16(3) German Law Review 179.

the Child[57]). Finally, as we showed in our article, legal action is also a growing form of mobilization by the younger generation. Three new cases are particularly telling: the case brought by young Portuguese people before the European Court of Human Rights[58], the case brought by Swiss senior citizens[59], who are particularly vulnerable to global warming and the case brought before the Montana Disctrict Court[60]. Still pending is the *Aurora* case, brought before the Swedish courts by young Swedes accompanied by Greta Thunberg[61]. The last hope remains in the request for an opinion from the International Court of Justice (ICJ) by the State of Vanuatu and 105 other states to question the Court on the nature and extent of international climate obligations so that young people generations and the most vulnerable states can be protected.[62]

Despite these relevant advances, the decisions are not yet numerous enough to build a general theory in this field, and remedies are not always in accordance with the importance of providing a sustainable life to future generations. However, we feel that the issue is gaining in importance, firstly through the growing number of legal cases, and secondly through media coverage and the sympathy of the public and young people concerned by the climate emergency. Yet, the Law (International and national) must be able to respond to these legitimate concerns quickly enough to avoid the worst possible future for the younger generations.

---

57 Greta Thunberg before United Nations Committee for the Rights of the child, <https://perma.cc/4VFN-CLVB>.

58 *Cláudia Duarte Agostinho et autres c le Portugal et 32 autres États* App No 39371/20 (ECtHR, 13 November 2020).

59 *Association Aînées pour la protection du climat c Suisse Klimat Seniorinnen* App No 53600/20 (ECtHR, 27 October 2020).

60 *Held v Montana* (n 53).

61 *Anton foley and others v Sweden (Aurora case,* introduced in 2022), pending. The plaintiffs argue that the state has failed to adopt sufficient and adequate procedural measures by not investigating, in line with the best available science. They also argue that the state has failed to take sufficient and adequate measures to implement Sweden's fair share, to reduce IPEJA emissions between 2019 and 2030, to reduce national IPEJA emissions between 2019 and 2030, to secure that GHG emissions reductions within one category is not achieved through increasing emissions in another category under any circumstances, and to compensate annual emissions that exceed the permissible emissions, by reducing the net emissions by an equivalent amount in the following period under any circumstances, starting in 2019. Ultimately, the case argues the violation of the European human Rights Convention.

62 United Nations, 'General Assembly Adopts Resolution Requesting International Court of Justice Provide Advisory Opinion on States' Obligations Concerning Climate Change' (29 March 2023) GA/12497 <https://perma.cc/BZ2L-36AJ>.

14. Mechanisms Available under the Law of the Sea to Speak on Behalf of Future Generations

Elena Ivanova[*]

Abstract: *The protection and preservation of the marine environment, the conservation of marine living resources, and the sustainable exploration and exploitation of marine resources more generally are of significance for food security and for the survival and health of future generations. Thus, the marine environment and the marine resources, including the Area and its resources, are valuable assets for future generations, which can only be preserved if current generations take action in this respect. It is the purpose of this contribution to examine and draw attention to the typology of these actions and the tools and mechanisms through which future generations' interests can be voiced in the law of the sea context. These include: interpretation; accessible dispute settlement mechanisms for the resolution of disputes concerning the protection of the marine environment and the conservation of marine living resources; procedures for rendering advisory opinions; and the principle of 'Common Heritage of Mankind'.*

1. Introduction

The seas and oceans cover a vast majority of the Earth's surface and form part of the ecosystem balance. They play a critical role is maintaining its life-support systems, in moderating the climate, in sustaining animals and plants, including oxygen-producing phytoplankton.[1] They constitute the natural habitat of fish, which are an important source of protein and whose very survival and conservation are of essential significance for food security and, hence, have intergenerational repercussions. The submarine areas subjacent to the water column are rich in non-living resources of tremendous economic significance which are heavily exploited in areas within national jurisdiction. This exploitation also has intergenerational repercussions, given the risks to the marine environment in terms of its degradation and by implication for the marine ecosystem and biodiversity.

---

* Dr Elena Ivanova worked as a Research Fellow at the Max Planck Institute Luxembourg for Procedural Law. Her doctoral dissertation examines the interaction between the dispute settlement mechanisms established under the UNCLOS and the WTO Agreement. Her research interests include law of the sea, WTO law, public international law, conflict of laws, international arbitration.

1 Report of the World Commission on Environment and Development: Our Common Future, Annex to UN Doc A/42/427, 258.

The submarine areas also embody the area of the seabed, the ocean floor and the subsoil thereof, beyond the limits of national jurisdiction, which the United Nations Convention on the Law of the Sea (UNCLOS or 'Convention')[2], the constitution for the seas and oceans, denotes as 'the Area', and the resources of that area. Furthermore, objects of an archaeological and historical nature found in the Area are to be preserved or disposed of for the benefit of mankind as a whole.[3] In addition, the Area is a home to genetic organisms whose importance for human health and medicine is yet to be established.[4]

The Area and its resources were the only areas of the planet which at the time of the UNCLOS negotiations had not been appropriated for national use.[5] The manner in which the Convention has dealt with these areas has a direct bearing on the interests of future generations. It declares the Area and its resources to be the common heritage of mankind, thus essentially recognising future generations, an inalienable part of 'mankind' or rather 'humankind',[6] as beneficiaries of the Area. UNCLOS subjects the activities taking place in that area to the principle of 'Common Heritage of Mankind'[7], while imposing an obligation upon the States parties to the Convention ('States Parties') to develop the said common heritage for the benefit of mankind.[8] The Convention addresses the legal status of the Area and its resources and brings deep seabed mining activities under the con-

2 United Nations Convention on the Law of the Sea (adopted 10 December 1982, entered into force 16 November 1994) 1833 UNTS 3.

3 Art 149 UNCLOS.

4 These are not covered by the utilisation regime embodied in Part XI UNCLOS. However, the negotiations on an international legally binding instrument under the UNCLOS on the conservation and sustainable use marine biological diversity of areas beyond national jurisdiction (BBNJ) are ongoing. See: <https://www.un.org/bbnj/> accessed 7 July 2023.

5 The oceans, outer space and Antarctica are usually regarded as the 'global commons', although there is some controversy as to whether Antarctica should be treated as part of the international commons, given the fact that some States maintain territorial claims. See Report of the World Commission on Environment and Development (n 1) 275. Whereas outer space and Antarctica are addressed by other treaties, the UNCLOS is concerned solely with the oceans.

6 The Convention utilises the term 'mankind', unlike the UNESCO Declaration of the Responsibilities of the Present Generations Towards Future Generation, adopted by UNESCO's General Conference at its 29th Session, 21 October-12 November, 1997, Paris, France (29 C Resolution/ 44). However, the terms 'mankind' and 'humankind' (being considered a gender neutral term) will be used interchangeably in this paper.

7 Arts 136 and 150 UNCLOS.

8 Art 150 (i) UNCLOS.

trol of an international organisation – the International Seabed Authority ('the Authority'), which acts as a proxy of mankind and is designed to ensure that the utilisation of the Area and its resources benefit mankind. Thus, the Convention not only treats humankind, and by logical implication future generations, as an addressee of rights under treaty law – a novelty in international law – but it establishes an institution and mechanisms to ensure that these rights are protected. As a result, the principle of 'Common Heritage of Mankind' as enshrined in the Convention envisages institutional co-operation among States Parties through the Authority for the management and use of the common heritage of mankind in the interest of mankind which has no analogue in treaty law. It constitutes one of the most important achievements of the UNCLOS in the law of the sea context, enables the protection of the interests of future generations in the Area, and will be given special consideration in this paper.

Against this backdrop, the protection and preservation of the marine environment, the conservation of marine living resources and sustainable fisheries, and the sustainable exploration and exploitation of the marine resources more generally (including the resources of the Area with a view to the conservation of the marine biodiversity), are of significance for food security and for the survival and health of future generations. In other words, the marine environment and the marine resources, including the Area and its resources, are valuable assets for future generations, which can only be preserved if current generations take action in this respect. Thus, positive action taken by present generations with a view to preserving these assets is a means to safeguarding the interests, including vital interests, of future generations.

It is the purpose of this contribution to examine and draw attention to the typology of these actions, the channels through which these interests can be voiced in the law of the sea context, the subjects who can take action, given the importance of the seas and oceans, and the legal regime developed under the UNCLOS for future generations.[9]

9 The term 'future generations' for the purposes of the current paper denotes cohorts of not yet born, i.e. hypothetical individuals, as opposed to past and present generations, including young people. This approach is premised on the view that such an understanding of the notion of 'future generations' encourages long-term thinking and thinking about intergenerational equity and the distant future (as opposed to the near future), which is likely to induce a greater effort and proactive steps (including by way of progressive development of the law through interpretation) on the part of the present generations to address tough challenges of the present so as to secure the ability

The tools and mechanisms through which intergenerational considerations can be taken into account, and the protection of the marine environment and the conservation of the marine resources can be enhanced and secured, are perceived in this paper as an important means through which the interests of future generations can be voiced and protected. These include: interpretation; accessible dispute settlement mechanisms for the resolution of disputes concerning the protection of the marine environment and the conservation of marine living resources; procedures for rendering advisory opinions; and the principle of 'Common Heritage of Mankind'.

The selection of some of the above mechanisms is premised on the view that, *first*, interpretation by courts and tribunals is a means for bringing intergenerational considerations into the decision-making, i.e. into the understanding and the application of the existing law, and an avenue for the development of the law relating to the protection of the environment, the preservation and conservation of its components and the common heritage of mankind. *Second*, since judicial decisions and advisory opinions normally have an impact on States' conduct, judicial interpretations which take into account intergenerational considerations and the latest developments in environmental law are logically likely to influence States' behaviour with a view to improving the performance of their obligations related to the environment and the conservation of living resources. As a result, interpretation, given in authoritative pronouncements on the state of the law (i.e. in judicial decisions and advisory opinions) is a tool to protect the interests of future generation and a subtle tool for voicing the foreseeable needs of future generations. However, the mechanisms through which the conduct of States can be scrutinised, the UNCLOS provisions interpreted and the performance of States ultimately improved in the interest of future genera-

---

of future generations to meet their own needs. Future generations thus fall within the broader scope of 'the absent'. The latter concept, given the normal meaning of the word 'absent' undoubtedly encompasses cohorts of individuals who do not currently exist such as past and (not yet born) future generations. However, this concept can be given a broader understanding in light of the purposes of the current project (which is concerned, among other things, with intergenerational equity and the possibility for taking representative action with a view to making decisions and achieving meaningful results with implications for those generations who cannot themselves take action and protect their interests in the present due to the fact that they do not currently exist or cannot vote) and can be extended also to young people, i.e. present generations who have not yet reached adulthood, and respectively cannot yet vote and participate in the decision-making. Under this conception, the guiding criterion for inclusion in the group of 'the absent' is the lack of capacity to participate in the decision-making.

tions are dispute settlement procedures and the procedures for rendering advisory opinions.

The Convention which has almost universal participation embodies a significant body of law aimed at the protection of the marine environment and the conservation of its living resources. The interpretation of the said provisions by UNCLOS courts and tribunals is therefore of crucial significance for the protection of the marine environment and the health of the oceans and hence for the interests of future generations and will be assessed in Section II of this paper. The purpose of this exercise will be to demonstrate how the latest developments in environmental law and intergenerational considerations have been (and can be) integrated into the understanding and the application of the law in practice through interpretation, to display the potential of the UNCLOS dispute settlement mechanism and the procedure for rendering advisory opinions for protecting the interests of future generations.

Section III will deal with the principle of Common Heritage of Mankind and will be concerned with the innovative institutional arrangements under the Convention aimed at the protection of the interests of future generations.

Section IV will address the dispute settlement procedure set out in Part XV UNCLOS. It is compulsory, i.e. proceedings can be initiated by way of unilateral application, which ensures both its efficacy and accessibility.[10] In addition, the Convention provides for a mechanism for the resolution of disputes concerning the activities in the Area which secures the application of the principle of common heritage of mankind enshrined in Part XI UNCLOS and the enforcement of the obligations therein. The discussion on the said dispute settlement procedures will focus on three aspects of the contentious jurisdiction of UNCLOS courts and tribunals: first, their jurisdiction *ratione materiae* over disputes with an environmental dimension, including disputes concerning the conservation of the marine living

10 For more details regarding the UNCLOS dispute settlement system, see Andronico Adede, *The System for Settlement of Disputes under the United Convention on the Law of the Sea: A Drafting History and a Commentary* (Martinus Nijhoff 1987); Rüdiger Wolfrum, 'The Settlement of Disputes Before the International Tribunal for the Law of the Sea – A Progressive Development of International Law or Relying on Traditional Mechanisms?' (2008) 51 Japanese Yearbook of International Law 140; Patibandla Chandrasekhara Rao, 'Law of the Sea, Settlement of Disputes' in Rüdiger Wolfrum (ed), *Max Planck Encyclopedia of Public International Law* (*MPEPIL*) (OUP 2011).

resources; second, the special jurisdiction of the Seabed Disputes Chamber (partly exclusive) over disputes concerning the activities in the Area; and, third, their jurisdiction *ratione personae.* In addition, attention will be drawn to the procedure for rendering advisory opinions and the advisory jurisdiction of the Seabed Disputes Chamber and the ITLOS.

2. Interpretation of the Obligations Concerning the Protection of the Marine Environment under the UNCLOS

The Convention embodies a significant body of law aimed at the protection of the marine environment and the conservation of marine living-resources, and, given its almost universal participation, constitutes one of the most important international legal regimes in this respect. Authoritative interpretations of the respective provisions given by UNCLOS tribunals are of crucial significance for the protection of the marine environment, the sustainable exploitation of marine living resources, the health of the oceans, and for the interests of future generations because they guide and have an impact on States' conduct in this respect. Since many of the UNCLOS provisions – including Article 192 -[11] are regarded as reflecting customary international law,[12] these interpretations have the potential to influence the understanding of the respective customary international law[13] and consequently the behaviour of the States Parties and of other States bound by that law. They set the tone and, depending on the approach chosen, can loosen the said protection or, conversely, discipline States and induce them into taking more active steps and adopting stricter measures with a view to ensuring better protection of the marine environment and preventing the over-exploitation of marine living resources with obvious implications for future generations.

---

11 See Detlef Czybulka, 'Article 192' in Alexander Proelss and others (eds), *United Nations Convention on the Law of the Sea: A Commentary* (Beck – Hart – Nomos 2017) 1284–1285.

12 See James Harrison, *Saving the Oceans through Law: The International Legal Framework for the Protection of the Marine Environment* (OUP 2017) 17. See also 'United States Ocean Policy' (1983) 77 AJIL 619–623, in which the president of the United States confirmed that the United States would not become a signatory to the Convention, owing to its concerns over the Convention's deep-seabed mining provisions, but it would 'accept and act in accordance with the balance of interests relating to the traditional uses of the oceans, such as navigation and overflight'.

13 This is so given the inclination of international courts and tribunals to look into each other's pronouncements and lean on earlier case law.

Since most of these provisions are framed rather broadly, UNCLOS tribunals' interpretations play a crucial role in clarifying and specifying the content of the relevant States' obligations and the level of protection due. Bringing these interpretations in line with the latest developments in international environmental law and integrating intergenerational considerations in them will logically benefit future generations because such interpretations are most likely to provide the highest protection of the marine environment and foster the sustainable use of the marine ecosystems. UNCLOS tribunals have indeed taken bold steps in this regard, while consistently holding that the existing corpus of international law related to the environment is to inform the meaning of the relevant conventional provisions. They have also contributed to the debate on the nature and content of the precautionary approach, while potentially facilitating the formation of customary international law, which has implications beyond the confines of the law of the sea and strengthens the environmental protection more generally and beyond the marine areas. Adherence to the above obligations, as interpreted, ensures a higher level of protection and maintenance of the marine environment in the long run with implications across generations.

Most relevant to the topic of this contribution are Articles 61 (2) requiring coastal States ensure that the maintenance of the living resources in the Exclusive Economic Zone (EEZ) is not endangered by over-exploitation through proper *conservation* and management *measures*; Article 62 (4) demanding the nationals of all States fishing in the EEZ to *comply with the conservation measures* of the coastal State; Article 117 UNCLOS which obliges all States to take *measures* with respect to their nationals for the *conservation* of the marine living resources on the high seas; and Article 192 UNCLOS imposing upon States the *general duty to protect and preserve the marine environment* which is applicable to all maritime areas,[14] whose interpretation will be given careful consideration in the subsequent paragraphs in light of the aforementioned observations.

14 See *Request for an Advisory Opinion submitted by the Sub-Regional Fisheries Commission (SRFC)*, Advisory Opinion, 2 April 2015, ITLOS Case No 21, para. 120, referring to *Southern Bluefin Tuna (New Zealand v Japan; Australia v Japan)*, Provisional Measures, Order, 27 August 1999, ITLOS Reports 1999, 280, at 295, para. 70.

2.1. The Obligation to Protect and Preserve the Marine Environment Under Article 192 UNCLOS

Under Article 192 UNCLOS 'States have the obligation to protect and preserve the marine environment'. According to Yankov, 'it is the first time that a legal rule of this kind has been incorporated in a multilateral treaty of a universal character'[15] and it 'should be considered as an important step in the codification and progressive development of the law of the sea'.[16] Article 192 is phrased in general terms and says nothing about the protection due. By reference to the ITLOS jurisprudence, however, the arbitral tribunal constituted for the purposes of the *South China Arbitration* affirmed that this provision 'does impose a duty on States Parties'[17] and that its content is informed by the other provisions of Part XII and the corpus of international law relating to the environment:

> [t]he corpus of *international law relating to the environment*, which informs the content of the general obligation in Art. 192, requires that States "ensure that activities within their jurisdiction and control respect the environment of other States or of areas beyond national control." Thus, States have a positive "duty to prevent, or at least mitigate" significant harm to the environment when pursuing large-scale construction activities [emphasis added].[18]

---

15 Alexander Yankov, 'The Significance of the 1982 Convention on the Law of the Sea for the Protection of the Marine Environment and the Promotion of Marine Science and Technology – Third Committee Issues' in Bernard H Oxman and Albert W Koers (eds), *The 1982 Convention on the Law of the Sea* (Law of the Sea Institute 1984) 75.

16 ibid., 76.

17 *The South China Sea Arbitration (Philippines v China),* Award, 12 July 2016, PCA Case No 2013–19, para. 941, referring to *M/V "Louisa" (Saint Vincent and the Grenadines v Kingdom of Spain)*, Provisional Measures, Order, 23 December 2010, ITLOS Reports 2008–2010, 58, at 70, para. 76; *Dispute Concerning Delimitation of the Maritime Boundary Between Ghana and Côte D'Ivoire in the Atlantic Ocean (Ghana/Côte D'Ivoire)*, Provisional Measures, Order of 25 April 2015, ITLOS Reports 2015, para. 69. Harisson supports the view that Art 192 is better characterised as a statement of principle whose primary function is to determine the scope of Part XII as a whole. See Harrison (n 12) 23.

18 *The South China Sea Arbitration* (n 17) para. 941, referring to *Legality of the Threat or Use of Nuclear Weapons,* Advisory Opinion, 8 July 1996, ICJ Rep 226, para. 29; *Indus Waters Kishenganga Arbitration (Pakistan v India)*, Partial Award, 18 February 2013, PCA 31 RIAA 55, para. 451, quoting *Arbitration Regarding the Iron Rhine ('IJzeren Rijn') Railway between the Kingdom of Belgium and the Kingdom of the Netherlands*, Award, 24 May 2005, PCA 27 RIAA 35, para. 59.

Drawing on the preceding jurisprudence of UNCLOS tribunals and the ICJ, it further clarified that the content of the obligation under Article 192 is given shape in Article 194 (5) UNCLOS and includes the obligation to adopt certain measures necessary to protect and preserve the rare and fragile ecosystems, and constitutes an obligation of conduct which as such requires due diligence.[19]

2.1.1. Due Diligence Obligation

In the *South China Sea Arbitration*, the Arbitral Tribunal stated that due diligence signifies that the obligation to adopt appropriate rules and measures goes beyond their mere adoption and necessitates a certain level of vigilance in the enforcement of these measures and in the exercise of administrative control.[20] As a consequence, it reached the conclusion that the obligation to preserve and protect the environment in Article 192 UNCLOS includes a *due diligence obligation* to *prevent* the harvesting of species that are recognised as being at risk of extinction and requiring international protection[21] as well as the obligation to *prevent* the harmful activities that would affect depleted, threatened, or endangered species indirectly through the *destruction* of their *habitat*.[22] In the process of elucidating the scope and meaning of Article 192 UNCLOS, the Arbitral Tribunal touched and elaborated on concepts and issues of relevance for international environmental law such as the concepts of 'due diligence' and 'obligation of conduct' and the link between them,[23] as well as the core content of the general obligation to protect and preserve the marine environment.

19 *The South China Sea Arbitration* (n 17) para. 956.
20 ibid.
21 ibid.
22 ibid., para. 959.
23 ibid., para. 941, referring to the *Request for an Advisory Opinion submitted by the Sub-Regional Fisheries Commission (SRFC)* (n 14) paras 118–136, and *Pulp Mills on the River Uruguay (Argentina v Uruguay)*, Judgment, 20 April 2010, ICJ Rep 14.

2.1.2. Preservation of the Environment – Maintaining and Improving the Present Condition

It is to be observed that Article 192 not only concerns the protection of the marine environment from future damage but also its preservation.[24] Preservation goes beyond protection and entails 'maintaining and improving its present condition' as explained by the Arbitral Tribunal in the *South China Sea Arbitration*.[25] In this respect, the Arbitral Tribunal also clarified that 'Article 192 thus entails the positive obligation to take active measures to protect and preserve the marine environment, and by logical implication, entails the negative obligation *not to degrade* the marine environment [emphasis added].'[26] This interpretation of Article 192 gives the obligation embodied in it a wide-ranging character requiring from States to prevent the negative changes of the marine environment through its use as well as taking active measures, i.e. positive action, to preserve the oceans as an ecosystem. This aim undoubtedly forms part of the aspirations of the present generations, and, hence, is in their interest, respectively in the interest of future generations. Such interpretations encourage and, indeed, induce States to take positive action of the kind discussed by the arbitral tribunal with a view to preserving the marine environment and engaging in sustainable fisheries so as to be in compliance with their international obligations.

2.1.3. Erga Omnes

Article 192 has often been assigned an *erga omnes* quality.[27] This is why, any State will have standing to sue for breach or non-compliance and this applies to the obligation to protect and preserve the marine environment, including in areas beyond national jurisdiction.[28] Arguably, the award rendered in the *South China Sea Arbitration* provides some tentative

24 See Czybulka (n 11) 1286.
25 *The South China Sea Arbitration* (n 17) para. 941.
26 ibid.
27 Alexander Proelss, *Meeresschutz in Völker- und Europarecht: Das Bespiel des Nordatlantiks* (Duncker & Humblot 2004) 82; Patricia Birnie, Alan Boyle and Catherine Redgwell (eds), *International Law and the Environment* (3rd edn, OUP 2009) 383; Czybulka (n 11) 1283; Elena V Ivanova, *The Competing Jurisdiction of the UNCLOS and the WTO Dispute Settlement Fora in the Context of Multifaceted Disputes* (Nomos 2022) 212.
28 See Birnie, Boyle and Redgewell (n 27) 234.

support for this view, although the Arbitral Tribunal did not deal with the said *erga omnes* quality of Article 192. In the *South China Sea Arbitration*, the Philippines brought claims relating to environmental harm caused by Chinese activities in various locations in the South China Sea. The Arbitral Tribunal held that it had jurisdiction to deal with these claims, although the Philippines did not argue that it had suffered damages in its own maritime zones. Neither did the Arbitral Tribunals require that the Philippines demonstrate that it had been specifically affected by the alleged environmental harm. In this respect, the Arbitral Tribunal highlighted that:

> because the environmental obligations in Part XII [starting with Article 192] apply to States irrespective of where the alleged harmful activities took place, its jurisdiction is not dependent on the question of sovereignty over a particular feature, on a prior determination of the status of any maritime feature, on the existence of an entitlement by China or the Philippines to an exclusive economic zone in the area or on the prior delimitation of any overlapping entitlements.[29]

2.2. Conservation of Living Resources in the light of Articles 61 (2), 62 (4), 117

Concerning the conservation of living resources, both Article 61 (2) and Article 117 impose upon the coastal State and upon all States, respectively, the obligation to take conservation measures, whereas Article 62 (4) prescribes that nationals of other States fishing in the EEZ *shall comply* with the conservation measures of the coastal State (i.e. it imposes a specific obligation on the flag State within the EEZ). Article 61 (2), which requires that coastal States '*ensure* through proper conservation and management measures that the maintenance of the living resources in the exclusive economic zone is not endangered by over-exploitation [emphasis added]', and Article 62 (4) apply to the EEZ, whereas Article 117, requiring that all States '*take*, or cooperate with other States in taking, *such measures* for their respective nationals *as may be necessary* for the conservation of the living resources of the high seas [emphasis added]', applies to the high seas.[30] All of these obligations concern the conservation of marine living resources and are incumbent upon different categories of legal subjects.

29 *The South China Sea Arbitration* (n 17) para. 927.
30 Art 117 UNCLOS.

2.3. Due Diligence Obligations

If regarded as due diligence obligations, their performance would necessitate greater effort and diligence on the part of States that goes beyond the mere adoption of measures for conservation of living resources and includes their enforcement and the exercise of administrative control. The Tribunal has had the opportunity to address the content of the broadly framed obligation under Article 62 (4) UNCLOS. In its *Fisheries Advisory Opinion* rendered upon the *Request for an Advisory Opinion submitted by the Sub-Regional Fisheries Commission (SRFC),*[31] the ITLOS characterised this obligations as on obligation of due diligence which entails the adoption by States of laws and regulations, *including enforcement procedures,* so as to ensure that their nationals comply with the coastal States' conservation measures.[32] Such an approach/interpretation ultimately serves the interests of future generation in so far as it effectively demands from States – and potentially secures – better performance, which ought to result in enhanced conservation of living resources. This is precisely the manner in which interpretation can be instrumentalised to protect the interests of future generations.

2.3.1. Conservation of the Living Resources as an Element in the Protection and Preservation of the Environment

While leaning on its earlier pronouncements, the ITLOS affirmed the interconnectedness and interdependence of the conservation of marine living resources and the protection and preservation of the marine environment by treating the former as a constitutive element of the latter: 'the conservation of the living resources of the sea is an element in the protection and preservation of the marine environment'.[33] Moreover, it held that Article 192 UNCLOS imposing the obligation to protect and preserve the marine environment applies to all maritime areas.[34] As a result, efforts for the conservation of living resources form a necessary part of the performance

31 *Request for an Advisory Opinion submitted by the Sub-Regional Fisheries Commission (SRFC)* (n 14).

32 ibid., paras 104, 134, 219.

33 ibid., para. 120, referring to *Southern Bluefin Tuna (New Zealand v Japan; Australia v Japan)* (n 14) para. 70.

34 ibid.

of the obligation to protect and preserve the environment in the marine space.

Another important aspect of the *Fisheries Advisory Opinion* is the discussion on the interaction between the conservation of the marine living resources and Illegal, Unreported and Unregulated (IUU) fishing.[35] The conservation of living resources is inextricably linked to the phenomenon of IUU fishing which heavily compromises States' conservation efforts. Indeed, IUU fishing is now well recognised as a key threat to the management and sustainability of fisheries and therefore a matter of global concern.[36] The Tribunal acknowledged the negative impact of IUU fishing on the conservation of marine living resources[37] and construed the obligations stemming from the Convention, while taking into account that IUU fishing heavily compromises States' conservation efforts.[38] As a consequence, flag States will have to engage more actively in the fight against IUU fishing, including through a higher degree of vigilance in law enforcement, in order to meet their obligations under the UNCLOS.

2.3.2. Implications

Although context specific and concerned with obligations within the EEZ, the *Fisheries Advisory Opinion* contains various declarations of a more general nature which can have implications in the future beyond the advisory proceedings and the maritime zone in question. These relate to the notion of 'conservation', the link between the obligation to protect and preserve the marine environment and the obligation to take measures for the conservation ofliving resources, the core content of the obligation to protect the marine environment. Concerning the latter, the Tribunal adopted a

---

35 See Hélène Ruiz Fabri, Makane M Mbengue and Brian McGarry (eds), 'Special Issue: Regime Convergence and Lex Ferenda in IUU Fishing Disputes' (2022) 22 (3–4) International Community Law Review 363.

36 Seokwoo Lee, Anastasia Telesetsky and Clive Schofield, 'Slipping the Net: Why Is It So Difficult to Crack Down on IUU Fishing?' in Myron H. Nordquist and others (eds), *Freedom of Navigation and Globalization* (Brill Nijhoff 2015) 88. According to the Food and Agriculture Organisation (FAO), it represents 20 % of the catches annually, and its value is estimated at up to USD 23 billion annually. See the official website of FAO <http://www.fao.org/iuu-fishing/en/> accessed 7 July 2023.

37 *Request for an Advisory Opinion submitted by the Sub-Regional Fisheries Commission (SRFC)* (n 14) paras 101–102.

38 ibid., paras 119–124.

strict approach with respect to the level of protection due, which would necessitate a higher degree of vigilance and engagement by States in enforcing the laws and regulations aimed at the conservation of marine living resources. It should be noted that advisory opinions are not binding,[39] but as authoritative legal pronouncements on the state of the law,[40] they have significant persuasive value and practical implications in that they are likely to be taken into account and influence the decision-making in subsequent international proceedings and the future conduct of States.[41] Thus, for example, the principled positions embodied in the *Fisheries Advisory Opinion* concerning the links among conservation of living resources, IUU fishing and the protection of the marine environment can be relevant in interpreting Article 117 UNCLOS which is applicable to the high seas. Article 117 imposes on '[a]ll States [...] the duty to take, or to cooperate with other States in taking, such measures for their respective nationals as may be necessary for the conservation of living resources'. This obligation can be interpreted as implying a duty to take measures to ensure that their nationals, i.e. natural or juridical persons, do not support or engage in IUU fishing. The wording of Article 117 UNCLOS ('*take* [...] measures' as opposed to *adopt* laws and regulations or measures) suggests that this obligation goes beyond the mere adoption of legal measures and involves a certain degree of vigilance in enforcing these measures,[42] i.e. it is a due diligence obligation.

---

39 See Interpretation of Peace Treaties with Bulgaria, Hungary and Romania, First Phase, Advisory Opinion, ICJ Reports 1950, 65, 71; Request for Advisory Opinion submitted by the Sub-Regional Fisheries Commission, Advisory Opinion, 2 April 2015, ITLOS Reports 2015, at 26, para. 76.

40 See *Dispute Concerning Delimitation of the Maritime Boundary between Mauritius and Maldives in the Indian Ocean (Mauritius/Maldives)*, Preliminary Objections, Judgement, 28 January 2021, ITLOS Case No 28, para. 203.

41 Elena V Ivanova, 'The Cross-Fertilization of UNCLOS, Custom and Principles Relating to Procedure in the Jurisprudence of UNCLOS Courts and Tribunals' (2019) 22(1) Max Planck Yearbook of United Nations Law 142, 154. Indeed, the ITLOS decision on preliminary objection in the maritime boundary delimitation dispute between Mauritius and Maldives in the Indian Ocean confirms the former point, given the ample reference in it to a preceding advisory opinion of the ICJ. See *Dispute Concerning Delimitation of the Maritime Boundary between Mauritius and Maldives in the Indian Ocean (Mauritius/Maldives)* (n 40) paras 168, 171, 174, 205 *et seq*.

42 In the same vein, Rosemary Rayfuse, 'Article 117' in Alexander Proelss and others (n 11) 809; *Fisheries Jurisdiction Case (Spain v Canada)*, Judgement, 4 December 1998, ICJ Rep 432, para. 84.

What is more, the broader interpretation of the term 'conservation' consistently adopted by the ITLOS suggests that ecosystem considerations (from which IUU fishing can hardly be delinked) have and will continue to play a role in the assessment of the performance of the obligations under Articles 61 (2), 62 (4), 117, 192 UNCLOS all of which concern the conservation of marine living resources. It should be noted that the UNCLOS adopts a species specific approach to the conservation of living resources[43] and does not cover all species which might be in need of conservation.[44] Yet, there are provisions within UNCLOS which allude to the ecosystem approach, i.e. to a more inclusive and homogenous approach to the protection and preservation of the marine environment.[45] Also, UNCLOS tribunals have consistently taken into account the intricate relationship of marine species, marine ecosystems and the marine environment that supports them. The ecosystem approach to the protection of the marine environment implies sustainable use of natural resources with implications across generations, i.e. implies taking intergenerational considerations into account. The ecosystem-based approach together with the precautionary approach are the main pillars supporting the international efforts for sustainable development, recognised in the Plan of Implementation of the World Summit on Sustainable Development.[46] It can be observed that the ecosystem approach is enshrined in post-UNCLOS instruments concerning the conservation of marine species.[47]

---

43 It provides different rules applicable to different marine species: shared fish stocks (Art 63(1)); straddling fish stocks (Art 63(2)); highly migratory species (Art 64); marine mammals (Arts 65 and 120); anadromous stocks (Art 66), catadromous species (Art 67), and sedentary species (Art 68).

44 Deep-sea species are highly vulnerable to fishing activities due to their exceptional longevity, slow growth, delayed maturity and low productivity and would need special conservation measure for which the UNCLOS does not expressly provide. See Julian Anthony Koslow and others, 'Continental Slope and Deep-Sea Fisheries: Implications for a Fragile Ecosystem' (2000) 57(3) ICES Journal of Marine Science 548, 550; Yoshifumi Tanaka, 'The Changing Approaches to Conservation of Marine Living Resources in International Law' (2011) 71 ZaöRV 291, 301; see also Rüdiger Wolfrum and Nele Matz, 'The Interplay of the United Nations Convention on the Law of the Sea and the Convention on Biological Diversity' (2000) 4(1) Max Planck Yearbook of United Nations Law 445.

45 For example, Arts 194(5) (providing for the protection of fragile marine ecosystems), 196(1) (on the introduction of alien species into marine ecosystems) UNCLOS.

46 See Plan of Implementation of the World Summit on Sustainable Development, paras 25, 25, 30, 109 <https://perma.cc/UUR2-FDVP>.

47 See the Preamble to the UNFSA, the Convention on Biological Diversity.

Although the term marine environment is not defined in the UNCLOS, the jurisprudence of UNCLOS tribunals suggests that it includes the concept of marine life, thus going beyond the anthropocentric understanding of the environment.[48] This is implied in the declaration of the ITLOS in *the Southern Bluefin Tuna* Cases that 'the conservation of the *living resources* of the sea is an *element* in the protection and preservation of the marine *environment* [emphasis added]'[49] which has been reiterated and incorporated in subsequent pronouncements of UNCLOS tribunals.[50] Moreover, in its *Fisheries Advisory Opinion*, the ITLOS explicitly stated that 'living resources and marine life are part of the marine environment.'[51] The Arbitral Tribunal in the *South China Sea Arbitration* has similarly determined that the general obligation to protect and preserve the marine environment under Article 192 'may be broadly enough worded to include the obligation to protect and preserve marine biodiversity'.[52] It also held that Article 192 which imposes the obligation to protect and preserve the environment includes a due diligence obligation to prevent the harvesting of species that are recognised internationally as being at risk of extinction[53] and covers not only the prevention of the direct harvesting of these species but '*extends* to the *prevention* of harms that would affect depleted, threatened, or endangered species *indirectly* through the *destruction of their habitat* [emphasis added]'.[54] Thus, the obligation to 'protect and preserve' refers to the all-encompassing living and non-living marine nature, its ecosystem and components.

---

48 Gerhard Hafner, 'Meeresumwelt, Meeresforschung und Technologietransfer' in Wolfgang Graf Vitzthum (ed), *Handbuch des Seerechts* (CH Beck 2006) 363.

49 *Southern Bluefin Tuna (New Zealand v Japan; Australia v Japan)* (n 14) para. 70.

50 *Request for an Advisory Opinion submitted by the Sub-Regional Fisheries Commission (SRFC)* (n 14) para. 110; *The South China Sea Arbitration (Philippines v China),* Award, 12 July 2016, PCA Case No 2013–19, 956.

51 *Request for an Advisory Opinion submitted by the Sub-Regional Fisheries Commission (SRFC)* (n 14) para. 216.

52 *The South China Sea Arbitration (Philippines v China),* Award on Jurisdiction and Admissibility, 29 October 2015, PCA Case No 2013–19, para. 284.

53 *The South China Sea Arbitration* (n 17) 956.

54 ibid., 959.

2.4. The Precautionary Approach

The UNCLOS does not mention the precautionary approach but UNCLOS tribunals and the Seabed Disputes Chamber have elaborated on it. In its *Advisory Opinion Concerning Responsibilities and Obligations of States with Respect to Activities in the Area*, the Seabed Disputes Chamber held that the precautionary approach is part of the aforementioned obligations. What is more, it explicitly stated that this approach is 'an integral part of the general obligation of due diligence of sponsoring States which is applicable even outside the scope of the Regulations' and which requires States Parties to take 'all appropriate measures to prevent damage that might result from the activities of contractors that they sponsor'.[55] It further clarified that '[t]his obligation applies in situations where scientific evidence concerning the scope and potential negative impact of the activity in question is insufficient but where there are plausible indications of potential risks', that this obligation would not be met if those risks are disregarded and that '[s]uch disregard would amount to a failure to comply with the precautionary approach'.[56] To support these findings, it referred to the earlier practice of the ITLOS, while noting that the 'link between due diligence obligation and the precautionary approach is implicit the Tribunal's Order of 27 August 1999 in the Southern Bluefin Tuna Cases (New Zealand v. Japan; Australia v. Japan)',[57] as well as to para. 164 of the ICJ judgment in *Pulp Mills on the River Uruguay,* stating that 'a precautionary approach may be relevant in the interpretation and application of the provisions of the Statute' (i.e., the environmental bilateral treaty whose interpretation was the main bone of contention between the parties).[58] The Seabed Dispute Chamber also acknowledged the existence of a trend towards making the precautionary approach part of customary international law, while indicating its incorpor-

55 *Responsibilities and Obligations of States with Respect to Activities in the Area (Request for Advisory Opinion Submitted to the Seabed Disputes Chamber*), para. 131.

56 ibid., paras 58–59. In the preceding paragraphs the Seabed Disputes Chamber also stated the 'due diligence' concept is a variable one and may change over time as measures considered sufficiently diligent at a certain moment may become not diligent enough in light of new scientific or technological knowledge, but, nonetheless the standard of due diligence has to be more severe for riskier activities. ibid., para. 117.

57 ibid., para. 132.

58 ibid., para. 135, referring to *Pulp Mills on the River Uruguay (Argentina v Uruguay)* (n 23).

ation into a growing number of international agreements.[59] Tentative steps in that direction were also made much earlier by the ITLOS in the *MOX Plant Case* and in the *Southern Bluefin Tuna Cases* which have contributed to its reputation as an environment-friendly dispute settlement forum.[60]

3. Common Heritage of Mankind

Pursuant to the UNCLOS, the principle of Common Heritage of Mankind is applicable to the Area. This principle is recognised in different treaties. Its nature of customary international law has also been discussed in the literature,[61] but the UNCLOS gives it a specific expression and content. One of its features is that it implies taking intergenerational considerations, i.e. sustainability.

3.1. Evolution of the Notion

3.1.1. UNCLOS III

The term common heritage of mankind (more recent terminology speaks of 'humankind'[62] instead of 'mankind') has been developed in connection with the codification activities concerning the progressive development of international law within the framework of the UNCLOS.[63]

During the Third United Nations Conference on the Law of the Sea, the anticipated scarcity of terrestrial resources triggered an increased interest in the possibility of mining the polymetallic nodules in the deep seabed, which were perceived as having significant economic value, whereas heavy exploitation was expected within a decade or so. This led to the development of a comprehensive legal regime governing the activities in the Area,

59 *Responsibilities and Obligations of States with Respect to Activities in the Area* (n 55) para. 135.

60 See *MOX Plant (Ireland v United Kingdom) (Order)* ITLOS Case No 10 (3 December 2001), at paras 84, 89; *Southern Bluefin Tuna Cases (New Zealand v Japan; Australia v Japan),* Provisional Measures, 27 August 1999, ITLOS Cases Nos 3, 4, at para. 77.

61 Rüdiger Wolfrum, 'Common Heritage of Mankind' in Rüdiger Wolfrum (ed), *MPEPIL* (OUP 2009); Silja Vöneky and Anja Höfelmeier, 'Article 136' in Alexander Proelss and others (n 11) 956.

62 See for example the Preamble to the Paris Agreement.

63 Wolfrum (n 61).

i.e. the only areas of the planet which had not then been appropriated for national use. The term common heritage of mankind was introduced by Malta in a *note verbale* of 18 August 1967 requesting the introduction of an agenda item: 'Declaration and treaty concerning the reservation exclusively for peaceful purposes of the seabed and the ocean floor, underlying the seas beyond the limits of present national jurisdiction, and the use of their resources in the interest of mankind.'[64] The invention of the concept is particularly attributed to Arvid Padro, representative of Malta at the General assembly of the United Nations.[65] While elaborating on the dangers of allowing the extension of national jurisdiction to the deep seabed,[66] Malta suggested a new approach through the prohibition of national appropriation, dedication to peaceful uses of the Area and shared and sustainable utilisation of its resources with consideration for developing countries.[67] Thus, the concept of common heritage of mankind was meant to counter the idea that the sea was *res communis* and the seabed *res nullius* open for appropriation.[68]

Against this backdrop, the implementation of the principle of common heritage of mankind in the UNCLOS differs historically to other novelties within the Convention such the EEZ legal regime. Whereas the latter is regarded as codification of naturally evolved international law, the principle of common heritage of mankind is rather revolutionary.[69] The common heritage of mankind is an essential principle under the UNCLOS implemented in Part XI which governs the activities and the exploitation of the resources of the Areas. Article 136 (entitled Common heritage of mankind) which is the starting provision of Part XI Section 2 (entitled Principles

64 UN Doc. A/6695.

65 See Tullio Scovazzi, 'The Conservation and Sustainable Use of Marine Biodiversity, Including Genetic Resources, in Areas beyond National Jurisdiction: A Legal Perspective' (Speech at the Twelfth Meeting of the United Nations Open-ended Informal Consultative Process on Oceans and the Law of the Sea, 22 June 2011) <https://perma.cc/7LCJ-ZRTD>; Vöneky and Höfelmeier (n 61) 952.

66 Including increased suspicions and tensions among the dominant marine powers resulting from the competition for the resources of the Area; militarization of the said area and growing danger of permanent damage to the marine environment. ibid., 952.

67 See UN Doc. A/6695 2.

68 Wolfrum (n 61).

69 Arvid Pardo, *The Common Heritage: Selected Papers on Oceans and World Order 1967–1974* (Malta University Press 1975) 16.

governing the Area) and Article 137 (entitled Legal status of the Area and its resources) are the key provisions.

From the UNCLOS it was then introduced into the national legislation pertaining to the activities in the Area. In 1967 it was also brought into the discussion on a legal regime concerning outer space[70] and Antarctica.[71] Attempts have been made to invoke this principle with respect to cultural property,[72] the protection of the environment.[73] The main impact of this principle is the establishment of an international administration for the areas beyond national jurisdiction, the so-called international commons.

---

70 See UNGA Res 1962 (XVIII) entitled 'Declaration of Legal Principles Governing the Activities of State in the Exploration and Use of Outer Space'; Art 1 Treaty on Principles Governing the Activities of States in the Exploration and Use of Outer Space, including the Moon and Other Celestial Bodies (Outer Space Treaty). See also Art 11 Agreement Governing the Activities of States on the Moon and Other Celestial Bodies (Moon Treaty) which entered into force in July 1984. The Moon Treaty though demands that the activities on the moon be carried out in the interest of promoting international co-operation and focuses on it.

71 Concerning Antarctica, the common heritage principle has been invoked to a lesser extent. At the Eleventh Consultative Meeting to the Antarctic Treaty, it was emphasized in para. 5 (d) Recommendation XI-1 that 'the Consultative Parties, in dealing with the question of mineral resources in Antarctica, should not prejudice the interests of all mankind in Antarctica'. See Recommendation XI-1 (ATCM XI – Buenos Aires, 1981. More recently, the Consultative Parties to the Antarctic Treaty, meeting in Santiago, Chile, in May 2016, reiterated that' the comprehensive protection of the Antarctic environment and dependent and associated ecosystems is in the interests of science and mankind as a whole'. See Santiago Declaration on the Twenty Fifth Anniversary of the signing of the Protocol on Environmental Protection to the Antarctic Treaty, adopted on 30 May 2016. See also the Preamble to the Protocol on Environmental Protection to the Antarctic Treaty.

72 The UNCLOS does not provide for a comprehensive regime on the underwater cultural heritage. Two provisions are devoted to 'archeological and historical objects': Art 149 concerns 'archeological and historical objects' found in the Area; Art 303 deals with 'archeological and historical objects' found at sea. Under Art 149, such objects must be 'preserved or disposed of for the benefit of mankind as a whole' which seems to be close to the objective for which the regime on the common heritage of mankind was established, although the latter does not apply to such objects. The subject matter of Arts 149 and 303 is also covered by the Convention on the Protection of the Underwater Cultural Heritage (CPUCH).

73 Environmental Law makes some allusion to the principle of common heritage of mankind. See for example Protection of Global Climate for Present and Future Generations of Mankind, UNGA Res 43/53 (6 December 1988) GAOR 43rd Session Supp 49 vol 1, 133. However, this resolution uses the term 'common concern of mankind' which seems to call predominantly for co-operation and does not cover the full spectrum of the common heritage principle.

The way this principle was implemented in the UNCLOS did not lack criticism and it is one of the main reasons why the United States did not become a signatory to the Convention.[74] Given this criticism, the Agreement Relating to the Implementation of Part XI of the United Nations Convention on the Law of the Sea of 10 December 1982 ('Implementation Agreement') did indeed modify this principle without, however, sacrificing its core.[75]

It has been discussed whether it is more appropriate to refer to it as a doctrine or a concept[76] but since it is installed in treaty law concerning common spaces and governs the regime on the deep seabed, it would be appropriate to speak of it as a principle.[77] No fully agreed definition of the notion exists, given that it varies across treaty regimes, and there is no unified State practice or express acceptance. However, it is possible to identify some common core elements.

3.2. Content of the Principle of Common Heritage of Mankind under the UNCLOS

The principle is set forth in different provisions within the UNCLOS. The Preamble refers to UNGA Res 2749 (XXV) of 17 December 1970 declaring *inter alia* that 'the area of the seabed and ocean floor and the subsoil thereof, beyond the limits of national jurisdiction, as well as its resources, are the common heritage of mankind, the exploration and exploitation of which shall be carried out for the benefit of mankind as a whole, irrespective of the geographical location of States'. The principle is highlighted in Article 136 and Article 311 (6). The latter provides *inter alia* that 'there shall be no amendments to the basic principle relating to the common heritage of mankind set forth in article 136' and thus attributes a special status to Article 136 elevating it above treaty law without qualifying it as *jus cogens*.[78] It proclaims the employment of the principle and declares the Area and its

74 See 'United States Ocean Policy' (n 12) 619–623, in which the president of the United States confirmed that the United States would not become a signatory to the Convention, owing to its concerns over the Convention's deep-seabed mining provisions.

75 For more details, see Wolfrum (n 61) and Ram Prakash Anand, 'Common Heritage of Mankind: Mutilation of an Ideal' (1997) 37 Indian Journal of International Law 1.

76 Kemal Baslar, *The Concept of Common Heritage of Mankind in International Law* (Brill 1998) 2–3.

77 Wolfrum (n 61).

78 Rüdiger Wolfrum with respect to the Kyoto Protocol. ibid.

resources the common heritage of mankind, whereas subsequent provisions install different aspects of it. They deal with the legal status of the Area and its resources and set out the regime for their utilisation.

3.2.1. Legal Status: Prohibition of Private and Public Appropriation or Sovereignty

Article 137 (1) prohibits the exercise of sovereignty or appropriation over any part of the Area and its resources by not only States but also by natural or juridical persons. The reference to all States instead of the States Parties could be seen as an implicit reference to customary international law. In addition, it imposes upon States Parties the obligation not to recognise any such act which operates as an important safeguard for the prohibition of appropriation and sovereignty.[79] The duty of non-recognition implies that States cannot take any action which implicitly or explicitly recognises the validity of the relevant claim.[80]

Complementarily, Article 137 (2) prescribes that all rights in the resources of the Area are vested in 'mankind as a whole' and specifies that the Authority is to act on behalf of mankind. The UNCLOS does not attach an international legal personality to 'mankind' but it does so with respect to the Authority.[81] However, the Authority rather serves as an advocate securing the needs and long term concerns of mankind. These include the foreseeable needs and interests of future generations implying aspects of the principle of sustainable development in the management of exhaustible resources and safeguards for the protection of the environment.

The resources of the Area are inalienable (Article 137 (2) second sentence), whereas the minerals recovered from the Area may be alienated but only in accordance with Part XI and the rules, regulations and procedures of the Authority. This arrangement is supplemented by Article 1 Annex III UNCLOS which states that title to minerals shall pass upon recovery. Thus,

79 Vöneky and Höfelmeier (n 61) 955.

80 The ICJ held that '[t]he member States of the United Nations were under an obligation to recognize the illegality and invalidity of South Africa's continued presence in Namibia': Legal Consequences for States of the Continued Presence of South Africa in Namibia [South West Africa] notwithstanding Security Council Resolution 276 (1970), Advisory Opinion, 21 June 1971, ICJ Rep 16, 54). See also Jochen A Frowein, 'Non-Recognition' in Rüdiger Wolfrum (ed), *MPEPIL* (OUP 2011).

81 Art 176 UNCLOS.

the Convention distinguishes between the legal status of the seabed and the recovered resources: unlike the seabed, minerals can be subject to appropriation. Acquisition of rights over minerals must be in accordance with the Convention, i.e. through contractual agreements with the Authority[82] where the activities are not carried out by the Enterprise.[83] Unilateral mining and appropriation of minerals is thus prohibited under the UNCLOS. As far as non-States Parties are concerned, there are good reasons to argue that customary international law hinders their claims to rights over the seabed and obliges them to not recognise any such claims.[84] It has widely been recognised that some general features of the principle of common heritage of mankind embodied in the UNCLOS, such as the prohibition of appropriation and sovereignty, peaceful use and utilisation for the benefit of mankind, have become customary international law. Ambiguity exists with respect to unilateral mining. Views have been expressed that it is to be carried out for the benefit of mankind as whole, although States would have the discretion to decide how the common benefit is to be effectuated.[85]

3.2.2. Regime of Utilisation

The regime of utilisation features several core components: *International Cooperation and International Management; Regulated Utilization; Intertemporal Dimension; Distributive Effect; Peaceful Use*[86], all of which to a varying degree secure the protection of the interests of future generations. However, the most distinctive and innovative achievement of the UNCLOS regime of utilisation is the creation of an international organisation – the International Seabed Authority or the Authority which is designed to ensure that the Area and its resources are being developed for the benefit of mankind and respectively for the benefit of future generations. The Authority exercises control over the activities in the Area and is vested with legal capacity, including the capacity to adopt regulations and institute and be a party to legal proceedings, which enable it take active steps in view of the interests of future generations. This will be given thorough consideration in the subsequent paragraphs. Also, attention will be drawn

82 Art 3(5) Annex III UNCLOS.
83 See Art 153(3) read in conjunction with para. (2) UNCLOS.
84 Vöneky and Höfelmeier (n 61) 956.
85 Wolfrum (n 61); Wolfgang Durner, *Common Goods* (Nomos 2000) 223.
86 Wolfrum (n 61). See also Vöneky and Höfelmeier (n 61) 955, whose description of the major components overlaps with the aforementioned ones to a significant extent.

to the intertemporal dimension of the utilisation regime in light of the objectives of the current project.

(a) The Authority – a Means for Achieving International Cooperation and International Management

Under the said regime of utilisation, States are obliged to co-operate internationally in the exploration and exploitation of the Area's resources.[87] In this respect the obligation to cooperate under the legal regime of the Area surpasses the general obligation to co-operate under international law.[88] International cooperation and management of the Area is achieved through the establishment of the Authority. All States Parties to the Convention are *ipso facto* members of the Authority[89] which acts on behalf of mankind as far as the deep seabed and the ocean floor are concerned,[90] and consequently represents those States which are not parties to the UNCLOS. Thus, 'States Parties are meant to act as a trustee on behalf of mankind'.[91]

The principal organs of the Authority are an Assembly (a plenary organ), a Council (an executive organ) and a Secretariat (an administrative organ),[92] whereas the Enterprise (also an operative organ but with a commercial purpose which in some aspects resembles a private corporation) is the organ through which the Authority is to carry out activities in the Area directly.[93]

Pursuant to Article 176 UNCLOS, the Authority has international legal personality thus becoming a member of the international community different from the States Parties and from other legal persons. It is vested with 'legal capacity as may be necessary for the exercise of its functions and the fulfilment of its purposes'[94], which includes: capacity to contract;[95] capacity

87 This duty is installed through various provisions under Arts 138, 150 UNCLOS.
88 See Rüdiger Wolfrum, 'Cooperation, International Law of' in Rüdiger Wolfrum (ed), *MPEPIL* (OUP 2010).
89 Art 156(2) UNCLOS.
90 Art 137(2) UNCLOS.
91 Wolfrum (n 61).
92 Art 158(1) UNCLOS.
93 Art 158(2) UNCLOS.
94 Art 176 UNCLOS.
95 Art 153(3) UNCLOS.

to acquire and dispose of immovable property;[96] capacity to institute or to be party to legal proceedings[97] and capacity to adopt regulations.[98] The last two aspects of the said legal capacity are particularly relevant to the topic of this contribution and shall be addressed further.

Similar to the Authority, the Enterprise is endowed with 'legal capacity as may be necessary for the exercise of its functions and the fulfilment of its purposes'[99], which entails capacity to contract, capacity to acquire and dispose of immovable property as well as judicial capacity.[100] Its legal personality differs from that of the Authority as it is confined to the specific functions and purposes of the Enterprise.[101] Moreover, the latter enjoys autonomy in the conduct of its operations.[102] The Authority and the Enterprise act and are obliged independently.[103]

Concerning the Authority's capacity to *adopt regulations*, Article 145 UNCLOS authorises and obliges[104] the Authority to adopt rules, regulations and procedures for the 'effective protection of the marine environment from harmful effects' which may arise from activities in the Area. This obligation of the Authority is further complemented by Annex III and the Agreement relating to the implementation of Part XI of the United Nations Convention on the Law of the Sea (1994 Implementation Agreement). Paragraphs (a) and (b) of Article 145 UNCLOS both specify harms and activities of particular concern which are to be addressed, '*inter alia*', by these regulations. The term '*inter alia*', however, makes clear that the listed harms and activities are not exhaustive and additional threats to the environment might be addressed by the said regulations.

The Authority is to *exercise control* over the activities in the Area and is responsible for ensuring that they are carried out in accordance with the relevant UNCLOS provisions and the rules, procedures and regulations issued by the Authority.[105] The key provision regarding the utilisation of

96 Art 176 UNCLOS. See Pablo Ferrara, 'Article 176' in Alexander Proelss and others (n 11) 1230–1231.
97 Arts 187 and 188 UNCLOS.
98 Art 145 UNCLOS.
99 See Art 170(2) UNCLOS, Art 1(1)(2) Annex IV UNCLOS.
100 See Art 13(2) Annex IV UNCLOS.
101 See Art 170(2) UNCLOS; Art 1(1)(2) Annex IV UNCLOS.
102 Art 2(2) Annex IV UNCLOS.
103 See Art 2(3) Annex IV UNCLOS.
104 ISA, written statement of the Proceedings in ITLOS Case No17 (2010), para. 4.25.
105 Art 157 UNCLOS.

the Area is Article 153 UNCLOS[106] which prescribes that the activities in the Area are to be carried out by the Enterprise or, in association with the Authority, by the States Parties, or state enterprises or natural or juridical persons which possess the nationality of the States Parties, through contracts with the Authority. As a result, the utilisation of the Area is subject to a specific regulation and is controlled by an international organisation through which States Parties are to take into account not only the interests of other States but mankind as a whole, and, by necessary implication, those of 'future generations' as part of 'mankind'.

Through its capacity to regulate and manage the utilisation of the Area and its resources, and given the wording of the relevant UNCLOS provisions, the Authority can ensure that the latest developments in international environmental law pertaining to the protection of the marine environment are reflected in the legal rules governing the activities in the Area and are observed by all the entities involved in the prospecting, exploration, and future exploitation of the resources of the Area, and ultimately that the common heritage of mankind is being developed in a sustainable manner for the benefit of future generations, among others. Indeed, in accordance with its obligation under Article 145 UNCLOS, the Authority adopted Regulations on the Prospecting and Exploration for Polymetallic Nodules in 2000,[107] Regulations on the Prospecting and Exploration for Polymetallic Sulphides in 2010[108] and the Regulations on Prospecting and Exploration for Cobalt-rich Ferromanganese Crusts in 2012,[109] which explicitly require the Authority, sponsoring States and contractors to apply the precautionary approach,[110] the best environmental practices,[111] and environmental impact

106 Although the utilization regime has been further elaborated and slightly modified by the 1994 Implementation Agreement, Art 153 was not affected.

107 Regulations on Prospecting and Exploration for Polymetallic Nodules in the Area, adopted in 2000, ISA Doc. ISBA/6/A/18 (2000).

108 Regulations on prospecting and exploration for polymetallic sulphides in the Area, adopted in 2010, ISBA/16/A/12/Rev.1 (2010).

109 Regulations on Prospecting and Exploration for Cobalt-rich Ferromanganese Crusts in the Area, adopted in 2012, ISBA/18/A/11 (2012).

110 Regulation 31(2) Regulations on the Prospecting and Exploration for Polymetallic Nodules; Regulation 5(1) Regulations on the Prospecting and Exploration for Polymetallic Sulphides; Regulation 2(2) Regulations on Prospecting and Exploration for Cobalt-rich Ferromanganese Crusts in the Area.

111 Regulation 5(1) Regulations on the Prospecting and Exploration for Polymetallic Sulphides; Regulation 5(1) Regulations on Prospecting and Exploration for Cobalt-rich Ferromanganese Crusts.

assessment[112] to their activities in the Area. Moreover, in its High-Level Action Plan adopted in 2019 by the Assembly, the Authority expressed a commitment to building 'a comprehensive and inclusive approach to the development of the common heritage for the benefit of mankind as a whole that balances the three pillars of sustainable development and adoption of regulations for exploitation reflecting best international standards and practices, as well as agreed principles of sustainable development.'[113]

Humankind-New Subject of International Law? It has been argued that the principle of common heritage of mankind resulted in the establishment of a new subject of international law – humankind.[114] Since international law is State-focused and has so far regulated relationships amongst States, treating humankind as an addressee of rights under treaty law is a novelty.[115] Yet, the UNCLOS does not vest humankind with international legal personality. Humankind as such is not capable of representative legal action such as international organisations. The Authority is an administration through which States Parties control the activities in the Area with a view to ensuring they are in line with the rules and principles established under the Convention and benefit mankind. The Authority has various means to achieve this target, two of them being its regulatory powers and its capacity to initiate proceedings before relevant dispute settlement fora with respect to disputes concerning the activities in the Area. Through its judicial capacity the Authority acts as a proxy of humankind and is in a position to take active steps in the interest of mankind. Indeed, one of the important achievements of the UNCLOS is the establishment of a mechanism through which the interests of humankind as a whole, including the populations of all States, comprised of present and future generations, can be taken into account in the process of utilisation of the seabed and the ocean floor and their resources. This translates into developing production policies and

112 Regulation 18(b) Regulations on the Prospecting and Exploration for Polymetallic Nodules; Regulation 20(1) Regulations on the Prospecting and Exploration for Polymetallic Sulphides; Regulation 20(1) Regulations on Prospecting and Exploration for Cobalt-rich Ferromanganese Crusts.

113 See Decision of the Assembly of the International Seabed Authority relating to the strategic plan of the Authority for the period 2019–2023 adopted on 27 July 2018 and High Level Action Plan of the International Seabed Authority and Priorities for the 2019–2023 Period, available at: <https://www.isa.org.jm/index.php/our-work/protection-marine-environment> accessed 7 July 2023.

114 See Christian Walter, 'Subjects of International Law' in Rüdiger Wolfrum (ed), *MPEPIL* (OUP 2007).

115 See Vöneky and Höfelmeier (n 61) 956.

regulations and exploitation with a long-term perspective, while assessing their potential impact upon future generations so as to ensure that seabed mining would benefit, *inter alia*, future generations. In this respect, the mentioning of mankind is not futile. It operates as a reference point for assessing all activities in the Area. As a reference group, mankind is wider than States and provides for the inclusion of those human beings, currently existing or not yet present, which are not represented by States.[116] Compared to other treaties alluding to the common heritage of mankind and concerning areas beyond national jurisdiction, the complex management and exploitation system developed by the UNCLOS is by far the most elaborate. Also, the manner in which the principle of common heritage of mankind was implemented in the UNCLOS differs from the approach adopted in other treaties. While the Convention established a complex international management system such as the Authority, the latter has no analogue in other treaties dealing with or alluding to the principle of common heritage of mankind.[117]

(b) Intertemporal Dimension

Neither Part XI nor the UNCLOS more generally make reference to the concept of sustainable development, whose core feature is its intertemporal dimension. Yet it is acknowledged that this concept is one of the important elements of the principle of common heritage of mankind.[118] The combined use of the terms mankind and heritage suggests that the interests of future generations as part of mankind are to be taken into account and respected in the utilisation of the Area and its resources, i.e. the international commons.[119] Articles 145 and 209 demand the marine environment be protected from harmful effects which *may arise* in the *future* from the activities in the Area. In addition, the aim of the prohibition of appropriation as the term 'appropriation' indicates, is to preserve indefinitely, i.e. over time, the

116 See Wolfrum (n 61).

117 ibid.

118 Baslar (n 76) 103; Wolfrum (n 61); Silja Vöneky and Anja Höfelmeier, 'Article 137' in Alexander Proelss and others (n 11) 963.

119 Wolfrum (n 61).

legal status of the international commons against all States and all private persons with implications for future generations.[120]

4. Dispute Settlement Mechanism under the UNCLOS

The legal regime concerning the activities in the Area and the obligations of States Parties with respect to the protection of the marine environment and the conservation of marine living resources were identified in this paper as the major elements of the Convention which directly concern the interests of future generations. In addition to this, the Convention creates a dispute settlement mechanism featuring a compulsory dispute settlement procedure and a procedure for rendering advisory opinions, a key tool for protecting the said interests. This mechanism is a means for scrutinising States' conduct, improving their performance in the realm of environmental protection and conservation of marine living resources, and ensuring proper implementation of the principle of Common Heritage of Mankind. The compulsory procedure regarding environmental disputes and disputes concerning the activities in the Area facilitates the activation of the said dispute settlement mechanism, which for its part, has the potential to deter non-compliance with the respective UNCLOS provisions. The exercise of the contentious and advisory jurisdiction of UNCLOS adjudicatory bodies, on the other hand, is a channel through which intergenerational considerations can be integrated in the interpretation of the conventional provisions and from there reflected in the application of the relevant law, national law and the conduct of States. The following paragraphs will address the advisory jurisdiction of UNCLOS adjudicatory bodies and three aspects of their contentious jurisdiction: first, their jurisdiction *ratione materiae* over disputes with an environmental dimension, including disputes concerning the conservation of marine living resources, second, the special jurisdiction of the Seabed Disputes Chamber (partly exclusive) over disputes concerning the activities in the Area, and, third, their jurisdiction *ratione personae.*

120 ibid.

4.1. Disputes Concerning Activities in the Area

The UNCLOS has established a special dispute settlement mechanism for the resolution of disputes concerning the activities in the Area detailed in Article 187 UNCLOS. The Seabed Disputes Chamber, composed of 11 members, operates as a court within a court and has compulsory jurisdiction, generally exclusive, over disputes concerning the activities of the Area.[121]

The jurisdiction *ratione materiae* comprises: disputes between States Parties concerning the interpretation and application of Part XI UNCLOS and the related Annexes;[122] disputes between a State Party and the Authority (types of non-contractual disputes arising from acts of omissions of the Authority or a State Party alleged to be in violation of Part XI UNCLOS and its related Annexes or of the rules, regulations and procedures adopted by the Authority or disputes marked by excess of jurisdiction or misuse of power by the Authority);[123] contractual disputes between States Parties, the Authority or the Enterprise, state enterprises, legal and natural persons which possess the nationality of a State Party or are effectively controlled by them or their nationals, when sponsored by such States) or between the Authority and prospective contractors;[124] disputes relating to the responsibility of the Authority[125] and other disputes for which the jurisdiction of the Seabed Disputes Chamber is specifically provided in the Convention.[126] However, disputes concerning the interpretation or application of a contract referred to in Article 187 (c) (i) may be submitted to binding com-

121 See Tullio Treves, 'Seabed Disputes Chamber: International Tribunal for the Law of the Sea (ITLOS)' in Hélène Ruiz Fabri (ed), *Max Planck Encyclopedia of International Procedural Law (MPEiPro)* (OUP 2019).

122 This jurisdiction is not exclusive as the parties have the other options to submit such disputes to a special chamber of the ITLOS or an *ad hoc* chamber of the Seabed Disputes Chamber. See Art 188(1) UNCLOS. See Elena V Ivanova, 'Special Chambers: International Tribunal for the Law of the Sea (ITLOS)' in *MPEiPro* (OUP 2019).

123 Art 187(b) UNCLOS.

124 See Art 187(c) and (d) UNCLOS. See also Joseph Akl, 'The Seabed Disputes Chamber' in Patibandla Chandraskhara Rao and Rahmatullah Khan (eds), *The International Tribunal for the Law of the Sea: Law and Practice* (Kluwer Law International 2001) 84.

125 Art 187(e) UNCLOS.

126 Art 187(d) UNCLOS.

mercial arbitration at the request of any party, unless otherwise agreed.[127] The commercial arbitral tribunal has no jurisdiction over questions of interpretation of the Convention: the Seabed Disputes Chamber retains its compulsory jurisdiction in this regard.[128]

4.2. Environmental Disputes

Disputes concerning the interpretation and application of the UNCLOS, including its provisions relating to the protection of the marine environment and the conservation of marine resources, are subject to the compulsory procedure under Part XV UNCLOS. Moreover, the ITLOS has established two standing special chambers, the Chamber for Fisheries Disputes and the Chamber for Marine Environment Disputes, available to deal respectively with disputes concerning the conservation and management of marine living resources[129] and with disputes relating to the protection and preservation of the marine environment.[130] In addition, the Seabed Disputes Chamber has exclusive jurisdiction over a major part of the disputes concerning the activities in the Area, including those with an environmental dimension.

---

127 See Art 188(2)(a) UNCLOS.

128 ibid.

129 These include disputes concerning the interpretation and application of any provision of the UNCLOS which relates to the conservation and management of marine living resources as well as disputes concerning any provision of any other agreement relating to the conservation and management of marine living resources which confers jurisdiction upon the Tribunal. See Resolution on the Chamber for Fisheries Disputes (adopted on 28 April 1997). ITLOS, *Yearbook International Tribunal for the Law of the Sea 1996–1997* (Brill 1999) 154.

130 These include disputes concerning the interpretation and application of any provision of the UNCLOS which relates to the protection and preservation of the marine environment; disputes concerning the interpretation and application of any provision of special convention and agreements relating to the protection and preservation of the marine environment referred to Art 237 UNCLOS, as well as disputes concerning any provisions of any other agreement relating to the protection and preservation of the marine environment which confers jurisdiction upon the Tribunal. See Resolution on the Chamber for Marine Environment Disputes (adopted on 28 April 1997). ibid. 156; Ivanova (n 122).

4.3. Advisory Jurisdiction

Under the UNCLOS, the Seabed Disputes Chamber is vested with jurisdiction to issue advisory opinions[131] which it has already exercised upon a request of the Council of the Authority.[132] Through this mechanism, the Seabed Disputes Chamber has the opportunity to pronounce itself on whether certain rules, procedures or regulations of the Authority are in conformity with the Convention, including the principle of common heritage of mankind and the rules concerning the protection and preservation of the environment, before they are adopted by the Assembly.[133]

Similar to the Seabed Disputes Chamber, the ITLOS can issue advisory opinions. Pursuant to Article 138 ITLOS Rules, the Tribunals may give an advisory opinion if an international agreement related to the purposes of the UNCLOS specifically provides for the submission to the Tribunals of a request for such an opinion.[134] Although the advisory function of the Tribunal and the adoption of Article 138 ITLOS Rules have been debated as neither the ITLOS Statute nor the UNCLOS expressly provide for the Tribunal to give advisory opinions,[135] the ITLOS rendered its first advisory opinion as a full court upon a request of the Sub-Regional Fisheries Commission (SRFC), thus confirming the compatibility of Article 138 ITLOS Rules with the UNCLOS.

The aforementioned advisory opinions addressed various legal questions pertaining to international environmental law, the precautionary approach, the content of the obligation to protect and preserve the marine environment, the fight against IUU fishing, the activities in the Area (in the case of the Seabed Disputes Chamber's advisory opinion) all of which concern and contribute to maintaining the 'health' of the seas and oceans, food security, respectively the sustainable use of marine resources with implications

---

131 Art 191 UNCLOS.

132 *Responsibilities and obligations of States with respect to activities in the Area*, Advisory Opinion, 1 February 2011 ITLOS Case No 17.

133 Akl (n 124) 86.

134 See Art 21 ITLOS Statute in conjunction with Art 138 ITLOS Rules. See Alexander Proelss, 'Advisory Opinion: International Tribunal for the Law of the Sea (ITLOS)' in *MPEiPro* (OUP 2019).

135 It has been questioned whether the adoption of Art 138 was a lawful exercise of the regulatory powers conferred on the Tribunal by Art 16 Annex VI. See Sotirios-Ioannis Lekkas and Christopher Staker, 'Annex VI Article 21' in Alexander Proelss and others (n 11) 2381.

across generations and across legal sectors. The advisory opinions were heavily relied on in the jurisprudence of UNCLOS Tribunals.[136] Indeed, both the ITLOS and the Seabed Disputes Chamber, have admitted and have taken into account that their advisory opinions would have practical significance as they 'would assist [the SRFC or the Council of the Authority as the case may be] in the performance of [their] activities and contribute to the implementation of the Convention'.[137] Notably, the advisory opinion of the ITLOS has already influenced the operation of the SRFMO which has taken steps for its effective implementation.[138] These observations confirm the point made in the initial paragraphs of this paper, namely that advisory opinions, albeit non-binding, can have an impact and indirectly induce States into compliance with their obligations under the UNCLOS, including under the common heritage principle, in a manner that would benefit future generations as part of humankind.

4.4. Locus Standi

Unlike the ICJ whose access, according to Article 34 (1) ICJ Statute, is limited to States, the ITLOS is also open to non-State entities, including natural and juridical persons and even entities which are not parties to the Convention in any case expressly provided for in Part XI UNCLOS or in any case submitted pursuant to any other agreement conferring jurisdiction on the Tribunal which is accepted by all the parties to that case.[139]

---

136 See *Request for Advisory Opinion submitted by the Sub-Regional Fisheries Commission* (n 39) paras 125, 128, referring to the *Advisory Opinion of the Seabed Disputes Chamber on the Responsibilities and obligations of States sponsoring persons and entities with respect to activities in the Area*; *The South China Sea Arbitration (Philippines v China)*, Award, 12 July 2016, PCA Case No2013–19, paras 743, 744, referring to *Request for Advisory Opinion submitted by the Sub-Regional Fisheries Commission* (n 39).

137 *Request for an Advisory Opinion submitted by the Sub-Regional Fisheries Commission*, Advisory Opinion, 2 April 2015, ITLOS Case No 21, para. 77; *Responsibilities and obligations of States with respect to activities in the Area* (n 132) para. 30.

138 Following the rendering of the requested opinion, the SRFMO organised various events, including national workshops to validate national and sub-regional action plans with a view to its effective implementation. More information is available on the official website of the SRFMO <https://spcsrp.org/en/harmonization-policies-and-legislation> accessed 7 July 2023.

139 Art 20(2) UNCLOS Annex VI. See also Elena V Ivanova, 'Intervention: International Tribunal for the Law of the Sea (ITLOS)' in *MPEiPro* (OUP 2019).

As a result, under certain conditions, **non-State entities** and even non-parties to the UNCLOS can submit a dispute concerning the *conservation of the marine living resources* and the *protection and preservation of the marine environment* (these are two categories of disputes which concern and are of essential interest for future generations). The accessibility of the dispute settlement mechanism for non-State entities results in a greater variety of actors capable of taking action with a view to scrutinising States' conduct and thus inducing States into compliance with their international obligations.

Disputes concerning the *activities in the Area* can be submitted to the Seabed Disputes Chamber, to a special chamber of the ITLOS or an ad hoc chamber of the Seabed Disputes Chamber not only by States, but also by non-State entities, including the Enterprise, the Authority, natural or juridical persons which possess the nationality of States Parties or are effectively controlled by them or their nationals, when sponsored by such States or any group of the foregoing which meets the requirements under the Convention.[140]

The UNCLOS has created new legal subjects vested with international legal personality. Given their legal capacity to contract and be a party to legal proceedings, both the Enterprise and the Authority have separate *locus standi* before the Seabed Disputes Chamber of the ITLOS as well as before commercial arbitral tribunals.[141] Notably, although the Seabed Disputes Chamber does not have jurisdiction with regard to the exercise by the Authority of its discretionary powers and cannot declare invalid or pronounce on the compatibility of the rules, regulations and procedures of the Authority, it can decide on claims concerning excess of jurisdiction or misuse of power by the Authority as well as claims that application of such rules, regulations and procedures would be in conflict with the contractual obligations of the parties in dispute or with the obligations

140 See Arts 187(c), (d), 188(2) UNCLOS.

141 Art 187(c) in conjunction with Art 188(2) UNCLOS enable the Enterprise and Authority to institute or be a party in legal proceedings before the Seabed Disputes Chamber or in commercial arbitration with respect to disputes concerning joint arrangements between contractors and the Enterprise, in the case of the Enterprise, as well as with respect to disputes concerning the activities in the Area between the Authority and: States Parties, contractors (States Parties; state enterprises, legal and natural persons which possess the nationality of a State Party or are effectively controlled by them or their nationals, when sponsored by such States) or prospective contractors, in the case of the Authority.

under the UNCLOS.[142] This litigation possibility provides a mechanism for monitoring and scrutinising the exercise of powers by the Authority in individual cases and give remedy for its eventual failures to comply with its contractual obligations or obligations under the UNCLOS.[143] Whereas the Authority enjoys immunity from legal process in the territory of its States, unless expressly waived by it,[144] actions can be brought against the Enterprise in a court of competent jurisdiction in the territory of a State Party in which it operates.[145] Further to the question of standing, it should be mentioned that, pursuant to Article 187 (c) UNCLOS, state enterprises, natural or legal persons referred to in Article 153 (2) (b) have standing before the Seabed Disputes Chamber of the ITLOS.

In sum, various types of non-State entities can institute proceedings with respect to disputes concerning the interpretation and application of relevant contracts or acts or omissions relating to the activities in the Area and affecting the interests of the other contracting party. Thus, not only States and States Parties but non-State entities, including the Authority acting on behalf of mankind as a whole, can control the execution of the said contracts and ensure through litigation that the activities in the Area conform to the rules and principles established by the UNCLOS, and by implication that the principle of common heritage of mankind (with all the implications for future generations discussed above) is respected. The UNCLOS effectively broadens the scope of entities capable of taking legal action with a view to ensuring that the obligations under the UNCLOS concerning the activities in the Area and the application of the principle of common heritage of mankind are met.

The same applies *mutatis mutandis* to advisory proceedings. Whereas the exercise of the advisory jurisdiction of the Seabed Disputes Chamber

142 Art 189 in conjunction with Art 187 UNCLOS.

143 This solution was a compromise at the UNCLOS III Conference between those who insisted on the necessity to allow a full judicial appreciation of the rules, regulations and procedures of the Authority and those who were in favour of its overriding power. See Akl (n 124) 85.

144 Art 178 UNCLOS. For more details, see Pablo Ferrara, 'Article 178' in Alexander Proelss and others (n 11) 1237.

145 Pursuant to Art 13(3) Annex IV UNCLOS, actions may be brought against the Enterprise in a court of competent jurisdiction in the territory of a State Party in which the Enterprise has an office, has appointed an agent for the purpose of accepting service or notice of process, has entered into a contract for goods and services, has issued securities, is engaged in commercial activity.

can be triggered by the Assembly or the Council,[146] a request for an advisory opinion of the Tribunal may be submitted 'by *whatever body* is authorised by or in accordance with [emphasis added]' an international agreement related to the purposes of the Convention specifically providing for such a submission.[147]

5. Conclusion

Although not yet present or not yet capable of taking legal action to protect their interests themselves, future generations are not devoid of voice. Their voice is echoed in the various provisions of the UNCLOS which oblige present generations to take active steps to protect and preserve the marine environment and develop the Area for the benefit of mankind. The UNCLOS offers a variety of mechanisms which could be utilised to this end. While imposing upon the States Parties the obligation to protect and preserve the marine environment and take measures for the conservation of marine living resources, it also creates a compulsory dispute settlement procedure through which the adherence to the said obligations can be secured. The latter constitutes a mechanism through which the conduct of the States Parties can be scrutinised and their performance improved. The exercise of the compulsory and advisory jurisdiction of UNCLOS adjudicatory bodies is a channel through which intergenerational considerations can be integrated into the interpretation and from there reflected in the application of the relevant law, national law and the conduct of States. Their broad jurisdiction *ratione personae* allows a greater variety of actors to take action and question by judicial means the legality under the Convention of States' acts and thus demand correction in their behaviour in line with the principles and rules of the Convention. However, its most innovative achievement is the development of the principle of common heritage of mankind and the creation of mechanisms, a compulsory dispute settlement procedure and a procedure for rendering advisory opinions, through which the efficient implementation of this principle is ensured. Through this principle, the UNCLOS recognises future generations, an inalienable part 'Mankind' or rather 'Humankind', as beneficiaries of the Area and its resources and imposes an obligation upon the States Parties

146 Art 191 UNCLOS.
147 See Art 21 ITLOS Statute in conjunction with Art 138 ITLOS Rules.

to the Convention to develop the said common heritage for their benefit. Under this principle, a complex international management system, the Authority, has been established which has no analogue in other treaties dealing with or alluding to the principle of common heritage of mankind. The Authority serves as an advocate securing the needs and long term concerns of mankind which include the foreseeable needs and interests of future generations. Thus, States Parties are meant to act as a trustee on behalf of mankind and hence on behalf of future generations.

15. Voice and No Votes for Future Citizens

Rudolf Schuessler and Fritz Gillerke***

Abstract: *This chapter discusses an important distinction in conceptions of the representation of future people in democratic decision-making processes.*
It thereby builds on the discussion of the All Affected Principle. Firstly, the authors argue that both of its predominant interpretations, the All Subjected Principle and the Principle of All Affected Interests, are complementing principles of democratic inclusion that correspond to different types of political representation. Secondly, the authors argue that the application of the All Subjected Principle can be further restricted under conditions of Political Modal Presentism. Political Modal Presentism prescribes that no hypothetical representative of an unborn person should hold more institutional political powers than is held by a representative of a living person with the same morally relevant characteristics. From Political Modal Presentism one can derive a narrow version of the All Subjected Principle.
Based on this line of argument, this chapter demonstrates that under a narrow conception of the All Subjected Principle, one should not grant voting rights to representatives of future citizens.

Modern democracies are representative democracies. Political decisions are taken by chosen representatives supposed to act in the interest of the people they represent. The representative element in modern democracies gives rise to the idea that future generations, whose lives and interests will be severely affected by present political decisions, should also be represented in present democratic processes.[1] It is not obvious, however, whether the representation of future persons can be rendered compatible with the

---

* Rudolf Schuessler is Professor of Philosophy at the University of Bayreuth (Germany).

** Fritz Gillerke holds a PhD from the University of Bayreuth. He works as public sector consultant in Berlin (Germany).

1 On political representation in general, see Hanna F Pitkin, *The Concept of Representation* (University of California Press 1967); Laura Montanaro, 'Representation', *The Encyclopedia of Political Thought* (Wiley-Blackwell 2015); Suzanne Dovi, 'Political Representation', *The Stanford Encyclopedia of Philosophy* (Spring 2017) <https://plato.stanford.edu/entries/political-representation/> accessed 12 September 2021. On representation of future people, see the papers in Jörg Tremmel, 'Institutionelle Verankerung der Rechte nachrückender Generationen' (2004) 37 Zeitschrift für Rechtspolitik 44; Kristian S Ekeli, 'Giving a Voice to Posterity – Deliberative Democracy and Representation of Future People' (2005) 18 Journal of Agricultural and Environmental Ethics 429; Kristian S Ekeli 'The Principle of Liberty and Legal Representation of Posterity' (2006) 12 Res Publica 385; Ludvig Beckman, *The Frontiers of Democracy: The Right to Vote and its Limits* (Palgrave Macmillan 2009); Dennis F Thompson, 'Representing Future Generations: Political Presentism and Democratic

present basic understandings of democracy.[2] To clarify this issue, some key questions about the representation of future persons need to be addressed. Who should represent the still unborn, and who should be represented? What kinds of rights or entitlements should representatives of future people have in present political processes? Here, we will mainly be concerned with this last question, assuming that representation of the yet unborn in democratic societies can, in principle, be justified.

Our considerations rely on a very general principle. A hypothetical representative of an unborn person should not be endowed with more institutional political powers than held by a representative of a living person with the same morally relevant characteristics. That is, an actually existing person should *ceteris paribus* be at least as well represented as a person only expected to come into being. Let us call this the principle of 'Political Modal Presentism' ('PMP') because it prefers the actual over the merely possible, or actual over merely expectable existence. Based on PMP, theories of democracy can be used to limit the entitlements of representatives of future people. We restrict our considerations to those yet unborn and somewhat distantly future persons (for instance, persons born 30 years from now).

If we speak of future generations, we, therefore, refer to persons born beyond the horizon of traditional (and especially pre-climate-crisis) political planning. By reducing the overlap between current and future generations

Trusteeship' (2010) 13 Critical Review of International Social and Political Philosophy 17; Ludvig Beckman 'Political Representation of Future Generations and Collective Responsibility' (2015) 6 Jurisprudence 516; Deryck Beyleveld, Marcus Düwell and Andreas Spahn, 'Why and How Should We Represent Future Generations in Policymaking?' (2015) 6 Jurisprudence 549; Axel Gosseries, 'Introduction: Representing Future Generations?' (2015) 6 Jurisprudence 492; Iñigo González-Ricoy and Axel Gosseries (eds), *Institutions for Future Generations* (OUP 2016); Lukas Köhler, *Die Repräsentation von Non-Voice-Partys in Demokratien: Argumente zur Vertretung der Menschen ohne Stimme als Teil des Volkes* (Springer Fachmedien Wiesbaden 2017).

2 It has been argued that representation of future people in present democratic decision processes would undermine our democratic systems. See eg, Ludvig Beckman, 'Democracy and Future Generations. Should the Unborn Have a Voice?' in Jean-Christophe Merle (ed), *Spheres of Global Justice* (Vol 2, Springer 2013); Berenice Bovenkerk, 'Public Deliberation and the Inclusion of Future Generations' (2015) 6 Jurisprudence 496; Karsten K Jensen, 'Future Generations in Democracy: Representation or Consideration?' (2015) 6 Jurisprudence 535. However, such concerns need not be decisive for the limited representation we suggest. We thus operate under the assumption that limited representation may not derail present democratic systems and ask how it might be justified.

we attempt to emphasise the particular conceptual challenges of adjudicating between the living and the not-yet-born. The present generation accordingly comprises all living persons. The representation of distant future persons may be specifically relevant for climate policies or population ethics. The issue of their representation is sufficiently different from the representation of already living minors to justify separate treatment. Adolescent children, for instance, might be granted voting rights and thus can be represented through existing channels. Young children might be represented by their parents by giving them an additional vote per child. None of this makes sense for the distant unborn. The representation of yet unborn future people is, therefore, an issue which deserves to be approached in its own right.

Applications of PMP can build on the observation that different categories of presently living persons are represented in different ways and with different powers in democratic political processes. It follows that future people in analogous classificatory categories should not possess greater powers than their actually existing predecessors. Take, for instance, the right to vote for a legislative assembly. Presently, this right is usually restricted to the citizens of a state. Hence, representatives of future citizens of the same state might obtain voting rights in present elections for a legislative assembly, but as long as the traditional distribution of voting rights is considered legitimate, representatives of future non-citizens should not obtain voting rights because the corresponding present non-citizens lack such rights. At least, this is what PMP implies. We will discuss further implications in the present paper.[3]

It is not enough for our considerations to extrapolate from existing political practices. We want to offer a normative analysis, and the actual practices of democracies are therefore only relevant inasmuch they can be normatively justified. Consequently, we need to discuss how present persons can be justly represented in democratic communities.

3 What so far has been said about 'present' persons shows that we count all potentially approachable people (eg, approachable with requests of consent) as relevantly present in the sense of Political Modal Presentism. Since we are concerned with democratic theory and not democratic practice, it does not matter much whether these are, in fact, approached. 'The absent' are people who cannot be approached, that is, mainly the dead and the unborn. PMP implies that representatives of the dead should not hold more power than representatives of analogous living persons. The too young, comatose, or mentally handicapped form a further category of concern for whom issues of representation arise. However, this class of people will not be discussed for the sake of simplicity.

1. Principles for the Ascription of Voting Rights in Democracies

It is widely assumed in political theory that being affected by certain state activities is a sufficient normative basis for demanding a say in the decisions that lead to these activities. The medieval juridical principle that all people should be allowed to have some say in matters that concern all (*quod omnes tangit, ab omnes approbari debet*) is an example in point.[4] Moral philosophers like Jürgen Habermas similarly assume that only those norms can aspire to be morally binding to which all persons affected by the norm can freely assent.[5] Such demands can be generalised to an 'All Affected Principle' ('AAP'), saying that whoever is affected by the activities of a state (or an institution or even an agent) should have a say in the decisions that lead to these activities.[6] AAP is a very broad principle and much in need of interpretation. It is, for instance, not immediately clear what being affected or 'having a say' is supposed to mean. Unsurprisingly, therefore, AAP has been subject to different interpretations. In any case, we regard AAP to be morally valid in at least some interpretation. AAP is at the heart of democracy, and those who accept (as we do) that people are entitled to democratic governance, must in some way endorse AAP.

Starting from this, two understandings of AAP may be distinguished, which apparently differ fundamentally. Some scholars regard the 'Principle

4 On '*quod omnes tangit*', see Gaines Post, 'Plena Potestas and Consent in Medieval Assemblies: A Study in Romano-Canonical Procedure and the Rise of Representation, 1150–1325' (1943) 1 Traditio 355; Gaines Post, *Studies in Medieval Legal Thought. Public Law and the State 1100–1322* (Princeton University Press 1964).

5 See Jürgen Habermas, *Moralbewußtsein und kommunikatives Handeln* (Suhrkamp 1983).

6 The AAP goes back to Robert A Dahl, *After the Revolution? Authority in a Good Society* (Yale University Press 1990); Robert E Goodin, 'Enfranchising All Affected Interests, and Its Alternatives' (2007) 35 Philosophy & Public Affairs 40; Robert E Goodin, 'Enfranchising All Subjected, Worldwide' (2016) 8 International Theory 365. See also Sfoia Näsström, 'The Challenge of the All-Affected Principle' (2011) 59 Political Studies 116; Zoltan Miklosi, 'Against the Principle of All Affected Interests' (2012) 38 Social Theory and Practice 483; David Owen, 'Constituting the Polity, Constituting the Demos: On the Place of the All Affected Interests Principle in Democratic Theory and in Resolving the Democratic Boundary Problem' (2012) 5 Ethics and Global Politics 129; Ben Saunders, 'Defining the Demos' (2012) 11 Politics, Philosophy & Economics 280; Matt Whitt, 'Democracy's Sovereign Enclosures: Territory and the All-Affected Principle' (2014) 21 Constellations: An International Journal of Critical and Democratic Theory 560.

of All Affected Interests' ('PAAI') as a correct specification of AAP.[7] According to PAAI, people should have a say in all decisions that affect their interests. This still needs further clarification because we still do not know what 'a say' is supposed to mean, and the concept of interests also needs elucidation and, last but not least, it should be specified how interests can be affected. Depending on the answers to these questions, the class of people affected by state activities can become very large. Examples offer some clarification. In the 1980s, German environmental regulations allowed German industries to emit sulfur oxides which harmed Swedish forests (and thus, indirectly, Swedish citizens).[8] Being harmed by acid rain clearly affects a person's legitimate interests. According to PAAI, the Swedish citizens should therefore have had a say in the German decisions that led to the emission of sulfur oxides.

Yet, democratic states usually restrict influence on political processes to their own citizens, and these exert their influence mostly through political representatives rather than directly. Such practices might rely on an alternative understanding of AAP. According to the 'All Subjected Principle' ('ASP'), only persons who are subject to the laws and institutions of a state are entitled to full (and equal) political influence on the said laws and institutions.[9] Since Swedes are not subject to German laws, they need not be allowed to have 'a say' in German environmental decision-making. ASP corresponds much closer than PAAI to the actual practices of modern democracies, but this does not imply that it is normatively justified. PAAI appears normatively more plausible to quite a few observers. In fact, there is a lively dispute in political philosophy about which of the two, PAAI or ASP, is better suited to ground representation in democracies.[10]

Our own position is that PAAI and ASP are not strict alternatives. They should rather be regarded as complementary. That is, both are normatively valid, but they call for different representative entitlements. PAAI entitles persons to 'voice' in processes that lead to activities which affect the interests of the said persons. Hence, the affected persons or their representatives

7 eg, Beckman, *The Frontiers of Democracy* (n 1); Goodin, 'Enfranchising All Affected Interests, and Its Alternatives' (n 6).

8 Goodin, 'Enfranchising All Affected Interests, and Its Alternatives' (n 6) 49. For a discussion of the case from a negotiation-analytic perspective, see Cecilia Albin, *Justice and Fairness in International Negotiations* (CUP 2001).

9 Goodin, 'Enfranchising All Affected Interests, and Its Alternatives' (n 6) 49; Beckman, *The Frontiers of Democracy* (n 1) 71; Näsström (n 6); Köhler (n 1).

10 See the literature quoted in the preceding footnotes.

should be heard, and their arguments and demands should be seriously considered. It is not enough if the interests of affected persons are merely considered by the decision-makers without any chance for the affected to voice them themselves or via representatives. In our acid rain example, the affected Swedish citizens should be able to voice their concerns in German decision-making processes, eg, through spokespersons chosen by the affected Swedes.

However, should not *all* persons be allowed to speak in democratic processes, regardless of their affectedness? If democratic processes are regarded as vehicles for making good decisions (as theories of epistemic democracy claim), these processes should be influenced by the best of arguments, and since we do not know in advance who is going to proffer the best argument, we should listen to all comers. It seems legitimate to call for such a broad sweep, but it also appears legitimate to further differentiate. All sorts of people may exert their influence through free media and open public hearings, but it seems reasonable to institutionally grant persons whose interests are seriously affected by a decision a stronger voice. Their representatives may be allowed to voice their concerns and arguments in parliaments or even closed caucuses and thus exert a more direct influence on decision-making processes than the general public. However, we propose not to extend PAAI-grounded influence to voting at any level of the democratic process. We thus accept the standing practices of democratic states to a significant degree as morally legitimate. This specific meaning of our voice/vote distinction should be borne in mind. Claims that future people should have a voice in present political processes often include voting as a form of voice.[11] In our terminology, by contrast, voice and vote are alternatives. 'Voice' encompasses all forms of influencing decision processes merely by communication, whether directly or via representatives, 'vote' refers to a decision by a vote in or for political institutions.

Moreover, we suggest allocating voting rights according to a very restrictive understanding of ASP.[12] That is, voting in democratic assemblies should

11 See eg, Ekeli, 'Giving a Voice to Posterity – Deliberative Democracy and Representation of Future People' (n 1); A Fung, 'The Principle of Affected Interests: An Interpretation and Defense', in Jack H Nagel J and Roger W Smith (eds), *Representation: Elections and Beyond* (University of Pennsylvania Press 2013).

12 This stands in contrast to authors who in the wake of Andrew Dobson, 'Representative Democracy and the Environment' in William M Lafferty and James Meadowcroft (eds), *Democracy and the Environment – Problems and Prospects* (Edward Elgar Publishing Limited 1996) already regard being affected as a sufficient condition for

be restricted to the elected representatives of people who, in a restrictive understanding, are subject to the laws and institutions of a state (or political community). The restrictiveness in question concerns the interpretation of the clause 'being subject to the laws and institutions of a political community'. In a straightforward sense, migrants who seek asylum or try to enter a state at the state's borders are subject to the state's laws.[13] They are surely treated according to these laws when they are allowed to enter and when they are rejected. It, therefore, seems to follow from ASP that migrants should have voting rights in the state to which they try to gain access. In fact, many persons who are not citizens of a state may claim voting rights in a community if we understand ASP as 'Simple ASP'.[14]

- *Simple ASP*: Persons have a moral right to vote for the legislative and political decision-making institutions of a political community if and only if the persons are subject to the laws of the community in the sense of being treated in ways specified according to these laws.

Against this, it may be objected that voting rights should only be granted to people who have no choice in being subject to the laws of a political community. According to this restrictive view, voting rights should only be granted to persons who, in a juridical sense, are subject to the laws of a political community without having the alternative to opt out. Persons able to evade subjection to the laws of a community simply by leaving the territory of a state or moving away from its borders are, on this view, not deeply enough subject to the coercion of law to be granted voting rights. This objection touches upon an important point. From a restrictive and if you like conservative perspective, voting rights to the main legislative or executive institutions of a state are such powerful vehicles of political influence that they should be granted only to people who are bound to feel the consequences of their decisions for the community. Whoever is allowed to make decisions of utmost importance for a community should, as far as practicable, also have to bear the consequences of their decisions, and negative consequences in particular. Moreover, from the restrictive perspective, we advocate that not any kind of consequence is relevant for the allocation

---

having a right to vote, and others who assume such rights on the basis of a generously applied ASP (see below).

13 See Claudio López-Guerra, *Democracy and Disenfranchisement: The Morality of Electoral Exclusions* (OUP 2014); H De Schutter and L Ypi, 'Mandatory Citizenship for Immigrants' (2015) 45 British Journal of Political Science 235.

14 See Goodin, 'Enfranchising All Subjected' (n 9); De Schutter and Ypi (n 13).

of voting rights in sovereign political communities. The consequences that matter pertain to the basic tasks of states (or sovereign political communities), such as the provision of internal and external security, civic freedoms and basic welfare. Since voters decide upon the provision of these goods, they should also not be legally allowed to evade the consequences of their decisions in this respect. If we accept these considerations as the basis for the ascription of democratic voting rights, Simple ASP fails because it grants voting rights to persons who at any time may legally dissociate themselves in crucial respects (subjection to police force, taxation, war) from the community in which they have voting rights.

Of course, citizens may, to some extent, evade the consequences of their votes by living abroad as expats.[15] However, expats remain subject to key laws of the state of which they are citizens. They may be taxed and thus remain potentially accountable for spending they caused by voting in their country of origin. They may also be drafted for military service and thus be held accountable for security policies they supported. Hence, modern states may, at least from a juridical point of view, establish a reasonable congruence of influence and legal affectedness for their citizens, even if the citizens live abroad.

What about resident non-citizens? Some resident non-citizens may lack the resources to leave a state, and some may even be barred from returning to their state of origin.[16] Hence, they also become willy-nilly subject to the decisions a community takes with respect to the basic tasks of states. For such reasons, communities may be obligated to take care of needy non-citizen residents, and communities may have good moral reasons for offering citizenship to practically permanent residents. However, an offer of citizenship is not the same as offering voting rights to non-citizens. The right to dissociate themselves from a community and its fundamental concerns, which resident non-citizens have even if they may at a given point in time lack the means to exercise this right, may therefore constitute the main guiding principle for a denial of voting rights to non-citizens.

This is not to say that this perspective is morally without alternative. More generous criteria, like Simple ASP, can coherently be postulated and used for the ascription of voting rights to resident non-citizens or even

15 On expats see eg, Claudio Lopez-Guerra, 'Should Expatriates Vote?' (2005) 13 Journal of Political Philosophy 216.

16 On non-citizen residents see ibid.; Lopez-Guerra, *Democracy and Disenfranchisement: The Morality of Electoral Exclusions* (n 13); De Schutter and Ypi (n 13), which hold a contrary position to ours.

representatives of migrants. We only insist that the extent to which a person needs to be subject to the laws of a community in order to ground voting rights is subject to competing interpretations. There is a considerable bandwidth of reasonably tenable interpretations, some being more inclusive or restrictive than others. If states opt for a restrictive interpretation, as they presently do by only granting voting rights to citizens, they remain normatively blameless as long as they act within the confines of reasonably adoptable interpretations. Therefore, states may adopt a reasonable interpretation of the ASP, which understands subjection to laws as juridically ineluctable subjection. Critics, of course, may legitimately try to politically change this state of affairs and push for a different moral majority opinion, but this does not render the existing practices of states morally wrong. In any case, here we will apply Political Modal Presentism based on the actual ascription of voting rights in modern democracies, which we regard as morally defensible. Consequently, we will rely on:

- *Narrow ASP*: Persons have a moral right to vote for the main legislative and political decision-making institutions of a political community if and only if the persons (a) are subject to the laws of the state in the sense of being treated by the state in ways specified by the laws, (b) cannot legally evade such subjection, and (c) a core set of their legitimate life concerns, which the state is supposed to effectively safeguard, is seriously affected by the laws.

Conditions (a) and (b) of Narrow ASP have already been discussed and justified. Condition (c) only spells out what has also been indicated above. There are clusters of concerns for the satisfaction of which people unite and form political communities. The concerns that the respective communities are supposed to secure or support in the European tradition are life, liberty, property, basic welfare, and protection against arbitrary violence, to name only the most prominent traditional issues. According to the narrow interpretation we adopt, only these concerns matter for calibrating ASP.

However, condition (c) also directs our attention to issues of environmental depletion and, above all, the emerging climate crisis. Since the environmental policies of states affect core concerns of human life on a global scale, one might think that condition (c) of Narrow ASP grounds demands of voting rights of all affected persons in existing states or even grounds calls for a world state.[17] Yet, this view relies on PAAI, not ASP. The affected persons are often not subject to the laws of the existing states in question (conditions (a) and (b)) but only affected by their policies and, if you like, by the outcomes of their laws' application to other persons. Moreover, as long as no alternative institutions exist that all reasonable persons ought to entrust with the task of safeguarding their core concerns of security, freedom, and welfare, nobody needs to abandon the state as a trustee of such concerns. All else may be a utopia, whether a remote or a more nearly realisable one, and nobody needs to entrust the foundations of their lives to untried institutions with uncertain viability and effectiveness. Hence, Narrow ASP can be upheld in the world as it is, and nothing more is required for our argument. Note that we do not deny the problematic global effects of state legislation. If procuring the core concerns of a decent life is the main constitutive reason for forming a political collective that does the job, states cannot succeed on their own, at least as far as climate policy is concerned. However, if no political organisation is available here and now, which may trustworthily implement responsible climate policies, we can, at best, have a moral duty to strive for one. In the meantime, the state need not be abandoned as a decision-maker because it still procures security, freedom, and welfare and can also be tasked with climate change mitigation.

If we start from the assumption of a predominantly state-based international order and regard it as morally legitimate to grant only citizens voting rights in states, Political Modal Presentism may be used to delimit the voting rights of future persons. Since future persons are not to be put in a better position than the presently living, only future citizens of existing states might, by proxy, attain voting rights. It suffices to discuss this category of future persons to determine whether future persons should be represented with voting rights in present democracies. However, before

17 AAP is sometimes used to argue for a 'world government' or a 'global democracy' (eg, Torbjörn Tännsjö, 'Future People, the All Affected Principle, and the Limits of the Aggregation Model of Democracy' in Toni Rønnow-Rasmussen and others (eds), *Hommage à Wlodek: Philosophical Papers Dedicated to Wlodek Rabinowicz* (Department of Philosophy Lund University 2007); Goodin, 'Enfranchising All Subjected' (n 9), and thus for abandoning the still prevailing statist international order. If such demands are considered as utopian and infeasible for at least the near future, the question arises how the representation of future people might be normatively justified under the political auspices of non-ideal, existing democracies. This is the question that preoccupies us here.

we deal with this issue, let us look at PMP a bit more closely to see why it is warranted. At first glance, PMP seems to privilege presently living persons over absent past and future persons by taking them as a standard for judging moral legitimacy. This view, however, is misleading. PMP is consonant with equality between persons regardless of the period in which they live.[18] In fact, the assumption of such equality is its driving concern because equality implies that we should only grant a future person a right under conditions XYZ if we also grant the same right to a presently living person under conditions XYZ. Simple logic then demands that if we deny a presently living person a right under conditions XYZ, a future person should also lack that right under the same morally relevant circumstances – and this is Political Modal Presentism.

Note that PMP is only *ceteris paribus* valid, i.e., it holds unless a moral difference between periods can be established. If it could be shown that a different global political order ought to be normatively presupposed in the future, we would not be entitled to argue on the basis of the present predominantly state-based international order and democratic institutions which grant voting rights only to citizens. It is, therefore, important that a different political order (eg, a world state or stronger international institutions) might, at best, be *ideally* demanded. By contrast, we engage in non-ideal considerations. Given that it cannot be concluded that an assumed ideal order would be achieved if all people do what is non-ideally morally required of them, we cannot presuppose that a world-state or stronger international institutions can and ought to be presumed at the future time we consider. PMP then encourages us not to speculate asymmetrically in favour of future persons. Future persons should not have more rights than analogously positioned present persons just because they might live under more ideal moral conditions. Unequal treatment needs to be justified by moral differences, which are not merely speculative and should not rely on risky bets on a better future.[19]

---

18 This claim does not preclude that at different times, different morally relevant conditions may hold. Eg, future societies may be much richer than presently existing ones and therefore grant more welfare rights. However, if we hold morally relevant conditions constant, a mere difference in time should be morally irrelevant. In other words, there should be no pure moral time preference.

19 Here, we assume uncertainty in the sense of lacking reliable numerical probability assessments. If it could be shown that a particular institutional arrangement will exist in the future with a reliable high probability p, it might become normatively authoritative (for instance, if p amounts to what traditionally is called 'practical

2. Narrow ASP and the Voting Rights of Future Citizens

We may expect that future persons will be affected by the consequences of present policies and laws, although it is less clear what kinds of people will be affected and to which extent. For the future effects, eg, of current greenhouse emissions, some broad categories of harm should nevertheless be foreseen. Hence, PAAI may be used to argue for the representation of future affected persons in present democratic processes.[20] However, we only admit to representation with voice. Consequently, representatives of future persons of which nothing more is known than that they are affected, future persons should, at best, have a voice but no voting rights in present political processes. However, there is a category of future persons which we may, as things stand, expect to fall under ASP. These are the future citizens of states.

If we operate under the premise that present states exist as sovereign political agents in the future, it may plausibly be assumed that they will have significant citizen populations. However, the conditional first part of this sentence, of course, engenders some uncertainty. It is, as outlined, possible that in the more or less distant future in which our future persons live, states are no longer the most important political agents in the international system. Global institutions may encroach on most of the traditional roles of states, including the procurement of basic concerns of life, and therefore global institutions might be the political units to whose laws the descendants of present citizens of states will be subject. Moreover, for European states, the EU might be the future political unit to which ASP refers. Yet, as argued, such possible political futures should not be used to

---

certainty'). However, we need not cater for this complication because distant political futures cannot be predicted with reliable high probability.

20 There is a worry whether future people can be affected by the policies of present states at all (Tannsjö (n 17); Clare Heyward, 'Can the All-Affected Principle Include Future Persons? Green Deliberative Democracy and the Non-Identity Problem' (2008) 17 Environmental Politics 625) especially in light of uncertainties about their effects and problems arising from the so-called *Non-Identity Problem* (see eg, ibid.; Bovenkerk (n 2)). However, there is a broad stream of literature showing that *NIP* does not rule out duties of justice towards future people (Melinda A Roberts, 'The Nonidentity Problem', *Stanford Encyclopedia of Philosophy* (Fall edn, 2019) <http://plato.stanford.edu/entries/nonidentity-problem/> accessed 12 September 2021 for an overview, and Rudolf Schuessler, 'Non-Identity: Solving the Waiver Problem for Future People's Rights' (2016) 35 Law and Philosophy 87 for the view of one of the present authors) and the discussion may be restricted to confidently expectable consequences (eg, flagged out as such in IPCC reports).

increase the political powers of future persons unless the relevant political developments can be predicted with high confidence. In this respect, it also needs to be accounted for that an assumed transition to alternative political systems would deprive present states of the obligation to cater for future people due to ASP. After all, future persons will, under this condition, not be subject to the laws of precursor states once a transition to new political systems has occurred.

For implementation in present states, accordingly, only voting rights for representatives of future citizens of these states need to be contemplated. One may object that the continued existence of the states in question cannot be taken for granted even if the international order remains state-based. Some states may simply cease to exist. Some regions of states may become independent or join another state (or be annexed). Against this, we maintain that states are persistent entities. Once created, most states persist for historically long periods. Most importantly, however, states operate under a legal fiction of their own persistence. International law does not proceed under the assumption of an expected decay of states but without temporal limits for their existence, and this assumption is commonly considered morally legitimate. For this reason, the possibility of a state's dissolution does not impugn our considerations concerning the rights of distant future citizens.

A further difficulty is that laws change more regularly and more often than states lose their legal authority. Certainly, legal systems also operate with a fiction of continued validity of laws without presuming any regularity of 'decay'. Yet, such fictions only make sense if they are not utterly unrealistic. In the case of state continuity, reality tendentially confirms the fiction. For laws, empirical studies are needed to show whether we can reasonably expect that distant future citizens (eg, born thirty years or more in the future) will live under the sway of present laws. Lacking such information, we may simply analytically distinguish between more and less persistent kinds of laws. Constitutional laws will probably belong to the former category.[21] In any case, ASP may only justify voting rights for future citizens with respect to laws which can reasonably be expected to be persistent. We should, therefore, at best, grant voting rights to representatives of future citizens in some domains of legislation but not in all.

21 Axel Gosseries, 'Constitutions and Future Generations' (2008) 17 The Good Society 32.

The practical application of this condition may appear difficult. In order to restrict voting rights for future citizens to persistent kinds of laws, an independent body must determine which laws can ultimately be deemed persistent. Given the encompassing consequences, decisions upon a law's persistence should then be made cautiously and by carefully safeguarding institutional integrity.

This caveat, however, only becomes relevant if we do not reject voting rights for representatives of future citizens altogether. In fact, we will now proceed to show that representatives of future citizens should generally not be endowed with voting rights. If Narrow ASP is accepted, its conditions (b) and (c) exclude future citizens from the domain of people who might claim voting rights by virtue of the principle.

Admittedly (b), the non-existence of a right to opt out appears complicated. For any given law, it is for future citizens expectably not more legal to evade being subject to the law by leaving the territory of a state than for presently living citizens. Thus, they seem in the same way subject as present citizens to condition (b) of Narrow ASP. However, we should remember that the underlying issue is that voters should not be able to avoid the coercion resulting from a law they pass, especially not if they impose the burden of the law on others. An issue of equality, therefore, becomes relevant here, which does not arise as long as Narrow ASP only applies to contemporaries. In this case, all persons subject to the law have an analogous and equal position with respect to the coercion that the law potentially exerts. However, this equality is violated for future citizens. Future citizens can abolish a law and thereby get rid of the coercion it implies, although present citizens have been subject to it.[22]

At first glance, this inequality may be considered as not very different from the inequality young and old persons face with respect to being subject to laws. At any point in time at which a law is abolished or changed, a younger person will expectably have been less long under its coercion than older persons. However, this is a fact that young people can hardly strategically exploit because at any time they abolish a law, they also abolish it for older persons. The situation is different if future citizens become represented by presently living caretakers. The representatives may be pivotal in introducing a law that is onerous for the presently living. Future citizens may then free themselves from the law as soon as they come to decide on

22 A similar argument against the binding force of present laws for future people is made by Beckman (n 2) 781.

it. Thus, representatives of future citizens with voting rights can exploit an asymmetry of power in favour of their future constituents. The said representatives may inordinately burden presently living persons who are subject to a law, knowing that their clients will in the future be able to throw off the burden.

We may conclude that an asymmetry of options for legally ridding oneself of subjection to laws exists between present and future citizens. Future citizens should, therefore, not be granted voting rights if the equality between all persons subject to a law is to be salvaged.

Condition (c) is beset by similar problems of asymmetry. The condition ensures that the persons falling under Narrow ASP form a community whose members are co-dependent on each other with respect to their chances of leading good lives. These chances are usually safeguarded by the core activities of states which traditionally comprise the provision of internal and external security (police and military), health care, old-age pensions, education, and basic social welfare. Taxation is the main instrument for financing the respective tasks, and thus the persons falling under Narrow ASP are also the persons that form the permanent tax base of a state. Narrow ASP claims that only persons who are in this way co-producers, co-benefiters, and risk sharers of basic activities of the state ought also to be co-deciders in the state's political processes. It is, therefore, important to note that future citizens are not subject to the mutual interdependence of deciding and being affected by the core tasks of the state, which characterises the community of present citizens. As persons that do not yet exist, future citizens cannot stand in the reciprocal relation to present citizens, which characterises the state as a community that shares benefits and risks from decisions concerning basic tasks.

The consequences of this asymmetry can be momentous. Representatives of future citizens might pave the way for decisions on the internal and external security of a state which might be of relatively small consequence for future citizens but affect the presently living momentously. The same is true for economic and welfare policies. Of course, it is plausible to assume that future citizens will in some way be also affected by the respective decisions, but the crucial point is that they will expectably be affected in crucially different ways than the presently living. There will therefore exist a massive asymmetry in consequences so that the persons falling under Narrow ASP would no longer form a co-dependent community with their presently living predecessors. Take the example of going to war. If we talk about an enemy that might destroy or impose heavy post-war burdens on a state, like in WWI or WWII, the decision to engage in war is existential for the presently living citizens. Their lives will expectably be severely affected by the war. The same does not necessarily hold for future citizens of the state. Wars like WWI and WWII had significant social and cultural impact. However, at the same time they had merely small long-term negative effects on the economies of the countries involved. Their economic success or relative failure was determined by factors that were, in the long run, independent of the wars. After WWII, the defeated and occupied aggressors, Germany and Japan, emerged as economically more powerful than ever.

One may, of course, object that such asymmetries between present and future citizens are precisely what representatives of future persons are supposed to balance. They might counterbalance the self-serving bias that the representatives of the presently living implement at the cost of future generations by overspending and turning a blind eye to environmental degradation.[23] On the whole, as might be argued, pro-present and pro-future biases counterbalance each other and thus produce a more or less fair result. This, however, is in no way warranted. A balancing effect is only to be expected in a few fields in which the interests of present and future citizens meet. The thrift of representatives of the future, for instance, might counterbalance the spending mania of present parliamentarians. Yet, in many respects, the interests of present and future people are not aligned and may well combine to produce lose-lose outcomes. Representatives of the future may, for instance, neglect present military security in favour of environmental protection. Representatives of the present may prefer the opposite. It is not clear, however, whether political logrolling can be expected to create a reasonable compromise by balancing these tendencies. Logrolling may lead to war *and* environmental depletion.

A particular problem exists with respect to social justice. Future citizens have no immediate interest in social justice for the presently living. Their representatives might vote for economic and environmental policies which favour the well-being of future generations regardless of the possible unfairness of these policies for the less well-off today. The political representatives of the worse-off thus face a political battle on two fronts, against economic neoliberals who do not care much about social policies and against representatives of the future who also do not care. There is no counterbalancing

23 On the assumption of intertemporal myopia in standard economics, see eg, Shane Frederick, George Lowenstein and Ted O'Donoghue, 'Time Discounting and Time Preference: A Critical Review' (2002) 40 Journal of Economic Literature 351.

here. Voting rights for representatives of future citizens straightforwardly lead *ceteris paribus* to a deterioration of the position of the socially weak. Hence, the expectation is unfounded that voting rights for representatives of future citizens would lead to a net gain of justice in present democracies. Counterbalancing may be expected for myopia concerning debt accumulation and environmental protection. However, this comes at the price of a devaluation of security and social policies in present societies. There is no accepted metric that might show whether these countervailing tendencies in sum produce a net gain or loss. It is not even possible to claim that environmental concerns should prevail because they amount to a life-or-death threat for humanity as a whole. Security issues invoke the same threat. A global nuclear war might also lead to the extinction of humanity. Therefore, in final consideration, we have no good reason to assume that a balancing of interests between present and future persons, which might justify the acceptance of inequality between them with respect to Political Modal Presentism, is possible.

3. Conclusion

We have shown why ASP should not be used for granting voting rights to representatives of future people. The version of ASP we apply is restrictive, reflecting legitimate present practices of allowing only the citizens of existing states and their representatives to vote in the major political institutions of a state. Future citizens of existing states are, by extrapolation from these practices, the only future people that might be given voting rights. However, this would violate two conditions of our restrictive Narrow ASP. Future citizens are, contrary to condition (b), asymmetrically able to evade subjection to laws of present political communities simply by changing the laws. Moreover, present and future citizens of states fail to share the basic risks and burdens of the provision of basic goods such as security, liberty, and help in need (condition c). Therefore, they do not form the sort of community to which ASP should be applied (hence, we also assume that *Simple ASP* is not a sufficient criterion for forming a demos).

In contrast to some other sceptics concerning the political representation of future people, we do not reject all kinds of their political representation. Distinguishing between voice and vote, we argue for institutionalised rights of voice for future people. PAAI is the adequate norm for granting rights to be listened to (with a suitable calibration of affectedness). However, PAAI should not be used for granting voting rights to representatives of future persons because, as PMP implies, this would lead to unacceptable consequences. PMP appeals to us as a very plausible principle, which claims that future persons should not have rights or entitlements which presently living persons with analogous roles or characteristics lack. Hence, Simple ASP and PAAI should not be applied to future persons without applying them to the presently living, and application today would lead to a huge extension of the electorate for the legislative and executive institutions of present states. Not only migrants who have no realistic chance to attain decent living conditions unless they migrate to a wealthy state would be entitled to a vote in this state. Military interventions would automatically entitle insurgents in the state in which the intervention occurs to vote in the intervening states. To sum up, a democratic order as we know it would have to be abandoned if voting rights were granted on the basis of Simple ASP and PAAI. Narrow ASP is the only principle that is consonant with current democratic practices, and it does not grant voting rights to representatives of future people.

16. Democratic Legitimacy, Institutions for Future Generations and the Problem of Constitutional Power

Ludvig Beckman[*]

Abstract: *Recognising widely held concerns regarding 'presentist' biases in democratic institutions, this chapter challenges the contention that democratic legitimacy inexorably requires the inclusion of future generations in democratic decisions. According to two requirements of democratic legitimacy – inclusion and constitutional empowerment – people should be empowered to participate in decisions about policy and law, and to determine the rules structuring the political framework. Drawing a distinction between these requirements, this chapter contends that though it may be feasible to 'include' future generations for proxy representation, future generations cannot enjoy 'constitutional power'.*

This chapter applies two separate understandings of constitutional power to future generations, the 'constituent power' to create constitutional frameworks, and the 'constituted power' to amend such frameworks' norms. It contends that neither is achievable for unborn people and that full intergenerational democratic legitimacy is therefore impossible. Reason for concern with the long-term effects of contemporary policies and political systems still remain, of course. But in attending to them, justice rather than democratic legitimacy should guide our judgments.

Introduction

Impending climate change and the apparent incapacity of democratic governments to act with sufficient resolve is a source of pessimism about democratic politics. Though there are many potential explanations for lethargic democratic politics, one of them is that representative systems are at fault by design. Electoral cycles incentivise governments and elected lawmakers to respond primarily to the short-term interests of the electorate. Hence, the lack of concern for future generations – here understood as people yet unborn and, more generally, as non-overlapping future generations[1] – is a predictable outcome of the political *presentism* that is an inherent feature of democratic systems.[2]

---

* Ludvig Beckman is a Professor in Political Science at Stockholm University and the Institute for Futures Studies.

1 On the significance of the distinction between overlapping and non-overlapping generations, see Axel Gosseries, 'Future Generations' Future Rights' (2008) 16(4) Journal of Political Philosophy 446.

2 Dennis Thompson, 'Representing Future Generations: Political Presentism and Democratic Trusteeship' (2010) 13(1) Critical Review of International Social and Political

A variety of remedies for political presentism have been proposed: the introduction of ombudsmen or special committees in parliaments with powers to propose policies benefiting the future; reform of parliamentary voting procedures that impede decisions affecting the future; stronger constitutional protection of future generations' interests. A more radical idea is to restructure the composition of legislative assemblies to include political representatives for future generations.[3] These representatives would be proxies for future generations as they are empowered to promote the interests of a group that is in fact absent. According to Michael Rose, proxies *represent* future generations if the relevant audience – i.e. the current members of democratic states – accept them as such.[4]

Here, I am not interested in the feasibility of proxy representation or the difficulties of identifying the interests that they should protect. For the sake of the argument, I will simply accept that institutions for the political representation of future generations (IFG) are feasible and that they serve to promote the interests of future generations. The question here is, instead, how to assess IFGs from the point of view of *democratic legitimacy.*

One's initial reaction is arguably to think that the democratic legitimacy of IFGs is debatable. After all, they attenuate the legislative powers of the living generation and reduce their powers to self-determination. Though it may be desirable to protect the interests of future generations, we might object that all peoples should be entitled to democratic self-rule. Even if the living are myopic and selfish, they are still entitled to a democratic process! Hence, as Ivo Walliman-Helmer suggests, there is reason to suspect that

---

Philosophy 17; David Runciman, 'Democracy Is the Planet's Biggest Enemy' *Foreign Policy* (Washington, 20 July 2019) <https://perma.cc/U58K-JB4L>.

3 For overviews, see: Inigo Gonzalez-Ricoy, 'Intergenerational Justice and Institutions for the Long Term' in Klaus Goetz (ed), *The Oxford Handbook of Time and Politics* (OUP 2020); Andre Santos Campos, 'Representing the Future: The Interests of Future Persons in Representative Democracy' (2021) 51(1) British Journal of Political Science 1; Bernice Bovenkerk, 'Public Deliberation and the Inclusion of Future Generations' (2015) 6(3) Jurisprudence 496.

4 Michael Rose, 'All-affected, Non-identity and the Political Representation of Future Generations: Linking Intergenerational Justice with Democracy' in Thomas Cottier, Shaheeza Lalani and Clarence Siziba (eds), *Intergenerational Equity. Environmental and Cultural Concerns* (Brill 2019).

IFGs that impair the ability of present people to rule themselves by democratic procedures are in 'conflict with claims about democratic legitimacy'.[5]

However, advocates of IFGs do have a powerful reply to this objection. They point out that the political representation of future generations is not contrary to the democratic process. IFGs improve the democratic qualities of political systems by making public decisions accountable to future interests.[6] This reply is premised on the notion that the democratic legitimacy of political systems should take into consideration the interests of both present and future generations.[7] Public decisions made today should be legitimate to members of present as well as future generations.

Democratic legitimacy is not the only potential justification of IFGs. A concern with *intergenerational justice* may also provide grounds for reforms that improve the extent to which political decisions take future interests into account. But reasons of intergenerational justice are arguably distinct from principles of democratic legitimacy. Public decisions that are just are not necessarily legitimate by democratic standards, and public decisions that conform to precepts of democratic legitimacy are not necessarily just.[8] The basis for the distinction between democratic legitimacy and justice is naturally complex and somewhat contentious as it relates to ongoing debates on the place of justified coercion and legitimate authority in accounts of political legitimacy.[9] These questions are bracketed in this paper, however. Democratic legitimacy is here simply understood as equal to the procedural preconditions for democratic rule. Public decisions are considered as legitimate if and only if they are made in accordance with the norms

---

5 Ivo Wallimann-Helmer, 'Can Youth Quotas Help Avoid Future Disasters?' in Igor Dimitrijoski and others (eds), *Youth Quotas? And other Efficient Forms of Youth Participation* (Springer 2015).

6 Simon Caney, 'Political Institutions for the Future: A Fivefold Package' in Axel Gosseries and Iñigo Gonzalez-Ricoy (eds), *Institutions for Future Generations* (OUP 2018) 135.

7 Axel Gosseries and Iñigo González-Ricoy, 'Designing Institutions for Future Generations' in Gosseries and González-Ricoy (n 6) 16.

8 For the distinction between democracy-based and justice-based argument for the political representation of future generations, see Ludvig Beckman, 'Do Global Climate Change and the Interest of Future Generations have Implications for Democracy?' (2008) 4 Environmental Politics 610, and Iñigo Gonzalez-Ricoy and Felipe Rey, 'Enfranchising the Future: Climate Justice and the Representation of Future Generations' (2019) 10 WIREs Climate Change 1, 2.

9 For an overview, see Fabienne Peter, 'Authority and Legitimacy' in Fred D'Agostino and Gerald Gaus (eds), *The Routledge Companion to Social and Political Philosophy* (Routledge 2013).

and rules required for them to be democratic. By contrast, justice refers to the moral justifiability of outcomes. Public decisions are on this simplistic view 'just' if and only if they produce results that align with principles of social justice.

Accordingly, the claim that IFGs are required for reasons of intergenerational justice is a claim about the kind of political institutions required to establish just outcomes. This claim has the obvious defect of ignoring the procedural requirements of democratic legitimacy. The more convincing basis for IFGs is consequently that they are required by principles of democratic legitimacy. The claim is that the political representation of future people's interests is necessary for democratic reasons rather than for reasons of justice.

Now, a popular understanding is that democratic legitimacy requires that anyone relevantly affected should be included in the democratic process. Provided that future generations *are* relevantly affected by public decisions, democratic legitimacy inexorably *requires* institutions that include future generations. The principle that all relevantly affected interests should be included in democratic procedures is the central premise for the democratic legitimacy of IFGs.

This paper challenges this specific attempt to defend institutions representing the interests of future generations. The argument advanced is that even if IFGs successfully include future interests in public decisions, they fail to empower future generations in all respects that are relevant for democratic legitimacy to be achieved. The people included in the democratic process should not just be able to partake in decisions of policy but also in decisions on the political framework. Such constitutional power is in other words a fundamental requirement for democratic legitimacy. Where the people included are unable to exercise constitutional power, their inclusion in the political process does not contribute to the realisation of democratic legitimacy. The central claim defended here is then that IFGs are unable to extend constitutional power to future generations. To illustrate this, this paper proceeds in three steps. The first dissects the argument for IFGs in further detail. The second addresses the relationship between democratic legitimacy, democratic inclusion and constitutional power. The final section explains why constitutional power cannot be adequately secured through the political representation of future generations.

1. Future Generations and Democratic Legitimacy

The argument for the political representation of future generations has the structure of a conclusion (3) that depends on two premises (1 and 2):

(1) The principle of democratic inclusion requires that the interests of future generations be represented by public institutions (IFGs).
(2) Principles of democratic inclusion are part of the principles of democratic legitimacy.
(3) The principle of democratic legitimacy requires that the interests of future generations be represented by public institutions (IFG's).

If these premises are accepted, the conclusion must also be accepted. The conclusion *is* a valid inference from the premises. But the premises themselves are not necessarily true. Let us therefore take a look at the grounds for accepting them.

The first premise is controversial as democratic standards for inclusion are contested. Thus, the very first premise of the argument that the interests of future generations should be represented by public institutions in order for democratic legitimacy to be achieved can be questioned. Yet, that is not the route taken here. In the following, I will proceed on the assumption that the first premise is true though some of the difficulties with this premise are discussed further below. For the sake of argument, I will accept that a plausible conception of democratic inclusion exists such that the interest of future generations should be included by means of political representation. What I want to focus on instead is the second premise.

Premise 2 does at first glance appear less controversial. Surely public institutions must be inclusive to be legitimate by democratic standards. This is true of most if not all conceptions of democracy.[10] We shall note though that this premise does not represent a complete account of democratic legitimacy and that democratic inclusion is not a sufficient condition. Of course, the fact that democratic legitimacy includes additional conditions does not automatically undermine the conclusion (3). After all, the conclusion of the argument does not state that the political representation of the interests of future generations is sufficient for democratic legitimacy – only that it is necessary. But the conclusion of the argument does depend on

10 This is not true for minimalist conceptions according to which the competitive selection of leaders exhausts the necessary and sufficient conditions for democracy. Adam Przeworski, 'Minimalist Conception of Democracy: A Defence' in Ian Schapiro and Casiano Hacker-Cordón (eds), *Democracy's Value* (CUP 1999).

the assumption that the political representation of future interests are *pro tanto* improvements in terms of democratic legitimacy. The assumption is in other words that democratic inclusion is a requirement of democratic legitimacy that applies independently of other requirements of democratic legitimacy. The validity of that assumption cannot be taken for granted, however. The alternative is that democratic inclusion is a conditional requirement of democratic legitimacy; that it contributes to democratic legitimacy only if other requirements of democratic legitimacy are also in place.

In sum, it is possible to distinguish between two versions of the claim that democratic legitimacy requires inclusion: (2a) that democratic legitimacy unconditionally requires democratic inclusion and (2b) that democratic legitimacy requires democratic inclusion only on condition that additional conditions apply. The difference between these versions can be illustrated by a simple analogy from a different context. Consider the difference between the claim (1) 'a good dinner requires a good wine' and the claim (2) 'a good dinner requires a good wine, but a good wine contributes to the goodness of the dinner only if the food is decent'. Both claims hold that a good wine is necessary for a good dinner; no dinner is good without a good wine. The difference though is that only (1) holds that a good wine unconditionally contributes to the goodness of a dinner. According to (2) a good wine contributes to make the dinner good only on condition that the dinner is decent.

In the present context, the point is that the second premise in the argument for the political representation of future generations can be read in two distinct ways. Either the claim is that the political representation of future generations contributes to the democratic legitimacy of political institutions even if other requirements of democratic legitimacy cannot be satisfied. Or, the claim is that the political representation of future generations contributes to the democratic legitimacy of political institutions only if other requirements of democratic legitimacy are satisfied. Both readings cannot be correct. If one of them is correct, the other is false, and vice versa. Consequently, the correct reading of premise two cannot be taken for granted.

The argument of this paper is that premise 2 should be read as the claim that the political representation of future generations enhances the democratic legitimacy of political systems only on condition that additional requirements are met. The further claim defended is that these additional requirements of democratic legitimacy cannot be met in relation to future generations. If correct, the conclusion is that the democratic argument for the political representation of future generations fails and that the conclusion above (3) is invalid. Notably, this refutation does not depend either on rejecting the claim that all 'relevantly affected' should be included, or on rejecting the claim that future generations are relevantly affected in the sense required for principles of democratic inclusion to apply.

2. Democratic Legitimacy

I take the received view of democratic legitimacy to be that it represents a moral standard such that public institutions are legitimate if and only if they are democratic.[11] The normative implications of legitimacy are nevertheless in dispute. Following what can be termed the justice-based account, the claim that public institutions are legitimate by democratic standards implies that they should be supported by duties of justice.[12] A second view is that democratic legitimacy represents a condition for political obligation. The subject population is not morally required to comply with the law unless public institutions comply with standards of democratic legitimacy. A third alternative is that democratic legitimacy is a necessary condition for permissible coercion. Public institutions are morally permitted to make decisions that are coercive only if they are democratic. Since democratic decisions are permissible, subjects have no right to interfere with or obstruct them.

The normative consequences of democratic legitimacy and failures thereof accordingly varies. If public institutions are not democratically legitimate with respect to future generations, it follows either that we have no reason to support them out of duties of justice, that we are not morally bound to comply with their decisions or that we do not have duties not to interfere with the decisions made.

For the purposes of this paper, we need not adjudicate between these accounts. The one claim that is essential to the argument in favor of IFGs is that democratic inclusion is a requirement for democratic legitimacy. In what follows, I first survey the usual objections against the claim that democratic inclusion applies to future generations. Next, I proceed to establish

11 Fabienne Peter, *Democratic Legitimacy* (Routledge 2009); Allen Buchanan, 'Political Legitimacy and Democracy' (2002) 112(4) Ethics 689.
12 Charles Beitz, *Political Equality* (Princeton 1989).

that democratic inclusion is conditional on the additional requirement for democratic legitimacy – the capacity for constitutional power.

2.1. Inclusion

Debates on the political representation of future generations are heavily influence by the theory according to which democratic inclusion is required for anyone relevantly affected by public decisions. This is reflected in the claim that future people's interests should be represented because they are affected.[13] Public decisions with significant impact on future generations 'cannot be regarded as legitimate' absent adequate representation of their interests.[14]

Even if democratic inclusion applies to all relevantly affected, it is not self-evident that future generations ought to be included. If future people are *not* relevantly affected by current decisions, it follows that they either need not or should not be included. The hypothesis that future people are not affected may of course seem preposterous at first glance – surely future people are affected by decisions made by current political systems! Yet, to be 'affected' is to be worse off *compared* to otherwise. A person is for this reason not 'affected' by actions that are preconditions for her existence – assuming that she is better off by existing than by not existing. Decisions that are conditions for the existence of a person does not make her worse off compared to what she would otherwise have been. Consequently, decisions with consequences for future generations do not 'affect' future generations if these decisions are also preconditions for their existence.[15]

A distinct objection is that 'relevantly affected' is not the correct criterion of democratic inclusion. Rather, the correct view is that the decision must only include the people that are 'subject' to decisions. A person is subject to decisions either if the decision claims the legitimate authority to regulate her behavior or if the decision subjects her to coercion. These are distinct

13 Jörg Tremmel, 'Parliaments and Future Generations – The Four-Power-Model' in Dieter Birnacher and May Thorseth (eds), *The Politics of Sustainability: Philosophical Perspectives* (Routledge 2015).

14 Kristian Ekeli, 'Constitutional Experiments: Representing Future Generations Through Submajority Rules' (2009) 17(4) Journal of Political Philosophy 440, 445.

15 Clare Heyward, 'Can the All-Affected Principle Include Future Persons? Green Deliberative Democracy and the Non-identity Problem' (2008) 17(4) Environmental Politics 625.

readings of the criteria for a person being subject to a decision but it is unclear that future generations are subject to decisions taken by political institutions today on either account. The decisions made by contemporary governments may not claim the legitimate authority to regulate the conduct of future people. And the decisions made by contemporary governments are unlikely to subject future people to coercion.[16] Of course, further reflection is required to demonstrate if future generations are subject to decisions in either of these senses.

The point here is not that these objections are conclusive but to demonstrate the current focus in debates on the political representation of future generations. Inadvertently, little attention is given to the basic premise that democratic legitimacy requires the inclusion of anyone to whom principles of democratic inclusion apply. But this is the premise that turns out to be less than convincing. To show this, we shall have to ignore the two objections just mentioned. The relevant question is not whether requirements of democratic inclusion apply to future people but whether these requirements apply to future generations independently of other requirements of democratic legitimacy.

2.2. Constitutional Power

Inclusion is but one criteria of a democratic process. Accordingly, democratic inclusion is a necessary but insufficient precondition for democratic legitimacy. In the following I focus on a particular important requirement that is often overlooked but that figures clearly in the account of the democratic process influentially presented by Robert Dahl. As Dahl makes clear, a democratic association is one where the people control the rules that both regulate and constitute the process of decision-making. The democratic idea is that the people should be empowered to decide not just the policies and rules that apply to them but also the rules that apply to the institutional framework of decision-making.[17] In state-like political units the institutional framework is regulated by 'higher laws that are usually (though not neces-

16 Ludvig Beckman, 'Power and Future People's Freedom: Intergenerational Domination, Climate Change, and Constitutionalism' (2016) 9(2) Journal of Political Power 289.

17 Robert Dahl, *Democracy and Its Critics* (Yale University Press 1989).

sarily) part of the constitution. Accordingly, a democratic process is one where *constitutional power* is vested, directly or indirectly, in the people.[18]

The significance of constitutional power can be explained by what David Miller has called the 'scope' issue. The scope of an association is equal to the 'range of issues'" on which it can make decisions.[19] The range of issues on which an association is able to make decisions depends importantly on the content of the rules that regulate the process of decision-making. The rules that regulate the decision-making process are constitutional rules. Hence, the scope of the association depends importantly on the content of the constitution. The democratic control of the constitution is consequently of immense importance. Only by the power to decide the content of the constitution are the members of associations able to decide the range of issues on which they can make democratic decisions.

If constitutional power is a precondition of a democratic process and a democratic process is a prerequisite for democratic legitimacy, it follows that democratic legitimacy requires that the power to determine the constitution belongs to the people. A political unit that is legitimate by democratic standards should not merely be inclusive; it should also be an association where constitutional power is subject to popular control.

Consider the following example to illustrate the significance of constitutional power to democratic legitimacy. Imagine an association (A) that is fully inclusive. Because it is fully inclusive, everyone that should be included can participate in decisions on the issues that are within the scope of the association. Now, the range of issues that can be decided by A is regulated by a rule (P) that limits the powers of A to decisions on X, Y, and Z. Imagine now that P is not subject to control by the members of the association. As a consequence, the members of A lack control over the range of issues they can decide. Instead, they are subjected to the powers of whomever is able to decide P. This is the basis for the contention that A does not fully qualify as ruled by a democratic process despite the fact

18 Dahl speaks of 'control of the agenda' and not 'constitutional power' though I take these expressions to be extensionally equivalent. Dahl explains control of the agenda in terms of the powers of 'sovereignty' (ibid., 107). Moreover, records on the terminology used in Ancient Greece confirms that 'control of the agenda' referred to demos as 'kurios tes politeias' ('in control of the constitution'). Matthew Landauer, 'Demos (a) kurios? Agenda Power and Democratic Control in Ancient Greece' (2021) European Journal of Political Theory 375.

19 David Miller, 'Reconceiving the Democratic Boundary Problem' (2020) 15(11) Philosophy Compass 1.

that A is fully inclusive. Thus, inclusion is not sufficient for a democratic process and since we have already accepted that a democratic process is both necessary and sufficient for democratic legitimacy, it follows that that inclusion is insufficient for democratic legitimacy. An association that is inclusive may still fail to be legitimate by democratic standards.

This observation is relevant to the argument that IFGs are necessary for democratic legitimacy. As already made clear, institutions for the political representation of future generations are justified by appeal to principles of democratic inclusion. But since inclusion is not sufficient for democratic legitimacy, it is unclear that IFGs are sufficient for democratic legitimacy. Public decisions are legitimate with respect to future generations only if future generations are both included and empowered to control the constitution.

3. *The Importance of Constitutional Power*

As explained earlier, the claim that democratic legitimacy requires democratic inclusion is either conditionally or unconditionally valid. The claim is conditionally valid if it is premised on additional requirements of democratic legitimacy. The claim is unconditionally valid if it is not premised on additional requirements of democratic legitimacy. In what follows, I venture to explain why democratic inclusion is a conditional requirement of democratic legitimacy. Inclusion contributes to the democratic legitimacy of an association only if the members included share in constitutional power. Hence, inclusion without constitutional power is pointless from the point of view of democratic legitimacy.

The reason why this should be so is not immediately obvious, of course. Even if an inclusive demos is not sufficient for democratic legitimacy, it seems natural to think that an association with an inclusive demos is necessarily more legitimate than an association with a less inclusive demos.[20] That judgment is premised on an *additive* understanding of the criteria for democratic legitimacy. If the criteria are additive, more is always better. Assuming that the criteria for democratic legitimacy are additive, it follows that an association that is fully inclusive but where members lack

20 Peter Lawrence, 'Global Guardians for Future Generations: Remedying a Blind Spot of Democracy?' in Nejma Tamoudi, Simon Faets and Michael Reder (eds), *Politik der Zukunft* (Transcript Verlag 2020) 197.

constitutional power is more legitimate by democratic standards than an association that is not inclusive and where members lack constitutional power.

The alternative is to assume that the criteria for democratic legitimacy are *multiplicative*. A multiplicative index is an equation where the total sum is zero if any factor in the equation is zero. If the criteria for democratic legitimacy are multiplicative, if follows that an association that scores zero on some criteria of democratic legitimacy is without democratic legitimacy even if it scores positively on some other criteria of democratic legitimacy.

It seems that at least some democratic criteria are multiplicative rather than additive. Consider two criteria of a democratic process: effective opportunities to political participation and informed understanding of the political alternatives. According to Dahl, both are fundamental requirements of a democratic process.[21] If these criteria are additive, we should be able to say that an association where members *either* enjoy effective opportunities to participation, *or* enjoy an informed understanding of political alternatives is more democratic than an association where neither condition is satisfied. However, that seems implausible. An association where members are unable to participate just does not seem democratic at all. The fact that they are informed about the political alternatives does not contribute to making it more democratic. Similarly, an association where members lack information and knowledge about the political alternatives would not be democratic in any sense at all, even if they do enjoy opportunities for political participation. Blindfolded participation is not democratic participation. There is consequently reason to conclude that at least some criteria for democratic legitimacy are multiplicative rather than additive. The question though is whether democratic inclusion and constitutional power also are.

The starting point is that the requirement of democratic inclusion applies to future generations and that this requirement can be satisfied by IFGs. If democratic inclusion and constitutional power are additive, it follows that IFGs do make a positive contribution to the democratic legitimacy even if future generations would lack constitutional power. The conclusion is different if the criteria are multiplicative. In that case, IFGs do make a positive contribution to democratic legitimacy only if they enable future generations to share in constitutional power.

The claim defended here is that inclusion without constitutional power does not contribute to democratic legitimacy at all. To see why, recall that

21 Dahl (n 17) 109–112.

constitutional power is the capacity to determine the scope of power of the association. Hence, members that lack constitutional power are unable to determine the range of issues on which the association can make decisions – they are powerless with respect to 'scope' of the association. In fact, absent constitutional power, the members are powerless in a dual sense: they lack the power to exclude issues from the scope of democratic control and they lack the power to include issues within the scope of democratic control.

Issues are excluded from the scope of democratic control if the constitution denies the association the power to make certain decisions. Sometimes, the members have strong interests in thus limiting the powers of their association. Imagine, for example, that there are good reasons to limit the powers of the government to enact policies that encourage the use of fossil sources of energy. One way to achieve this is by constitutionally disempowering the government in relevant respects. Constitutional constraints that limit the powers of the government restrict the scope of issues that can be decided by citizens through democratic procedures. Arguably, however, such constraints are legitimate by democratic standards only if they are subject to democratic control by the citizenry, either directly or indirectly. Hence, democratic constitutional power is a precondition not just for the ability to limit the scope of the association but also for the democratic legitimacy of such limits.

The effectiveness of democratic control is expanded when constitutional constraints are lifted. Evidently, the members of an association may have strong interests in expanding 'democratic control' over issues previously excluded by the constitutional framework. Imagine that a majority of the citizens of a European country want to leave the EU. A decision to that effect is likely to require amendments to the constitutional framework and is therefore beyond the scope of both the parliament and the government to take through ordinary legislative procedures. Under these circumstances, the decision to leave the EU is premised on democratic exercises of constitutional power. Hence, democratic constitutional power is a precondition not just for the ability to expand the scope of the association but also for the democratic legitimacy of decisions to that effect.

These examples lend support to the claim than an inclusive demos risks ending up virtually powerless unless they are empowered to control constitutional norms. Citing Dahl, members that lack the power to control the rules that regulate the scope of the association may in the end be disenfranchised on all issues 'other than those the rulers had allowed to remain on the pitifully shrunken agenda'.[22]

The situation described is not unusual in political and historical contexts. It is manifested in cases of colonial domination, foreign occupation, and military tutelage. No matter how free and inclusive the elections are in such regimes, they fall short of democratic legitimacy as constitutional power remains vested in bodies that are unaccountable to the people. The lack of popular constitutional power is reflected in the labels that figure among scholars of democratisation: 'tutelary democracy'[23] or 'protected democracy'[24]. Indeed, the epithet 'democratic' should arguably be avoided for such regimes.[25]

4. Future Generations and Constitutional Power

The argument so far is that constitutional power is necessary for democratic legitimacy and that it represents a precondition for democratic inclusion. Unless the population subjected to or affected by public decisions can influence the scope of the decisions that they can make, the extent of democratic inclusion is of no avail. It should now be clear why this point is relevant to the argument that democratic legitimacy requires political representation of future generations. The political representation of future generations is a requirement of democratic legitimacy only on condition that constitutional power can be attributed to future generations.

The final and crucial question then, is whether it can. Answering this question is confounded by the fact that the institutional requirements for democratic constitutional power are both unclear and controversial even in intra-generational settings. Hence, we need to begin by reflecting on the very notion of democratic constitutional power.

Constitutional power is the capacity to introduce, revise or abolish rules that regulate the powers of political institutions. The claim that the people should control the constitution is equivalent to the claim that the people

22 Dahl (n 17) 113.

23 Adam Przeworski, 'Democracy as a Contingent Outcome of Conflicts' in Jon Elster and Rune Slagstad (eds), *Constitutionalism and Democracy* (CUP 1988).

24 Brian Loveman, '"Protected Democracies" and Military Guardianship: Political Transitions in Latin America, 1978–1993' (1994) 36 Journal of Interamerican Studies and World Affairs 105.

25 David Collier and Steven Levitsky, 'Democracy with Adjectives: Conceptual Innovation in Comparative Research' (1997) 49(3) World Politics 430.

should be able to participate, directly or indirectly, in decisions on constitutional norms.

A body with constitutional power is able to regulate the scope of its own power – the powers it possesses are limited only by rules of its own making. A body thus empowered is in effect 'the sovereign' within the domain. In the context of the state, the requirement that constitutional power is vested in the people is in other words equivalent to the requirement that sovereignty belongs to the people. That idea is familiar from the constitutional provisions to the effect that public power 'derives from' or 'belongs to' the people, epitomissed in the principle of popular sovereignty.[26] Although popular sovereignty is a familiar constitutional principle, its meaning is far from clear. The democratic tradition is split between two rival perspectives on what it means for the people to partake in constitutional decision-making.

Some believe that sovereignty resides in the people to the extent that they have the political power to replace the constitutional framework. The people show themselves as the 'sovereign' in extra-legal moments of action. Constitutional power is 'constituent power', a capacity that is not subject to legal limitations. Sovereignty accordingly belongs to the people only if the people are able to overturn the constitutional order by means of force.

Others insist that constitutional power necessarily depends on legal power. For the people to determine the constitution, they must possess the legal power to participate in the process of constitutional decision-making. The people control the constitution only if a rule exists such that the people are legally authorised to revise, create or abolish constitutional norms.

We are now in a better position to grasp what is involved in the question whether constitutional power can be attributed to future generations. Future generations share in constitutional power only if it is true either that future generations share in 'constituent power', or that future generations are legally authorised to partake in the process of constitutional decision-making.[27]

---

26 Denis Galligan, 'The People, the Constitution, and the Idea of Representation' in Denis Galligan and Mila Versteeg (eds), *Social and Political Foundations of Constitutions* (CUP 2013).

27 Note that this question is distinct from traditional concerns with 'generational sovereignty' made famous by Thomas Paine's and Thomas Jefferson's assertion that 'the earth belongs to the living'. Whereas they worried that rigid constitutions would subjugate future peoples to the 'tyranny of the past', the question we are interested in is the possibility of extending constitutional power to future peoples. On generational sovereignty, see Maior Felt, 'For the Living: Thomas Paine's Generational

4.1. Future Generations as 'Constituent Power'

The idea of 'constituent power' has a long pedigree and is not uniquely attributable to democratic states.[28] According to the democratic interpretation, constituent power serves as the basis for the claim that democratic legitimacy must extend to the legal system in its entirety.[29] Democratic legitimacy requires that constituent power is vested in the people such that the people assume 'supreme authority of the state'.[30]

Accordingly, democratic legitimacy with respect to future generations is premised on the possibility of constituent power being shared with future people. The constitutional framework through which public bodies are empowered to make decisions today is democratic with respect to future interests only if future generations can be part of 'constituent power'.

How constituent power is exercised is disputed in the literature. For some writers, constituent power is exercised when the people enact a constitution 'by revolutionary means or otherwise'.[31] The extension of constituent power to future generations is clearly unattainable if constituent power is exercised only through political revolutions. Revolutionary action is evidently undertaken only by the living. However, others envisage the exercise of constituent power through constitutional referendums and constituent assemblies.[32] That alternative seems more hospitable to future generations. Though future generations do not yet exist, their interests can be rendered politically present in referendums and constituent assemblies through various forms of proxy representation.

Yet, the claim of democratic constituent power is that the people should have unlimited authority to make or amend the constitution. Since all legal

---

Democracy' (2016) 48(1) Polity 59, and Axel Gosseries, 'Generational Sovereignty' in Gosseries and Gonzalez-Ricoy (n 6).

28 Joel Colón-Ríos, 'Five Conceptions of Constituent Power' (2014) 130 Law Quarterly Review 306.

29 Andreas Kalyvas, 'Popular Sovereignty, Democracy, and the Constituent Power' (2005) 12(2) Constellations 223; Joel Colón-Ríos, 'The Legitimacy of the Juridical: Constituent Power, Democracy, and the Limits of Constitutional Reform' (2010) 48 Osgoode Hall Law Journal 199.

30 Paulina Ochoa Espejo, 'Popular Sovereignty' in Michael T. Gibbons (ed), *The Encyclopedia of Political Thought* (Wiley-Blackwell 2015).

31 Hans K Lindahl, 'Constituent Power and the Constitution' in David Dyzenhaus and Malcolm Thorburn (eds), *Philosophical Foundations of Constitutional Law* (OUP 2016).

32 Andreea Ana-Maria Alexe, 'Constituent Power – the Essence of Democracy' (2015) 47 Revista de Ştiinţe Politice. Revue des Sciences Politiques 316.

powers are limited by the legal framework that define them, the exercise of constituent power requires recourse to non-legal powers. But proxy representation through institutions for future generations are legal constructs that depend for their existence on legal rules. IFGs are legally defined instruments of power that are therefore limited. Hence, the powers of IFGs do not permit the attribution of constituent power to future generations. The upshot is that we are at pains to imagine the circumstances that allow for the extension of constituent power to future generations.

4.2. Future Generations as the Legal Sovereign

The alternative is to deny that constitutional power depends on the exercise of non-legal powers. The power to partake in constitutional decision-making is a legal power that is attributed to legal institutions and offices – the legislature, the electorate, etc. *The people* hold the power to determine the constitution only if they are included in legally constituted institutions to which the constitutional framework has conferred the requisite legal powers.

Indeed, following predominant theories of legal positivism, the power to revise or create law is necessarily a legal power. The power to make constitutional decisions is an 'office' or 'institution' within the legal system. No agent that is not already empowered *by* the legal system can be a source of power *of* the legal system. That was the insight that in various stages developed from Kelsen to Hart.[33] The only conceivable meaning of 'popular sovereignty' is that the people are empowered by the legal system to participate in constitutional decision-making.

The objection that future generations are 'absent' loses its force if one accepts that the powers required for democratic legitimacy are legal powers. The fact that the political representation of future generations is limited by the extent of the legal powers vested in IFGs is no different from how contemporaries are empowered. Hence, we are perfectly entitled to imagine legal institutions designed to represent present and future interests that are empowered to partake in the process of constitutional decision-making.

But here is the catch. The powers vested in legally empowered institutions are not unlimited. They unavoidably depend on mechanisms for legal

33 Pavlos Eleftheriadis, 'Law and Sovereignty' (2010) 29 Law and Philosophy 535; David Dyzenhaus, 'Constitutionalism in an Old Key: Legality and Constituent Power' (2012) 1 Global Constitutionalism 229.

validation. For ordinary decisions, the nature of this mechanism is not difficult to understand. The legal validity of a decision made by a legal authority is conditioned by the possibility that the decision can be validated as consistent with the hierarchy of norms in the relevant legal system. For example, a decision taken by an administrative body is valid on condition that it can be validated by appeal to the legal provisions that apply to that body. These legal provisions are in turn valid to the extent that they are enacted by bodies with the proper legal authorisation in the legal system, and so on.

But the chain of validation by appeal to *higher* laws inevitably comes to an end at some point. The question then is how to validate the highest norms of the legal system? Unless they are valid by virtue of *something*, it appears that the chain of validation is without foundation. The influential reply to this question given by HLA Hart is that the 'rule of recognition' serves as the ultimate standard of legal validity. The rule of recognition confers legal validity to the highest legal norms and to the legal system as a whole.[34]

The rule of recognition is not a rule enacted by the lawmaker. Indeed, it could not be that since any rule enacted by the lawmaker is subject to the need for validation. Rather, the rule of recognition is embedded in the judgments of higher legal officials. These social practices reproduce the rule of recognition, and because they are social practices – not explicit rules of the system – the rule of recognition neither is, nor can be, determined by the law maker. The ultimate standard of legal validity consequently remains beyond democratic control. Whatever is meant by 'the people' or 'the people's will', it is 'not part of the ultimate rule of recognition for the legal order'.[35]

The relevant point in this context is that the judgments of legal validity are independent from the legal powers of law-making. This is relevant because it means that mechanisms for legal validity occupy a space in the legal system that is not accessible to institutions for the political representation of future generations. The rule of recognition is a social practice that remains divorced from the legal powers attributed to institutions for political representation.

34 Herbert L A Hart, *The Concept of Law* (Clarendon Press 1962) 255; Gerald Postema, *A Treatise of Legal Philosophy and General Jurisprudence* (Springer 2011) 311; John Gardner, *Law as a Leap of Faith* (OUP 2012) 107.

35 Kent Greenawalt, 'The Rule of Recognition and the Constitution' (1987) 85 Michigan Law Review 621.

It is not really clear what follows from this observation. One possibility is that it is irrelevant due to the distinction between the legal power to make decisions and the validation of legal decisions. What matters for democratic legitimacy is that future generations are made present in some legally constituted body empowered to decide on the constitutional framework – not if they are made present in the process of validation of such decisions. Properly empowered IFGs that include future generations are sufficient to establish a democratic process that renders public decisions legitimate with respect to future people. There is in other words no 'catch'.

The alternative conclusion is that 'presentism' in a different key remains a feature of legally constituted political systems. All decisions that are made by political bodies depend on mechanisms for legal validation that exclude future generations. However strongly the interests of future generations are included in the process of law-making, the ultimate power to control the constitution depends on a process of legal validation that belongs to the living.

5. Conclusions

An influential argument for institutions for future generations is that they are necessary for democratic legitimacy. Future generations should be included because future people are significantly affected by the decisions made by governments today. In the first part of this paper I argued that democratic inclusion is conditioned by access to constitutional power – a distinct requirement of democratic legitimacy. For future people to be included in the demos we must also be able to recognise future people as equally entitled to participate in constitutional decision-making. The second part of the paper argues that this requirement is a serious limitation on the argument that institutions representing future generations are required by democratic legitimacy. Whether constitutional power is understood in terms of constituent power or in terms of legal power, there is reason to doubt that future generations can be acknowledged as democratic co-authors of the constitutional framework. If constitutional power cannot include future generations, the argument that their political representation is required by principles of democratic legitimacy ultimately fails.

The wider implication of this conclusion is that democratic legitimacy may not be a relevant standard for intergenerational relationships. If democratic legitimacy cannot be achieved with respect to people yet unborn, there is no longer reason to worry about the democratic status of our political systems in relation to future people. This is, of course, no reason to conclude that there are no moral concerns raised by the long-term effects of current policies and political systems, only that democracy is not one of them.

17. Representing the Interests of Present and Future Generations at the Same Time – A Case Study of the Hungarian Ombudsman for Future Generations

Marcel Szabó[*]

Abstract: *In human history, the moral responsibility for future generations was linked relatively early to the idea that we must pass on our Earth in good shape (as unchanged as possible) to the generations of our children, grandchildren, and other descendants. Section I of this chapter presents how the Hungarian law protects the rights and interests of future generations – through the institution of the Hungarian Ombudsman for Future Generations (historical background, powers, the legal relationship between the Ombudsman and the Hungarian Constitutional Court). Sections II and III deal with the theoretical considerations regarding the legal personality of future generations and the presence of the interests of future generations at the level of international law, respectively. Section IV introduces the ethical, economic and legal aspects of the protection of interests of future generations. As a conclusion (Section V), the chapter argues that the activities of future generation institutions should mainly focus on the 'conservation of options'.*

Introduction

The responsibility of humankind for their descendants is one of the most ancient moral norms. In human history, the moral responsibility for future generations was linked relatively early to the idea that we must pass on our Earth in good shape (as unchanged as possible) to the generations of our children, grandchildren, and other descendants. Dinah Shelton and Alexandre Kiss trace this moral command directly back to the Old Testament's story of Noah.[1] According to that story, the Lord entrusts humanity with the Earth after the flood and enters a covenant with humans and other living beings. Based on specific interpretations, this command creates a form of guardianship over the Earth's natural resources, defined by the Old Testament as a religious precept. Therefore, the rights of future generations initially prevailed in the form of human responsibility for protecting the

---

* Marcel Szabó is a Professor of Law (Pázmány Péter Catholic University, Budapest), a Justice (Constitutional Court of Hungary), and a former Hungarian Ombudsman for Future Generations (2012–2016).

1 Alexandre Kiss and Dinah Shelton, *Guide to International Environmental Law* (Martinus Nijhoff Publishers 2007).

natural environment. At the end of the 18th century, a new concept further extended the scope of intergenerational equity to cover the State's obligation to prevent the unfair transfer of debt to subsequent generations. Just days following the adoption of the Declaration of Human and Civil Rights, Thomas Jefferson wrote to James Madison to draw his attention to the fact that members of the present generation have no right to take on more debt than they can repay in their own lifetime. Otherwise, the present generation would restrict the right of future generations to self-determination.[2] This study examines the institutional interpretation and implementation of the interests of future generations, with particular consideration to the institution of the Hungarian Deputy Commissioner Responsible for the Protection of the Interests of Future Generations.

1. Protecting the Interests of Future Generations in Hungarian Law

1.1. The Constitutional Framework Established by the Hungarian Fundamental Law

The Hungarian Fundamental Law, which entered into force in 2012, enshrines not only the right to a healthy environment (in Article XXI) but also contains several key provisions for the protection of the interests of future generations. According to the National Avowal:

> [w]e commit to promoting and safeguarding our heritage, our unique language, Hungarian culture, the languages and cultures of nationalities living in Hungary, along with all man-made and natural assets of the Carpathian Basin. We bear responsibility for our descendants; therefore, we shall protect the living conditions of future generations by making prudent use of our material, intellectual and natural resources.

In this context, the National Avowal also declares that the Fundamental Law 'shall be an alliance among Hungarians of the past, present and future'. Thus, even the National Avowal shows that the decisions adopted by incumbent governments also affect future generations. Therefore, any incumbent government and legislature's decisions shall also consider future generations' interests. This also means that the cited provision of the Na-

2 Thomas Jefferson, *To James Madison From Thomas Jefferson, 6 September 1789* <https://perma.cc/7VRP-AYUA>.

tional Avowal sets out a framework for interpreting the Fundamental Law and, thus, the Hungarian legal system. According to such a framework of interpretation, the interests of future generations shall generally be taken into account with the same weight as, and simultaneously with, current needs.

> According to Article P(1) of the Fundamental Law:
> [n]atural resources, in particular arable land, forests and the reserves of water, biodiversity, in particular native plant and animal species, as well as cultural assets shall form the common heritage of the nation; it shall be the obligation of the State and everyone to protect and maintain them, and to preserve them for future generations.

Article P(1) identifies, in the case of the natural and cultural resources of the nation's common heritage,[3] the behaviour expected of 'the State and everyone': (i) protection, (ii) maintenance, and (iii) preservation for future generations. In preserving natural resources for future generations, the present generation is responsible for preserving choice, quality, and access.[4] These principles help to assess the interests of present and future generations from the same point of view and to strike a balance between them. Article P(1) of the Fundamental Law is a forward-looking provision in several respects. On the one hand, based on the concept of the common heritage of humankind, it has created the category of 'common heritage of the nation', which includes both natural and cultural values.

On the other hand, it also stated that protecting these values is 'the responsibility of the State and everyone', including civil society and every citizen.[5] However, while this obligation only requires natural and legal persons to comply with the legislation in force, the State may already be expected to clearly define the legal obligations that both the State and private parties must comply with for the values referred to in Article P(1) to be effectively protected[6] and that these, if necessary, be enforced. 'Thus, Article P of the Fundamental Law also implies an absolute and substantive

3 Decision No. 3104/2017 (V. 8.) AB of the Hungarian Constitutional Court, Reasoning [37]-[39].

4 Decision No. 28/2017 (X. 25.) AB of the Hungarian Constitutional Court, Reasoning [33].

5 Decision No. 16/2015 (VI. 5.) AB of the Hungarian Constitutional Court, Reasoning [92].

6 Decision No. 28/2017 (X. 25.) AB of the Hungarian Constitutional Court, Reasoning [30].

measure concerning the State of natural resources which imposes objective requirements on the current activities of the State.'[7] In decision No 14/2020. (VII. 6.) AB, the Constitutional Court also confirmed that:

> Article P(1) of the Fundamental Law is based on the constitutional formulation of the concept of public trust about environmental and natural values, the essence of which is that the State treats the natural and cultural treasures entrusted to it as a kind of trustee for future generations as beneficiaries and allows present generations to use and exploit these treasures only to the extent that it does not jeopardize the long-term survival of natural and cultural values as assets to be protected for themselves. The State must consider the interests of present and future generations when regulating these treasures and adopting the applicable laws and regulations. The rule of preservation of natural and cultural resources for future generations in the Hungarian Fundamental Law may thus be considered part of the newly formed and consolidated universal customary law and expresses the constitutional commitment to the importance and preservation of environmental, natural, and cultural values.[8]

Article P provides a robust constitutional mandate to the Ombudsman for Future Generations (one of the very few national institutions dealing with the rights and interests of future generations at national level) to take action for the benefit of future generations and the protection of Hungary's natural and cultural resources. Generally speaking, the Fundamental Law entrusts the Deputy Commissioner[9] with the protection of the interests of future generations. At the same time, the Act on the Commissioner for Fundamental Rights refers to the rights of future generations as the object of protection.

7 Decision No. 28/2017 (X. 25.) AB of the Hungarian Constitutional Court, Reasoning [32].

8 Decision No. 14/2020 (VII. 6.) AB of the Hungarian Constitutional Court, Reasoning [22].

9 The first Hungarian ombudsman for future generations was Sándor Fülöp (2008–2011). Between 2012 and 2016, Marcel Szabó (the author of the present article) served as ombudsman for future generations. The current ombudsman is Gyula Bándi (2017-present), Professor of Environmental Law at Pázmány Péter Catholic University, Budapest.

1.2. The Hungarian Deputy Commissioner for Fundamental Rights and Ombudsman for Future Generations

The Hungarian Ombudsman institution came into being during the democratisation process of the late 1980s and early 1990s. The Hungarian Parliament adopted the first Ombudsman Act in 1993,[10] and the first Ombudsmen were elected in 1995.[11] The former Constitution adopted a model of the ombudsman system in which separate Commissioners could be elected to protect individual constitutional rights. Although the former Ombudsman Act directly referred to the Commissioner for Civil Rights and the Commissioner for the Rights of National and Ethnic Minorities only, Section 32/B(4) allowed for the election of additional ombudspersons for the protection of other fundamental rights. Applying this Section, in 1995, the Ombudsman for Data Protection and later, in 2007, the Ombudsman for Future Generations were elected. All the Ombudsmen were nominated by the President of Hungary and subsequently elected by the Parliament for a 6-year term. Before the establishment of the Ombudsman for Future Generations, it was the Commissioner for Civil Rights in Hungary who was responsible for the protection of the right to a healthy environment.

The Fundamental Law (which entered into force in 2012) represented a paradigm shift in the Hungarian Ombudsman system, changing the status and constitutional role of the Ombudsman for Future Generations. Since 1 January 2012, the independent Ombudsman Offices have been merged into one, creating a new institution: the Office of the Commissioner for Fundamental Rights.[12] Under the new structure, the Commissioner is responsible for protecting human rights in general. At the same time, the two Deputies are entrusted with protecting the rights of national minorities and future generations, respectively. In questions concerning the natural envir-

10 Hungarian Act LIX of 1993 on the Parliamentary Commissioner for Civil Rights.

11 Hungarian Parliament Decree No. 84/1995 (VII. 6.).

12 According to Gabriele Kucsko-Stadlmayer's classification of various powers, the Hungarian Ombudsman's Office belongs to the institutional 'Human Rights Model', where powers related to fundamental rights protection dominate the mandate of the Ombudsman. Based on the Ombudsman's powers, Kucsko-Stadlmayer differentiates between 'Basic Models', 'Rule of Law Models', and 'Human Rights Models'. The first is characterised by wide investigative powers, while the second's main priority is to monitor the lawful and proper operation of authorities. The protection of fundamental rights is prioritised in the third, Human Rights Model. Gabriele Kucsko-Stadlmayer (ed), *European Ombudsman-Institutions – A Comparative Legal Analysis Regarding the Multifaceted Realisation of An Idea* (Springer 2008) 59–66.

onment and the interests of future generations, the Ombudsman for Future Generations (Deputy Commissioner) has the right to act independently from the Commissioner. Although his office is structurally incorporated under the Office of the Commissioner for Fundamental Rights and may serve as Deputy when necessary, his unit is procedurally autonomous in its area of expertise. This is also reflected in the institution's designation: the Ombudsman for Future Generations (*a jövő nemzedékek szószólója*), an office with the power to carry out activities in its own right.[13] In this regard, the Ombudsman is most similar to institutions entrusted with protecting children's rights,[14] which are either part of the general ombudsman system or its function identity of it.[15] The critical question is not necessarily the institutional structure but the legislative background that determines and circumscribes the powers and responsibilities of the Ombudsman.

The current framework of functions of the Ombudsman for Future Generations is laid down in Article 30(3) of the Fundamental Law. Pursuant to that law, the Ombudsman for Future Generations 'shall protect the interests of future generations'. At the time of its establishment, the mandate of the Ombudsman was primarily geared toward protecting the right to a healthy environment, leaving the institution with a narrower focus and authority.[16] However, as of 2012, the mandate of the Ombudsman for Future Generations is not only restricted to the enforcement of this right. Institutional protection is extended to all fundamental rights which can, directly or indirectly, affect the interests of future generations. Since the Fundamental Law considers the protection of the nation's common heritage to be part of the interest of future generations, the Ombudsman can undertake action in all questions concerning the nation's common heritage. This way, the Fundamental Law provides real power to the Ombudsman, for, in practice, nearly all decisions may impact the interests of the unborn. The economy, education, health care, or State debt are all issues that inevitably affect the

13 Section 3(4) of the Hungarian Act CXI of 2011 on the Commissioner for Fundamental Rights.

14 As an example, the European Network of Ombudspersons for Children (ENOC) established in 1997, links 43 offices for children from 34 states in Europe <http://enoc.eu> accessed 24 November 2021.

15 For instance, ENOC works together with independent children's rights institutions: children's ombudspersons, commissioners for children, or focal points on children's rights in national human rights institutions or general ombudsman offices <http://enoc.eu/?page_id=8> accessed 24 November 2021.

16 Section 27/B(1) of the Hungarian Act LIX of 1993 on the Parliamentary Commissioner for Civil Rights.

conditions, financial burden, and well-being of future generations and are, therefore, in need of institutional protection. Hence, according to Article P, consideration for future generations should become a part of every decision taken by the Hungarian legislature and enforcement bodies. There are no conceptual obstacles to prevent the Ombudsman from taking action on any of the aforementioned questions. However, acting upon such a broad interpretation of its mandate will only be possible after the institution's further consolidation into the Hungarian political and institutional system.

One of the most powerful features of the Office of the Commissioner for Fundamental Rights is its publicity and transparent operation. Every year, the Commissioner and the two Ombudsmen (the Ombudsman for Future Generations and the Ombudsman for National Minorities) report on and prepare a statistical analysis of the cases and petitions they have handled. These reports serve as important indicators of environmental policy-making and are highly relevant for the future work of the Office.

Pursuant to the new Act on the Ombudsman adopted in 2011,[17] the Ombudsman for Future Generations can draw the attention of the Commissioner, other affected institutions, and the public to any suspected infringement of the interests of future generations.[18] This direct channel to the public can help influence public perception of risks and long-term consequences. To enhance the efficiency of its work, the Ombudsman can use various communication tools, including patronage of noble causes, operation of an official Facebook page,[19] and extensive media coverage that can reach broad segments of the population. A successful example of the latter was raising public awareness of air quality standards through the Ombudsman's cooperation with civil society organisations, governmental bodies, and local municipalities.

According to the Ombudsman Act, only the Commissioner for Fundamental Rights has the right to carry out investigations (based on *ex officio* proceedings, public complaints, or individual petitions) but the Ombudsman for Future Generations can also initiate and partake in the inspections.[20] If the Commissioner rejects an investigation requested by

---

17 Hungarian Act CXI of 2011 on the Commissioner for Fundamental Rights.

18 ibid., section 3(1)(a).

19 See Jövő Nemzedékek Szószólója <www.facebook.com/J%C3%B6v%C5%91-Nemzed%C3%A9kek-Sz%C3%B3sz%C3%B3l%C3%B3ja-885959088173953/?fref=ts> accessed 24 November 2021.

20 Section 3(1)(c)-(d) of the Hungarian Act CXI of 2011 on the Commissioner for Fundamental Rights.

the Ombudsman, he must note the refusal and explain it in his annual Parliamentary report. This provides an important safeguard mechanism for *ex officio* proceedings of the Ombudsman for Future Generations. The excellent professional and institutional relationship between the Ombudsman and the Commissioner is reflected in the fact that the Commissioner has never rejected any investigations initiated by the Ombudsman to date.

Should the Commissioner and the Ombudsman for Future Generations find an instance of maladministration, they issue a *joint report*. The joint reports present the results of the investigation, reveal any noted maladministration, and, if necessary, formulate general or specific recommendations to the legislator or law enforcement authorities to remedy the harm done. Reports by the Commissioner for Fundamental Rights and the Ombudsman for Future Generations are not binding upon the Parliament, the Government, or any other addressee. However, when an infringement constitutes a violation of the Fundamental Law, i.e., the adopted regulation is not only harmful to the interests of future generations but also constitutes a breach of the Fundamental Law, the Ombudsman for Future Generations may turn to the Commissioner for Fundamental Rights to propose the submission of a petition to the Constitutional Court, requesting the annulment of the legal provision in question.[21] Joint reports are critical when the remedy of the cases concerned can ensure the realisation of both inter-generational and intra-generational justice. In 2020, the Ombudsman and the Commissioner published 13 joint reports that concerned, in particular, the issue of noise pollution, waste management, air quality control, and environmental damage.[22]

---

21 Decision No. 14/2020 (VII. 6.) AB of the Hungarian Constitutional Court, in which the Constitutional Court stated that several elements of the 2017 amendment of the Act on Forests is unconstitutional. The case was initiated by the Commissioner for Fundamental Rights, in agreement with the Ombudsman.

22 Joint Reports No. 540/2019, 94/2020, 385/2020, 642/2020, 669/2020, 1025/2020, 1026/2020, 1073/2020, 1100/2020, 1365/2020, 1371/2020, 2037/2020, 4642/2020. All the Joint Reports are available (in Hungarian) at the website of the Office of the Commissioner for Fundamental Rights.

1.3. The Legal Relationship between the Ombudsman for Future Generations and the Constitutional Court

The Ombudsman for Future Generations turned to the Constitutional Court in several cases *via* the Commissioner for Fundamental Rights to contribute to the protection of Hungary's natural resources. For example, in *Decision No. 14/2020. (VII. 6.) AB*, the Constitutional Court stated that several elements of the 2017 amendment of the Act on Forests are unconstitutional. The Commissioner for Fundamental Rights initiated the case in agreement with the Ombudsman for Future Generations. The Constitutional Court fully agreed with the petition that the amendment to the Forest Act primarily served the interests of forest owners by overshadowing key environmental considerations.[23]

The Ombudsman for Future Generations also assists the Constitutional Court by filing *amicus curiae* briefs. *Amici curiae* may help the Constitutional Court develop its interpretation regarding the environmental provisions of the Fundamental Law. The Ombudsman can act as a guardian for future generations representing their long-term interests and influencing the decisions of the Constitutional Court by providing important legal interpretations and reasoning. In a landmark decision in 2015, the Constitutional Court annulled certain clauses of an Act which had not been promulgated at the time. The clauses in question would have made it possible for government-run authorities, whose primary responsibility was not environmental protection, to take over the management of nature conservation areas from national park directorates. Following an extensive investigation, the Ombudsman for Future Generations issued an independent Statement entitled 'National Parks as safeguards of natural and cultural values for future generations'.[24] His Statement concluded that pursuant to the Fundamental Law, the protection and maintenance of biodiversity and its preservation for future generations was, among others, the obligation of the State, and that the responsibility for this was best fulfilled by the exist-

---

23 Regarding the decision see eg Katalin Sulyok, 'The Public Trust Doctrine, The Non-Derogation Principle and the Protection of Future Generations' (2021) 1 *Hungarian Yearbook of International Law and European Law* 359; Attila Pánovics, 'Decision No. 14/2020 (VII. 6.) of the Hungarian Constitutional Court on the Protection of Forests' (2021) 1 *Hungarian Yearbook of International Law and European Law* 376.

24 *National Parks as safeguards of natural and cultural values for future generations*, Statement of the Ombudsman for Future Generations (in Hungarian), issued on 16 December 2014, 2.

ing national park directorates. The Ombudsman highlighted that the land management activities of national parks are characterised by the highest standards of preservation, stemming from their primary task to protect the natural environment. Deviating from this arrangement, therefore, would be unconstitutional.[25] This Statement influenced the decision of the Constitutional Court, which referred to the Ombudsman's brief as a persuasive source on the constitutional protection of the environment.

Besides *amici curiae*, based on Section 57(3) of the Act on the Constitutional Court, the Constitutional Court has the right to invite State bodies and authorities to make a declaration, send documents or give an opinion in pending cases. In 2017, the Hungarian Constitutional Court took a huge step towards the general recognition of the protection of the interests of future generations in the Hungarian legal system in an ex post review case initiated by Members of Parliament. In this case, the Constitutional Court had to evaluate whether the privatisation of certain Natura 2000 sites without sufficient environmental guarantees may be considered a violation of the core obligation of the State under the Fundamental Law to preserve natural resources, including biodiversity. Applying Section 57(3) of the Act on the Constitutional Court, this was the very first case in which *the Constitutional Court invited the Ombudsman to submit his detailed opinion.*[26] In its landmark decision, the Constitutional Court stated that:

> the core obligation to protect biodiversity as the UN Convention on Biological Diversity (ratified by 196 parties, including Hungary) prescribes, is a peremptory norm of general international law accepted and recognized by the international community of States as a whole from which no derogation is permitted.[27]

25 ibid.

26 In 2018 the Constitutional Court again invited the Ombudsman to submit his opinion in a preliminary norm control case, in which the President of Hungary stated that an adopted but not yet promulgated Act on groundwater is unconstitutional. See Decision No. 13/2018 (IX. 4.) AB of the Hungarian Constitutional Court. About the Decision: Marcel Szabó, 'The Precautionary Principle in the Fundamental Law of Hungary – Judicial Activism or an Inherent Fundamental Principle? An Evaluation of Constitutional Court Decision No. 13/2018 (IX. 4.) AB on the Protection of Groundwater' (2019) 1 *Hungarian Yearbook of International Law and European Law* 67–83; Gábor Kecskés, 'The Hungarian Constitutional Court's Decision on the Protection of Groundwater – Decision No. 13/2018 (IX. 4.) AB of the Constitutional Court of Hungary' (2020) 1 Hungarian Yearbook of International Law and European Law 371.

27 Decision No. 28/2017 (X. 25.) AB of the Hungarian Constitutional Court, Reasoning [38].

2. Behind the Institution – Theoretical Considerations Regarding the Legal Personality of Future Generations

While the representation of the interests of future generations is gaining clout in both international law and the national laws of different States, the question may nevertheless be raised whether, today, we can speak about the rights of future generations in a legal sense or merely about their interests.[28] The answer depends in no small part on what exactly is meant by 'rights' in the theoretical approach. According to the will theory of rights approach,[29] rights provide freedom of choice between different options. In this framework, even the rights of the child may be questioned (due to their limited judgment), just like the fact that there is no separate legal entity for future generations, which is independent of that of the present generations, could be a justification for negating next generations' rights. This is because members of the present generation must merely preserve freedom of choice for future generations. However, were we to adopt an interest-based approach to rights, it may correctly be assumed that there are fundamental interests, the safeguarding of which is desirable since these may coincide with future generations' likely choice of values. Therefore, maintaining such freedom of choice coincides with future generations' interests and, at the same time, protects their rights.

In this context, the question of who precisely the members of future generations cannot be avoided. Are we to understand the members of future generations as specific individuals who may have rights? Or do they make up a group that has collective rights instead? Or, on the contrary, are future generations a general concept most characterised by potential advocacy? While many authors reject the application of collective rights to future generations, I am convinced that the rights or interests of future generations may only be perceived as group rights or collective interests. Of course, we may never be sure whether a specific member of the present generation shall have descendants or not. However, the birth and future existence of an entire next generation, at least at the level of our current scientific knowledge, is near certain. Thus, by recognising the collective

28 By way of example, Beckerman and Pasek deny the recognition of the rights of future generations in the present, but at the same time, they recognise that there is a moral obligation to take into account the interests of future generations. Wilfred Beckerman and Joanna Pasek, *Justice, Posterity and the Environment* (OUP 2001) 28.

29 Bernhard Windscheid, *Lehrbuch des Pandektenrechts I-III* (Rütten und Loening 1906).

nature of future generations' interests or rights, we do not have to consider the individual and varied decisions of specific members of the present generation. Instead, the interests or rights of future generations may be protected by relying on predictable average human behaviour based on rational situational awareness and decision-making.

The relevant literature reveals that future generations may have different rights in relation to each other. Therefore, the issue that their rights may conflict must also be addressed.[30] To solve this conundrum, some suggest we only owe a duty of care to the generation following us. Otherwise, the future is uncertain; we do not influence the fate of further generations. In my opinion, however, the present and the future are separated by this exact moment when this paper was written, which is the only certainty in the relationship between the present and the future. I am convinced that the members of this current generation should recognise future generations' fundamental interests, with the ensuing ethical conclusions to be drawn by humanity.

3. The Interests of Future Generations in International Law

Issues related to future generations appeared in the system of international law quite early on, with the emergence of international environmental law. For example, the first principle of the Declaration adopted at the 1972 UN Conference on the Human Environment[31] states that humanity must take responsibility for protecting and improving the environment for present and future generations. Twenty years on, in 1992, the Rio Declaration[32] reaffirmed this concept in its third principle stating that '[t]he right to development must be fulfilled so as to equitably meet developmental and environmental needs of present and future generations.' A similar example in international law is the obligation enshrined in the Framework Convention on Climate Change,[33] according to which parties must preserve the climate system for the benefit of present and future generations of humankind.[34]

30 László Sólyom, 'A jövő nemzedékek jogai és ezek képviselete a jelenben' in Benedek Jávor (ed), *A jövő nemzedékek jogai* (Védegylet, Budapest 2000) 38.
31 United Nations Conference on the Human Environment, Stockholm, 15–16 June 1972.
32 1992 Rio Declaration on Environment and Development.
33 United Nations Framework Convention on Climate Change, UNFCCC. The Convention was adopted on 9 May 1992 in New York.
34 Article 3(1) of the Convention.

On 26 February 1994, experts from UNESCO and the Cousteau Society adopted the Universal Declaration of the Human Rights of Future Generations in Laguna. This is, of course, not an interstate declaration but a mere scientific expert background document, a tool to influence legal development.[35] Then, on 12 November 1997, UNESCO's General Conference adopted the Declaration on the Responsibility of the Present Generation Towards Future Generations.[36] The first article of the Declaration States that present generations are responsible for ensuring that the needs and interests of present and future generations are fully safeguarded. According to Article 4 on the Preservation of life on Earth, the present generation inherited the Earth temporarily. It should take care to use natural resources reasonably and ensure that harmful modifications of the ecosystems do not prejudice life and that scientific and technological progress in all fields does not harm life on Earth. According to Article 5 on the Protection of the environment, present generations should preserve the quality of the environment, natural resources, and living conditions. They should ensure that future generations are not exposed to pollution, which may endanger their health or even survival. Before any changes are carried out, present generations should consider the possible consequences of major projects for future generations. The declaration adopted within the framework of UNESCO may only be regarded as a soft law norm in the international law sense. Still, at the same time, it expresses the position of the States and the direction of international law development.

In international law, talking about the rights of future generations is problematic – even compared to national law. According to the traditional international law approach, the primary subjects of international law are States. Legal personality has been extended to international organisations only after the gradual development of international law. Meanwhile, in certain cases, individuals may only be subjects of international law. According to relevant jurisprudence, in particular situations, the concepts of 'common heritage of mankind' and 'common cause of humanity' may confer legal personality on the whole of humanity. In this respect, future generations, i.e., humanity on Earth, may even be considered a special subject of international law. Still, this approach is far from being generally accepted

35 La Laguna declaration on human rights by the 1st International Colloquium on Human Rights, La Laguna, Tenerife (Spain), 1–4 Nov. 1992. A/CONF.157/LACRM/7.

36 The General Conference of the United Nations Educational, Scientific and Cultural Organization: Declaration on the Responsibilities of the Present Generations Towards Future Generations, 12 November 1997.

in international law. In light of the foregoing, it is understandable why UNESCO has chosen humanity's responsibility in the present as the basis for their approach towards future generations and why they were silent on rights and obligations.

4. Some Aspects of Taking the Interests of Future Generations into Account

I am convinced that the (legal and political) representatives of the present generations shall (or, at least, may) also consider future generations' interests within the framework of ethics, economics, and law.

4.1. Ethical Aspects

For centuries, the main driving force behind human history was the idea that the world is gradually developing and improving the standard of living. Technical means are constantly being refined, the environment surrounding us is continuously enhanced, and the quality of life is improving, with the result that everyone will live a better life and have more to consume. This approach, however, is only valid until it is assumed that resources are endless and can be exploited without limits.

The climate change phenomenon shows that this assumption does not hold water. Future generations will hardly be able to increase the use of resources and consume more than today's generations. On the contrary, a significant decrease in available resources and consumption is expected in terms of both their absolute value and their value *pro capita*. However, it follows from our responsibility towards future generations that we raise the question: if it is already certain that we cannot improve our lives and living conditions, what sacrifice should we make in order not to impair the living conditions of our children, grandchildren, and other members of the future generations and to provide them with the opportunity of free choice? Even though today's generation's responsibility for future generations is set out in an increasing number of legal documents, this responsibility is considered an ethical problem.

Responsibility for future generations sheds light on a further issue. The next generations belong to specific societies instead of specific individuals. Therefore, responsibility for future generations can be understood at the level of the whole society rather than that of particular individuals. However, the question may be raised whether preserving the living conditions for future generations requires the same level, or at least the same proportion, of sacrifice from all members of today's generations – regardless of whether they are citizens of an industrialised or a developing country. Regarding the fact that today's countries' financial and other opportunities differ significantly, I believe that such differences between actual living conditions should also be considered when determining our scope of responsibility for the next generations. Intra-generational equity requires each country to ensure the survival of its descendants. This is in the knowledge and hopes that other countries also undertake a similar responsibility and sacrifice towards their future generations. While from an ethical point of view, we may expect everyone to take all necessary measures in the interest of their descendants, the approach requiring action from today's generations in the interest of future generations in other parts of the world is already doomed to fail, on account of overriding economic, geographical, political and other objective differences.

The cornerstone of thinking about our responsibility for future generations is that the members of a nation can give a uniform answer to the question of who we are, what cultural and ethical values we subscribe to, what we want to leave to our children, grandchildren, and other members of the future generations, and how should we change our current consumption and everyday life to achieve this end. In his encyclical letter 'Laudato si', Pope Francis underlines that the sense of today's generations' life may be questioned if they leave an uninhabitable world to subsequent generations.[37]

In general, we may say those countries are willing to make a more significant sacrifice where for certain reasons (like belonging to the same country), there is already a direct and institutionalised link between today's generation and future generations. Although international law introduced *inter alia* the category of inter-generational equity, it still lacks any actual means to affect the implementation of such equity. By contrast, the national law of certain States already contains institutions (mostly falling within the scope of the social care system) that are aimed at achieving inter-generational cooperation. Such institutions include, for example, old-age pensions or childbirth allowances, although these institutions only tangentially address the long-term framework for cooperation between present and future

37 Encyclical Letter Laudato si' of the Holy Father Francis on Care for Our Common Home, 2015, para. 206.

generations. Therefore, we may conclude that while the institutions of international law are suitable for designating the scope of inter-generational equity, it is up to the States to determine its content.

4.2. Economic Aspects

The current economic model is based on increasing consumption and production and the idea that their continuous development can satisfy the needs of a growing world population. The greatest weakness of this model is that our Earth's resources are limited. While the citizens of industrialised States already exploit natural resources intensively to ensure their well-being and quality of life, citizens in developing countries also seek to reach such a level of well-being. This effort, however, will result in an unsustainable situation, already in the short term (by 2050, according to certain pessimistic forecasts).[38]

According to Principle 8 of the 1992 Rio Declaration, 'to achieve sustainable development and a higher quality of life for all people, States should reduce and eliminate unsustainable patterns of production and consumption and promote appropriate demographic policies.'

This means that due consideration of the interests of future generations and the responsible management of the Earth's resources requires revisiting our basic economic approach. In my opinion, a key element may be decoupling,[39] that is, separating the economic concept of growth from natural growth (in terms of consumption). While statistically, growth is virtually unlimited (at least in theory), our Earth's limited resources constitute an absolute limit for physical growth. The institution of decoupling is not unprecedented in economic history. For example, the quantity of cash issued by national banks no longer corresponds to the quantity and value of gold, serving initially as a coverage for the money issued.

In my view, the implementation of decoupling, in this case, is by no means impossible. Decoupling would be supported, for example, by making public administration eco-friendly, by prescribing the obligatory

38 See eg the 2022 Report of the UN FCCC titled 'Nationally determined contributions under the Paris Agreement'. FCCC/PA/CMA/2022/4.

39 The OECD Environment Programme, Indicators to measure decoupling of environmental pressure from economic growth. Executive Summary <https://perma.cc/2Z9V-PMSD>.

recycling of raw materials in the construction of infrastructure, or by the mandatory consideration of calculations regarding the efficiency of certain investments and their proper accounting. However, the issue in this respect (similar to carbon dioxide emissions) is obtaining stakeholders' joint support. Market players will refrain from adopting a different market practice if they consider its introduction a competitive disadvantage; otherwise, they would threaten their own market position.[40]

On a smaller scale, institutions following the concept of sustainable development already exist. Such institutions include community banks that support and finance specific green activities (even from their profits).[41]

According to this thinking, we should not consider ecological services as externalities when establishing product value.[42] For example, when developing countries make their raw materials available to industrialised countries today, economic calculations almost ignore the extent to which the ecological service value in the State concerned decreases as a result of the production of the specific raw material (for example, in case of exhaustion of mines or excessive use of soils, etc). While economic thinking is based on the law of supply and demand, States (or the community of States) may establish a legal framework that duly considers the costs of production, which should also be reflected in pricing. These costs include the destruction of important ecological services to support restoration and the reasonable use of such ecological services. In addition to the legal framework, ethical considerations should not be ignored either. The laws of supply and demand (that is, a more advantageous offer) shall not undermine ecological aspects, even exceptionally, not only because it is prohibited by law but also because such offers are unacceptable from an ethical point of view. Considering the different weights of market players, the world's leading economic powers should cooperate in imposing such an approach on the market as a whole. This holds true because the long-term interests of States are the same in this respect (even though this may not always be obvious, when one considers short-term political interests).

---

40 *Decoupling Natural Resource Use and Environmental Impacts from Economic Growth* (UNEP 2011).

41 *Green Investment Banks – Policy Perspectives* (OECD 2015); *Greening the Banking System – Taking Stock of G20 Green Banking Market Practice* (2016) 12(16) UNEP Inquiry Working Paper 1.

42 TEEB, 'The Economics of Ecosystems and Biodiversity' (2010) TEB Reports for Business <https://perma.cc/FB2S-4SB2>.

Furthermore, discounting also plays an essential role in today's economic thinking. By recognising future damage at a smaller current value, discounting creates a link between (ecological) damage arising in the distant future and a financial advantage that may be realised in the immediate future.[43] However, this approach prioritises current economic advantage over mid-term and long-term damage.[44]

Meanwhile, the concept of so-called green economics[45] already exists. Green economics also considers ecological services and assigns a value to them, including them in the analysis of economic processes. While today this approach is pushed into the background by mainstream economic thinking, it is clear that reform ideas that would be suitable for applying the concept of sustainable development and the responsible management of environmental resources against the unconditional achievement of short-term economic advantages also exist in the field of economics.

4.3. Legal Aspects Flowing from the Ethical and Economic Aspects

Our responsibility for future generations may primarily be assessed at the national (Member State) level. Nevertheless, we must apply an approach that reaches beyond the Member State level when protecting human rights, particularly the so-called second and third generation of human rights.[46] Article 1 of the International Covenant on Economic, Social and Cultural Rights sets out that '[a]ll peoples may [...] freely dispose of their natural wealth and resources [...]. In no case may a people be deprived of its means of subsistence.' Although each State ensures the enforcement of fundamental human rights within their territories (with due regard also to their legal systems and cultures), they typically fail to take into account whether economic operators (including, in particular, multinational companies)

---

43 Cedric Philibert, 'Discounting the Future' (*Internet Encyclopaedia of Ecological Economics*, June 2003) <https://perma.cc/MN5C-779M>.

44 Joseph H Guth, 'Resolving the Paradoxes of Discounting in Environmental Decisions' (1995) 18(95) Transnational Law & Contemporary Problems 95.

45 Cameron Allen and Stuart Clouth (eds), *A Guidebook to the Green Economy* (UN Division for Sustainable Development 2012).

46 Regarding the current concept of the development and possible categories of human rights, see eg Spasimir Domaraczki and Margaryta Khvostova, 'Karel Vasak's Generations of Rights and the Contemporary Human Rights Discourse' (2019) 20 Human Rights Review 423.

within their jurisdiction respect fundamental human rights in their foreign operations. The reason may be that such regulation does not consider the global processes it may trigger. Such a direct link exists where rules on water resources impact neighbouring countries using the water base[47] or where emissions of pollutants affect the territory of neighbouring States (transboundary effect). An indirect link exists, however, when the said effect on other States and their citizens can only be construed indirectly. I believe that an (international) legal environment that allows for establishing legal responsibility not only in the case of direct links but also in the case of scientifically substantiated indirect links would also be suitable for enforcing responsibility for future generations and promoting responsible management of resources.[48] Taking into account the 2001 Articles on the international legal responsibility of States for wrongful acts,[49] State responsibility would be based on non-compliance with the so-called due diligence obligation.[50]

Certain international agreements (primarily those with the environment or human rights as their subject) already apply to monitoring mechanisms and from time to time investigate the Contracting Parties' practice of implementation.[51] Extending this monitoring to all areas related to climate change and the issue of responsibility for future generations may contribute to establishing the foundations of global solidarity and reducing intra-generational inequality.

Furthermore, setting forth legal consequences is a significant element of regulating responsibility for future generations. The current rules of international law, particularly those relating to climate change, are much more directed towards managing damage that has already occurred than

---

47 See eg *Handbook on water allocation in a transboundary context* (United Nations 2021).

48 Katalin Sulyok, *Science and Judicial Reasoning* (CUP 2020).

49 For completeness, it is worth mentioning that the Trail Smelter arbitration case (16 April 1938, and 11 March 1941) has played an important role in influencing the development of international environmental law, and the (customary) law of state responsibility. *Reports of International Arbitral Awards, Vol. III* (United Nations 2006) 1905–1982. Rebecca M Bratspies and Russell A Miller (eds), *Transboundary Harm in International Law. Lessons from the Trail Smelter Arbitration* (CUP 2006).

50 Timo Koivurova, 'Due diligence' in *Max Planck Encyclopedia of Public International Law* (OUP 2010).

51 Examples of monitoring: regular country visits by elected or appointed experts; *ad hoc* inspections on-site by experts; evaluations based on questionnaires; written reporting, done by the member states (self-assessment).

preventing it or restoring the original condition (where possible). So, for example, receiving persons fleeing from uninhabitable areas requires significant economic and social resources from the States concerned. With careful planning, these resources could also be used to prevent the causes of environmental degradation, solving problems at the source. This is also important because while climate change may render the environment of billions of people uninhabitable, the European Union, a leading economic power of the world, may only be capable of receiving some ten million refugees.

Intra-generational solidarity, as mentioned above, requires that we change our current perspective primarily (and, in many cases, exclusively) based on economic interests. The classic liberal economic policy of Adam Smith and David Ricardo is based on the self-regulating power of the market. It assumes that free market processes, which are free from government intervention, create an economic order yielding ideal outcomes for everyone. While it is unquestionable that the extension of economic cooperation was a success in many areas (for example, the European Union or the WTO was also established and operated based on this idea), intra-generational solidarity requires State (and international legal) intervention and subjecting classic free market processes to legal and ethical limits. In my view, two issues arise in this respect.

On the one hand, legal and ethical limits are not applied. It is hardly justifiable from a legal or ethical point of view that within the framework of the WTO, (mineral) water is considered a commodity just like any other product.[52] Therefore, according to market processes and interests, the water resources of a developing country may also be used for supplying an industrialised country, allowing the latter to save its own water resources. On the other hand, State legislation (or, as the case may be, the community of States) should be resilient enough to withstand lobbying even when, due to the rationalisation of economic processes and the increased efficiency of production, the business interests of market players come into conflict with legal and ethical rules.

Similar trends also apply where agricultural land (arable land on the territory of the relevant State) is acquired or leased by foreign market players. As both international law and EU law, as well as the national law

52 Mike Muller and Christophe Bellmann, *Trade and Water – How Might Trade Policy Contribute to Sustainable Water Management?* (International Centre for Trade and Sustainable Development 2016) 14–17.

of several countries, allow for the lease and acquisition of arable land by foreigners, certain industrialised countries may satisfy the needs of their citizens by using the resources of other States, sparing the use of their own arable land.[53] The relevance of this topic is well demonstrated by the fact that, for example, within the European Union, arable land is considered an investment within the scope of the free movement of capital, which the Member States may only exceptionally restrict. Furthermore, under EU law, Member States allow for the acquisition of their arable land by the citizens of other Member States (and non-EU countries).[54]

Another example of the conflict between legal and ethical aspects is the regulation and practice concerning the prohibition of child labour.[55] Although, in principle, all States of the world support the ban on child labour, certain States and international organisations have failed to take efficient action against multinational companies that obtain advantages on the market through the indirect use of child labour. Currently, action against such market players is primarily based only on the ethical values of society.[56]

The European Union achieves its most important economic objectives from a budget corresponding to hardly 1 % of the Member States' budget. Thus, if we spent only 1 % of the world trade turnover to mitigate inter-generational and intra-generational inequalities, significant progress could be achieved in preserving natural resources for future generations and, ultimately, in the fight against climate change.[57] Given that, I believe that

53 The law of foreign investments deals with this question in detail. Generally speaking, human rights law may support the right of foreigners to acquire property. Within the EU, there are specific rules concerning agricultural land (under the legal regime of the freedom of capital).

54 Case C-52/16, SEGRO, Judgment of 6 March 2018, ECLI:EU:C:2018:157.

55 The ILO Conventions and Recommendations concerning child labour are available at <https://www.ilo.org/ipec/facts/ILOconventionsonchildlabour/lang--en/index.htm> accessed 24 November 2021

56 See eg the class action lawsuit against Nestlé, Hershey, Cargill and other companies, in which the plaintiffs (eight citizens of Mali) alleged that the respondent companies were using child labour on Ivory Coast cocoa farms. The lawsuit was dismissed in 2022 for procedural reasons <https://www.reuters.com/business/hershey-nestle-cargill-win-dismissal-us-child-slavery-lawsuit-2022-06-28/> accessed 14 March 2023.

57 On the other hand, one can argue that it is mostly western and colonial states that are responsible for the current (and possible future) environmental crisis. For this reason, according to the above mentioned articles of state responsibility, these states should bear the burden but they are the most reluctant to change the current course of events despite the fact that the priority for many populations is to survive now.

the current regulatory environment should be revisited based on ethical aspects. This also holds true for the obligation to preserve natural resources for future generations. Several natural resources may be fully exhausted within a couple of decades if the current depletion rate is maintained. While a couple of decades is a very short period compared to the history of humanity, in the world of short-term political objectives, it is long enough to be put into the focus of political thinking. For example, in its decision No. 28/2017. (X.25.) AB, the Hungarian Constitutional Court found that the obligation to preserve biological diversity is 'a necessarily applicable rule of the international law, and it also reflects the intention of the international community as a whole.'[58] Legal solutions engaging similar, existing legal means to preserve natural resources may be an example for legislators, those applying the law, and (constitutional) courts globally.

Long-term thinking is already used in legislation when adopting professional strategic plans for several years or decades, typically. What is common to such plans is that they are elaborated primarily based on expert aspects instead of political ones. Furthermore, while they are not directly binding, their continuous consideration and application by the legislator are (or would be) desirable. In most countries, such strategies cover the development of road networks, the use of water resources, flood protection or the preservation of biological diversity. While an ideal legislative process would entail full consideration of strategic findings, certain States, as compared to their current practices, would already make significant progress if they specified in their constitutional rules that, in accordance with the precautionary principle, rules jeopardising the achievement of strategic objectives shall not be enacted in legislation. In this vein, in its decision No. 13/2018. (IX.4.) AB concerning the protection of groundwater resources, the Hungarian Constitutional Court pointed out that:

> for mid-term and long-term planning and foreseeable legislation, certain strategies [...] are deemed to be professional starting points which should be taken into account also with regard to the precautionary principle and the principle of prevention [...], accordingly, the failure to take into

58 Decision No. 28/2017 (X. 25.) AB of the Hungarian Constitutional Court, Reasoning [38].

account such professional strategies shall be assessed separately during the assessment of unconstitutionality of legislative changes.[59]

Further to strategic documents, several national parliaments have a body that is mainly responsible for taking into account sustainable development (or, in a broader sense, the interests of future generations), such as all the 54 members of the Global Network of the National Councils for Sustainable Development.[60] What is common to those bodies is that their members come from professional and scientific research institutes, universities, and civil society organisations in addition to politics, and they are responsible for *inter alia* taking a position on whether legislative bills comply with the concept of sustainable development. They may also initiate legislation (where applicable).

Even though such institutions exist in several states, in many cases, legislators do not accept their recommendations (primarily for budgetary reasons). Therefore, it would be desirable to ensure that the legislator does not ignore the experts' position of bodies responsible for enforcing sustainable development. (It is worth noting that adopting the national budget in several countries is subject to a supporting opinion from the court of auditors or the budgetary council).[61] Such strategic bodies may also become entitled to assess the practical implementation of laws already adopted and to propose legislative amendments where necessary.

While certain strategic documents are to be adopted only at the national level, the protection of the interests of future generations may be implemented globally. Several international civil society organisations requested the creation of a position similar to that of an ombudsman or the UN High Commissioner for Human Rights as an element of the UN's reform at the Rio+20 summit. The person filling that position would be specifically responsible for protecting the interests of future generations.[62] Even though this institution has not been established yet, the UN Secretary-General was

---

59 Decision No. 13/2018 (IX. 4.) AB of the Hungarian Constitutional Court, Reasoning [40].

60 Global Network of National Councils for Sustainable Development and Similar Bodies, *Country Profiles* <https://www.ncsds.org/index.php/sustainable-development-councils/country-profiles.html> accessed 14 March 2023.

61 Within the EU, see eg the research report of the IMF <https://blog-pfm.imf.org/en/pfmblog/2019/05/how-parliamentary-budgets-are-set-and-managed-in-europe> accessed 14 March 2023.

62 World Future Council, *Bringing Added Value to the High Level Political Forum: A High Level Representative for Future Generations* <https://perma.cc/KS46-GQPT>.

invited to prepare a report on the situation of future generations within the auspices of the UN.[63] The report specified that a position responsible for future generations might be set up within the UN, and national institutions specifically responsible for the protection of the interests of future generations were presented as models to be followed by the UN Member States. The UN Secretary-General's report highlighted eight national institutions as examples: the Secretary-General considered the institutions of Canada, Finland, Germany, Israel, Hungary, Norway, New Zealand, and Wales as pioneers in promoting sustainable development and inter-generational solidarity.[64] Below, among these model institutions, I will describe the framework for the operation of the Ombudsman (and also the Deputy Commissioner for Fundamental Rights) responsible for the protection of the interests of future generations in Hungary, highlighting the elements that may serve as a model for other States in protecting the interests of future generations.

5. Concluding Remarks

Scholars generally agree that the institutional representation of future generations should not be uniform across different countries and regions. It is argued that such efforts must be tailored to the specific characteristics of the inter-generational issues at hand and each country's cultural and legal specificities.[65] The effectiveness of future generations' institutional representation depends on many factors, only one of which is the institutional framework. This framework can be filled with substance based on the perspectives, available tools, and opportunities for cooperation between individual representatives. The model institutions with the most freedom to interpret their mandate are usually Ombudsman institutions. Therefore, in the case of this establishment, it is essential to how the holder of the office interprets the norms regulating its powers and how it uses the oppor-

63 *Intergenerational Solidarity and the Needs of Future Generations*, Report of the Secretary General, A/68/100, 2013.

64 ibid., para. 39.

65 Boldizsár Nagy, 'Speaking Without a Voice' in Emmanuel Agius and Salvino Busuttil (eds), *Future Generations and International Law* (Earthscan 1998) 62.

tunities afforded to it.[66] So far, all Ombudsmen for Future Generations have sought to take advantage of the broad spectrum of opportunities, exploiting the potential in this unique institution. They truly aspired 'to make human responsibility felt in all [areas] of State and civil life, with respect to the conservation of natural values ... for the sake of protecting the next generations.'[67]

One of the most important guarantees of the success of the Hungarian Ombudsman for Future Generations is the public's support and participation in its activities. Environmental concerns raised by the Ombudsman are often met with a strong response from the crowd, urging decision-makers to re-think the problem and potential solutions. However, it is essential to point out that the intensity of the public response directly connects with the amplification of the Ombudsman's message by the media. Since long-term thinking is not a typical feature of the press, it is difficult to publicise issues concerning the interests of the unborn. It is primarily issues that have day-to-day relevance that is taken up by the media. In cases where no acute event draws attention to the importance of a cause, the biggest supporter of the Ombudsman is the scientific sphere. If the Ombudsman wants to prove that certain decisions and processes cause permanent environmental damage, it is much easier to achieve progress if the Ombudsman works in close cooperation with the Hungarian Academy of Sciences and professional NGOs. Supported by sufficient scientific evidence, it is harder for the political sphere to disregard the assertions of the Ombudsman.

The change in the institutional set-up of the Office of the Commissioner for Fundamental Rights in 2012 resulted in a number of positive changes. With the adoption of the Fundamental Law of Hungary, the constitutional powers of the institution were considerably widened. The Fundamental Law entrusted the Ombudsman for Future Generations with protecting the interests of future generations, while the Ombudsman Act refers to the rights of future generations as the object of protection. Cooperation with the Commissioner for Fundamental Rights is critical in a number of cases in which the given problem only partially concerns the protection of future generations. Coordinated, joint action can therefore be valuable or may even become an essential source of legal protection. In accordance

---

66 Bernadette Somody, 'Jogállami paradoxon – A sikeres ombudsmani jogvédelem sajátosságai' in Éva Heizerné Hegedűs (ed), *Az ombudsman intézménye és az emberi jogok védelme Magyarországon* (OBH 2008) 101–106.

67 See the Comprehensive Summary of the Parliamentary Commissioner for Future Generations of Hungary <https://perma.cc/4223-F8TF_>.

with the precautionary principle, the Ombudsman for Future Generations frequently relies on early warnings. He presents his position in the earliest stages of a potentially unlawful activity when the Commissioner is not entitled to act.

The example of the Hungarian Ombudsman for Future Generations shows that while the protection of future generations could potentially affect all policies, their representation cannot be effectively expanded to all fields of legislation and governance. No national institution to protect future generations will ever be mandated to act as a branch of power taking action on behalf of future generations. Therefore, the activities of future generation institutions should mainly focus on the 'conservation of options', as Brown Weiss put it. That is to say, they must concentrate their efforts on helping maintain the quality of the environment and ecology to whatever degree possible, acting for the preservation of biodiversity, clean air, soil, water, and other natural resources.

18. How to See the Invisible? The Recognition of the 'Rights of Nature' to Represent Future Generations

Silvia Bagni and Michele Carducci***

Abstract: *Is it possible to ignore Nature in discussions about future generations? Nature is the ontological and biophysical unit that marks life. Therefore, excluding Nature's rights means not representing the future. This study proposes the recognition of the 'rights of Nature' as a hermeneutic tool to represent and protect the rights of future generations. The proposal is based on three elements. This generation must take great responsibility for safeguarding the ecological conditions that will ensure the stability of the One Earth System. The intertemporal integrity of natural processes is the determining variable of climate control. The qualification of the interdependence between Nature and future generations is coherent with the transformative changes recently invoked by the 2019 IPBES Global Assessment Report to achieve sustainability.****

1. Introduction

In legal terms, investigating the way in which the absent can be represented implies addressing two consequential research questions: first of all, to identify the 'absent', in opposition to the 'present'; secondly, once the absent has been defined as a subject, to select the interests he/she can be entitled to.

As for the first research question, both the editors and the other authors of this book have been focussing on humans, individuals or people who are not here at this moment, so hypothetical legal subjects that have been identified as past or future generations. In this chapter, we will broaden the scope of the 'absent', in order to include also non-human legal subjects, which will be identified with the common name of 'Nature', in the ecological sense that will be further explained.

The second research question involves trying to list the specific interests and rights that the absents could claim, in order to make the process of

* Silvia Bagni is Associate Professor in Comparative Public Law at the University of Bologna.

** Michele Carducci is Full Professor of Comparative Constitutional Law at the University of Salento.

*** §§ 1 and 9 were written by both authors; §§ 7 and 8.1 by Silvia Bagni; all other §§ by Michele Carducci.

recognizing a 'present' legal representative for them more objective. In fact, recognizing absents' rights makes sense only if they could be revindicated by someone who is present. We will try to demonstrate that assumption, starting from what humans and non-humans have in common, that is the interdependent relationship that connects their existence. From an ecosystem perspective, there is one main and basic substantive right that must be guaranteed: the right to a safe and balanced One Earth System; that stands as a pre-requisite for all other rights of past, present and future generations, both humans and non-humans. This right is very peculiar with respect to other traditional substantive rights, because it is multidimensional. What does it mean? Usually, claiming a right consists in revindicating a space, tracing a border where an individual or a group can stand without interference from the outside. So, we could say that rights have a spatial dimension: they could be geometrically represented within the space. As for the right to a safe and balanced One Earth System, we will try to show that it is built both on spatial and temporal coordinates. First of all, it represents the common space where every other claim can be presented.[1] This means that it is an inclusive space, which is also a relational space, where every single entity is somehow connected to the others. In addition, these connections are not merely instantaneous, but persist in time through feedback loop mechanisms, bridging past, present and future. The temporal dimension, which we will refer to as 'natural time', is the fundamental characteristic of this relation.

Conceiving such a right is the epistemological consequence of a holistic and multi-disciplinary approach to life on Earth, that requires an effort on the part of legal scholars in order to rethink traditional legal concepts and adapt them to a broader reality. This new legal paradigm has been theoretically discussed by a minority group of legal scholars since more than a decade[2] and has become a normative reality since the adoption of

1 Like relational values, it is everywhere, see Kai MA Chan and others, 'Why Protect Nature? Rethinking Values and the Environment' (2016) 113(6) Pnas 1462.

2 Academic literature on rights of Nature is now very wide. The first attempts at theorization were the seminal article by Christopher D Stone, 'Should Trees Have Standing? Towards Legal Rights for Natural Objects' (1972) 45 Southern California Law Review 450 and the works of Thomas Berry <https://thomasberry.org/category/publications/> accessed 7 July 2023. Publications on the subject matter have flourished in the last decades. The reader can find a vast bibliography in the following two reports: Michele Carducci and others, *Towards an EU Charter of the Fundamental Rights of Nature* (*EESC* 2020) <https://perma.cc/FM22-327Q>; Jan Darpö, *Can Nature Get It*

the 2008 Ecuadorian Constitution, which incorporated the rights of Nature and paved the way for a Copernican revolution in law.

In this chapter, we will try to explain its theoretical basis, rooted in ecological concepts, and we will also attempt to draft the legal fundamental principles that derive from it. In § 2, we focus on the definition of the 'absent', supporting the need to widen its scope, including also non-humans and natural relations, so advocating for the use of 'Nature' as a comprehensive expression. In § 3, we will concentrate on the temporal dimension that connect past, present and future generations as a whole subject. In § 4, we analyse how the relations between nature, human actions and climate have been regulated thus far, in particular through the UN Framework Convention on Climate Change (UNFCCC). In § 5, we move to the identification of the subjective rights of the absent, pinpointing the need to guarantee a safe and balanced One Earth System. In § 6, starting from the bias of Western culture about a holistic concept of Nature, we introduce the idea of 'sympoiesis', a heuristic that means 'co-production' and is useful to understand why, in the 'rights of Nature' approach, nature is a subject, like humans. In § 7 we advocate for the adaptation of the environmental legal system to the natural laws that govern the Earth System. This requires, on the one hand, the formulation of a new *Grundnorm* and different set of conflict resolution rules; on the other, the implementation of an ecological analysis of law by enforcers and decision-makers; a multidisciplinary attitude to the formation of institutional bodies; an update in democratic processes. In § 8 we introduce the relational approach to law as a methodology that can be applied to reconcile the concept of 'right' with the sympoietic heuristics we have described in § 6. The article ends with some concluding remarks on the challenges that this approach implies with respect to Western legal dogmas about right-holders.

Right? A Study on Rights of Nature in the European Context (Policy Department for Citizens' Rights and Constitutional Affairs Directorate-General for Internal Policies 2021) <https://perma.cc/RQ9Z-WS68>. See also the monographic issue: (2022) 13(1) Revista Catalana de Dret Ambiental. As for the Earth System Law, the main reference is Luis J Kotzé, 'Earth System Law for the Anthropocene' (2019) 11(23) Sustainability 6796 <https://perma.cc/F7V7-X3MX>; Louis J Kotzé and others, 'Earth System Law: Exploring New Frontiers in Legal Science' (2022) 11 Earth System Governance 1 <https://doi.org/10.1016/j.esg.2021.100126> accessed 7 July 2023. See also Timothy Cadman, Margot Hurlbert and Andrea C Simonelli (eds), *Earth System Law: Standing on the Precipice of the Anthropocene* (Routledge 2022).

2. Step One: Defining the Absent in Broader Terms

Our contemporary condition is characterised by two unprecedented features in legal terms:

- on the one hand, the fusion of human destiny with the non-human destiny of the planet (the thermodynamic equilibrium of the climate system on which our future depends);[3]
- on the other, the irreversible biophysical and spatial disconnection of human beings from the climate system on which they depend.[4]

In the Anthropocene, the Cartesian dualism between nature and society has broken down, resulting in a deep intertwining of the fates of nature and humankind.[5] However, this plot is paradoxical. We no longer consider Nature to be a factor hostile to our plans of development, but we define what nature is or must be (natural capital, ecosystem service, asset, resource, subject). We continue to regard nature as an 'external object', even though it has been 'manipulated' by our definitions and classifications. Today, the climate and environmental crisis requires us to rethink this paradox and build a different narrative and regulatory relationship with nature.

In the online version of the Oxford Dictionary, nature is defined as follows: 'all the plants, animals and things that exist in the universe that are not made by people'. This definition creates a clear opposition between humanity and nature, which seems to recall Renaissance philosophical ideas about human domination over nature, and that has been refuted by ecology and the Earth sciences. In contrast, the definition of 'environment' that the Oxford Dictionary offers is more inclusive, considering humans and non-humans on the same level: 'the natural world in which people, animals and plants live'. From a scientific point of view, the environment is part of a natural ecosystem, the space in which countless relationships of mutual interdependence between biotic and abiotic elements, as well as the exchange of energy and matter, produce stability in the life of our planet. So, by using the expression 'rights of Nature' we will refer to this ecological

3 John Barry, Arthur PJ Mol and Anthony R Zito, 'Climate Change Ethics, Rights, and Policies: An Introduction' (2013) 22(3) Environmental Politics 361.

4 Christian Dorninger and others, 'Assessing Sustainable Biophysical Human–nature Connectedness at Regional Scales' (2017) 12 Environmental Research Letters.

5 Eva Lövbrand and others, 'Who Speaks for the Future of Earth? How Critical Social Science can Extend the Conversation on the Anthropocene' (2015) 32 Global Environmental Change 211.

definition. The international community has been aware of this relational concept of nature for some time. The Preamble of the World Charter for Nature, proclaimed by the United Nations (UN) General Assembly in 1982, states that 'mankind is a part of nature and life depends on the uninterrupted functioning of natural systems' and that 'civilization is rooted in nature'. Moreover, the adoption of the Charter was justified in the interests of present and future generations. Unfortunately, the Charter has no binding force, and this holistic idea of nature very soon gave way to the concept of sustainable development.

Our approach finds some correspondence in another soft law document, the Universal Declaration of Rights of Mother Earth, approved in Cochabamba by the World People's Conference on Climate Change and the Rights of Mother Earth in 2010.[6] The preamble states that 'we are all part of Mother Earth, an indivisible, living community of interrelated and interdependent beings with a common destiny'. As humans are a constitutive element of natural ecosystems and, ultimately, of the Earth System (ES), the concept of 'rights of Nature' is also comprehensive of human interests. As we will see, the recognition of 'rights of Nature' is relational, meaning that the focus is on the protection of the relationship, and the harmony and balance of all nature's components.

The Western idea of separation between humans and nature is the consequence of our disconnection from the climate system. As we know, humans are biophysically connected to the biosphere through the flows of materials and energy appropriated from ecosystems. While this connection is fundamental for human well-being, modern societies have disconnected themselves from the natural productivity of their immediate regional environment. This disconnection operates through two historical processes. The first occurred through the use of energy inputs from outside the biosphere (non-renewable minerals, such as fossil fuels, metals and other minerals) and caused the 'biospheric' human-nature disconnection. The second occurred with the 'spatial' disconnection caused by international trade, which resulted in the import and export of biomass products and mineral resources from different ecosystems. We therefore live in an era where the destiny of humanity is fused with the destiny of the climate system, while humanity lives 'disconnected' from it. The challenge of the future is to reconstruct a common space-time between humanity and nature. In this

---

6 Declaración Universal de los Derechos de la Madre Tierra <www.rio20.net> accessed 7 July 2023.

perspective, the discourse on the rights of nature has also become central to the debate on future generations. In fact, attributing legal subjectivity to nature means recognising legal value to the rules of functioning of natural systems in their intertemporal and thus intergenerational perspective.

3. *'Natural Time' as the Key Dimension for Understanding the Absent as Nature*

As we have clarified that the 'rights of Nature' approach is relational and includes the interests of humanity, we can now consider the projection of this relationality into the fourth dimension, that of time. This book looks at past and future generations as the absent and investigates how they can be represented. As already mentioned, the recognition of the rights of nature allows us to consider the importance of the different time scales of ecosystems and the entire climate system. Intertemporality is a determining factor for the existence of all forms of life, including human life. Consequently, respecting the rights of nature also means representing the intergenerational dimension of human rights and responsibilities.[7] This perspective has always been accepted by indigenous peoples, who consider themselves part of the natural system and understand life as relation, and time as non-linear, so that 'generations', past and future, are always present at the same moment (in the cult of their ancestors, in the propitiatory rituals for the harvest, in the passage of seasonal celebrations...). The flux of time in the natural scale produces the fading of boundaries between past, present and future generations.

On the contrary, in the Western legal tradition, humans 'have' time, as an object of possession (so much so that we say 'time is money'). In the chthonic legal tradition, humans 'are' in the flux of time. Quite paradoxically, this 'to have-to be' opposition with respect to time has long been accepted by the Western system of scientific knowledge: for instance, Odum ironically stated that we all know we are born and will die, and therefore that we 'are' before we even 'have', but our society denies this ontology, fostering the illusion that we can 'grow' forever by accumulation. In physics, the epistemological framework changed with the shift from Newtonian physics to thermodynamics, with the discovery of entropy. Instead, the Western legal paradigm simply ignores all these scientific findings.

7 Drew Purves and others, 'Time to Model all Life on Earth' (2013) 493 Nature 295.

As all current global environmental law is based on a different anthropocentric paradigm, to give way to the nature's rights approach, legal scholars have been focussing on the issue of attributing legal personhood and standing to nature. Obviously, as should be clear from what we have said up to now and from what we will try to explain further in the following paragraphs, the recognition of the 'rights of Nature' is wider in scope.

4. Current International Regulation on Climate Change: Nature as a Stone Guest

International regulation on climate change offers some legal basis to the rights of Nature approach that we have presented.

Article 1 of the UNFCCC reproduces definitions of biophysical and earth sciences precisely on the complex temporal relationship between spheres of the climate system and human action. Article 2 recognises that dangerous human interference affects ecosystems and their timing, also compromising human interests, starting with food. Ultimately, the Convention qualifies the problematic nature of the temporal relationship between human action and nature.

Secondly, the Framework Convention bases its regulations on the assumption that human action has made the climate system 'unstable'. For this reason, in Article 2, it identifies the objective of 'stabilising' the entire climate system to exclude 'dangerous anthropogenic interference with the climate system'. This means adapting the legal rules of human behaviour to the timescales of the climate system, i.e., the 'natural' timescales of the ES, governed by thermodynamic and biophysical laws. It is no coincidence that the Convention adds this clarification again in Article 2: the stabilisation of the entire climate system 'should be achieved within a time frame sufficient to allow ecosystems to adapt naturally to climate change, to ensure that food production is not threatened and to enable economic development to proceed in a sustainable manner'.

It is important to note that the entire Framework Convention on Climate Change combines the consideration of the timing of the climate system with the protection of the interests of present and future generations.

In this perspective, the 'rights' of future generations focus not only on their social or political content, but on the permanence over time of the natural cycles of functioning and adaptation of all spheres of the climate system, without which human life itself cannot remain stable.

5. Step Two: Identifying the Subjective Rights of the Absent

The expression 'subjective rights' can have different meanings. Let us try, for example, to use the so-called 'Hohfeldian' scheme, developed by the American jurist Wesley Newcomb Hohfeld,[8] which is still considered valid today.[9] According to Hohfeld, discourses formulated in terms of rights always refer to four distinct elementary legal positions, defined as: claim, privilege, power, immunity. Where does nature as 'subject' fit into this classification? Apparently, it only fits into the 'claim', i.e., the fact that someone is obliged to behave actively, or by omission, towards the holder of the claim. The other elementary legal positions of the subjective right presuppose a capacity for action which nature, as such, has neither in terms of 'privilege', nor in terms of 'power', nor in terms of 'immunity'. However, if we instead consider the time factor in the thermodynamic and biophysical flow of the climate system, we discover that nature has not only 'claims', but also 'powers'. In the 'Hohfeldian' scheme, power is the possibility, on the part of its holder, to modify the legal position of others, or even one's own, so that the correlative legal position of power is subjection, and the inability of others to prevent it as its negation. In the field of the laws of thermodynamics and biophysics, this is exactly how it is: the temporal dynamics of nature prevail over human laws and we humans are incapable of preventing it. So, paraphrasing the well-known song by Patty Smith, 'Nature has the power'.

Ultimately, there is a correspondence between respect for the rights of nature as power and the representation of the rights of future generations. If nature is respected in its times of functioning within the climate system, the rights of human beings are guaranteed not only in the present but also in the future. By subjectivizing nature, it is possible to give voice and visibility to future generations.

This close correlation between times of nature and future human life has become evident with the climate emergency. The formula developed by Lenton, Rockström *et al*[10] summarizes the concept: E = R *x* U. The emergency exists (E) because the risks of degeneration of the entire climate

---

8 Wesley Newcomb Hohfeld, 'Some Fundamental Legal Conceptions as Applied in Judicial Reasoning' (1913) 23(1) The Yale Law Journal 16.

9 Herbert LA Hart, 'Are there any Natural Rights?' (1955) 64(2) The Philosophical Review 175.

10 Timothy M Lenton and others, 'Climate Tipping Points – Too Risky to bet Against' (2019–2020) 575 Nature 592.

system (R) increase over time. The time of the climate system has become the factor of urgency (U) to which human action must adapt to protect its future. Humans, to ensure their future, must protect nature within its times. So, the maintenance of a safe and balanced One Earth System is the precondition of any other right for present and future generations and the principle claim in representing the absent, as we have defined it above. However, the rights of Nature approach, that would be implied by the application of the ecosystemic principles to the legal paradigm, would drive major institutional and systemic changes to the legal system, that we will try to illustrate in the following paragraphs.

6. Sympoietic Heuristics and the Legal Status of Nature as a Subject

The intergenerational and interspatial dimension of the rights of nature bring with her the need to experiment with new 'legal approaches' to natural and social phenomena. As a matter of fact, urgency for a shift in the legal paradigm can be perceived also in numerous international documents. According to UN Resolution A/69/322 of 18 August 2014, these approaches should draw 'from the holistic scientific knowledge provided by earth system science to develop laws and policies that better manage human behaviour in light of the interconnections between people and nature'.[11] The Paris Climate Agreement, in Article 6 no. 8, also suggests holistic approaches. More recently, even the Human Development Report 2020 has recognized that long-term sustainability should involve more than meeting quantitative targets of the reduction of carbon dioxide emissions or of biodiversity loss: 'We need to aim for transformative changes in how societies relate to the biosphere [...]. The goals of sustainable human development must be rooted in integrated, transdisciplinary understandings of the connections of societies in the biosphere'.[12]

Moreover, holistic, interactional and systems-oriented ontologies are inherent in many indigenous cosmologies that have long preceded the emergence of systemic approaches in modern social and natural sciences.[13] This

11 UN General Assembly, Resolution A/69/322 of 18 August 2014, para. 50.

12 Human Development Report 2020 (UNDP 2020) 98.

13 Iván Dario Vargas Roncancio, 'Plants and the Law: Vegetal Ontologies and the Rights of Nature. A Perspective from Latin America (2017) 43(1) Australian Feminist Law Journal 67; Iván Dario Vargas Roncancio, *The Legal Lives of Forests: Law and the*

also explains the link between the rights of nature and the question of the recognition of indigenous rights.

It is true that a systems-based and complex approach to earth sciences has emerged in the Western tradition, especially when oppositions to mechanistic and Newtonian views of natural phenomena began to become prominent. However, Western thought has privileged a vision of complexity, as a product of exclusively social and anthropocentric processes, within which law has become an instrument for governance, indifferent to the complexity of nature. Therefore, the Western legal tradition has not elaborated the 'sympoietic' perspective of indigenous cosmogonies. 'Sympoiesis' is a heuristic of the whole ES. Heuristics provide essential tools for understanding living systems, their characteristics and their behaviour. However, 'autopoietic' heuristics are very different from 'sympoietic'. The term 'sympoiesis' was created by the environmental scientist Dempster[14] to argue, in the light of ecosystem studies, that complexity consists of a collective production of actions and feedbacks that have neither spatial nor temporal boundaries that can be controlled by a single subject. In 'sympoiesis', there is no 'subject' and no 'object'... After all, the term 'sympoiesis' derives from Greek and means, 'doing together'. 'Doing together' does not mean 'interacting' but 'co-acting', in a real 'symbiogenesis' of creation of matter and energy.[15] In 'sympoiesis', everyone is a 'subject' that produces consequences on others and therefore relationships that can also be governed by law.

The autopoietic perspective imagines a process of 'self-regulation' of a plurality of different elements, some of which are 'created' by human action, such as law, and therefore remain separate from the 'natural' ones. In this way, human 'self-regulation' and natural 'self-regulation' are not framed as a single system but as two different 'entities'. Consequently, complexity would operate as a plurality of systems with three fundamental characteristics: they are self-reproducing in an independent and closed manner (eg, law produces law, economy produces economy, etc); they have a self-defined and autonomous content (eg, law is not the economy, the economy is not society, society is not the family, etc); they have different functioning mechanisms (eg, law functions differently from the economy, the economy functions differently from society, etc). These allow each system to repro-

other-than-human in the Andes-Amazon, Colombia (An Anthropological and Legal Theory Approach) (PhD thesis, McGill University 2021).

14 M Beth and L Dempster, *A Self-Organizing Systems Perspective on Planning for Sustainability* (Master Thesis, University of Waterloo 1998).

15 Lynn Margulis, *Symbiotic Planet: A New Look at Evolution* (Basic Books 1998).

duce and control itself independently of the others. In practice, autopoietic heuristics totally ignore thermodynamics and the biophysical fact that everything is matter and energy, regardless of the living 'system' considered (legal, economic, social, human, etc).

On the other hand, a 'sympoietic' heuristic interprets complexity as an integrated ecosystem of non-separable subjects, all composed of matter and energy, just like the climate system. Just as the climate system has no boundaries because it involves the entire ES, so the idea of non-separability of human matter, energy and 'nature' suggests that there are no boundaries within the climate system. With this heuristic, there is no contraposition between subjects and objects. There is a sharing of biophysical conditions, which affect all subjects, human and non-human. Biophysical protection concerns everyone because everyone is 'matter' and 'energy' in the climate system. A 'biophysical' law cannot disregard this 'sympoiesis'. In this perspective, we can understand why the recognition of the rights of nature does not produce the invention of a new subject as opposed to the human subject. Instead, it is a cultural and legal approach that reveals the common biophysical conditions of matter and energy between humans and non-humans.

In practice, by recognising the rights of nature, we recognise the 'sympoietic' heuristics of the climate system. The rights of nature are the 'magnifying glass' of this heuristic. Within the climate system, all subjects contribute to its dynamics. Nevertheless, not all actors play the same role.[16] Once again, the UNFCCC reminds us of this difference in its Preamble and Article 2. Only humans have produced 'dangerous' interference in the climate system, not other actors. Then humans must re-establish a responsible synergy with the other actors in the system, eliminating 'dangerous interference'. Human beings have only one way to achieve this 'responsible symmetry': re-establishing the connection of their actions with the times of nature, that is, of the different spheres of the climate system.

---

16 Marie-Catherine Petersmann, 'Sympoietic Thinking and Earth System Law: The Earth, its Subjects and the Law' (2021) 9 Earth System Governance 1 <https://www.sciencedirect.com/science/article/pii/S2589811621000185> accessed 21 July 2023.

7. The Relational Approach to the Law as a Methodology to Reconcile the Concept of 'Right' with Sympoietic Heuristics

The sympoietic heuristics shows that the stability of relations of interdependence and co-creation among individuals, species, communities and ecosystems should be the main goal of policies and rules. So 'relation' must shift from the periphery of the law to the centre of its institutional tools.

However, from a legal point of view, this goal is difficult to reach with existing legal instruments, because the concept of 'right' has been defined in terms of individual or collective 'claims' that clash with the opposing claims of other subjects. So, the concept of 'rights' generates an adversarial and confrontational system of dispute resolution, where (usually) one party wins and the other succumbs. As stated in the European Economic and Social Committee Report *Towards an EU Charter of the Fundamental Rights of Nature. Study* 'We also need to reframe rights from adversarial to synergistic, moving from "rights" to "right relationships", a "right relationship" being one that supports the wellbeing of the whole'.[17]

So, how can we legally protect the relationship between the parties instead of focusing only on their individual claims? To answer the question, we will try to analyse different academic contributions to the idea of a 'relational approach to law'. Even if the concept has mainly been applied to solve intercultural conflicts between humans, its premises can offer meaningful insights into the process of shifting to an ecological legal paradigm.

In the introduction to her seminal book *Law's Relations: a Relational Theory of Self, Autonomy, and Law*, Jennifer Nedelsky hopes that environmentalists will be among her readers because, as she stresses, 'The very concept of ecology is relational'.[18] Meeting those expectations, her arguments will be applied to our proposal, as a powerful step in the direction of a re-orientation in how we shape and understand our world. By re-defining the self from a relational perspective, she supports a new concept of law and a new language for rights[19]: 'A relational analysis provides a better framework for identifying what is really at stake in difficult cases and for

17 Carducci (n 2) 10.

18 Jennifer Nedelsky, *Law's Relations: a Relational Theory of Self, Autonomy, and Law* (OUP 2011) 12.

19 'My point throughout is that law needs an alternative conceptual framework to do its work optimally, and new concepts need to be given life in the law' (Dorninger and others (n 4)).

making judgments about the competing interpretations of rights involved [...] Both law and rights will then be understood in terms of the relations they structure – and how those relations can foster core values, such as autonomy'.[20] In fact, the author tries to defend a relational concept of autonomy, that generates from the relationships in which the self is always re-created.[21]

Nedelsky also takes into consideration the consequences that relational autonomy project onto the paradigm of equality, with respect to non-human entities. Even if, for her purposes, she maintains the idea of the inherent equality among humans as the basis of her discourse, she also underlines that the relational approach would foster a redefinition of our relationship with nature, on a stance of mutual respect, concern, care, interdependence and responsibility. In fact, her analysis of the situation of conflict of values in difficult cases is really straightforward. The relational approach suggests that, instead of looking at which value stands higher in a hierarchy, we should change the question, and look at an alternative method of conflict resolution, which could correctly evaluate the relationship existing among all the actors, so that a choice between two evils (the complete sacrifice of one value) is no longer the only option.[22]

She also advocates a relational approach to rights, which means that their enforcement must be considered in terms of 'the ways rights structure relationships'.[23] A legal controversy is usually seen by lawyers as a conflict of rights. Conceiving rights in a relational perspective would imply considering that there is a mutual relationship between the rights' bearers, which makes them also reciprocally responsible towards one another.[24] Responsibility, accountability, sense of care, are the dimensions missing in the liberal theory of rights. Rights rhetoric appears to be universally accepted

---

20 ibid.

21 'Autonomy is made possible by constructive relationships – including intimate, cultural, institutional, national, global, and ecological forms of relationship – all of which interact' (ibid., 118).

22 'Finally, inspired by Amy, I realized that the contribution of my relational approach to this problem of inclusion could not come from figuring out a rank ordering among different life-forms. Amy kept trying to tell her interviewer that he was asking the wrong question (while, with increasing impatience, he kept trying to get her to answer it). The most important ethical question is not how to choose between two bad options, but how to change the situation (often by restructuring the relations) so that those are no longer the only options' (ibid., 196).

23 ibid., 235.

24 ibid., 248.

and applied, even in an undemocratic context. The relational approach can be used to enhance some core values, such as autonomy and equality, as well as producing some new values, such as care.[25]

In her studies about Singapore's relational constitutionalism, Li-ann Thio considers the Singapore experience as a valuable and original product of a different cultural and legal sensitivity, based on non-liberal views: 'to be is to exist in relation to other beings and relationalism prioritises the longevity or durability of mutually dependent relationships, rather than treating relationships as discrete short-term transactions'.[26]

Even if the main objective of relational constitutionalism in Singapore is to manage inter-group conflicts and assure religious harmony, its cultural basis and the methods followed to reach its goal can offer food for thought on how to shape the ecological legal paradigm: 'The vision of the individual within a relational framework is not the vision of an atomistic rational being asserting rights against the state, which many liberal theorists favour. Instead, individuals are situated in communities, shaped and constituted by the network of relationships they interact with and are fundamentally connected to'.[27]

Following Thio's arguments, we could consider the stability of the ES as the common value at the basis of a sustainable and harmonic society, where people are aware of their vulnerability and interdependency with respect to other non-human lives, and the matter and energy we co-produce by our interactions. This idea corresponds to the interpretation Silvia Bagni gave of the constitutional architecture of the State designed by the new Constitutions of Ecuador and Bolivia in 2008 and 2009, that she called the Caring State. In fact, this concept emerged as attached to experiences that were incorporating the Rights of Nature into the legal system, both at the constitutional and legislative level. The Caring State is based on two main pillars: environmental and social justice. These goals are to be understood in the light of what we have called in this article a 'sympoietic' perspective. In fact, 'environmental justice' is intended in a broader sense, as opposed to the international idea of the 'environment'.

A slightly different version of relational constitutionalism has been re-conceptualised by Elizabeth Macpherson, where she defines Australasian

25 ibid., 82.

26 Li-ann Thio, 'Singapore Relational Constitutionalism: the "Living Institution" and the Project of Religious Harmony' (2019) Singapore Journal of Legal Studies 204, 233.

27 ibid., 206–207.

Environmental Constitutionalism as Relational Legal Pluralism.[28] She has studied the cases of recognition of ecosystem rights in New Zealand and Australia, and she considers that they represent an innovation in the context of environmental constitutionalism, specifically because of their relational function. Macpherson indicates that Australasian Environmental Constitutionalism is indeed an example of the 'relational turn' in socio-legal theory, which departs from static notions of law to a focus on the relational processes of dialogue and negotiation in plural, multicultural legal settings'.[29]

Finally, a different legal paradigm based on the principle of 'relationality' comes from indigenous jurisprudence and political movements in the Global South. Comparing Andean indigenous perspectives with the Western legal tradition, Maria Elena Attard Bellido imagines a dialogue on legal pluralism based on a pluri-national, communitarian and decolonized perspective.[30] This alternative jurisprudence rejects the binary code of legal disputes in favour of solutions that defend harmony and sustain '*vivir bien*'. Within this understanding of the law, jurists are called on to 'feel the reality', before 'knowing' or 'thinking' it[31]. Knowledge is the result of collective experiences and practices, transmitted through generations. The author proposes applying to the analysis of legal conflicts the methodology of the *chakana*, which represents the Andean Cosmovision. The *chakana*, as an intercultural interpretative tool, invites the lawyer to consider the legal facts from four dimensions: being (*ser*), knowing (*saber*), doing (*hacer*) and power (*poder*). This multidimensional approach (*sentipensar*, 'thinking with our feelings') guarantees the harmony of humankind with its environment and aims at the realization of *vivir bien*.

We are sure that a relational approach to law could be seen by many as a dangerous erosion of individual rights and freedoms; by others it could

28 Elizabeth Macpherson, 'Ecosystem Rights and the Anthropocene in Australia and Aotearoa New Zealand' in Domenico Amirante and Silvia Bagni (eds), *Environmental Constitutionalism in the Anthropocene. Values, Principles and Actions* (Routledge 2022) 168.

29 ibid., 171.

30 Maria Elena Attard Bellido, 'Entre la diosa Themis y Mama Ocllo: la propuesta de argumentación jurídica plural desde la filosofía intercultural andina de la Chakana' (2019) 50 Diálogo de Saberes 79.

31 'Desde esta ética aymara, el runa/jaqi — el ser humano como parte de la naturaleza— siente la realidad, más que conocerla o pensarla' (Josef Estermann 2009, cited by Attard Bellido (n 30) 93).

seem utopic. As for the first critique, we have tried to explain with the concept of 'sympoiesis' and in the next paragraph with the new hierarchy of conflict resolution criteria, that the individual is not erased by our proposal, but empowered by its relational dimension, which can foster a more inclusive and respectful community. Relationality applied to human-human relations integrates the dogmatic structure of rights, trying not only to solve a conflict, but also to advance workable solutions to complex social problems, encouraging social transformation.[32]

As for the second critique, we are strongly convinced that our mental thought structures produce a strong impact on how we behave. Additionally, our language, as a product of our thinking, shapes our behaviour. So, we absolutely need to create a 'habit of relational thinking'. This could generate a shift in our epistemological paradigm, from a liberal to a relational/ecological one, to request from humanity a real change in the pattern of consumption and exploitation of our planet and our fellows. As was asserted in the 2020/2021 UN University Interconnected Disaster Risk Report 'changing the underlying systems that create disastrous situations can only begin when individuals recognize their part in the larger, whole iceberg, rather than just the tip'.[33]

8. *Adapting Legal Systems to the Recognition of the 'Rights of Nature'*

8.1. The Grundnorm of the Integrity of the ES and new Conflict Resolution Rules

From the above discussion, it is clear that legal science should be shaped by the new knowledge emerging from the ES sciences; but also, from the ancestral knowledge transmitted through centuries by the chthonic legal tradition that still survives within indigenous peoples.[34] In fact, indigenous customary law is based on natural laws and on principles that aim to maintain a harmony among all the members of the community, humans and non-humans.[35]

32 Nedelsky (n 18) 342.
33 UN University Interconnected Disaster Risk Report 2020/2021, 88.
34 Nicole Redvers and others, 'The Determinants of Planetary Health' (2021) 5 The Lancet e156.
35 For Latin American, African and Australasian indigenous traditions see respectively Ramiro Ávila Santamaría, 'Rights of Nature vs. Human Rights? An Urgent Shift of

The sympoietic heuristics described above require legal scholars to re-interpret the hierarchy of values at the basis of sixteenth century social contract philosophy, from which constitutionalism derived. In that period, the abundance of natural resources, capitalism in its early stages, and ignorance about the homeostatic mechanisms of the ES represented the perfect scenario for human domination of the planet.[36] The impact of the industrial revolution on the ecosystem and climate was at that time unimaginable. Consequently, the legal status of natural elements as objects and resources was coherent with the social, cultural and economic premises. The stability of the Holocene era was taken for granted.

The situation has dramatically changed, and the law should in turn also change. The fundamental goal of a constitutional system should be the preservation of the integrity of the Earth System (see above, § 5).[37]

Kim and Bosselmann propose considering the protection and restoration of the integrity of the Earth's life-support system 'as a potential Grundnorm or goal of international environmental law'.[38] Nature as 'Grundnorm' could guide the evolution of global constitutionalism[39] as a set of rules on the permanence of rights over time (in Cooter's 'strategic' meaning of Constitution[40]). As Schmidt notes, the protection of the ES is a goal, from which to extrapolate a new *Grundnorm*, as a criterion of the validity of the system's sources of production.[41] The validity of norms no longer coincides with compliance with internationally assumed constraints (as in the Kelsenian *Stufenbau*), but with their conformity to the 'natural' rules that guarantee the stability of the ES.[42] So, when conflict of rules occur, norms' legitimacy

---

Paradigms' in Amirante and Bagni (n28), Kyriaki Topidi, 'Ubuntu as a Normative Value in the New Environmental World Order' in Amirante and Bagni (n28) and Macpherson (n28).

36 Fritjof Capra and Ugo Mattei, *The Ecology of Law. Toward a Legal System in Tune with Nature and the Community* (Berrett-Koehler 2015).

37 Quirino Camerlengo, *Natura e potere. Una rilettura dei processi di legittimazione politica* (Mimesis 2020).

38 Rakhyun E Kim and Klaus Bosselmen, 'International environmental law in the Anthropocene: Towards a purposive system of multilateral environmental agreements' (2013) 2 Transnational Environmental Law 285, 305.

39 Michele Carducci and Lidia Patricia Castillo Amaya, 'Nature as "Grundnorm" of global constitutionalism: contributions from the Global South' (2016) 12(2) *Revista Brasileira de Direito* 1.

40 Robert D Cooter, *The Strategic Constitution* (Princeton University Press 2000).

41 Jeremy J Schmidt, 'The Moral Geography of the Earth System' (2019) 44 Transactions of the Institute of British Geographers 728.

42 Michele Carducci (n 2) 170 ff.

should first be measured, bearing in mind the tipping points that scientists have indicated with respect not only to climate stability, but to ES resilience, that is, the capacity of maintaining or recovering the equilibrium that allows life to prosper on our planet. Climate change is, in fact, one of the nine indicators of the Planetary Boundaries Framework, even if, together with biosphere integrity, both have been considered the two core indicators, through which the other boundaries operate.[43]

Moreover, the same concept of 'right' could appear inappropriate. The ecosphere, the ecosystems and non-human species do not have any claims to make to the legislator. They simply exist and follow the intrinsic rules of survival in their DNA and the interdependency paths that evolution has forged. How humanity represents itself inside this framework, either as an insider or an outsider, does not depend on Nature's claims, but on our own cultural understanding.

This analysis is complemented by the concept of 'emergent property',[44] which means that each level gains some additional characteristics from the layers below. Following Odum, emergent properties do not correspond to the sum of the characters of all inferior unities but are the product of their interrelationships.[45] As already stated in § 3, all the players in the game of life have different roles, but a hierarchy among the layers remains, and generates increasing complexity in the organization of living and non-living matter. From a legal point of view, this hierarchy is relevant when applying dispute resolution criteria to legal conflicts.

The ecological *Grundnorm* we have recognized obliges us to prohibit any action or omission that affects the safe operating space for humanity[46] (identified by the planetary boundaries framework or by the overcoming of the tipping points of the ES). This means that the balance of the ES should always prevail over the other legal subjects' rights. This same rule

43 Will Steffen and others, 'Planetary Boundaries: Guiding Human Development on a Changing Planet' (2015) 347 (6223) Science 736.

44 George W Salt, 'A Comment on the Use of the Term Emergent Property' (1972) 113 (1) The American Naturalist 145; see also Rom Harré, *The Philosophies of Science* (OUP 1985).

45 Eugene P Odum and Gary W Barrett, *Fundamentals of Ecology* (5th edn, Thomson 2004) 8.

46 Johan Rockström and others, 'A Safe Operating Space for Humanity' (2009) 461 Nature 472; Paulo Magalhães, 'Common Home As a Legal Construction Based on Science' in Silvia Bagni (ed), *How to Govern the Ecosystem?* (Dipartimento di Scienze giuridiche 2018).

was included in art. 1, § 7 of the Universal Declaration of Rights of Mother Earth[47] and corresponds in legal terms to the application of the '*in dubio pro natura*' principle, where 'Nature' is holistically interpreted as the eco-sphere.

Many scientific reports and studies have denounced that we have already crossed the safe operating space for humanity, at least in the two core indicators of climate change and biological integrity. Consequently, the '*in dubio pro natura*' criterion must be declined in two sub-principles: '*in dubio pro clima*' and '*in dubio pro conservatione*'. The latter was already recognized by the CITES with respect to biodiversity and in principle 5 of the ecosystem approach endorsed by the COP of the Convention on Biological Diversity (UNEP/CBD/COP/5/23). Biodiversity is the engine of evolution on the planet. Moreover, we are still unable to understand all the complex relationships and feed-back loops deriving from the interaction of all the levels of organization of the ES, so the precautionary principle should aim to justify not only the preference assigned to the protection of species from extinction, but, in general, the preference of the solution that guarantees the highest rate of biodiversity, even when not at risk of extinction.

If ecosphere stability is not endangered, to determine which competing right must prevail, we have to look at the status of the legal subjects involved, following the hierarchy of the living and non-living components of the ecosphere. Ecosystem stability must prevail over species and individual rights; and species existence must prevail over individual rights.

Only when the previous conditions are satisfied, should a safeguard clause in favour of human rights apply. The common condition of the vulnerability of all individuals and species when faced with a planetary ecological disaster justifies a restriction of the 'pro-homine' principle. But from a 'sympoietic' perspective, even when only human interests are in conflict, dispute resolution principles must be applied, taking into consideration the fact that human actions are never ecologically neutral and always co-create relationships with other forms of matter and energy. For this reason, proportionality should become 'eco-proportionality' (proposed by Winter) and the defence of the 'essential core' of human rights must

---

47 '(7) The rights of each being are limited by the rights of other beings and any conflict between their rights must be resolved in a way that maintains the integrity, balance and health of Mother Earth' (Universal Declaration of Rights of Mother Earth, World People's Conference on Climate Change and the Rights of Mother Earth).

always try to reach a reasonable balance with Nature's rights and preserve the fundamental right to life of non-human subjects.

8.2. Introducing Science-Based Processes of Democratic Decision-Making and the Ecological Analysis of Law

In the previous sub-paragraph, we have defended that 'sympoietic' heuristics requires an important discussion of modern legal categories. Additionally, it requires a reorganisation of legal procedures and deliberative bodies. By way of example, judging bodies should become multidisciplinary with equal discussion rights: involving not only judges, but ecologists, geologists, physicists, and so on. Their function should be not merely advisory but should make it possible to promote the ecological analysis of law in terms of consideration of the intertemporal consequences of human action on natural systems. Moreover, the reasons for the acts should not be exclusively legal but also scientific. This approach would favour a new 'holistic' episteme of a non-autopoietic kind.

In addition, a multidisciplinary perspective would make it possible to know the facts in their biophysical dimension and not only with regard to human interests. It would not be a matter of entrusting decisions 'to' scientists, but of deciding 'with' scientists in a dimension of equal discussion (precisely through the right of concurrent or dissident decision). Scientific knowledge allows us to understand how nature works and what its times are compared to the times of human action. In this way, the democratic method would also evolve as a method of knowledge of the complexity of reality and of discussion of the interdependencies between times of nature and human times.

The interpretation and application of the law should take into account the acquisitions of thermodynamics and biophysics on the times of functioning of the different spheres of nature. In this perspective, an 'ecological analysis of law' becomes opportune. This means assessing the effectiveness of the legal rules with regard both to their effects on human expectations, as already provided for in the economic analysis of the law, with its postulate of efficiency, and to the processes generated on the climate system, in terms of energy consumption (emergy and exergy) that conditions the determinant vectors of the emergency.[48]

It is interesting to note that this perspective of the ecological analysis of law and policy seems to emerge also in the European context on two fronts. The first is the new double constraint of 'do no significant harm' (DNSH) and compliance with the 'environmental objectives' as common denominators of any economic activity (the double constraint was introduced by European Regulation no. 2020/852). The second is the affirmation of the '*net-gain principle*' to give nature back more than it takes, established by the EU Biodiversity Strategy for 2030 (entitled 'Bringing nature back into our lives') and reiterated in other documents of the European Green Deal.

The principle of DNSH to the environmental objectives of the European Union implies the need not to irreversibly compromise the natural cycles of reproduction and equilibrium of the different spheres of the climate system.

The 'net gain' criterion suggests that economic action must not simply 'compensate' for any loss of biodiversity produced by its impacts, but, on the contrary, contribute to increasing biodiversity within the European Union.

9. *Conclusion*

In our research, we have proposed the 'Rights of Nature' approach as a legal paradigm justifying the representation of absent generations (past and future) through the juridification of the 'invisible', which we have indicated as nature in its twofold dimension, spatial and temporal. In fact, the ecological crisis we are facing can be tackled only if we recognize that the current timeline of human actions to combat climate change does not correspond to the temporal dimension of natural phenomena, such as the climate itself, or bio-geo-physical cycles, on which the stability of the ES depends. As human beings are part of the ES, they should live 'reconnected' with nature. This assumption produces many relevant consequences with respect to the issue of representing the absent. First of all, in the natural timescale, the borders between past, present and future generations fade. From an ecological point of view and accepting the integrity of the ES as a new *Grundnorm*, there are no qualitative differences, as far as the interests

48 Analisi ecologica del diritto <https://www.analisiecologicadeldiritto.it> accessed 7 July 2023.

of present and future generations are concerned. They converge on the same goal, and are interconnected and interdependent, not only intra- and inter-generation, but also intra- and inter-species.

So, theoretically speaking, the legal problem should no longer be one of representation, but of scientific knowledge, enabling us to choose the interests to be taken care of, having as a starting point the interconnectedness of all the components of the ES. As we have underlined in § 8.2, the processes of decision-making and enforcement of the law should be reshaped, giving voice and space to scientific findings. Responsible research and innovation should not only include ethical and methodological issues, but also ask itself 'how to care' in the definition of research topics[49]. This same path has been followed by the IPBES (Intergovernmental Science-Policy Platform on Biodiversity and Ecosystem Services) in its last Global Assessment Report on Biodiversity and Ecosystem Services. The IPBES was created in 2012 to provide policy-makers, the private sector and society at large, with scientifically credible assessments on the state of knowledge on the planet's biodiversity. In its last Report, the IPBES adopted an intercultural and inclusive approach, merging for the first time ever, data coming from scientific literature and from indigenous and local knowledge and practices, as our own approach has tried to suggest.

However, the relevance we recognize to science should not be misunderstood. We do not support technocracy: we advocate responsible democratic methods of decision-making.[50] This is coherent with the sympoietic heuristics described in § 6, and implies, as we have tried to show in § 7, a rediscovery of the relational approach to law and the reincorporation of the ethics of care in politics.

If, in theory, the representation issue could be considered as resolved, in practice we do not expect that the paradigm shift we propose could happen rapidly. If we come back to the IPBES Report mentioned above, and we move to the possible solutions, it suggests that, considering the current status of the planet in term of biodiversity and ecosystem services, the objective of a sustainable use of nature can be reached only by implementing a 'fundamental system-wide reorganization across technological,

---

49 Ângela Guimarães Pereira and Andrea Saltelli, 'Post-normal Institutional Identities: Quality Assurance, Reflexivity and Ethos of Care' (2017) 91 Futures 53, 59.

50 Sergio Messina, *Eco-democrazia. Per una fondazione ecologica del diritto e della politica* (Orthotes 2019).

economic and social factors, including paradigms, goals and values'.[51] In fact, the approaches for sustainability proposed in the Report[52] correspond to a large extent to our own definition of the 'rights of Nature' approach. Specifically, in the legal field, from a sympoietic (co-creative) perspective, we have invited legal scholars to reshape the law on the basis of new ecological and relational values.[53]

In the 'rights of Nature' approach, the representation issue is solved with the recognition of legal personhood and standing to natural elements, the implementation of new rules of conflict resolution, the incorporation of the ecological analysis of law and the creation of eco-democratic decision-making processes, as we have proposed in § 8.

Our approach to the research topic of representation of the absent has transformed the research question from a matter of procedure to a substantive question about the fundamental values on which our human society must be founded. Our hope is that this debate will attract more and more researchers, eventually involving the whole community.

---

51 IPBES, *Summary for policymakers of the global assessment report on biodiversity and ecosystem services of the Intergovernmental Science-Policy Platform on Biodiversity and Ecosystem Services* (IPBES Secretariat 2019) 14.

52 Enabling integrative governance to ensure policy coherence and effectiveness; Promoting inclusive governance approaches through stakeholder engagement and the inclusion of indigenous peoples and local communities to ensure equity and participation; Practicing informed governance for nature and nature's contributions to people; Promoting adaptive governance and management (Global Assessment Report to achieve sustainability (IPBES 2019) 44).

53 Chan and others (n 1).

19. The Recognition of the Rights of Nature in Latin America – The Lost Linkage with the Rights of Future Generations

Luis A. López Zamora[*]

Abstract: *This Chapter involves a study on the Rights of Nature (RoN). RoN comprehends the establishment of a set of specific rights, as well as the recognition of a new legal subject (nature) at the national and at the international levels. For example, on the international level, various international forums slowly envision nature as a potential right holder. Even though this has yet to transpire in formulating and adopting an international treaty establishing that, the language of the RoN now commonly appears in different international soft law documents. Latin American jurisdictions have served as inspiration for those documents, since the recognition of RoN in the region has been considered as paradigmatic. However, the regional recognition of nature's rights has not been free of ambiguities, especially when it is considered together with the recognition of another new legal entity: the Future Generations. The interactions between those new right holders in Latin America have been scarcely studied; this contribution seeks to fill that gap.*

1. Introduction

Recognising the Rights of Nature (RoN) is part of a global trend, in which Latin America has been considered a success story. Specialised scholarship highlights that in some Latin-American jurisdictions, the recognition of RoN has been enshrined at the constitutional level or, alternatively, proclaimed by constitutional courts or tribunals. According to the scholarship on the subject, such recognition entailed a breakthrough in protecting nature as it extends legal protection to the environment for its intrinsic value.[1] The purpose of this Chapter is to subject that statement to critical analysis. Unlike much of the regional and international scholarship that has studied the rise of the RoN in Latin America, we will not assume that such recognition has occurred innocuously or that – in any case – it

* Luis A. López Zamora is a Research Fellow at the Max Planck Institute Luxembourg for Procedural Law and a Doctoral Researcher at Christian-Albrechts-Universität zu Kiel (Germany).

1 The terms 'nature' and 'environment' are different. While 'environment' refers to nature's attributes that human beings need to live, 'nature' also includes elements that, without directly benefiting humans, are part of the integrated cycles where living and non-living organisms develop and that make life possible. Although this differentiation can have philosophical significance (and even legal consequences) in this contribution we will use 'environment' and 'nature' synonymously.

has not caused complications in the legal systems where RoN have been incorporated.

To demonstrate our position, we will take into account two tendencies we have observed during the course of this research:

(a) Recognition of the RoN in the region has been executed without a detailed explanation of why this process was necessary. Some of the questions that remain unanswered are: Was the recognition of the RoN vital, bearing in mind that there were already legal frameworks in place in the Region protecting the environment? Was the recognition of the RoN warranted, bearing in mind the cost of implementing a new set of rights?
(b) It is a fact that that recognition usually occurs in connection with the implementation of the rights of future generations. It should be borne in mind that in both scholarship and adjudication these two sets of rights have been considered together as if they were part of a similar phenomenon. Indeed, the proclamation in the region of the RoN is usually followed by references to the rights of future generations. Are those two sets of rights connected? Furthermore, if they are connected, how does their normative interplay transpire?

To find answers to these questions, we will consider the legal reasons behind the recognition of the RoN in Latin America. This issue has scarcely been explored. That exercise will allow us to observe that the primary reasons for recognising the RoN have been procedural-based. For example, the proclamation of the RoN leads to the recognition of nature as an entity capable of holding rights – therefore – as a legal subject. As a result, nature has access to proceedings that are capable of protecting its interests, which were previously non-existent. Some of these proceedings are constitutional remedies which can protect nature directly. Another example of the procedural reasons behind the recognition of the RoN is that through those rights, the rights of future generations can be made effective. To explain this, it is important to bear in mind that the implementation of the rights of future generations faces theoretical and practical limitations. For example, in a dispute settlement context it is difficult to concretely determine the rights or interests of future generations. Without that determination, these rights and interests are merely rhetorical recognitions with no practical application.

After reviewing the procedural reasons for the recognition of the RoN mentioned above, we have found that in both cases the RoN have been formulated directly or indirectly in connection with the rights of future generations and -in some cases- with the sole purpose of making the implementation of those rights possible. This suggests that the recognition of the RoN in Latin America has not been based on the value nature possesses in and of itself, but for the service it can provide to human interests. We will consider the inconsistency of that outcome, and the theoretical incompatibility between the Latin American practice in the matter and the reasons why the RoN were formulated in scholarship in the 1970s.

To explore all these points, we will begin (in Section 2 of this Chapter) by describing the emergence of the RoN in law and the particular theoretical discourse that promoted its recognition. At the same time, we will consider a similar trend that led ultimately to recognising the rights of future generations. In Section 3, we will describe the emergence of the RoN in Latin America and the considerations that scholarship has given to that process. With that in mind, we will revise the antecedents that allowed nature's personhood to be recognised in the region, such as the relativisation of humans' monopoly on the legal subjectivity given the recognition – to a certain extent – of animals' rights. In Section 4 we will review the recognition of the RoN in the jurisdictions of Ecuador, Bolivia and Colombia, and inquire into the reasons that led to that process. This exercise will allow us to see that the recognition of the RoN and its utilisation for procedural reasons is due to the lack of theoretical differentiation between the interests protected through the RoN and those protected through the rights of future generations. We will then explain how that lack of differentiation can have theoretical and practical implications.

2. Setting the Stage: The Rights of Nature and the Rights of Future Generations as Distinctive Discourses

The argument that nature can hold rights appeared in legal discourse 40 years ago.[2] The discussion centered on analysing the feasibility of the existence of those 'rights' on philosophical and legal grounds. An example

2 Nonetheless, this had some precedents. In this regard, Kauffman and Martin recalled that '[w]hile RoN law only emerged recently, RoN's normative foundations have developed over centuries in both Western and non-Western cultures.' See: Craig M Kauffman and Pamela L Martin, 'Constructing Rights of Nature Norms in the US, Ecuador and New Zealand' (2018) 18 Global Environmental Politics 47.

of this was the attempts to articulate the subjectivity of nature (or the subjectivity of sections of nature such as rivers, seas, lakes and land among others) in the 1970s. In the case of forests, that defense was made in the writings of Professor Christopher D Stone.[3] His thesis influenced legal scholarship in the United States, igniting a debate about the feasibility of recognising the RoN in the legal sphere. An important aspect of Stone's thesis is that it was a first defense of the existence of the RoN using normative language and not merely arguments based on environmentalist ethics. This made it possible to consider broadening the notion of legal personhood and, as a result, the reformulation of rights theory.[4]

After that first impulse, the existence of the RoN was received – albeit tenuously – in some individual votes of judges from the United States.[5] Thus, it became necessary not only to defend the existence of the RoN but also to clarify their content. Environmental ethics,[6] which is the discipline that influenced the formulation of the RoN in law, had already proposed three possible aspects of those rights by proposing that nature could have '(...) the right to exist, the right to continue to exist, and the right, if degraded, to be restored.'[7] These postulates were later transferred to the legal field.

---

3 Christopher D Stone, 'Should Trees Have Standing? – Towards Legal Rights for Natural Objects' (1972) 45 Southern California Law Review 450.

4 Stone mentions how in ancient times, children, women, enslaved people, or people with disabilities, hardly had the status of subjects of law; and that for their full recognition it was necessary to expand the notion of legal personhood. He also recalled that the next step in that direction was the recognition of the personhood of nonhuman entities, like corporations or companies. His statements are an accurate account of the expansion of legal subjectivity in the history of law. However, there is an element that is not sufficiently highlighted: the fact that whether in the case of children, women, enslaved people, or corporations, the legal interests protected by the Law always involved human beings. In the case of corporations, the presence of human interests is the reason for creating such fictions. This is fundamental since – as we shall see in subsequent sections of this Chapter – it is the human interest which seems to be behind the recognition of nature's personhood in Latin America.

5 For example, in the dissenting opinion of Justice Douglas, in the case Sierra Club v Morton (Secretary of the Interior), Certiotari to the United States Court of Appeals for the Ninth Circuit, No 70–34, 19 April 1972.

6 Andrew Brennan and Norva Y S Lo, 'Environmental Ethics' in Edward N Zalta (ed), *The Standford Encyclopedia of Philosophy* (Summer 2022 Edition) <https://perma.cc/U85H-D2VJ>. See, also: Roderick Nash, *The Rights of Nature: A History of Environmental Ethics* (University of Wisconsin Press 1989).

7 Olivier A Houck, 'Noah's Second Voyage: The Rights of Nature as Law' (2017) 31 Tulane Environmental Law Journal 31.

An example of the reception of those propositions in law is Article 4 of the Ugandan National Environmental Act of 2019, which states: '(...) nature has the right to exist, persist, maintain and regenerate its vital cycles (...).'[8] This also happened in the United States with the enactment of the Lake Erie Bill of Rights which stated that the lake had the right '(...) to exist, flourish, and naturally evolve.'[9] However, the most striking examples of the reception of the content of the RoN come from Latin America where that language was enshrined in provisions at the highest hierarchical level such as the Constitution of Ecuador. The reasons why the language of the RoN gained traction in this part of the world come down to several factors. One factor was the regional trend of expanding the theory on legal personality (which happened with the recognition – to a certain extent – of the legal subjectivity of certain animals). Another factor was that the language around RoN offered regional political parties the necessary legitimacy to implement social reforms by differentiating themselves from previous political models.

Be that as it may, the fact that Latin America is where the RoN have been most clearly recognised, and where the RoN have been codified more precisely (by explicitly pronouncing their content), does not mean that the process has been straightforward (this will be discussed in Section 4 of this contribution).

It is important to point out at this juncture that at the same time as the discussions on the RoN unfolded, the debate on the existence of obligations of current generations *vis-à-vis* future generations also arose in law. The theoretical problem linked to the acceptance of obligations towards future generations revolves around the feasibility of those obligations being able to operate in a legal system. That limitation results from the fact that those obligations would need to be fulfilled to benefit a group that may or may not exist in the future, and whose interests are not determinable in the present.[10] The task of defining who makes-up that group and their legal interests are enormous. Furthermore, the existence of obligations of one generation with respect to another forces the formulation of those obligations in a way that speaks of an entity capable of holding rights that

8 Mentioned in the Report of the Secretary-General, Harmony with Nature, Seventy-Fourth Session, Sustainable Development, A/74/236, 26 July 2019, para. 33.

9 ibid., para. 35.

10 See: Wilfread Beckerman and Joanna Pasek, *Justice, Posterity and the Environment* (OUP 2001) 11–28.

can be claimed. That leads to asserting the existence of a new subject of law (future generations).[11]

Therefore, the discussion regarding the recognition of nature's personhood runs parallel with the debate on the existence of the rights of future generations.[12] In fact, in Latin America, the discourse that defends the existence of the obligations of current generations *vis-à-vis* future generations cannot be separated from the RoN's discourse since – as we shall see below – both were formulated in a close and even intermingled manner (Section 4.1). One of the reasons for this is that the rights of future generations were expressed in such a way as to be placed close to the RoN.[13] This is because realising both notions required the expansion of the theory of legal subjectivity, and because both are linked to environmental matters.

However, it is crucial to bear in mind that both notions are still different. Both have particular theories supporting their existence and – thereupon – they legally materialize with different scopes of protection. For example, the rights of future generations do not aim at protecting only future generations' interests on environmental matters. The rights of future generations can encompass the protection of the interests of that group in other areas.[14] On the other hand, both of these new 'typologies of rights' adopt different

11 Regarding this discussion, see: Hendrik Philip Visser't Hooft, 'The Theory of Justice and our Obligations Towards Future Generations' (1987) 73 *Archiv für Rechts- und Sozialphilosophie* 30 and Bruce R Reichenbach, 'On Obligations to Future Generations' (1992) 6(2) Public Affairs Quarterly 207.

12 An example of this is the Constitution of Norway, which states that '(...) [n]atural resources should be managed on the basis of comprehensive long-term considerations whereby this right will be safeguarded for future generations as well.' See: Axel Gosseries, 'On Future Generations' Future Rights' (2008) 16(4) Journal of Political Philosophy 446, 448. In the case of Latin America, the Constitution of Bolivia is to be highlighted. For some authors, that Constitution recognizes the RoN while recognizing – at the same time – in its Article 33, the rights of future generations. Article 33 of that instrument asserts that people have the right to a healthy, protected, and balanced environment, adding that its exercise should allow individuals and communities of present and future generations to develop in a normal and permanent way (Constitution of Bolivia of 2009). The parallel development of the right of future generations (to a healthy environment), with the RoN is not a coincidence; both appeared when environmental concerns acquired global prominence.

13 On both topics, see: Nuria Belloso Martin, *El Debate sobre la Tutela Institucional: Generaciones Futuras y Derechos de la Naturaleza* (Universidad de Alcalá 2018).

14 An example of this can be seen in the UNESCO Declaration on the Responsibility of the Present Generations Towards Future Generations of 1997. In that instrument, there is a recognition of future generations' interests to freedom of choice, human genome and biodiversity, cultural diversity, and cultural heritage. See: Declaration on

strategies when defending their existence, as each of them is supported by different philosophical theories. In fact, both notions respond to a different view on the paradigm shift around the relationship of human beings with nature; therefore, they are constructed differently in normative language.

To understand this claim, it is necessary to keep in mind that in the field of environmental ethics, the view that human beings are the only entity of value, and nature only an object of exploitation, is called the anthropocentric approach. There are also non-anthropocentric views, which include the biocentric and ecocentric approaches. RoN and the rights of future generations are expressions of the last two approaches respectively and – to some extent – use them as justification for their legal crystallisation.[15] Biocentrism refers to the protection of living beings for their intrinsic value. Part of this theory defends the attitude that not only humans but also other beings (especially sentient beings) require protection,[16] which leads to the recognition of animal rights. Furthermore, since that theory disconnects the legal protection to be afforded from the immediate benefits individuals would receive, it served as a basis for recognising environmental rights for those who are not yet born. On the other hand, ecocentrism argues that living beings and natural processes are worthy of protection[17], which served as the basis for the formulation of the RoN.

Over the years, the philosophical approaches that forged the new relationship between human beings and nature achieved greater clarity. In contrast, legal scholarship faced complications in achieving similar results.[18] The reason for this is that the incorporation of the RoN and the rights of future generations in law is an intricate exercise. For example, legal scholarship would need to incorporate both new sets of rights in a way that continued to respect the coherence of how law has traditionally worked. To achieve that, the legal scholarship would need to explain why it is indis-

---

the Responsibilities of the Present Generations towards Future Generations, Adopted by the General Conference of UNESCO, 29th Session, 12 November 1997.

15 Although these acronyms cause certain problems, we use them for practical reasons. See: Lars Samuelsson, 'At the Center of What? A Critical Note on the Centrism-Terminology in Environmental Ethics' (2013) 22(5) Environmental Values 627.

16 See: Eduardo Gudynas, 'La Senda Biocéntrica: Valores Intrínsecos, Derechos de la Naturaleza y Justicia Ecológica' (2010) 13 Tabula Rasa 45, 50.

17 See: Francesco Allegri, 'Exploring Non-Anthropocentric Paradigms' (2019) 7 Relations: Beyond Anthropocentrism 7, 9.

18 María V Berros, 'Challenges for the Implementation of the Rights of Nature. Ecuador and Bolivia as the First Instances of an Expanding Movement' (2021) 48(3) Latin American Perspectives 192, 196.

pensable to recognise new subjects of law and also give concrete content to their emerging rights. Finally, the recognition of those subjectivities would need to be carried out in such a way as to respect the ethical reasons that propelled their recognition in the first place. Although this may not generate significant complexities at first glance, it could create several strains should any consequences of their recognition face adjudication.[19]

The Latin American experience in the matter is an example. The experience gained in the region shows that it is insufficient to simply recognise nature's and future generations' subjectivity for their rights to harmonise in the legal systems where they are incorporated. That means it is important to consider that those new subjects of law and their associated 'rights' have the potential of clashing with several institutions already in place. This has led some authors to consider that

> (...) experience with rights for nature has shown that their conceptual deficiencies have led to confusion, inefficiency, and arbitrariness,without any obvious environmental benefit. Multiple litigants pursuing conflicting goals have come to court claiming to speak on behalf of nature's rights, forcing courts not only to balance heterogeneous effects of policy choices but also to arbitrate between alternative plausible representational claims. Where nature's rights have been litigated, courts have struggled mightily to make sense of the inquiry before them.[20]

In this contribution, we will refer primarily to the recognition of RoN. Therefore, our focus will be on them and only incidentally on the problems linked to the rights of future generations. Thus, the theory behind the recognition of the right of future generations will not be dealt with in depth.

Ultimately, our goal is to elucidate the RoN through posing specific questions. For example, how should the defense of RoN be conducted from a procedural point of view? Who is entitled to initiate proceedings to defend those rights? What type of proceedings are viable for the protection of the RoN? Why are existing proceedings (established by administrative law or based on the protection of diffuse rights) insufficient to protect the environment? Moreover, why is it that the recognition of future generations' rights

19 In the Latin American adjudicative practice, those two sets of rights have faced challenges. That has made evident that their recognition, albeit in principle novel, requires adjustment or – at least – clarification.

20 Mauricio Guim and Michael A Livermore, 'Where Nature's Rights Go Wrong' (2021) 107(7) Virginia Law Review 1347, 1352.

to a healthy environment is not enough to protect nature? Furthermore, if nature's subjectivity is accepted, should its rights be defended by constitutional means – for example – through a writ of amparo (*accion de amparo* – action of protection)? These questions are fundamental and will be analysed by considering the practice and the legal instruments developed in Latin America.

The strategy we will follow will be to review the provisions and/or jurisdictional decisions adopted in three Latin American States: Ecuador, Colombia and Bolivia. In doing so, we will try to find answers to the above questions.

3. *The Emergence of the Rights of Nature in Latin America and the Scholarship Explaining that Trend*

In this section, we will revise the Latin American scholarship that deals with the recognition of the RoN. We will first describe the process by which the theory of legal personality has expanded in the region. Then, we will give an overview of the legislative techniques used to recognise the RoN, and finally, we will examine the regional adjudicatory practice highlighting the way academia has understood that process.

3.1. On the Dilution of the Monopoly of Human Legal Subjectivity in the Region

The theory of legal personality or theory of legal subjectivity enquires about who should be recognised as an entity capable of holding rights and duties in a specific legal framework. In this contribution, we will deal with that theory. The reason for this is that when the RoN and the rights of the future generations are seriously considered, they involve the recognition of legal entities entitled to a new set of rights; however, that exercise is one that faces complications. For example, recognising new subjects in law (like nature or the future generations) clashes with the classical theory of legal personhood. Regarding future generations, their incorporation implies the recognition of rights belonging to non-existing humans, creating several theoretical problems. For them to work, it will be necessary – as a first step – to determine who are or who could be considered part of those groups; an answer that is still much debated. On the other hand, their recognition would need to be followed by giving content to their rights using today's standards, a job that could end up in the protection of interests that could turn out to be irrelevant for the future generations when they exist.

The RoN generate their own complications in that they allude to rights that are held by 'nonhumans.' How can law recognise rights belonging to nonhuman entities? Is the recognition of nature's subjectivity (through the RoN) based on technical legal reasons or does it happen for rhetorical reasons?

Furthermore, before incorporating those new legal entities into a particular legal system, it would be necessary to demonstrate that the classification of legal personhood recognised in law up until now is insufficient to protect one or more relevant societal interests.[21] And connected to that, any attempt to recognise any new legal entities would face the fact that, since the theory of subjectivity was framed in modern terms several institutions have been built on the presumption that (existing) human beings are directly or indirectly the only ones holding rights and duties in a legal system. As a result, expanding who or what can be considered a subject of law ends up affecting a normative system in its entirely.

For those reasons, it seems fair to say that with the inclusion of nature and future generations in certain legal systems, the traditional theory of legal personhood is progressively being eroded. Moreover, some would argue that the recognition of those new legal subjectivities exerts adverse effects on the predictability of the legal systems where they have been included, since who or what may or may not hold subjective rights becomes relativised.

21 These latter criticisms in turn face the fact that law is a human construction, and therefore humans will determine what law should encompass. Thus, humans decide who should be considered a rights holder. As Tur notes, '(i)f legal personality is the legal capacity to bear rights and duties, then it is itself an artificial creation of the law, and anything or anyone can be a legal person.' See: Richard Tur, 'The "Person" in Law' in Arthur Peacocke and Grant Gillet (eds), *Persons and Personality. A Contemporary Inquiry* (Blackwell 1988) 121. For a contrary position, see: Visa Kurki, *A Theory of Legal Personhood* (OUP 2019) 127–152. This reasoning is behind some of the decisions expanding the theory of legal personhood in Latin America. Examples of this, can be seen in the judgments recognising that certain animals have the status of subjects of law (i.e., the case of the chimpanzee Cecilia – Chimpanzee Cecilia case (2016) Tercer Juzgado de Garantías, Poder Judicial de Mendoza, P-72.254/15, (2016), and the orangutan Sandra – Orangutan Sandra case (2015) Poder Judicial, Ciudad de Buenos Aires, A2174–2015/0 (2015).

Bearing this in mind, we ask: why have RoN gained acceptance in some Latin American jurisdictions even though this acceptance could produce complications? We believe that the reasons for this can be better understood when it is recalled that in Latin America there are some precedents regarding the expansion of the theory of legal personhood. As a result, the expansion of legal subjectivity in the region by recognising nature's and the future generations' personhood has not been considered taboo. One should remember that legal personhood saw its expansion in law with the full recognition of children, women and the disabled, as well as with the recognition of legal entities and the recognition of States as sovereign entities. However, it also expanded (in more recent times), due to the impulse exerted by the recognition – up to certain limits – of animals' subjectivity. This tendency gained strength with the emergence of sectors defending animal welfare. Eventually, animals will start benefiting from protections that came close to some benefits humans enjoy as rights.[22] Those normative protections (whether recognising subjectivity or not to animals) were developed in the United States[23] and in Europe, generating doctrinal debates. In Latin America, a similar trend occurred; however, due to the region's need to solve problems speedily (because of the crises it constantly faces), those innovations were not backed up by scholarship. Be that as it may, it has been in Latin America where the recognition of animals' subjectivity has been more strikingly enunciated.[24] This helped the

22 However, whether such protection implies rights in their favour and therefore whether they can be subjects of law remains a matter of scholarly debate. For example, this issue is being analysed by the Max Planck Institute for Comparative Public Law and International Law <https://www.mpil.de/en/pub/research/areas/public-international-law/global-animal-law.cfm#head> accessed 28 September 2022. For an introduction to the matter, see: Anne Peters (ed), *Studies in Global Animal Law* (Springer 2020) and Saskia Stucki and Visa Kurki, 'Animal Rights' in M Sellers and M Kirste (eds), *Encyclopedia of the Philosophy of Law and Social Philosophy* (Springer 2020).

23 In the United States, legal actions (i.e., *habeas corpus*) have been filed with the intention to free captive apes. The results, however, were not successful. Nonetheless, the position of some judges showed a desire to protect those animals even when it was no possible due to procedural limitations. Those limitations arose since the proceeding used to air those claims required that the beneficiaries had legal subjectivity. On this, see: David Boyd, *Los Derechos de la Naturaleza. Una Revolución Legal que Podría Salvar el Mundo* (Santiago Vallejo trar, Heinrich Boll Stiftung 2020) 61–66.

24 See: Anne Peters, 'Rights of Human and Nonhuman Animals: Complementing the Universal Declaration on Human Rights' (2018) 112 AJIL Unbound 355, 356-ff.

regional judiciary to see that the classical theory of legal personality was not immovable, leading to further relaxations.[25].

An example of this happened in Argentina, where the legislation applicable to security dogs provided that after a certain time of service they could retire, receiving housing, health care and food at the expense of the State. The same happened with emotional support dogs, which were granted working conditions, schedules and vacations.[26] These advances were used to issue a ruling on the matter in Argentina. In that case, the plaintiffs asked the Court to grant a *habeas corpus* in favour of the orangutan Sandra. After some deliberation, the judiciary decided to grant the *habeas corpus*.[27] This was endorsed by the Judiciary of Buenos Aires,[28] which recognised '(...) the orangutan Sandra as a subject of law'.[29] Some Colombian courts

25 A former judge of the Inter-American Court of Human Rights, Zaffaroni, recalls that in the case of criminal law, animals have had an ambiguous position vis-à-vis the law. An example is the 'animal trials' where, among other curiosities, the confession of a sow was obtained. Zaffaroni's comments remind us that the theory of personhood, where the human being is the only subject of law, was formulated more recently than we thought. See: Eugenio Zaffaroni, 'La Pachamama y el Humano' in Alberto Acosta and Esperanza Martínez (eds), *La Naturaleza con Derecho. De la Filosofía a la Política* (Universidad Politécnica Salesiana 2011) 30.

26 Mentioned by: Alejandra Molano Bustacara and Diana Murcia, 'Animales y Naturaleza como Nuevos Sujetos de Derecho: Un Estudio de las Decisiones Judiciales más Relevantes en Colombia' (2018) 13(1) Revista Colombiana de Bioética 82, 93. Regarding the judgment of the ape Sandra, see: Maria V Berros, 'Breve Contextualización de la Reciente Sentencia sobre el Habeas Corpus en Favor de la Orangutana Sandra: Entre Ética Animal y Derecho' (2015) 41 Revista de Derecho Ambiental 154.

27 Orangután Sandra case (2014) Cámara de Casación Penal, Sala II, CC-C688321/2014/CFCI (2015).

28 Orangután Sandra case (2015) Poder Judicial, Ciudad de Buenos Aires, A2174–2015/0 (2015).

29 ibid., this trend was ratified during a proceeding initiated on behalf of a chimpanzee. In that case, the Mendoza Judiciary granted a *habeas corpus* to protect a chimpanzee and recognised thereto that it was undeniable that great apes (among which chimpanzees were included) were sentient beings and that therefore they could be considered nonhuman subjects of law. See: Chimpanzee Cecilia case (2016) Tercer Juzgado de Garantías, Poder Judicial de Mendoza, P-72.254/15, (2016) 30. In that decision, the tribunal added that great apes should be considered subjects of law, with legal capacity, but factually incompetent (ibid., 40). Regional scholarship has echoed the decisions taken by the Argentinian tribunals. See: Raúl Campusano Droguett, 'Sentencia de Alto Tribunal que Abre la Posibilidad de Reconocer Derechos a Animales de Acuerdo con Doctrina de Derecho Internacional' (2017) 36 Actualidad Jurídica 423; María Carman and María Valeria Berros, 'Ser o no Ser un Simio con Derechos' (2018) 14(3) Revista Direito GV 1139; Daniel J García López, 'Has de Tener un Cuerpo que Mostrar: El Grado Cero de los Derechos Humanos' (2018) 59 Isegoría 663; Visa

faced similar cases. One of those cases involved a request for a *habeas corpus* in favour of Chucho the bear.[30] At first instance, the *habeas corpus* was denied; however, in the second instance, it was granted.[31] The case reached the Constitutional Court of Colombia where the *habeas corpus* was overturned.[32]

In Latin America, it can be said that the recognition of animal 'rights' is still in the making; however, such progress has helped to relativise the traditional theory of legal personality. It is in this context that the recognition of RoN took place.

3.2. The Recognition of the Rights of Nature

In Latin America, the RoN have been recognised through legislation and jurisprudence.

3.2.1. The Case of Ecuador

The first legislative step to recognise the RoN happened in the Constitution of Ecuador of 2008 (currently in force). Article 71 of that instrument states that nature has the right to its existence and to the maintenance and regeneration of its vital cycles. In addition, Article 72 states that nature has the right to be restored. If those provisions seem equivocal on the establishment of the RoN, this is cleared up by Title II Chapter VII of the Constitution of Ecuador where the rights enunciated in Articles 71 and 72 are labeled as RoN. This is also confirmed by Article 10. That provision states that '(n)ature will be subject to those rights recognised by the Con-

---

Kurki, 'Legal Personhood and Animal Rights' (2021) 11(1) Journal of Animal Ethics 47, and Juan Camilo Herrera and Saskia Stucki, 'Habea(r)s Corpus: Some Thoughts on the Role of Habeas Corpus in the Evolution of Animal Rights' (*IConnect Blog*, 4 November 2017) <https://perma.cc/6FXY-M2ZT>.

30 For an analysis of this case, see: Macarena Montes Franceschini, 'Legal Personhood: The Case of Chucho the Andean Bear' (2021) 11(1) Journal of Animal Ethics 36.

31 See: Chucho the Bear case (2017) Sala de Casación Civil y Agraria, AHC4806-2017 – Radicación No 17001-22-13-000-2017-00468-02 (2017).

32 Insofar as the Court considered that, that would result in a breach of the right to due process as it would amount to using a manifestly inconsistent proceeding. See: Chucho the Bear case (2020) Constitutional Court of Colombia, SU016/20 (2020).

stitution'.[33] Then the remaining question is whether that recognition was only rhetorical or if it indeed intended to establish actionable rights. The Constitution of Ecuador opted for the latter option, insofar as the RoN in that jurisdiction can be protected through an action for protection and precautionary measures.[34]

Latin American scholarship highlighted the novelty of recognising the RoN at the constitutional level in Ecuador. That scholarship emphasised that the monopoly held by humans regarding who should be considered subjects of law ended up being relativised. Contrarily, the regional scholarship that criticised that recognition repeated the doubts cast in other parts of the world regarding the recognition of the RoN. For example, it was pointed out that that recognition would imply breaking the 'rights-obligations' structure every subject of law has to face. This is because nature cannot have nor make any obligation effective, and because it cannot enforce its rights. Ecuadorian scholarship has offered convincing counter-arguments to those critics, and has[35] highlighted that the recognition of those rights was intended to leave behind the anthropocentric view of the relationship of human beings with nature. According to those views, the recognition of the RoN was justified by giving relevance to the indigenous vision of the relationship with nature, which was made possible thanks to the incorporation in the Constitution of notions such as the *Pacha Mama*

33 Constitution of Ecuador of 2008, Title II Chapter VII.

34 It must be borne in mind that although the Constitution of Ecuador mentions who can request protection for nature (art 71) it does not expressly indicate the avenues that can be activated to that end. The Ecuadorian doctrine agrees that the writ of *amparo* (action of protection proceeding) would be the suitable and appropriate way to do so. The Ecuadorian jurisprudence has endorsed this. In this regard, the Loja Provincial Court of Justice (LPCJ) in the Vilcabamba River case (Vilcabamba River case (2011) Provincial Court of Justice of Loja (Criminal Chamber), 11121–2011–0010 (2011) stated that the action for protection proceeding was the only suitable and effective way to put an end to the damage done to nature. In addition to that, precautionary measures have been granted for the protection of the rights of nature, for example in the Galapagos Islands' case. See: Rene Patricio Bedón Garzón, 'Aplicación de los Derechos de la Naturaleza en Ecuador' (2018) 14(28) Veredas do Dereito 13.

35 See: Ramiro Ávila Santamaría, 'El Derecho de la Naturaleza: Fundamentos' in Acosta and Martínez (n 25); Diana Murcia Riaño, *La Naturaleza con Derechos. Un Recorrido por el Derecho Internacional de los Derechos Humanos, del Ambiente y del Desarrollo* (Instituto del Estudios Ecologistas del Tercer Mundo 2012); Edwin Cruz Rodríguez, 'Derechos de la Naturaleza, Descolonización e Interculturalidad. Acerca del Caso Ecuatoriano' (2014) 31 Verba Iuris 15.

or the *Sumak Kawsay*.[36] However, those academics have offered little or no account of the practical implications of the recognition of the RoN in the Ecuadorian legal system. As a result, several questions have remained unanswered. For example: How should a court decide when the protection of the RoN comes at the expense of the protection of the rights of individuals? Furthermore: How should an Ecuadorian court decide when a dispute involves the clash of the RoN with the rights of future generations[37] (a situation that cannot be ruled out given the recognition of the rights of future generations in Articles 317 and 395 of the Ecuadorian Constitution)?[38]

3.2.2. The Case of Bolivia

Bolivia is the second State where the RoN were 'incorporated'. However, the Constitution of Bolivia of 2009 (currently in force) did not include them in its text. What was included in that instrument is the notion of *Buen Vivir – Vivir Bien* ('Good Living' – 'Live Well').[39] That concept has

36 See: Daniel E Bonilla Maldonado, 'El Constitucionalismo Radical Ambiental y la Diversidad Cultural en América Latina. Los Derechos de la Naturaleza y el Buen Vivir en Ecuador y Bolivia' (2019) 42 Revista Derecho del Estado 3; Edwin Cruz Rodríguez, 'Del Derecho Ambiental a los Derechos de la Naturaleza: Sobre la Necesidad del Diálogo Intercultural' (2013) 11(1) Jurídicas 95.

37 This can happen because the expansion of the theory of legal personhood affects the legal system as a whole. Furthermore, since several legal institutions are already in place based on the conviction that human beings are the sole subjects of the legal order, that situation is able to create tension. Then the inclusion of the RoN forces a systematic review of the existing legal institutions in the legal orders that have included nature's subjectivity. The regional scholarship has given little thought to the matter; however, some authors noticed the need to harmonise their constitutional provisions while including the RoN. In this last regard, see: Carla Cárdenas, 'Los Derechos de la Naturaleza y la Constitución en el Ecuador. Interrogantes sin Respuesta' (2009) 15 Revista de Bioética y Derecho 24.

38 Constitution of Ecuador of 2008, art 317: 'Nonrenewable natural resources are part of the unalienable heritage of the State and are not subject to a statute of limitations. In the management of these resources, the State shall give priority to responsibility between generations, the conservation of nature, the charging of royalties or other non-tax contributions and corporate shares; and shall minimize the negative impacts of an environmental, cultural, social and economic nature.'

39 Article 8.1 of the Constitution of Bolivia states: 'The State adopts and promotes the following as ethical, moral principles of the plural society: ama qhilla, ama llulla, ama suwa (do not be lazy, do not be a liar or a thief), suma qamaña (live well), ñandereko (live harmoniously), teko kavi (good life), ivi maraei (land without evil) and qhapaj ñan (noble path or life).'

environmental implications and is conceptually similar to the notion of *Sumak Kawsay*[40], which was enshrined in the Constitution of Ecuador and helped in the recognition of the RoN in that jurisdiction. For some authors that parallelism would make it possible to conclude that the RoN were recognised in Bolivia.[41] However, as Gudynas mentions, although the mandate of Good Living was included in the Bolivian Constitution, neither nature nor the *Pachamama* were recognised as subjects of rights there.[42] To the contrary, some articles of the Bolivian Constitution mandate the State with achieving the industrialisation of nature. Attempts were made to correct that public policy with the issuance of two infra-constitutional provisions.

Consequently, on 21 December 2010, the Bolivian Legislative Assembly enacted Law No. 071 (Law of the Rights of Mother Earth).[43] However, the language used to structure that norm was not clear. Scholarship considers that issuing this norm implied the establishment of the RoN in Bolivia; nonetheless, such a statement must be taken with caution. Article 1 (object of the law) indicates that that instrument has '(...) the purpose of recognizing the rights of Mother Earth, as well as the obligations and duties of the State (...)'.[44] Mother Earth is defined as a dynamic living system made up of the indivisible community of all living beings.[45] That definition points to the notion of nature, so up until that moment it was reasonable to conclude that Law No. 071 intended to regulate the RoN. However, a doubt remained:

40 Article 14 of the Constitution of Ecuador states: 'The right of the population to live in a healthy and ecologically balanced environment that guarantees sustainability and the good way of living (sumak kawsay), is recognized.' For its part, Article 275 states that: 'The development structure is the organized, sustainable and dynamic group of economic, political, socio-cultural and environmental systems which underpin the achievement of the good way of living (sumak kawsay). The State shall plan the development of the country to assure the exercise of rights, the achievement of the objectives of the development structure and the principles enshrined in the Constitution. Planning shall aspire to social and territorial equity, promote cooperation, and be participatory, decentralized, deconcentrated and transparent.'

41 See: Fernando Huanacuni, 'Los Derechos de la Madre Tierra' (2016) 3(4) Revista Jurídica Derecho 157, 166. From other latitudes, see: Cletus G Barié, 'Nuevas Narrativas Constitucionales en Bolivia y Ecuador: El Buen Vivir y los Derechos de la Naturaleza, Latinoamérica' (2014) 59 Revista de Estudios Latinoamericanos 9.

42 Eduardo Gudynas, 'Por que Bolivia no Reconoce los Derecho de la Naturaleza?' *Rimay Pampa* (La Paz, 4 June 2018) <https://perma.cc/5W9M-NXRA>.

43 Law No 071, Law of the Rights of Mother Earth, 21 December 2010.

44 ibid., art 1.

45 ibid., art 3.

Was the intention of the Bolivian legislator to establish a right holder or was the reference to nature's personhood only rhetorical? Law No. 071 seems to opt for the first option, since its Article 5 (legal character of Mother Earth) indicates that Mother Earth adopts the form of a collective entity of public interest.[46] However, it remains unclear as to what should be understood by a collective entity of public interest.

In our opinion, defining nature as a collective entity of public interest represents a middle ground formula. In other words, with the recognition of nature as a collective entity, the interests of nature are legally covered; however, nature's autonomy is not declared. This last step could not be taken given the obstacles of creating a legal person that is incapable of claiming their rights and due to the limitations to determining the scope of their particular interests. Because of that limit, nature was recognised as a legal entity, but a collective one where humans participate. For this reason, Law No. 071 added that Mother Earth and all its components (including humans) are holders of all the rights it recognises.[47]

Consequently, the RoN are also assigned to individuals, in what we label as a twist towards realism, as it is impossible for nature itself to claim its rights and express its interests. The result of that technique leads to the intermingling of humans' and nature's interests, making Law No. 071 a hybrid regulation in the matter. This becomes more apparent when Principle 4 of Law No. 071 is considered. That principle indicates that the State and any person shall respect, protect and guarantee the rights of Mother Earth with a view to achieving the well-being of current and future generations.[48] As we have explained, the philosophy that underlines the recognition of the rights of future generations (in its environmental facet) and that of RoN are different. If we consider Principle 4 of Law No. 071, the outcome is that the RoN end up subjected in their entirety to the benefit of current and future generations. This ends up subordinating the RoN to human interests. Bearing that in mind, it is not necessary to dwell on the specific rights recognised by Law No. 071 belonging to Mother Earth, since it subordinates them to individuals and it remains therefore doubtful that Law No. 071 truly recognises nature as an autonomous legal entity.

On 15 October 2012, Law No 071 was complemented with Law 300 (Framework Law on Mother Earth and Integral Development to Live

46 ibid., art 5.
47 ibid.
48 ibid., art 2.4.

Well).[49] This norm, far from establishing that the RoN are rights autonomously held by Mother Earth, stated that these rights were limited by the existing rights in the Bolivian legal system.[50] Along these lines, Article 15 of Law 300 established that the State had to promote the use and exploitation of the renewable natural resources of Mother Earth.[51] The provision added that to that end the State would implement actions for the progressive increase in the use and sustainable exploitation of nature's nonrenewable components.[52] In other words, Law 300's purpose was to promote a balanced exploitation of nature's resources rather than clarifying the scope of nature's personhood or how its rights should be understood or claimed. It must be said that the fact that the norm regulates the exploitation of natural resources does not imply by itself – as some authors assert – the denial of the possible recognition of the RoN in Bolivia. This is not an automatic conclusion that can be reached since all rights are limited and – in certain circumstances – need to be limited (even constitutional and fundamental ones). What can be drawn from the experience in Bolivia is that the RoN were recognised in a particular way, with certain subordination of those rights to the interest of human beings.

After considering both the Ecuadorian and Bolivian experiences, we can conclude that the recognition of the RoN by legislative means occurred without adequately considering the effects this would exert in those legal systems. Therefore, it falls to case law to fill that gap by explaining how the RoN can work coherently. Additionally, if the true intention of the legislators was to recognise nature as a subject of law, we should be able to witness

49 Law No 300, Framework Law on Mother Earth and Integral Development to Live Well, 15 October 2012.

50 For this reason, Article 4.1 of Law 300 (Principles – Compatibility and Complementarity of Rights, Obligations, and Duties) provides that the rights found in the legal system cannot be materialised without the others, and that no right can be above the others. Law 300 mentions that the rights referred to by Article 4.1 are the Rights of Mother Earth, Collective and Individual Rights, Fundamental Rights, and the Rights of the Urban and Rural Population to live in a just, equitable and solidary society (ibid., art 4.1). By 'just, equitable and solidary society', the norm states that means a society in which all people have sufficient capacities, conditions, means, and income to satisfy their material and social needs, without social class differences and poverty. That last section of the regulation points out the need to access nature to propel the economic development of the State, a goal that implies some restrictions to the RoN as its exploitation is needed to achieve those purposes.

51 ibid., art 15.1.

52 ibid., art 15.3.

the adjustment of the norms already in place in those jurisdictions in line with the new philosophy embodied by these new sets of rights. However, in neither of those two legal orders does that seem to have occurred.[53] In Ecuador, legislation has not only failed to implement the constitutional mandate embodied by the RoN; it has also privileged traditional pre-existing extractive conceptions. This led some environmental sectors to express critical views on the value of the recognition of RoN in Ecuador.[54] What is more, the recognition of the RoN – at a constitutional level – in that jurisdiction has not prevented an increase in environmental conflicts, given the State's interest in exploiting natural resources.[55] Something similar has occurred in Bolivia.[56] Regarding Bolivia, Murcia Reaño points out that '(t)he promotion of Mother Earth's rights has permeated little into domestic policy – in fact, the Defensoría de la Madre Tierra was never created – but it was a key element in the Bolivian environmental diplomacy, along with the discourse of good living.'[57] This last point is key – in both Ecuador and Bolivia – as it points out the recognition of the RoN for political reasons. For example, in Ecuador that might have happened to obtain support for the approval of the new Constitution of 2008, and in Bolivia that could

53 Contrary to that, the environmental legal framework in those States has not been adjusted to the recognition of nature's personhood. That is why Murcia Riaño iterated that in Ecuador no consistent case law was formed after the recognition of the RoN. Although the constitutional procedural mechanisms used in Ecuador to protect the RoN were copied from the Colombian constitutional model, in practice the Ecuadorian judiciary did not develop the judicial activism that happened in Colombia. See: Diana Murcia Riaño, 'Estudio de la Cuestión en los Ámbitos Normativo y Jurisprudencial' in Esperanza Martínez and Adolfo Maldonado (eds), *Una Década con Derechos de la Naturaleza* (Instituto de Estudios Ecologistas del Tercer Mundo 2019) 57.

54 Those groups have indicated that – in contrast – the laws that have been drafted and enacted since the approval of the 2008 Constitution, have aimed at guaranteeing control over the environment (i.e., by the issuance of Land Laws, Food Sovereignty Laws, Mining Law, Water Law, among others) guaranteeing in that way, the economic model needed by international capital. See: Natalia Sierra, 'La Avanzada del Post-Neoliberalismo Encubierta en un Usurpado Discurso de Izquierda' in *Sumak Kasay o Plan Nacional del Buen Vivir: ¿Que está Detrás del Discurso?* (Acción Ecológica 2012). Cited by: Diana Murcia Riaño (n 53) 58.

55 Rickard Lalander, 'Entre el Ecocentrismo y el Pragmatismo Ambiental: Consideraciones Inductivas sobre Desarrollo, Extractivismo y los Derechos de la Naturaleza en Bolivia y Ecuador' (2015) 6(1) Revista Chilena de Derecho y Ciencia Política 109, 114.

56 ibid., 135 and ff. See also: Marco Aparicio, 'Nuevo Constitucionalismo, Derechos y Medio Ambiente en las Constituciones de Ecuador y Bolivia' (2011) 9 Revista General de Derecho Público Comparado 1.

57 ibid., 60.

have happened for the strengthening of the government of Evo Morales. A review of this trend needs to be carried out by scholarship.

That said, the second way the RoN have been recognised in the region has been through case law. One of the Latin American legal systems with the highest judicial practice in the matter is Ecuador. One reason for that is that the RoN are expressly recognised there. We will review the decisions adopted by its courts in later sections of this contribution. For its part, due to the ambiguous recognition of the RoN, Bolivia has not developed relevant jurisprudence on the matter.

Despite this, it is worth noting that the reception of the RoN in a legal system does not depend on the legislative enshrining of those rights.

3.2.3. The Case of Colombia

Colombia is where, despite the lack of constitutional or infra-constitutional recognition of the RoN, their proclamation has been the most strongly made. The jurisprudence of various Colombian ordinary courts (as well as its Constitutional Court) has shaped the recognition of those rights.

The first decision on the matter was taken by the Constitutional Court of Colombia in the Atrato River case.[58] On that occasion, the Constitutional Court recognised the existence of the RoN based on the 'ecological constitution'. According to the Court, the 'ecological constitution' is made up of the constitutional provisions that deal with environmental matters and that, as a whole, support the recognition of the RoN and other environmental rights.[59] The Constitutional Court recognised the river's personhood due to the pollution and environmental degradation the river had suffered, as well as because of the government's inaction to stop that situation. From that moment on, a series of acknowledgements of nature's personhood followed; for example, the acknowledgement of the personhood of the Amazonia. This was declared by the Supreme Court of Justice (SCJ). The SCJ recognised the '(...) Colombian Amazonia as a 'subject of rights', entitled

58 Atrato River Case (2016) Constitutional Court of Colombia, T-622/16 (2016).

59 On the notion of the ecological constitution, see: José Humberto Ospina Herrera (2007) Constitutional Court of Colombia, T-760/07 (2007) and Demanda de inconstitucionalidad contra los parágrafos 6º (parcial) y 7º (parcial) del artículo 1º de la Ley 507 de 1999 (2000) Constitutional Court of Colombia, C-431/00 (2000). See also: Oscar Darío Amaya Navas, *La Constitución Ecológica de Colombia* (3rd edn, Universidad Externado de Colombia 2016).

to actions of protection, conservation, maintenance and restoration which would be performed by the State and the territorial entities comprising the State'.[60] For its part, the Administrative Court of Boyacá (ACB), while solving a dispute involving the Paramos (moorlands), took into account the decisions concerning the Atrato River and the Amazonia cases. The ACB indicated that the protection granted to the Paramos is '(...) self-executing, that is, as an autonomous fundamental right (...) for its protection there is no need for provisions prohibiting activities that threaten its conservation as a subject entitled to constitutional protection (...)'.[61] Another decision along the same lines was taken by the Superior Court of Medellín (SCM) – Fourth Civil Chamber, where the legal personhood of the Cauca River was declared.[62]

From the review we have made of the Colombian case law, it can be concluded that recognition of the RoN has permeated into different jurisdictional levels in Colombia. The decisions cited here are not all the decisions taken in that jurisdiction as far as the RoN are concerned; however, there is no doubt that in Colombia, the recognition of nature's personhood has been achieved thanks to the activism of the courts. An advantage of this way of right recognition is that – from the beginning – the rights have been formulated considering the practical and procedural dimensions involved in that exercise. That is why the recognition of RoN in Colombia shows that nature's personhood was produced with the intention of making its rights actionable.

The recognition of the RoN in Ecuador, Bolivia, and Colombia has been highlighted by scholarship as a breakthrough. However, the account given by scholarship to that experience describes that process as if it had occurred flawlessly[63] when that is not the case. The experience in Ecuador and Bolivia illustrates a series of theoretical problems. For example, in Bolivia, the

60 Amazonia case (2018) Supreme Court of Justice – Sala de Casación Civil, STC4360–2018, Radicación No 11001–22–03–000–2018–00319–01 (2018) 45.

61 Paramos case (2018) Administrative Court of Boyacá, 15238–3333–002–2018–00016–01, 9 (2018) 35.

62 Cauca River case (2019) Superior Court of Medellín – Fourth Civil Chamber, 2019–076 (2019).

63 Luisa Gomez-Betancur, 'The Rights of Nature in the Colombian Amazon: Examining Challenges and Opportunities in a Transitional Justice Setting' (2020) 25(1) UCLA Journal of International Law and Foreign Affairs 41, 72-ff; Elizabeth Macpherson, Julia Torres Ventura and Felipe Clavijo-Ospina, 'Constitutional Law, Ecosystem, and Indigenous Peoples in Colombia: Biocultural Rights and Legal Subjects' (2020) 9(3) Transnational Environmental Law 521, 532-ff.

recognition of the RoN exhibits limitations to the point that it is not possible to conclude that a real legislative recognition of nature's personhood happened there. In Ecuador, although the recognition of the RoN is clear, on the jurisdictional level it is difficult to see how those rights could be implemented coherently. In Colombia, we find similar contradictions when the cases involving the establishment of nature's personhood are analysed in detail.

As indicated in the introduction of this contribution, the approach we will use to assess the recognition of the RoN in the region will be to consider the procedural reasons that lead to that outcome, and from there we will determine if their implementation has been carried out in line with the philosophical values underpinning the incorporation of those sets of rights.

4. Unveiling the Reasons for the Implementation of the Rights of Nature in the Region

As we have indicated earlier, we believe that the recognition of the RoN in Latin America has not been performed consistently. We believe that there is a discrepancy between the procedural reasons that have pushed their recognition forward and the ethical reasons that sustain the RoN's formulation. It should be borne in mind that the ethical discourse that defends the incorporation of the RoN argues that their recognition should happen with a view to protecting nature for its value in itself; in other words, it is believed that nature should be protected based on the mere fact that it exists. However, after examining the case law in the region, we find that the ethical discourse that sustains the RoN, is at odds with the normative reasons behind the incorporation of those rights. In order to test our assertion, we will examine the procedural dimension behind the RoN's recognition in more depth.

After reviewing the case law in the matter, we have found at least two procedural reasons for the recognition of the RoN: (a) in order to channel certain environmental concerns through constitutional avenues (so nature's interest can be directly actionable), and (b) to allow the rights of future generations to work in practice. Concerning the first procedural reason, we see that through the recognition of nature's personhood it became possible to protect it through constitutional means. This happens because with such recognition, nature becomes worthy of protection for its own value. In other words, nature can now be protected independently of the service provided to human beings. As a result, certain constitutional proceedings now can be initiated to protect nature's concerns without the mediation of a violation of the fundamental right of individuals to a healthy environment. For its part, the second reason for the RoN's recognition is that it helps to make the rights of future generations effective. In this latter scenario, there is an instrumentalisation of the RoN which could be at odds with the underlying ethical idea that has fostered nature's rights.

We will analyse in further detail the two procedural reasons for the recognition of the RoN.

4.1. Recognising Nature's Legal Subjectivity to Grant it Access to Constitutional Procedures

After considering the judgments adopted by some Latin American courts on the matter, we can confirm that in several cases the recognition of the RoN has been aimed at granting nature access to constitutional proceedings. It must be borne in mind that constitutional avenues have not been able to be directly activated to protect nature's interests. An example of this happened in Colombia as its courts could not provide protection to nature through those means, since they were considered to be used only for infringements of fundamental rights (which were considered to be held only by legal subjects in that jurisdiction). The disagreement with that limitation is one of the reasons why the great majority of the RoN in the region have been aired in the context of constitutional disputes. Plaintiffs have repeatedly tried to initiate constitutional processes to protect nature's interests using action of protection proceedings due to their promptness and the more straightforward way they are structured.

An example of that can be seen in the ruling handed down by the Constitutional Court of Colombia when the Atrato River was recognised as possessing legal personhood. The case began with a request filed before the Administrative Tribunal of Cundinamarca (ATC). The ATC decided not to process the request (*tutela action* – writ of *amparo*) since the petition was considered inadmissible. The ATC argued that the writ of *amparo* was intended to protect collective rights and not fundamental ones. That was a relevant argument that created a procedural obstacle. The ATC considered that there were other proceedings capable of protecting nature (or its components). According to the ATC, the appropriate procedure to be activated was the popular action procedure (*proceso de accion popular*) and not an *amparo* procedure. The Council of State (Second Section) agreed and confirmed that decision. The Council of State recalled that the plaintiffs could present their claim before the 'popular judge' and that it was improper to attempt – through a writ of *amparo* – to substitute the applicable proceeding.

Deciding against that line of argumentation, the Constitutional Court of Colombia considered that the writ of *amparo* was appropriate, insofar as the rights involved were not only collective but also fundamental (such as the right to health and the principle of human dignity). The Constitutional Court considered as incorrect the argument held by the ordinary judges, that there were other applicable proceedings, such as a 'popular action procedure'. The Court considered the argument flawed on two grounds: (a) the harm under analysis involved both collective and fundamental rights, and (b) there were doubts about how effective a popular action proceeding would be in solving the problem. In this context, the Constitutional Court developed the existence of the RoN.

However, it should be noted that with the admissibility of the writ of *amparo* the possible harm to a fundamental individual right could have been determined. If that was correct, why did the Court consider it necessary to additionally recognise the RoN? The Court gives no straightforward answer. However, what should be kept in mind is that after establishing the legal personhood of the Atrato River, the Constitutional Court mentioned certain actions that the competent authorities had to implement. Was the recognition of the river's personhood done to make the authorities implement those actions? In our opinion, that is not very convincing; insofar as there are already means in place in the Colombian legal order that would have made it possible for the competent authorities to act with the sole order of the Constitutional Court.[64]

64 In this regard, it must be borne in mind that in Colombia, Ecuador and Bolivia (as in other States of the region), different mechanisms protecting the environment already exist. Indeed, Latin American States have established a convoluted legal framework that protects nature. This protection is exercised by specialised entities such as the ministries of environment, ministries of energy, mines and natural resources, supervisory bodies, or by the regional or local governments. Those entities are responsible for supervising any activity that might damage the environment. Furthermore, those same entities can issue precautionary measures, order the shutdown of works, and apply urgent measures, among other actions. Moreover, if those entities determine the responsibility of an individual or a company, they have the power to impose

Therefore, the reasons for recognition of the Atrato River's personhood should be looked for elsewhere.

As already mentioned, the reason behind that recognition seems to be rooted in the goal to make the activation of constitutional proceedings (such as a writ of *amparo*) possible in the name of the river. Once the river's legal personhood was recognised, that entity became a holder of rights (even fundamental ones) and – therewith – it became possible to activate constitutional proceedings directly in its favour. There are benefits for nature to have access to those procedures, compared to other avenues. For example, if we follow the position of the ordinary judiciary in the case, an alternative procedure to air the legal problem at stake could have been a popular action proceeding; however, that road faces limitations. First, a popular action proceeding is activated when there is a possible damage to a collective right (held by humans) and not to determine the possible infringement of the interests of nonhuman entities. Even if a popular action proceeding could be used to protect nature's interests, those proceedings entail longer procedural stages than those applicable to a writ of *amparo* proceeding which is urgent by nature.[65] Let us suppose another option is chosen, such as commencing administrative proceedings. In that case, those proceeding will require the presentation of evidence and the initiation of steps that could take years – due to its technicality – and the right of the other parties to appeal the decision before judicial instances.

---

penalties and order the remediation of the environment. Then: what was the reason to extend legal personhood to nature if the governmental entities could carry out most of the measures that the Court determined? One possibility is that, even though national authorities had the competencies to act, they did not exercise them, so the problem needed to be solved innovatively. However, in different Latin American States the inaction of a governmental entity can be tackled through an 'enforcement action'. Moreover, if the Constitutional Court found a tendency of governmental agencies not to fulfil their duties (or where certain public policies had generated lack of protection for the environment) that Court had at hand constitutional procedures such as the declaration of an unconstitutional state of affairs (created by that Court itself and adopted by other of its peers in the region) to order an entity to modify or implement actions destined to stop a situation of structural unconstitutionality. Regarding this topic, see: Luis A López Zamora, 'Constitutional Tribunal of Peru' in Rainer Grote, Frauke Lachenmann and Rüdiger Wolfrum (eds), *Max Planck Encyclopedia of Comparative Constitutional Law* (OUP 2021). Finally, if there was collective environmental damage, the Colombian legal system offered the possibility of starting a popular action (class action).

65 See: Hector Fix-Zamudio, 'The Writ of Amparo in Latin America' (1981) 13(3) University of Miami Inter-American Law Review 361 and Jose Maria Serna de la Garza, 'Amparo' in Grote, Lachenmann and Wolfrum (n 64).

It is in this context that the recognition of the RoN's happened in the Atrato River case. The decision to grant legal personhood to the river comes close to recognising rights for nature due to its intrinsic value. This is so because the dispute was solved with the admissibility of the plaintiff's writ of *amparo* (and the subsequent declaration of the violation of their right to water). The declaration of the river's subjectivity (RoN) is a step that was taken only to disconnect the constitutional protection of the river from any human interest that could be at stake. The judgment on the Atrato River case is an important step in the recognition of the RoN in Latin America; however, it is just as important to mention that the Constitutional Court referred to future generations' rights, and how they would benefit from the recognition of the river's personhood. Therefore, the RoN's proclamation in that case seems to have happened not only to protect nature for its own sake but also because of the service it could provide.

4.2. The Recognition of Nature and its Role in Making the Legal Personality of Future Generations Work

What we have just mentioned leads to the second procedural reason why the RoN might possibly have been recognised in Latin America. We said that in the regional experience, one of the newly recognised subjectivities (nature or future generations) had been used to make the other work. The utilisation of a subject of law in that way has gone unnoticed due to the lack of theoretical differentiation that exists between those two categories in Latin American scholarship[66] and in the jurisprudence of their tribunals. The result is the subordination of the values underlying the recognition of one legal personhood for the benefit of the values underlying the other.

66 In one of the most important books about the RoN from the region, references are made to those rights together with a plethora of allusions to the right of future generations, as if they would be necessarily interconnected. In other sections, it is implied that one could be a tool to ensure the enforcement of the other but without indicating the differences that those two sets of rights have. See the presentation and prologue of the book: Carlos Espinosa Gallegos-Anda and Camilo Pérez Fernández (eds), *Los Derechos de la Naturaleza y la Naturaleza de sus Derechos* (Ministerio de Justicia, Derechos Humanos y Cultos 2011). This lack of delimitation overlooks the fact that both sets of rights have a different view on the relationship that human beings should have with the environment.

In Ecuador, where the recognition of both sets of rights has been expressly included in the Constitution, the reference in its case law of both rights together is the result of the theoretical difficulty of dissecting the RoN from the rights of future generations.[67]

In Colombia, this has happened because of (a) the theoretical difficulty of differentiating both notions, but also due to (b) practical reasons.

---

67 In the case of Ecuador, this can be observed in the judgment adopted by the Civil and Mercantile Chamber of the Provincial Court of Azuay (PCA), Ecuador. See: Rio Blanco case (2018) Provincial Court of Azuay – Civil and Mercantile Chamber, 01333201803145 (2018). The PCA emphasised the reform undertaken by the Constitution of Ecuador through which a new economic model was imposed. That new economic paradigm established a non-extractive model based on the indigenous worldview of Good Living (*Sumak Kawsay*). That principle sought to find harmony between the person/community and the environment. In the PCA's view, the constitutional reform that happened in Ecuador aimed to end the extractive economic model, a shift that was vital for future generations so that they could enjoy the same quantity and quality of natural resources as we do. The Court added that based on that, the Constitution recognised different rights such as the RoN, land rights, and protection of biodiversity (ibid., 19). In this judgment, the PCA referred to the RoN together with future generations (although without necessarily referring to future generations as rights holders). Another example is the judgment taken by the Criminal Chamber of Loja (Ecuador), Judgment in Trial No 11121-2011-0010 (See: Vilcabamba River case (2011) Provincial Court of Justice of Loja (Criminal Chamber), 11121-2011-0010 (2011)). In that case, the Court enforced the RoN through an action of protection proceeding. As mentioned before, Ecuador is one of the jurisdictions where the RoN have been enshrined at the constitutional level; therefore, the Court could delve into certain considerations. The Court stated that nature's importance is so evident and indisputable that any discussion in that regard was redundant; however, it noted that it should not be forgotten that some damage caused to nature is 'intergenerational', consisting of damage that due to its magnitude has repercussions not only on the current generation but on future generations (ibid.). In a recent decision, the Constitutional Court of Ecuador referred to the RoN (in the Bosque Protector Los Cedros case). See: Bosque Protector Los Cedros case (2021) Constitutional Court of Ecuador, 1149-19-JP/20 (2021). The Constitutional Court recalled that the RoN include nature's right to (a) have its existence fully respected and to (b) maintain and regenerate its natural cycles (ibid., para. 25). The Court added that the RoN, like all constitutional rights, have full normative force and were autonomous (ibid., para. 35). Although the Constitutional Court did not elaborate on the autonomy of the RoN, it made it clear by the way it structured its judgment that those rights needed to be considered through a separate analysis than the one the human right to a healthy environment would require. This last judgment is important; however, the tendency in Ecuador so far is to analyse the RoN considering the damage their breach would entail to human interests. See: Girard D Vernaza Arroyo and Danelia Cutie Mustelier, 'Los Derechos de la Naturaleza desde la Mirada de los Jueces en Ecuador' (2022) 16(49) Revista IUS 285.

Examples of the first scenario can be spotted in the judgment delivered by the SCJ in the Amazonia case.[68] In that case, the SCJ stated that the protection afforded by the Constitution aims at benefiting each person individually but also the 'others'. By 'others', the tribunal meant the other people inhabiting the planet and the unborn,[69] therefore, referring to the rights of future generations. According to the Court, those rights were based on: (i) the ethical duty of solidarity between members of the human species and (ii) the intrinsic value of nature.[70] The Court's reasoning is – to say the least – confusing. Several contradictions arise. The one to be highlighted now is that the Court seemed to be able to make a connection between the RoN and the rights of future generations without giving any explanation.

The second reason why the RoN have been linked with the rights of future generations in Colombia is due to the difficulties of realising the right of future generations to a healthy environment. This is rooted in the fact that it is not possible to know today what the future generations (in the future) will consider relevant. The impossibility of accessing the content of the environmental rights of future generations (that is, what should be protected in concrete terms) makes the RoN an important device. The RoN can work as a conceptual tool that helps to abstractly objectify nature's value making some of its characteristics immovable. Then, what at first sight looked like the protection of nature for the value it had in itself, ultimately appears as a recognition destined to guarantee some of nature's features in order for those to be enjoyed by future generations.

68 Amazonia case (2018) Supreme Court of Justice – Sala de Casación Civil, STC4360–2018, Radicación No 11001–22–03–000–2018–00319–01 (2018). The proceeding started with an action of protection that sought to stop the degradation suffered by the Amazonia. Twenty-five children brought the case, so the dispute – at first view – involved the rights of future generations. However, in its decision, the Court went on to recognise the personhood of the Amazonia. How did the connection between the rights of future generations and the RoN develop? Was the recognition of the RoN necessary in the case? What analysis did the Court carry out and what distinctions did the Court make between both notions? According to the Court's reasoning, how do the two new legal personhoods articulate? The Court did not provide answers to those questions. On the contrary, in its reasoning it is evident that the Court intermingled the RoN with the rights of future generations as if both were implied, giving no explanation of why they both needed to be considered at the same time.

69 ibid.,18–19.

70 ibid., 19.

That reasoning can be found in the decision of the SMC in which the subjectivity of the Cauca River was proclaimed. On that occasion, the SMC drew a connection between the recognition of the RoN with the implementation of the rights of future generations. To that end, the SCM reviewed the constitutional provisions supporting the recognition of the rights of future generations, pointing out that they regulated the territorial transformation of Colombia in order to optimise the use of natural and human resources in pursuit of a decent existence for current and future populations. The SMC added that the Constitution implicitly recognised the dignity of future generations, which is a distinctive feature of the subjects of law. According to the Court, that implied not only the recognition of future generations' personhood, but also the possibility of their rights being protected through constitutional proceedings. To that end, the SCM concluded that there were no doubts about the crisis that affected the river's ecosystem, which needed to be preserved for the benefit of future generations so that, in front of that subject of rights (future generations) emerged another subject of law of no less importance: the river itself.[71]

A similar trend happened in the judgment of the SCJ in the Amazonia case. As previously mentioned, the SCJ recognised the RoN when considering the legal personhood of future generations. The Court left unclear the connection between the plaintiffs' request and the recognition of the RoN.[72] However, it added that the RoN is the central concept on which the intrinsic value of the environment is based, which led it to conclude that 'respect for itself' (intrinsic value) implied a respect for the parts that correspond to nature itself and of which – in turn – future generations will be part of.[73]

71 Cauca River case (2019) Superior Court of Medellín – Fourth Civil Chamber, 2019–076 (2019) Consideration No 8. Taking into account the Court's considerations in the case, it becomes impossible to understand the reasoning behind recognising the subjectivity of the Cauca River. That lack of clarity has procedural implications (given the possible lack of motivation of the judgment), but also makes it difficult to understand the reasons for recognising a new subjectivity. The lack of reasoning of the Court makes it difficult to refute or agree with its decision.

72 Amazonia case (2018) Supreme Court of Justice – Sala de Casación Civil, STC4360–2018, Radicación No 11001–22–03–000–2018–00319–01 (2018) 21. The Court limited itself to referencing the judgment issued by the Constitutional Court of Colombia in the Atrato River case and the case where the subjectivity of the Amazonia was recognised. ibid., 39 and 45.

73 ibid., 21.

The recognition of the RoN together with the recognition of the rights of future generations can also be seen in the judgment delivered by the Constitutional Court of Colombia in the Atrato River case. Early in the judgement, the Constitutional Court defined both sets of rights, clearing the way to make their differentiation possible.[74] Consequently, this case was an ideal occasion to elucidate the interaction between future generations' subjectivity and the RoN personhood. Nonetheless, this did not happen. On the contrary, in later sections of the judgment it is possible to observe that the Court subordinated the recognition of the Atrato River subjectivity to human needs. For example, the Court, in order to argue the need to proclaim the river's personhood[75], referred to the right to water and how illegal mining harmed food production (trees, crops, and fish), the sanitary conditions, and the cultural practices of the area,[76] all elements associated with the satisfaction of human beings. The Court finished by including

74 Atrato River Case (2016) Constitutional Court of Colombia, T-622/16 (2016). In this case, the communities living in the Atrato river basin filed a request before the Constitutional Court of Colombia. This decision has been highlighted as a fundamental decision in the recognition of the RoN; however, it is important not only because of the recognition of the river's personhood but also for the reasoning that the Court set out. In its reasoning, the Court clarified – albeit tenuously- the possible relationship between the rights of future generations and the RoN. The Court stated that the existing provisions and the pluralistic approach promoted by the Colombian Constitution made the relationship with the environment one in permanent evolution. From there, the Court added that at least three theoretical approaches could explain the transition towards protecting nature's interests in that legal system. At first, the relationship with nature was based on an anthropocentric approach, which conceived of human beings as the only *raison d'être* of the legal order and nature as a mere object. Subsequently, a biocentric approach appeared which claimed more solidarity and human responsibility. This approach advocated for the existence of man's duties towards nature and future generations. Finally, an ecocentric approach, which conceived nature as an authentic subject of rights emerged in scholarship (ibid., 5.5 and 5.6). The Court recalled that the biocentric vision derived at first from an anthropocentric conception, since at that time nature's protection was formulated to avoid a catastrophe that could extinguish human beings. Under this interpretation, nature was not a subject of rights, but an object at man's disposal; however, it differed from the purely anthropocentric approach insofar as it considered that the environment of a country did not belong exclusively to the people who inhabit it, but also to future generations and humanity in general (ibid., 5.8). As for the ecocentric vision, the Court indicated that based on that, nature's personhood was recognised, and that this last approach was grounded in the Colombian Constitution.

75 ibid., section 9.32.

76 ibid., section 9.30.

in its reasoning the importance of protecting the biological and cultural diversity of the nation for future generations.[77]

The question that immediately arises in all of those cases, is: Why did the courts find it necessary to recognise nature's personhood together with the subjectivity of future generations?

As already mentioned, one key issue in the recognition of the rights of future generations is the determination of who should be considered part of that group (whether those who have not yet been born or – at the same time – those who currently do not have the legal stand to protect their rights effectively, such as children). Another issue that arises is what is the exact scope of the rights of future generations? To say that future generations are subjects of law does not conclude their inclusion in a legal system. On the contrary, it is necessary to continue and determine the specific content of their rights. There is no doubt that future generations can regard some interests as valuable for their future existence included among which is enjoying a healthy environment. However, the environmental protection granted today in the light of today's values and concerns may be irrelevant for those groups in the future. In other words, the scope given to future generations' rights might be wrong from a historical perspective. Furthermore, if the legal maxim which states that all rights (even the constitutional ones) are not absolute is valid,[78] then a possible conflict between future generations' rights and individuals' rights now emerges. In those cases, a balancing exercise would need to be performed. However, a judge faced with that dilemma would need access to the specific content on future generations' interests. Only then would he or she be able to carry out a balancing exercise.

---

77 ibid.

78 That is part of a broader debate. In that debate, some scholars argue that all rights – even constitutional ones – are limited. According to that view, rights are legal recognitions that need to be contrasted and delimited by the other rights and values recognised in a legal order. Consequently, if they enter into conflict *inter se*, a proportionality test would be necessary. That exercise comes into play when a conflict between rights or between a right and a constitutional value arises. This does not exclude the possibility that in particular situations some rights can be formulated in such a way as to be absolute, such as the right not to be tortured or enslaved. Be that as it may, the possibility of enunciating absolute rights is exceptional, and to that end a precise technique is required. On this, see: John Finnis, 'Absolute Rights: Some Problems Illustrated' (2016) 61(2) American Journal of Jurisprudence 195 and Martin Borowski, 'Absolute Rights and Proportionality' (2013) 56 German Yearbook of International Law 385.

One of the conclusions of this contribution is that in some Latin American jurisdictions, the recognition of the RoN has been initiated to solve the obstacle mentioned above. To that end – in a legal system – a field of evident interest for future generations is recognised, and then is 'objectified' by granting it legal personhood. With that strategy, the new subject of law ends up with an area of protection that safeguards some of their minimal characteristic (their rights). The way nature's personhood has been recognised in Latin America demonstrates that its recognition has happened not for its intrinsic value, but for the service it can provide to human beings. That pattern can be observed in the case law of both Ecuador and Colombia. In those jurisdictions, the RoN are used as a bridge connecting the rights of future generations and the existing world. This seems to be the reason for the recognition of the RoN together with the rights of future generations in several judgments. Then, it is fair to call out the inaccuracy of the scholarship assertion that the recognition of the RoN in the region has occurred with the aim of recognising nature's rights autonomously. On the contrary, the judgments delivered by the Latin American courts demonstrate that the RoN play a role in making others' rights operative.[79]

5. Conclusions

In this contribution, we have explained that the RoN emerged in the legal discourse with the aim of protecting the interests of nature because of its intrinsic value. For its part, the rights of future generations (to a healthy environment) were recognised so as to prevent environmental degradation as that would benefit a collectivity that does not yet exist. In Latin America, those two categories – even though distinctive – have faced the tendency of being considered as expressions of a same phenomenon.

We have observed through our research that in Latin America the premises for the formulation of the RoN (nature's intrinsic value) have

79 Part of the Ecuadorian scholarship has indirectly recognised this, when stating that 'the tendency (...) to legally treat environment [nature] not as an object but a subject of law, constitutes a progress in Law. However, it has also been configured as a limitation of the power of the State concerning the indiscriminate use of renewable resources, which are fundamental for future generations'. See: Frank Mila and Karla Ayerim, 'El Constitucionalismo Ambiental en Ecuador' (2020) 97 Actualidad Jurídica Ambiental 5, 12. See also: Mario Aguilera and Mercedes Cóndor, 'La Iniciativa Yasuni ITT como Materialización de los Derechos de la Naturaleza' in Gallegos-Anda and Pérez Fernández (n 66) 213.

not been followed insofar as they have been subordinated to the rights of other legal subjects. That fact has created a fundamental inconsistency, which could end in the mimicry of those rights, if they were subjected – fundamentally – to the interests of others entities. If that were so, nature would remain an object in a legal system, and not a subject of Law. Thus, to maintain coherence with the ethical foundations that underline the recognition of nature's personhood, nature's rights should be – at least theoretically – conceptualised and articulated as autonomously assigned to nature. However, the review of the case law in Latin America shows that this has not been the case. In contrast, we have detected a conceptual confusion between the scopes of the RoN and the rights of future generations on environmental matters, and – even more – a trend of instrumentalising the RoN.

We concluded that the lack of honouring the ethical basis for the recognition of nature's personhood (i.e., by subordinating it to the rights of future generations) is rooted in the theoretical difficulty of differentiating the scope of nature's and future generations' rights, and in the need to overcome some of the procedural barriers that the rights of future generations face. Another factor that has made the autonomous implementation of the RoN difficult in Latin America, is the fact that if nature is released from the service it provides to human beings, that fact would lead to inevitable outcomes. For example, if nature were to be incorporated in a legal order autonomously, that would imply that nature's rights would shape the rights of the other legal subjects; situation that results from the fact that the rights of all right holders gain contour when contrasted with the rights of the other legal entities in a legal order. When this is considered together with the topic analyzed in this Chapter, the recognition of RoN would result in the re-shaping and reformulation of the individual environmental rights of human beings (including that of future generations) in accordance with the scope of the content of nature's rights. That would lead to other entanglements. For example, if we consider that the philosophical foundation for the recognition of RoN and the rights of future generations is different, then the possibility of conflicts between their rights could not be discarded. When all of these are considered, a fair conclusion is that using the RoN to make the rights of future generations effective, should not be considered a harmless exercise.

Doing so conceals that both set of rights could come into conflict, a situation which cannot be ruled out since their scopes are different. In this contribution, we have highlighted that, while the purpose of the RoN is to protect nature in terms of existing and/or maintaining its vital cycles, the rights of future generations are not limited to environmental concerns. The rights of future generations include different facets of human life, such as the possible right to minimum social security, public medical care, and technology with respect for fundamental rights, among others.[80] To fulfil those other interests held by the future generations, nature's rights would need to be balanced inasmuch as all rights (even constitutional ones) face limitations when encountering coexisting rights worthy of protection.

Therefore, the recognition of RoN in conjunction with the rights of future generations – in some instances – could generate tension, and their instrumentalization as has happened in Latin America, requires a more critical assessment.

80 See: Gosseries (n 12).